Annotated Bibliographies of Old and Middle English Literature

VOLUME V

OLD ENGLISH WISDOM POETRY

This volume offers an introduction to the scholarly literature (mainly but not exclusively between the years 1800 and 1990) on Old English wisdom poetry. This genre is here defined to include (in the ASPR classification and title system) the metrical Charms, *The Fortunes of Men*, *The Gifts of Men*, *Homiletic Fragments I* and *II*, *Maxims I* and *II*, *The Order of the World*, *Precepts*, the metrical Proverbs (Latin-English and Winfrid), the Riddles of the Exeter Book, *Rune Poem*, *Solomon and Saturn*, and *Vainglory*. The General Introduction considers some broad issues in the history of scholarship on Old English wisdom poetry and the methodological problems involved in its research. The ensuing General Bibliography is divided into chapters. The first two chapters cover general and miscellaneous works respectively and the remainder each deal with a major text or collection of texts. Aside from the first two, each chapter contains a brief introduction, in which an overview of research on the relevant text is provided. Thus the chapter detailing the specialist bibliography of metrical charms is preceded by an introduction on scholarship concerning the charms. Topics covered in these chapter introductions include the manuscript provenance; editorial policies and debates; datings, localizations, and attributions; sources and analogues; genre affiliations; literary-critical evaluations; place in the context of Anglo-Saxon poetry; and contribution to our understanding of Anglo-Saxon culture. Within chapters, the General Bibliography is chronologically arranged. Two indices are supplied, the first an Index of Scholars and the second a Subject Index: both are keyed to the General Bibliography.

Dr RUSSELL POOLE teaches in the School of English and Media Studies at Massey University.

Annotated Bibliographies of
Old and Middle English Literature

ISSN 1353–8675

General Editor: T. L. Burton

Editorial Assistants:
Sabina Flanagan and Rosemary Greentree

Already Published

VOLUME I
The Language of Middle English Literature
David Burnley and Matsuji Tajima

VOLUME II
Ancrene Wisse, the Katherine Group, and the Wooing Group
Bella Millett

VOLUME III
Visions of the Other World in Middle English
Robert Easting

VOLUME IV
Old English Prose of Secular Learning
Stephanie Hollis and Michael Wright

Annotated Bibliographies of Old and Middle English Literature

VOLUME V

OLD ENGLISH WISDOM POETRY

RUSSELL POOLE

D. S. BREWER

First published 1998
D. S. Brewer, Cambridge

ISBN 0 85991 530 1

D. S. Brewer is an imprint of Boydell & Brewer Ltd
PO Box 9, Woodbridge, Suffolk IP12 3DF, UK
and of Boydell & Brewer Inc.
PO Box 41026, Rochester, NY 14604–4126, USA

A catalogue record for this book is available
from the British Library

Library of Congress Cataloging-in-Publication Data available

This publication is printed on acid-free paper

Printed in Great Britain by
St Edmundsbury Press Ltd, Bury St Edmunds, Suffolk

Contents

General Editor's Preface   vii

Acknowledgements   ix

Abbreviations   xii

Bibliographical Introduction   1

Aims
Coverage of Texts
Coverage of Bibliographic Items
Principles of Annotation
Methods of Organization
Methods of Reference

General Introduction   7

General Bibliography   37

Bibliography of General Items   39

Bibliography of Miscellaneous Items   62

The Metrical Charms   154

The Fortunes of Men   191

The Gifts of Men   195

Homiletic Fragment I   199

Homiletic Fragment II   202

Maxims I and *II*   204

The Order of the World   234

Precepts   237

The Metrical Proverbs (Latin-English and Winfrid)   240

The Exeter Book Riddles   244

The *Rune Poem*   333

Solomon and Saturn   350

Vainglory   372

List of Works Cited   376

Index of Scholars   377

Subject Index   385

Haere e whai i te waewae o Uenuku, kia ora ai te tangata.

('By going to the feet of Uenuku [the source of wisdom], it may be well for a person': Māori proverb cited by John Patterson, *Exploring Maori Values*, Palmerston North: Dunmore, 1992, 56.)

Kāore te tohunga e whai mātauranga i a ia anake, engari he mana i tukua iho e rātou ma.

('The mana of the expert comes not just from his learning but from the people who gave that learning': Māori proverb cited by Patterson, 95.)

Descripsi in Novembr. 1864. Medicinam adhibui: sulphuret. ammonii. W.G.P.

(W.G. Pluygers, recording his transcription of the Leiden Riddle, cited by A.H. Smith, **777**, 9.)

Of course, these will not do in Leipzic, Bonn, or Kiel, for either they contain 'zu wenig' or 'zu viel'. One 'Kenner' adds some words, who subtly thinks he can, another simply 'tilgt', a third 'nimmt Lücken an'.

(Ernst A. Kock, **163**, 185–6.)

One criticism we may as well anticipate. It may very justly be brought against us that we 'do not know the [modern] literature of the subject' – or rather of the various subjects included in this volume. In order to save critics the trouble of looking for references we may state at once that we do not know the literature of any of the subjects treated in this book. We have read some books which happen to have come in our way; and to some of these we refer occasionally. But we do not for a moment claim to have made any exhaustive examination of the modern literature bearing on these subjects. We have doubtless missed many important works, and thereby failed to obtain much valuable information. If we had read more widely we should not have completed the book – which perhaps might have been the better course.

(H. Munro and N. Kershaw Chadwick, **183**, xix.)

General Editor's Preface

The last two decades have seen an explosion in the production of annotated bibliographies in the humanities, motivated in part by the sheer impossibility of keeping up with the mass of critical literature produced since the fifties. They fill a need, felt by students and teachers at all levels, for reliable, concise, yet detailed guides to what has been written. Medieval English literature has been no exception to this general trend, with annotated bibliographies of many of the major authors and areas appearing in the last twenty years, or being now in preparation.

The primary aim of the current series of some two dozen volumes is to produce an annotated bibliography for every area of medieval English literary studies for which such a tool is not already in existence or in preparation. One of the major benefits of the series is thus to focus attention not only on those of the more popular areas not covered in other bibliographies, but also on those hitherto marginalized. The individual volumes contribute to our knowledge of our cultural heritage by showing, through a summary and evaluation of all known writings on the area in question, why that area is worthy of closer study, what sorts of interest it has already provoked, and what are the most fruitful directions for future research in it.

One of the distinguishing features of this series is the chronological arrangement of items, as opposed to the alphabetical arrangement more commonly adopted. Chronological arrangement facilitates the reading of annotations in the same order as the publication of the items annotated, and thus gives readers at one sitting a sense of the development of scholarship in the field. At the same time, the convenience of alphabetical arrangement is retained through the index of scholars and critics, which allows readers to locate with ease all items by a particular writer.

Each bibliography in the series is concentrated on a relatively small, reasonably self-contained area, defined on generic lines. This concentration leads to a second distinguishing feature of the series: the fullness and detail both of the annotations themselves and of the introductory sections. With the aim of letting the original authors speak for themselves the authors of the bibliographies keep their annotations as neutral as can reasonably be hoped; in the introductory sections, however, they offer critical analyses of the works annotated, drawing attention to the major trends in scholarship, showing which approaches have been most influential, which are exhausted, and which are most in need of further development.

The editorial work for the series has been assisted since 1991 by grants from the Australian Research Council and the University of Adelaide, to both of which bodies grateful acknowledgement is made here.

T.L. BURTON

Acknowledgements

Where else to start but by paying tribute to the scholars themselves, who have explored and cultivated this region of Old English poetry? Only a catalogue in the style of *The Fortunes of Men* will do them justice. Some quested for ancient rituals, some deciphered runic messages, some stumbled upon analogues, some went crazy over riddles, some hacked at hypermetric lines, some assayed herbal medicines, some spotted oral formulas, some carved messages on kelp, some compiled word-lists, some dabbed reagents on manuscripts, some blew the dust off apocrypha and patrologias, some went nativist, some gazed up into the clouds for solutions, and some aesthetically sniffed at literary flowers and flourishes. All entered into the continuing debate, sometimes amicably, sometimes not, and initiated students into further explorations. These predecessors should be present to us and even where they lapse into excess or foolishness or bigotry we may learn from them to recognize kindred errors in ourselves.

Among my more particular debts, I am grateful to the bibliographers and editors who have contributed to such works as *Anglo-Saxon England*, the *Cambridge History of English Literature*, the *Old English Newsletter*, *The Year's Work in English Studies*, and *The Anglo-Saxon Poetic Records*. Without the bibliographical contribution of Stanley Greenfield and Fred Robinson in particular (*A Bibliography of Publications on Old English Literature from the Beginnings to the End of 1972, Using the Collections of E.E. Ericson*), writings on Old English wisdom poetry would be much harder to document. Other individual scholars whose contributions on these or related fronts spring to mind are Angus Cameron and Roberta Frank, Donald K. Fry, Neil Ker, George Krapp and Elliott Van Kirk Dobbie, Patrizia Lendinara, John Lindow, Eric Stanley, Patrick Stevens, and Craig Williamson. The editors of Volume 4 of the present series, along with the series editor, Tom Burton, helped to make key decisions as to the contents and format of this volume. I owe a great deal to Tom Burton, not merely for initiating the bibliographic series of which this volume forms a part but also for his prompt advice and rulings on a whole range of thorny problems and for his careful checking of the format of my manuscript.

I am indebted to the following bodies for financial assistance towards the costs of computing and of library visits: the New Zealand Lottery Science Fund; the Massey University Research Fund (for a University Research Fellowship and other awards); the Massey University Leave Fund; the Massey University Department of English; the New Zealand Vice-Chancellors' Committee (for the award of a Claude McCarthy Fellowship); the New Zealand–United States Educational Foundation (for the award of a Fulbright Travel Award); and the Humanities Research Centre, Australian National University (for the award of a visiting scholarship).

The following institutions have generously provided study and research facilities: Clare Hall, University of Cambridge; the Centre for Medieval Studies, the Pontifical Institute of Mediaeval Studies, and the Dictionary of Old English,

University of Toronto; the Humanities Research Centre, Australian National University; and the Department of Scandinavian, University of California Berkeley. The English Department of Harvard University and the organizers of the 1996 conference of the Australia and New Zealand Association for Medieval and Renaissance Studies gave me welcome opportunities to try out preliminary versions of parts of the General Introduction; I am grateful to those who attended for their comments and responses.

Any compiler of a bibliography will appreciate how much the helpfulness of library personnel can contribute to a project like this one, particularly when it is undertaken by a compiler who is not a professional bibliographer. The inter-library loan staff at Massey University Library have efficiently accessed numerous items. In addition, I have visited many libraries, both in New Zealand and overseas. I should like to mention specifically libraries at the following institutions: in New Zealand, the Universities of Auckland, Canterbury, and Otago, Victoria University of Wellington, Waikato University (along with the New Zealand National Library); in Australia, the University of Sydney, the University of Melbourne, the Australian National University; in Canada, the University of Toronto, Pontifical Institute for Mediaeval Studies, University of Western Ontario; in the United States of America, Cornell University, Harvard University, Stanford University, University of California Berkeley, University of Denver, University of Illinois; in Britain, the University of Cambridge, Oxford University English Faculty Library, the British Library. Among individual library personnel I am especially grateful to David Lowe, of the University Library, Cambridge, and Heinz Fuchs, of the Niedersächsische Staats- und Universitätsbibliothek, Göttingen, who assisted me with German dissertations.

Numerous scholars have given me invaluable assistance, some by replying to enquiries about their own work, some by assisting me to access the work of others, and some by providing me with research facilities (or a combination of these things). I hope that the following is a complete list: Theodore M. Andersson, Graham D. Caie, Carol Clover, Margaret Clunies Ross, Susan Deskis, Matthew Driscoll, Ralph Elliott, Teresa Fiocco, Leonard Forster, Thomas Forster, Roberta Frank, Shiona Grant, Joseph Harris, Ruth Harvey, Toni Healey, Connie Hieatt, Tom Hill, Stephanie Hollis, Gregory Jember, Marianne Kalinke, Simon Keynes, Patrizia Lendinara, John Lindow, David and Ian McDougall, Philip Mitchell, Haruko Momma, Marie Nelson, Heather O'Donoghue, Marijane Osborn, Hiroshi Ozawa, Derek Pearsall, William Schipper, Paul Sorrell, Eric Stanley, Patrick Stevens, Paul Beekman Taylor, Jane Toswell, Raymond P. Tripp, Jr., Greg Waite, Hideki Watanabe, and Michael Wright. I am also grateful to the denizens of ANSAXNET and OLDNORSENET for some useful leads. Any errors and omissions in this bibliography are my responsibility alone.

Here at Massey I am indebted to Professor R.P. Corballis and other colleagues in the English Department, who relieved me from some teaching and administrative tasks while I was engaged in research overseas. Mike West, then a senior student of the Department of Information Systems, helped me with technical aspects of the data-base on which the bibliography is built, and Julie McKenzie, of the Department of English, solved some word-processing problems. I am also grateful to Lynda Burch and Richard Scott and their colleagues at, respectively, Computing Services and the Centre for University Extramural Studies for some last-minute technical assistance.

I should like finally to thank Roger and Wendy Browne, Warwick Slinn, and most of all Debbie Rayner for their personal support and friendship during the time I have been working on this project.

Abbreviations

MANUSCRIPTS

British Library Add. MS 9067	British Library, Additional Manuscript 9067
CCCC	Cambridge, Corpus Christi College
Cotton Caligula A.vii	London, British Library, Cotton Caligula A.vii
Cotton Domitian A.ix	London, British Library, Cotton Domitian A.ix
Cotton Faustina A.x	London, British Library, Cotton Faustina A.x
Cotton Otho B.x	London, British Library, Cotton Otho B.x
Cotton Tiberius A.iii	London, British Library, Cotton Tiberius A.iii
Cotton Tiberius B.i	London, British Library, Cotton Tiberius B.i
Cotton Vitellius A.xv	London, British Library, Cotton Vitellius A.xv
Harley 585	London, British Library, Harley 585
Royal 2 B.v	London, British Library, Royal 2 B.v
Royal 4 A.xiv	London, British Library, Royal 4 A.xiv
Royal 12 D.xvii	London, British Library, Royal 12 D.xvii
Vossianus Lat. 4to 106 106	Leiden, Rijksuniversiteit, Vossianus Lat. 4to 106

LITERARY WORKS

Fortunes	*The Fortunes of Men*
Gifts	*The Gifts of Men*
Maxims	*Maxims I* and *II*
Order	*The Order of the World*

PERIODICALS, REFERENCE WORKS, AND INSTITUTIONS

ASPR	Anglo-Saxon Poetic Records
EETS	Early English Text Society
ELH	*English Literary History*
JEGP	*Journal of English and Germanic Philology*
NS	New Series
PMLA	*Publications of the Modern Language Association of America*
YWOES	*The Year's Work in Old English Studies*

OTHER

ae	alt-englisch
MS	manuscript
OE	Old English
OEW	Old English wisdom (poetry)

Bibliographical Introduction

AIMS

This bibliography is intended for all those interested in Old English wisdom poetry and the works associated with it, both within and outside English studies. Its principal aim is to provide a helpful bibliographical guide to the scholarly literature. Secondary aims are to give a survey of the research on Old English wisdom poetry, tracing its development over approximately the past two centuries and reviewing our current state of knowledge, and to draw attention to the methodological pitfalls which researchers are likely to encounter in this multi-disciplinary area.

COVERAGE OF TEXTS

This volume covers the following poems or groups of poems (as defined in ASPR): the metrical Charms, *The Fortunes of Men, The Gifts of Men, Homiletic Fragments I* and *II, Maxims I* and *II, The Order of the World, Precepts,* the metrical Proverbs (Latin-English and Winfrid), the Riddles of the Exeter Book, *Rune Poem, Solomon and Saturn,* and *Vainglory* (in that order). As has been many times observed, Old English poetry, not to say Old English literature in general, resists classification. Some duplication with other volumes in this series could scarcely be avoided. An example is the scholarly literature on magico-medical texts, which often and rightly deals with both poetic and prose texts within the one discussion. It must be admitted that the separation of the supposedly metrical from the supposedly unmetrical has had many unfortunate effects, not least the wholesale emendation and conjectural correction of the texts classed as metrical, so as to bring them into conformity with the usage of *Beowulf* and other undoubtedly poetical works. Nevertheless, a bibliography is not the place to devise new classifications and I have worked within the inherited system throughout.

All the texts covered in this volume are based on wisdom of some kind. The core type of text is secular, impersonal, and non-narrative. These considerations exclude *Soul and Body, Deor,* and *Beowulf,* among many others. Despite this appearance of system, it is nevertheless very difficult to distinguish core from periphery. Narrative is found in the metrical Charms, Christian doctrine is found in *Solomon and Saturn,* and a personalized speaker is found in the Exeter Book Riddles – to mention only some obvious exceptions. Since all Old English poetry smacks of wisdom, the criteria for exclusion can only be artificial and often relate more to a modern intuitive sense of literary classification than to anything Anglo-Saxon. I have tried to redress this artificial selectiveness somewhat in the General Introduction, where I relate the texts surveyed in the General Bibliography to the broader manifestations of wisdom in Old English poetry.

COVERAGE OF BIBLIOGRAPHIC ITEMS

The texts discussed in this volume have fared very unevenly at the hands of scholars. A few have scarcely seemed to merit separate chapter status here, thanks partly to their brief or fragmentary compass and partly to the inattention of scholarship. Others, such as the Riddles, have at times been overdone, whether by the textual critic, zealous to undo the effects of bookmoths, beer-mugs, and red-hot pokers upon the precious manuscript; by the curious solver, determined to wrench all clues into conformity with a preconceived solution; or by the neophyte aesthete, who fancies that here is a field never previously harvested by literary criticism. But whether overdone or underdone, each of these texts has been accorded its own chapter, if only as a means of conspicuously representing the extent of either solicitude or neglect. Since much of the scholarly literature is topic-based rather than text-based, many entries are cited once and for all in the chapters devoted to respectively the Bibliography of General Items and the Bibliography of Miscellaneous Items: the relevance of these works to specific texts can be determined by a perusal of the individual entry and the Subject Index. Cross-references have not been used.

In the following paragraphs I shall outline the principles of selection as to content. The present volume focuses on the period 1800–1990. I have systematically omitted all publications prior to 1800, regardless of their scholarly interest. Likewise, publications subsequent to 1990 are generally not listed. I have annotated material in other languages, indicating the language used where necessary. All translations are my own unless otherwise stated.

My coverage of the scholarship is literary in its focus, with the Greenfield/Robinson bibliography as its central resource. When possible, however, I have attempted to follow the material wherever it led – into linguistics, history, archaeology, folklore, anthropology, theology, medicine, and science. In the General Bibliography I have avoided evaluative comments and insinuations about the quality of the scholarship, even in the most trying cases. Readers of the volume will appropriately form their own judgements as to the worth of the items documented between these covers. To someone whose chief interest lies in the development of our discipline every item included here will seem to justify attention. Nevertheless, I have in extreme cases indicated where a contribution is wholly or largely derivative from previous scholarship or, conversely, proceeds in apparent ignorance of earlier contributions. In the General Introduction I have allowed myself greater subjectivity in reacting to previous scholarship.

With certain classes of item the decision to include or exclude is inevitably subjective and personal. I have tried to incorporate anthologies, readers, and translations, in order to take account of the valuable annotations that sometimes crop up in the most unexpected of places. Literary histories and surveys are also included, on the grounds that to eliminate them would be to eliminate some of the most interesting sources of insights and commentary on the minor poems. But since not all such surveys merit close attention, comprehensiveness has not been aimed at or attained here. I have on the whole avoided citing items that reflect upon gnomic poetry or wisdom literature in general, unless they make specific reference along the way to one of the texts with which this volume concerns itself. Entries in general reference works and brief references (i.e. less than a page) in books are included only if, in my judgement, they add significantly to the scholarship on the subject, or the work itself is of general relevance.

Linguistic, lexicographical, and word studies are included where, in my judgement, they embody a substantive discussion of specific elements of one of our texts. Although the standard dictionaries, grammars, encyclopaedias, and other reference works are normally excluded, on the grounds that the reader should hardly require to be reminded of their existence, on the other hand lesser-known glossaries and grammars are cited where they have something pertinent to offer. I have also made partial exceptions of a few bibliographic works, though without necessarily noting their contents in much detail. Articles largely devoted to the minutiae of textual criticism, specific emendations, restorations of lacunae, and disputes over readings and palaeography are not always fully excerpted if the information can be recovered from the apparatus in ASPR and other editions. What I have tried to convey in this category of contribution is the philosophy and method underlying the specific comments. A full listing of Riddle solutions is likewise not attempted, although I have tried to capture all solutions that either were new at the time of proposal or have been advocated with new arguments by subsequent scholars. Reviews are not systematically listed but a few that seemed especially noteworthy, in terms of furnishing new arguments and documentation or revealing interesting and characteristic attitudes towards OEW poetry, have been allowed in. Thesis material is almost entirely excluded, except where the thesis has been published or by other means entered into scholarly debate. I have provided most guidance with early German theses, since they have often played a major part in the development of scholarship and yet experience has taught me that they can be very difficult to access. I hope that the net effect of these policies will be neither minimalism nor clutter but rather a broad documentation of the reception of Old English wisdom poetry.

Many items, especially translations of texts into languages other than modern English, have proved elusive and completeness was not aimed for in this respect. The same can be said for items in Japanese periodicals. All too many of these items are of limited distribution and unavailable even to scholars who enjoy the use of very large libraries. I have for this reason decided not to encumber the bibliography with large quantities of 'unseen' fugitive items. Enquirers are referred to the year-by-year bibliographies in *Anglo-Saxon England*, which provide thorough documentation. In the case of a very few items which will be readily available to many readers but through one misfortune or another have not been accessible to me, I have tried to give some notion of their content from secondary sources.

PRINCIPLES OF ANNOTATION

Following the general policy of the series, I have aimed to annotate fully enough to provide a usable summary of the content and argument of each item. Where possible, I have let the authors speak in their own words or have paraphrased minimally, to give the reader an idea of the tone of the original. The scale of annotation, however, is not always directly proportional to the length or importance of the work annotated; sometimes, indeed, it is inversely proportional. I have worked on the principle that in the case of long and detailed works (such as Storms's *Anglo-Saxon Magic*) the main need is for a concise overview, but with short articles a detailed annotation may show the reader that the contribution is essentially irrelevant to his or her own project and thereby obviate the trouble of accessing the original.

The names of authors are normalized as far as possible, so that Klaeber, for example, always gets cited with the one given name (Frederick, not Friedrich), regardless of its form in the actual publication. Where it was necessary to list an author under more than one name in the General Bibliography, I have included a cross-reference from the earlier name in the Index of Scholars. Where possible, pagination is indicated for one-volume publications; in multi-volume works, only the number of volumes is stated. Cyrillic, Greek, and runic characters are converted to their closest Roman-alphabet equivalents, macra are used only in the context of etymological discussions, and Icelandic words and titles are cited in their modern Icelandic form.

METHODS OF ORGANIZATION

Entries in the General Bibliography chapters are listed in chronological order, by year of publication; within years, they are listed alphabetically by author except in rare cases where the chronological sequence of articles within the year was of special importance. Reviews are listed separately from the book reviewed, since the items chosen for coverage often tackle other aspects of the subject as well as those covered in the work under review. As noted, the two initial chapters list, respectively, general and miscellaneous treatments of Old English wisdom poetry. 'General' means that the item in question offers broad coverage of Old English wisdom poetry as a genre. 'Miscellaneous' means that the item deals with two or more types of wisdom poetry. In practice it has occasionally been difficult to keep these two categories apart. In the remaining chapters, I have classified by work (so that, for example, all items exclusively on the metrical Charms are listed in the relevant chapter). To form a clear view of the historical development of any particular topic, the reader should consult all three chapters (i.e. general, miscellaneous, and specialist), using the Subject Index.

The remainder of the book is designed to provide various types of guidance through the General Bibliography. The General Introduction discusses some important issues and assumptions that pervade scholarship on Old English wisdom poetry. The General Bibliography is followed by a List of Works Cited, an Index of Scholars, and a general Subject Index.

METHODS OF REFERENCE

References To Edited Texts

I have used the titles and line numbers established by the ASPR edition. References to other editions in quotations and paraphrases have been silently adjusted in accordance. Except where otherwise stated, all quotations from the Old English are taken from the ASPR edition. All translations from the Old English, except where otherwise stated, are my own.

References To Books And Articles

References with a number in bold type (e.g. 'Ettmüller, 1') are to the numbered entries in the General Bibliography. References with a date but no number (e.g.

'Hickes 1705') are to the List of Works Cited following the General Bibliography. Page references to books are to the latest edition cited, unless otherwise indicated.

General Introduction

In this introduction I shall begin by describing in some detail a few salient features of Old English versified wisdom as we find it in the context of the poetic corpus as a whole. My attention will be focused principally upon the body of knowledge, the implied audience, and the teaching strategies that this admittedly heterogeneous group of poems seems to presuppose. I shall continue by attempting to show that these features engender characteristically conflicting attitudes and responses on the part of scholarship, as it has been conducted since the early nineteenth century. Finally, I shall analyse what I see as the general scholarly movements and trends that result from these conflicts.

I

With Richard Dawkins, we might see the 'meme', or self-replicating unit of cultural inheritance, as collaborating in the determination of human evolution with the gene, or self-replicating unit of biological inheritance.[1] The meme carries information about cultural artefacts from one brain to another, much as biological genes carry information about the physical structure of an organism from one body to another. In psychology, sociology, anthropology, and other social sciences, it has been traditional to ask how people acquire ideas. The newly-emerging study of memes, or memetics, turns the question on its head and asks: how do ideas acquire people?[2] From the vantage-point of this volume, we can supply the answer that although all discourse participates in the perpetuation of memes, wisdom literature is a medium specifically designated for that purpose. During the span of history that we can reconstruct from oral and written records, it has been instrumental in the continuance of human culture. According to Morton Bloomfield (44), it has as its function to suggest a scheme of life in the broadest sense of the word, to ensure its continuance, to predict its variations, and to associate humanity with the rhythms of nature. It is an attempt to control life by some kind of order, to reduce the scope of the unexpected and sudden. Viewed in this fashion, it clearly has 'survival value' in a sense that Darwinians would recognize.

Wisdom texts in Old English may run to as much as four hundred lines or as little as two. It is characteristic of the longer texts, such as *Solomon and Saturn* or *Maxims I*, that they break up readily into smaller components, which in certain cases give the impression of having at one stage or other led an independent existence. Typically these components consist of a series of comparatively short

---

1   *The Selfish Gene* (Oxford: Oxford UP, 1976) 202–15.
2   John L. Casti, 'The Meme is the Message', *New Scientist* 153 no. 2072 (8 March 1997): 42–3.

gnomic statements on one or other topic. The statement may be as brief as a line or even a half-line, perhaps a proverb or aphorism, or it may extend to a riddle or short homiletic piece or a charm. Any attempt – and there have been many – to 'totalize' a wisdom poem as serving one function and one function alone is rendered perilous by the slippery evanescence of their topics and concerns.

If we go on to consider the content of these individual statements we find that some simply observe that a given entity or phenomenon exists. Although there may additionally be an indication of where this object belongs in a hierarchy, there is no connection to the concerns of human beings. *Rune Poem* provides examples. The *ur* ('wild ox', 'aurochs') is mentioned for its fighting capacities: the human use of its horns is left unstated. Hail is placed in an implicit hierarchy where it is the 'hwitust corna' ('whitest of grains'): its capacity to hurt human beings, poignantly registered in *The Wanderer* line 105, is not mentioned. The poplar gains its strophe chiefly on account of its method of reproduction, as contrasted to the oak, yew, and ash, whose usefulness to human beings is specifically registered. Here, as Margaret Clunies Ross has said **(1044)**, *Rune Poem* is using a human cultural instrument, the runic alphabet, as a means of ordering nature. A similar observation would apply to a few of the Exeter Book Riddles, such as those on the swan (7), the cuckoo (9), and the jay (24). The functions of the text are a blend of the taxonomic and the celebratory.

Beyond these functions, wisdom literature shows a capacity to mediate between the realm of phenomena and the realm of cultural goods. Already to note the beauty of ice (as in *Rune Poem*) or to describe the iceberg in anthropomorphic terms (as in Riddle 33) is to initiate the process, with human beings in their 'experiencer' role as the target of mediation.[3] To extend from that so as to say that ice forms a bridge (a commonplace found in both *Maxims I* line 74 and *Solomon and Saturn* line 306) intensifies the role relationship, in that the mediation is then addressed to human beings as 'agents'. Ice is a physical phenomenon. A bridge belongs in the realm of cultural goods. In connecting the two concepts, the wisdom text links a physical phenomenon to the satisfaction of a cultural need. Accordingly, W.F. Bolton **(246)** and Maureen Halsall **(1033)** identify the chief concern of *Rune Poem* as human use of earthly prosperity. In Andreas Heusler's view **(166)**, not merely *Rune Poem* but also the Exeter Book Riddles and the Anglo-Latin riddle collections have that function. Heusler has, I think, somewhat exaggerated this aspect, but certainly some of the Exeter Book Riddles do describe how an object is adapted by human beings to suit their needs, examples being the honey that becomes mead (27), the hide that becomes a book (26), the tree that becomes a battering ram (53), and the horn that becomes a drinking receptacle (14). Accounts of the exploitation of animate objects also feature in wisdom poems. *Fortunes*, characterized by Levin Schücking **(177)** as a stark commentary on everyday human need, includes an account of the taming of the hawk (lines 85–92). The bird is converted from its natural state, 'wildne fugel wloncne' ('wild, proud bird'), so that it becomes 'wynsum' ('obedient') and will return to its owner's hand or, as noted in *Maxims II* lines 17b–18a, sit on his

---

3   Here I take my analysis of role relations from Fillmorean case grammar: C.J. Fillmore, 'The Case for Case', *Universals in Linguistic Theory*, ed. E. Bach and R.T. Harms (New York: Holt, 1968) 1–88.

glove. We find a counterpart in Charm 8, which shows how to keep bees working to fulfill human needs. Charm 2 represents the esoteric end of this process, invoking a use of herbs for which the authority is Christ himself.

Conversely, the poet's mediation may have a cautionary message, addressing human beings in their role as 'patients'. We are warned off entities within Nature that engender need or even loss of life rather than satisfying needs and fostering life. Thus in *Rune Poem* line 29 ice is described in terms of its beauty but with the warning that it is 'ungemetum slidor' ('exceedingly slippery'). Likewise, the thorn (line 7), as something 'ðearle scearp' ('very sharp'), is not good to grasp. Similarly in *Maxims I* line 176 the bear is described as 'sliþhende' ('possessing cruel paws').

The ordering and utilizing of Nature is complemented in these poems by the satisfaction of needs within society, 'from man to man', as Olive Schreiner phrased it. In *Rune Poem* we are enjoined to give *feoh* 'wealth' away, *gyfu* 'gift' is noted as a source of pride, *os* ('god' or 'mouth'?) generates wisdom, and *mann* 'man' offers love for a member of his kin. The possessors of endowments, natural or acquired, are typically shown in *Gifts* as deploying them for the benefit of others. In *Maxims I* lines 100–6 we learn of the duties of a wife, in *Maxims II* lines 14–15 of the duties of good companions towards a young prince. In the Exeter Book Riddles human usefulness encompasses the dark Welsh slaves, the kneader of dough, and maybe even the one-eyed seller of garlic. If we examine Old English wisdom poetry with the psychologist Abraham Maslow's empirically-derived hierarchy of human needs in mind, we can see that all the needs he cites (for food, shelter, safety, sexual intercourse, love, esteem, self-actualization, intellectual satisfaction, and aesthetic gratification) are dealt with at one point or another.[4]

Characteristically, though, wisdom poetry examines the problematic status of natural and human resources more thoroughly than I have yet shown. My example of ice will serve to demonstrate this. Ice, as a state of matter, is normally transitory. This month's rain, in autumn, may in a positive turn of events pave the way for a useful ice-bridge in winter, when we might hope to cross to some other territory. Conversely, this month's ice may form next month's flowing river and the following month's rain. That might mean a negative turn of events if it barred you from making a journey that had been possible before the thaw. We could call these events favourable and unfavourable transience respectively. Transience is, to be sure, not a totally satisfactory term. As Christine Fell has recently reminded us, it does not accurately reproduce the native terminology, which relates instead to the contrast between that which is on loan (*læne*) and that which is eternal (*ece*).[5] We might prefer to speak more neutrally, with Peter Clemoes, of 'the junction between one action and a differing one' and agree with him that this was an aspect of life and existence upon which Anglo-Saxon attention was 'sharply focused'.[6] Nevertheless, and with these cautions, I shall continue with the term 'transience', as convenient for my purposes here.

---

4 *Motivation and Personality* (New York: Harper, 1954) 80–98.
5 'Perceptions of Transience', *The Cambridge Companion to Old English Literature*, ed. Malcolm Godden and Michael Lapidge (Cambridge: Cambridge UP, 1991) 172–89, at 173.
6 *Interactions of Thought and Language in Old English Poetry* (Cambridge: Cambridge UP, 1995) 89.

An emphasis upon transience, both favourable and unfavourable, can be seen foregrounded in *Beowulf*, where the *edwenden*, 'turn of events', is explicitly thematized (lines 280, 1774, and 2188) and where the shifts between one state and another are abrupt and (for us) even confusing. One of the fittes, for example, opens with what we should naturally interpret as a subordinating conjunction, *oþþæt* (line 1740). Often, as Raymond Page points out (**271**, 10), the poet gives a hint of future darkness amidst his descriptions of brightness and gaiety. At the moment of the creation of the great hall Heorot the poet reminds his audience of how short the life of the hall is to be. He also speaks of the likelihood that as the years of our lives accumulate we shall experience a diversity of circumstances (lines 1060b–2):

> Fela sceal gebidan
> leofes ond laþes   se þe longe her
> on ðyssum windagum   worulde bruceð.
>
> 'Anyone who makes use of the world for long here in these days of strife experiences much to love and much to hate.'
>
> (Clemoes translation, 113)

In *The Dream of the Rood*, with its riddle-like transformations and paradoxes, the adverb *hwæþre* insistently emphasizes the notion of unexpected change. As a striking example of the focus upon the antithesis between successive states Fell cites (185) the *Anglo-Saxon Chronicle* for AD 1011, with its famous words 'Wæs ða ræpling se þe ær wæs Angelcynnes heafod ond Cristendomes. Þær man mihte þa geseon earmðe þær man ær geseah blisse' ('He was then a prisoner who previously had been the head of English Christianity. There misery could then be seen where previously joy was seen'). A standard syntactical pattern, where deictic adverbs are heavily correlated so that every *ða* inevitably leads to its *ær*, magnifies the rhetorical effect.

That our own perceptions are inextricably part of the diversity, shifting from day to day, also constitutes a topic of interest for the poet. The 'rad' strophe of *Rune Poem*, for example, is most readily understood as meaning that 'riding is pleasant in prospect but hard when one has to do it', as Tom Shippey (**300**) suggests. Andrew Breeze has refined this with the proposal that here the poem is playing with two contrasting perceptions of war (**1045**).

Old English poetry is notoriously rich in sentiments about unfavourable transience. Typical are the admonitions in *The Seafarer* lines 88b–90:

> Blæd is gehnæged,
> eorþan indryhto   ealdað ond searað,
> swa nu monna gehwylc   geond middangeard.
>
> 'Splendour is humbled. Earth's nobility ages and grows sear just as each man now does throughout the middle-earth.'
>
> (Bradley translation, **317**, 334)

The 'wise man's' suspicious and slightly cynical posture is attributed by Shippey (**300**) to the experience of chronic uncertainty. The best strategy is to expect unfavourable events and to guard against them. Maslow has commented, in the context of modern empirical psychology, that unfavourable events are not necessarily distressing so long as one has previously been inducted into the knowledge that they will come and then usually go: 'throughout life it may be said that one of the main conative functions of education is this neutralizing of apparent dangers through knowledge' (85). It is as if Old English wisdom poetry were adhering to the same educational programme. The 'nyd' strophe in *Rune Poem* warns us to be aware of possible future adversity even as we live in prosperity. In *Gifts* lines 47b–8 the builder is praised because he knows how to reinforce the structure securely against sudden subsidence ('Con he sidne ræced/ fæste gefegan wiþ færdryrum'). The word *fær*, seen here, is one of the key lexical elements used to denote catastrophic turns of events. In *The Ruin* the imagery centres upon the deserted and decaying city. Where *Solomon and Saturn* is concerned, A.R. von Vincenti (**1061**) hazards the opinion that the poem represented a warning about the transitory nature of life aimed at heathen Anglo-Saxons, although it is more straightforwardly construed as another routine assertion for the benefit of an already Christian audience.

Of course, unexpected changes might be for the good, and hence the wise person issues warnings against premature despair. The speaker in *Deor* famously consoles himself with the refrain 'Þæs ofereode, þisses swa mæg' ('That passed; this also may': lines 7, 13, 17, 20, 27, and 42). The idea of encountering a good unexpected thing or event is instrumental to the structure of *The Descent into Hell*, which seems to start off-topic with the spectacle of the Marys coming to Christ's tomb only to be surprised at his resurrection (cf. Shippey **300**, 38–9). In *Maxims I* lines 39b–44 we are told that blind persons may unexpectedly recover their sight. This is of course true in a perfectly routine medical sense, though the possibility of a spiritual interpretation has been canvassed by Frederick M. Biggs and Sandra McEntire (**625**).

> Blind sceal his eagna þolian.
> Oftigen biþ him torhtre gesihþe,   ne magon hi ne tunglu bewitian,
> swegltorht, sunnan ne monan.   Þæt him biþ sar in his mode,
> onge þonne he hit ana wat,   ne weneð þæt him þæs edhwyrft cyme.
> Waldend him þæt wite teode,   se him mæg wyrpe syllan,
> hælo of heofodgimme,   gif he wat heortan clæne.
>
> 'A blind man must do without his eyes. He is deprived of clear sight, his eyes cannot perceive the stars, bright in the sky, nor the sun and moon. This is painful to him in his mind, distressing when he knows this one thing alone, and does not expect any change in it will come to him. The Ruler fixed this torment for him, and can give him recovery, a cure for the jewel in his head, if he knows the man's heart is pure.' (Shippey text and translation, **300**, 66–7)

The advice in *The Wanderer* line 113 to 'know the remedy' can be seen as relating to this general aspect of transience. Conversely, identification of an incorrect remedy spells doom, as we are assured in *The Seafarer* lines 100–01:

> Ne mæg þære sawle   þe biþ synna ful
> gold to geoce   for godes egsan.
>
> 'Gold cannot benefit the soul that is full of sins in face of the fear of God.'

The ultimately certain remedy, so *The Seafarer* advises us (line 109), is to 'stieran . . . strongum mode, ond þæt on staþelum healdan' ('steer a wilful heart and keep it fixed on stable points': Bradley translation, **317**, 334). These stable points appear to be the 'eorþan sceatas ond uprodor' ('corners of the earth and the heavens above': line 105).

Unexpectedness and diversity may express themselves spatially as well as temporally. The vast diversity of creation is directly thematized in some poems. Clemoes comments that 'over the world at large the diverse *æþelu* of all beings amounted to a huge fruitfulness which was quite beyond calculation' (76). The power of Nature in its sheer copiousness to surpass our human understanding is the first theme touched upon in *The Panther* (lines 1–3):

> Monge sindon   geond middangeard
> unrimu cynn,   þe we æþelu ne magon
> ryhte areccan   ne rim witan.

> 'Many are the countless species throughout the world whose noble qualities we cannot rightly recount, whose numbers we cannot know.'   (Bradley translation, **317**, 353)

In *Maxims I* lines 12b–15a the world is envisaged as containing a series of 'islands', each replete with its own unknowable multiplicity of kinds:

>   He us geþonc syleð,
> missenlicu mod,   monge reorde.
> Feorhcynna fela   fæþmeþ wide
> eglond manig.

> 'He [God] grants us rationality, diverse tempers and many tongues. Many an island broadly embraces a profusion of kinds of life.'
>   (Bradley translation, **317**, 346)

No doubt the practical experience of many travellers and voyagers is reflected in the literary theme of travelling from island to island augmenting one's knowledge. In *Solomon and Saturn* the 'islands' traversed by Saturn may equate with the multitude of heathen nations (Charles Wright, **340**). Alternatively, such nations as Lybia, Greece, and India may even have been regarded as islands in the conventional sense, as proposed by Dennis Cronan (**1107**). In the prose text *The Wonders of the East* the phrase 'ðonne is sum ealand' ('then there is an island', translating the Latin 'est et alia insula') recurrently preludes the account of some new prodigy.[7] In *The Phoenix* the Earthly Paradise is presented as the ultimately miraculous island, differing from the rest in that transience is outlawed. So bizarre is this notion that the poet can only express it negatively, invoking seasons, features of topography, and other transient features familiar from his England. Altogether, the diversity of this world is such that only the wisest and best-informed can hold it all in their heads.

Diversity extends itself into a formal principle. In the two sets of *Maxims* the shifts of subject matter are so frequent as to suggest a random conspectus of the world. The alliterative associativeness tends to emphasize diversity even where it is not explicitly thematized – as in *Maxims II*, where every type of location, whether hall, fen, or glove, is appropriate for somebody's or something's needs and one never can tell which type will be mentioned next. The Exeter Book

---

[7]   Andy Orchard, *Pride and Prodigies. Studies in the Monsters of the Beowulf-Manuscript* (Cambridge: Brewer, 1995) 183–203.

Riddles form a rich and randomly-ordered catalogue of diversity and they do it, moreover, without any demonstrable ventures into the more genuinely esoteric solutions, such as 'hippopotamus', favoured by Aldhelm and Eusebius. These enigmas repeatedly conjure up new 'wonders' for us to contemplate (e.g. Riddle 47 line 2). The same unsystematic awe infects *Solomon and Saturn*: 'Ac hwæt is þæt wundor ðe geond ðas worold færeð' ('But what is that wonder that travels throughout this world?': line 280). Andy Orchard's analysis makes it clear that *The Wonders of the East* is essentially comparable to the poetic texts in possessing no fixed principle for the ordering of its numerous prodigies (26–7). Only occasionally in our texts do the juxtapositions arise from a predictable collocation of lexical items or *topoi*, as in *Gifts* lines 68b–70a:

> Sum biþ þegn gehweorf
> on meoduhealle. Sum biþ meares gleaw,
> wicgcræfta wis.
>
> 'One is a servant appointed in the mead-hall. One is discerning over a horse and experienced in equestrian skills.'
>
> (Bradley translation, **317**, 327)

We find the same 'hall/horse' juxtaposition thematized in the 'rad' strophe of *Rune Poem* (lines 13–15), where, as we saw, there is a cryptic contrast between sitting in the hall fancying riding an easy pursuit and the uncomfortable jolting reality on the horse's back.

It follows from this spectacle of diversity and the unexpected that our arrival at means of satisfying our needs is not necessarily achieved by a superficial contemplation of phenomena. Although we might expect fire to 'meltan' wood, a truism enshrined in *Maxims I* line 71, yew-wood is an exception, in that it resists fire and is slow to burn away: these properties are, as Roberto Solari observes (**1042**), the subject of special attention in *Rune Poem*. A reputation for certain bad qualities on the part of any object or person may lead the unwise to ignore potential good qualities. We are assured in *Gifts* lines 31b–3a that

> Sum biþ wonspedig,
> heardsælig hæle, biþ hwæþre gleaw
> modes cræfta.
>
> 'One is unsuccessful, an ill-fortuned man, but yet he is skilful in the arts of the mind.' (Bradley translation, **317**, 327)

More fundamentally, surface phenomena do not point directly to what in human culture we enshrine as abiding truths because the world as a whole is constantly in a flux of change and entropy. The statement in *Maxims II* line 10 that 'soð bið swicolost' expresses aphoristically the notion that the truth is tricky to arrive at.

Accordingly, wisdom and the getting of wisdom are graded in our texts according to a definite hierarchy. At the bottom of the hierarchy are Grendel-like beings, who do not recognize bounties when they see them (*Beowulf* line 681). Then come babes and children, who need parental guidance, as is noted in *Fortunes* lines 7–8a:

> Fergað swa ond feþað fæder ond modor,
> giefað ond gierwaþ.

'Thus his father and mother lead him along and guide his footsteps
and provide for him and clothe him.' (Bradley translation, **317**, 341)

As young adults they move up to the next step in the hierarchy, but still fall
noticeably short in their capacity to recognize their duties and the ways of this
world. *Maxims I* (lines 45b–7) counsels us to train a young man rather as we
might a hawk:

> Læran sceal mon geongne monnan,
> trymman ond tyhtan   þæt he teala cunne,
> oþþæt hine mon atemedne hæbbe.

'A young man must be taught and encouraged and persuaded in order
that he be thoroughly competent, until he has been tamed.'

(Bradley translation, **317**, 347)

Admittedly an exceptional few can be simultaneously young and wise. *Beowulf*
lines 1925–9 testifies to the precocious wisdom of Hygd.

> Hygd [wæs] swiðe geong,
> wis welþungen,   þeah ðe wintra lyt
> under burhlocan   gebiden hæbbe,
> Hæreþes dohtor.

'Hæreth's daughter Hygd [was] very young, wise, accomplished,
though she had lived few winters within the enclosed stronghold.'[8]

The hero himself, though no *senex*, earns praise from Hroðgar for his *sapientia* as
well as his *fortitudo* (lines 1841–5):

> Þe þa wordcwydas   wigtig Drihten
> on sefan sende;   ne hyrde ic snotorlicor
> on swa geongum feore   guman þingian.
> Þu eart mægenes strang,   ond on mode frod,
> wis wordcwida.

'The all-knowing Lord sent those utterances into your mind. I have
never heard a man speak in public more wisely at so young an age.
You are strong in might and also mature in mind, prudent in speech.'

(Burrow text and translation, **333**, 132)

An Anglo-Saxon idealization of the *senex puer*, or prematurely wise boy (or
young man), is cited by Burrow (**333**) from Alcuin's *Life of Willibrord*, which
describes how the missionary saint showed from early boyhood such virtue and
good sense 'that you might think that our times had seen the birth of a new
Samuel. . . . Thus every day this boy of virtuous disposition advanced, so that he
might transcend the tender years of his boyhood in the seriousness of his
behaviour; and he became like an old man in wisdom, though slight and frail in
body' (100). God himself, appearing as a ship's captain to St Andrew in *Andreas*
(lines 505–9), is taken by the apostle for a *juvenis senex*:

8   Michael Swanton, *Beowulf edited with an Introduction, Notes, and New Prose Translation* (Manchester: Manchester UP, 1978) 127.

Þu eart seolfa geong,
wigendra hleo,   nalas wintrum frod;
hafast þeh on fyrhðe,   faroðlacende,
eorles ondsware.   Æghwylces canst
worda for worulde   wislic andgit.

'You are yourself young, leader of men, and not at all old in years;
yet you have the power of mind, seafarer, to reply like a grown man.
You can judge the true significance of every man's worth in the
world.' (Burrow translation, **333**, 103)

If precocious youths flourish from time to time, so too do retarded adults. Some
never reach the stage of recognizing the instability and full diversity of this
world. Ignorant of possible changes and fluctuations, like stockmarket investors
in the late 1980s, they display an overweening confidence in the present state of
affairs. They understand how to meet their needs only in terms of what
Providence happens to be currently furnishing. Even Beowulf, so wise before his
time, receives a sharp reminder from Hroðgar that sorrow is always apt to be in
the offing: 'Ne frin þu æfter sælum! Sorh is geniwod/ Denigea leodum' ('Do not
enquire after happiness! Sorrow is renewed for the Danish people': 1322–3a).
Admittedly, there were decided disincentives against augmenting one's stock of
wisdom, as Clemoes has pointed out (344): 'To be wise down here was not
merely to be simple. As the father in *Precepts* observed in a gnomic saying with
echoes of the Old Testament, "Seldan snottor guma sorgleas blissað,/ swylce dol
seldon drymeð sorgful/ ymb his forðgesceaft, nefne he fæhþe wite." ("Rarely is
the wise man glad without sorrow, and likewise the fool seldom tempers joy with
sorrow about his destiny, unless he knows of hostility.")' Indeed, the father in
Precepts is characterized as a man weighed down by vexations and sorrows
('tornsorgna full': line 76). He would presumably agree with the speaker in *The
Wanderer* that there is no reason why the mind should not grow dark, in view of
all the sad things it knows (lines 58–62a: cf. Shippey **300**, 27) and with the
speaker in *Maxims II* that 'wea bið wundrum clibbor' ('grief is amazingly
clinging': line 13).

But if one triumphs over these deterrents, a fuller recognition of the true
nature of the world will come normally with one's advanced years. *The Wanderer*
proclaims (lines 64–5a) that 'ne mæg weorþan wis wer, ær he age/ wintra dæl in
woruldrice' ('a man cannot become wise, before he possesses his share of years
(literally, winters) in the kingdom of the world'). Hroðgar in *Beowulf* (lines
1724a and 2114a) is just such a 'wintrum frod' person. *Maxims II* lines 10b–11
declares:

gomol [biþ] snoterost,
fyrngearum frod,   se þe ær feala gebideð.

'An old man knows most things, a man made wise by distant years,
who has experienced a great deal before.'
(Shippey text and translation, **300**, 76–7)

What role for wise women in this hierarchy? We have already seen Hygd placed
in the same *juvenis senex* group as Beowulf. Wealhþeow in *Beowulf* gains praise
as 'cynna gemyndig', 'expert in lineages' (line 613). St Helen, the eponymous
heroine of *Elene*, matches wits with Jewish men of learning in a particularly

confrontational series of dialogues. Helen Damico points out detailed similarities in the attributes of Wealhþeow and Helen, among them acuity, wisdom, tenacity of memory, and strength of mind.[9] Analysing the treatment of Judith in the poem of that name, Orchard notes (9) a change from her characterization in the Vulgate and in Ælfric's homily: in *Judith* we are expressly invited to consider her beauty, courage, and wisdom. She is among other things a 'snoteran idese' ('wise lady': line 55) and a 'gleawhydig wif' ('prudent woman': line 148). Additionally, Fred Robinson has conjectured (352) that, where the *Maxims* are concerned, we might well envisage a woman composing a poem that transmits various kinds of folk wisdom to one's people, especially when that wisdom encompasses a sensitive comment on child-rearing and an account of a Frisian woman welcoming her husband home from the sea. Disappointingly, however, these are mere wishful speculations that cannot be confirmed from documentary evidence.

True wisdom will come the more readily if the elderly person has not simply lived for many winters but also as a matter of deliberate policy cultivated an awareness of vicissitudes, mutability, and the world's few stable principles. The poems dramatize this process by staging a dialogue between one wise person and another, as they match wits, compare notes, and pass on traditions. *Vainglory* opens with a speaker who by implication is himself elderly passing on wisdom from an elderly informant:

> Hwæt, me frod wita   on fyrndagum
> sægde, snottor ar,   sundorwundra fela

> 'Lo! a sage counsellor in days long gone, a wise informant, told me many unique wonders.'
>   (Modified from the Bradley translation, 317, 335)

The opening of *Maxims I* (1–4a) presupposes a more active dialogue:

> Frige mec frodum wordum!   Ne læt þinne ferð ontælne,
> degol þæt þu deopost cunne.   Nelle ic þe min dyrne gesecgan,
> gif þu me þinne hygecræft hylest   ond þine heortan geþohtas.
> Gleawe men sceolon gieddum wrixlan.

> 'Sound me out with shrewd words. Let your own intellect not be hidden, nor that of which you have deepest understanding be kept secret. I will not speak my mystery to you if you hide from me the faculty of your reason and the reflections of your heart. Discerning people must exchange maxims.' (Bradley translation, 317, 345–6)

This is to establish both a subject position and an interlocutor position at the outset, and they are refreshed in the audience's memory by a later reprise (lines 18b–23a):

> Þing sceal gehegan
> frod wiþ frodne;   biþ hyra ferð gelic. . . .
> Ræd sceal mid snyttro,   ryht mid wisum

---

9   *Beowulf's Wealhþeow and the Valkyrie Tradition* (Madison, WI: U of Wisconsin P, 1984) 28.

'Wise men hold meetings together. Their minds are similar. . . . Good
advice goes with wisdom, justice with the wise.'

(Clemoes translation, 113)

Solomon and Saturn confronts Solomon in all his wisdom with a travelling wise
man who engages in learned disputations – a motif derived, Katherine O'Brien
O'Keeffe (1110) believes, from the *Cosmographia* of Æthicus Ister. In the Exeter
Book Riddles the implicitly wise speaker of Riddle 1 addresses the enigma to a
'þoncol mon' (line 12) who can guess the answer. Such dialogues are implicitly
or explicitly extended to the audience. The speaker's self-alignment with wisdom
reflexively invites the audience to perform the same act of alignment.

Beyond the wise old people are the prophets. A mysterious and unnamed
prophet ('se wit(e)ga': lines 50 and 81) is entrusted with the moral message of
Vainglory. A native liking for the figure of the 'ancient sage' may well have been
reinforced, in poems like *Solomon and Saturn*, *Daniel*, *Elene*, or *Exodus*, by
Christian learning: Anglo-Saxon poets provide a liberal representation of
prophets, wise men, and soothsayers among their heroes from Christian history,
as noted by Shippey (47). In his analysis of the characterization of Daniel, Paul
G. Remley notes how he emerges in the poem as a figure of judgement and good
counsel:[10]

> witga cwom,
> Daniel to dome,   se wæs drihtne gecoren,
> snotor and soðfæst.
>
> 'A wise man came to judgement, Daniel, who was favoured by God,
> a wise and truthful man.' (Remley text and translation, 247)

As Remley goes on to show, collocations of poetic vocabulary running through
the entire poem celebrate the prophet's acumen, drawing on terms relating to
counsel and wisdom, law and covenant.

Beyond the prophets in turn is God, with his divine foreknowledge and a total
command of predictive statements that far outgoes all others in the hierarchy.
Continuing from the lines I have already quoted about parental care of the child,
Fortunes lines 8b–9 remarks that

> God ana wat
> hwæt him weaxendum   winter bringað.
> 'Only God knows what the years will bring him as he grows up.'
>
> (Bradley translation, 317, 341)

Maxims I informs us that only the Lord knows where the plague will go after it
departs from our country (lines 29–30; cf. Shippey 300, 64). According to
Maxims II lines 61–6 nobody but God knows where the soul goes after death:

> Meotud ana wat
> hwyder seo sawul sceal   syððan hweorfan,
> and ealle þa gastas   þe for gode hweorfað
> æfter deaðdæge,   domes bidað

---

10 *Old English Biblical Verse. Studies in Genesis, Exodus, and Daniel*, Cambridge Studies in Anglo-Saxon England 16 (Cambridge: Cambridge UP, 1996) 247.

on fæder fæðme.   Is seo forðgesceaft
digol and dyrne;   drihten ana wat,
nærgende fæder.   Næni eft cymeð
hider under hrofas,   þe þæt her for soð
mannum secge   hwylc sy meotodes gesceaft,
sigefolca gesetu,   þær he sylfa wunað.

'Only the Ruler knows where the soul must turn to then, as with all
the spirits who go before God after the day of their deaths, and wait
for judgement in their father's embrace. One's future fate is dark and
hidden. Only the Lord knows, the father who saves us. No man
comes back again under our roofs to tell men here for sure what the
Ruler is really like, or to describe the homes of the conquerors, where
he lives himself.' (Shippey text and translation, **300**, 78–9)

God's home is thereby distinguished from those distant 'islands' that can be
visited by merchants and travellers. This is the bourne from which no traveller
returns. Clearly statements such as those I have quoted above are not some
acknowledgement of an existential mystery or complexity at the heart of human
life but rather a conceding of ultimate wisdom to the supernal being, symmetrical
with the acts of deference required at the lower levels of the hierarchy of wisdom.
Given its expressly Christian message, *Order* is to be understood in the same
sense when it insists that nobody is so wise as to know the start or finish of the
sun's path (lines 78–81: cf. Shippey **300**).

The discourse of wisdom, as we see it in our extant texts, defines itself as the
voice of experience speaking to inexperience. Its tendency is to privilege the old
over the young, the wise over the foolhardy, humility over pride, and
contemplation over action. From *Maxims I* lines 45b–7 and Hroðgar's speech to
the hero in *Beowulf* (lines 1840–5) we gather that it was customary for young
persons to be indoctrinated with the wisdom of their elders. Sometimes the
subject position is overt, as in *Precepts*, and sometimes merely implied. Either
way, the discourse lays claim to a comprehensive but compendious wisdom. It
attempts to convey in a nutshell the full range of spatial and temporal diversity.
Spatial breadth is as crucial to *Solomon and Saturn* and *The Seafarer* as it is to
Widsith. Temporal depth is as crucial to Charm 2, *Vainglory, Beowulf*, and *The
Wanderer* as it is to genealogical treatises. Hugh Magennis documents an
Anglo-Saxon preoccupation with the past and a notion of a shared Germanic
heritage.[11] It is a related impulse, I would urge, that motivates the sporadic
heathen allusions in our texts. Ing, Wyrd, and even Woden were not utterly
excluded; instead they underwent marginalization or re-interpretation. Wyrd
could be conveniently rationalized as subject to God and therefore as an example
of order (cf. Barbara Raw, **54**). Yet simultaneously Wyrd is accorded what could
be interpreted by anyone who chose as pre-Christian significance in *Maxims II*
lines 4–5 (cf. Stanley, **296**). In   *Rune Poem*, with its paronomasia and
etymological play,   the text equivocates between pagan atavism and
Latin-Christian mimicry in the possible denotations of *os* ('god' and 'mouth'
respectively, the former cognate with Old Norse *áss*): two different systems of

---

11 *Images of Community in Old English Poetry*, Cambridge Studies in Anglo-Saxon England 18 (Cambridge: Cambridge UP, 1996) 5.

wisdom compete for the one lexical item. In Charm 8 the use of the term *sigewif* for the bees imposes mythological depth upon its commonplace referent. The speaker's self-construction of aged wisdom is reinforced by these allusions to the long ago and far away. Invoking whole realms of lived experience, the discourse is so framed as to exceed the competence of its youthful target audience. Add to this cultural construction the biological probability that only the exceptional Anglo-Saxon survived into old age (cf. Page, **271**, 9–12) and we can grasp two key factors in the speaker's sense of empowerment, entitlement to respect, and rhetorical effectiveness.

II

Given these pretensions it is decidedly embarrassing that the extant manifestations of the discourse frequently appear so platitudinous as positively to bring discredit upon George Eliot's 'men of maxims'. Shippey has made a number of interesting observations on this score (**300**). He notes how difficult it is for us to tell whether the sayings in *Maxims* represent traditional received truths or personal discoveries on the part of the poet, banal statements of fact or invitations to read significance into cryptic remarks. Equally, he thinks, the meaning seems either obfuscated or platitudinous to us nowadays in *Order* and *Precepts*. In *Order* the poet, having made the ambitious declaration that he will tell us more about God than we can understand, balks at his task, and comes out only with the flat statement that 'His power is very great': his wisdom tells us very little more than we might have realized for ourselves, though it does so with tremendous assertiveness (3). Susan Deskis, pondering the failure of scholars to identify the full range of possible analogues for proverb-like statements in *Beowulf*, attributes some of the blame to a besetting ambivalence about the gnomic passages: 'Unsubtle pronouncements like "All men must die" have been considered unworthy of the *Beowulf*-poet, and hence ignored.'[12] Other scholars evaluating other poems have been equally unflattering. Bruce Dickins (**1004**) describes *Rune Poem* as a child's mnemonic not more pregnant with occult significance than 'Thirty days hath September'; Kemp Malone compares its value for rune-masters with that of ABC poems for learners of the alphabet (**30**). The Exeter Book Riddles, though certainly elusive enough on occasion and often (as we have seen) addressed to the wise, descend to the commonplace when they virtually solve themselves. Marjorie Anderson and Blanche C. Williams (**189**) feel impelled to defend them as charming short poems and, as we shall see later, many other scholars have been driven to similar apologies.

    In the midst of these worries, let us not forget that platitude can have clear social functions. Like many a platitudinous speech nowadays, expressions of poetic wisdom in Anglo-Saxon times may have been simultaneously expected and resented, respected and quietly ignored. Statements of the banal may have served a purpose that it is difficult for us to reconstruct or envisage. In particular, they may have indicated a specific subject position – one of authority, addressing

---

12 *Beowulf and the Medieval Proverb Tradition* (Tempe, AZ: Medieval and Renaissance Texts and Studies, 1996) 2.

itself to perennial human goods and needs and reiterating truths that all children need to be taught and which have served society well down the generations. The insertion of *Maxims II* into a *Chronicle* manuscript is plausibly explained by Frederic Cassidy and Richard Ringler (273) on the basis that it satisfied Anglo-Saxons as a solemn, profound, and fittingly sententious prologue to a serious historical work. The sententious generalizations which Beowulf uses to preface his speech of consolation to Hroðgar after the death of Æschere (lines 1384–94) establish him as a virtual 'frod guma', as noted by Burrow (333, 133). We could offer a similar justification for the coastguard's formulaic utterance to Beowulf:[13]

> Æghwæþres sceal
> scearp scyldwiga   gescad witan,
> worda ond worca,   se þe wel þenceð.
>
> 'A sharp shield-fighter who thinks clearly must know the difference between the two things: words and deeds.'
>
> (*Beowulf* lines 287–9: Swanton text and translation, 48–9)

Likewise, Byrhtwold gains authority from traditional wisdom in his famous speech 'hige sceal þe heardra . . .'.[14] As M.A.L. Locherbie-Cameron points out, the generalized nature of the half-lines places them in the tradition of proverbs or maxims (78). In the words 'A mæg gnornian/ se þe nu fram þis wigplegan wendan þenceð' ('He may grieve forever, who means now to turn from this battle': lines 315–16), Byrhtwold may be quoting a well-known proverb and then applying the quotation to his particular situation. Like Polonius, this old warrior had an apt word or saying for the occasion; unlike Polonius, he could translate proverb into action in a manner the poet presents for admiration (80). Our conclusion can only be that platitude constitutes an intrinsic element in the hegemonic discourse of wisdom.

David Lawton finds a similar blend of platitude and authority in English fifteenth-century poetry: 'the currency of "conventional platitudes" suggests a wide-spread interest in them; that is, it says more about a culture than about a dull author'.[15] In Lawton's postulated culture 'lord and servant share the same concerns and a similar, Boethian, frame of reference' (789). At the top of their society, 'fifteenth-century magnates seem to have taken a gloomy pleasure in the laws that bound them, more than the least of their subjects, to Fortune's wheel. The more they could find out about those laws, the better; hence the demand for encyclopedias of mutability and tips on others' mistakes, compilations of what are commonplaces to us but may have appeared to them as political philosophy.' Here is an analysis that can readily be applied to the Old English scene, with its Alfredian translation of Boethius, its cautionary tales of royal errors in *Beowulf* and scriptural verse, and its corpus of wisdom poetry, notably *Fortunes*.

To that analysis, however, I would add that utterances of wisdom must always be considered in their dialogic context, not in themselves. Like other cultural

---

13 Cf. Tom Shippey, *Beowulf* (London: Arnold, 1978) 12–15.
14 M.A.L. Locherbie-Cameron, 'Some things the *Maldon* poet did not say', *Parergon* NS 13.1 (July 1995): 69–80.
15 'Dullness and the Fifteenth Century', *ELH* 54 (1987): 761–99, at 775.

goods, they are not something that transcends the culture but rather an element located within culture. Some scholars have erroneously characterized wisdom texts as embodying a monolithic 'wisdom of the people', co-extensive with the society as a whole. Margaret Williams, for instance, considers them in a chapter revealingly titled 'A Pondering People' (28). Raw sees (54) their gnomic and predictive statements as conveying an agreed view of both nature and human behaviour. In fact, though, what constitutes wisdom must have had to be renegotiated in successive generations and modes of production. *Maxims II* sagely warns that youth will oppose age in parallel fashion to the opposition between good and evil, life and death, and light and darkness (lines 51–2); aged wisdom might indeed find the linkage of polarizations in this aphorism disconcerting. As if to confirm the aphorism, sometimes in our Old English texts we can hear the voice of normally repressed inexperience asserting itself. An undercurrent of youthful defiance emerges in Beowulf's self-defence against the accusations of Unferð:

> Wit þæt gecwædon   cnihtwesende
> ond gebeotedon   – wæron begen þa git
> on geogoðfeore –   þæt wit on garsecg ut
> aldrum neðdon,   ond þæt geæfndon swa.   (*Beowulf* lines 535–8)

> 'As boys we two came to an agreement and boasted – we were both then still in our youth – that we would risk our lives out on the ocean; and we did just that.' (Swanton translation, 59)

We can infer that youth has its own imperatives, in respect of which the hegemonic wisdom purveyed in our texts possesses only limited understanding and control. Perhaps youthful resentment was also whetted on occasions when, as in some other societies, age chose to withhold its secrets jealously, rather as presupposed in the opening to *Maxims I* cited above. The conversion of the conveniently titled Symphosius Enigma 95, 'luscus allium vendens', into the potentially baffling Riddle 86 that we encounter in the Exeter Book may offer a hint in that direction. The riddler jealously guards his secret, a stance that might even remind us, if we are nativistically inclined, of the dangerous one-eyed riddler in *Hervarar saga ok Heiðreks*. Easy associations may have linked this type of jealousy and grudging, where the dispensing of wisdom was concerned, with that of the stereotype niggardly king, who evades the sharing of treasure with his warband.

Attitudes which by way of shorthand we can call 'young' and 'old' must have waged a perpetual contest not just within the community as a whole but also within the individual subject and the heteroglossia of the individual text. The various attestations of the word *wlonc* provide us with a case study of the dialogism to which I am referring. Attempts to construct a univocal significance for this lexical item have inevitably proved unsuccessful. For instance, Frank H. Whitman (899) unduly privileges the notion of 'pride', Bogislav von Lindheim (815) that of 'lust' or 'greed' in their respective studies. When Bernard F. Huppé (270) asserts that the phrase 'wlonce wigsmiþas' in *Vainglory* was striking enough, with its encapsulation of heathen and warrior values, to be borrowed by the poet of *The Battle of Brunanburh*, this is to make unjustified assumptions about both semantic univocality and direct literary influence. Michael von Rüden (308) does better when he suggests that the semantic imprecision attaching to *wlonc* is symptomatic of cultural tensions within Anglo-Saxon society as a whole. Taken together, the attestations reveal a contest between (negatively – a wise old person's natural view) 'vainglorious, presumptuous' and (positively – an ambitious young person's natural view) 'splendid, confident'. The modern English words 'proud' and 'bold' are the sites of comparable contestations.

Similarly, there is no need to invent a special contextual meaning for *druncen*, such as 'having consumed alcohol, having drunk', to explain its apparently neutral use in *Beowulf* line 1231. The word means 'drunk', 'drunken', just as now: what is crucial is the social ambivalence toward drunkenness. Erich Budde (**124**) points out that the admonitions in *Precepts* and in *Fortunes*, where a drunkard's fate is described in chilling terms, sit side by side with the flippancy of Riddle 27. Deplorable to a homilist, drunkenness is functional if it spurs a young man to make a boast that, once carried through successfully, will result in good for the community as a whole. Young men, after all, have perennially been deemed expendable by society – and have acquiesced in that judgement.[16]

Thus wisdom literature exists within and to some extent consists of a dialogism between experience and inexperience. Add to this picture Fell's observation that 'whether we are talking about poets writing in Latin or the vernaculars, in England of the eighth century onwards or Europe in the sixth century, one link between them is the anguished affection with which a Christian poet regards those lovely things of the world that the preachers tell him to despise' (177). In a dialogic system the poet and the preacher inhabit the same discourse and even the same individual subject. As we read our texts, therefore, two sentiments conflict with each other. We sometimes find the phenomena of the world registered and even glorified and cherished in a fashion consonant with the immediate impressions and enthusiasms of what Blake called Innocence. But simultaneously they are set in a context of Experience that reveals their impermanence, along with our human inability to know them in their full diversity or to predict the precise moment of their decline and fall.

III

If the esteem in which wisdom poetry is held has varied sharply, epoch by epoch, the explanation lies in the dialogic process which I have been describing. The works of Chaucer and the generation of poets that followed him exhibit analogous tensions. At first sight Chaucer might seem to be a debunker of wisdom. The youthful protagonist in *The Book of the Duchess* brings salutary consolation yet he is characterized as maladroit and glib and is definitely given no credit for speaking as a *puer senex*. The narrative framework within which Chaucer places his *Monk's Tale* has the effect of calling down ridicule upon Boccaccio's copious wisdom on 'men's falls'. A generation later, then, the

---

16 Cf. Dorothy Whitelock's comment that 'whether terms such as "wlonc" ("proud") or "wingal" ("drunken" or at best "having abundantly drunk") are pejorative will depend upon the moral seriousness of the poem in which they occur' ('*The Wanderer, The Seafarer*, and the Genre of *Planctus*', *Anglo-Saxon Poetry. Essays in Appreciation. For John C. McGalliard*, ed. Lewis E. Nicholson and Dolores Warwick Frese (Notre Dame: U of Notre Dame P, 1975) 192–207, at 204).

reverential amplification of the same Boccaccian wisdom in Lydgate's *Fall of Princes* seems to betoken a conservative's reaction against Chaucer's irreverence. But closer scrutiny shows that debunking was not the totality of Chaucerian attitudes. For example, Egeus in *The Knight's Tale* may strike us as platitudinous and plethoric, yet no hint is given that the characters find him so, or would wish him absent from the scene. Lawton (780) comments on 'the tenacity of the Chaucer received by the fifteenth century, a Chaucer radically different from ours. The works most often cited by fifteenth-century poets are, in rough order, *Troilus*, *Melibeus*, the Clerk's Tale, the Monk's Tale, *Boece*, the Knight's Tale and the Parson's Tale (seven uniformly serious works followed by the Wife of Bath and the Man of Law). Most of them are emphasized by Lydgate in the prologue to the *Fall of Princes*.' This wisdom-loving Chaucer evidently coexisted with the debunker both *in propria persona* and in the literary tradition of his successors.

Wisdom is no less a contested element in the plays of Shakespeare. In the spirit of western individualism that informs the play *Hamlet*, the hero occupies the position of restless, sceptical, intellectual youth, whereas Polonius is identified with complacent, platitudinous, unenquiring age. At first sight, then, the play has marginalized the wisdom of the old. Yet the Polonius of *Hamlet* compares favourably in wisdom with the speaker of *Precepts* (7, 31) or *Maxims*. Furthermore, how many in the audience, even in our sceptical modern age, have gratefully internalized the following Polonian doctrine (I.3.75–7)?

> Neither a borrower nor a lender be,
> For loan oft loses both itself and friend,
> And borrowing dulls the edge of husbandry.

Within our selves we are both Hamlet and Polonius.

The picture that emerges from these examples is that, all along, whether in Cynewulf's or Chaucer's or Shakespeare's England, the expression of wisdom has held a characteristically ambiguous place in society. Similar ambivalences to those I have just described find themselves mirrored in the judgements of the scholars of the last two hundred years, as they contemplate the whole corpus of Old English poetry, since much if not all of it contains strongly gnomic or moralistic or didactic elements. Largely on the positive side have been characterizations that reify and emphasize such aspects as profundity, childlike spontaneity and directness, the self-expression of the folk, and fidelity to paganism. Largely on the negative side have been characterizations that reify and emphasize such aspects as platitudinousness, conventionality, the ventriloquy of a colonized mentality, and compliance with Christianity. In the ensuing paragraphs I shall take these positions up and show how, with all their conflicting implications, they permeate scholarship on Old English wisdom poetry.

The characterization of Anglo-Saxon wisdom as truthful, simple, fresh to the point of childlikeness, and directly responsive to personal observation of Nature and other forces in the universe pervades nineteenth-century scholarship and is not dead even now. Our own consciousness is seen as having forfeited its pristine native wisdom, which is the object of a keen nostalgia in some segments of nineteenth- and twentieth-century thought, and as having come to depend upon mediation, impersonality, dissimulation, false sentiment, mystification, hypersensitivity, and so on. The scholarly processes involved here can be likened to attempts on the part of colonizers to comprehend the culture of the native peoples. Misrecognition on the part of the observer can occur at any point in either situation.[17] Despite the loudly proclaimed self-criticism, the modern attitude toward the ancient 'natives' has about it a goodly amount of *de haut en bas*. Gary Kelly speaks of a similar ambivalence between nostalgia and patronage in discussing the British nineteenth-century reception of the *Thousand and One Nights*: 'While many critics and intellectuals saw these Arabian tales as the childish extravagances of a childish culture, appealing to the childish in the West (mostly women and children), others . . . argued that the tales, especially the adventures of Sinbad, had the simplicity and force of epic literature that only a vigorous, youthful culture could produce.'[18]

I shall cite only a few such characterizations here, since they are too familiar to need full documentation. For George Anderson the childlike love of sound, rhythm, and fancy that is habitually associated with an isolated people is exhibited in the metrical Charms, the Exeter Book Riddles, and the gnomic verses (**31**). For Agop Hacikyan (**846**) the temper and the philosophy of a young, virile race is attested in the Exeter Book Riddles. For some critics the attribute of spontaneity is evident in the uncontrolled use of imagistic language. Albert H. Tolman believes that 'simile and allegory are too conscious and elaborate for the Anglo-Saxon mind'; 'they were too vitally interested in what they said to be able to hold it off and examine it coolly with a view to the most effective presentation'.[19] Francis Gummere (**629**) argues that the juxtaposition of three different metaphors in *Order* line 19, 'bewritan in gewitte wordhordes cræft' ('to write the power of the word-hoard in the mind'), attests to a stage prior to conscious attempts at figurative language. For Elizabeth Deering Hanscom the lack of mediation in Old English poetry is the crucial feature: poets 'looked at nature through their own eyes, without artistic and literary mediators' (**120**). Similarly R.A. Kissack (**175**) writes that 'the poet who scanned [the turbulent sea] stood upon the bosom of a high-prowed ship in the very midst of the element about which he sang. He was one of the valiant sea warriors who helped to push out the hardy vessel into the foaming breach of a northern sea' (388). In sum, then, we have an image of the Anglo-Saxon poet as direct, spontaneous, and unsophisticated.

These constructions and idealizations are closely integrated into the supposedly empirical work of the editor and textual critic. One temptation for the editor is to eliminate anything that appears incongruously sophisticated or complex and impose a logic of the purportedly appropriate simplicity and transparency by recourse to emendation. A striking example is the sentence 'wea bið wundrum clibbor' ('grief is amazingly clinging') in *Maxims II* line 13. Puzzling over it, Peter Cosijn (**536**) felt that a kind of sense did emerge, particularly for a critic prepared to adopt an 'anomalist' standpoint, where

---

17 Simon During, 'Waiting for the Post: Some Relations between Modernity, Colonization, and Writing', *Ariel* 20.4 (1989): 31–61, at 41.

18 'Social Conflict, Nation and Empire: From Gothicism to Romantic Orientalism', *Ariel* 20.2 (1989): 3–18, at 9.

19 'The Style of Anglo-Saxon Poetry', *PMLA* 3 (1887): 17–47, at 28 and 31.

apparent eccentricities in expression are not automatically emended away but attributed to an eccentric author's style or vision. Ill-luck tends to dog, i.e. 'cling to', a person. But since such a notion seemed foreign to the common-sense mentality that allegedly informs the *Maxims*, Cosijn thought an empirically verifiable comment on a material substance preferable. The outcome was the tentative and quite unnecessary conjecture 'wea*x* bið wundrum clibbor' ('wax is amazingly clinging'). It was ignored by other scholars until Elliott Van Kirk Dobbie (**203**) came to its rescue in spite of the declared conservative policy of the ASPR edition.

Another salient instance occurs in *Maxims II* line 10, where, as noted above, the manuscript reads 'soð bið swicolost', 'truth is most deceptive'. The thought that the truth is deceptive or otherwise 'swicol' may, as Robinson suggests (**617**), have struck scholars as too anticipative of our own epistemologically insecure age, because certainly the line has been subjected to a long series of emendations. In earlier attempts the attack fell on 'soð'. E.A. Kock compounded conjectural emendation with conjectural etymology when he argued for 'swæð', with a meaning 'slippery place' that has to be inferred from Old Norse *svað* (**147**). Ferdinand Holthausen rejected Kock's 'swæð' in favour of 'seað' ('pit') (**150**). Both operated on the unspoken assumption that the abstractness and subtlety of the text were inappropriate and that the aphorism required a concrete noun. More recent editors, including Dobbie (**203**), have felt that some form of 'sweotolost', 'clearest', would yield better sense. An intermediate form 'switolost' recommended itself as offering a palaeographical explanation of the supposed scribal error. But, defending the manuscript reading, Robinson (**617**) points out that 'switolost' is not a plausible form in light of historical phonology. The alleged palaeographic straightforwardness of the conjecture was therefore itself 'most deceptive'.

Scholarly attempts to find cohesion in the *Maxims* and some other gnomic texts, notably *Gifts*, are particularly revealing as to the bias of the searcher. These texts could be described without much exaggeration as literary Rorschach blots. At one extreme, Nicholas Howe (**328**) argues that attempts to credit them with unity or coherent development are bound to be frustrated by their essential function as collections of sayings that could be free-standing. At the other extreme we find scholars, such as Patrizia Lendinara (**590**), who can trace a coherent programme, if not precisely a sentence-by-sentence progression, in for instance *Maxims II*. For the editor an extremely difficult, if not intractable, problem is to decide exactly where emendation might be justified in order to obtain what we would see as a coherent flow of logic from one sentence to the next. In *Maxims I* line 152, for example, the manuscript reads 'wræd sceal wunden' ('a bandage shall be bound'), which would be perfectly satisfying were the next phrases not 'wracu heardum men,/ boga sceal stræle' ('strife [appertains] to a brave man, the bow [appertains] to an arrow'). The ASPR editors, George Krapp and Elliott Van Kirk Dobbie (**194**), print the manuscript reading, in accordance with normal ASPR policy, whereas most readers are likely to be tempted by Cosijn's 'wræd sceal wundum' ('a bandage appertains to wounds/wounded people') (**536**).

A little later in *Maxims I* (lines 154–7), we have this passage (as printed unemended in the ASPR edition, **194**, 162):

. . . maþþum oþres weorð,   gold mon sceal gifan.
Mæg god syllan   eadgum æhte ond eft niman.
Sele sceal stondan,   sylf ealdian.

'One precious thing is worth another, gold is to be given away. God can give possessions to the fortunate and take them back again. A hall must stand, and itself grow old.' (Shippey translation, **300**, 71–3)

Ettmüller (**68**), presumably finding this sequence too loosely associative, emended 'sylf' to 'silfer' ('silver'). In cases where a clear underlying logical link could not be discerned, it is evident that sometimes even the ASPR editors felt dissatisfied with a purely associative linking. Consider line 34 in *Maxims II*. Krapp and Dobbie present the text (**203**, 56) 'beorh sceal on eorðan/ grene standan', which can be translated unproblematically as 'a tumulus shall stand green upon the earth'. But in the notes (175) a change from 'beorh' to 'beorc' ('birch-tree') is proposed, with query. The reason for change, I imagine, would be to forge a primarily rational link with the preceding lines, which read: 'Wudu sceal on foldan/ blædum blowan' ('On the earth a wood must bear blossoms and fruit': Shippey translation, **300**, 77). The fact that the linking is actually almost independent of sequential logic and owes much to verbal association and paronomasia, as indicated by Roberta Frank (**281**), can be seen from the lines that precede 'wudu': 'Treow sceal on eorle,/ wisdom on were' ('Truth/loyalty must be in a warrior, wisdom in a man').

Assumptions about Anglo-Saxon directness and simplicity combine with modern standards of logic to encourage the removal of what seem to us inconsistencies of perspective. In Riddle 40 the narrator is supposed to be the solution of the riddle, 'Creation'. But in line 73, 'þone we wifel wordum nemnað' ('which we call the dung-beetle'), the pronoun 'we' presumably means not Creation but the reciter of the riddle, along with the audience. To remove the inconsistency of speaker, Holthausen (**756**) suggested 'þone þe wifel wordum wise nemnað'; Moritz Trautmann (**758**) refined this to 'þone wise wifel wordum nemnað'. An analogue, which occurs in *Precepts* lines 83–5, was similarly rejected by James Bright (**634**, 187), on the grounds that it involved an 'impossible change of person'. By contrast, Hans Pinsker (**938**) adopted a more anomalist approach when he resisted Craig Williamson's (**916**) emendation in Riddle 86 of 'ic' (line 7) to 'hio'. In light of my earlier speculations on this teasing riddle, Pinsker's editorial anomalism has something to recommend it. With modern narrative theory in mind we might be inclined not to discard but to attach significance to these readings, arguing that a fluid narrative movement from the subject of the enounced to the subject of the enunciation and vice versa is perfectly possible.

Paradoxes have also been the target of conjecture, again presumably because they negated expected qualities of directness and straightforwardness. Thus in Riddle 27 ('mead') a succession of scholars found fault with the manuscript reading in line 13 'strengu bistolen, strong on spræce' ('robbed of strength, strong in speech'). Their objections seem surprising, since the paradox is a familiar one: drunken people can often be physically weak yet vocally strong, as noted by Frederick Klaeber (**752**). Perhaps the asyndetic construction characteristic of Old English poetic style obscured the relative simplicity of the logic. As a remedy Christian Grein (**75**) proposed 'strengu bistolen, strongan spræce', i.e. 'robbed of strength [and] of strong speech'. If empiricism were the be-all and end-all in this type of conjecture, Grein could have noted the palaeographical minimalism of his emendation and its conformity with variation technique; if nothing else, he certainly should have attempted to justify the weak form of the adjective. In fact, the emendation is simply announced without explanation or commentary. Still not satisfied with the second half-line, Trautmann (**751**) opted for palaeographic adventurism by substituting 'bistroden spræce', 'robbed of speech'. Holthausen countered with 'unstrong spræce' (**751**, 89). Meanwhile, Kock returned to Grein's 'strongan spræce', explaining the phrase as instrumental-case (**761**). Revealingly, with Kock an honourable exception, these scholars paid little overt attention to empirical matters such as palaeography, syntax, or stylistics: rather, they left their emendations to stand or fall on the criterion of conformity to the supposed rules of Anglo-Saxon logic.

Riddle 33 (solved as 'iceberg') provides a parallel example. Georg Herzfeld (**684**) stigmatized 'hilde to sæne' ('slow to battle') in line 5 as implausible because the phrase seemed to him to contradict 'hetegrim' ('fierce in hatred') and 'biter beadoweorca' ('biting in its battle-actions'), which also describe the iceberg. His solution was to invent the word **tosæge* ('inclined'). This opened the way for a succession of scholars to propose emendations of their own: Klaeber (**122**); Holthausen (**128** and **756**); and Trautmann (**751**). Meanwhile, Stopford Brooke (**13**), followed by Frederick J. Tupper (**727**) and Alfred Wyatt (**737**), defended the reading on the grounds that an iceberg might well be spoken of as slow in engaging in hostilities but implacable once it did attack. Surprisingly, Krapp and Dobbie (**194**) sided with Herzfeld, holding to the manuscript reading only because no convincing alternative had been proposed. It is important to bear in mind here that these assaults upon paradox proceeded in defiance of its admitted status as a generic feature of the Exeter Book Riddles.

We have seen that idealizations of directness and simplicity have proved deeply attractive to scholars, to the point where they would alter manuscript readings without sufficient justification. To some extent supportive of these idealizations but also to some extent conflicting with them is another set of idealizations to the effect that profundities and hidden truths lurk in the same body of texts. A prevalent approach has been to enhance apparently banal or over-obvious passages into greater subtlety by recourse to textual interventionism (*via* either conjectural emendations or a vigorously anomalist approach), ingenious literary criticism, and elaborate sociological or historical contextualization.

On the literary-critical side, genre theory is often invoked. A look at two rival responses to Riddles 1–3, usually solved as 'storm', will illustrate the point. Pinsker (**939**) argues that these texts cannot qualify as true riddles because the subject is too obvious. Instead they should be assigned to a different genre, that of hymns glorifying the power of the Creator. Stephen Mitchell (**942**) prefers to defend the traditional genre affiliation. He disposes of the alleged obviousness by ascribing it to defective modern scholarship. If the clues supplied are in terms of 'storm' then in a properly constructed riddle the solution must be something else, such as 'army'. His hypothesis takes much for granted about the riddle genre and comes at the additional price of an emendation in Riddle 1 line 10a, where Mitchell alters the manuscript reading 'holme' to 'helme' so as to obtain the picture of two clashing armies. Another recourse to genre taxonomy can be seen in Ann Harleman Stewart's (898) suggestion that the real purpose of Riddle 47 was not to mystify but to construct a parody of Old English heroic poetry. Nigel Barley's (49) exposure of the ethnocentrism that has led to the imposition of such terms as 'riddle', 'lyric', 'elegy', and 'proverb' as universal categories in the first place has come as a much needed corrective.

We can here briefly review some other deployments of literary criticism in its various Protean shapes. Using the close-reading approach, Robinson (896) seeks to rehabilitate Riddle 47 by an elaborate demonstration of its complexity of meaning. He suggests that the poet used a series of verbal ambiguities to thematize the simultaneous reality and insubstantiality of language. Reflexive interpretations can also help in the recuperative enterprise. Seth Lerer (981) avails himself of one when he argues that in Riddle 42 the reader's attention is diverted from the ostensible solution to the real topic, which is interpretation itself. *Precepts*, dismissed by Derek Pearsall (52) and Stanley Greenfield and Daniel Calder (60) as a rather uninspired series of admonitions, finds a defender in Elaine Tuttle Hansen (637), who sees it as reflecting and celebrating the human capacity to structure reality and organize experience into an ethical and epistemological system. Still another approach is offered by allegorical exegesis. Marie Nelson contends (881) that Riddle 34 ('rake') may refer to an anagogical harrowing of sinners as well as to a literal raking up of weeds. For Riddle 33 she posits (991) a primary solution 'iceberg' combined with a secondary solution 'hatred'. Patrizia Lendinara (892) solves Riddle 9 as both 'cuckoo' and 'ingratitude', Riddle 17 as both 'fortress' and 'soul'. Outside the Riddles, Dammers (502) argues that the taming of the hawk in *Fortunes* summarizes in small the Christianizing of human beings.

A second common type of defence against charges of platitudinousness involves historical or social contextualization. Hugo Müller (540) takes the view that apparent truisms in the *Maxims* were historically not truisms at all but freshly minted observations, which he situates in an epoch when human beings were seeing and classifying the world freshly. Another approach has been to argue that apparent platitudes conceal arcane and esoteric founts of wisdom. Thus Leslie Whitbread (567) credits the Frisian sailor passage in *Maxims I* with a traditional, indeed ritual, content on the basis that it describes a custom comparable to 'special taboos and ceremonies of purification' observed in Papua New Guinea. Lynn L. Remly (591) asserts that *Maxims I* lines 23b–9a, along with other passages, represents the original 'sacred experience' and reveals a fascination with the central mystery of the world, namely the appearance of life: necessarily, then, the passage emphasizes bare facts and irreducible reality, in a way that could be confused by a modern scholar with sheer banality. Loren C. Gruber (603, 606, 608), although conceding that many aphorisms represent observations of mundane affairs, finds that others encode an ancient Scandinavian epistemology or conceal a mode of access to the supernatural. Gregory Jember (911) argues that traditional rational-empirical approaches to riddles cannot provide verifiable exclusive solutions because riddles are not themselves consistently rational or empirical. Would-be solvers must stand outside their own consciousness and history. Such invocations of alterity, however imaginatively compelling, usually smack of over-interpretation.

Textually more intrepid are Karl Schneider's endeavours (226) to demonstrate that *Rune Poem*, along with its partial counterparts in Old Norse and Old Icelandic, is no mere childish mnemonic but preserves relics of early Germanic heathen cults, mythologies, and fertility rituals. Reconstruction of an originary text is crucial to his approach, as we shall see if we consider his handling of the 'thorn' strophe (lines 7–9). In the ASPR edition (203) it reads as follows:

> [ðorn] byþ ðearle scearp;   ðegna gehwylcum
> anfeng ys yfyl,   ungemetun reþe
> manna gehwylcun   ðe him mid resteð.

> '[The thorn] is very sharp; contact [with it] is bad for any person; it is exceedingly severe to anyone who rests with it.'

On the face of it, what we have here is a sardonically platitudinous description of the thorn. Schneider reaches for more arcane knowledge by emending 'ðegna' (line 7) to 'þyrsa', 'giants', and 'manna' (line 9) to 'mægþa', 'maidens'. The result is a depiction not of 'thorn' but of Þunor the thunder-god, who fights the giants and brings fertility to maidens. Working from a radically different viewpoint, but also with the aim of detrivializing the poem, Marijane Osborn and Stella Longland (1036) advocate its potential to provide a fresh approach to the problems of individuality and existence: the runes were thought of as not merely an archaic 'alphabet' but rather an old system of the wise, which found refuge, in a censored form, with the new.

So far I have been documenting a tension in scholarship between perceptions of simplicity and profundity. Let us now move to a different though related set of conflicting perceptions. Bloomfield speaks (44, 5) of a debate in the nineteenth century where poetic texts found explanation as either 'a mysterious product of the Volkgeist' or 'the product of a poet trying to express his feelings, as a romantic poet might, in verse'. In our own more abstract version of scholarship what is at stake is the role of collectivity and individual author respectively as key players in the textual process. Where candidacy for folk authorship among the wisdom corpus is concerned, the Charms have been treated as the only obvious candidate. As to the other wisdom poems, many nineteenth- and early twentieth-century scholars went to the opposite extreme, ascribing as much of the corpus as possible to Cynewulf. This fad, characterized by Eric Stanley (316) as the supreme example of biographical folly, encompassed even the apparently very loose-knit *Maxims I*, which was attributed to Cynewulf by Franz Dietrich (71), Max Rieger (72), Gregor Sarrazin (95), and Joseph Strobl (537), along with other scholars. Naturally *Fortunes*, *Gifts*, *Precepts*, and *Rune Poem* conveyed a much clearer impression of a single, structuring hand and so they too went the Cynewulfian route. Rieger (76) associated *Fortunes* specifically with a youthful Cynewulf's secular recitations in the mead-hall. Still more strongly suggestive of individual authorship have been the *Homiletic Fragments*, the Exeter Book Riddles, the *Solomon and Saturn* fragments, and *Vainglory*. Thus, although scholars such as Tupper and Archer Taylor have investigated folkloristic traits in the Exeter Book Riddles, an actual attribution of these texts to the folk at large has never been favoured. Rather, being literary products of a kind that could easily be misrecognized as nineteenth-century lyrics, they have naturally been drafted into the ranks of single-author works. Similarly, the two *Solomon and Saturn* poetic texts, in virtue of their perceived eccentricity, have each been ascribed to individual authors. Broad, vague assumptions like these inevitably feed into textual criticism. The editorial treatment of *Vainglory*, for instance, shows a correlation between assumptions of highly individuated authorship and the assertively anomalist textual criticism seen in the treatments by Huppé (**270**) and T.E. Pickford (**1115**).

In spite of this hankering after a prototype of modern individual authorship, some folk participation in wisdom texts has seemed axiomatic. A typical nostalgia can be seen in Francis P. Magoun's (**234**) assumption that an identification of joy with musically accompanied song, such as we see in *Gifts*, points to an early unlettered peasant society. It is also evident in Raw's view (**54**) that most of the control over the logical progression of the *Maxims* must have been ceded to the audience, implying a trust which could only have existed within a close-knit group with a common literary culture. Carolyne Larrington has posited 'a body of folk-wisdom, not yet in metrical form, a body which can be sensed as a living, pulsing, gnomic background to all Germanic poetry'.[20] From these visions of the collectivity it is an easy step to assume that the wisdom transmitted is perennial rather than conditioned by particular eras and modes of production. Henry Sweet is in company with many other scholars when he compares *Maxims* with the Old Norse *Hávamál*, arguing that both belong to the earliest stage of poetry, despite possible later alterations (**77**). Karl Helm (**420**) seeks to bolster the claims of Charm 1 by pointing to the presence of obsolescent lexical items such as *folde*, while wilfully ignoring the conservatism of diction throughout the Old English poetic corpus. Significant for Aldo Ricci's (**181**) discussion of the Charms is not the extant form in the manuscripts but the type of text, since in his opinion the original version would have undergone centuries of oral transmission before being first recorded. Invocations of an organic community, endowed with spontaneity and immediacy of communication, have also lent powerful aid to oral-formulaic theory. Here too, unhappily, logic has often been forgotten or jettisoned. Magoun (**425**), for instance, applies the theory to the metrical Charms, arguing that except for amulet charms and the like it is not plausible that they had a fixed text. But the opposite argument could equally well be made from basic axioms or assumptions, namely that a charm depends for its efficacy upon exact, ritualized repetition. On just such an assumption Malone (**30**) envisaged a series of monastic scribes who copied charms with the traditional wording for fear that they would otherwise prove ineffective.

I can here mention only a few of the critiques and rebuttals that the folk and oral hypotheses have provoked. J.W. Rankin (**550**) criticizes Blanche Williams (**547**) for attempting to separate heathen material from Christian and for not taking Latin didactic prose and verse into account in her discussion of sources. Ashley Crandell Amos (**56**) excludes Ricci's approach to dating on the grounds that it lacks any basis in linguistic or prosodic evidence. Barley (**278**) emphasizes the international character of Anglo-Saxon medicine, pointing out that the small self-contained world that we would ideally hope for in investigating the Anglo-Saxons has already been shattered by contact with Romania: although the Germanic peoples might have developed a native 'gnomology', he doubts that the surviving maxims belong to this stock. B.K. Martin (**584**) points to a potential

---

[20] *A Store of Common Sense: Gnomic Theme and Style in Old Icelandic and Old English Wisdom Poetry*, Oxford English Monographs (Oxford: Clarendon, 1993) 18.

error of primitivism when motifs such as ice forming a bridge (already referred to above) or land and water being 'bound' by cold are ascribed to Germanic antiquity, since the same motifs were current in Latin literature. In the process of digesting several centuries of speculation about oral poetry, Roberta Frank mordantly contextualizes the latest outbreak: 'when a new communications technology appeared to be accelerating out of control, so was the academy's nostalgia for a bookless past, for non-élitist culture, for personal voice'.[21]

The scholarly wavering between the rival attractions of the folk and the individual author can be partially illustrated by the controversy concerning the attribution of the Exeter Book Riddles. On the single-author side the leading hypothesis, almost from the first, has been that originated by Heinrich Leo (**657**), namely that the Cynewulf whose runic signature figures in *Elene* and three other poems also composed the Riddles. Although the opposite hypothesis, pure folk authorship, has never to my knowledge been advocated, we have a near approach in a theory espoused by Karl Bülbring (**685**), to the effect that the Riddles originated with a variety of poets and contained a strong folk element. The ambivalence within scholarship as a whole is encapsulated in various publications by Herzfeld. In an 1891 contribution (**684**) he ascribed virtually all the Riddles to a youthful Cynewulf on the basis of congruity in a great number of characteristic expressions and attitudes, methods of handling source-material, and linguistic, rhetorical, and prosodic features. Within ten years, however, he had reversed his position (**699**), so as to propose that many of the Riddles derive from popular origins and that a variety of authors contributed to the Exeter Book collection. The publications of Tupper provide another illustration of the competition between different kinds of assumptions concerning Riddle authorship. He begins from the notion that the Riddles evince a very complex interdependence between artistic and folk invention, although conceding that on the whole the composition represents literary rather than folk endeavours (**706, 707**). In his edition of the Riddles (**727**), he rejects Leo's theory of Cynewulf's authorship in favour of multiple authorship by unknown poets. But then, later in the same year, he publishes an article (**728**) which uses supposed runic clues to reinstate Cynewulf's claim to authorship. Empirical principles are flouted in this publication, which sweeps aside Sievers's (**683**) linguistic criteria for dating and draws far-fetched inferences from Renaissance Icelandic runic signatures.

To take a final instance of long-lived rival hypotheses and the concomitant fluctuations in scholarship, we might mention the search for what Bloomfield (**44**) described as 'the original Germanic pagan spirit in Old English literature'. This tendency can be found in various forms in the contributions itemized in this bibliography. Runes have proved a natural attractant. Schneider (**594**) argues that the pagan significances of runes are cryptically concealed in two passages, *Maxims I* lines 71–80 and *II* lines 1–13. Elémire Zolla (**1083**) analyses the Paternoster section of *Solomon and Saturn* to demonstrate that each word or phrase in the prayer is assigned a rune with an appropriate meaning: thus the phrase 'qui es in coelis' is represented by *ac* (line 93), signifying the oak as pillar of the cosmos and as source of nutriment. Other variants on this approach to

---

[21] 'The Anglo-Saxon Oral Poet', *Bulletin of the John Rylands University Library of Manchester* 75.1 (1993): 11–36, at 12–13.

Solomon and Saturn are offered by Schneider (**226**) and by Günter Kellermann and Renate Haas (**1100**). C.L. Wrenn (**245**) suggests that a traditional use of the *r*-rune to symbolize the occupant of the divine chariot may survive in *Solomon and Saturn* line 99, where the leader of the Paternoster runes is R, 'bocstafa brego' ('prince of letters'). (A less fanciful explanation would link *r* with Latin *rex*.) Vestiges of animism are another source of fascination. F.W. Moorman (**711**) believes that the Exeter Book Riddles continue the primitive view of elemental forces, sea and wind, for instance, as conscious beings. Similarly, Edith Whitehurst Williams (**900**) sees the personifications in the Riddles as founded upon a pre-Christian animism. With greater plausibility John Niles (**357**) points to Charm 12 lines 6–7, where he believes that the 'wolf's paw, eagle's feather, and eagle's claw' allude to tokens of power that the shaman wears or brandishes, and to *Maxims II*, where the wild boar is mentioned in company with two other creatures admired for their fierce independence, the hawk and the wolf. Vestiges of actual cults of deities have also been traced. Charm 2 has often been reconstructed as an account of Óðinn's self-sacrifice. Raymond Tripp (**503**) interprets the tree-climbing section in *Fortunes* (lines 21–6) as an allusion to the same mythic episode. (Meanwhile, less speculatively, Edwin Howard (**499**) had pointed out that since the other deaths in this poem do not seem to have been unusual ones a reference to falconry might have been intended; another possibility would be the harvesting of green leaves for fodder, as suggested by J.E. Cross (**229**), or of wild honey.) Jacob Grimm (**363**), followed by John Kemble (**66, 1047**), uses *Solomon and Saturn* to construct a place for Saturn in the Germanic pantheon. Wrenn (**43**) traces a connection between this Saturn and Woden. Whitehurst Williams points to the word 'meotud' in Riddle 3 line 54 as an indication of continued belief in Fate as a relentless spirit, who cannot be reconciled with a beneficent God (**900**). Fate, in the semblance of Wyrd, has of course been the subject of speculations too numerous to be entered into here.

Meanwhile, a less romantic strain has been striving to make itself heard. Romanticism on the runes in *Solomon and Saturn* has been rebutted by René Derolez (**216**), who sees them as not intrinsic to the poem but purely ornamental with at the most an archaic, pagan, or cryptic, flavour. Audrey Meaney (**262**) cautions against quarrying Old English poetry for traces of heathen mythology and doubts that the poet of *Maxims I* possessed substantial information about Woden. Thomas Hill (**457**) argues that although diachronic inquiry into Charm 1, attempting to discriminate pagan from Christian, has its legitimacy, interpretation and discussion inevitably suffer if there is no concern for the meaning and significance of the text in its present form. Damico (**468**) takes de-mythologization to an extreme when she attempts a literary (rather than religious-historical) study of the Valkyries: the horde of malevolent spear-throwing female riders in Charm 4 becomes in her interpretation a metaphor for a sudden pain. Yet, despite all the rebuttals, Stanley acknowledges in his *The Search for Anglo-Saxon Paganism* (**296**, ix) that 'something of what I was writing about is still with us, at least in some measure'.

My own impression is that students often come to Old English, as to Old Norse, in the hopes of discovering a fully-fledged heathen mythology. Sustained investigation would demonstrate that such hopes and dreams continue to be nurtured in popularizing articles and lectures, television programmes, CD-ROMs, historical fiction, mythopoeic writings, reconstituted pagan cults, and sundry other fugitive or fringe manifestations. Nowadays, of course, the Internet is conferring ever greater visibility on these 'para-scholarly' activities and concomitantly providing us with new insights into the phenomenology of our discipline. Sometimes, to be sure, these ephemera may not achieve a fully published or even written form. Nevertheless, they represent a kind of 'writing', in the Derridean sense, because they help to structure the discourse of this discipline, validating and perpetuating certain hopes, dreams, and *idées fixes*. The general moral that we can draw is that although discountenanced ideas and hypotheses may undergo repression into what we might term, with apologies to Fredric Jameson, a 'scholarly unconscious' they cannot be utterly extinguished. To the contrary, scholarship is forever witnessing the return of the repressed. Indeed, repressed models and theories can be described as a Derridean 'supplement' from which so-called serious scholarship cannot be sequestered.

IV

When we consider the history and evolution of studies in Old English wisdom poetry we should recur to the question with which I began this introduction: how do ideas acquire people? Or, in my present context, how do conceptions concerning Old English wisdom poetry acquire currency and allegiance among scholars? Let us start on a positivist note with the assertion that discoveries can be made and do sometimes nudge our discipline into an altered set of perceptions, maybe even a 'paradigm shift'. As an outstanding discovery we could cite John C. Pope's disclosure (**307**) that in the Exeter Book a gap occurs in quire xvi in the midst of what had passed for a single riddle but now stands revealed as two unrelated fragments. In consequence, earlier attempts to emend the so-called Riddle 70 were proved to be delusory and that in itself greatly benefited scholarship. But discoveries can be problematic too. For one thing, anti-discoveries (or rebuttals of the supposed discoveries) often prove quite as decisive, or even more so. We could cite here Page's careful demonstration (**1027**) that George Hempl (**1002**) had leapt to conclusions about the origins of the runes in Hickes's print of *Rune Poem* (1705). Vincenti's discovery (**1061**) that the lost final section of *Solomon and Saturn* II is partly preserved in some earlier lines in the manuscript fragment has likewise been picked apart by Dobbie (**203**), though the latter oddly attributes the discovery to Robert Menner (**1073**). Discoveries of sources, such as some of Thomas Hill's and James Cross's listed in this bibliography, are likely to remain a matter of opinion, as subsequent research has tended to demonstrate. Uncertain too is the genre classification of *Wulf and Eadwacer*, despite the plausibility of Henry Bradley's assertion (**678**) that here we are dealing with a dramatic monologue rather than the riddle which his predecessors thought they had detected. The status of Riddle 60 continues to be contested, despite the 'discovery' of its cohesion with *The Husband's Message* (Strobl, **537**: cf. the comments of Fell, 173).

Discoveries of solutions to the Riddles constitute an especially problematic category. Once devised, they may seem as inevitable as a correct solution to a crossword puzzle and yet they can also be overthrown by a new suggestion: the long history of attempts on Riddle 39 by one confident solver after another supplies us with an object lesson here. Sometimes archaeological evidence or specialist methodologies have been called into requisition, but in the last analysis successful solutions continue to be serendipitous as often as they are empirical. At one of the Old English sessions of the MLA convention of December 1995 I experienced vicariously the moment of serendipity when someone solved Riddle 5 extempore as 'whetstone'. This answer is unquestionably superior to Ludwig Müller's very long established solution 'shield' (655), since it explains the clues 'anhaga' (line 1) and 'dagum ond nihtum' (line 14) in a way that 'shield' cannot. (Trautmann's 'chopping block' can safely be dismissed.) Whether the new solution will emerge into the light of day in a published form and gain acceptance for as long as Müller's will make an interesting sequel to this story.

Ultimately, then, empirical investigation and discovery play a restricted (though honourable) role. Ours is not simply some 'discipline' where literature is scientifically analysed in dispassionate, clinical isolation from vaguer, undefineable passions and sentiments. As scholars of literature read any given set of manuscript words they are invariably forming hypotheses on both a large and a small scale. We must form hypotheses in order to read at all. Stretches of text may be classified as poetry or prose, as oral or written. We may integrate them with or separate them from other stretches of text in the manuscript context.[22] Rival genre classifications of the text may be devised. We may speculate about the type of authorship. Other classificatory polarities that may enter into hypotheses about the text are impersonality versus personal involvement, communicativeness versus solipsism, tradition versus innovation, paganism versus Christianity, Germanicism versus Graeco-Latinity, formularity versus individualism, *pensée sauvage* versus colonial mimicry, aristocratic versus folk orientation, and so forth. These classificatory principles, all of them represented in the works documented in this bibliography, constitute facets of the continuing discourse that centres itself upon Anglo-Saxon texts and cultural goods. Behind each of them lies some wish or hope, some emotional or imaginative investment, some gesture of (mis)recognition, on the part of scholars and the social context within which they live and work.

The positivist vision of hard-won small gains in knowledge, let alone of 'paradigm shifts', though significant to the rhetoric of scholarship, is not then the whole of its essence. Such a statement should come as no surprise, after the general studies of disciplines and fields undertaken by Michel Foucault.[23] Although gratitude is owing to Allen Frantzen for his book *Desire for Origins*,[24] which has usefully challenged some assumptions concerning the ideology and methodology current in Old English teaching and research, he slides into excess when he construes scholarly developments as dominated, determined even, by a fiercely empirical or positivist philology. In the numerous examples that I have

---

22 For salutary recent reminders of the complexities and uncertainties attaching to these tasks see Fred C. Robinson, *The Editing of Old English* (Oxford: Blackwell, 1994) and Carol Braun Pasternack, *The Textuality of Old English Poetry* (Cambridge: Cambridge UP, 1995) 199.

23 See in particular *The Archaeology of Knowledge and the Discourse on Language*, trans. A.M. Sheridan Smith (New York: Pantheon, 1972).

24 *Desire for Origins. New Language, Old English, and Teaching the Tradition* (New Brunswick, NJ: Rutgers UP, 1990).

adduced in this introduction it is manifest that the contrary holds true: scholars have felt entitled at a certain point to evade or even defy empirical considerations as the attraction of a hypothesis proved overpowering. To my mind, Malone was closer to the heart of the matter when he wrote, over sixty-five years ago, that the 'tendencies of philological research, like everything else, are mainly determined by the fashions which happen to be prevalent'.[25] The word 'drift', he thought, was 'not inappropriate as a description of our activities, however full of purpose they may seem to us as individuals'.

Constitutive of the 'drift', I believe, is the presence within the discourse of antithetical assumptions and hypotheses such as those documented above. These can be envisaged (to indulge in a little harmless mathematical modelling) acting as powerful and countervailing 'attractors'. Between these 'attractors' we can trace a scholarly wavering, usually involving a multiplicity of scholars and over a comparatively lengthy period but occasionally within the mind of a single scholar at a single phase of that person's career. Dialogues between and within scholars mean that research is necessarily not a matter of linear progress – or indeed of linear regress. We all need to be mindful of our subject positions as participants in the general oscillation. Traditionally, practitioners have been viewed as sovereign in respect of the discourse, reaching conclusions on a basis of a reasoned choice among the different possibilities offered by the evidence. The opposite view would be to see the discourse as possessing total power over practitioners – as a kind of machine that determined their intellectual moves. Both views are of course simplistic. Rather, we can say that vis-à-vis the discourse the individual scholar has the function of *agent*, in both senses of the word. The discourse speaks and reproduces itself through the individual scholar, who to that extent is its agent. And yet the scholar also modifies the discourse by placing observations, ideas, and hypotheses in new contexts and combinations, and to that extent has his or her status as a qualifiedly 'free agent'.

The foregoing analysis suggests that we ought to contemplate the notion of limits to scholarship in our field, in rough analogy to current probings into the limits of science.[26] We might see our field, like many of those in the Humanities, as configured by a long-term oscillation between compelling but mutually contradictory hypotheses, none of them guaranteed by unassailable evidence. The discoveries, empirical or otherwise, are of course significant but only as one element within this much more complex and inscrutable total dynamic.

[25] 'Studies in Old English Poetry, 1920–30', *Philological Quarterly* 10 (1931): 400–03, at 400.
[26] Ian Stewart, 'Crashing the Barriers', *New Scientist* 153 no. 2075 (29 March 1997): 40–4.

General Bibliography

Bibliography of General Items

1 **Ettmüller, Ludwig.** *Vorda Vealhstôd Engla and Seaxna: Lexicon Anglosaxonicum ex poëtarum scriptorumque prosaicorum operibus nec non lexicis anglosaxonicis collectum cum synopsi grammatica.* Quedlinburg: Basse, 1851. lxxi + 767 pp.

This very detailed glossary, arranged not alphabetically but on phonological principles, includes discussion of items in the OEW poems. For example, 'scirenige' in Riddle 8 line 9 is explained as a variant of *scericge* and *scearecge*, all equivalent to Latin *mima* (693).

2 **Grein, Christian W.M.** *Bibliothek der angelsächsischen Poesie in kritisch beabeiteten Texten und mit vollständigem Glossar.* 2 vols. Kassel: Wigand, 1857–8.

An edition and translation of virtually all the OEW poems are included. Grein was unable to see the Exeter Book and therefore made the text of Thorpe (**65**) his basis for poems contained in that manuscript. The total number of Riddles is reckoned at 89. This includes *Wulf and Eadwacer* but combines Riddles 68 and 69 and excludes Riddles 67, 78, 82, 92, and 94. As to editorial policy, Grein is conservative, particularly in rejecting the conjectures of Bouterwek (**69**). Nevertheless, he attempted to emend and to fill up the manuscript lacunae in the text of the Riddles on the basis of the information supplied in Thorpe's edition. *Solomon and Saturn* is printed, minus the prose section, from Kemble's text (**1047**) and with his normalizations, since here too Grein was unable to inspect the manuscripts personally. He does, however, add some emendations of his own to the text. The literal translation into German is meant to substitute for notes and commentary, which accordingly are very sparing, though they include such particular points as 'scirenige' in Riddle 8 line 9 (373–4). A brief survey of manuscripts and scholarship relating to each poem is appended. Riddle 2 is solved as 'anchor', 3 as 'hurricane', 47 as 'bookmoth', 68–9 as 'winter', 75 as 'dog', and 87 as 'cask and cooper'. Grein comments that the exchange of speeches in *Solomon and Saturn* II lacks logical coherence.

3 ——. *Sprachschatz der angelsächsischen Dichter.* 2 vols. Cassel: Wigand, 1861–4. Rev. edn. J.J. Köhler, with F. Holthausen. Heidelberg: Winter, 1912.

These volumes are intended as the glossary to **2**. Among its entries are notes on difficult or dubious readings in OEW poems. Grein suggests the emendation 'þe swa scire nige' in Riddle 8 line 9 (296 and 410). Under *neómian* he suggests 'neómegende' for manuscript 'neome cende' in *Fortunes* line 84 (290). Some brief commentary is also included. Under *Vôden* he notes that 'alwalda' in *Maxims I* line 132 refers to the Christian God (730). In Riddle 72 the phrase 'feower broþor' in lines 6–7 is explained as 'mamillas vaccae', i.e. 'udders' (527). Other entries presuppose but do not explicitly state a specific interpretation: for instance, under *vyn* [i.e. *wyn*] he cites *Maxims I* line 106 in the form 'mere hafað mundum mægð, êgsan . . .' (757). [For a review see M. Trautmann, **140**.]

4	**Leo, Heinrich.** *Angelsächsisches Glossar.* Alphabetischer Index dazu von Walther Biszegger. Halle: Waisenhaus, 1872–7. 2 parts in 1 vol.

Some difficult vocabulary items in OEW poems are the subject of brief notes and comments. Thus for Riddle 8 line 9 Leo suggests a verb *scirenian* or *scirenigan* 'shine, sparkle' (640). For the reading 'neome' in *Fortunes* line 84 he proposes *nemian*, a causative 'to name, call, prompt' (138). For 'wearnung' in *Solomon and Saturn* line 429a he suggests the gloss 'resistance' (16).

5	**Brink, Bernhardt A.K. ten.** *Geschichte der englischen Literatur.* Vol. 1. *Bis zu Wiclifs Auftreten.* Berlin: Oppenheim, 1877. 2 vols. 1877–93. Trans. Horace M. Kennedy. *History of English Literature.* 2 vols. New York: Holt; London: Bell, 1883–96. Rev. edn. of the translation of Vol. 1, New York: Holt, 1889; London: Bell, 1895–6. Rev. edn. of the German text by Alois Brandl. 2 vols. Strassburg: Trübner, 1899–1912.

This survey of Anglo-Saxon literature includes the OEW poems. The Exeter Book Riddles are the sole surviving vestige of Cynewulf's production as an itinerant singer. Cynewulf followed the Latin originals of his riddles with varying degrees of freedom but always with lifelike and spontaneous treatment. Some themes, nevertheless, derive not from the Latin but from oral tradition. Riddle 14 is quoted and translated into German verse. Gnomic verse is to be seen as having adapted itself to the metrical system of epic poetry, though evidence exists of isolated attempts at strophic division. The poet seems to have combined a number of aphorisms or propositions with no linkage other than chance sequence of thought, which was often suggested solely by the alliteration. A translation of *Maxims I* lines 71–99 is appended, with comments. *Rune Poem*, though not of great antiquity in its present form, can be seen as the most closely related to the old popular poetry among extant texts. *Fortunes* and *Gifts* are less primitive in form: in this type of text we detect a direct reciprocal influence between secular and religious poetry. *Precepts* is similar to the *Disticha Catonis* and perhaps influenced by the *Proverbia Salomonis*. Though *Solomon and Saturn* has its basis in an ancient and deep-rooted Germanic custom of oral contest in speaking aphorisms, its material is ultimately derived from an oriental legend that included Moloch. Moloch should be regarded as the Oriental counterpart of Saturn, since Marcol[f] = Malcol = Moloch = Kronos = Saturn. Kemble (**1047**) is right to see the two poetic sections as representing two separate poems, the first later than the second. The poetic style in *Solomon and Saturn* II is closer to older poetry in its observance of the rules of alliteration than it is to the *Metres of Boethius*. Commenting on Charms 4 and 8, ten Brink notes that they would be difficult for the Church to censor when used *in extremis*.

6	**Wülker, Richard P.** *Bibliothek der angelsächsischen Poesie, begründet von Christian W.M. Grein, neu bearbeitet, vermehrt und nach eignen lesungen der handschriften herausgegeben von Richard Paul Wülker.* Vol. 1 *Das Beowulfslied nebst den kleineren epischen, lyrischen, didaktischen und geschichtlichen Stücken.* Vol. 2 *Die Vercelli-Handschrift; die Cambridger Handschrift des*

Corpus Christi Collegs No.CCI; Judith; der Hymnus Cædmons und die Geschichte der sogen. Cædmonhandschrift nebst kleineren geistlichen Dichtungen. Vol. 3 (ed. Bruno Assmann) *Die Handschrift von Exeter* [i.e. those Exeter Book poems not included in vols. 1 and 2]; *Metra des Boetius; Salomo und Saturn; die Psalmen.* 3 vols. Kassel: Wigand, 1881–98.

Text, notes, and bibliography are included for all OEW poems. The material is distributed as follows: 1.2: Metrical Charms, *Homiletic Fragments I* and *II*, *Rune Poem*, *Maxims I* and *II*, and *Precepts*. 2.1: Charm 11, in a transcription of the manuscript text (202–3). 2.2: *Winfrid Proverb* (315). 3.1: *Fortunes*, *Gifts*, *Vainglory*, *Leiden Riddle*, and Exeter Book Riddles. On an unnumbered page at the end of this volume, notes are appended on the text of *Maxims I*. 3.2: *Solomon and Saturn*, minus the prose section (ed. Assmann). The edition includes an extensive critical apparatus, with the editor's own emendations. A bibliography of previous editions and translations is provided but no notes or glossary. All texts are based on fresh investigation of the manuscripts. This edition takes in all the Exeter Book Riddles, including fragments. [For a review see F. Holthausen, **112**.]

7 Robinson, William Clarke. *Introduction to Our Early English Literature, from the Earliest Times to the Norman Conquest.* London: Simpkin, Marshall, 1885. xliv + 217 pp.

This student textbook follows ten Brink (**5**) in endeavouring to emphasize the literary interest of the texts. The excerpts are based on the text of Grein (**2**). Introductions and translations are supplied, but no notes or glossary. The texts include Exeter Book Riddle 14 and the metrical Charms, along with excerpts from *Fortunes*, *Gifts*, *Homiletic Fragment I*, *Maxims*, *Order*, *Precepts*, *Rune Poem*, *Solomon and Saturn*, and *Vainglory*. Robinson comments on many of these texts. He argues that the Charms would have been efficacious in their Anglo-Saxon cultural context. *Gifts*, *Fortunes*, *Vainglory*, and *Homiletic Fragment I* may be the work of one author, possibly Cynewulf, who also composed the Riddles. *Precepts* resembles the speeches of Polonius. Old Testament analogues and sources, notably the Book of Job, can be identified for *Solomon and Saturn*. *Order* is a joyful and poetic meditation on the wonders of Creation. *Homiletic Fragment I* is remarkable for its freedom from antifeminism, as contrasted with the *Maxims*. Although the Frisian wife welcomes her sailor-husband home upon the beach, she makes love to another man when he sails away again. Robinson points out, however, with self-confessed national pride, that this unfaithfulness is attributed not to the [Anglo-]Saxon, but to the Frisian wife. Reflecting on anti-Frisian stereotypes, Robinson suggests that it was very probably among the Frisians that Wagner's famous 'Flying Dutchman' received his first impressions of the inconstancy of the sailor's bride but notes also that the Frisians helped considerably in the conquering and peopling of Britain.

8 Wülker, Richard Paul. *Grundriss zur Geschichte der angelsächsischen Litteratur: Mit einer Übersicht der angelsächsischen Sprachwissenschaft.* Leipzig: von Veit, 1885. xii + 532 pp.

Each section of this manual is a review of editions, translations, and scholarly studies of relevant literary texts. Wülker sometimes appends brief comments and evaluation, sometimes also lengthy citations. Included are the metrical Charms, with a detailed discussion of the names of herbs in Charm 2 (347–55), *Maxims* (228–30), *Order*, where the text in the Exeter Book should be regarded as an abridged version (234–5), *Precepts* (230–1), Exeter Book Riddles, classed as certainly the authentic work of Cynewulf (165–70), *Rune Poem* (355–6), and *Solomon and Saturn* (360–7). Generally Wülker endorses the summation of the Cynewulfian oeuvre given by Grein (**84**). On *Solomon and Saturn* he agrees with ten Brink (**5**), *contra* Vogt (**1053**), that the two poetic sections preserved in CCCC 422 have nothing in common beyond the names of the interlocutors. It was this commonality that was instrumental in their being brought together in a single manuscript compilation. Being, formally speaking, a true dialogue, *Solomon and Saturn* II has more in common with the Solomon:Marcolf/Saturn tradition than *Solomon and Saturn* I, but neither this nor any other consideration justifies an earlier dating for *Solomon and Saturn* II than for *Solomon and Saturn* I (366).

9 **Körting, Gustav.** *Grundriss der Geschichte der englischen Literatur von ihren Anfängen bis zur Gegenwart.* Münster: Schöningh, 1887. xvi + 412 pp. Rev. edn. 1893.

Körting deals very briefly with all the OEW poems. He gives brief reviews of previous scholarship. In later editions, following Trautmann (**673**), he casts doubt on Cynewulf's authorship of the Riddles and advocates multiple authorship as a stronger possibility.

10 **Kail, J.** 'Über die Parallelstellen in der angelsächsischen Poesie.' *Anglia* 12 (1889): 21–41.

Kail follows up Sarrazin's work (**95**) on parallels. Whereas Sarrazin had excluded Charms and *Precepts*, along with other poems, from the Cynewulf/*Beowulf* nexus, Kail argues that all Old English poems participate in a system of formulas, though some are more formulaic than others. He sees didactic poems, including *Gifts* and *Order*, as being poorest in formulas, though not devoid of them. By way of conclusion, he discountenances the assumption that a single author such as Cynewulf was responsible for the bulk of the Anglo-Saxon poetic corpus, arguing that a scenario where poets heavily imitate each other is more plausible.

11 **Lüning, Otto.** *Die Natur, ihre Auffassung und poetische Verwendung in der altgermanischen und mittelhochdeutschen Epik.* Zürich: Schulthess, 1889. iv + 314 pp.

In this comparative study, Lüning makes little comment on the individual occurrences of a motif but places them in a broad context that includes Old Norse and Middle High German as well as Old English. He stresses the vividness of natural description in early Germanic poetry. From the OEW poems he cites *inter alia* the mentions of sun and light in *Order*, fen and river in *Maxims II*, and the constellation *Tir* and the ash-tree in *Rune Poem*.

12 **Meyer, Richard Moritz.** *Die altgermanische Poesie nach ihren formelhaften Elementen beschrieben.* Berlin: Hertz, 1889. xx + 549 pp.

Meyer attempts a complete compilation of apparently formulaic material in Old English and other Germanic poetry. Included are scattered references to OEW poetry, traceable through the index.

3   **Brooke, Stopford A.** *The History of Early English Literature.* 2 vols. London: Macmillan, 1892. Repr. 1899 as 2 vols. in 1. xiv + 502 pp.

This history contains brief coverage of almost all OEW poetry. In his discussion of the Exeter Book Riddles (367–70) Brooke upholds the attribution to Cynewulf, though acknowledging that good evidence for it is lacking. What he finds important is the genius of some of the Riddles, not who wrote them. Notable in the Riddles is the inception of the English tradition of poems about animals. This tradition is distinctive in that the poet evinces empathy with these creatures on their own terms rather than making them act like human beings, as in e.g. the beast fables of Henryson. The anticipations of modern English poetry (e.g. in Riddle 7) and the independence from the Latin sources, which lack any sort of poetic dimension and which may have done no more than supply the initial ideas, strikingly demonstrate the strengths of the poet. Brooke provides a series of illustrative translations, of which the following is a sample (from Riddle 29 lines 1–3): 'I have seen a wight wonderfully shapen,/ Bearing up a booty, in between his horns,/ A Lift-Vessel flashing light, and with loveliness bedecked.' Brooke makes very full use of literary texts as a source of information on social and environmental conditions. Thus in his Chapter 8, 'Armour and War in Poetry', he draws on *Gifts* and some relevant Riddles (14, 20, 23, 35, and 53). In Chapter 9, 'The Settlement in Poetry', he draws on the following Riddles: 7, 8 'nightingale', 15 'badger', 21, 27, 28, 29, 38, 40, 56, and 80. The following Riddles are cited with new solutions: 57 'martins', 60 'reed', and 72 'ox'. Also used are *Fortunes* and metrical Charms 1, 4, 7, 8, and 9. In Chapter 10 'The Sea' he solves Riddle 10 as 'barnacle-goose' and also discusses Riddles 1–3 and 33. In Chapter 11 'Christianity and Literature' he discusses Riddle 66. In Note E (to Chapter 9) he analyses the folklore elements in Charms 2, 3, and 11. In Chapter 25 he suggests that the *Maxims*, in their original form, probably represent the collecting activity of some literary person at York, during Ecgberht's or Æthelberht's time, who was interested in heathen verse and customs and borrowed from *Beowulf* and *The Seafarer*: subsequently a scribe misplaced some lines. *Fortunes* is a better poem than *Gifts*. *Rune Poem* and *Solomon and Saturn* are also mentioned.

4   **Sarrazin, G.** 'Parallelstellen in altenglischer Dichtung.' *Anglia* 14 (1892): 186–92.

Sarrazin replies to Kail (**10**), expressing gratitude for some hitherto unnoticed parallels but rejecting his theory of poetic imitation.

5   **Kaluza, Max.** 'Die Schwellverse in der altenglische Dichtung.' *Englische Studien* 21 (1895): 337–84.

Kaluza discusses in detail the diversity of opinions concerning hypermetric verses. He defends the notion that these verses had the status of a recognized metrical form and a special significance in context. Among his citations are passages from *Maxims I*, where half-lines like 41a and 175a clearly have three lifts and occur in well-defined series (338–40). Sievers's exclusion (92) of *Solomon and Saturn* from his investigations is criticized and some suggestions are put forward on possible approaches to an analysis (347–8). A list of hypermetric verses is appended, organized by metrical types and including citations from the metrical Charms, *Fortunes, Maxims I, Maxims II, Order, Precepts,* Exeter Book Riddles, *Rune Poem,* and *Solomon and Saturn.* Verses such as 'þeof sceal gangan þystrum wederum' (*Maxims II* line 42a) are to be classed as hypermetric despite the fact that the first four syllables form a normal half-line (383). Sievers's poem-by-poem list of hypermetric verses is emended in the light of the foregoing analysis: these alterations affect Charms, *Fortunes, Maxims I* and *II, Order, Precepts,* Riddles, *Rune Poem,* and *Solomon and Saturn* (375–6). In a final note some emendations are mentioned as having been assumed for the present, with the detailed defence being reserved for a later publication: lines in *Maxims I* and *Solomon and Saturn* are cited here.

16 **Wülker, Richard Paul.** *Geschichte der englischen Litteratur von den ältesten Zeiten bis zur Gegenwart.* Vol. 1. Leipzig and Vienna: Bibliographisches Institut, 1896. viii + 422 pp. Rev. edn. Leipzig and Vienna, 1900.

Volume I contains a general survey of Old English literature, including the OEW poems. Wülker starts with portions of Charm 1, as representing the oldest Old English literature extant, once Christian interpolations stemming from an eighth- or ninth-century monk have been eliminated. Next come the other metrical Charms. The author speculates that Aldhelm may have written some of the Exeter Book Riddles, Cynewulf others. He mentions *Rune Poem* only in passing. The *Maxims* may owe their format to drinking contests, where each participant had to contribute a maxim in succession, following the rules of versification, or else pay a forfeit: this would account for an observed pattern where the linkage between one maxim and the next is determined by alliteration rather than by content (51). *Solomon and Saturn* is interesting as documenting numerous superstitions. Wülker goes against his earlier opinion (8) in identifying *Solomon and Saturn* II as the older of the two verse sections.

17 **Trautmann, Moritz.** 'Kynewulf der Bischof und Dichter.' *Bonner Beiträge zur Anglistik* 1 (1898): i–viii and 1–123.

Trautmann specifically excludes a large number of OEW poems from the Cynewulf canon: *Fortunes, Gifts, Maxims, Order, Precepts,* Exeter Book Riddles, *Solomon and Saturn,* and *Vainglory.* Among the criteria he uses are uncontracted forms of words like *beon* and monosyllabic forms of words like *clibbor.* He argues that the Riddles are heterogeneous as to date and authorship and that an ascription to Cynewulf can be upheld for only a few of them. In the chronological table of Old English poetry (appended) the Riddles are shown as mostly between AD 700 and 740, along with *Fortunes, Gifts,* and *Vainglory.*

18 **Wülker, Richard P.** Rev. of *Altenglische Spruchweisheit,* by Leon Kellner [108]. *Anglia Beiblatt* 9 (1899): 166–7.

Wülker complains that Kellner's edition contains only three small excerpts from *Solomon and Saturn* and one from *Precepts,* the other OEW material being completely ignored by the compiler.

9   Brandl, Alois. *Die angelsächsische Literatur.* Hermann Paul, ed., *Grundriss der germanischen Philologie.* 2nd edn. improved and enlarged in four volumes. Strassburg: Trübner, 1901–9. Also published as a separate edition with the title *Geschichte der altenglischen Literatur*: 1. *Angelsächsische Periode bis zur Mitte des zwölften Jahrhunderts.* Sonderausgabe aus der zweiten Auflage von Pauls Grundriss der germanischen Philologie. Strassburg: Trübner, 1908. [x] + 941–1134 + 10 pp. [i.e. continuously paged from the previous volume].

Brandl includes a survey of the following OEW poems under the heading 'Altheimische Dichtung vor Alfred': metrical Charms, *Maxims*, and *Precepts* are seen as belonging to heathen and/or ritual genres). The *Proverbs*, Exeter Book Riddles, and *Rune Poem* belong to early secular genres. *Fortunes, Gifts, Order,* and *Vainglory* are classed among pre-Alfredian Christian poetry. Brandl deals with the metrical Charms, *Fortunes, Gifts, Maxims, Order, Precepts, Rune Poem,* and Riddles in a general survey fashion, with some notes on metrics and style. His classification of the metrical Charms is formalistic in its basis. He dates *Maxims I*A and B as eighth-century, C as Alfredian. In *Maxims II* he sees two disparate elements combined according to a more or less conscious design: a heathen or heroic core and a Christian or pietistic set of additions. The Christian redactor was not concerned about the creation of internal inconsistencies. Brandl argues for a late (tenth-century) dating for *Solomon and Saturn*, partly because of its possible relation to the Benedictine Reform in England. He suggests that the second part of *Fortunes* may be a later continuation and reinterpretation of a heathen fragment.

20   Ward, A.W., and A.R. Waller. *The Cambridge History of English Literature.* Vol. 1. Cambridge: Cambridge UP, 1907. 13 vols. 1907–27.

The authors include a brief treatment of OEW poetry. They use metrical Charm 1 to argue that the gift of song was by no means confined to professionals but could extend to the 'plough-lad'. This text, perhaps the oldest in the language, reveals the ceorl's capacity for song and his nature-worship, with faint (if any) traces of Christianity. The writing down of the metrical Charms occurred at a comparatively late period, when the heathen practices which survived among the peasantry were no longer regarded as dangerous. *Solomon and Saturn* provides a clear illustration of the way in which Christianity combatted pagan beliefs, substituting the Paternoster for the ancient heathen war-spell. Saturn is a docile learner and mild disputant as contrasted with the saucily witty Marcolf of other traditions. The peculiarly English tone and character of the Exeter Book Riddles is in some measure due to Aldhelm's example. *Gifts* can be traced back to the 29th homily of Pope Gregory. The form of *Precepts* is compared to that of the Old Norse *Sigrdrífumál* and the last part of *Hávamál*.

21   Rankin, J.W. 'A Study of the Kennings in Anglo-Saxon Poetry.' *JEGP* 8–9 (1909–10): 357–422 and 49–84.

For the purposes of this investigation, Rankin uses the word *kenning* simply as a convenient designation of a metaphorical, a periphrastic, or a more or less complex term employed in the Anglo-Saxon poems instead of the single, specific name for a person or thing. Rankin seeks to show that the great majority of the

Anglo-Saxon kennings occur as a result of direct translation, close imitation, or freer variation and proliferation of the many Latin terms for God. These terms are found abundantly in the Vulgate Bible, the church hymns, and other Christian Latin literature. Rankin lists all kennings in Old English poetry under four headings: (1) for the Deity (1908, 410–22), (2) for ancillary religious concepts (heaven, hell, angel, devil, etc.), (3) for human beings and human activities, and (4) for the natural world (1909, 51–80). Latin influence is most marked with the first of these categories, least marked with the last. OEW poems are included in the lists but are not the subject of sustained discussion.

22 **Richter, Carl.** *Chronologische Studien zur angelsächsischen Literatur auf Grund sprachlich-metrischer Kriterien.* Studien zur englischen Philologie 33. Halle: Niemeyer, 1910. xii + 101 pp.

Richter includes various OEW texts in his chronology. He assigns *Fortunes*, *Gifts*, *Precepts*, the *Leiden Riddle*, and *Vainglory* to the period before Cynewulf, though some of these texts seem to belong more securely to that period than others. Among his criteria are the absence of the definite article, the treatment of intervocalic *-h-*, and monosyllabic realization of final liquid and nasal consonants. He agrees with Trautmann (**673**) in rejecting the attribution of the Riddles to Cynewulf and thinks it very likely that the collection of riddles in the Exeter Book stems from a variety of poets and even periods. Nevertheless, many of the Riddles, perhaps the majority, are to be assigned to the period of Cynewulf, i.e. the early eighth century. The chief linguistic criterion here is the treatment of intervocalic *-h-*. *Solomon and Saturn* is to be dated as late as the tenth century. Significant here is the disyllabic treatment of words with final liquid or nasal consonants, together with the predilection for end-rhyme and assonance. The metrical Charms elude a precise dating, though their general character speaks for the first half of the eighth century.

23 **Paetzel, Walther.** *Die Variationen in der altgermanischen Alliterationspoesie.* Palaestra 48. Berlin: Mayer, 1913. iv + 216 pp. [Part 1 appeared as the author's inaugural dissertation, Berlin 1906.]

Paetzel includes a list of variations in OEW poetry (133–5). OEW poetry is not specifically mentioned in his concluding summary (213–16).

24 **Heusinkveld, Arthur H., and Edwin J. Bashe.** *A Bibliographical Guide to Old English: A Selective Bibliography of the Language, Literature, and History of the Anglo-Saxons.* University of Iowa Humanistic Studies 4.5. Iowa City: U of Iowa P, 1931. 153 pp.

The bibliography includes works up to 1930. All OEW poetry is covered selectively, with very brief evaluative comments. Also included are bibliographies on relevant aspects of Old English culture, e.g. magic and medicine.

25 **Bartlett, Adeline Courtney.** *The Larger Rhetorical Patterns in Anglo-Saxon Poetry.* Columbia University Studies in English and Comparative Literature 122. New York: Columbia UP, 1935. 130 pp.

Among the rhetorical patterns detected by Bartlett is the 'envelope', where words used at the beginning of a passage recur at the end: this pattern can be seen in Riddles 13, 15, 42, 47, 48, 49, 51, and 56, with some other less definite possibilities. In *Gifts* we see 'an obvious and not very skilful use of the pattern' (23). Among the types of parallelism is repeated *hwilum* as the carrier of anaphora: this can be seen in Riddles 3, 12, 14, 24, 80, and 93 and in *Solomon and Saturn* lines 151b–60. A similar use of *oðer* occurs in *Solomon and Saturn* lines 367–9 and 488–96. For *sum* see *Fortunes* lines 10–63 and 71b–92 and *Gifts* lines 30–96 and 106–9, the last of these instances being without complete syntactic parallelism (42–3). The parallelism is of a rudimentary nature in Riddle 40 and *Rune Poem* (44). The handling of antithesis tends to be mechanical, as in *Gifts* lines 8–26, or rhetorically loose and inept, as in *Solomon and Saturn* lines 367–9 (46–7). Expanded lines mark a 'central' point in *Precepts* lines 17b–19, among other poems (64), but conversely can often be 'heaped' at the beginning or end of a 'long logical group', as in *Order* lines 98–102 (68). 'Because of the nature of the gnomic poems, their groupings can have little significance. The thorough-going irregularity of *Solomon and Saturn* and its dialogue plan make that poem also insignificant for rhetorical groups' (70). Bartlett suggests that 'the moralizing strain beloved by the Germans in heathendom and taking there a gnomic form was perpetuated under Latin Christianity in the less aphoristic, more hortatory (but not perhaps more didactic) form which is termed homiletic' (73). In her discussion of homiletic passages she includes *Fortunes*, *Gifts*, *Order*, *Precepts*, and *Vainglory*. She finds the Exeter Book also 'coloured by the moralizing strain' (75–6). Her discussion of 'decorative inset' includes a category of 'runic and macaronic', in which *Solomon and Saturn* lines 84–140 and Exeter Book Riddles 24, 42, 58, and 90 are briefly mentioned (84–5). 'The art of the [metrical] Charms is so chaotic that no patterns in their use of Latin words can be determined' (85). In the discussion of introductory formulas *Vainglory*, *Precepts*, *Maxims I*, *Fortunes*, *Gifts*, *Order*, and *Homiletic Fragment I* are mentioned. In her table of opening formulas in the Riddles Bartlett dissents from Tupper's (727) application of the term (91–6). Closing formulas are also discussed (96–100), with the Riddles again shown in a table. The discussion of the speech includes an analysis of the structure of *Vainglory* (104).

26   Wardale, Edith E. *Chapters on Old English Literature.* London: Kegan Paul, 1935. x + 310 pp.

Wardale includes scattered, brief comments on the OEW poems. She sees the *Maxims* as trite and commonplace but interesting on account of their popular origin. The metrical Charms are characterized by a standard tripartite form, as is demonstrated by a brief analysis of Charms 4 and 8. Their strophic form points to an early date of composition. The brief discussion of the Exeter Book Riddles includes a review of the controversy concerning Cynewulf's authorship. Wardale suggests that *Rune Poem* might be an early effort composed to assist the monks in learning the native alphabet; this would explain the presence of the learned word 'os'. She criticizes the lack of any plan of arrangement and the juxtaposition of heterogeneous skills in *Gifts*. *Fortunes* is a more original poem, though it overlaps with *Gifts* in content. A brief description of *Solomon and Saturn* is also included.

27 **Renwick, W.L., and Harold Orton.** *The Beginnings of English Literature to Skelton 1509.* London: Cresset, 1939. Rev. edn. 1952. 450 pp.

This bibliography is prefaced by a general introduction, which does not specifically mention OEW poems. The bibliography proper consists of a brief discussion of each genre, followed by a selection of readings. Included are metrical Charms (170–1), *Gifts* (184–5), *Precepts* (185), *Fortunes* (188–9), *Maxims I* (189), *Order* (189–90), Exeter Book Riddles 1–59 (195–6), *Homiletic Fragment II* (200), Riddle 30b and Riddle 60 (200), Riddles 61–95 (202), *Leiden Riddle* (211–12), *Rune Poem* (215), *Solomon and Saturn* (215–6), and *Homiletic Fragment I* (221). The Exeter Book is dealt with in a separate entry (177–9). [References here are to the revised edition.]

28 **Williams, Margaret.** *Word-Hoard: Passages from Old English Literature from the Sixth to the Eleventh Centuries.* New York: Sheed and Ward, 1940. xvi + 459 pp.

Williams considers much of OEW poetry in a chapter called 'A Pondering People', discussing it in its social and historical context. The numerous illustrative translations are intended to be as literal as possible. The section on the Exeter Book Riddles (134–44) includes quotations from Riddles 3, 7, 9, 14, 20, 21, 26, 29, 47, 48, 60, 85, 86, and 91. Williams argues that the Old English Riddle poet, as contrasted with Symphosius, develops his subject by means of a sort of dramatic insight into the human qualities of the object of which he writes. She also comments more briefly on *Rune Poem* (144–6), metrical Charms 1, 4, and 8 (150–6), *Solomon and Saturn* (158–65), *Maxims* (167–70), *Gifts* (170–2), and *Order* (176–8). Sample translation, from *Rune Poem* lines 27–8: 'Need presses on the heart, yet oft to the children of men/ it is help and heal, if they first bend before it.'

29 **Kennedy, Charles W.** *The Earliest English Poetry: a Critical Survey of the Poetry Written before the Norman Conquest with Illustrative Translations.* London: Oxford UP, 1943. Repr. 1972 with a new foreword by James P. Pettegrove. viii + 375 pp.

This survey includes coverage of virtually all the OEW poems. Kennedy sees the *Maxims* as having little central unity; they can be analysed to produce a taxonomy of aphorisms. He discusses *Gifts* as a Christian gnomic poem. *Fortunes*, though superior to *Gifts*, contains a slight blurring of the theme brought about by the poet's references to crafts in contexts where the central stress is upon varieties of human fortune. *Solomon and Saturn* is interesting for its pervasive sense of Necessity and Law and for its kinship to medieval contests of wit. In *Order* Kennedy criticizes a lack of balance in the treatment of Creation, whereby precisely half the passage is devoted to a glorification of light. *Precepts* appears to be indebted to the biblical Book of Proverbs. In the metrical Charms, the sutures by which the ancient pagan and later Christian elements became united are often easily discernible. The continued use of pagan elements can be associated with the policies of Pope Gregory. In metrical Charm 4 the reference to the smith is a survival from the legend of Weland the smith. *Rune Poem* should be seen as a mnemonic, not a literary composition. The Exeter Book Riddles are somewhat influenced by their Latin analogues and by learned writings. Such influence appears very strikingly in Riddles 1–3, with their indebtedness to Pliny and Lucretius. In their essence, though, the Riddles constitute a mosaic of the actualities of daily experience.

0 Baugh, Albert C. *A Literary History of England.* London: Routledge, 1948. xv + 1796 + lxxx pp. Rev. edn. *A Literary History of England.*Vol. 1 *The Middle Ages.* New York: Meredith, 1967. ix + 312 pp. + unpaginated bibliographical supplement.

The section entitled 'The Old English Period (to 1100)' is covered by Kemp Malone (1–105 in the second edition, to which all subsequent references are keyed). In Chapter 3 'The Old Tradition: Poetic Form' (20–31) Malone notes that only relics of the postulated original end-stopped versification remain in Old English poetry, examples being in the *Leiden Riddle*, the metrical Charms, and *Maxims I* (26). In Chapter 4 'The Old Tradition: Popular Poetry' (32–44) Malone discusses *Rune Poem*, Charms, the *Maxims*, and the *Winfrid Proverb* with wide-ranging comparisons to quasi-metrical passages from legal and other documents. Metre is given special attention throughout. On *Rune Poem* he comments that 'its practical value for would-be runemasters is comparable to that of ABC poems for learners of the alphabet. The runes were learned by name, and in a fixed order. It seems altogether likely that the runes from the first were learned by means of a poem in which each rune-name began a section. . . From this original poem the three runic poems extant were presumably descended' (34). As mnemonic verse *Rune Poem* is to be compared with *Widsith* and other 'thulas' [i.e. the Old Icelandic *þulur*, singular *þula*]. Like them, it 'started as a speaking, but in its present form it is better classified as a writing' (34). The structural resemblance to riddles indicates that the literary elaboration of *Rune Poem* may have been influenced by the Exeter Book Riddles. 'Versified wisdom . . . is old in English, older than the language, indeed. But it had to pay for the privilege of written record. The clerics who wrote down what we have of it made fewer changes, interestingly enough, in the spells than in the sayings. They presumably feared that a spell would not work unless they kept the old wording, while they knew a saying would hold good whatever the wording' (38). The metrical Charms reflect a tradition independent of classical Old English poetry, but allied to legal verses and to pre-classical end-stopped linear verse in their freedom. They 'vary much in literary merit, but they all have freshness and go' (39). A strictly Christian charm like the hypothesized archetype represented by Charms 5 and 10 may 'go back to a heathen original, but we need not make this presumption, since such spells might perfectly well have come into being in Christian times' (39). But Charm 10, as contrasted with its variant, Charm 5, has been altered by a medieval redactor to create a more classical verse-form. 'Evidently a Christian spell could not always hold its own against the classical tradition' (40). In Charm 9 the original heathen addressee might have been Godmund, not Garmund. The lists of 'biblical worthies' in Charm 11 are reminiscent of *þulur* (41). Charm 2 might always have been in a state of disorder. By contrast, Charm 4 is 'well built as it stands' and 'a little masterpiece of its kind' (42). The *Winfrid Proverb*, described as 'bookish', with its use of variation, is cited as comparable to the expression 'bugge spere of side oððe bere' ('buy spear from side or bear') quoted by the compiler of Latin laws attributed to Edward the Confessor (43). Although the *Maxims* are primarily compilations of traditional sententious wisdom, the clerical compilers have more or less remodelled their material to make it fit the classical run-on linear style and 'not a few passages are homiletic or reflective rather than gnomic in character' (44). In Chapter 8 'Religious Poetry: Poems on Various Themes' (78–87) Malone includes *Solomon and Saturn*, remarking that *Solomon and Saturn* II is superior to (and somewhat earlier than) *Solomon and Saturn* I and 'makes a worthy example of reflective religious poetry' (83). *Fortunes, Gifts, Homiletic Fragment I, Order, Precepts*, and *Vainglory* are also briefly mentioned in this chapter. In Chapter 9 'Secular Poetry' (88–95) Malone emphasizes the literary character and poetic value of the Riddles, noting that Riddle 47 does not even attempt to be enigmatic: 'the riddle form was stretched to include something merely paradoxical, and even this only by identification of the ink-marks with the words they symbolize' (89). Riddle 60 should probably be seen as forming part of *The Husband's Message*.

31 **Anderson, George K.** *The Literature of the Anglo-Saxons.* Princeton, NJ: Princeton UP, 1949. Rev. edn. 1966. ix + 444 pp.

In his Chapter 2 'A Foreword to the Literature of the Anglo-Saxons' (40–55) Anderson enunciates some 'axioms of Old English literature' (42). In his opinion, those features of Old English literature which are most comprehensible to a present-day layperson are those which pertain most clearly to the pagan sphere. One representative of this Old English pagan literature is the scattered residuum of folklore, such as the metrical Charms, most of the Exeter Book Riddles, and a great deal of the proverbial, sententious ('gnomic') verse and prose. The poetic form of these texts exhibits the 'childlike love of sound, rhythm, and fancy that is habitually associated with an isolated people' (45). OEW poetry is specifically covered in the chapter 'Miscellaneous Old English Poetry' (154–205), with notes and select bibliography appended. Anderson entertains the possibility that some lines in the *Maxims* are directly influenced by the Book of Proverbs, but thinks they are more probably mere analogues. He regards the 'general colouring' of even the 'quite pagan apothegms' as mainly Christian (170–1). *Gifts* and *Fortunes* are in essence also gnomic verses, though devoted to a particular subject. In *Fortunes*, 'as elsewhere, we are struck by the rarity of a natural death in Anglo-Saxon literature when the writing is not of definitely clerical origin' (171). The Exeter Book Riddle collection 'is the work of several writers, some laymen and some educated, some earls, some clerics, some even churls' (172). All the Riddles 'have a certain relation to the kenning, which imparts to the imagery of Old English verse its typical qualities' and many are 'nothing more than elaborate, successive kennings' (173). Anderson views the riddle and the kenning as precursors of medieval allegory. He dismisses the *Winfrid Proverb* with the comment, 'Only the pedant would be interested in its discussion here' (174). He finds *Homiletic Fragment I*, with its echo of Psalm 28: 3–4 (quoted here in English: 174–5), more interesting than the thematically related *Vainglory*. The speaker in *Precepts* is compared with Polonius: 'it is barely possible that the poem was in use in the church schools of the time' (176). The content of this poem is compared to *The Proverbs of Alfred. Order* is probably fragmentary, certainly incoherent, and less communicative on the topic of Creation than the much shorter *Caedmon's Hymn*. The metrical Charms are summarized and very briefly discussed. 'One should no doubt relegate such manifestations of the older order to the anthropologist, but the spirit which prompts these manifestations is also the spirit which produces Old English literature' (179). In the title of Charm 3 (as conventionally translated) the words 'against a dwarf' presumably mean 'against the illnesses which in popular fancy could be blamed upon the influence of a dwarf – lameness, faintness, epilepsy, and convulsions' (180). *Rune Poem* is dated at approximately 775, though with the acknowledgement that some scholars would place the poem earlier (182). It is explained as parallel to the treatment of the alphabet in present-day children's books. Despite the presence of a prose section, *Solomon and Saturn* is to be kept separate from the prose (Cotton Vitellius A.xv) *Dialogues of Solomon and Saturn*: 'it might be defined as an abstract discourse . . . upon the divinity of Christ' (184). Agreeing with Morley **(74)** concerning the 'non-Anglo-Saxon qualities' of *Solomon and Saturn*, Anderson remarks that its 'rather mature mysticism and scholasticism bespeak rather the Continental churchman' (184). A dating of between 800 and 850 seems appropriate. *Homiletic Fragment II* is 'quite negligible' (186). The metrical Charms are further discussed at 391–3 in Chapter 13 'Scientific Writing in the Old English Period' (384–402). Anderson sees Charm 2 as evidence of the loose bonds in which Christianity before the Norman Conquest held the English people.

2 ———. *Old and Middle English Literature from the Beginnings to 1485*. Oxford: Oxford UP, 1950. New York: Collier, 1962. 318 pp.

Anderson points out that English literature as a whole has been thoroughly impregnated with teaching and aphorism. Indeed, he alleges, English literary criticism has been prone to base judgements more on the meaning of a literary work than on its aesthetics. This tendency he relates back to the remarkable predilection for moralizing in Anglo-Saxon literature. The *Maxims* and other associated poems in the Exeter Book are not significant as *belles lettres*, since they are, in general, bald prosaic statements: *Precepts* and *Order* are 'negligible'. Rather their importance lies in yielding us half-opened vistas of the life of the common people of the time. The metrical Charms, for example, are the kind of thing an ignorant churl would remember from his grandmother and employ in situations not precisely covered by the Scriptures. He sees the Exeter Book Riddles as prefiguring later medieval literature, in that the type of mind that can develop a kenning and a riddle can soon make the transition to allegory.

3 **Magoun, Francis P., Jr.** 'Abbreviated Titles for the Poems of the Anglo-Saxon Poetic Corpus.' *Études Anglaises* 8 (1955): 138–46.

In Magoun's opinion, the poems of the Old English corpus, being oral or composed in an oral tradition, cannot be expected to possess contemporary titles. Texts so recorded would scarcely be felt as 'fixed' and thus something to which a 'title' would seem particularly meaningful to a singer. The singer's song of the occasion would be in response to a request 'Sing us about so-and-so or about such-and-such.' Magoun's proposed abbreviations for the OEW poems are as follows: *Fortunes* = FtM; *Gifts* = GfM; *Homiletic Fragment I* = HomI; *Homiletic Fragment II* = HomII; *Latin-English Proverbs* = LEP; *Leiden Riddle* = LdR; *Maxims I* = MxmI; *Maxims II* = MxmII; Metrical Charms = MCh; *Order* = OrW; *Precepts* = Prc; *Winfrid Proverb* = PrW; Exeter Book Riddles = Rdl; *Rune Poem*

= Run; *Solomon and Saturn* = SmS; *Vainglory* = Vgl. Grein's abbreviations, where available, are appended.

34 **Schlauch, Margaret.** *English Medieval Literature and its Social Foundations.* Warsaw: Państwowe Wydawnictwo Naukowe, 1956. xvi + 366 pp. London: Oxford UP, 1967. New York: Cooper Square, 1971.

Schlauch includes various OEW texts in her coverage. Some, such as *Order, Vainglory, Rune Poem*, and *Homiletic Fragment I* and *II*, are merely mentioned, without elaboration. Others are the subject of brief comments. Schlauch locates the chief interest of *Solomon and Saturn* in its revelation of the varied materials contributing to Old English didactic literature. In this respect she likens it to *Physiologus* and other learned texts. The metrical Charms are discussed as incorporating early, pagan material. In terms of their origin the *Maxims* may well represent the product of versified peasant experience; nonetheless, their extant form, not least the rather artificial breaks in midline, shows signs of literary redaction. Although *Fortunes* and *Gifts* are of Christian origin, the type they represent appears to antedate Christianity. The Exeter Book Riddles impart a learned conception of Nature, transmitted ultimately from Athens and characterized by a hierarchy of ranks of being. The theology served by this conception is, however, left largely implicit.

35 **Bonser, Wilfrid.** *Anglo-Saxon and Celtic Bibliography.* 2 vols. Oxford: Blackwell, 1957.

This vast compilation (through to 1953) includes selected references to 'general culture' that are pertinent to OEW poetry: magic and medicine, proverbs, and riddles.

36 **Ker, Neil R.** *Catalogue of Manuscripts Containing Anglo-Saxon.* Oxford: Clarendon, 1957. lxiii + 567 pp.

Ker discusses the date, palaeography, provenance, history, and condition of the manuscripts in which the OEW poems appear. Item 32: Cambridge, Corpus Christi College 41. This manuscript contains metrical Charms 8, 9, 10, and 11 and part of *Solomon and Saturn*. The manuscript is dated at the first half of the eleventh century. Item 70: Cambridge, Corpus Christi College 422. This manuscript contains *Solomon and Saturn*. Ker dates it as mid-tenth-century. Item 116: Exeter, Cathedral 3501, ff.8–130 (The Exeter Book). This manuscript contains the great bulk of OEW poems, namely (in order) *Gifts, Precepts, Vainglory, Fortunes, Maxims I, Order,* Riddles 1–59, *Homiletic Fragment II,* Riddle 30b, Riddle 60, and Riddles 61–95. Ker dates it at the second half of the tenth century: the hand is the same throughout. Item 137: Cotton Caligula A.vii. This manuscript contains metrical Charm 1 and dates from the first half of the eleventh century. Item 154: Cotton Faustina A.x. This manuscript contains one version of the *Latin-English Proverbs* and dates from the second half of the eleventh century. Item 179: Cotton Otho B.x, the leaf, now lost, containing the text of *Rune Poem.* Ker follows Hempl (**1002**) in his reconstruction of Hickes's methods in assembling his materials (1705). Item 191: Cotton Tiberius B.i. This manuscript contains *Maxims II*, written in a mid-eleventh-century hand. Item 231: Harley 585. This manuscript contains metrical Charms 2, 3, 4, 5, and 6. It dates from the end of the tenth century or the beginning to middle of the eleventh century. Item 249: Royal 2 B.v. This manuscript contains a variant version of the *Latin-English Proverbs* and dates from the mid-tenth century, with Old English annotations from the eleventh century. Item 250: Royal 4 A.xiv. This manuscript contains metrical Charm 12 and dates from the mid-twelfth century. Item 264: Royal 12 D.xvii. This manuscript contains metrical Charm 7 and dates from the mid-tenth century. Item 394: Vercelli, Biblioteca Capitolare CXVII (The Vercelli Book). This manuscript contains *Homiletic Fragment I*. Ker dates it at the second half of the tenth century. Appendix 19: Leiden, Rijksuniversiteit, Vossianus Lat. 4to 106. This manuscript contains the *Leiden Riddle*. The manuscript as a whole dates to the earlier ninth century, with the Old English text as a contemporary addition. Appendix 37: Vienna, Nationalbibliothek 751. This manuscript contains the *Winfrid Proverb*. Ker dates the manuscript as ninth-century.

7 **Wrenn, Charles L.** 'On the Continuity of English Poetry.' *Anglia* 76 (1958): 41–59. Repr. in C.L. Wrenn. *Word and Symbol: Studies in English Language.* London: Longmans, 1967. 78–94.

Wrenn does not refer specifically to any OEW poems, but identifies gnomic moralizing as the one perennial element in English poetry.

8 **Zesmer, David M.** *Guide to English Literature from Beowulf through Chaucer and Medieval Drama.* College Outline Series 53. New York: Barnes, 1961. xi + 397 pp.

Zesmer offers a brief introduction to 'charms, riddles, and gnomic verse' (74–7). He quotes excerpts from Gordon's **(174)** translation of some of the relevant texts and comments briefly on a few specific texts, e.g. *Maxims I* and metrical Charm 4.

9 **Dubois, Marguerite Marie.** *La Littérature anglaise du Moyen Age (500–1500).* Paris: Presses Universitaires de France, 1962. 174 pp.

Dubois offers brief summaries and comments on OEW poetry in this introductory survey of early English literature.

0 **Greenfield, Stanley B.** *A Critical History of Old English Literature.* New York: New York UP, 1965. London: U of London P, 1966. xi + 237 pp. + 2 maps.

Greenfield discusses and quotes translated passages from *Rune Poem* (191–3), metrical Charms 1, 4, and 8 (193–6), *Maxims I* (197–8), *Maxims I and II* (196–9), *Fortunes* and *Gifts* (199–201), the Exeter Book Riddles (204–8), and *Solomon and Saturn* (208–12). *Order, Precepts,* and *Vainglory* are more briefly dealt with. Greenfield argues that *Homiletic Fragment II* is a complete poem as it stands. He draws attention to the informative and hortatory nature of *Rune Poem*, but also to humour in the 'rad' strophe and a possible 'double entente' in the 'os' strophe. As contrasted with the *Maxims*, the metrical Charms contain a very specialized wisdom: they possess a certain magic in their occasional imagery, in their genuineness of sentiment, and in the suspense created by their ritualistic intention and structure. The author of the *Maxims* was undoubtedly a cleric who fused, in however ill-made a way, ancient and more contemporaneous aphoristic lore.

Greenfield resists the idea that the connections between aphorisms are simply a matter of alliteration. He finds *Fortunes* a better-integrated poem than *Gifts*: though the former perhaps deviates from an original intention of depicting the destinies of men, both the themes developed in the text (gifts and destinies) are drawn together at the conclusion. The variety and heterogeneity of the Riddles are emphasized. *Solomon and Saturn* II is compared with the elegiac poetry.

41 Schubel, Friedrich. *Englische Literaturgeschichte.* I. *Die alt- und mittelenglische Periode.* Sammlung Göschen 1114. Berlin: De Gruyter, 1954. Rev. edn. 1967. 168 pp.

Schubel makes brief comments on the OEW poems. He sees the metrical Charms, *Maxims*, and catalogue verse (e.g. *Rune Poem*) as representing essentially heathen genres, despite the outwardly Christian appearance of the extant examples. He attempts to distinguish different compositional strata in the *Maxims*. He emphasizes the heterogeneity of the Exeter Book Riddles in form and origins. Scholars, in his view, have concentrated unduly on the quest for Riddle solutions, at the expense of other types of investigation.

42 Standop, Ewald, and Edgar Mertner. *Englische Literaturgeschichte.* Heidelberg: Quelle und Meyer, 1967. 755 pp. 4th rev. edn. 1983.

The authors provide a brief introduction to the OEW poems, emphasizing the demarcation between Christian and pagan.

43 Wrenn, Charles L. *A Study of Old English Literature.* London: Harrap, 1967. x + 283 pp.

OEW poetry is considered principally in Chapters 9 'Lyric, Elegy, and Miscellaneous Minor Poems' and 10 'Learning and Folk Poetry', the latter comprising *Solomon and Saturn*, *Rune Poem*, Exeter Book Riddles, the metrical Charms, and the *Maxims*. These are presented as poems which all evince pleasure in the ingenious display of antiquarian learning. The rival claims of the various editorial titles of these poems are briefly commented on. Remarking on the scarcity of Anglo-Saxon love poetry, Wrenn takes the 'Frisian sailor' passage in *Maxims I* (lines 94–9) as suggesting 'rather the practical Germanic attitude toward marriage as described by Tacitus' (150). Problems with inconsistency make a combined Riddle 60 and *The Husband's Message* less likely than two separate poems, despite the prosopopoeic parallel offered by Riddle 30 (152). Wrenn notes the similarity in tone in the prologues of *Vainglory, The Wanderer,* and *The Seafarer* (157). In *Order* and *Precepts*, by contrast, the opening is a mere device for the homilist to make the exhortation seem more personal (158). The gnomic poems 'clearly contain in fossilized forms elements of the traditional Germanic practice of a type of mnemonic versifying combining didactic aims with the kind of pleasure to be had from old-fashioned nursery rhymes' (161). Wrenn sees Saturn in the two *Solomon and Saturn* poems as 'doubtless related to the Germanic god Woden ultimately, as well as to some Germanic representative of the Roman god Mercury' (162). *Solomon and Saturn* furnishes much material for the study of Old English and Germanic folklore and the Christianization of Germanic magic. The constituent strophes of *Rune Poem* may originally have been conceived of as riddles, with the rune name as the answer (163). Wrenn translates samples of the *Maxims*, contending that *Maxims II* is marginally more organized than *I*, where the ecclesiastical compiler 'seems merely to have set down whatever occurred to him of the heterogeneous gnomic and sententious material he remembered' (164–6). The metres of the Charms are to be regarded as pre-dating those of classical Old English poetry (166). The Riddles range in date from the composition of the *Leiden Riddle* down to the time when the Exeter Book was being assembled: the formula 'frige hwæt ic hatte' is as old as the Vedic Hymns. Most of the poetic power in the Riddles is found in their descriptions of the sea. Riddle 75 ('dog') is comparable to Riddle 47 in stating its solution at the outset. Riddle 28 suggests the quality of a harp through the repetition of sounds which are only very loosely related to meaning (170–5). The other OEW poems are all mentioned, but without substantive comment.

4 Bloomfield, Morton W. 'Understanding Old English Poetry.' *Annuale Mediaevale* 9 (1968): 5–25. Repr. in *Essays and Explorations: Studies in Ideas, Language, and Literature*. Cambridge, MA: Harvard UP, 1970. 58–80.

Bloomfield places Old English wisdom poetry in a very broad context of comparable medieval and classical, European and near-Eastern literature. He criticizes what he sees as a lack of serious attention to the genre in Old English studies. The poems conventionally categorized as Old English wisdom poetry represent no more than a sample of the wisdom literature represented by many Old English poems. For instance, the so-called elegies are really an extension of wisdom poetry. The purpose of wisdom and its literature is to suggest a scheme of life in the broadest sense of the word, to ensure its continuance, to predict its variations, and to associate humanity with the fundamental rhythms of nature. It is an attempt to control life by some kind of order, to reduce the scope of the unexpected and sudden. The genre consists of proverbs, riddles, fables, anecdotes, exempla, dialogues, list science, didactic rules, aphorisms, charms, and reflective poems. It is ethically, not ritually, oriented. The 'scientific' aspect of wisdom, as it contemplates the nature of things, has not always been recognized. The role of the teacher is simulated by the prevalence of direct address or dialogue form.

5 Cross, J.E. 'The Old English Period.' *The Middle Ages.* Ed. W.F. Bolton. History of Literature in the English Language 1. London: Barrie, 1970. 12–67. Rev. edn. Sphere History of Literature 1. London: Sphere, 1986. 29–80 and 403–4.

Cross makes very brief remarks on most OEW poems. *Fortunes* and *Gifts* are mentioned for their rhetorical repetitions and their vignettes of Anglo-Saxon life, *Precepts* for its usefulness in shedding light on Anglo-Saxon manners, *Vainglory* for its effective fulmination, *Order* for its model of the universe, the Exeter Book Riddles as an unexpected facet of the scholarly life, and *Solomon and Saturn* as an example of the eclectic learning to be found in Anglo-Saxon England. *Rune Poem, Maxims*, metrical Charms, and *Homiletic Fragment I* and *II* are also the subject of brief comment.

6 Peltola, Niilo. 'Observations on Intensification in Old English Poetry.' *Neuphilologische Mitteilungen* 72 (1971): 649–90.

Peltola's analysis includes the OEW poems. He studies the incidence of intensifying words such as *ful* and *oft*, together with the metrical constraints upon their use.

47 Shippey, T.A. *Old English Verse.* London: Hutchinson, 1972. 220 pp.

Most of the OEW poems are discussed or at least mentioned in passing in chapter 3 'Wisdom and Experience: the Old English "Elegies" '. They are depicted as alien to modern taste but as potentially revelatory concerning the nature of Old English elegies. The elegies indeed could be subsumed under 'wisdom literature', as the bias in the selection of poems in the Exeter Book tends to suggest. *Maxims I* lines 169–71 points to the idea that 'the poet gains experience, and is saddened by it; expresses himself, and gives cheer' (55–6). A principle of alternation between spontaneous reaction and conscious control in the elegies can be inferred. The taste for wisdom poetry in Anglo-Saxon England is attested by the poets' selection of prophets, wise men, and soothsayers among their heroes from Christian history (61). A native liking for the figure of the 'ancient sage' may well have been reinforced, in poems like *Daniel*, *Elene*, or *Exodus*, by Christian learning. To appreciate the elegies, it helps to find out what associations and linkages are consistent or latent in gnomic verse. Notable in this respect is *Solomon and Saturn* II, in whose 'half-agreements and cryptic modifications' something of the 'deeper reaches of Anglo-Saxon philosophy can be glimpsed' (63). The word 'warnung' in line 429a should be interpreted not as 'free-will' but as 'warning, advance intimation', reached through the application of wisdom. Detailed analysis of the poem shows that Solomon presents a picture of intense struggle in the universe and in people's minds, 'a struggle that produces suffering of all kinds' (66). With its emphasis on the Fall of the Angels rather than original sin as the source of this struggle, this text helps to explain the popularity of the Fall of the Angels as a theme in Old English poetry. A kinship with the elegies can be seen in the account of motherhood in *Solomon and Saturn* II lines 372–87.

48 Cameron, Angus. 'A List of Old English Texts.' *A Plan for the Dictionary of Old English.* Ed. Roberta Frank and A. Cameron. Toronto: U of Toronto P, 1973. 25–306.

Cameron lists the manuscripts and printed editions (among them those of the OEW poems) upon which the *Dictionary of Old English* will be based. Notices of editions in dissertation form, of editions in progress, and of proposed editions are given wherever possible. Reviews which include collations or lists of corrections are mentioned.

49 Barley, Nigel. 'The Proverb and Related Problems of Genre-Definition.' *Proverbium* 23 (1974): 880–4.

Barley points out that paremiologists have long sought for an adequate cross-cultural definition of the proverb, but no such thing exists. 'We do much better to forget the genres and concentrate on the features . . . and processes' (880–1). Old English proverbs resist definition according to a semiotic analysis based on modern English because they 'were included in the Anglo-Saxon category of *cwidas* along with wills and legal pronouncements, "maxims", and various other forms of oral statement. It is clear that legal principles such as *Kinsmen shall have property in common* are to be applied by particularizing synecdoche and the use of previous cases as precedent by metaphor. Thus, these semiotic processes do not suffice to characterize genres that are distinct for us. Moreover, they do not suffice to delimit Anglo-Saxon genres' (882). Although the Anglo-Saxon word *gealdor* may suggest a functional category of 'incantation' to us, texts so designated use precisely the same semiotic processes as the Anglo-Saxon 'proverbs'. Barley urges that we overcome the ethnocentrism that has led to the imposition of 'proverbs', 'riddles', and so forth as universal categories and avoid the fallacy that simply because we have a word it necessarily corresponds to a discrete aspect of reality.

0 Watson, George. *The New Cambridge Bibliography of English Literature.* Vol. 1 600–1660. Cambridge: Cambridge UP, 1974. 5 vols. 1969–77.

This bibliography is very brief but comprehensive. Page references are not given. For works on other than strictly literary topics, such as the magico-religious aspects of the metrical Charms, references to specialist bibliographies are supplied, e.g. to Storms (**418**).

1 Beale, Walter H. *Old and Middle English Poetry to 1500: A Guide to Information Sources.* American Literature, English Literature, and World Literatures in English Information Guide Series 7. Detroit: Gale Research, 1976. xiii + 454 pp.

Beale's plan is to present a selective but extensive and representative list of editions and criticism. In practice the presentation is highly selective: for instance, only six items on the metrical Charms are cited. Beale favours recent, English-language publications. Most titles are accompanied by descriptive and critical annotations.

2 Pearsall, Derek. *Old English and Middle English Poetry.* London: Routledge, 1977. Vol. 1 of *The Routledge History of English Poetry.* xiv + 352 pp. 4 vols. to date. 1977–.

This survey includes brief comments on OEW poetry. In his chapter 1 'Beowulf and the Anglo-Saxon Poetic Tradition' (1–24) Pearsall notes that the incidence of apparently primitive features such as end-stopped lines in the metrical Charms and gnomic poems does not mean that the poems themselves are necessarily of early date (6–7). In his chapter 2 'Anglo-Saxon religious poems' (25–56) Pearsall comments briefly on the *Homiletic Fragments. Homiletic Fragment I*, like all the other poems in Vercelli Book, is overshadowed by the twenty-two prose homilies which occupy the bulk of the volume and seem to have been regarded as intrinsically more important (48). *Vainglory* offers a schematic doctrinal commentary on what elsewhere, in *Beowulf* or *The Battle of Maldon*, is more complexly registered as deplorable or suspect as a pattern of human behaviour not essentially Christian (48–9). The envelope dramatic structure in *Order* clearly derives from an extension of sermon techniques, but the potential for a richer poetic development is nevertheless there (49). The compiler of Exeter Book includes material which can only be regarded as the débris or spoil-heaps of the

monastic tradition: *Fortunes, Gifts, Maxims I, Precepts,* and the Riddles, which
are a perverse encyclopaedia. This type of text is the raw material of poetry rather
than poetry itself and testifies to the monastic educational system (51). In chapter
3 'Late Old English Poetry and the Transition' (57–84) Pearsall comments that
Solomon and Saturn is one of the few poems outside the codices to preserve the
traditional poetic style and with it something of the generosity of temper and
range of interests of the older poetry. The first poem in this set may echo Hisperic
tradition in its eccentricity: Ælfric and Wulfstan would hardly have countenanced
the strange mingling of oriental, Germanic, and Christian elements (63). In the
second poem the contrast with Ælfric, for whom Wyrd is simply a false belief, is
as striking as the comparison with Alfred, grappling equally with the problems of
the powerful Wyrd that he substitutes for Boethius's more manageable Fortuna
(64). The metrical Charms and some of the gnomic poetry, which, along with
other texts, exhibit looser alliteration, stronger end-stopping, simpler and more
repetitive syntax, and, occasionally, relics of strophic form and refrain, testify to
a popular tradition which persisted alongside the classical style, ultimately to
outlive it.

53 **Nöth, Winfried.** 'Systems Analysis of Old English Literature.' *PTL: a Journal
for Descriptive Poetics and Theory of Literature* 3 (1978): 117–37.

Expressing dissatisfaction with standard genre demarcations, Nöth attempts a
taxonomy of Old English poetry according to the methods of systems theory. In
this taxonomy *Gifts* and *Order* represent the phase of equilibrium, *Fortunes* the
opposition between the two phases of equilibrium and disequilibrium, and the
metrical Charms a single-phase genre of the transitory phase. The Exeter Book
Riddles and gnomic verses represent two other major single-phase text types. The
Riddles, unlike the *Maxims,* can be considered a typical paradigm of a text in a
state of linguistic disequilibrium.

54 **Raw, Barbara.** *The Art and Background of Old English Poetry.* London: Arnold,
1978. 148 pp.

In Chapter 1 'The manuscripts of Old English poetry: the material and its
limitations' Raw groups *Homiletic Fragment I, Soul and Body I,* and *The Dream
of the Rood* as copied into the Vercelli Book from a single earlier manuscript (2).
Chapter 2 'The art of poetry' makes incidental reference to *Fortunes, Gifts,* and
Maxims I. Exeter Book Riddle 8 lines 1–3 is used as a contemporary attestation
of the variation technique (17). The power of poetry as consolation is attested in
Maxims I lines 169–71 (26). Chapter 3 'The poet and his audience' mentions
Precepts and *Solomon and Saturn* among the Old English poems that 'quote an
authority beyond that of the poet' (42). In Chapter 4 'The poet and his world'
Raw points out that the predictive statements to be found in gnomic poetry
suggest that there was an agreed view of nature and of landscape as well as of
human behaviour and goes on to show how narrative poems such as *Beowulf*
exhibit this view (48–50). Even in Riddles 1–3 the focus is on universals, not
upon a specific place (51). *Maxims, Order,* and *Solomon and Saturn* depict a
world controlled by God: Wyrd is subject to God and therefore an example of
order (60–4). In Chapter 5 'Poetic form' Raw documents the traditional linking of
judgement and wintry weather in *Solomon and Saturn* and other poems (68).

Gifts draws on the Parable of the Talents and Rom. 12: 3–8 to form a 'hymn', praising God's generosity and discretion. The form imposed by the poet derives from the opening and closing lines and from a linkage of different sections by logic and syntax (69–73). The main theme of *Fortunes*, also a hymn, is human helplessness: all fates, even death, are equally an expression of God's merciful care for men (73–4). In the *Maxims* most of the control over the logical progression of the poem is ceded to the audience, for them to construct as they please. This sharing of poetic creation implies a trust which could only have existed within a close-knit group with a common literary culture. In *Maxims I* there is a certain coherence: unities between 'man and nature' and parallels between 'man and God' gradually emerge (74–81).

5 Pilch, Herbert, and Hildegard Tristram. *Altenglische Literatur.* Anglistische Forschungen 128. Heidelberg: Winter, 1979. 261 pp.

The survey includes a general discussion of the Exeter Book Riddles, emphasizing the demarcation between those with Latin sources and those with Germanic sources. The rhetorical device of digression is seen at work in Riddle 55 (33). Similarities between the metrical Charms and material in Old Irish, Icelandic, and German point to a common European origin (35). Many dicta in *Maxims I* and *II* must have been intended allegorically, to judge from the anthropomorphic treatment of Nature (37). *Precepts* is to be distinguished from *Maxims* on the grounds that the former describes life as it should be rather than as it is. The *Winfrid Proverb* acts, however, as a reminder of the fragility of this distinction (38–40). *Rune Poem* is a mixture of proverb, maxim, and riddle, the last type approximated in the 'beorc' strophe (40–2). *Solomon and Saturn* is also to be associated with the riddle genre. The prose section in CCCC 422 is probably a continuation of *Solomon and Saturn* I, since the subject (the Paternoster) is the same. As with Riddle 56, some of the allusions in *Solomon and Saturn* resist definite solution (72–4 and 133). *Gifts*, *Fortunes*, and *Vainglory* show a mixture of homily and proverb. Appended is a review of recent scholarship that includes some comments on work on Old English wisdom poetry.

6 Amos, Ashley Crandell. *Linguistic Means of Determining the Dates of Old English Literary Texts.* Medieval Academy Books 90. Cambridge, MA: Medieval Academy of America, 1980. xiii + 210 pp.

Amos surveys a wide range of possible linguistic tests for the dating of Old English texts, including OEW poems. She excludes the sort of dating attempted by Ricci **(181)**, who assumed that the metrical Charms underwent centuries of oral transmission before they were first recorded. The linguistic tests applied in her book 'make no claim to detect that sort of prehistory in a text' (10). She finds that texts of any reasonable length that record only short vowels in words with loss of *h* should be considered later in general than texts that record both long and short forms or only long forms. Only *Cædmon's Hymn*, *Gifts*, *Juliana*, and *Precepts* contain exclusively long forms: such texts seem likely to be earlier than those with some short forms (33–4). The *Leiden Riddle* must be later than apocope of -*u* (25); the end-stopping in this text is modelled on its source (98). For additional material on OEW poems see Charts 2 'Metrically Attested Uncontracted and Contracted Forms of Words' (50–63) and 4 'Metrically

Attested Forms of Words Containing Syllabic Consonants with or without Parasiting' (78–9).

57   Greenfield, Stanley B., and Fred C. Robinson. *A Bibliography of Publications on Old English Literature from the Beginnings to the End of 1972, Using the Collections of E.E. Ericson.* Toronto: U of Toronto P, 1980. xxii + 437 pp.
This work is intended as a complete record of all relevant books, articles, and reviews, arranged by topics and with selective annotations.

58   Calder, Daniel G. 'Histories and Surveys of Old English Literature: A Chronological Review.' *Anglo-Saxon England* 10 (1982): 201–44.

In the course of this review Calder makes passing mention of various treatments of OEW poetry. He sees in particular Brandl (**19**) and Heusler (**166**) as breaking new ground in the discussion of wisdom poetry.

59   Alexander, Michael. *Old English Literature.* Macmillan History of Literature. London: Macmillan, 1983. xv + 248 pp.

This student introduction to Old English literature is liberally illustrated with free translations. In Chapter 4 'The world's wonder: riddles' (72–89) Alexander focuses on religious awe and the wisdom of the poem's commentary on its events as key features of *Beowulf.* Similar features are evident in much Old English verse, where traditional Germanic and Old Testament wisdom complement each other. Excerpts from Exeter Book Riddles 1, 3, and 29 are quoted in translation to exemplify religious awe (76–9). Awareness of the limits of human knowledge is a standard element in the Riddles. Other Riddles quoted in the chapter are 7, 25, 27, 28 ('barley'), 30, 47, 51, 71, 85, and 92. A sample translation from Riddle 25 lines 1–3: 'I'm the world's wonder, for I make women happy/ – A boon to the neighbourhood, a bane to no one,/ Though I may perhaps prick the one who picks me' (79). Riddle 60 is compared with Symphosius 2 ('reed') to show how thoroughly the English poet has naturalized and expanded his original (81). This text, along with Riddles 35 and 84, illustrates the danger of always associating what is animistic and heathen with the Old English tradition and what is sophisticated and Christian with the Latin (82). The 'pregnant brevity and enigmatic allusiveness' of the Riddles 'give them a certain formal similarity to the Imagist poems of Ezra Pound' (85). The chapter also contains Alexander's translation from *Maxims I* side by side with a translation by the Australian poet A.D. Hope (86–8). The beginning of *Order* is quoted to show how wisdom verse links with religious verse (88). Other OEW poems are mentioned in passing. Riddle 26 is quoted separately (32–3) as an example of clerical recreation.

60   Greenfield, Stanley, and Daniel Calder. *A New Critical History of Old English Literature.* New York: New York UP, 1986. xiii + 372 pp.

The book offers brief comments and evaluations concerning virtually the full range of OEW poems. [Much of this commentary differs only slightly from that in Greenfield's original *A Critical History of Old English Literature* (**40**).] In *Rune Poem* the circular structure of the poem and the humour in the 'rad' strophe are remarked on. Metrical Charms 1, 4, and 8 are analysed. An envelope pattern is suggested for *Maxims I*. The problem of the auxiliary *sceal* is discussed with special reference to *Maxims II*. The authors find *Fortunes* more graphic and detailed than *Gifts* and therefore better. *Precepts* is a rather uninspired series of admonitions, whereas *Vainglory* is richer, both in diction and in interpretive problems. In *Order* the sun-symbol unifies the basic ideas. *Homiletic Fragment II* is seemingly addressed by way of consolation to one in distress and, to judge from the thematic and verbal linking, should not be regarded as a fragment. Isaacs's (264) views on *Homiletic Fragment I* are accepted. As to the Exeter Book Riddles, we are urged to bear in mind the multiplicity of dates of composition, authors, themes, and types of source. Riddle 11 is solved as a 'cup or beaker of wine'. The second poetic section of *Solomon and Saturn* is preferred to the first, since it constitutes a true dialogue where Saturn propounds riddles in his own right.

1 **Hansen, Elaine Tuttle.** *The Solomon Complex: Reading Wisdom in Old English Poetry.* Toronto: U of Toronto P, 1988. ix + 228 pp.

Hansen argues that in OEW poetry the traditional communicative process is constructed and (usually) valorized as a collaborative effort. The emphatically abstract nature of the father's advice in *Precepts* requires that we make sense of the poem by reading it not as the incomplete and inadequate record of an outdated code of ethics, but as one manifestation of the human need for order. *Vainglory*, with its structural resemblances to *Precepts* and to Hroðgar's sermon in *Beowulf*, is to be seen not as vague but as an intentionally difficult poem, with an intimation of the limitations of human knowledge. *Order* is like *Vainglory* in characterizing and exploiting the audience's involvement in the creative process; it celebrates creation theology. In *Fortunes* and *Gifts* the various endowments and fortunes listed should not be construed as mimetic descriptions of actual experience but as instances of the generic and the typical, chosen for their cultural significance. In reading the Exeter Book Riddles we should look for the possibility of mutually exclusive interpretations and unresolved contradictions. Many of the Riddles seem to reflect a concern with potential sources of social conflict. They may address the tension between the affirmation of order and justice, on the one hand, and the experience of evil, suffering, and instability, on the other. Like the Riddles, the metrical Charms depend on a double process of breaking down certain conventional categories in order to make a renewed affirmation of structure. *Solomon and Saturn* evokes and then modifies a specific tradition, the Germanic flyting (or verbal contest); as in *Precepts*, the focus is not on content but on the traditional situation that is the framework for the poem. In *Maxims I* each section opens with a generic signal, introducing us to the rules of interpretation and encouraging us to affirm that there can be design in apparent chaos.

Bibliography of Miscellaneous Items

62 **Conybeare, John Josias.** *Illustrations of Anglo-Saxon Poetry.* Ed. with additional notes and introductory notices by his brother William Daniel Conybeare. London: Harding and Lepard, 1826. New York: Haskel, 1964. xcvi + 287 pp.

The selected texts, with verse translations, include excerpts from *Maxims I* and *II*, e.g. 'Again shall summer shine, again/ Shall winter weave his icy chain . . .' (*Maxims I* lines 76–7) (228–31). Other illustrations comprise *Fortunes* (204), *Order* (205–7), and two excerpts from *Solomon and Saturn*, lines 1–6a from CCCC 41 and lines 314–22 from CCCC 422 (lxxxiii–lxxxv). For the text of these latter two excerpts Conybeare draws on transcriptions by Wanley (1705) and a Mr Shelford, a Fellow of Corpus Christi College Cambridge. Despite the statement that the Exeter Book Riddles are 'so extremely obscure that they might well suffice to damp the ardour of a Saxon Oedipus', Riddles 2 and 3 (excerpts), 32, 46, 66, and 90 are included (208–13). The following solutions are mooted: Riddles 2 and 3 'sun', Riddle 32 'wagon', Riddle 46 'Adam and Eve with two sons and a daughter', and Riddle 66 'the Divine Power, comprehending at once the most minute and vast portions of his creation'.

63 **Kemble, John.** 'On Anglo-Saxon Runes.' *Archaeologia* 28 (1840): 327–72.

Kemble prints relevant excerpts from the Paternoster portion of *Solomon and Saturn*. In his view, it is the Roman letters that are essential, whereas the runes are dispensable. The absence of the letter *i* suggests the loss of some verses. Kemble also supplies a text and translation of *Rune Poem*. In his opinion, blunders such as 'segel' for 'sigel' in line 45 point to late composition. Significant in the same direction is the interpretation of the word 'os' as 'mouth', with the eclipse of its traditional sense. The use of runes in the Exeter Book Riddles is compared to Cynewulf's practice in his runic signatures. Riddles 19 and 75–6, the latter taken as one riddle, may contain mythological allusions.

64 **Wright, Thomas.** *Anglo-Saxon Period.* Vol. 1. of *Biographia Britannica Literaria; or Biography of Literary Characters of Great Britain and Ireland, arranged in chronological order.* London: Parker, 1842. 554 pp. 2 vols. 1842–6.

In a comparatively extensive discussion of the Exeter Book Riddles (79–82), Wright points out that although many of them are at present unintelligible (e.g. Riddle 18) they are by no means devoid of beauty or interest. He solves Riddle 13 as 'the Aurelia of the butterfly, and its transformations'. Riddle 28, to be solved as 'John Barleycorn', exemplifies how certain ideas run through the popular literature of different nations, regardless of period. Wright notes the sporadic use of rhyme in this riddle. Riddle 46 is to be solved as 'the patriarch Lot and his two daughters and their two sons'. The *Winfrid Proverb* is cited after Kemble (**641**). *Solomon and Saturn* is compared to the Latin *Disputatio inter Pippinum et*

Alcuinum, with the suggestion that it was designed for recitation to the common people. The use of runes in the Exeter Book Riddles, *Rune Poem*, and *Solomon and Saturn* is noted.

5 **Thorpe, Benjamin.** *Codex Exoniensis: A Collection of Anglo-Saxon Poetry, from a manuscript in the Library of the Dean and Chapter of Exeter, with an English translation, notes, and indices.* London: Pickering (for Society of Antiquaries of London), 1842. xiv + 546 pp.

The text and translation are arranged in double columns. Brief textual notes are placed at the foot of each page; fuller endnotes are also supplied. Thorpe's policy is to translate as literally as possible. The introduction (viii–x) contains some remarks on OEW poetry, excerpted below. Included in this edition is virtually the entire collection of Exeter Book Riddles (381–441, 470–2, and 479–500). Thorpe omits or curtails only those passsages which he regards as mutilated beyond restoration (Riddles 67, 78, 82, 89, 92, and 94). Riddle 88 is divided into two parts, the second beginning at line 17b. Thorpe comments on the Riddles in general as follows: 'Of the "Riddles" I regret to say that, from the obscurity naturally to be looked for in such compositions, arising partly from inadequate knowledge of the tongue, and partly from the manifest inaccuracies of the text, my translations, or rather attempts at translation, though the best I can offer, are frequently almost, and sometimes, I fear, quite, as unintelligible as the originals' (x). Although the *ænigmata* of Symphosius, Aldhelm, Bede, and others may occasionally have supplied the poet with topics, the Riddles are too essentially Anglo-Saxon to be viewed as other than original productions. Resemblances can be pointed out between *Maxims I* (333–46) and the *Sentences* of Theognis and the *Works and Days* of Hesiod, but rather than envisaging the Greek poems as a source we should see these and other similar productions as all having originated in a state of society common to all peoples at a certain period of civilization. Though in its present form subsequent to the introduction of Christianity, *Maxims I* constitutes a virtually unique vestige of the earliest kind of learning. Comparable are *Hávamál*, which also undoubtedly owes its preservation to oral tradition, and *Fortunes* (327–33), whereas *Order* (346–52) is apparently a later attempt at this style of composition. Texts and translations of *Gifts*, *Precepts*, and *Vainglory* are located at 293–300, 300–5, and 313–18 respectively.

6 **Kemble, John Mitchell.** *The Saxons in England: a History of the English Commonwealth till the Period of the Norman Conquest.* 2 vols. London: Longmans, 1849. Rev. edn. Walter de Gray Birch. London 1876.

Interpreting the 'ear' strophe in *Rune Poem*, Kemble suggests that 'our forefathers contemplated the personal intervention of some deity whose contact was death' (353–4). He cites *Solomon and Saturn* in support of the idea that we can detect 'ancient heathendom' in Old English depictions of the Devil and Hell (379–89, 394–5). Metrical Charms 4 and 8 allude to Valkyries (403–5). The texts of Charms 6, 4, and 1 are printed on 528–9, 530–1, and 532–5 respectively, using the edition of Grimm (**363**).

67 Klipstein, Louis F. *Analecta Anglo-Saxonica: Selections in Prose and Verse, from the Anglo-Saxon Literature.* 2 vols. New York: Putnam, 1849.

Klipstein offers texts and brief notes for various OEW poems, along with an introductory ethnological essay. The chosen poems include metrical Charm 1, at 1.251–4, following the edition of Grimm (**363**); *Gifts*, at 2.209–16; *Fortunes*, at 2.216–21; *Precepts*, at 2.222–6; and Exeter Book Riddles 13, 28, 46, 57, 61, and 74, at 2.337–40. Riddle 19 is solved as 'horse, man, wagon, and hawk'.

68 Ettmüller, Ernst Moritz Ludwig. *Engla and Seaxna Scôpas and Bôceras: Anglosaxonum Poëtae atque Scriptores Prosaici, quorum partim Integra Opera, partim Loca Selecta collegit, correxit, edidit.* Quedlinburg: Basse, 1850. Amsterdam: Rodopi, 1966. xxiv + 304 pp.

Most of the OEW poems are included, with texts based on the editions of Thorpe (**65**), Hickes (1705), Conybeare (**62**), and Grimm (**363**). The selected poems are metrical Charms 1, 4, and 11 (300–4); *Fortunes* (249–51); *Maxims I* lines 60–190 (281–3 and 285–6); *Maxims II* (283–4); *Precepts* (246–8); Exeter Book Riddles 2–5, 7, 8, 10, 12, 14, 15, 19, 22, 26–9, 31–3, 35, 37, 46, 60, 66, 80, and 86 (289–300); *Rune Poem* (286–9); and *Vainglory* lines 13–73 (248–9). The book includes an introduction and some brief notes. A few textual problems, e.g. the repetition of 'hand ofer heafod' in Charm 11 lines 24 and 27, are discussed. Ettmüller regards the *Maxims* as of popular origin and as a series of genuine proverbs which have been chained together ('tantum vinculo conjuncta') by alliteration.

69 Bouterwek, Karl W. *Caedmon's des Angelsachsen biblische Dichtungen.* 2 vols. Elberfeld: Bädeker, 1849–51. Rev. edn. Gütersloh: Bertelsmann, 1849–54. [Vol. 1 of the rev. edn. bears the Bädeker imprint.]

The first edition contains text only. The introduction to the revised augmented edition (i–ccxxxviii) focuses on cults of the heathen gods and the heavenly bodies among the Anglo-Saxons and contains passing comments on OEW poetry. Included are text and translation of *Maxims I* lines 125–37 (xcvii–xcviii). The text of metrical Charm 4 (lxxxv–lxxxviii) is based on Grimm (**363**). The excerpts from *Solomon and Saturn* (lxiv–lxix) are based on Kemble (**1047**) and are here translated into German for the first time. The exchange on Wyrd in *Solomon and Saturn* II lines 426–506 is used to illustrate the Anglo-Saxon belief in an inexorable Fate. Also cited is the passage in the prose section of *Solomon and Saturn* where the Paternoster attacks the devil with glowing arrows: Bouterwek comments on points of detail in Kemble's edition. He proposes the solutions 'hemp' for Riddle 25 (310–11) and 'millstone' for Riddle 32 (cix).

70 Grein, Christian W.M. *Dichtungen der Angelsachsen stabreimend übersetzt.* 2 vols. Cassel: Wigand, 1857–9.

These translations of Old English poetry into German alliterative verse include *Fortunes*, Exeter Book Riddles, and *Vainglory*.

1   **Dietrich, Franz.** Rev. of *Commentatio quae de se ipso Cynevulfus . . . tradiderit*, by Heinrich Leo **[657]**. *Jahrbuch für romanische und englische Literatur* 1 (1859): 241–6.

Dietrich comments on the cryptographic use of runes in the Exeter Book Riddles and *Solomon and Saturn*. He agrees with Leo that the text now known as *Wulf and Eadwacer* is a 'charade' on the name 'Cynewulf'. If this is so then it is reasonable to regard *Wulf and Eadwacer* as the introduction to Cynewulf's Riddles and to ascribe most of the riddles that follow in the Exeter Book to him, particularly those containing runes. Dietrich notes the archaic language found in the Riddles as additional support for the ascription to Cynewulf. He emphasizes, however, that not all the Riddles can be by Cynewulf. The Riddles confirm Grimm's **(363)** conjecture of a link with Aldhelm rather than Leo's assumption of a Northumbrian connection.

2   **Rieger, Max.** *Alt- und angelsächsisches Lesebuch nebst altfriesischen Stücken mit einem Wörterbuche.* Giessen: Ricker, 1861. xxviii + 353 pp.

The reader includes the *Leiden Riddle*, with textual notes (xxii–iii); the *Winfrid Proverb* (129n.); *Maxims I* lines 71–137 (129–31); Exeter Book Riddles 2, 5, 14, 26, 29, 35, and 47, with an attribution to Cynewulf (132–6); *Rune Poem* (136–9); *Solomon and Saturn* lines 1–20, 146–69, and 282–301 (139–42); and metrical Charms 1, 4, and 8 (142–6). All the texts are based on previous editions, notably those of Grimm **(363)**, Kemble **(1047)**, Thorpe **(65)**, and Wright and Halliwell **(364)**, but with occasional suggested emendations, e.g. 'wæpan wigan' in Riddle 14 line 1. A glossary is appended.

3   **Heyne, Moritz.** *Über die Lage und Construction der Halle Heorot im angelsächsischen Beovulfliede. Nebst einer Einleitung über angelsächsischen Burgenbau.* Paderborn: Schöningh, 1864. x + 60 pp.

Heyne uses the *Maxims* and Exeter Book Riddles to document Anglo-Saxon customs and such artifacts as the battering ram, hand-mill, and key. The antler is identified as an architectural feature (44). The Riddles principally drawn on by Heyne are 4 (27), 29 (14), 53 (20), 88 (44), and 91 (30). The meaning of Riddle 29 line 7b 'wealles hrof' is discussed (14). In *Maxims I* line 63, 'at hire bordan' is explained as 'at her house', parallel to Frisian *bort* in *bort-magad*. Heyne cites *Maxims I* line 90 for the custom of the queen serving the king with the first drinking-cup.

4   **Morley, Henry.** *The Writers before Chaucer, with an Introductory Sketch of the Four Periods of English Literature.* London: Chapman, 1864. Vol. 1 Part 1 of *English Writers*. 2 vols. 1864–7. 2nd rev. edn. *From Caedmon to the Conquest.* London: Cassell, 1888. Vol. 2 of *English Writers: An Attempt towards a History of English Literature.* 11 vols. 1887–95.

The first edition offers a brief review of Old English poetry. In his discussion of runic inscriptions, Morley develops the notion that runic messages could be inscribed on pieces of wood, some of them quite large. 'A long letter from her lover might be as much as a strong girl could carry in her arms' (247). The 'obvious solution' to Riddle 60 is that a 'writer – it might be a sweetheart who had many vows to send to a fair Saxon maid – took for his letter beam the stump of an old jetty' (248). A translation of Riddle 60 follows. Very brief descriptions of some other OEW poems are given, for instance *Gifts* and *Precepts* (325–26), which both exhibit a pure 'Christian spirit'. Also mentioned are *Fortunes, Order,* and *Maxims I,* the latter described as Anglo-Saxon proverbs: the Frisian sailor passage 'may have been a small strain of domestic song, heard now and then on shipboard' (326). Charm 1 is summarized with the remark that 'here is enough to keep a day busy from dawn to dusk' (326). The Exeter Book Riddles have a moral and religious purpose in common with the other poems that provide the immediate context in the manuscript (327). *Solomon and Saturn* I and II are treated as a single work. Morley highlights the Oriental hyperbole, humour, and other non-Anglo-Saxon qualities of *Solomon and Saturn,* concluding that the poem exhibits none of the characteristics of the Anglo-Saxon mind. He suggests that it may have been a version of 'a *Contradictio Salomonis,* withdrawn from the Canon in the fifth century by Pope Gelasius' (328). The dialogue in *Solomon and Saturn* II shows no sustained attempts at coherence. The second edition is greatly modified. A translation of *Fortunes* is added (2.32–37). Morley contends that too much ingenuity has been applied to the solution of the Exeter Book Riddles, especially by Leo (**657**) and Dietrich (**658**): to be correct, a solution should be simple. He modifies his solution to Riddle 60 to a 'letter-beam cut from the stump of an old jetty' (2.38). Additionally, he solves the so-called first riddle [*Wulf and Eadwacer*] as 'the Christian preacher', Riddle 90 as the 'lamb of God who overcame the Devil and destroyed his power', and Riddle 95 as the 'word of God' (2.224–5). He sees these solutions as militating against Cynewulfian authorship and follows Wülker (**83**) in also questioning other Cynewulf attributions, e.g. *Maxims I* and *II.* [For a review of the 2nd edn. see Bradley, **678.**]

75 Grein, Christian W.M. 'Zur Textkritik der angelsächsischen Dichter.' *Germania* 10 (1865): 416–29.

Grein makes a series of emendations in *Fortunes; Gifts; Homiletic Fragment I; Maxims I* and *II; Order; Precepts;* Exeter Book Riddles 1, 2, 3, 8, 9, 10, 11, 13, 14, 15, 17, 20, 21, 22, 23, 26, 27, 29, 30, 31, 32, 35, 36, 37, 39, 40, 42, 44, 47, 51, 53, 55, 58, 60, 62, 64, 66, 68, 72, 73, 83, 84, 88, 91, and 95; *Rune Poem; Solomon and Saturn;* and *Vainglory.* The emendations are listed without explanation or commentary.

76 Rieger, Max. 'Über Cynewulf. III, IV, V.' *Zeitschrift für deutsche Philologie* 1 (1869): 313–34.

Rieger notes similarities between *Gifts* and *Christ* lines 659–90 in their lists of gifts. He argues that Cynewulf, the supposed author of *Gifts,* here radically distorted the spirit of 1 Cor. 12: 8–10. In so doing Cynewulf was influenced by a theme current in traditional vernacular poetry, with which he was familiar before he became a cleric. The God described in the poem as dispensing the gifts could equally well be Woden, were it not for Cynewulf's inclusion of a few *cræftas* from the ecclesiastical sphere. If *Gifts* is a work attributable to Cynewulf's secular youth and mead-hall recitation, then *Fortunes* must be so too. Rieger sees the ending, with an emphasis on aristocratic gifts and virtues, as a compliment to the court. He points out resemblances between these two poems and *The*

Wanderer, The Seafarer, and the *Maxims. Maxims I* is attributable to Cynewulf on the basis of almost verbatim correspondences to *The Seafarer.* Rieger sees the popular content and brevity of these shorter poems as testifying to the form taken by entertainment in the hall.

77 Warton, Thomas. *History of English Poetry from the Twelfth to the Close of the Sixteenth Century.* Rev. edn. Ed. W. Carew Hazlitt, with a preface by Richard Price. 4 vols. London: Reeves, 1871. Microcard edn. Louisville, KY: Lost Cause, 1958.

Vol. 2 of this edition contains a chapter by Henry Sweet entitled 'Sketch of the History of Anglo-Saxon Poetry'. Included within it are brief comments on OEW poetry (3–19). Sweet compares the *Maxims* with *Hávamál,* arguing that although both texts may have been altered in later times, they belong to the earliest stage of poetry. He sees *Solomon and Saturn* as also containing a variety of gnomic sentences, which however are intermixed with other kinds of material within the dialogue form. Much of the poem is of foreign origin, and often wildly extravagant. Nevertheless, many passages have a strongly heathen character and probably represent fragments of some older text resembling the Eddaic *Vafþrúðnismál.* Sweet accepts Cynewulfian authorship of the Exeter Book Riddles.

78 Schipper, Julius. 'Zum Codex Exoniensis.' *Germania* 19 (1874): 327–38.

Schipper offers new readings, derived from a fresh scrutiny of the manuscript, in *Fortunes, Maxims I, Order, Precepts,* Exeter Book Riddles, and *Vainglory.* In the case of the Riddles and other fragmentarily preserved poems, he seeks to supply more information about manuscript readings and lacunae than Thorpe (**65**) had done. Additionally, he confirms a few of the emendations and restorations suggested by previous scholars.

79 Ebert, Adolf. *Allgemeine Geschichte der Literatur des Mittelalters im Abendlande.* Vol. 3. Leipzig: Vogel, 1887. 3 vols. 1874–87.

Brief comments on some OEW poems are included in this history. Ebert attributes the Exeter Book Riddles to Cynewulf, as a youthful composition, while admitting the possibility that some of them might represent the work of other poets. Though far from being slavish re-workings of any of the Latin riddles, the Exeter Book Riddles are closest to Aldhelm. The author of the Riddles was a 'germanische Romantik' (40–5). The section on didactic poems (84–96) includes coverage of gnomic poetry, a genre concerning which Ebert is very dismissive. *Fortunes* at least possesses greater poetic merit than *Gifts,* which has no poetic merit whatever. *Precepts* contains too many repetitions. The *Maxims* could be explained as a poetic game, where one participant recited a proverb and the next player had to tack another on to it with the correct alliteration. The influence of the Exeter Book Riddles can be traced in *Solomon and Saturn.* In its archaic, serious character, this work reveals its oriental background. It derives proximately from a lost Latin source which in turn was derived from Old Testament apocrypha in Greek. That the entire original may have been in prose form is indicated by the presence of a prose section in the Old English redaction.

Although not necessarily the work of the same poet, the two verse dialogues were mutually influenced and stem from a common source. Saturn is to be seen as not the Roman god but the leader of the Chaldeans (91–6).

80 **Rieger, Max.** 'Die alt- und angelsächsische Verskunst.' *Zeitschrift für deutsche Philologie* 7 (1876): 1–63.

Rieger discusses irregular versification in Old English, with passing attention to OEW poetry (*Maxims, Order,* Exeter Book Riddles, *Rune Poem,* and *Solomon and Saturn*). He uses the *Maxims* to exemplify *ljóðaháttr* in Old English, the Riddles and *Solomon and Saturn* to exemplify lines where the second lift in the second half-line alliterates, and *Order* and *Rune Poem* to exemplify quadruple alliteration over the whole line. His examples of total failure of alliteration include *Maxims I* line 117 and some lines from the Riddles; here, he suggests, rhyme sometimes seems to function as a substitute. He detects a metrical irregularity in *Maxims I* line 79 and suggests emendation of 'holen' to 'ele' to improve both versification and sense.

81 **Sweet, Henry.** *An Anglo-Saxon Reader in Prose and Verse with Introduction, Notes and Glossary.* London: Macmillan, 1876. Oxford: Oxford UP, 1879. Rev. edn. C.T. Onions, 1922. Rev. edn. Dorothy Whitelock, 1967. xi + 408 pp.

The Reader as currently published contains the following OEW texts: metrical Charms 4 and 8; *Maxims II*; and Exeter Book Riddles 7, 9, 14, 26, 29, 47, and 57.

82 **Kern, H.** 'Angelsaksische Kleinigheden.' *Taalkundige Bijdragen* 1 (1877): 193–209.

Kern suggests substituting 'foldgæg' for the supposed manuscript reading 'foldgræg' in *Maxims II* line 31. [Early editions all incorrectly read 'foldgræg' for 'flodgræg' here.] The second element *gæg would be identical to the first word in the Otfrid phrase *gahez wazzer* 'decurrens aqua'. Indeed, the form *græg* may represent a by-form of *gæg*. The compound would have a similar structure and meaning to *grundfus* and *helfus*. In Exeter Book Riddle 23 line 9 'ealfelo' should be explained as 'completely pale or bleak'. In *Maxims I* line 117, 'adl' should be emended to 'hald'.

83 **Wülker, Richard P.** 'Über den Dichter Cynewulf.' *Anglia* 1 (1878): 483–507.

Wülker argues for a firm ascription of the Exeter Book Riddles to Cynewulf, who describes himself as 'indryhten' in Riddle 95 line 1. The concealment of Cynewulf's name in Riddle 90 suggests that he had some familiarity with Latin. The Riddles date from his youthful stint as an itinerant singer (506–7). On the other hand, the dialect of the *Leiden Riddle* cannot be used to prove that Cynewulf was a Northumbrian (500) and the attribution to him of *Fortunes, Gifts, Maxims, Order,* and *Vainglory* should be rejected.

84 **Grein, Christian W.M.** *Kurzgefasste angelsächsische Grammatik.* Kassel: Wigand, 1880. iv + 92 pp.

In a brief survey of Anglo-Saxon literature Grein dates *Maxims, Precepts,* and

Solomon and Saturn to the beginning of the eighth century, *Rune Poem* conjecturally to the seventh. He finds *Solomon and Saturn* II lacking in cohesion (9). He attributes the complete collection of Exeter Book Riddles to Cynewulf and praises their poetic qualities: they are no mere guessing game but embody an evocation of Nature. Also Cynewulfian are *Gifts, Order, Precepts,* and *Vainglory* (11–15).

35 Wülker, Richard Paul. *Kleinere angelsächsische Dichtungen: Abdruck der handschriftlichen Überlieferung mit den Lesarten der Handschriften und einem Wörterbuch.* Halle: Niemeyer, 1882. vi + 169 pp.

Included here are metrical Charms 1, 2, 4, and 8; *Maxims I* and *II; Precepts*; and *Rune Poem.* Wülker supplies conservative texts, with very brief textual notes and glossary.

36 Lefèvre, P. 'Das altenglische Gedicht vom Heiligen Guthlac.' *Anglia* 6 (1883): 181–240.

Lefèvre rejects Cynewulfian attributions of *Fortunes, Gifts, Maxims I, Order,* and *Vainglory* as unsupported by evidence or argument. He regards Exeter Book Riddles 1–60 as among the secure attributions, the remainder of the Riddles being highly probable. Passages from the Riddles are cited in passing, to illustrate alliterative and rhyming patterns, caesura, end-stopping, and other features of versification. Despite these arguments, Lefèvre leaves the Riddles aside in the ensuing discussion of the literary affiliations of *Guthlac,* referring solely to the signed Cynewulfian poems *Juliana, Christ,* and *Elene.*

37 Merbot, Reinhold. *Ästetische Studien zur angelsächsischen (altenglischen) Poesie.* Diss. U Breslau. Breslau: Koebner, 1883. 37 pp.

Merbot's discussion of the profession of poet includes detailed word studies (e.g. *gied, scop,* and *woðbora*) with citations from OEW poems. He argues that the words *woðbora* and *scop* should be differentiated, the one being primarily religious and the other primarily secular in their respective semantic ranges. He discusses the concept of *cræft* in relation to *Gifts.* Poetic performance in general is examined with reference to *Gifts* and *Fortunes.*

38 Earle, John. *Anglo-Saxon Literature.* London: SPCK, 1884. vi + 262 pp.

Earle includes brief comments on some OEW poems in this introductory survey. Although some of the strophes in *Rune Poem* are possibly ancient, much of the poem must be regarded as late and dilettante work. Not all the rune names are clearly authentic. Most of the Exeter Book Riddles show the influence of Symphosius and Aldhelm, though some are of native origin. The metrical sections of Charm 1 probably include some fragments from a genuinely ancient heathen charm. The poetic sections of *Solomon and Saturn* are rather insipid. So extravagant, by contrast, is the prose section that the reader suspects a 'tinge of drollery'. 'The earliest laughter of English literature is ridicule; and if this ridicule seems to touch things sacred, it will, on the whole, I think, be found that not the sacred things themselves, but some unreal or spurious use of them, is really attacked. So here, if there is any appearance of a sly derision, the thing derided is not the Paternoster, but the vain and magical uses which were too often ascribed to the repetition of it' (210–12).

89   Merbach, Hans Johann. *Das Meer in der Dichtung der Angelsachsen.* Diss. U Breslau. Breslau: Gutenberg, 1884. 59 pp.

In this study of lexical items and sets relating to 'sea' in Old English poetry Merbach traces instances of the notion that the sea 'covers' the earth in Exeter Book Riddle 16, *Maxims I,* and elsewhere (10). Also included is a brief discussion of 'warig' (*Maxims I* line 98) in relation to other *war-* words (28–9).

90   Sievers, Eduard. 'Zur Rhythmik des Alliterationsverses II.' *Beiträge zur Geschichte der deutschen Sprache und Literatur* 10 (1885): 451–545.

In this article Sievers extends his five-type metrical system from *Beowulf* to other Old English poetry. Taking some emendations proposed by previous scholars in the texts of *Order,* Exeter Book Riddles, *Rune Poem, Solomon and Saturn,* and *Vainglory,* he tests them against his system and shows that many of them have to be rejected (512–20).

91   Sweet, Henry. *The Oldest English Texts.* EETS 83. London: Oxford UP, 1885. vii + 668 pp.

Sweet's compilation includes the text of the *Leiden Riddle* and Exeter Book Riddle 35 (149–51). In his brief account of the manuscript and its editors, he notes Bethmann's ignorance of Old English (**65**), Rieger's (**72**) use of and emendations to Dietrich's transcript (**659**), and Pluygers's entirely objective and very valuable reading (cf. **720**), correcting Dietrich. Sweet lists the differences between Dietrich's transcript and the results of his own independent investigation of the manuscript. He sees the text as a direct copy of an original Old Northumbrian one. Also included is the *Winfrid Proverb,* based on Massmann's facsimile (**642**) of the Vienna manuscript. The word 'dædlata' points clearly either to a West Saxon original or to a West Saxon scribe (151–2).

92   Sievers, Eduard. 'Zur Rhythmik des germanischen Alliterationsverses III: Der angelsächsische Schwellvers.' *Beiträge zur Geschichte der deutschen Sprache und Literatur* 12 (1887): 454–82.

The discussion includes hypermetric verses in *Maxims, Order, Precepts,* Exeter Book Riddles, and *Rune Poem. Solomon and Saturn* is excluded, on the grounds that the irregular metrical structure of this work separates it from other Old English poetry. Indeed it is often difficult to determine if a given passage consists of poetry or prose. Nevertheless, some preliminary comments towards an analysis of the metrical system in *Solomon and Saturn* are appended. Emendations in *Order* line 77 and *Precepts* line 31 are attempted, to create a normal hypermetric half-line. In *Maxims I* a form similar to *ljóðaháttr* can be discerned, but some other lines, especially the three-syllable ones, do not fit any attested system. These irregularities can be attributed to the influence of actual proverbs in everyday use and have no evidential value for the Old English metrical system. A comprehensive list of hypermetric verses is included.

3 **Sweet, Henry.** *A Second Anglo-Saxon Reader: Archaic and Dialectal.* Oxford: Clarendon, 1887. Rev. edn. T.F. Hoad 1978. xii + 237 pp.

Texts of the *Leiden Riddle* and *Winfrid Proverb* are included. The editor of the revised edition comments that the principal concern has been to make the various texts as accurate as possible. Notes and glossary are not included.

4 **Kluge, Friedrich.** *Angelsächsisches Lesebuch zusammengestellt und mit glossar versehen.* Halle: Niemeyer, 1888. Rev. edn. 1897, 1902, and 1915. ii + 206 pp.

This reader comprises critical apparatus and extensive glossary but no annotations or introduction. In the fourth edition the selected texts include metrical Charms 4 and 8 (114–15), *Rune Poem* (138–40), and *Maxims II* (141–2). The first three editions additionally contained metrical Charm 1, along with 4 and 8 (20–3 of the second and third editions). In *Rune Poem* line 73 Kluge emends 'bleadum' to 'bleaðum'.

5 **Sarrazin, Gregor.** *Beowulf-Studien. Ein Beitrag zur Geschichte altgermanischer Sage und Dichtung.* Berlin: Mayer, 1888. vii + 220 pp.

Sarrazin canvasses the possible attribution of some OEW poems to Cynewulf. He traces verbal resemblances in *Fortunes*, *Gifts*, *Order*, *Vainglory*, *Maxims*, and *Solomon and Saturn*. Cynewulf's role in poems like these might have been that of a redactor or interpolator or perhaps an influence upon a later poet. Strong similarities can be detected between *Beowulf* and the signed works of Cynewulf on the one hand and *Maxims II* on the other, suggesting that if *Maxims II* is not by the same author then at the least this text must originate with a sensitive imitator. Sarrazin defends Cynewulfian authorship of the Exeter Book Riddles against Trautmann (**673**), adducing new parallels both with the signed works and with *Beowulf*.

6 **Cook, Albert S.** 'The Affinities of the Fata Apostolorum.' *Modern Language Notes* 4 (1889): 7–15.

Cook compares the vocabulary of *Fata Apostolorum* with that of *Vainglory* and the Exeter Book Riddles. The attribution of the Riddles to Cynewulf is dubious.

7 **Gummere, Francis B.** *On the Symbolic Use of the Colors Black and White in Germanic Tradition.* 1889. 52 pp. [No further publication details are available.]

In some passing comments, Gummere proposes that the expressions 'to the north' and 'to the mountains' in metrical Charm 12 line 3 equate with 'to the devil'. The motif of a cold hell, found in *Solomon and Saturn* line 469, should be seen in the context of medieval visions of hell. Gummere collects references in the Exeter Book Riddles to dark hair and complexion.

8 **Hoops, Johannes.** *Über die altenglischen Pflanzennamen.* Diss. U Freiburg. Freiburg: Lehmann, 1889. 84 pp.

Chapter 1 (12–41), dealing with references to plants in Old English poetry, makes scattered mentions of OEW poems. Hoops proposes a more scientifically and historically oriented approach than that of Lüning (**11**). Relevant are the following comments: the use of *wlite, torht,* and their derivatives to mean 'beautiful' rather than simply 'bright', illustrated from *Rune Poem* and the Exeter Book Riddles (20–1); words for 'sea-weed', with citation of *Maxims I* (25); 'eolxsecg' in *Rune Poem* line 41 (26); rose and lily in Riddle 40 as among nature descriptions influenced by classical literature (28–9); thorn in *Rune Poem* (30); trees in the Exeter Book Riddles (31 and 35); the utilitarian attitude to the oak in *Rune Poem*, with the comment that in northern Europe ground acorns are still used in food for human consumption (35); the ash in *Rune Poem* and Riddle 42 (36–7); the birch and yew in *Rune Poem* (37–8); the beech in Riddle 40 (37–8); the four woods in Riddle 55, with a query as to why the 'holen' would be described as 'fealwa' in line 10 (38); and the formula 'swa breþel swa þystel' in metrical Charm 9 line 17 (41). In Chapter 2, which deals with superstitions relating to plants, Hoops mentions Charm 1 (55) and provides a complete edition, with new emendations, translation, and notes, of Charm 2 (55–64).

99   Cosijn, Peter J. 'Cynewulf's Runenverzen.' *Verslagen en Mededeelingen der Koninklijke Akademie van Wetenschappen. Afdeeling Letterkunde.* 3rd ser. 7 (1890): 54–64.

Cosijn discusses the meaning of 'yr' in *Rune Poem* line 84, expressing dissatisfaction with all existing theories. He assumes Cynewulfian authorship of Exeter Book Riddle 90 and of *Wulf and Eadwacer.*

100   Meyer, Elard Hugo. *Germanische Mythologie.* Lehrbücher der germanischen Philologie 1. Berlin: Mayer, 1891. xii + 354 pp.

Meyer cites individual words from the metrical Charms and other OEW poetry, but does not comment on the texts as such.

101   Sievers, Eduard. *Altgermanische Metrik.* Sammlung kurzer Grammatiken germanischer Dialekte, Ergänzungsreihe 2. Halle: Niemeyer, 1893. xvi + 252 pp. Abridged version: 'Altgermanische Metrik.' *Grundriss der germanischen Philologie.* Ed. Hermann Paul. Vol. 2a. Strassburg: Trübner, 1893. 861–97. 3 vols. 1891–93. Rev. edn. improved and enlarged. Vol. 2b. 1905. 1–38. 4 vols. 1901–9. Trans. in abridged form by Gawaina Luster as 'Old Germanic Metrics and Old English Metrics'. In *Essential Articles for the Study of Old English Poetry.* Ed. J.B. Bessinger and S.J. Kahrl. Hamden, CT: Archon, 1968. 267–88.

Sievers observes that although most Old English poetry is not strophic, a strophe-like pattern emerges in *Maxims I* and *Wulf and Eadwacer,* where the smooth succession of regular bipartite long-lines is repeatedly interrupted by undivided long-lines. Both poems also contain *ljóðaháttr*-like formations. From the sporadic occurrence of lines without caesura in *Maxims I* and elsewhere we may infer that the origin of the Old Norse *ljóðaháttr* stanza goes back to the common Germanic period. But these vestiges are too scanty to permit secure conclusions concerning either the structure of the undivided line or the extent of strophic formations in Old English gnomic poetry. Quasi-stanzaic formations, as seen in *Rune Poem*, should be compared to French *tirades* rather than to true stanzas. Sievers notes instances of end-rhyme combined with internal rhyme, as in *Vainglory* and *Rune Poem*, but ascribes much of it to chance.

2 **Abbey, C.J.** *Religious Thought in Old English Verse.* London: Low, Marston, 1892. xiii + 456 pp.

Abbey passes brief opinions on some OEW poems. He comments, partly following Kemble **(1047)**, that the strong religious feeling of the Anglo-Saxons preserved *Solomon and Saturn* from the coarse and flippant humour that characterizes European treatments of the material. *Precepts* is a didactic poem which inculcates sound religious morality. *Gifts* is like a Christian version of a Greek choral hymn, with *Fortunes* as a companion-piece. *Order* shows a mind keenly alive to the beauty of created things. Excerpts from each poem (in translation) are appended.

3 **Gummere, Francis B.** *Germanic Origins: A Study in Primitive Culture.* New York: Scribner, 1892. viii + 490 pp. Rev. edn. F.P. Magoun, Jr. *Founders of England.* New York: Stechert, 1930.

Gummere discusses *Solomon and Saturn* and metrical Charm 4 in relation to the cult of 'mighty women' or *dísir*, with an annotated translation of Charm 4 (372). He discusses Charm 1 in relation to the worship of Nature, again with an annotated translation (405). On the literary-critical front, he praises the evocation of sword and hilts in *Solomon and Saturn* lines 223–4, finding in it 'something of the later romantic shudder' (312).

4 **Schröder, Eduard.** 'Über das Spell.' *Zeitschrift für deutsches Altertum* 37 (1893): 241–68.

This article has some general relevance to the metrical Charms and *Precepts*. Schröder comments that the word *spell*, as used in *Precepts* line 25, relates to the 'instruction' part of that word's semantic range, not the 'narrative' part. He also discusses lexical items with relevance to the Charms, e.g. *sang* and *gealdor*.

5 **Holthausen, Ferdinand.** 'Beiträge zur Erklärung und Textkritik altenglischer Dichtungen.' *Indogermanische Forschungen* 4 (1894): 379–88.

Holthausen supplies brief textual notes on and emendations to *Homiletic Fragment II* and various Exeter Book Riddles, mostly with the aim of improving the versification. He solves Riddle 58 as 'well-sweep'. The Old English word for this device would have been *rod*, not *rad*, the reading contained in the manuscript (line 15).

6 **Kögel, Rudolf.** *Geschichte der deutschen Litteratur bis zum Ausgange des Mittelalters.* Vol. 1. *Bis zum Mitte des elften Jahrhunderts.* Part 1. *Die stabreimende Dichtung und die gotische Prosa.* xxiii + 343 pp. Strassburg: Trübner, 1894. 2 vols. 1894–7.

Kögel includes scattered remarks on OEW poetry. In the course of discussing the early Germanic charms, he uses some of the Old English metrical Charms as illustrative material. Charm 4, which he translates, receives special attention. Lines 20–6 should be excised as an interpolation, which originated as a parallel composition designed to replace lines 3–19 (93–5). Charm 1 contains an ancient heathen core which has its origins in continental Europe and can be compared

with the myth of Freyr and Gerðr in *Skírnismál*. The offering to the soil can be
construed as a form of rune magic where the Christian symbols function merely
as substitutes for heathen precursors. Lines 30–1 represent another interpolation.
The word 'erce' is to be explained as 'earth' (39–42). Kögel uses the Old English
texts as a means of inferring the form of Germanic gnomic poetry. He thinks that
the material underlying *Maxims I* was converted into the standard long-line
scheme carelessly, hence the presence of so many irregular lines. In discussing
the versification, he places special emphasis on *ljóðaháttr*.

107 **Gollancz, Israel.** *The Exeter Book, Part I, Poems I–VIII.* EETS 104. London:
Oxford UP, 1895. viii + 305 pp.

Included in this volume are texts and parallel translations of *Gifts* (292–9) and
Precepts (300–5). In his 'Prefatory Note' (vii) Gollancz announced a plan to
issue the present edition in three parts, with Parts II (remaining text and
translation) and III (notes, introductions, and indexes) to follow shortly. [In fact
they were never completed: for further information see Mackie's completion
(**188**).] Gollancz announces a conservative editorial policy: the readings of the
manuscript have been preferred to plausible emendations. He notes that it is
surprising how often the manuscript is correct. Annotations are restricted to
variations from the manuscript readings. A sample translation, from *Gifts* (lines
72–7): 'One understandeth the laws, when people/ seek counsel. One is expert at
dice./ One is witty at wine bibbing,/ a good beer-keeper. One is a builder,/ good at
raising a house. One is a general,/ a bold leader of the host. One is a senator.'

108 **Kellner, Leon.** *Altenglische Spruchweisheit: Alt- und mittelenglischen Autoren
entnommen.* Programm der K.K. Realschule zu Wien. Vienna: Gerold, 1897. 26
pp.

Kellner collects snippets of wisdom from Old English and Middle English
literature and arranges them under such headings as 'Wechselfälle des Lebens',
'Weisheit und Bildung: Bücher', and 'Klugheit, Vorsicht, Schweigsamkeit'. He
includes one brief excerpt from *Precepts* and three from *Solomon and Saturn*; his
texts are taken respectively from Gollancz (**107**) and Kemble (**1047**). There are
no notes or discussion. [For a review see Wülker, **18**.]

109 **Brooke, Stopford A.** *English Literature from the Beginning to the Norman
Conquest.* London: Macmillan, 1898. ix + 340 pp.

This book represents an abridged and re-worked version of the Old English
section of Brooke (**13**). The text is liberally illustrated with translations from the
Old English. In his Chapter 2 'Old English Heathen Poetry', Brooke presents
metrical Charm 1 lines 51–8 as part of an ancient lay sung by ploughmen in the
Germanic continental homelands. He translates lines 69–70 as 'Hale be thou
Earth, Mother of men!/ Fruitful be thou in the arms of the god', commenting that
these lines may be the oldest 'stave' in any 'modern language' (43–4). Other parts
of Charm 1 have undergone Christian revision. Charm 4 offers a clear reference
to Valkyries, whereas in Charm 8 'sigewif' as addressed to the bees is better
understood as a term of endearment (44–5). Charm 2 represents a later stage than
Charm 1, since in it the 'mythical Heaven and Earth, the nature deities', are

succeeded by 'the far more personal Woden of the third century' (45). In Chapter 5 'Semi-heathen poetry' Brooke expresses the view that 'a good deal of poetry among the people', including 'the Riddles of Cynewulf', was 'scarcely touched by Christianity' (86–7). Brooke here gives a literary appreciation of many of the Exeter Book Riddles. The strongly felt impersonation of sword, shield, helmet, and bow in the Riddles bespeaks the tenacity of the ancient warrior ethos (87–8). The descriptions of nature for its own sake that we find in the Riddles are quite singular in early modern poetry: the 'power of clouds' (Riddle 7 line 5) is 'a phrase Wordsworth might have used' (91). The spirit of audacious lordship over the sea has been replaced by the 'agriculturist's' fear in texts like Riddle 4 (94), yet this poem, along with Riddle 33 ('iceberg'), represents a high reach of the imagination and some of the finest sea-descriptions in English literature. Riddle 29 ('sun and moon') is a true piece of nature poetry, built on an ancient nature myth (96). The imaginative qualities of the Riddles cannot be attributed to their direct Latin analogues but may be influenced by Virgil or, in view of their Northumbrian homeland, by Celtic nature poetry. In Chapter 10 'The Elegies and the Riddles' Brooke is not categorical about Cynewulf's authorship of the Riddles but inclines to the view that the best ones represent the work of his youth (151 and 160–2). The other OEW poems are dealt with in Chapter 13 'Other Poetry before Alfred'. *Gifts* may be a 'Christian working up of a heathen poem from which Cynewulf in the *Christ* also drew his passage on the Gifts of Men' (207). *Fortunes* has more literary qualities than *Gifts* (208). The *Maxims* are thrown together, without any order, by redactors at York and (later) in Wessex; they include quotations from the poets (e.g. from *Beowulf*) and *Maxims I* ends with a late addition (208–9). *Rune Poem* is eighth- or ninth-century, though the 'Ing' strophe incorporates pre-Christian, mythological material. *Solomon and Saturn* consists of two dialogues (plus the prose), of which the second is the older, as we can gauge from the vigorous fashion in which it begins. The somewhat anti-aristocratic and anti-clerical levity of the later Solomon and Marculf tradition in Europe is not permissible in the Old English redaction. The 'wonders' in the prose section are 'so heaped up and amazing that they may have had their origin in Eastern imagination' (210–11). Translations of Exeter Book Riddles 1–3 are appended (309–11), along with excerpts in translation from *Maxims I* and *II* (317–18).

0 Cosijn, Peter J. 'Anglo-Saxonica IV.' *Beiträge zur Geschichte der deutschen Sprache und Literatur* 23 (1898): 109–30.

Cosijn points out the similarities between the lists of occupations in *Gifts* and *Christ* (125). He contributes textual, editorial, and explicatory notes on *Fortunes*, *Gifts*, *Order*, *Vainglory*, and some of the Exeter Book Riddles, notably 1 (125–30). In reference to Riddles 23 and 24 he remarks that grammatical gender within the riddle is kept in conformity to the gender of the solution.

1 Becker, Ernest J. *A Contribution to the Comparative Study of the Medieval Visions of Heaven and Hell with Special Reference to the Middle-English Versions.* Baltimore: Murphy, 1899. ii + 101 pp.

Becker includes *Solomon and Saturn* lines 451–76 and Exeter Book Riddle 40 lines 40–1 in his survey of early English impressions and conceptions of Hell. He argues that these conceptions were derived from Christian teachings, not from pagan beliefs.

112 **Holthausen, Ferdinand.** Rev. of *Bibliothek der angelsächsischen Poesie III.1*, by Richard P. Wülker [6]. *Anglia Beiblatt* 9 (1899): 353–8.

Specific mentions of OEW poems from the Exeter Book are included in this review. Holthausen praises the accuracy of Assmann's reporting from the Exeter Book, remarking that significant new readings have been recovered thanks to his work. On the other hand, insufficient attention has been paid to earlier editors' emendations. Holthausen also puts forward various corrections and new emendations, often with the object of improving the versification (357–8). He briefly discusses the manuscript runes and annotations associated with the Exeter Book Riddles. Other texts referred to are *Gifts*, *Order*, and *Vainglory*.

113 **Mead, William E.** 'Color in Old English Poetry.' *PMLA* 14 (1899): 169–206.

Mead arranges the colour-words in groups, specifying the frequency with which they are used and to what objects they are applied. His citations are brief but aim at completeness and include material from the metrical Charms, *Maxims*, Exeter Book Riddles, *Rune Poem*, and *Solomon and Saturn*. He finds the fondness for mixed and neutral colours remarkable: especially picturesque is the mention in Riddle 3 line 19 of 'flintgrægne flod'. The word *haso* is used, he thinks, with apparent definiteness of colour feeling, as contrasted with the indefinite *brun*. But conventionality plays a large part in the selection of colour words: green seems to be the favourite.

114 **Roeder, Fritz.** *Die Familie bei den Angelsachsen. Eine kultur- und litterarhistorische Studie auf Grund gleichzeitiger Quellen.* I. *Mann und Frau.* II. *Kinder.* Studien zur englischen philologie 4. 2 vols. Halle: Niemeyer, 1899.

This general study contains passing references to OEW poems. Roeder draws on *Maxims II* lines 43–5 to illustrate the betrothal process. Love generally had no place prior to betrothal or outside of marriage, which was regarded from a characteristically practical point of view. Poems that emphasize sexuality, such as Exeter Book Riddle 63, are likely to be indebted to Latin models. *Maxims I* and the Riddles can be used to document the Anglo-Saxon criteria of female beauty. The adjectives 'frysan' (*Maxims I* line 95) and 'hwitloccedu' (Riddle 80 line 4) are interpreted as describing women's hair. Passages in *Maxims I*, *Fortunes*, and Riddles have evidential value for Anglo-Saxon marriage customs.

115 **Cook, Albert S., and Chauncey B. Tinker.** *Selected Translations from Old English Poetry.* Boston: Ginn, 1902. Rev. edn. 1926. xi + 195 pp.

These translations are aimed at intelligent students of English literature, to encourage them to read works earlier than Chaucer. The editors see Old English poetry at its best as characterized by the sense of reality and the instinct of reverence. The translations are by various hands, including Tennyson, William D. Stevens, and the editors. Represented are Exeter Book Riddles 1, 2, 7, 14, 23, 26, 27, and 80; excerpts from *Maxims I* and *II*; and metrical Charms 1, 2, 4, 5, and 8.

The editors follow Strobl (**537**) and Blackburn (**698**) in integrating Riddle 60 into *The Husband's Message*.

6 Anderson, L.F. *The Anglo-Saxon Scop.* Philological Series 1. Toronto: U of Toronto P, 1903. 45 pp.

Anderson illustrates from *Order* and *Maxims I* how intimately the art of poetry was associated with learning and wisdom in the Anglo-Saxon mind. The Exeter Book Riddles and *Order* are classified as catalogue poetry. Further information about the *scop* is drawn from *Fortunes*.

7 Jordan, Richard. *Die altenglischen Säugetiernamen.* Anglistische Forschungen 12. Heidelberg: Winter, 1903. xii + 212 pp. Amsterdam: Swets, 1967.

In this series of word studies on the names of mammals Jordan includes references to *Fortunes*, the Exeter Book Riddles (e.g. 15, 22, 24, and 40), *Rune Poem* (for *eoh*, 'horse', and *ur*, 'aurochs'), *Solomon and Saturn*, and the *Maxims* among his citations, but normally without any discussion of the context. The section on (e.g.) the wolf and related words includes various occurrences in OEW poetry. Among them is 'wulfheafodtreo' in Riddle 55 line 12, which Jordan tentatively solves as a richly decorated stand. Here he argues against Dietrich's 'shield' (**658**) and takes his cue from Grein's 'cross' and 'gallows' (**3**). The stand would have resembled a cross or gallows, in that weapons were hung upon it much as a criminal is hanged on the gallows (62). The reading 'frid-hengest' in Riddle 22 line 4 is unclear and perhaps arises through an error for 'fierd' (107). The word 'sceamas' (also line 4) is explained (115–16). The word 'eolh(x)secg' in *Rune Poem* line 41 is discussed (181), with a rejection of Grienberger's (**1000**) suggested variant form **eolhs*, parallel to *fox*. Schipper's reading (**1052**) 'hwælen' is tentatively accepted for *Solomon and Saturn* line 264 in the sense 'of whales' (209).

8 Krackow, Otto. *Die Nominalcomposita als Kunstmittel im altenglischen Epos.* Diss. U Berlin. Weimar: Wagner, 1903. iv + 88 pp.

Krackow makes some passing mentions of OEW poetry. He argues that the metrical Charms are closer to the vernacular in the use of compounds than is *Beowulf*. He traces the influence of interlinear glosses in compound formations such as those exemplified by 'un-ræd-siðas' (Exeter Book Riddle 11 line 4) and 'eges-ful-licran' (*Solomon and Saturn* line 46). Statistics document the incidence of compounds in poetic works.

9 Strunk, William. 'Notes on the Shorter Old English poems.' *Modern Language Notes* 18 (1903): 72–3.

Strunk proposes the following emendations: in *Gifts* line 93 'hafað' to 'hefeð', in *Fortunes* line 8 'giefað' to 'giemað', and in *Order* line 85 'flode' to 'foldan'.

0 Hanscom, Elizabeth D. 'The Feeling for Nature in Old English Poetry.' *JEGP* 5 (1903–5): 439–63.

Hanscom believes that the Anglo-Saxons looked at nature through their own eyes, without artistic and literary mediators, such as characterize present-day Western culture. She sees this immediacy in the treatment of the storm theme in Exeter Book Riddles 1–3, in the description of foul weather in *Solomon and Saturn*, and in the description of ice in *Rune Poem*. In this latter case, the glint and gleam of the ice attracted the poet's attention, and, with that quickness to see light rather than colour that characterized the sight of the early English, he composed a brilliant piece of verse. She cites the 'þorn' strophe from *Rune Poem* as evidence that the Anglo-Saxons, though insensitive to the beauty and fragrance of flowers, were impressed by tougher plants, such as the thorn and briar. Mentions of trees, e.g. in *Maxims I* and the Riddles, are more typically utilitarian. Noting the rarity of references to flowers in Old English verse, she suggests that Riddle 40, which mentions the lily and the rose in a purely conventional passage, may be of late and perhaps secondary origin.

121   Ker, W.P. *The Dark Ages.* Periods of European Literature. London: Blackwood, 1904. Rev. edn., with a foreword by B. Ifor Evans. London: Nelson, 1955. xviii + 361 pp.

In his chapter on 'The Elements', i.e. the central preoccupations and conventions of Dark Age literature (24–95), Ker briefly puts *Solomon and Saturn* in a European context of dialogue and riddle writing, mentioning the riddling enquiry and answer as key features and noting their resemblance to the kenning (86–8). He characterizes Solomon as 'still invincible in knowledge' and Saturn as 'a gentle opponent', in contrast to later European developments of the Salomon and Marcolf tradition (89). Ker traces a process where, following the composition of Latin riddles in Anglo-Saxon England, Old English becomes applied to riddle composition 'with a surprising difference in literary effect, and no change at all in the general principles regarding the matter of the poems' (92). 'It was partly, no doubt, the English taste for rhetorical efflorescence that led Aldhelm and Alcuin to their Latin riddles' (93). 'In some of the riddles the miracle takes place which is not unknown in literary history elsewhere: what seems at first the most conventional of devices is found to be a fresh channel of poetry. Many of these quaint poems, taking their start from a simple idea, a single term, expatiate, without naming it, over all the life of their theme, and the riddle, instead of an occasion for intricate paraphrase, becomes a subject of imaginative thought. The poets of the riddles are not content with mere brocading work, though they like that well enough: but, besides, they meditate on their subject, they keep their eye on it. The riddle becomes a shifting vision of all the different aspects in which the creature may be found – a quick, clear-sighted, interested poem. Though it is only a game, it carries the poetic mind out over the world' (93).

122   Klaeber, Frederick. 'Emendations in Old English Poems.' *Modern Philology* 2 (1904): 141–6.

Klaeber suggests new interpretations and emendations in *Gifts* line 2 ('ginra geofona'), Exeter Book Riddle 3 lines 31 and 32 (tentatively 'rince' and 'fere' respectively), Riddle 33 line 5 (tentatively 'hilde on wene'), Riddle 48 line 1 (suggesting that 'ændean' = 'ærendian'), Riddle 53 line 10 (emending 'an yste' to 'anes'), and *Vainglory* line 12 (emending 'rice' to 'ricene').

3 Holthausen, Ferdinand. 'Zur altenglischen Literatur. 1. Das XI. Rätsel. 2. Zum Neunkräutersegen.' *Anglia Beiblatt* 16 (1905): 227–31.

Holthausen proposes the solution 'water-lily' for Exeter Book Riddle 10, pointing out that at least part of the plant is black, in keeping with the adjective in line 7. He suggests emendations in metrical Charm 2 and confirms previous scholars' interpretations of *weden-* (lines 48 and 50) as 'blue'.

4 Budde, Erich. *Die Bedeutung der Trinksitten in der Kultur der Angelsachsen.* Diss. U Jena. Duisburg, 1906. 105 pp.

Budde points out the warnings against drunkenness in *Precepts* line 34 and in *Fortunes* lines 51–7. In the latter passage a drunkard's fate is described. He posits the influence of popular, more flippant attitudes to drink in Exeter Book Riddle 27. A long series of citations from other OEW poems, e.g. *Fortunes*, *Vainglory*, and *Gifts*, is used to provide further evidence on Anglo-Saxon drinking customs. Budde documents a custom of reciting riddles at feasts and discusses problematic references to drunkenness in Riddles 12 and 60.

5 Cortelyou, J. Van Zandt. *Die altenglischen Namen der Insekten, Spinnen- und Krustentiere.* Anglistische Forschungen 19. Heidelberg: Winter, 1906. vii + 124 pp. Amsterdam: Swets, 1969.

The sources listed for this study of Old English names for insects include the Exeter Book Riddles and other poetic works. Cortelyou regards Anglo-Saxon knowledge of insects as marking little real advance on that shown by Greek and Latin writers, though one exception is the recognition of the 'queen' bee as female (9). Specific references to OEW poems are scattered through a genus-by-genus treatment of the material; only those citations that are accompanied by a discussion or interpretation of the word in a specific OEW context are noted here. The expression 'gores sunu' in Riddle 40 lines 72–3 is explained as a kenning for 'beetle' (19 and cf. 23). The meaning of the word *moþþe* is problematic: does it correspond to Modern English *moth* or to German *Motte* 'member of the Familia Tineidae' (56–7)? [Cortelyou does not mention any specific implications for Riddle 47 here, but does note that most of his citations refer to the clothes moth.] The family of hydrometridae (pond skaters) is attested only in Riddle 40 lines 76–7 in the circumlocution 'þes lytla wyrm, þe her on flode gæð fotum dryge' (96). Cockayne's (**365**) reading 'spider' in metrical Charm 3 line 9 (for 'spiden') is used as the basis of an emendation to 'spiðer', in the sense of modern English 'spider'. Cortelyou interprets the manuscript title of this Charm as 'wið weorh', i.e. 'to counter a swelling' (108–9). Lexical items in Riddle 40 are also cited: 'beobread' in line 59 (28–9) and 'hondwyrm' in line 96 (114–15).

6 Geldner, Johann. *Untersuchung einiger altenglischer Krankheitsnamen.* Braunschweig: Westermann, 1906. x + 50 pp.

This glossary of terms for diseases includes 'æradl' (*Maxims I* line 31) and makes reference to the metrical Charms.

127 **Warren, Kate M.** *A Treasury of English Literature from the Beginning to the Eighteenth Century; selected and arranged with translations and glossaries.* With an introduction by Stopford A. Brooke. London: Constable, 1906. 6 vols. in one. lviii + 973. I *Old English Literature from its Beginning to the Eleventh Century.* Issued as a separate vol. London: Constable, 1908. xxv + 112 pp.

The anthology includes some OEW poetry based on (respectively) the text of Grein (2) and Assmann's revision (6) of Grein. English translations appear on facing pages. The selected texts comprise metrical Charm 8; excerpts from *Gifts* and *Rune Poem*; and Exeter Book Riddles 1, 2, 5, 7, and 29. Sample translation (from Riddle 7 lines 1–4): 'My raiment is still when I tread the earth, or rest in the dwelling, or drive the water. Sometimes my trappings and this high air upraise me over the houses of men.'

128 **Holthausen, Ferdinand.** 'Zur Textkritik altenglischer Dichtungen.' *Englische Studien* 37 (1907): 198–211.

Holthausen contributes textual notes, many of them to tidy up the versification. The passages dealt with are as follows: In *Precepts* line 87 he defends the manuscript reading. In *Maxims I* he deals with lines 37–8, 79 (suggesting 'ofen' for 'holen'), 106–7, 117 ('hadl' for 'adl'), 164 (reorganizing the verse into a *ljóðaháttr* pattern), 165–6, 174–5, 179, and 183. In *Homiletic Fragment I* he discusses lines 28 and 43. In *Solomon and Saturn* he deals with lines 299 and 367–9. As to the Exeter Book Riddles, he deals with Riddle 3 line 45 (suggesting 'dreorgum' for 'dreontum'), Riddle 9 lines 1 and 10, Riddle 15 (noting new analogues for Walz's (693) suggested solution, 'porcupine', but also suggesting 'hedgehog'), Riddle 24 line 2, Riddle 27 lines 7–8 (suggesting 'weorpe' for 'weorpere' and 'esne' for 'efne'), Riddle 29 line 5, Riddle 33 line 5 (suggesting 'cene' for 'sæne'), Riddle 35 line 8, Riddle 36 lines 4–5, Riddle 38 line 2 ('-myrþe' for '-myrwe') and lines 5–7, Riddle 39 line 26, Riddle 40 line 84, Riddle 53 line 2, Riddle 54 line 2, Riddle 55 lines 14–16, Riddle 71 line 6, Riddle 77 lines 7–8 (attempted restoration, rejecting his own previous attempt, 700), Riddle 84 lines 22–3, Riddle 87 lines 4–5, Riddle 88 line 5 (restoration), Riddle 90 (restoration of the Latin), Riddle 91 line 8, Riddle 92 lines 1 and 3 (suggesting the solution 'ash-tree'), and Riddle 94 line 3.

129 **Whitman, Charles H.** 'The Old English Animal Names: Mollusks; Toads, Frogs; Worms; Reptiles.' *Anglia* 30 (1907): 380–93.

These word studies take in a number of passages in OEW poems. Whitman explains the *hapax legomenon* 'fenyce' in Exeter Book Riddle 40 line 71 as 'fen-frog', 'marsh-frog', from simplex *yce/ice*. As to *Rune Poem*, he explains the manuscript readings 'wynan' in line 37 as from *wyna*, 'name of an animal or plant', and 'ea fixa' in line 87 as from *eafisc* 'river-fish'. The *hapax* 'laguswemmend-' in *Solomon and Saturn* line 290 also means 'a fish'.

130 **Jost, Karl.** *Beon und Wesan. Eine syntaktische Untersuchung.* Anglistische Forschungen 26. Heidelberg: Winter, 1909. Amsterdam: Swets, 1966. vi + 141 pp.

Jost comments briefly on the use of *beon* and *wesan* in *Fortunes, Gifts,* and *Vainglory* (183–6).

1 **Williams, Owen Thomas.** *Short Extracts from Old English Poetry.* Bangor: Jarvis and Fisher, 1909. viii + 93 pp.

[Not seen: information from ASPR 2: lxxxiii **(520)** and ASPR 3: xciii and 303 **(194).**] The anthology includes *Homiletic Fragment I,* along with *Fortunes* lines 1–61 and *Gifts* lines 44–96. Among the emendations suggested in this edition is 'brond aswencan' for manuscript 'brondas þencan' in *Fortunes* line 43.

2 **Holthausen, Ferdinand.** 'Zu altenglischen Literatur XI. 34. Zu den Gnomica Exoniensia; 35. Zu Salomon und Saturn.' *Anglia Beiblatt* 21 (1910): 174–6.

Rejecting analyses and emendations put forward by Wülker **(6),** Sievers **(92),** and Kaluza **(15),** Holthausen regularizes *Maxims I* line 46 by deleting 'and tyhtan', which he sees as a scribal addition (175). He regularizes *Solomon and Saturn* line 460b by positing a lacuna after 'Ðæt sindon' and filling it with the words 'ða feondas' (176).

3 **Schmitz, Theodor.** 'Die Sechstakter in der altenglischen Dichtungen [I].' *Anglia* 33 (1910): 1–76.

Schmitz seeks to identify the secure examples of hypermetric lines in Old English poetry and, where possible, to suggest literary motivations for their use. His identifications differ in detail from those of Sievers **(92).** He argues that *Vainglory* line 71a is corrupt but that the length of line 82a is justifiable, since the poem here takes on an admonitory tone. In *Fortunes,* lines 15–16 are secure examples. In *Maxims I* analysis is complicated by the need to reckon with irregular versification in the original text; indeed, a few lines defeat any attempt at metrical analysis. In view of the possibly 'folk' character of the *Maxims,* emendation is not a sound policy, though in fact Schmitz does offer a few conjectures. Schmitz also resists Müller's **(540)** arguments that some especially irregular lines should be classified as prose. He points out that it is in the nature of maxims that their key word should occupy a focal position at the beginning of the sentence, which in turn affects versification. Schmitz identifies numerous hypermetric lines here, as contrasted with *Maxims II,* where he finds comparatively few. He sees some merit in the notion that certain sets of hypermetric lines may represent an older compositional layer within the compilation. In *Precepts* he sees the hypermetric verses as emphasizing the idea of divine punishment (line 19). In Exeter Book Riddle 16 they contain motifs crucial for an identification of the solution. The other apparent examples in the Riddles (40 line 5b and 48 line 2a) are ascribed to textual corruption. In *Rune Poem* hypermetric verses tend to coincide with the beginning and end position of the strophe. Schmitz takes issue with Sievers's assertion **(92)** that *Solomon and Saturn* is too problematic to permit metrical analysis, pointing out that the *Maxims* (which Sievers did analyse) contain still greater irregularities. Emendations are suggested to dispose of some of the apparent examples in *Solomon and Saturn;* likewise, some hypermetric passages in *Solomon and Saturn* seem to be rhetorically motivated, e.g. by a reference to the Last

Judgement (lines 327–31), though others seem more random. In *Order*, the entire conclusion would originally have been hypermetric, so reinforcing an admonition to abjure worldly pleasures.

134 ———. 'Die Sechstakter in der altenglischer Dichtung II.' *Anglia* 33 (1910): 172–218.

Schmitz examines previous scholars' studies of hypermetric verses. He argues that some examples, such as *Solomon and Saturn* lines 312–13, represent a licence whereby the poet was enabled to incorporate material that would have resisted standard versification. By contrast, some lines (including examples in *Rune Poem*) may owe their form to the fact that the preceding lines had established a hypermetric pattern. The high incidence in *Maxims I* could point to the existence of entire poems composed in this form, though none survive. The incidence of hypermetric lines within a poem can be used as a guide to attribution. *Maxims I*, for example, is too irregular in versification to fit a Cynewulf ascription. Likewise, the two poetic sections of *Solomon and Saturn* show such marked differences that they cannot originate with the same author.

135 Holthausen, Ferdinand. 'Zu den altenglischen Rätseln.' *Anglia* 35 (1912): 165–77.

Although welcoming Tupper's edition (**727**), Holthausen contends that a more consistent programme of metrical emendations would have been appropriate. Elementary blunders are more likely to stem from the scribe of the Exeter Book than from the poet of the Riddles. In particular, Tupper should have adopted the improvements that had already been put forward by Sievers (**92**) and other scholars, as in Riddle 42 line 2. Holthausen reviews numerous contentious lines, occasionally to defend the manuscript reading but more commonly to suggest metrical improvements: some examples are Riddle 14 line 14, Riddle 15 line 2, Riddle 17 line 11, Riddle 42 line 11, Riddle 46 line 6, and Riddle 93 line 12. Parallel examples are cited from some other OEW poems (*Fortunes*, *Order*, and *Solomon and Saturn*). Holthausen explains Riddle 62 as alluding to the branding of slaves. In a second section of the article, he takes up the problem of the rune-name *yr*, pointing out that phonological considerations preclude any equation of this word with Old Norse *ýr* 'bow'. The contexts in *Rune Poem* and *Elene* suggest a meaning 'horn' and an etymology as a formation from *ur* 'aurochs'.

136 Ker, William P. *Medieval English Literature.* London: Oxford UP, 1912. 192 pp.

Ker makes passing comments on the Exeter Book Riddles and *Solomon and Saturn*. He describes *Solomon and Saturn* as part of a common European fashion for dialogue literature. This literature, partly didactic and partly comic, was useful in the Middle Ages in providing instruction along with varying degrees of amusement.

137 Tupper, Frederick. 'Notes on Old English Poems.' *JEGP* 11 (1912): 82–103.

Note 5 (97–100) deals with the phrase 'hand ofer heafod' as it occurs in *Maxims I* lines 67–8 and metrical Charm 11 line 24a. Tupper traces an allusion to the 'commendation', a ritual by which the vassal pledged his loyalty and trust in return for his chief's gold and protection.

Bartels, Arthur. *Rechtsaltertümer in der angelsächsischen Dichtung.* Diss. U Kiel. Kiel: Donath, 1913. 117 pp.

Bartels makes passing references to OEW poems in which key legal terms such as *eorl* and *gesiðas* appear. He notes that the only occurrence of *ceorl* in the sense of 'husband' is in *Maxims I* line 96. He compares 'ceorles dohtor' in Exeter Book Riddle 25 line 6 with the '*bóndi*'s daughter' in an Icelandic riddle. He uses Riddle 12 line 4 to shed light on the position of the Wealas. An examination of *esne* as it occurs in the Riddles shows that it may be used neutrally, without reference to social class. Riddle 20 line 18 and Riddle 93 line 21 provide evidence on the code of vengeance.

Helm, Karl. *Altgermanische Religionsgeschichte.* II. *Die nachrömische Zeit.* 2. *Die Westgermanen.* Germanische Bibliothek 1.v.2: Religionswissenschaftliche Bibliothek 5. Heidelberg: Winter, 1937. 2 vols. 1913–37.

Helm attempts to reconstruct Germanic fatalism on the basis of *Maxims II* lines 1–5. Citing Brandl (**19**), he argues that if Wyrd was seen as a mightier force than Christ in this passage, it must be as a relic of the heathen belief that Fate was stronger than the gods (284–5). In his discussion of magic (117–57), Helm notes the brevity of the commands in the Anglo-Saxon metrical Charms and the emphasis on the speaker's powers.

Trautmann, Moritz. Rev. of *Sprachschatz der angelsächsischen Dichter,* by Christian W.M. Grein, rev. edn. by J.J. Köhler [3]. *Anglia Beiblatt* 24 (1913): 36–43.

Trautmann raises a few points of detail. A distinction needs to be made between the two words *gedræg* 'hiding place' and *gedreag* 'turmoil', the latter of which occurs in Exeter Book Riddle 6 line 10. The runic letters in Riddle 24 lines 7–9 show that the form *higore*, not *higora*, should be cited. If, as Trautmann suspects, 'flitan' in *Solomon and Saturn* line 179 is a verb rather than a noun, Köhler has erroneously altered Grein's original entry.

Funke, Otto. *Die gelehrten lateinischen Lehn- und Fremdwörter in der altenglischen Literatur von der Mitte des x. Jahrhunderts bis um das Jahr 1066.* . . Halle: Niemeyer, 1914. xviii + 210 pp.

Funke discusses the vowel quantities and scansion of Latin words in Old English poetry. The survey includes *calend, cantic, istoria, prologus,* and other Latin words which occur in *Solomon and Saturn.* Also mentioned is *zefferus* in Riddle 40 line 68. [For a review see Hüttenbrenner, **1066.**]

Olivero, Federico. *Traduzioni dalla poesia anglosassone con introduzione e note.* Bari: Laterza, 1915. 279 pp.

Olivero's introduction contains a brief discussion of *Fortunes, Gifts, Maxims I* and *II, Precepts,* Exeter Book Riddles, *Rune Poem, Solomon and Saturn,* and

Vainglory. He emphasizes the poetic qualities of the Riddles, in which force of imagination is combined with the delicacy of a miniature. Of OEW poetry, only the Riddles feature among the translations. Included are Riddles 2 and 3 ('hurricane'), 7, 16, 23, 26, 29, 33, 48, 53, and 55, all translations being based on Tupper (727). The annotations are mostly from the same source.

143 **Schücking, Levin Ludwig.** *Untersuchungen zur Bedeutungslehre der angelsächsischen Dichtersprache.* Germanische Bibliothek 2. Untersuchungen und Texte 11. Heidelberg: Winter, 1915.

Submitted to detailed scrutiny here are some words that occur in *Fortunes, Order,* Exeter Book Riddles, *Rune Poem,* and *Solomon and Saturn:* examples are *superne* (Riddle 62 line 9) and *wægfæt* (Riddle 3 line 37).

144 **Holthausen, Ferdinand.** 'Zu altenglischen Denkmälern.' *Englische Studien* 51 (1917): 180–8.

Holthausen contributes textual notes on various passages, some as a reaction to Trautmann's edition of the Exeter Book Riddles (751): attempts to defend the manuscript reading against Trautmann or to improve the versification are not noted in detail here. The passages dealt with are: *Solomon and Saturn* line 269 (suggesting 'wylteð' for 'wylleð'); Riddle 3 line 17; Riddle 4 (suggesting the solution 'lock'); Riddle 5 line 3; Riddle 11 line 9; Riddle 20 lines 16–17, 20–1, and 29; Riddle 23 lines 3, 8, and 14; Riddle 40 line 65; Riddle 41 line 7; Riddle 55 line 14; Riddle 64 (an attempt to interpret the runes); Riddle 67 lines 2–3 (attempt at restoration); Riddle 72 lines 4 (restoration) and 12; Riddle 81 lines 11–12 (restoration; similarly all the following); Riddle 82 line 2; Riddle 84 line 45; Riddle 85 lines 1–2; Riddle 89 line 3; and Riddle 93 line 4.

145 **Pontán, Runar.** 'Three Old English Textual Notes.' *Modern Language Review* 12 (1917): 69–72.

The author points out that in *Maxims I* line 176 the manuscript reads not 'sliþ herde', as hitherto thought, but 'sliþ hende'. Although a *hapax,* the word is a transparent formation, meaning 'provided with grim paws'. In Exeter Book Riddle 20 line 11, the reading 'wordlofes' should be taken as a compound, not as two words.

146 **Faust, Cosette, and Stith Thompson.** *Old English Poems, Translated into the Original Meter together with Short Selections from Old English Prose.* Chicago: Scott, Foresmann, 1918. 198 pp.

[Note that in library catalogues Faust is normally indexed under 'Newton'.] Translations of the following OEW poems are included: metrical Charms 1 and 4, based on Kluge's edition (94) (38–43); *Fortunes,* based on the Grein-Wülker edition (6) (58–61); excerpts from *Maxims I,* based on the edition of Blanche Williams (547) (56–7); and Exeter Book Riddles 1–3 ('storm'), 5, 7, 8 ('nightingale'), 14, 15 ('badger'), 23, 26, 45, 47, and 60 ('reed'), based on Wyatt (737) (44–55). An attempt is made to reproduce Old English metre in the translation. The following is a sample, from *Fortunes* lines 21–4: 'One from the top of a tree in the woods/ Without feathers shall fall, but he flies nonetheless,/

Swoops in descent till he seems no longer/ The forest tree's fruit . . .' (59). The above texts are grouped under the heading 'Pagan Poetry', though with the caveat that such artificial divisions as 'pagan' and 'Christian' are inexact (11).

7 Kock, Ernst A. *Jubilee Jaunts and Jottings: 250 Contributions to the Interpretation and Prosody of Old West Teutonic Alliterative Poetry. Lunds Universitets Årsskrift* NS 1, 14, no 26 (1918). Lund: Gleerup, 1918. iv + 82 pp.

Kock's brief comments on individual textual problems take in the following poems: *Fortunes, Gifts, Precepts,* Exeter Book Riddles, *Solomon and Saturn,* and *Vainglory.* The Riddles covered are 3, 6, 11, 15, 22, 26, 28, 38, 81, and 83. In Riddle 28 Kock sees the series of rhymes as an allusion to the chords of a stringed instrument. He tries to analyse the antithesis in *Precepts* lines 5–8. In *Maxims II* line 10 he proposes substituting 'swæð' ('slippery place') for 'soð', on the grounds that the concept of truth clashes in its abstractness with the general tenor of ancient wisdom. *Maxims I* line 78 is to be compared with the modern English proverb 'still waters run deep'. He sees 'mægðegsan wyn' (line 106) as a three-membered kenning, in skaldic style, where the 'dread of nations' ('mægðegesa') is a Viking and his 'joy' ('wyn') is his ship. Lines 177–80 are analysed as a regular *ljóðaháttr* strophe. Kock speculates concerning the references to animals in *Solomon and Saturn* lines 264–5. He seeks to explain apparently aberrant syntactic constructions in *Vainglory* lines 4, 44, and 59. [For reviews see Holthausen, **150**; Klaeber, **760**.]

8 ———. 'En misskänd ordfamilj.' *Studier tillegnade Esaias Tegnér den 13 Jan. 1918.* Lund: Gleerup, 1918. 298–303.

The article argues for three principal meanings of Germanic **ðómjan-*, (1) 'decide', (2) 'judge', and (3) 'pronounce, speak'. Kock mentions the use of *dom* in *Maxims I* in passing, noting that it often occurs in the same context as *beag* and *gifu* and their hyponyms and synonyms. In Exeter Book Riddle 73 Kock suggests completing line 10 to read 'oþþe æfter dome <d>ri<ogan wylle>' and argues that 'dom' should not be translated as 'custom, what is fitting'. In Riddle 28 line 11 'deman' should be translated as 'speak', not 'judge' or 'celebrate'.

9 ———, 'Interpretations and Emendations of Early English Texts.' *Anglia* 42 (1918): 99–124.

Kock summarizes his earlier arguments **(148)** concerning the interpretation of the verb *deman* as 'talk, speak' in Riddle 28 line 11 (113). In *Solomon and Saturn* line 130 he construes the noun 'flana' as accusative (122–3).

0 Holthausen, Ferdinand. Rev. of *Jubilee Jaunts and Jottings,* by Ernst A. Kock **[147]**. *Anglia Beiblatt* 30 (1919): 1–5.

Holthausen sees Kock's repunctuations and reinterpretations as more successful than his emendations. Earlier scholarly emendations, including Holthausen's **(128)** own 'hadl' in *Maxims I* line 117, have been neglected by Kock. Holthausen rejects Kock's 'swæð' in *Maxims II* line 10 in favour of 'seað'. In *Maxims I* line 38 he argues against 'nefre' and 'nearo' in favour of 'næfig' ('poor'). The undue shortness of *Maxims I* line 179 indicates emendation to 'næfre hy mon<na>

man<e> tomelde', where 'mane' could be either an adverb or an instrumental of *man*. In Exeter Book Riddle 81 line 5 emendation to 'middan' is recommended.

151 **Keiser, Albert.** *The Influence of Christianity on the Vocabulary of Old English Poetry.* Illinois Studies in Language and Literature 5: 1 and 2. Urbana: U of Illinois P, 1919. 150 pp.

The book consists of studies of the Old English poetic lexicon, mostly without close reference to context. Some specific references are the following: a discussion of terms for 'Lord's Prayer' in *Solomon and Saturn* (49); brief mention of possible allusions to the paten or communion plate in Exeter Book Riddles 48 and 59, both centring on the word 'hring' (55); discussion of the meaning of 'godspel' ('good tidings'?) in *Solomon and Saturn* line 65 (58); and discussion of Wyrd in the *Maxims* and *Solomon and Saturn* (59–62 and 95). Keiser advocates an identification of Wyrd in *Solomon and Saturn* lines 437 and 440 with the 'fallen angel'.

152 **Kock, Ernst A.** 'Interpretations and Emendations of Early English Texts V.' *Anglia* 43 (1919): 298–312.

Note 145 (307–8) analyses the meanings of *wist* and its compounds in relation to *Rune Poem* lines 19–21 and Exeter Book Riddle 53 line 10. When *wist* appears as a simplex, the basic meaning of 'existence' can extend to 'sustenance'. In compounds, by contrast, the meaning of this element is limited to 'presence' or 'residence'. These considerations lead Kock to support Trautmann's **(751)** emendation in Riddle 53 but not his interpretation. Note 148 (309) supports the interpretation 'Frisian' in *Maxims I* line 95, on the grounds that the *Maxims* may partly be traced back to the Saxon and Frisian shores and that Frisian texts show great fondness for their national name. Note 149 (309) argues that 'cypeþ' means 'buys' in *Maxims I* line 108. Note 152 considers Tupper's **(727)** and Trautmann's **(751)** solutions to Riddle 19, pointing out that the stress on the last rune in line 6 may represent poetic licence rather than a copyist's error.

153 **Wyatt, Alfred John.** *An Anglo-Saxon Reader edited with Notes and Glossary.* Cambridge: Cambridge UP, 1919. x + 360 pp.

The texts chosen include Exeter Book Riddles 9, 10, 16, 21, 27, 40 (lines 42–85), 47, 57, and 60; *Maxims I* (lines 50–99 and 118b–31); *Solomon and Saturn* (lines 282–301); and metrical Charms 1 and 9. The Reader contains introduction, notes, and glossary. Among his comments, Wyatt suggests that the word *erce* is mere gibberish and that Charm 1, in which it occurs, is still fully pagan; so too Charm 9, if the Christian introduction is explained as an addition. The 'Garmund' mentioned in this charm is to be explained as a locally recognized magician, who invented the charm. Dissenting from Tupper **(727)**, Wyatt regards Riddle 16 ('anchor') as originally an English folk-riddle, which became embellished by sporadic borrowings from Symphosius.

154 **Holthausen, Ferdinand.** 'Zu altenglischen Dichtungen.' *Anglia Beiblatt* 31 (1920): 25–32.

From this article-length collection of textual notes the following points may be mentioned as typical. In *Precepts* line 55 'drymeð' should be emended to 'dreorgað', although the source of the error is hard to explain (26). In *Solomon and Saturn* line 478 'man man' is an error for 'naman': Holthausen restores 'ðara ðe age naman' (27). The notes on the metrical Charms (30–2) mostly comprise changes to regularize line division, alliteration, and metre. In Charm 4 line 19 we should read 'hat sceal gemyltan'. In Charm 11 lines 36–7 the suggested reconstruction is 'swiðrendes wæteres, simble <me> gehealde,/ wið eallum feondum, freond ic gemete.' In Charm 1 line 55 Schlutter's postulation (375) of Old English **herse* is to be rejected.

5 **Kock, Ernst A.** 'Interpretations and Emendations of Early English Texts VI.' *Anglia* 44 (1920): 97–114.

Note 176 comments on *Maxims I* lines 54–5, 161–3, 177–80, and 187–90. Kock argues that much early Germanic wisdom was expressed in characteristically short, pithy sentences. Because of their prosodic shape, these utterances did not fit readily into the later systems of West Germanic or Norse versification. Anglo-Saxon and Scandinavian poets nonetheless incorporated them into their oeuvre as best they could. Hence we find short lines tacked on to metrically regular lines in both the *Edda* and the *Maxims*. Kock cites examples of *ljóðaháttr* from *Hávamál* as parallel to passages of irregular versification in *Maxims I*. Defending the Old English lines against metrical emendations, he characterizes attempts to force the usual ninth-century scheme on to such 'ancient reliques' as equivalent to 'dressing up Vikings in frock-coats' (108–10). Note 182 attempts a restoration of Riddle 31 lines 4–7, adding 'neol wæs hnæcca' in line 6 on the basis of partial parallels elsewhere in the Riddles. Line 4a becomes 'wiht <ne> wæs <þæs> on<wene>', on the basis of an observed 'wiht <no> wæs <þæs>' (or 'never so') construction. In line 7a 'folme' is replaced by the more logical 'feðre'. Note 183 attempts a restoration of *Solomon and Saturn* line 478, conjecturing '*endeman' ('final pain') as an emendation for 'man' and 'man man' of the manuscripts. This formation would be analogous to 'endedeað' and 'endelean'.

6 **Brandl, Alois.** 'Zu Vorgeschichte der *Weird Sisters* in "Macbeth".' *Texte und Forschungen zur englischen Kulturgeschichte. Festgabe für Felix Liebermann zum 20. Juli 1921.* Ed. Heinrich Boehmer et al. Halle: Niemeyer, 1921. 252–70.

Brandl discusses Wyrd as depicted in the *Maxims* (252–8). In *Maxims II* lines 1–5 the following powers are characterized: the king, in whose veins, according to early Anglo-Saxon belief, the blood of gods flowed; the giants; wind and thunder; Christ; and Fate. These were all powers that still possessed a mythic dimension. Consistent with the missionary ethos of this period, the powers of Christ are singled out for mention. As in *Beowulf*, Fate stands below divine rank and yet is 'very powerful' (translating 'swiþost'). Although it does not call up miracles, it does contribute to their fulfilment. Brandl also discusses *Maxims I* line 173. He notes that Wyrd is mentioned pejoratively in *Solomon and Saturn*, as the origin of all strife and misery. Systematic depreciation of the concept explains the glossing of *Parcae* as 'wyccan'. This paved the way for the transformation of Wyrd into the figure of the witch, identified in early Anglo-Saxon times as a wind-goddess and controller of Nature.

157 Holthausen, Ferdinand. 'Zu altenglischen Gedichten.' *Anglia Beiblatt* 32 (1921): 136–8.

Note 3 (136) replies to Kock's (**155**) attempts at restoration in Exeter Book Riddle 31 lines 4–6. Holthausen proposes 'niþerweard wæs neb, hyre <neoðan wæron>' instead of Kock's '<neol wæs hnecca>'. He defends his 'wiht næs <on wonge>' against Kock's 'wiht <ne> wæs <þæs> on <wene>', on the grounds that Kock's emendation is unduly complex and makes poor sense. Note 4 (137) defends his emendation (**154**) 'þara þe age naman' in *Solomon and Saturn* line 478. Kock's (**155**) conjectured 'endeman age' is suspect because it entails double alliteration in a b-verse.

158 Jente, Richard. *Die mythologischen Ausdrücke im altenglischen Wortschatz. Eine kulturgeschichtlich-etymologische Untersuchung.* Anglistische Forschungen 56. Heidelberg: Winter, 1921. xx + 344 pp.

Jente examines OEW poetry, along with other Anglo-Saxon literature, as a source of information on early English mythology. The OEW poems surveyed are *Fortunes, Gifts, Order, Precepts*, Exeter Book Riddles, *Rune Poem, Solomon and Saturn*, and *Vainglory*. Topics treated are pagan cults, pagan deities, beliefs in spirits and demons, fate and death, divination and prophecy, and magic. Jente examines the incidence and etymology of numerous words, including *ælf, draca, dweorh, ent, erce, feond, hægtesse, regen(meld), tan, þyrs*, and others that occur in OEW poems. Metrical Charm 1 is treated as evidence for earth-worship, with mention of other examples of this cult. The word *erce* is merely a personification of the earth, equivalent to *folde* and *eorðe*. The discussion of *wyrd* includes references to various OEW poems, and six senses are distinguished. A brief discussion of the word *forscrifan* takes account of *Solomon and Saturn* line 162. The word *os*, as used in *Rune Poem*, is identified with Woden.

159 Klaeber, Frederick. 'Zu altengl. *ændian: ær(e)ndian.*' *Anglia Beiblatt* 32 (1921): 37–8.

Taking his cue from Holthausen (**388**), Klaeber suggests that 'ændian' is equivalent to 'ærendian' in metrical Charm 2 line 24a. He notes that 'ærndian' is a frequent by-form of the latter and that examples of loss of -*r*- (cited) occur in similar phonetic environments. The original meaning would have been 'fulfil a mission', as in 'hwæt þu geændadest æt Alorforda'. In line 34 the meaning approximates to 'obtain by negotiation', as for *geærendian* in Bosworth-Toller (1882–98). From such a sense the meaning could easily have been extended to 'speak', 'inform' in general. Klaeber explains Exeter Book Riddle 48 line 1 similarly, dissenting from Trautmann's (**751**) equation with 'endian'.

160 Sedgefield, Walter J. 'Suggested Emendations in Old English Poetical Texts.' *Modern Language Review* 16 (1921): 59–61.

Sedgefield provides annotations on *Vainglory* lines 25 and 28; *Fortunes* lines 83 and 93; Exeter Book Riddle 1 line 10; Riddle 3 line 24; Riddle 15 lines 15 and 16; and Riddle 55 line 15. Despite the title, some of these notes defend the manuscript readings.

Spaeth, John Duncan. *Old English Poetry: Translations into Alliterative Verse with Introductions and Notes.* Princeton: Princeton UP; Oxford: Milford, 1921. xii + 268 pp.

Spaeth's reader is designed primarily for English literature survey courses in colleges and high schools. He wants his translations to be judged chiefly by their effect when read aloud. The selected texts include metrical Charm 4 and excerpts from Charm 1 (149–51); *Fortunes* (159–62); *Maxims II* and excerpts from *Maxims I* (155–9); and Exeter Book Riddles 5, 7, 10, 16, 21, 27, 47, and 57 (151–5). A sample translation from Riddle 57 lines 1–2: 'There's a troop of tiny folk travelling swift/ Brought by the breeze o'er the brink of the hill . . .' Spaeth considers that the Riddles should not be viewed as a random collection. They show the workmanship of a single poet, though identifications with Cynewulf are unjustified. Spaeth also suggests that alliteration functions to assist the memory in the *Maxims*.

Holthausen, Ferdinand. 'Studien zur altenglischen Dichtungen.' *Anglia* 46 (1922): 52–62.

In Note 1 Holthausen documents alliterative technique in Old English poetry. He compiles examples of deviant initial half-lines consisting of a verb plus a substantive, where the verb carries the alliteration instead of the substantive. He cites seven examples from the Exeter Book Riddles, three from *Solomon and Saturn*, and three from metrical Charm 2. He doubts that they carry any significance for dating. Emendation does not seem called for. In Note 2 he proposes a restoration in Riddle 47 line 2 and a new expansion of the runic abbreviations in Riddle 64.

Kock, Ernst A. 'Interpretations and Emendations of Early English Texts X.' *Anglia* 46 (1922): 173–90.

Note 279 includes Exeter Book Riddle 31 line 4 and *Solomon and Saturn* lines 149–50 in a tabulation of examples of the 'never so' construction drawn from various Germanic languages. In Note 314H Kock argues that the hypothetical compound '*weggar', posited to explain the runes in Riddle 19 lines 5b–6a, is a 'spear with ornaments like those on a *wægsweord*'. Note 316 defends hypermetric lines, including those in *Maxims II*, against emendation: 'Of course, these will not do in Leipzic, Bonn, or Kiel, for either they contain "zu wenig" or "zu viel". One "Kenner" adds some words, who subtly thinks he can, another simply "tilgt", a third "nimmt Lücken an" ' (185–6). Notes 317 and 318 point out that both Holthausen and Trautmann, despite the protestations of the latter, are responsible in their various works for numerous emendations in the name of metrical improvement. Riddle 27 lines 13 and 14 and Riddle 39 line 10 are among the passages mentioned. Kock concedes, however, that simple transposition of words is a comparatively minor intervention in the text. Indeed, transposition may seem quite tempting in cases where the scribe's word-order is commoner than that supposed to be the poet's (186–8).

Sedgefield, W.J. *An Anglo-Saxon Verse-Book.* Publications of the University of Manchester, English series 13. Manchester: Manchester UP, 1922. 248 pp. Rev.

edn. *An Anglo-Saxon Book of Verse and Prose.* Manchester: Manchester UP, 1928.

Sedgefield prints text and notes for the following poems: *Fortunes*; *Vainglory* lines 1–50a; *Maxims II*; *Gifts*; *Precepts*; metrical Charms 1, 2, 3, 4, 7, and 8; and Exeter Book Riddles 1, 3, 12, 15, 22, 32, 35, 39, 55, and 60. Among other comments and suggestions, Sedgefield sees the latter part of *Fortunes* as inferior to the former and therefore as a possible addition. The monks who wrote *Maxims II* and *Gifts* may have been meeting a popular taste for 'such saws' by grouping them together into alliterative verse. The Exeter Book Riddles show no trace of pre-Christian folklore. [For reviews see Crawford, **167**; Klaeber, **767**.]

165 **Craigie, William A.** *Specimens of Anglo-Saxon Poetry.* The Awle Ryale Series. Vol. 1. *Biblical and Classical Themes.* Edinburgh: Hutchen, 1923. Vol. 3. *Germanic Legend and Anglo-Saxon History and Life.* 1931. 3 vols. 1923–31.

In Vol. 1 Craigie arranges somewhat normalized excerpts from various texts, including *Solomon and Saturn* lines 451–76, to illustrate how the Fall of the Angels and other themes are treated in Anglo-Saxon poetic tradition. Vol. 3 contains metrical Charms 1, 2, 4, and 8; *Fortunes*; *Gifts*; *Maxims I* and *II*; *Precepts*; *Rune Poem*; and *Vainglory*. A bibliography is appended but no notes or glossary.

166 **Heusler, Andreas.** *Die altgermanische Dichtung.* Handbuch der Literaturwissenschaft. Ed. Oskar Walzel. Potsdam: Akademische verlagsgesellschaft Athenaion m.b.h., 1923. Rev. edn. 1941. iv + 250 pp. Darmstadt: Gentner, 1957.

In his 'Vorwort von Freundeshand' Hans Naumann gives an account of Heusler's methods in revising this handbook. In his chapter 1, on the scope and sources of early Germanic poetry (1–8), Heusler comments on the rapidity of the rise of Old English literature, so soon after the Conversion. The emphasis on the vernacular and on secular topics of composition, as seen in some of the wisdom poetry, is surprising (3–4). He defines 'altgermanisch' as a cultural concept without chronological demarcations: it embraces those traits which cannot be ascribed to Christianity or the classics and which in many cases extend far into the Middle Ages. Few manifestations of it survive equally in all the Germanic regions, but spells and charms, along with heroic poetry, are an exception (8). Heusler operates in a broadly comparative Germanic context throughout, with especially full consideration of non-skaldic Icelandic material. He discusses the mixture of different verse lengths in gnomic and dialogue poetry, suggesting that in primitive Germanic poetry (as in Old English) it was a sporadic feature, later to be regularized in early Norwegian poetry (34). Heusler discusses OEW poetry under the categories of 'ritualdichtung', 'zauberdichtung', 'spruchdichtung', and 'merkdichtung'. In the category 'ritual poetry' Heusler includes Charm 1 (48–9), noting that in style and prosody alike it is much closer to gnomic poetry than to epic. He points out the multifaceted nature of Charm 1 (charm, praise-poem, and prayer) and the persistence of end-stopped lines. He regards this and the other metrical Charms as being for the most part only superficially Christianized. Differences from the early German material are, however, marked, for instance in the looser structure and in the commands, which are much less formulaic and apt to be expressed in the weaker form of wishes. Charms 2 and 4 may represent semi-learned conflations of originally separate folk texts. In their present form they are a product of the scribal era. Charm 2 is possibly the work of a female herbalist (cf. 110). Charm 4 was intended to counter head-aches, as is indicated by the last line. Almost shamanistic in its trance-like narrative, it bears comparison with Finnish charms, which combat headaches by describing their supernatural origins. Old Norse charms may have acted as intermediaries between Finnish and Old English. The mingling of prose and verse seen in the Old English Charms can be paralleled in Indian material (60–3). Gnomic poetry is discussed under the term 'Spruchdichtung' (66–79). Heusler distinguishes between mere compilations of maxims ('Spruchhaufen') and the more coherently and artistically organized admonitory texts ('Sittenlehren'). *Maxims I* and *II* are literary compilations of the most padded and uninspired kind, and were perhaps designed for school use (74). *Precepts*, by contrast, is a completely Christian, clerical composition (75). The Riddle genre in England is an outcome of Latin influence, not a genuinely Germanic or folk feature. The Exeter Book Riddles are learned and clerical, after the style of the book-epics (77–9). The term 'Merkdichtung' encompasses list and catalogue poetry (79–97). Here the purpose of the verse form is mnemonic rather than aesthetic. A salient example is *Rune Poem*. Heusler minimizes the links of Riddles and *Rune Poem* with popular poetry and emphasizes their links to each other. Along with the Latin riddle collections, they can be seen as Christian works that highlight the utility of natural phenomena to humankind. Other elements in *Rune Poem*, however, go back to a common Germanic rune poem, on whose form Heusler offers some speculations (88–9). In Chapter 12 'Rückblick auf die niedere Dichtung' Heusler comments on the possible circumstances of composition and performance for these genres of poetry (108–13). They are to be seen as the possession of all the social classes and not, anachronistically, as folk poetry.

Crawford, Samuel J. Rev. of *An Anglo-Saxon Verse Book*, by W.J. Sedgefield [**164**]. *Modern Language Review* 19 (1924): 104–8.

Crawford appends some detailed notes. For *Fortunes* lines 52–3 he offers the translation 'He knows no moderation, to put restraint upon his language (mouth) with his mind.' On *Maxims II* lines 43–5, he suggests that 'þæt hi man beagum gebicge' is equivalent to 'get married'. He translates *Precepts* lines 4–7 as 'Do ever what is good, and thy deserts will be good. God will be ever thy protector and support in all good things, (but will be) a foe to the other (i.e. the bad man) who is inferior in deserts.' In Exeter Book Riddle 55 line 9 he confirms the vowel quantity and meaning of 'hlin'.

Legouis, Émile, and Louis Cazamian. *Histoire de la littérature anglaise*. Paris: Hachette, 1924. Trans. H.D. Irvine. *A History of English Literature: The Middle Ages and the Renascence*. London: Dent, 1926. Rev. edn. 1940. xxiii + 1395 pp.

The authors see the Exeter Book Riddles as fitting naturally into an Anglo-Saxon poetic which prizes the enigmatic. Key features are the denotation of an object by qualities rather than an exact name, the cultivation of periphrasis, and the pursuit of verbal subtleties. As riddles in the conventional sense, they are failures, being too diffuse and vague, but they make up for technical defects when the poet, inspired by his subject, forgets to appeal to the intellect and instead speaks to the imagination. Riddles 1–3, on the wind or the storm, are among the most original and most modern of short Anglo-Saxon poems. Such OEW poems as *Fortunes*, *Gifts*, and *Precepts* receive short shrift, as being overly sententious, but *Solomon and Saturn* appeals more, because its didacticism is leavened by elements of the fantastic.

169 **Singer, S.** 'Stil und Weltanschauung der altgermanischen Poesie.' *Vom Geiste neuer Literaturforschung. Festschrift für Oskar Walzel.* Ed. Julius Wahle and Victor Klemperer. Wildpark-Potsdam: Akademische verlagsgesellschaft Athenaion m.b.h., 1924. 9–21.

Taking his cue from Löwenthal **(744)**, Singer compares the Old English and Old Norse riddles for 'shield'. The Old Norse exemplars emerge as more dramatic and vivid. Overall, the Old Norse *gátur* seem more integrated in style than the Exeter Book Riddles. The distinct stylistic features of the Old English texts can be ascribed to eastern Christian influence, mediated through the Celts. *Solomon and Saturn* exemplifies this process.

170 **Heusler, Andreas.** *Deutsche Versgeschichte, mit Einschluss des altenglischen und altnordischen Stabreimverses.* Vol. 1. Grundriss der germanischen Philologie 8. Berlin: De Gruyter, 1925. 3 vols. 1925–9.

In Vol. 1 Heusler discusses the structure of early Germanic verse, pointing out resemblances to *ljóðaháttr* in the metrical Charms and *Maxims II*. He argues that in compilatory poems like these the freedoms of the gnomic aphorism had not been completely outgrown. The norm was therefore an agglomeration of long and short lines, some paired, some not. This mixture was an authentic feature of the original versification, not an outcome of textual corruption. He notes that when *ljóðaháttr*-like lines are embedded in prose, as in the metrical Charms, it can be difficult to decide whether a preceding phrase should be read as prose or verse. Thus in Charm 4 lines 25–6 the phrase 'þis þe to bote' may lie outside the verse framework, with the series of phrases based on 'X gescotes' functioning as the metrical core (244–7).

171 **Holthausen, Ferdinand.** 'Anglosaxonica Minora.' *Anglia Beiblatt* 36 (1925): 219–20.

Holthausen construes '*inspiderwiht', the postulated original reading in metrical Charm 3 line 9, as a compound referring to a house-spider. In Exeter Book Riddle 56 line 12 he restores to 'þara flan<þraca>', *metri gratia*. He solves Riddle 74 as 'swan', reading 'dreag mid fiscum' in line 4. In Riddle 84 line 33a he explains 'swa þæt wuldor wifeð' as 'as that weaves glory'. In Riddle 91 line 8a 'under bæc' should read 'on bæcling', again *metri gratia*. He solves Riddle 95 as 'thought', citing a Frisian parallel.

172 **Pons, Émile.** *Le Thème et le Sentiment de la Nature dans la Poésie anglo-saxonne.* Publications de la Faculté des Lettres de l'Université de Strasbourg 25. Strasbourg: Istra, 1925. 160 pp.

Pons discusses tone and feeling in the Exeter Book Riddles on 'swan' (7) and 'iceberg' (33). He finds pagan attitudes in Riddle 7 fused with the Christian attitude to death, within the intense realism of the poem. The affection displayed in Riddle 57 towards the creatures it describes constitutes one means by which the Anglo-Saxon poet attains to the high peaks of inspiration and penetrates to the very soul of Nature. Other Riddles discussed in this light are 8 ('thrush'), 10, 15, 23, 24, and 47. Pons finds that although the treatment of inanimate objects in the Riddles can be heroic or lyrical, it can also be somewhat conventional. He singles out Riddles 19, 21, 27, 34, and 56 as exhibiting a lapse into puerility on the part of the poet. Other Riddles evaluated are 6, 11 ('night'), and 29. Pons also comments on metrical Charms 1, 3, and 4. He notes the poet's emphasis, in *Order*, on ideas rather than images: what strikes the poet most, he thinks, is the rigorous order that reigns in the universe.

3 **Wyld, H.C.** 'Diction and Imagery in Anglo-Saxon poetry.' *Essays and Studies* 11 (1925): 49–91. Repr. in *Essential Articles for the Study of Old English Poetry.* Ed. J.B. Bessinger and S.J. Kahrl. Hamden, CT: Archon, 1968. 183–228.

In the course of this broad survey, Wyld makes passing mentions of *Order* for its striking description of the sun (60 and 66); of *Rune Poem* line 66 for its meaningful use of the metaphor 'brimhengest' (62); and of *Fortunes* lines 33–42 for the graphic and terrible description of a dead man on the gallows, enveloped in a deadly mist (89).

4 **Gordon, Robert K.** *Anglo-Saxon Poetry.* Everyman's Library. London: Dent; New York: Dutton, 1926. Rev. edn. 1954. xii + 334 pp.

Gordon supplies prose translations of the following OEW poems, with brief individual introductions and a general introduction: some metrical Charms, *Fortunes, Gifts, Maxims,* and some Exeter Book Riddles. Excluded are Charms 5, 6, 7, and 10, likewise Riddles 4, 10, 12, 13, 18, 19, 25 and many others, among them most of the fragmentary Riddles. *Maxims I* and *II* appear under the heading of 'Gnomic Poetry'. A sample translation from Riddle 20 lines 1–8a: 'I am a wondrous creature, shaped in strife, loved by my lord, fairly adorned; my mailcoat is motley; also a bright wire lies round the gem of death which my master gave me, who sometimes in his wanderings guides me myself to the fight. Then I bear treasure through the bright day, the handiwork of smiths, gold through the dwellings.'

5 **Kissack, R.A.** 'The Sea in Anglo-Saxon and Middle English poetry.' *Washington University Studies. Humanistic Series* 13.2 (1926): 371–89.

Kissack notes in passing that Exeter Book Riddles 2 and 3 and *Maxims I*, with its interesting sea simile, describe the sea for its own sake rather than as part of a narrative poem.

6 **Wyatt, Alfred John.** *The Threshold of Anglo-Saxon.* Cambridge: Cambridge UP; New York: Macmillan, 1926. xvi + 126 pp.

Wyatt prints the texts of metrical Charm 9 (32–3) and *Maxims II* lines 5–40a

(33–4), with very brief notes (81–2). He attempts to tidy up the versification of the Charm.

177 **Schücking, Levin L.** 'Die angelsächsische und frühmittelenglische Dichtung.' Part 1 of Hans Hecht and L.L. Schücking. *Die englische Literatur im Mittelalter.* Handbuch der Literaturwissenschaft. Ed. Oskar Walzel. 1–35. Wildpark-Potsdam: Akademische verlagsgesellschaft Athenaion m.b.h., 1927. iv + 191 pp.

This monograph is designed to complement Heusler's *Die altgermanische Dichtung* (**166**) in the same 'Handbuch' series: accordingly, poetry classed as 'Germanic' (e.g. the *Maxims* and metrical Charms) is not covered here. Schücking makes a series of scattered remarks on OEW poems. He comments on the difficulties in dating and localizing texts, noting that older works, such as the *Leiden Riddle*, could be quite freely adapted, without the regard for individual authors and the sanctity of their work that would be felt nowadays (1–2). Schücking postulates a shift in cultural values between Offa's time and Æthelstan's, perhaps under feminine influence and to the betterment of women's position in society. The warrior ethos is de-emphasized, so that in late poems like *Fortunes* it is the callings of goldsmith, singer, and falconer that attract detailed description (5–6). Nonetheless, the Anglo-Saxon poet is most at home when describing battles in the heroic manner. This is evident in Exeter Book Riddles 1–3, where the storm becomes a savage Viking, burning halls and plundering houses (8). Schücking notes that the wisdom literature of early Christian England is closely related to the gnomic poetry covered by Heusler in the earlier volume. *Gifts* and *Fortunes* stand in the same relation to each other as do Milton's 'Il Allegro' and 'Il Penseroso'. The poet of *Gifts* evinces contentment with God's dispensation of blessings and a naively egalitarian refusal to privilege one calling over another. *Fortunes* speaks starkly of everyday human need and suffering, in contrast to the high heroic pathos of *Beowulf*. *Fortunes* marks a distinct poetic advance towards naturalism and secularism, eschewing, as it does, the obvious Christian message and the demonology to be seen in its analogue in *Juliana* lines 468–505 (30–1). *Solomon and Saturn* I, along with the prose section, exhibits oriental spirituality, whereas *Solomon and Saturn* II is interesting as pressing further the abortive attempt to convert gnomic poetry into a debate format which we see at the start of *Maxims I*. The succession of urgent questions about the basic dilemmas of human life is enough to suggest what a receptive audience Alfred's translation of Boethius must have found. Among the less interesting wisdom poetry is *Vainglory*, an advocacy of humility which digresses into a realistic description of drunken behaviour in the mead-hall. *Precepts* is remarkable for an emphasis on self-control and resolution comparable with that seen in *The Wanderer* (31–2).

178 **Kittredge, George Lyman.** *Witchcraft in Old and New England.* Cambridge, MA: Harvard UP, 1929. New York: Russell, 1956. 641 pp.

In Chapter 2 'English Witchcraft before 1558' Kittredge provides a brief survey of some OEW texts as part of a demonstration that 'the Elizabethans did not import their ideas or practices [on witchcraft] from the Continent' (23). The tradition is continuous, not merely from the Anglo-Saxons to the present time but from 'remote ages and from conditions of all-but-primitive barbarism' (23). 'So intertwined were Christianity and paganism [in Anglo-Saxon times] that even the Paternoster itself was treated by learned and pious men in a manner that approaches witchcraft. This comes out grotesquely in [*Solomon and Saturn*]' (31). The actions on the part of the fiends of inscribing (runic) letters and fettering a fighting man's hands are a manifest transference from the runic sorcery of heathen days. Kittredge goes on to mention some of the metrical Charms (1, 2, 5, 6, 8, 9, 10, and 11) as connected with practices of witchcraft (32). Scattered through the other chapters are brief mentions of OEW poems in a broadly comparative light. Charm 4 is cited in a discussion of 'elfshot' (133), Charm 6 as 'a grisly act of black magic' loosely comparable to later magical practices with the remains of the dead (143). Charm 11 can be regarded as either a charm or a prayer (152). Charm 1 is placed in a context of spells against ruin of crops or soil (171–2), Charm 9 in a context of spells against theft, with the comment that 'on the whole, these Anglo-Saxon spells differ in no essential from the illicit formulas which white witches were and are accustomed to mutter' (191). Charm 3 concerns the nightmare, who takes her victim on a 'wild witch-ride' (218). Parallels are cited for the motif seen in *Solomon and Saturn* line 151, where a fiend assumes the form of a bird (494).

9 Krapp, George P., and Arthur G. Kennedy. *An Anglo-Saxon Reader.* New York: Holt, 1929. cxiv + 359 pp.

The selected works include *Latin-English Proverbs* (138); metrical Charms 3, 5, and 8 (139–41); *Maxims II* lines 21b–36a (141); and Exeter Book Riddles 5, 7, and 47 (142–3). The editors note that Charm 3 does not observe 'the customary rules of good verse' (206).

0 Philippson, Ernst. *Germanisches Heidentum bei den Angelsachsen.* Kölner anglistische Arbeiten 4. Leipzig: Tauchnitz, 1929. 238 pp.

Philippson seeks to distinguish between the practices of magic that the Anglo-Saxons brought with them from the continent and those that evolved subsequently, through Danish and other influences. An oriental origin is suggested for the magical use of the Paternoster in *Solomon and Saturn*. In the metrical Charms, examples are noted of the performer addressing the object to be charmed, e.g. a wen or a spear. Philippson emphasizes the heathen aspects of Charm 1. [For a review see Klaeber, **400**.]

1 Ricci, Aldo. 'The Chronology of Anglo-Saxon Poetry.' *Review of English Studies* 5 (1929): 257–66.

Ricci evaluates the use of linguistic and metrical tests to reach a chronology of Old English poetry. He argues that the mechanical application of these tests has led Richter (**22**) to place the date of composition of the metrical Charms incorrectly in the first half of the eighth century. In fact the Charms must have undergone centuries of oral transmission before being recorded (261). The value of Richter's tests is further undermined by the scribal practice of translating texts into a different dialect, evidenced by the different versions of the *Leiden Riddle*. Would-be daters of such texts must reckon with the resultant alterations in the syllable count and even in whole words. When one considers the type of text, as distinct from its extant form in the manuscripts, the Charms and *Maxims I* and *II* emerge as amongst the earliest Old English poems.

182 **Flom, George Tobias.** *Introductory Old English Grammar and Reader.* Boston: Heath, 1930. xiv + 423 pp.

The reader contains the following OEW texts: Exeter Book Riddles 7 and 29 (257–8); *Maxims II* lines 38b–57a (280); and metrical Charms 4 and 8 (281–2). A note on Riddle 29 line 7b explains 'wealles hrof' as 'horizon', comparable to 'himinjøður' in *Völuspá* verse 5 (336). A note on 'sigewif' in Charm 8 states that 'the bees must not be named by the regular word; the charm would not work if they were' (340).

183 **Chadwick, H. Munro, and N. Kershaw Chadwick.** *The Growth of Literature.* I. *The Ancient Literatures of Europe.* Cambridge: Cambridge UP, 1932. xx + 672 pp.

Some of the OEW poems, notably *Maxims I* and *II*, are treated according to comparative methods as the authors develop a typology of gnomic poetry in a variety of 'heroic age' societies (Greek, Roman, English, Irish, Welsh, and Scandinavian). In Chapter 12 'Gnomic Poetry' (377–403) the gnomes are classified, building on Aristotle's distinctions, into (1) gnomes of action and conduct (included by Aristotle in his *Rhetoric* II.21) and (2) gnomes of observation (excluded by Aristotle). The gnomes of Type 2 typically result from observation and cannot be converted into precepts. Type 1 may be regarded as the beginning of ethical literature, Type 2 as the beginning of scientific literature. In Old English the formulaic 'sceal' may be used for both types, so that in *Maxims II* lines 14–15 ('geongne æþeling sceolan gode gesiðas/ . . .') it might be translated either 'ought to' (Type 1) or 'it is characteristic of' (Type 2) – more probably the latter. Altogether Type 1 is rare in *Maxims I* and *II* but well represented in *Precepts*, which, as a later, more thoroughly Christian variety of poetry, is outside the immediate focus of this monograph. Type 1 is also well exemplified in various Old Norse poems, such as *Hávamál*, and in the Irish and Greek traditions. The Type 2 gnomes in Old English are best paralleled in Old Norse legal formulas, such as *Tryggðamál*, and in Welsh poetry. The Old English *Maxims* often expand into fuller descriptions which can be equated with the early types of descriptive poetry, such as the Exeter Book Riddles, and in this expandability (though not in gnomic typology) resemble Hesiod's *Works and Days*. Resemblances of versification, syntax, and substance make it likely that the Old English and Old Norse gnomic poems have a shared early Germanic origin, though in their subsequent development they have diverged considerably. Both show greater cohesion than Irish gnomic discourses, which are often a series of concatenated but syntactically unintegrated gnomes. Otherwise it is doubtful that the history of gnomic poetry followed the same lines in the various languages. In Chapter 13 'Descriptive Poetry' (404–22) the Exeter Book Riddles are included, with the comment that in the riddle genre solutions are not necessarily obscure or difficult. Many of the Riddles are adapted from Latin originals but many too are of native origin, though collected in religious houses. The Riddles can be distinguished into descriptive poems (third person) and speeches in character (first person); it is not always clear that the latter are intended as true riddles. Riddles in the Old Norse form do not occur in the Exeter Book collection, but are represented in *Solomon and Saturn* II, e.g. lines 282–4: 'ac hwæt is ðæt wundor . . .'. The formula seen here may be taken from a Scandinavian source or (more likely) was originally common to English and Scandinavian. Descriptive, gnomic, and antiquarian poetry may have been cultivated by the same class of poets in early societies. *Rune Poem* mostly takes the form of descriptive Type 2 gnomes; the Icelandic and Norwegian rune poems, though very late, may have some remote connection with *Rune Poem*. The Greek Simonides fragment 1 is cited as an analogue to *Fortunes* (along with a similar list in *Juliana* lines 468–505); Solon's fragment 13 is treated as an analogue to *Gifts*. In Chapter 15 'Mantic Poetry' (445–74) metrical Charms 1–6 and 8–10 are briefly mentioned in a comparative light. Charm 4 might have been intended to counter sunstroke. In Chapter 18 'Recitation and Composition' (569–91) *Fortunes*, *Gifts*, and *Maxims I* are briefly cited.

4 Golding, G.F. *Records and Songs of Saxon Times*. London: Bell, 1932. viii + 165 pp.

Golding includes translations of selected Exeter Book Riddles: 1, 7, 9, 14, 15 ('badger'), 26, and 47 (93–7). Also included are metrical Charms 1, 4, 5, and 8 (155–60). Sample translation from Riddle 1 lines 1–2: 'Where is the man so wise, so subtle of mind,/ That he may say of a truth who set me on my journey?'

5 Chambers, R.W., Max Förster, and Robin Flower. *The Exeter Book of Old English Poetry*. Introductory chapters by R.W. Chambers, Max Förster and Robin Flower and a Collotype Facsimile of the Exeter Book. London: Bradford, Percy Hund, Humphries for the Dean and Chapter of Exeter Cathedral, 1933. 94 pp. + facsimile.

This facsimile edition includes the OEW poems in Exeter Book. The introductory chapter by R.W. Chambers, 'Modern Study of the Poetry of the Exeter Book', gives a brief review of the history of scholarship on the Exeter Book poems. Discussing the edition of Thorpe (**65**), Chambers observes that its major deficiency lies in the editor's careless treatment of the mutilated passages. 'When there was not enough preserved to make continuous sense, Thorpe often did not trouble to transcribe such words or portions of words as *could* be read; and when he indicated a gap by asterisks, he did not give any indication of the size of the gap' (35). Max Förster, 'General Description of the Manuscript', provides a discussion of cryptic script as found in the marginalia to the Riddles and elsewhere. R.W. Chambers and Robin Flower, 'Transcription of the Damaged Passages of the Exeter Book', aim to put on record exactly what letters could currently be seen: portions of *Homiletic Fragment II* and some Riddles are transcribed. With this objective, backing strips and glue were removed from portions of the damaged folios so that as much as possible of the text could be photographed. As a result, occasionally more is visible in the facsimile than in the Exeter Book itself, since its rebinding.

186   Mackie, W.S. 'Notes on the Text of the Exeter Book.' *Modern Language Review* 28 (1933): 75–8.

Mackie provides new readings from the manuscript, textual emendations, and notes on *Fortunes* lines 43–4 and 83 (in the latter emending manuscript 'gearo' to 'sceacol', in the sense 'plectrum'), *Maxims I* lines 176 and 179, and *Order* line 41. Also covered are Exeter Book Riddles 3, 8 (where he interprets the runic letter C above the riddle as standing for *ceo* 'chough or jackdaw'), 28 (to be solved as 'stringed instrument'), 31, 39, 75 (where he interprets the runes as an anagram on the consonants of *hælend* 'saviour'), 90 (where he interprets 'obcubuit agnus <rupi>' as a reference to Matt. 16: 18), and 94 (with the suggested new solution 'Nature').

187   Stern, Gustav. 'Old English "Fuslic" and "Fus".' *Englische Studien* 68 (1933): 161–73.

Stern makes passing references to OEW poems in the course of his survey. He suggests that the phrase 'fus forðweges' in Exeter Book Riddle 30 line 3 may belong to a group represented by *forðsiðes fus* 'dying' (167). In *Maxims I* line 27, the phrases 'fus feran' and 'fæge sweltan' may be synonymous, both contributing to the idea that 'the doomed shall die' (168).

188   Mackie, W.S. *The Exeter Book Part II, Poems IX–XXXII.* EETS 194. London: Oxford UP, 1934 (*for* 1933). vii + 245 pp. + 2 plates. New York: Kraus, 1987.

In his 'Preface' (v–vii) Mackie notes that Gollancz's projected Part 2 (**107**) had proceeded far enough to include a text and translation of *Fortunes* and *Vainglory*, in uncorrected proofs. Mackie presents an entirely new text and (facing-page) translation of the Exeter Book poems. The text admits emendation only when the original gives no coherent sense or when it unaccountably violates the most elementary principles of Old English metre. Limited restoration of lacunae is attempted. Full descriptions of damaged passages are given in notes below the text. In dealing with these passages previous editors had been handicapped by the fact that a parchment binding round the edges of the holes concealed a good many letters or parts of letters that would otherwise have been visible. With the removal of this binding, it is possible for Mackie to decipher rather more of the original text, e.g. 'obcubuit' (not 'obcurrit') in Riddle 90. A reduced facsimile of page 125a shows the end of Riddle 62, Riddles 63–5, and the beginning of Riddle 66. OEW poems figure as follows: *Vainglory*: 10–15, *Fortunes*: 26–31, *Maxims I*: 32–47, *Order*: 48–55, Riddles Group I: 88–151, *Homiletic Fragment II*: 188–9, Riddles Group II: 190–1, and Riddles Group III: 202–39. Appendix A lists the various suggested solutions for the Riddles. Riddle 3 should be divided into three sections: lines 1–16 describing a land earthquake, lines 17–36 describing a storm at sea, and lines 37–67 describing a thunderstorm. Additionally Mackie proposes some new solutions: 'two men, woman, horses, dog, bird on ship' for Riddle 36, 'Nature' for 66, 'cross' for 67, 'gold' for 83, and 'horn' for 88. Appendix B is a very select list of suggested emendations, mostly from previous scholars. It includes Mackie's earlier suggestion (**186**) that the runes in Riddle 75 represent the consonants of 'Hælend' ('Saviour'), in reverse order. Sample translation, from *Fortunes* (lines 21–6): 'Another shall fall from a high tree in the forest/, having no wings; yet shall he be in flight,/ will sail through the air, until he is no longer/ a fruit hanging from the tree, and will then drop/ to its roots, hopeless and lifeless,/ will fall to the ground – his soul passes away.' [For a review see Holthausen, **192**.]

9 Anderson, Marjorie, and Blanche C. Williams. *Old English Handbook.* Boston: Houghton Mifflin; London: Harrap, 1935. vii + 503 pp.

The texts are taken from the manuscripts, in consultation with the modern editions. Included are metrical Charms 2 and 8 (283–6), excerpts from *Maxims II* (287–9), and Exeter Book Riddles 1, 2, 14, 27, and 80 (279–82). The Riddles do not constitute very satisfactory puzzles for modern readers and are better seen as charming short poems. *Maxims II* was probably written at a time when Christianity was still a new religion and when old pagan memories were easily awakened. This suggests a West Saxon compiler, given that in Wessex the fusion of Christianity and heathendom occurred late. It may have been the work of some monk, who put together the two elements, his own contribution being the Christian.

0 Bright, James Wilson. *An Anglo-Saxon Reader edited with Notes and Glossary.* Rev. edn. with new material ed. J.R. Hulbert. New York: Holt, 1935. cxxxii + 395 pp.

No OEW poetry was included by Bright in the original edition (James W. Bright, *An Anglo-Saxon Reader,* New York: Holt, 1891) or his subsequent revisions. The *Reader,* as revised by Hulbert, takes in *Maxims II* lines 1–45a (177–8); metrical Charms 1 and 4 (179–82); and Exeter Book Riddles 7, 8 ('nightingale'), 26, 28, 47, and 57 (174–6). Bibliographical references are supplied in the headnotes to these readings. In his introductory 'Sketch of Anglo-Saxon Literature' the editor avers that although this literature has no artistic value its study can be defended in terms of an investigation into the national psychology. Some of the ensuing remarks relate to OEW poetry. Hulbert notes that we do not know exactly how extant sets of gnomic poetry assumed their extant form but surmises that some versifier joined them, introducing such padding as was necessary for metre. The presence of proverbs in all Anglo-Saxon poetry shows that they pervaded the thinking of the time. In his discussion of the Charms Hulbert emphasizes the tolerance shown towards them by Christianity. The inclusion of the Riddles in the Exeter Book can be accounted for on the assumption that the scribe was impressed by the psalm-like storm riddles with which the collection starts, and doubtless not always aware of just what particular riddles meant. [For a revised and updated edition of the *Reader* see **273**.]

1 Hodgkin, Robert H. *A History of the Anglo-Saxons.* 2 vols. London: Oxford UP, 1935.

Hodgkin attempts to use OEW poems, along with other literary genres, as a means of determining the attitudes of the ordinary Anglo-Saxon. The closest we can get to the viewpoint of the *ceorl* is in the *Maxims* and Exeter Book Riddles. Riddle 21 ('plough') evokes the toil of those who settled and broke in new land, *Maxims I* the apprehension felt by them in their isolated communities. By the time the *Maxims* were composed the typical sailor had become a Frisian (1.230–1). Metrical Charms 1 and 4 suggest that ordinary people regarded Christianity as little more than a new charm (2.466–8). Excerpts from these texts are quoted in translation. [Citations from the third edition (1952).]

192 **Holthausen, Ferdinand.** Rev. of *The Exeter Book Part II, Poems IX–XXXII*, by W.S. Mackie **[188]**. *Anglia Beiblatt* 46 (1935): 5–10.

Holthausen takes exception to Mackie's editorial procedures as typical of Anglo-American inconsistency. Instead of using metrical criteria as a guide in the restoration or emendation of evidently corrupt passages, Mackie is eclectic in his approach. Holthausen lists emendations and restorations, some of them new, which he regards as consonant with modern editorial practice. In *Order* line 89 he emends 'sy' to 'ys', in *Fortunes* line 73 'weorþeð' to 'weorþað'. Other texts specifically mentioned are *Maxims I*, Exeter Book Riddles, and *Vainglory*.

193 **Jackson, Kenneth.** *Studies in Early Celtic Nature Poetry.* Cambridge: Cambridge UP, 1935. xii + 204 pp.

Part I is an anthology of early Irish and Welsh poetry. Jackson makes detailed reference to this anthology in Part II, 'Studies on the Poems'. The result is a comparative study of Old English, Old Norse, Irish, and Welsh nature poetry. Jackson argues that observation of nature expressed itself in the Western languages as gnomic poetry, riddle poetry, and catechisms of physical lore. Many of the Exeter Book Riddles, for example Riddle 29, are little nature poems on animals, elements, and similar topics. In *Rune Poem*, nature poetry enters when the subject is a natural one, as with 'ice' and 'newt' (86). Sea-descriptions, rare in Welsh, appear frequently in Old English poetry. The mentions of the sea in *Rune Poem* testify to the 'grim pleasure in its moods' that the Anglo-Saxons took (91). The 'gnome' is defined as 'a sententious statement about universals, as well about the world of nature . . . as about the affairs of men' (127). Jackson makes detailed comparisons between the Welsh and Old English material, with emphasis on *Maxims I* and *II*. Unlike the Welsh gnomic poems, the Old English counterparts 'show no trace of conflation with the elegies' (131). The simile of the falling leaf in *Solomon and Saturn* lines 314–22 is noted as a rare example of the use of a 'nature gnome' to illustrate a 'human gnome', a practice more common in Old Norse poetry. 'In spite of the differences, it is probable that the Norse and Anglo-Saxon gnomes go back to a common Germanic origin and are therefore following a tradition of considerable antiquity' (131–2). The gnomic observation of the seasons in *Maxims II* lines 5–9 can be paralleled in Irish prose and (partially) in four Irish seasonal poems included in Jackson's anthology. The characteristic Irish use of lists can be paralleled in *Maxims II* and *Solomon and Saturn*. Gnomic poetry is to be seen as 'the beginning of science, where the nature gnomes are the rudiments of physics and botany and zoology, and the human gnomes a crude psychology' (136). It would have been adapted not by the poets of the epics but by poets in touch with the folk. In turn, the gnomic collections became a source for Anglo-Saxon and Welsh composers of elegies.

94 Krapp, George Philip, and Elliott Van Kirk Dobbie. *The Exeter Book.* Vol. 3 of *The Anglo-Saxon Poetic Records: A Collective Edition.* London: Routledge; New York: Columbia UP, 1936. cxvii + 382 pp. 6 vols. 1931–53.

This edition includes texts of the following OEW poems: *Gifts, Precepts, Vainglory, Fortunes, Maxims I, Order, Riddles,* and *Homiletic Fragment II.* In the Preface (v–vi) Dobbie states that the text is based on the 1933 facsimile edition of the Exeter Book (**185**). In the Introduction (ix–lxxxviii) he suggests that Leofric may have included the Exeter Book in his donations because the content of the manuscript was in large part religious and the first text in it was *Christ.* In his detailed description of the manuscript, Dobbie notes that the poetic texts are written in a single hand. In the latter part of the manuscript the spacing between poems is frequently lacking, perhaps because of a desire to save space. Three pairs of riddles which are written together are 2 and 3, 42 and 43, and 47 and 48. The documentation of accent marks in the manuscript (xxiv–xxv) contains examples from the OEW poems. In the introductory section on the poems *Gifts, Vainglory, Fortunes,* and *Order* are treated together as possible examples of the 'school of Cynewulf' (xxxix–xlii). Dobbie supplies and justifies his choice of titles. The poet of *Gifts* may have been inspired by the list of gifts in *Christ* to devise a more elaborate treatment of the theme, in less specifically Christian terms. The ultimate source may have been Paul in 1 Cor. 12: 4–11 (perhaps as summarized by Gregory the Great in his twenty-ninth homily on the Gospels). In *Vainglory* and *Order* the autobiographical introduction seems to bear no organic relationship to the rest of the poem. No single source for *Vainglory* is apparent. On *Fortunes,* Dobbie resists Brandl's argument (**19**) that the second part of the poem is a later continuation and reinterpretation of a heathen fragment. 'The two parts of the poem complement each other admirably, and lines 93ff go well with both' (xli). *Order* is so loosely structured throughout that the doubts expressed by Wülker (**8**) and Brandl (**19**) as to the genuineness of the closing lines lose their force (xli). The author may have been familiar with the works of Cynewulf. Although the content of *Precepts* is not always specifically Christian, Brandl (**19**) is mistaken in classifying it with *Maxims I* as the product of pre-Christian moral teaching influenced by Christian doctrine (xlii–xliii). On *Maxims I* (xlv–xlvii) Dobbie comments that it is impossible to tell with any certainty whether the three sectional divisions indicated in the manuscript were intended by the scribe to be taken as three parts of a single poem, or as three separate poems. From line 3 onwards there is an almost complete lack of ordered arrangement. Classifications of portions of the text as 'heathen' and 'Christian', as by Brandl (**19**), are of little value. Williams's (**547**) speculation about Alfredian authorship is interesting but unprovable. *Homiletic Fragment II* is classified as a consolation and dated to the tenth century. The poem is probably fragmentary as it stands in the manuscript. The three groups of Riddles are discussed together (lxv–lxvii). Dobbie regards the burden of proof as being upon those who would demonstrate unity of authorship. In most cases it is impossible to tell whether similarity between an Exeter Book riddle and a Latin riddle rests upon conscious imitation of the Latin riddle or upon the use of the same traditional material. Also provided are tabulations of accents and other manuscript features, a bibliography, text, and notes. The solutions to the Riddles are discussed in the notes.

195 Pfeilstücker, Suse. *Spätantikes und germanisches Kunstgut in der frühangelsächsischen Kunst: Nach lateinischen und altenglischen Schriftquellen.* Diss. U Bonn. Kunstwissenschaftliche Studien 19. Berlin: Deutscher Kunstverlag, 1936. 244 pp.

The literary sources on early Anglo-Saxon art and technology surveyed here include OEW poems. Exeter Book Riddle 28 is cited as evidence for Anglo-Saxon methods of book production: the individual motifs in the riddle can be correlated with aspects of extant books. *Gifts* is cited to illustrate methods in metal-work, *Fortunes* for gold-smithing, *Maxims I* for the manufacture of weaponry, and various Exeter Book Riddles for other technological processes, with brief comments and translations into German.

196 Bracher, Frederick. 'Understatement in Old English Poetry.' *PMLA* 52 (1937): 915–34. Repr. in *Essential Articles for the Study of Old English Poetry.* Ed. J.B. Bessinger and S.J. Kahrl. Hamden, CT: Archon, 1968. 228–54.

Bracher tabulates the incidence of understatement in OEW and other poems (reprint, 233–4). The seven instances in *Maxims I* amount to a very high incidence, typical of the early pagan and heroic poems. By contrast, a low incidence is typical of the later Christian poems, both narrative and didactic. In a few cases, such as *Maxims I* lines 150–1, understatement becomes almost ludicrous (231). In the Exeter Book Riddles only ten instances of understatement are to be found.

197 Von der Leyen, Friedrich. *Die Götter der Germanen.* Munich: Beck'sche Verlagsbuchhandlung, 1938. xii + 322 pp. + 12 ill.

In passing, references are made to various OEW poems. Brief accounts of metrical Charm 1 and *Rune Poem* are given (68 and 52 respectively). The testimony of *Rune Poem* on Ing is mentioned (146). Charm 4 is cited as testimony to Anglo-Saxon belief in witches and valkyries, with reference to the resemblances between this text and the Merseburger Spruch (147–8). The *Maxims* are also briefly mentioned (145–52).

198 Marquardt, Hertha. *Die altenglischen Kenningar. Ein Beitrag zur Stilkunde altgermanischer Dichtung. Schriften der Königsberger gelehrten Gesellschaft* 14 Jahr. Geistes-Wissenschaftliche Klasse Heft 3 (1938). Halle: Niemeyer, 1938. xvi + 238 pp.

Marquardt cites many passages in the Exeter Book Riddles and elsewhere as containing virtual kennings, i.e. clauses that could easily be compressed into kenning format. She offers new interpretations of passages in *Maxims I*; Riddle 3; *Rune Poem* line 36, where 'hyrde fyres' = 'yew wood'; *Solomon and Saturn* line 25a, where 'windes full' = 'sky'; and *Vainglory* (on 'winburg-' in line 14 and 'æscstede' in line 17). She rejects Kock's (**147**) interpretation of *Maxims I* line 106, 'mægðegsan wyn', arguing that 'wyn' is not part of the kenning.

199 Hotchner, Cecilia Audrey. *Wessex and Old English poetry, with Special Consideration of The Ruin.* Diss. New York U. Lancaster, PA: Lancaster, 1939. vi + 146 pp.

Hotchner seeks to correct a perceived tendency, on the part of Stopford Brooke (**13, 109**) and others, to over-emphasize Northumbria as the home of Old English poetry. She argues that while Northumbria was producing *Beowulf* and similar masterpieces Wessex was fostering other types of poetry, which centred on the elegy. She identifies a strong elegiac element in *Fortunes* and *Homiletic Fragment II*, in common with *The Wanderer* and *The Seafarer*. Detailed verbal resemblances exist between *Fortunes*, *Gifts*, and *Homiletic Fragment II* on the one hand and *The Wanderer* on the other. *Maxims II* and *The Ruin* are similarly linked. The elegiac genre is not native to England but borrowed from such Latin poets as Ovid and Venantius Fortunatus. As to the original home of the Exeter Book Riddles, no one dialect can be identified as original for the entire corpus. Although some riddles certainly represent copies from Northumbrian originals, the translations of Aldhelm 33 and 100 at least are most likely to be local Wessex productions.

0 Juzi, Gertrud. *Die Ausdrücke des Schönen in der altenglischen Dichtung: Untersuchung über ein sprachliches Feld.* Zurich: Aschmann, 1939. 139 pp.

Juzi analyses the concept of the beautiful, with some reference to OEW poems. Her general contention is that the poetic need for an abundance of synonyms has triumphed over any need for finely differentiated shades of meaning. On points of detail, she interprets the first element of 'frid-hengest' in Exeter Book Riddle 22 line 4 as cognate with Old Norse *friðr*. The word *fæger* is used abnormally in *Precepts* line 12 ('fægerwyrde'), to denote not 'beautiful' but 'circumspect'. Juzi also notes some peculiarities in the usage of the words *torht*, *wrætlic*, *wuldor*, and *wundorlic* in OEW poetry, notably the Riddles.

1 Gross, Erika. *Das Wunderbare im altenglischen geistigen Epos.* Diss. U Frankfurt. Bottrop i. W.: Postberg, 1940. 171 pp.

In passing, Gross makes two references to OEW poems. Whereas *Maxims II* reflects early Germanic tradition by showing individual objects in their essential aspects, e.g. 'wudu sceal on foldan/ blædum blowan' (lines 33–4), the focus in the *Metres of Boethius* is on the way these objects combine to form the world as a whole (101). The description of fire in *Christ* 3 lines 972–6 is reminiscent of the description of the storm in Exeter Book Riddle 3, since both emphasize vivid movement. Gross argues that poetry on religious themes draws on the diction of purely descriptive poetry, such as Riddle 3 (147).

2 Timmer, Benno J. 'Wyrd in Anglo-Saxon Prose and Poetry.' *Neophilologus* 26 (1940–1): 24–33, 213–28. Repr. in *Essential Articles for the Study of Old English Poetry.* Ed. J.B. Bessinger and S.J. Kahrl. Hamden, CT: Archon, 1968. 124–59.

Timmer finds the idea represented by *wyrd* of special interest in Anglo-Saxon literature because of its continued use after the conversion to Christianity. The majority of scholars, he thinks, consider *wyrd*, even when used in Christian texts, as having some more or less remote association with the heathen belief in Fate. Only a minority see the use of the word as being wholly Christian, betokening Fate as subordinated to Divine Providence. Timmer's objective is to determine the meaning of *wyrd* in the texts as we have them. He omits the three instances of *wyrd* in the Exeter Book Riddles, on the grounds that the Riddles are strongly influenced by Latin. On the *Maxims* Timmer comments that had the Christian redactor posited by Brandl (19) and many other scholars understood the word in the heathen sense, it would have been excised (219–20). In *Maxims II* lines 4–5 the redactor probably intended the following sense: 'however great the powers of Christ may be, the order of events as ordained by God's Providence is mightiest.' At the same time it may be admitted that, if the words 'wyrd byð swiðost' actually belonged to the poem in its pre-Christian form, they must have referred to Fate. The plural *wyrda*, seen in *Maxims I* line 9 and *Solomon and Saturn* line 440b, means simply 'events'. In *Solomon and Saturn* lines 437–50, where Saturn is a heathen who is going to be converted, *wyrd* refers to the heathen goddess.

203 **Dobbie, Elliott Van Kirk.** *The Anglo-Saxon Minor Poems.* Vol. 6 of *The Anglo-Saxon Poetic Records: A Collective Edition.* New York: Columbia UP, 1942. clxxx + 220 pp. 6 vols. 1931–53.

The volume includes *Rune Poem, Solomon and Saturn, Maxims II, Winfrid Proverb,* the *Leiden Riddle, Latin-English Proverbs,* and the metrical Charms. Dobbie notes in the Preface (v–vii) that the texts of the poems edited here are based on photostats, supplemented in each case by a first-hand examination of the manuscript. An exception is the *Leiden Riddle*, where the text is based on the readings of earlier editors. The Introduction proceeds poem by poem, with brief descriptions of the relevant manuscripts. In the introduction to *Rune Poem* (xlvi–l) Dobbie accepts Hempl's (1002) argument that Hickes (1705) was indebted to Cotton Domitian A.ix, fol.10a. Detailed similarities in format and phrasing to the two Scandinavian rune poems are noted: despite Brandl (19), the explanation is not an original Germanic rune poem but rather the independent use of traditional popular material. *Rune Poem* gives the impression of being a miscellaneous compilation from all kinds of sources, both literary and popular. Some of the strophes may have been written as riddles, others resemble proverbs or maxims. The hypermetric stanzas ('hægl' and 'nyd') may have been derived from some other source than the stanzas written in normal verse. 'But in the form in which we now have it, it gives the impression of a complete and unified work by a single compiler, who drew from a variety of materials but adapted and revised these materials to suit his artistic purposes' (xlix). An eighth- or early ninth-century date is probable. In the introduction to *Solomon and Saturn* (l–lx) Dobbie suggests that *Solomon and Saturn* II probably represents an imitation of *Solomon and Saturn* I. 'It is most likely that the rather fanciful description of the Pater Noster, presented in dialogue form in lines 1–169 and in the prose fragment, inspired a second poet to put together, in the form of a riddle contest elsewhere widely known in Old Germanic tradition, the miscellaneous material of lines 179–506, derived in part from traditional gnomic literature, in part from Latin works on theology and demonology' (lix). Dobbie demurs at Menner's (1073) use of verbal parallels to place lines 170–8 after line 506. The frequent use of Latin words in both of the Anglo-Saxon poems seems to imply an (unknown) Latin source or sources. A late ninth-century or very early tenth-century date of composition is indicated. The *Menologium* and *Maxims II* are taken together in the Introduction (lx–lxvii). Dobbie regards them as originally separate from each other and from the redaction of the *Anglo-Saxon Chronicle* that follows them, though in the eyes of the scribe the two poems may have functioned as preliminary matter to the Chronicle. '*Maxims II*, like *Maxims I* in the Exeter Book, has no relationship in subject matter to either the *Menologium* or the Chronicle' (lxi). Dobbie notes the advantages of Müller's (540) purely formal analysis of *Maxims II* but points out that it 'does not tell us anything about the origins of the various component parts of the poem, and an attempt to classify according to subject matter tells us very little more' (lxvi). Lack of unity in style and content does not necessarily, despite Williams (547), indicate diversity of origin. *Contra* Brandl (19), attempts to divide the heathen from the Christian elements do not prove that we have here a heathen text reworked by a Christian poet. The *Winfrid Proverb* (lxvii–lxix) may be from a longer Anglo-Saxon poem, as suggested by Wülker (8), or it may have been an independent composition with the same sententiousness of tone seen in the virtually contemporaneous *Bede's Death Song*. Commenting on the *Leiden Riddle* (cviii–cx), Dobbie regards historical probability as favouring the conclusion that the translations of Aldhelm 33 and 100 were made by a Northumbrian and in the Northumbrian dialect. The *Latin-English Proverbs* (cx–cxii) are of interest as illustrating the informal use of the alliterative line. Imitation of the *Rhyming Poem* is a possibility. The metrical Charms (cxxx–cxxxviii) are placed in the order in which they appear in the manuscript, without classification as to form or content. Distinctions between heathen and Christian material are difficult to justify. Dobbie briefly reviews the history of identifications of the herbs mentioned in Charm 2. *Contra* Kögel (106) and Horn (392), the entirety of Charm 4 may well have been composed at the one time. In Charm 9 line 6 'Garmund, godes ðegen' probably belongs with the prose introduction rather than with the metrical section. Charm 6 probably consists of three originally separate texts. The other Charms are also the subject of brief comments. Documentation on accent marks in the manuscripts (cxxxix–cxlv), bibliography (cxlix–clxxx), texts, and notes are provided.

4 **Pope, John C.** *The Rhythm of Beowulf: An Interpretation of the Normal and Hypermetric Verse-Forms in Old English Poetry.* New Haven: Yale UP, 1942. Rev. edn. 1966. xxxvi + 409 pp.

Part 2 'The Hypermetric Verses' (99–158) includes OEW poetry in a discussion of all the Old English material. A caveat is issued, however, that the text of *Solomon and Saturn* is exceptionally corrupt and that *Maxims I* and *II* show certain tendencies that distinguish them from the epic tradition. Pope's list of hypermetric verses, correcting Sievers's (92), identifies 5 verses in *Precepts* (lines 17b–19), 4 in *Fortunes* (lines 15–16), between 145 and 152 in *Maxims I*, 9 in *Order* (lines 98–102), 7 or 8 in Exeter Book Riddle 16 (lines 1–4, possibly excluding 2a), 17 in *Maxims II* (lines 1–4, 42–5, and 47a), 8 in *Rune Poem* (lines 25–8), and between 44 and 46 in *Solomon and Saturn*. *Maxims I* and *Solomon and Saturn* are discussed in detail (102 and 104 respectively). In *Order*, line 102 should include 'sigan'. In Riddle 40, line 5b is corrupt. In *Solomon and Saturn* line 453b Pope suggests substituting 'worhte' for 'ongan wyrcan' so as to reduce the undue length of the verse, which 'can scarcely be read in the allotted time' (129 n. 15 and 134 n. 21). Problematic hypermetric verses in the *Maxims* are separately discussed (150–2): Sievers may be right to see them as the vestiges of a strophic formation but equally the transition from a genuine hypermetric to a pair of normal verses is extremely easy. Discussing the incidence of double alliteration in hypermetric verses, Pope registers a temptation to substitute 'cynedom' for 'rice' in *Maxims II* line 1a (154).

205 Bone, Gavin David. *Anglo-Saxon Poetry: An Essay with Specimen Translations in Verse.* Oxford: Clarendon, 1943. 79 pp.

Bone comments that the qualities common to all Old English verse greatly outnumber those peculiar to each poet. Much in the same way, he thinks, all tunes on the bagpipes sound the same to an Englishman. The translations include *Fortunes* and *Gifts* under the heading 'The Fates and Gifts of Men' (45–8); *Maxims II* (49–50); Exeter Book Riddles 29 and 47 (51); and metrical Charm 4 (52). A sample translation from *Maxims II* lines 13–14: 'Woes are catching: clouds are fading./ If you should ever advise a great lord,/ Urge him to giving and not to invading.' From Charm 4 the following free rendition (lines 7–11?): 'When the Fates ran amuck,/ Those mighty old hags on their green-crested nags/ Pressing horribly near, and couching their spear,/ I stood under cover and darted one over,/ An excellent arrow, its aim was so narrow.'

206 Malone, Kemp. 'Notes and Observations: Plurilineal Units in Old English Poetry.' *Review of English Studies* 19 (1943): 201–4.

Malone argues that end-stopped verse was characteristic of the earliest Old English poetic style. The *Leiden Riddle* is loosely representative of this style, where every line ended with a syntactical pause and every sentence made either a line or a couplet. Although the *Maxims* have been remodelled by clerical writers they retain traces of one- or two-line units.

207 Mossé, Fernand. *Manuel de l'anglais du Moyen Âge des origines au XIVe siècle.* Vol. 1: *Vieil-Anglais.* i *Grammaire et textes,* ii *Notes et glossaire.* Paris: Aubier, 1945. 2 vols.

Included, with brief annotations, are metrical Charms 8 and 9 and Exeter Book Riddles 14 and 35 (the latter also printed separately as the *Leiden Riddle*). These poems are collectively classed as 'poésie didactique'.

208 Sisam, Kenneth. 'Notes on Old English Poetry. On the Authority of Old English Poetical Manuscripts.' *Review of English Studies* 22 (1946): 257–68. Repr. as 'The Authority of Old English Poetical Manuscripts'. Kenneth Sisam. *Studies in the History of Old English Literature.* Oxford: Clarendon, 1953. 29–44.

Sisam uses the existence of duplicate manuscript versions of some poems, such as the *Leiden Riddle* and *Solomon and Saturn*, to show that the general level of scribal accuracy in copying was not exemplary. Variations in inflection and even in wording are readily documented. The *Leiden Riddle* texts contain half a dozen variants of some importance in sixteen corresponding lines, a degree of variation similar to that exhibited in Exeter Book Riddle 30. As compared with the variants in classical texts, these Anglo-Saxon manuscript versions show a laxity in reproduction and an aimlessness in variation which are more in keeping with the oral transmission of verse.

9 **Whitelock, Dorothy.** 'Anglo-Saxon Poetry and the Historian.' *Transactions of the Royal Historical Society* 4th ser. 31 (1949): 75–94. Repr. in *From Bede to Alfred: Studies in Early Anglo-Saxon Literature and History.* London: Variorum Reprints, 1980. 368 pp. ['Anglo-Saxon Poetry and the Historian' appears as article 3, with original pagination.]

Whitelock demonstrates that Old English poetry supplies much valuable historical information. OEW poems occur frequently among her examples. A vivid, if one-sided, picture of the fighting classes, especially the 'joys of the hall', can be obtained (91). The law which imposes heavy fines for fighting in other people's houses sheds light on the fate of the man who was 'too hasty of speech' in *Fortunes* lines 48–50 (92). *Fortunes, Gifts,* the *Maxims,* Exeter Book Riddles, and *Rune Poem,* along with other poems, usefully correct the heroic emphases of so much extant Old English poetry by describing the peace-time activities of ordinary men and women. The sketches of various occupations include the 'man who knows the laws'; 'he must have known that mass of customary law that has not come down to us' (92). The Exeter Book Riddles mention black, dark-hued, or dark-haired 'Wealas' doing menial work and *Fortunes* lines 33–42 contains a grim description of the thief on the gallows (93).

0 **Magoun, F.P., and J.A. Walker.** *An Old-English Anthology: Translations of Old-English Prose and Verse.* Dubuque, IA: Brown, 1950. x + 108 pp.

The translations are made as literal as possible, as an aid to beginners. Included in the anthology are Exeter Book Riddles 7, 8 ('jay, jackdaw, or the like'), 26, 28, 47, and 57 ('jackdaws') (89–91); *Maxims II* (91–2); and metrical Charms 1 and 4 (92–5). A sample translation from Riddle 47 lines 1b–3: 'That seemed to me a rare fate, when I learned of that remarkable occurrence, (namely,) that the larva swallowed up the writing of a certain man (literally, someone of men).'

1 **Young, Jean.** 'Glæd wæs ic gliwum: Ungloomy Aspects of Old English Poetry.' *The Early Cultures of North-west Europe. (H.M. Chadwick Memorial Studies.)* Ed. Cyril Fox and Bruce Dickins. Cambridge: Cambridge UP, 1950. 275–87.

Young notes the failure of *Gifts* to mention a chef and suggests that this omission is typical of the general emphasis on drink rather than food as epitomizing life in the 'beer-hall' in Old English poetry. Exeter Book Riddle 27 'dwells affectionately on the metamorphosis of mead from its green and salad days, when it flies through the air on the "feathers" of bees as honey, to the hour of its maturity and triumph over unwary youth' (276). As to music, she notes the idea in *Maxims I* lines 169–70 that 'for the musician (as for the poet) desire has less torment than for other mortals' (276). Riddle 8 'analyses with great accuracy of detail the performance of a real bird to which the poet must often have listened' (278) – i.e. the song-thrush. Riddles 15 ('weasel'), 40, and 42 suggest similar first-hand observation (279 and 281–2). Also noted are the references to animals in *Rune Poem* (281). The description of the Vasa Mortis in *Solomon and Saturn* belongs 'to the realm of demonology rather than ornithology' (278). Significant is the juxtaposition of falconer and harper in *Fortunes* lines 80–92 as sources of pleasure (279). As to the kenning for God in *Solomon and Saturn* lines 81–2, 'a protection for poor fishes and worms', the author inquires whether the author had heard of 'St Brandan's experience when chanting the Office of St Paul on the high seas' (280). In *Order*, lines 57–81 constitute 'a veritable Old English hymn to the sun' (283). *Gifts* reveals 'what store our ancestors set on manual skill' (285). 'The value set on simple human happiness by Anglo-Saxon poets explains that part of their poetry, and it is a larger part than is often realized, which is in the truest sense of the word philosophical. It enabled them to take life sometimes at least lightly and tolerantly' (286).

212   **Holthausen, Ferdinand.** 'Zur Textkritik alt- und mittelenglischer Gedichte.' *Archiv für das Studium der neueren Literaturen* 188 (1951): 98–107.

In a response to the editions by Menner (**1073**) and Dobbie (**203**), Holthausen proposes a series of emendations, most of them designed to improve the versification in various ways. In *Solomon and Saturn* he adds 'geneahhe' in line 7; reads 'swat', as a variation on 'dropan', in lines 44–5; deletes 'on' and reads 'westennes' in line 83; takes 'fif' and 'mægnum' separately in line 136 (as referring to the five senses); suggests replacing 'H' with 'I' in line 138; reads 'wynrode' and deletes 'lixan' in line 236; suggests 'næssas' instead of 'niehtes' in line 339; and restores line 465 to 'and him <beorhta> bebead bealdor heofonwara'. He also contributes minor notes on lines 360, 369, and 478. In metrical Charm 3 line 11 'lande' should be emended to 'tune' to avoid double alliteration in the second half-line. In Charm 4 short half-lines could be filled out as follows: 'sæt smið ana, sloh an seax lytel,/ wælspere isern' (lines 13–14) and 'fleoh þær to fenne on fyrgenheafde' (line 27). Holthausen also proposes various lexical substitutions in the text of the Charms. In the *Winfrid Proverb* he takes 'foreldit' as an intransitive verb: thus 'often the tardy are too old for fame'. In Exeter Book Riddle 19 he restores 'mearh' in line 2, in accord with the masculine-gender form 'hygewloncne', and moves the runic 'hægel' back to line 1, which he thinks otherwise too short. He also suggests two other minor emendations for sense and versification.

213   **Timmer, Benno J.** 'Expanded Lines in Old English Poetry.' *Neophilologus* 35 (1951): 226–30.

Timmer sees expanded lines as used for emphasis at the opening or close of certain poems. Relevant here are *Maxims I* and *II*, Exeter Book Riddle 16, and *Order*. Gnomic poetry and lines with gnomic content are emphatic by virtue of their proverbial character: examples cited include *Solomon and Saturn* lines 312–13 and *Fortunes* lines 15–17a.

214   **Brady, Caroline.** 'The Old English Nominal Compound in "rad".' *PMLA* 57 (1952): 538–72.

In the course of this study Brady makes sporadic references to OEW poems. In the 'rad' strophe of *Rune Poem* she argues for a contrast between notions held of 'riding' by respectively an occupant of a seat in a hall and someone actually astride a horse (540). The full primary meaning of *eorod* 'band of horsemen' has been preserved in Exeter Book Riddle 3 line 49 and Riddle 22 line 3 and, with emendation, in *Maxims I* line 62 (542–3). Precise contextual senses of *rad* or its cognates are deduced for *Fortunes* line 33 and for Riddles 19 line 5 ('journey') and 20 line 14 ('being carried'). The compound 'streamrade' in *Gifts* line 54 refers to the movement of the currents, not to the sea in general.

5 **Sisam, Kenneth.** 'Dialect Origins of the Earlier Old English Verse.' *Studies in the History of Old English Literature.* Oxford: Clarendon, 1953. 119–39. Repr. in *Essential Articles for the Study of Old English Poetry.* Ed. J.B. Bessinger and S.J. Kahrl. Hamden, CT: Archon, 1968. 74–95.

Countering Menner's arguments **(1073)** concerning the localization of *Solomon and Saturn,* Sisam points out that several words in this poem are absent from Anglian prose but present in Alfred's West Saxon prose. Menner's supposed distinctively Anglian words are also unsafe as evidence. Generally, vocabulary remains unsatisfactory or inconclusive as evidence of the original dialect of poems presumed to be early and it is best not to form a bias in favour of Anglian origin and against West Saxon or Kentish origin. Sisam uses the 'lorica' riddle (Exeter Book Riddle 35) as an example of literary or learned communication, arguing that there are no historical reasons why poems composed in the South should not pass to the North and Midlands, assume an Anglian dress or colouring there, and subsequently return to the South (122–3).

6 **Derolez, René.** *Runica Manuscripta: the English Tradition.* Rijksuniversiteit te Gent. Werken uitgegeven door de Faculteit van de Wijsbegeerte en Letteren, Aflevering 118. Bruges: De Tempel, 1954. lxiv + 455 pp. + 8 plates.

Derolez's survey includes the various OEW poems which contain runes or whose text is associated with runes. In his account of *Rune Poem* (16–26), he discusses the lost manuscript text, along with the Hickes print (1705). Since Smith (1696) did not mention *Rune Poem* in his catalogue of the manuscript (Cotton Otho B.x), the single leaf containing the poem must have been inserted between the time Smith saw the manuscript and Wanley described it in his catalogue (1705). Hickes's print is not a very trustworthy substitute for the manuscript evidence. The additional runes in the print are meaningless, have no connection with *Rune Poem,* and represent no more than a *probatio pennae.* Derolez agrees with Hempl **(1002)** in the hypothesis that Hickes found a set of rune-names with *Rune Poem,* but thinks that these names were probably not due to the scribe of the poem itself. The abnormal linguistic forms of the names are hardly surprising if we keep in mind the long evolution indicated by the text of *Rune Poem.* Derolez contends, in discussing the 'os' strophe, that the name was so essential a part of the rune that neither the name nor its meaning could be changed arbitrarily. *Rune Poem* was used as a means of teaching the runes. The runological value of the strophes in *Rune Poem* varies considerably: although some of the poetic definitions seem to contain a good deal of genuine runic lore, others must have been thoroughly modernized. In discussing the Exeter Book Riddles with runes (417–19), Derolez begins by noting cases where the rune indicates its name, as in Riddle 91 line 7 and in Riddle 19. He also discusses Riddles 64 and 75, noting that in the latter the third rune is a poorly made *u,* not an *l.* He compares the cryptic function of the runes in these riddles with that of the *notae* in Riddle 36. The differences between the scribbled runes associated with Riddles 5, 6, and 7 and the firmly inscribed runes used elsewhere in the Exeter Book need to be borne in mind in reaching an interpretation. The function of the runes in *Solomon and Saturn* I (discussed 419–21) seems to be purely ornamental with at the most an archaic, pagan, or cryptic, flavour. They do not fit the alliterative scheme and therefore could not have been read aloud. They probably were not the work of the original poet but belong to a later period.

217   **Kaiser, Rolf.** *Alt- und mittelenglische Anthologie.* Berlin: Kaiser, 1954. Rev. edn. *Medieval English: An Old and Middle English Anthology.* 1958. xi + 592 pp. + 24 plates.

This self-published student reader includes metrical Charm 1 (74–5); excerpts from *Maxims I* and *II* (75–6); Exeter Book Riddle 1, an excerpt from Riddle 3, Riddle 7, Riddle 9, Riddle 28 ('John Barleycorn', '?wine-cask', 'some kind of stringed instrument'), and Riddle 47 (77–8); an excerpt from *Vainglory* (88); *Fortunes* (91–3); excerpted strophes from *Rune Poem* (111); the *Leiden Riddle* side by side with Exeter Book Riddle 35 and Aldhelm 33 (131); and metrical Charm 12 (144). The text of *The Husband's Message* (90) excludes Riddle 60. Kaiser supplies an apparatus of select variant readings and emendations but no other annotations.

218   **Quirk, Randolph.** *The Concessive Relation in Old English Poetry.* Yale Studies in English 124. New Haven: Yale UP, 1954. xiv + 148 pp.

Quirk comments in detail on the syntax of Exeter Book Riddle 48 line 2, which he finds unusual in several respects. Also idiosyncratic is the use of 'ac' in *Solomon and Saturn* lines 336, 340, 344, and 348: it represents a subject-changing use, parallel to modern 'but' at the head of the sentence. He discusses concessive 'gif' in Riddle 72 line 18 and metrical Charm 4, along with the text of *Order* lines 23–6.

219   **Elliott, Ralph W.V.** 'The Runes of "The Husband's Message".' *JEGP* 54 (1955): 1–8.

Elliott sees several good reasons for regarding Exeter Book Riddle 60 as in reality part of *The Husband's Message*. The so-called Riddle does not read like a riddle: in content these seventeen lines are unmistakably related to what follows in the manuscript. Formally, the direct address in the second person carries through from the 'riddle' into *The Husband's Message*. Additionally, Elliott argues that the word 'dæg' in *Rune Poem* line 74 still possesses some of the traditional associations of fruitfulness and prosperity inherited from its pagan Germanic source. He interprets the 'iar' strophe in *Rune Poem* to refer to the sea – a river of fishes, and yet it always feeds upon the land.

220   **Greenfield, Stanley B.** 'The Formulaic Expression of the Theme of "Exile" in Anglo-Saxon Poetry.' *Speculum* 30 (1955): 200–6. Repr. in *Essential Articles for the Study of Old English Poetry.* Ed. J.B. Bessinger and S.J. Kahrl. Hamden, CT: Archon, 1968. 352–62.

Greenfield briefly mentions *Maxims II* line 19a and Exeter Book Riddle 39 as containing versions of the exile theme.

1 **Lehnert, Martin.** *Poetry and Prose of the Anglo-Saxons: A Text Book with Introductions, Translations, Bibliography and an Old English Etymological Dictionary.* Vol. 1. *Texts, translations, introduction, bibliography.* Vol. 2. *Glossary.* Berlin: VEB Deutscher Verlag der Wissenschaften, 1955–6.

The selected works include excerpts from metrical Charms 1, 4, and 8 (4–5); *Fortunes* (8–10); *Gifts* (7–8); *Maxims I* lines 81–106 and *II* lines 1–13 (6–7); Exeter Book Riddles 2, 5, 7, 8 ('jay'), 28 ('beer'), 34, 35, 47, and 60 (18–21); and *Rune Poem* (14–17). The reader also contains an introduction, bibliography, and notes. The English translations are by various hands, including Gordon (**174**) and Mackie (**188**) (74–9 and 83–7). On *Rune Poem*, the editor comments that certain strophes contain real poetry and are related to the Exeter Book Riddles.

2 **Mittner, Ladislaus.** *Wurd: Das Sakrale in der altgermanischen Epik.* Bibliotheca germanica 6. Berne: Francke, 1955. 204 pp.

Mittner makes scattered references to OEW poetry. He argues that the adjective *swið* is applied to *wyrd* only in poetry influenced by Christianity, such as *Maxims II* line 5 (89). He takes up the problem of whether God or Wyrd is stronger, citing *Maxims II* and *Solomon and Saturn* (106). He sees the description of Lucifer's fall in *Solomon and Saturn* lines 451–76 as 'epic' (113).

3 **Stanley, Eric G.** 'Old English Poetic Diction and the Interpretation of the "Wanderer", the "Seafarer" and the "Penitent's Prayer".' *Anglia* 73 (1955): 413–66. Repr. in *Essential Articles for the Study of Old English Poetry.* Ed. J.B. Bessinger and S.J. Kahrl. Hamden, CT: Archon, 1968. 458–514.

Stanley comments in passing on *Maxims I* and *II* (426, 432, 442, and 444). He notes the editorial tendency to begin a new sentence with the word 'fus' in *Maxims I* line 27, but points out that it is in the nature of the *Maxims* to combine things in contrast, whether or not it is customary to compare and contrast them in ordinary discourse. Nevertheless, it is possible that the compiler of *Maxims II* thought of some of the individual maxims as no more than disjointed truths. Stanley also discusses the use of the first person singular in the Exeter Book Riddles, especially 35 and 86 (447–50).

4 **Wahrig, G.** 'Das Lachen im Altenglischen und Mittelenglischen.' *Zeitschrift für Anglistik und Amerikanistik* 3 (1955): 274–304 and 389–418.

This is a general survey of laughter in early English culture. In passing (280–1) Wahrig mentions some of the Exeter Book Riddles, particularly the obscene ones, as instances of Anglo-Saxon humour. He points out, however, that these poems were not necessarily popular in composition and orientation. The contemporary audience might not necessarily have found them readily comprehensible. The Riddles would therefore probably not have been typical of Anglo-Saxon humour, but rather appealed to aristocratic and clerical taste. Wahrig also mentions *Rune Poem* in passing (283), to observe that there, as in

Beowulf, laughter is associated with feasting and noise in the mead-hall, all three being aftermaths of battle.

225 **Magoun, Francis P., Jr.** *Anglo-Saxon Poems Represented in Bright's Anglo-Saxon Reader Done in a Normalized Orthography.* Cambridge, MA: Department of English, Harvard U, 1956. [vii] + 49 pp.

Magoun uses the texts of ASPR (**194, 203**), converting them into his normalized spelling. The selected OEW poems are metrical Charms 1 and 4 (41–5); *Maxims II* (40–1); and Exeter Book Riddles 7, 8 ('jay, jackdaw'), 26, 28 ('John Barleycorn'), 47, and 57 (24–6). There is no introduction or annotation.

226 **Schneider, Karl.** *Die germanischen Runennamen: Versuch einer Gesamtdeutung. Ein Beitrag zur idg./germ. Kultur- und Religionsgeschichte.* Meisenheim-am-Glan: Hain, 1956. xii + 635 pp. + 7 diagrams.

Numerous citations of OEW poems are given as part of the detailed discussion of rune names: an instance is Charm 1 (247–8). Schneider regards *Rune Poem* (preliminarily discussed on 17–18 and 45–6), along with the Old Norse and Old Icelandic rune poems, as preserving relics of early Germanic heathen cults, mythologies, and fertility rituals. He points out the likelihood that the rune poems represent a much modified and corrupt tradition, though he declares a policy of not deviating from the manuscript readings unless absolutely necessary. His investigation is based on Grein-Wülker (**6**). Of the numerous references to *Rune Poem* scattered through the text, the following examples will serve to illustrate his approach. He reconstructs the 'þorn' strophe, emending 'ðegna' (line 7) to 'þyrsa' and 'manna' (line 9) to 'mægþa'. The result is a depiction of the thunder-god, who fights the giants and brings fertility. The god is aided by his phallic hammer, which is suggested by the shape of the rune (þ). The 'cen' strophe refers to the fire used in the cremation of chieftains, hence line 18 'þær hi æþelingas inne restaþ'. In the 'eoh' ('yew') strophe Schneider emends 'hyrde fyres' (line 36) to 'hyrde fe(o)res' ('guardian of life'), equating the yew with the Yggdrasil of Old Norse mythology. In the 'eoh' ('horse') strophe (line 56) he emends 'hors' to 'horsu' and understands 'hofum' as 'dwellings', not 'hooves', so revealing an allusion to the Indo-European archetype of young fraternal deities who are present at battles. Here they are represented in the form of architectural ornaments. The rune-name *is* denotes the primordial material of the cosmos. In line with his identification of Tacitus's *Mannus* with 'Father Heaven', who marries Mother Earth, Schneider emends 'on myrgþe' (line 59) to 'on moldan'. The 'ior' strophe is a description of the Miðgarðsormr familiar from Scandinavian mythology. In his chapter on the runic letters in the CCCC 422 text of *Solomon and Saturn* (558–69), Schneider again bases his investigation on Grein-Wülker (**6**). He argues that too much emphasis has been placed on oriental magic in previous scholarship on this poem. In many cases the original conceptual value behind the rune-names was still understood. He attempts to demonstrate this by applying the supposed traditional heathen interpretations of the runes in the context of *Solomon and Saturn*. Some of the names and meanings are straightforward, thus *is* 'ice', *lagu* 'lake', *feoh* 'cattle', and so forth, but others are more esoteric. The testimony of *Solomon and Saturn* lines 89–92 is crucial for the understanding of the rune *peorð*. It is to be interpreted as 'almighty Fate' and has a central role, in accordance with its position as the 'central rune'. The rune *eoh* 'horse' is to be construed as a dual, consistent with the interpretation in *Rune Poem* lines 55–6. *Ræda* is personified as the steerer of the chariot of the sun, namely 'Wodan'. *Nyd* refers to fire derived from friction, by means of a phallic fire-drill, and in *Solomon and Saturn* line 107 should be associated with a reading 'tunas', emended from 'twinnas'. The rune *cweorð* can be explained as the 'membrum virile' and *hægl* as 'Hagal-Ymir-Tuisto', and here too the testimony of *Solomon and Saturn* is crucial. The poet of *Solomon and Saturn*, lacking full conviction of the magical powers of the Paternoster against the Devil, sought to reinforce them by incorporating into the poem an adaptation of an ancient Germanic charm, which was originally intended to afford protection from demons of darkness who were inimical to Life.

Bliss, Alan J. *The Metre of Beowulf.* Oxford: Blackwell, 1958. ix + 170 pp.

In Chapter 14 'Hypermetric Verses' Bliss critiques the systems propounded by Sievers **(92)** and Kaluza **(15)** and offers a new one. Individual lines from OEW poetry discussed include *Order* line 102a (corrupt?), *Solomon and Saturn* line 334a (lacunose?), and *Maxims I* lines 35a, 111a, 113a, 124a, and 198a. Bliss points out that *Maxims I* and *II* and *Solomon and Saturn* agree in an unusual distribution where a high proportion of normal and heavy verses occurs in the b-verse. The *Maxims* are further bound together by the presence of double hypermetric verses. *Maxims I* is exceptional for the number of metrically obscure verses it contains. Clearly, Anglo-Saxon gnomic poetry belonged in some respects to a different tradition from the remainder of Old English poetry (96–7). Bliss's index to the scansion of hypermetric verses includes *Fortunes, Maxims, Precepts, Order,* Exeter Book Riddle 16, *Rune Poem,* and *Solomon and Saturn* (162–8).

Chadwick, Nora Kershaw. 'The Monsters and Beowulf.' *The Anglo-Saxons: Studies in Some Aspects of Their History and Culture presented to Bruce Dickins.* Ed. Peter Clemoes. London: Bowes, 1959. 171–203.

Chadwick cites *Maxims II* lines 26b and 42b, along with place-name evidence, to demonstrate that according to Anglo-Saxon tradition the abode of a dragon is in a barrow, whereas that of a *þyrs,* a monster such as Grendel, is in the fen (175). Metrical Charm 4, which is of unknown date but undoubtedly belongs to the heathen milieu, is used to demonstrate that the Valkyries (*wælcyrge*), identified in the poem as 'hægtessan' (line 19) and 'ða mihtigan wif' (line 8), had evil associations in Anglo-Saxon England (176).

Cross, J.E. 'On The Wanderer Lines 80–4: a Study of a Figure and a Theme.' *Vetenskaps-societeten i Lund. Årsbok* 35 (1959): 77–110.

Cross seeks to show that repeated 'sum' is a figure of diction derived ultimately from pre-Christian Greek and Latin rhetorical teaching. In patristic writings the figure of *repetitio,* e.g. 'alii . . . alii', abounds to introduce many different lists. It may be the source for 'sum . . . sum' in *Fortunes* and *Gifts,* though we should bear in mind that these are thematically simple poems that do not otherwise demonstrate a close knowledge of Latin Christian writings. Evidence for repeated 'sum' in other early Germanic lists is lacking. The deaths listed in *Beowulf* lines 1763–8 and *Fortunes* have a great deal in common and appear to be extensions on a distinct theme found in Christian works. Cross provides a line-by-line analysis of *Fortunes*, showing that the text is a tissue of Christian commonplaces. Nevertheless, some of the deaths are made more realistic for Anglo-Saxon conditions. The fall from a high tree (lines 21–6) can be accounted for as a failed initiative to gather tender green leaves for animal fodder.

230 **Elliott, Ralph W.V.** *Runes.* Manchester: Manchester UP, 1959. xvi + 124 pp. + 24 plates. 2nd corrected printing. *Runes: An Introduction.* 1963.

Elliott regards the allusion to 'wuldortanas' in metrical Charm 2 and the letters making up the Latin Paternoster in *Solomon and Saturn* as rune-magic. *Solomon and Saturn* shows a learned adaptation to Christian use of the age-old belief in the magic efficacy of runes. Shorthand and acrostic uses of runes in the Exeter Book Riddles are discussed. *Rune Poem* preserves most of the older rune-names well. The word 'iar' in *Rune Poem* line 87 is explained as an adoption from proto-Scandinavian *jár* 'year'; *eolhx* is due ultimately to a Germanic *algiz* 'protection, defence'. The poet overcame the difficulty of meaningless 'ior' (or 'iar') by simply attaching to it the first of the two meanings of *ear*, namely 'ocean, sea'.

231 **Habicht, Werner.** *Die Gebärde in englischen Dichtungen des Mittelalters.* Bayerische Akademie der Wissenschaften, philosophisch-historische Klasse, Abhandlungen NF 46. Munich: Verlag der bayerischen Akademie der Wissenschaften, in Kommission bei Beck, 1959. 168 pp.

In this study of the motif of noise in medieval English poetry, Habicht makes brief references to *Precepts* (on anger and lust), Exeter Book Riddle 27 ('mead'), and *Vainglory*.

232 **Kellermann, Günther.** 'Wandlung und Fortwirken des germanischen Weltbildes in den religiösen Vorstellungen der angelsächsischen Stabreimdichtung.' *Zeitschrift für Missionswissenschaft und Religionswissenschaft* 44 (1960): 241–56.

Taking his cue from the work of Schneider (226), Kellermann includes in his survey an analysis of how Christianity co-opted and adapted traditional Germanic lexis and poetic techniques in order to insinuate Christian concepts into the world-view of the aristocratic audience. Thus in *Maxims I* lines 132–7 the words 'soþ' and 'sylfa' are attached to the presentation of God as a divine 'cyning' and he is contrasted with Woden (242–3). The description in metrical Charm 9 of Garmund as 'godes ðegen' (line 6) testifies to a primitive Germanic view of the gods as subservient to the primal being (249). *Maxims I* line 73 testifies to the original sense of the word *wundor*: 'wall of twigs, partition', consistent with the sense of the verb *windan* (250–1). The power of *wyrd* is seen in *Maxims II* lines 4–5 as constraining the power of the deity (253). *Maxims I* lines 71–80 are quoted in translation as an excellent example of the enduring influence of Germanic cosmology upon the Anglo-Saxon Christian world-view (256).

Kennedy, Charles W. *An Anthology of Old English Poetry Translated into Alliterative Verse.* New York: Oxford UP, 1960. xvi + 174 pp.

Kennedy includes translations of metrical Charms 1 and 4; *Maxims II*; excerpts from *Fortunes* and *Maxims I*; and Exeter Book Riddles 2–3 ('wind'), 5, 7, 9, 14, 16, 21, 27, 47, and 85, with brief introductions. A sample translation from *Maxims I* lines 94–7: 'loved one is welcome/ To Frisian wife when his boat stands in./ His ship is come and her sailor home,/ Her own food-winner.'

Magoun, Francis P., Jr. 'Conceptions and Images Common to Anglo-Saxon Poetry and the *Kalevala*.' *Britannica: Festschrift für Hermann M. Flasdieck.* Ed. Wolfgang Iser and Hans Schabram. Heidelberg: Winter, 1960. 180–91.

In a section entitled 'Joy = Music' (188–91) Magoun notes that in both Anglo-Saxon poetry and the *Kalevala* a common word for 'joy' is used in the sense of '(the playing of) music'. He cites *Order* lines 11–12 and *Maxims I* lines 169–71 as instances where *glieg* specifically means 'music'. To this list he adds the occurrences of the compounds *glieg-mann* in *Maxims I* line 166 and *glieg-beam* in *Gifts* line 50 and elsewhere. [The normalizations here are Magoun's.] Such a close identification of joy with musically accompanied song is perhaps most readily understandable in the framework of an unlettered peasant society of earlier times.

Raffel, Burton. *Poems from the Old English.* Lincoln, NE: U of Nebraska P, 1960. Rev. edn. 1964. xii + 121 pp.

The first edition contains free translations of Exeter Book Riddles 8, 11, 14, 29, 32, and 60, along with an excerpt from metrical Charm 1 (lines 69–71). Raffel suspects that Riddle 60 represents a love message in the form of a riddle. A sample translation, incorporating material from Riddle 29 lines 1–4: 'I saw a silvery creature scurrying/ Home, as lovely and light as heaven.' In his foreword, Robert P. Creed discusses the relation between the original Old English texts and Raffel's translations. The revised and enlarged edition adds the following Riddles: 1, 2, 3, 7, 15 ('hedgehog'), 26, 33, 47, and 66.

Diamond, R.E. 'Theme as Ornament in Anglo-Saxon Poetry.' *PMLA* 76 (1961): 461–8. Repr. in *Essential Articles for the Study of Old English Poetry.* Ed. J.B. Bessinger and S.J. Kahrl. Hamden, CT: Archon, 1968. 374–93.

Diamond includes citations from the Exeter Book Riddles and other OEW poems as supporting evidence for the formulaic status of certain half-lines in *Elene* and other poems. The mentions of sea-voyaging in *Gifts* and *Christ II* constitute 'clear cases of a familiar theme being introduced in telescoped form into a long catalogue of parallels' (reprint, 386).

Derolez, René. 'Anglo-Saxon Literature: "Attic" or "Asiatic"? Old English Poetry and its Latin Background.' *English Studies Today.* 2nd series (1961): 93–105. Fourth Conference of the International Association of University Professors of English. Ed. G.H. Bonnard. Berne: Francke, 1961. Repr. in *Essential Articles for the Study of Old English Poetry.* Ed. J.B. Bessinger and S.J. Kahrl. Hamden, CT: Archon, 1968. 46–62.

Surveying possible classical features in Old English poetry, Derolez notes the reluctance of Old English poets to avail themselves of homoeoteleuton. Exceptional in this regard are the *Latin-English Proverbs*. Derolez compares the regular rhythmic pattern in the Old English version of these *Proverbs* with the Irish-Latin *Carmen ad Deum*, suggesting that for rhyme to become fully effective in Old English poetry a regularization of the number of syllables per half-line had to occur (55–6). The internal rhymes in Exeter Book Riddle 28 are associated with verse-filling asyndeton.

238   Campbell, Jackson J., and James L. Rosier. *Poems in Old English.* New York: Harper, 1962. ix + 147 pp.

This edition contains the Old English text of *Fortunes*, *Maxims I* lines 71–106, and Exeter Book Riddles 26 and 27. The introduction points out some leading characteristics of Old English poetry. In *Fortunes* imagination and doctrine are fused into an effective whole: the man falling to his death from a tree (lines 21–6) becomes almost simultaneously a fruit and a featherless bird. Notes to the individual poems explain idioms and signal emendations. *Maxims I* line 78 is left unemended and explained as 'the deep way of the dead'. In Riddle 26 line 17 'dolwite' is explained as 'pain of a wound'. A glossary is appended.

239   Cross, James E. *Latin Themes in Old English poetry, with an Excursus on the Middle English* Ubi Sount qui ante nos fuerount. Bristol, [1962]. 16 pp. [No date or publication information provided.]

Cross notes that the list in *Fortunes*, along with that in *Beowulf* lines 1763–8, possesses analogues in Latin and Greek texts. All exemplify the theme of the 'ways of death', often untimely death. He summarizes the results reached in his separate article on *Gifts* **(240)**.

240   Cross, J.E. 'The Old English Poetic Theme of "The Gifts of Men".' *Neophilologus* 46 (1962): 66–70.

Cross contends that the most appropriate term to describe the differing mental endowments or natural abilities enumerated in *Fortunes*, *Gifts*, and other such lists is 'talents'. In considering these lists we need to take account not merely of the Parable of the Talents (Matt. 25: 14–30) but also of the commentaries upon it. These comprise Pauline comments (Rom. 12: 6–8; 1 Cor. 12: 8–10; Eph. 4: 8) and the Patristic writings, especially Gregory's *Homily 9* from the *Forty Homilies on the Gospels*. Gregory's sermon contains the rhetorical figure of *repetitio*, like the Old English poems on this theme. Comparable also is the mention of two attributes, earthly possessions and acquaintance with a rich man, that would not nowadays be classed as talents. Another analogue is contained in a sermon for the common of saints on confessors by the ninth-century bishop, Haymo of Halberstadt.

241   ———. 'Aspects of Microcosm and Macrocosm in Old English Literature.' *Comparative Literature* 14 (1962): 1–22. Repr. in *Studies in Old English Literature in Honor of Arthur G. Brodeur.* Ed. Stanley B. Greenfield. Eugene, OR: U of Oregon, 1963. 1–22.

Cross makes passing reference to *Homiletic Fragment II* and *Order* in the course of a discussion mainly devoted to the *Rhyming Poem*. Lines 6–7 of *Homiletic Fragment II* are reminiscent of the Christian idea of the declining world in its sixth age, whereas *Order* praises the fixed order of the world. In this respect *Order* conforms with other Anglo-Saxon writings, including those of Ælfric. Accordingly, an ambivalent attitude towards the work of creation seems to characterize early Christian thought.

Ellis Davidson, H.R. *The Sword in Anglo-Saxon England: Its Archaeology and Literature.* Oxford: Clarendon, 1962. xxvii + 237 pp. + 16 plates.

Ellis Davidson discusses the descriptions of swords and how they are worn in *Maxims* and *Solomon and Saturn*. She suggests that the warning against lightly drawing the sword and the need for a ritual before battle in *Solomon and Saturn* lines 163–9 reflect pre-Christian practice. The phrase 'meces mærðo' in *Solomon and Saturn* line 163 may be a reference to the pommel. On Exeter Book Riddle 20 she notes that 'hawk' and 'sword' are almost equally possible as solutions. Riddle 70 may embody a system of imagery where the sparks struck from the piece of iron on the anvil are compared to plants in a field. The solution to Riddles 79–80 may be 'the sword in its scabbard'.

Gillam, Doreen M.E. 'The Connotations of Old English *fæge*, with a Note on Beowulf and Byrhtnoð.' *Studia Germanica Gandensia* 4 (1962): 165–201.

Gillam notes that 'a poetic term such as *fæge*, carrying its tantalizing hints of pagan lore over into such irreproachably Christian texts as *Christ* and *Guthlac*, challenges those who respond strongly to its presence in Old English poetry to discover more precisely how the strength of this effect is achieved and how it continues to operate over so many centuries' (165). Her exploration of the significance of *fæge* in relation to its contexts takes in metrical Charm 6, *Fortunes*, *Maxims I*, and *Solomon and Saturn*. She finds 'traces of magic' in *Solomon and Saturn* line 158 (172). A dichotomy of feeling, partly pagan pessimism and partly Christian optimism, exists in *Fortunes*, where the gloom of lines 1–57 is scarcely dispelled by the comforting reflections that God is responsible for all (175). The Christian idea of the wounds caused by sin may be behind the obscure reference to 'niehtes wunde' in *Solomon and Saturn* lines 338–9, since the fate of a *fæge* man and Judgement Day have just been mentioned (189). Gillam queries Menner's (**1073**) pagan explanation of the 'fæges rapas' in this context (193). She adds the Christian motif of inundation by the sea to the nexus of ideas, noting parallels in the scriptural poetry (199).

Wrenn, C.L. 'Two Anglo-Saxon Harps.' *Comparative Literature* 14 (1962): 118–28. Repr. in *Studies in Old English Literature in Honor of A.G. Brodeur.* Ed. Stanley B. Greenfield. Eugene, OR: U of Oregon, 1963. 118–28.

Wrenn describes the Sutton Hoo and Taplow harps. In his discussion of the music possibly produced on these instruments, he alludes to Grein-Köhler's (**6**) suggestion of 'modulatio' as the meaning of *rad* in *Rune Poem*. He finds a traditional association of the rising and falling of music with the motion of riding not implausible. The description of harp-playing in *Fortunes* lines 80–4 implies that, in playing, the Old English harp normally rested on the knees of the scop. Motifs in Exeter Book Riddle 70 suggest the general rectangular shape and ornamented appearance of the harp, which is therefore proposed as the solution of the Riddle.

245 ————. 'Magic in an Anglo-Saxon Cemetery.' *English and Medieval Studies Presented to J.R.R. Tolkien on the Occasion of his Seventieth Birthday.* Ed. Norman Davis and C.L. Wrenn. London: Allen, 1962. 306–20.

In passing, Wrenn comments that the 'os' strophe in *Rune Poem*, though influenced perhaps by association with Latin *os* 'mouth', still preserves a memory of Woden as the originator of speech and wisdom (315). Taking his cue from Schneider (**226**), Wrenn suggests that a traditional use of the *r*-rune to symbolize the occupant of the divine chariot may survive in *Solomon and Saturn* line 99. The leader of the Paternoster runes is R, 'bocstafa brego' ('prince of letters').

246 Bolton, W.F. *An Old English Anthology.* London: Arnold, 1963. xii + 178 pp. Rev. edn. Evanston, IL: Northwestern UP, 1966.

The anthology contains Old English texts, glossary, and brief introductions to each selection. OEW texts included are Exeter Book Riddles 6, 66, and 35 (in that order), along with the *Leiden Riddle* (7–9); *Rune Poem* (13–17); Riddle 60 (38–9); and *Maxims II*B (41–3). On the Riddles Bolton notes how the Exeter Book collection includes both 'thing' riddles (translatable from one language to another) and 'word' or 'charade' riddles (dependent on the vocabulary of a single language). He sees *Rune Poem* as really a set of *biþ*-maxims organized upon the runic alphabet. The poem is actuated chiefly by concern for man's use of earthly prosperity. The *Maxims* are comparable to the Riddles in respect of their oblique or figurative language and their often puzzling juxtaposition of subjects. [For a review see Vermeer, **853**.]

247 Quirk, Randolph. 'Poetic Language and Old English Metre.' *Early English and Norse Studies presented to Hugh Smith in Honour of his Sixtieth Birthday.* Ed. Arthur Brown and Peter Foote. London: Methuen, 1963. 150–71. Repr. in Randolph Quirk. *Essays on the English Language: Medieval and Modern.* London: Longmans, 1968. 1–19.

Among the extended lexical collocations cited by Quirk is that of *hand, hearp, gretan, gleo,* and *God*, seen in *Maxims I* lines 170–1 and *Gifts* lines 49–50. Another collocation is *earm, an-,* and *wineleas*, seen in *Maxims I* lines 172–3 (reprint, 3). Collocations of *eorl* and *æþeling* can be observed in *Rune Poem* (lines 55 and 84). A sense of satisfaction in the observance of traditional correspondences manifests itself in *Maxims II* (4).

248 Gillam, Doreen M.E. 'A Method for Determining the Connotations of Old English Poetic Words.' *Studia Germanica Gandensia* 6 (1964): 85–102.

Gillam explores the connotations of the verb *sceacan*, citing *Fortunes* line 39 and Exeter Book Riddles 20 line 14 and 93 line 13.

Grinda, Klaus R. 'Einige Handwerke in der altenglischen Dichtung und in zeitgenössischen Inschriften: Gesichtspunkte der Darstellung und soziale Wertung.' *Festschrift für Walter Hübner.* Ed. Dieter Riesner and Helmut Gneuss. Berlin: Schmidt, 1964. 77–90.

Grinda attempts to assemble references to crafts and skills in Old English poetry but finds them few and far between, as is natural in a literature with a distinctly aristocratic bias. An example is the mention of the smiths in metrical Charm 4. Often the poetic texts imply an attitude of admiration for crafts: typical are Exeter Book Riddle 70, *Fortunes*, and *Gifts*. Riddle 14 lines 1–3 may represent an isolated reference to a warrior who processes the horn on an amateur basis in his spare time. Exceptional in their detailed references to crafts are such Riddles as 21, 26, 27, 35 and 56. Riddle 54 can be seen as alluding to the preparation of butter.

Crossley-Holland, Kevin, and Bruce Mitchell. *The Battle of Maldon and Other Old English Poems.* London: Macmillan, 1965. xi + 138 pp.

This collection of translations contains a general introduction to Old English poetry and additional brief introductions to each group of poems. Included are *Maxims I* (excerpt); metrical Charms 8, 9, and 12; and Exeter Book Riddles 3, 5, 7, 9, 15 ('badger'), 16, 19, 26, 27, 29, 30, 33, 34, 37, 47, 50, 51, 53, 55, 57 ('swallows'), 66, 68–9, 77, 80, 81, 85, and 86. Sample translation from Riddle 27 lines 13–15a: 'Deprived of his strength, and strangely loquacious,/ He's a nincompoop, who rules neither his mind/ Nor his hands nor his feet.'

Manganella, G. 'Gli animali nella poesia anglosassone.' *Annali Istituto Universitario Orientale di Napoli* 8 sezione germanica (1965): 261–84.

Manganella translates in summary the various Old English poems that mention animals. He sees the Exeter Book Riddles as emphasizing the rapport between animals and human beings. Although some riddles draw their subjects from Symphosius, they add elements from other sources. An example is the sense of wonder in Riddle 47. Manganella enters into the debate over riddle solutions, opting for Young's solution (**789**) of Riddle 8.

Mitchell, Bruce. 'Some Problems of Mood and Tense in Old English.' *Neophilologus* 49 (1965): 44–57.

Mitchell seeks to account for the unexplained subjunctive in Exeter Book Riddle 70 line 4 by supposing that the main clause verb should also be subjunctive. The reading should be 'dreoge', rather than the 'dreogeþ' of the manuscript. Similarly in *Order* line 1 'wilt þu' is the equivalent of an imperative, hence is followed by the subjunctive 'bringe'. He lends guarded support to Holthausen's (**192**) emendation of 'sy' to 'ys' in *Order* line 89.

———. 'The Status of "hwonne" in Old English.' *Neophilologus* 49 (1965): 157–60.

In *Maxims I* line 104, Mitchell prefers Grein's (**2**) punctuation to that of ASPR (**194**): 'hwonne' is much more likely to introduce a noun clause of dependent question than an adverb clause of time. Likewise in Exeter Book Riddle 31 line 13, the interrogative origin and function of *hwonne* are still clearly to be seen.

254   **Schabram, Hans.** *Superbia: Studien zum altenglischen Wortschatz.* I *Die dialektale und zeitliche Verbreitung des Wortguts.* Munich: Fink, 1965. 140 pp. + 1 ill.

Schabram lists *Solomon and Saturn* and *Vainglory* as among the poetic texts containing the lexical items *oferhygd* and *ofermod* (123–9). As to *Solomon and Saturn*, Sisam's **(215)** negative assessment of Menner's **(1073)** arguments for Northumbrian origin should be discounted: the occurrence of *oferhygd* in this text should be explained as due to a later southern scribe. The case of *ofermod* in *Vainglory* is similar.

255   **Shook, L.K.** 'Old English Riddle No. 20: *Heoruswealwe.*' *Franciplegius: Medieval and Linguistic Studies in Honor of Francis Peabody Magoun, Jr.* Ed. Jess B. Bessinger, Jr. and Robert P. Creed. New York: New York UP, 1965. 194–204.

Shook defends Trautmann's **(751)** solution for Exeter Book Riddle 20, arguing that the Riddle's precise title should be *heoruswealwe* 'sword-swallow'. This is a kenning attested in *Fortunes* line 86, with the meaning 'hawk'. The proposed solution gives real significance to all the clues in the Riddle, whether they refer to the sword or the hawk. Shook also discusses *Fortunes* lines 85–92 (the 'fowler' passage), where the word *heoruswealwe* occurs

256   **Wrenn, C.L.** 'Some Earliest Anglo-Saxon Cult Symbols.' *Franciplegius: Medieval and Linguistic Studies in Honor of Francis Peabody Magoun, Jr.* Ed. Jess B. Bessinger, Jr, and Robert P. Creed. New York: New York UP, 1965. 40–55.

Wrenn takes up the idea of *mana* as an element in ancient Germanic culture. Included in the discussion is the following explanation of the *t*-rune in *Rune Poem*: 'here the Germanic and most auspicious war god Tiw . . . is confused, naturally enough, with *tir* "glory" ' (41). The rune *rad* in *Solomon and Saturn* I (lines 98–106) is also instanced. Wrenn regards the 'os' strophe in *Rune Poem* as definitely fixing the divine origin of writing 'in a way very much parallel to the Eddaic tradition' (42). He voices qualified endorsement of Schneider's assertion **(226)** that the runes are primarily a cult script.

257   **Alexander, Michael J.** *The Earliest English Poems.* London: Penguin, 1966. 160 pp. Rev. edn. 1967. Berkeley: U of California P, 1970.

This book of translations was in its first edition a bilingual text, with the Old English original and a facing translation. In the revised edition the Old English text was dropped. All editions contain a general introduction, along with introductions and notes to the separate poems. *Maxims I* is represented by lines 71–99. Here Alexander sees vestiges of ritual usage in the celebration of natural forces – Frost, Fire, Earth, and Ice. The Exeter Book Riddles included are 7, 9, 12, 25, 26, 29, 30, 35, 38, 42, 44, 47, 57, 68, 70 ('shepherd's pipe'), 74, 80, 81, and 86. Alexander compares the dislocation of perspective in the Exeter Book

Riddles to the modern theatrical device of alienation. The Riddles suggest a vestigial Anglo-Saxon consciousness that every created thing had its own personality, which the poet could assume. They embody 'thorough-wrought construction and that feeling between delight and horror which qualifies a human product as Art, and not just as evidence for social historians' (92). The notes take up some points of detail about the Riddles. In Riddle 30 Alexander dissents from Blackburn (698) concerning line 3a, which refers to the 'branch of a tree', not a 'ship', and line 5, which refers to a 'cup', not a 'harp'. On Riddle 70, he argues that a shepherd's pipe is more likely to have been hung up by the wayside than a harp. If Riddle 74 is not to be solved as 'siren', then perhaps 'nature' or 'life' might be appropriate solutions. In Riddle 35 line 9b 'wyrda cræftum' is translated 'with skill given by the Wierds'. Sample translation from Riddle 7 lines 1–4: 'When it is earth I tread, make tracks upon water/ or keep the houses, hushed is my clothing,/ clothing that can twist me above house-ridges.'

Campbell, Jackson J. 'Learned Rhetoric in Old English Poetry.' *Modern Philology* 63 (1966): 89–101.

Campbell discusses *Solomon and Saturn* line 12 in passing, noting that it might be considered a very awkward line in a poem full of metrical peculiarities, only some of which are due to bad textual transmission. Nevertheless, the learned, non-Germanic elements which it incorporates could have been assimilated into fluent verse by a suitably skilled traditional poet. He compares line 39 in this respect. He also comments on the translator's methods in Exeter Book Riddle 35. Such rhetorical patterns as anaphora and polysyndeton are carried over from the Latin and even expanded, but the overall organization of the poem is improved by a change in the sequence of lines.

Henry, Patrick L. *The Early English and Celtic Lyric.* London: Allen, 1966. 244 pp.

In his chapter 5, 'The gnomic manner and matter of Old English, Irish, Icelandic, and Welsh', Henry enters into a detailed discussion of parallels between Old English and Welsh gnomic poetry (his treatments of Irish and Old Norse poetry do not refer to Old English). He regards *Maxims I* and *II* as the 'chief gnomic collections', but also takes into account *Fortunes, Gifts, Order, Precepts,* and *Vainglory,* noting the Christian doctrinal elements. The meaning of the word *sceal* is investigated in a close analysis of *Maxims I* and *II.* Henry's conclusion is that 'gnomic *sceal* typically expresses the notions of customary action or state, inherent quality and characteristic property, passing over on the one hand to ideal or hortatory action (state), expressing on the other that sense of certainty which current dialectal varieties of the future (with *will*) bring out . . .' (103). Awareness of this principle may help us to define the genre of the so-called *Maxims* and also may enhance our sense of logical coherence in this genre. In *Maxims II* lines 43b–5, for instance, the idea that the girl who does not wish to prosper among her people and be sought in marriage frequents her lover secretly can be seen as fitting into a sequence of thief in darkness and demon in a marsh. The Icelandic material sets the Germanic background of the English gnome in relief. The Irish material, for its part, shows further possibilities in the way of approach and technique. The Welsh texts, by contrast, are of 'immediate and constant value as a criterion or standard of the English gnome and as a touchstone for its interpretation' (124–5). Particularly Welsh in manner is the nature vignette formed by *Maxims I* lines 50b–5, describing the violent and serene sea in illustration of human gnomes. Exeter Book Riddles 1–3, as a fine example of the man-nature synthesis, are compared with a Welsh riddle on the wind by Dafydd ap Gwilym.

260   **Sanesi, Roberto.** *Poemi anglosassoni: Le origini della poesia inglese (VI–X secolo).* Milan: Lerici, 1966. Rev. edn. Milan: Guanda, 1975. 181 pp.

[Not seen.] According to Lendinara (**463** and personal communication), the first edition contains translations of sundry Exeter Book Riddles and metrical Charms 4, 3, 12, 8, 1, 11, 9, and 2, in that order (173–87). The second (enlarged) edition adds ten riddles.

261   **Bessinger, Jess B., Jr.** 'The Sutton Hoo Harp Replica and Old English Musical Verse.' *Old English Poetry: Fifteen Essays.* Ed. R.P. Creed. Providence: Brown UP, 1967. 3–26.

Bessinger cites evidence from *Gifts* (lines 49–50) in an attempt to define the timbre of the Anglo-Saxon harp. It possessed a sharper, more reverberant, middle-frequency brilliance than the modern harp. He also cites evidence for use of the plectrum from *Fortunes* line 83, using Mackie's emendation 'sceacol' (**186**). He sees this passage as a brief realistic description, crammed with detail, of a virtuoso harp soloist at work – a piece of musical criticism written by a poet. The word 'neomegende', conjectured for *Fortunes* line 84 by Grein (**2**) and subsequent editors, means 'sounding', not 'sounding sweetly'.

262   **Meaney, Audrey L.** 'Woden in England: A Reconsideration of the Evidence.' *Folklore* 77 (1967): 105–15.

Meaney argues for caution in quarrying Old English poetry for traces of heathen mythology. Philippson (**180**) is right to see a reference to Psalm 96: 5 in *Maxims I* line 132. Nevertheless, in the Old English Woden is making idols, not being one himself. This difference may be due to misunderstanding or to the exigencies of alliteration. Meaney doubts that the poet of *Maxims I* possessed substantial information about Woden. Metrical Charm 2 requires us to posit a more fully informed poet, who at the least knew of Woden as a powerful wizard. The hanging in *Fortunes* lines 33–42 cannot be connected with Woden ritual by direct inference from the text. Nor can Exeter Book Riddles 1–3 be used to establish an early English version of the 'Wild Hunt' or a connection between the Hunt and Woden.

263   **Whitbread, Leslie.** 'The Doomsday Theme in Old English Poetry.' *Beiträge zur Geschichte der deutschen Sprache und Literatur* 89B (1967): 452–81.

Whitbread comments on the placing of *Homiletic Fragment II* in the Exeter Book. He suggests that knowledgeable poets made it a deliberate point of technique to introduce at or near the end of their work some more or less explicit reference to Doomsday. Even the heterogeneous *Maxims II* ends with an allusion to the mystery of souls after death. The references to Doomsday in *Solomon and Saturn* are typical of most Old English treatments in their vagueness.

4 Isaacs, Neil D. *Structural Principles in Old English Poetry.* Knoxville, TN: U of Tennessee P, 1968. xiii + 197 pp.

In a chapter entitled 'The Old English Taste of Honey', Isaacs argues that only lines 9–15a of *Homiletic Fragment I* closely parallel Psalm 28 (100). Here he differs from Krapp (520). He views this fragment as unique in Old English poetry for its metaphor-based structure. It is true that the opposition of spiritual love and earthly pleasure in the final lines may seem quite remote from the earlier oppositions of lying and faith, appearance and reality, and sweetness and stinging. Nonetheless, the controlling metaphor quite naturally expands and supports the shifting statement. In the chapter entitled 'The exercise of art, part II: the order of the world', Isaacs argues that *Order* is framed by a dramatic monologue. Within the frame a poet talks to a prospective poet about poetry and then creates a sample poem. This sample text both demonstrates the proper subject for poetry and makes a statement about poetry by using poetic creation as a submerged point of reference for the Creator's Creation. Isaacs finds many echoes of the Psalms in this poem-within-a-poem.

5 Whiting, Bartlett Jere. *Proverbs, Sentences, and Proverbial Phrases from English Writings Mainly before 1500.* With the collaboration of Helen Wescott Whiting. Cambridge, MA: Belknap–Harvard UP, 1968. li + 733 pp.

Whiting's search for proverbial material included OEW poetry, and some excerpts are cited. Three examples will suffice here. Under F284 'as hard as (the, any, a) flint' is cited 'Flinte ic eom heardre' (Exeter Book Riddle 40 line 78). Under F285 'flint-gray' is cited 'flintgrægne flod' (Riddle 3 line 19). Under W332 'to row (sail, strive) against (with) the wind' is cited 'werig scealc (MS sceal se) wiþ winde roweþ' (*Maxims I* line 185).

6 Jabbour, Alan. 'Memorial Transmission in Old English Poetry.' *Chaucer Review* 3 (1969): 174–90.

Jabbour examines the extant multiple copies of Old English poems and poetical passages to determine the role played by memorial transmission. He cites Sisam (208), who had compared the text of *Solomon and Saturn* to orally transmitted texts, and argues that enough variation is present in the two witnesses to suggest at least the possibility of memorial transmission. As to Exeter Book Riddle 30, whose two texts contain nine substantive variants in a nine-line poem, it is hard to avoid the hypothesis that these are oral variants. So too the pair *Leiden Riddle* and Riddle 35, though Jabbour regards the evidence as inconclusive.

7 Weber, Gerd Wolfgang. *Wyrd: Studien zum Schicksalsbegriff der altenglischen und altnordischen Literatur.* Frankfurter Beiträge zur Germanistik 8. Bad Hamburg: Gehlen, 1969. 175 pp.

Weber discusses *wyrd* as the principle of earthly transience and mutability. The following are among the points that he makes in his detailed study of this and related lexical items. The personification of *wyrd* does not imply a belief in it as a deity any more than does the personification of *yldo* in *Solomon and Saturn* lines 282–301. The Drawing attention to parallels between *Maxims I* lines 8–9 and *Wanderer* line 107, where *wyrd* is evidently subordinate to God, he supports Timmer's **(567)** translation of the *Maxims I* passage. The word *wyrd* tends to subsume all things that occur in this fallen world, and so tends to develop connotations of evil. He argues that in *Maxims II* line 5 the statement 'wyrd biŏ swiŏost' does not contradict Christian doctrine but rather expresses a heightened awareness of transience. In *Fortunes* line 41 'wyrde' signifies the Last Judgement. In Riddle 35 line 9 he opts for Sweet's **(91)** emendation of 'wyrda cræftum' to 'wynde-cræftum'. The auxiliary *sceal* in the *Maxims* and elsewhere has no necessary connection with any Germanic notion of Fate. Phrases such as 'swa him bebead meotud' refer to the Christian God and occur too frequently in the *Maxims* to be explicable as later Christian interpolations into a heathen poem. He combats the notion that elegiac sadness in Old English poetry is part of the heathen heritage: rather, the elegiac retrospect provides an incentive or rationale for turning to the Christian God. *Homiletic Fragment I* is to be compared with *The Wanderer* in its urging to avoid the sin of *tristitia* and to cultivate hope in God (lines 43–7). *Maxims II* belongs with Boethius in emphasizing the contradictory elements of which the world is composed. The attitude to Fate in *Solomon and Saturn* should be seen not as native Germanic but as a blend of Stoic and Christian. Similarly, Weber resists the theory that *Fortunes* should be split up into Christian and heathen portions. He discusses the logical cohesion between sentences in the *Maxims*. He notes parallels between *Maxims II* and certain passages in the *De Consolatione Philosophiae*, though a direct literary connection is not necessarily to be assumed.

268 Schabram, H. 'Kritische Bemerkungen zu Angaben über die Verbreitung altenglischer Wörter.' *Festschrift für Edgar Mertner.* Ed. Bernhard Fabian and Ulrich Suerbaum. Munich: Fink, 1969. 89–102.

Schabram comments on the incidence of the word *wlanc* (100–1). He dissents from Lindheim's **(815)** statement that *wlanc* is a distinctively poetical word, noting that this misleading impression is given by the standard dictionaries but could be corrected by recourse to the prose texts themselves. Also missed by Lindheim are the occurrences in *Rune Poem* line 56 and Exeter Book Riddle 30 line 6. Among the possible meanings of *wlanc* in the Riddles is 'mighty', despite Lindheim's statement to the contrary.

269 Hamer, Richard. *A Choice of Anglo-Saxon Verse Selected with an Introduction and a Parallel Verse Translation.* London: Faber, 1970. 207 pp.

Hamer notes that although some of his texts are taken verbatim from ASPR **(194, 203, 520)**, others are the result of his comparison of earlier editions. The selection includes metrical Charm 12; *Maxims II*; and Exeter Book Riddles 5, 7, 9, 11, 12, 14, 21, 26, 34, and 60. Sample translation from Riddle 7 lines 1–6: 'My dress is silent when I tread the ground/ Or stay at home or stir upon the waters./ Sometimes my trappings and the lofty air/ Raise me above the dwelling-place of men,/ And then the power of clouds carries me far/ Above the people. . .'

Huppé, Bernard F. *The Web of Words: Structural Analyses of the Old English Poems Vainglory, The Wonder of Creation, The Dream of the Rood, and Judith.* Albany, NY: State U of New York P, 1970. xxi + 197 pp.

Chapter 1 'Two reflective poems from the Exeter Book' presents a text and facing-page translation of *Vainglory* and *Order*, followed by analyses. In *Vainglory* the high incidence of uniquely attested lexical items suggests the poet's propensity to word creation and to word-play, as evidenced by 'scyldum' (line 8) and 'læteð' (line 10). Accordingly, we should be suspicious of even long-established emendations. The phrase 'wlonce wigsmiþas' (line 14) was striking enough, with its encapsulation of heathen and warrior values, to be borrowed by the poet of *The Battle of Brunanburh*. Huppé follows ASPR (**194**) in arguing that the word 'fintan' in line 32 means 'consequences', rather than literally 'tail'; nevertheless its choice is designed to evoke the serpent, that is, the devil, whose poisoned tail wounds himself. The vocabulary and syntax provide an effective metaphysical design. The poet thereby succeeds in inculcating a time-worn truth so as to make it vivid and impressive. A two-part structure can be demonstrated, with constituent periods and clausules. Excerpts from Cassiodorus, Ambrose, and Augustine provide a background for understanding the workings of the poet's mind. Sample translation from lines 1–4: 'Lo! a wise messenger old in wisdom/ revealed many mysteries to me long ago,/ he opened a locked tale the herald's foretelling/ this man informed in prophetic teachings.' The lexis of *Order* is less remarkable. Salient in this poem is its sustained metaphor of journey – notably the sun's journey and the mystery that attaches to it. The structure is tripartite. Huppé analyses line by line in great detail, explicating lexis, sources, rhetorical devices, and other features along the way. The range of connotations of 'woðboran' (line 2) includes the three Magi and suggests an analogue in the patristic reading of Psalm 18: 1. In the central part, the 'tale of creation', a military-epic colouring is supplied by 'herespel' (line 37). The account of creation is influenced by patristic constructions. The image of light is elaborately developed.

Page, Raymond I. *Life in Anglo-Saxon England.* English Life Series. London: Batsford, 1970. xii + 179 pp.

Page discusses the metrical Charms and refers to the *Maxims* and *Rune Poem* in the course of Chapter 3, 'Gods and Demons, Witches, Magicians and Monsters'. The female demons mentioned in Charm 4 might be equated with local or minor deities or supernatural beings of lesser standing than the principal pagan gods. The Charm was possibly intended to counter rheumatism. Page comments on the manuscript contexts of the metrical Charms. Charm 8, described as 'probably pagan in origin', is quoted in translation (38). Additionally, OEW poems are referred to in passing throughout the book to document aspects of Anglo-Saxon life. Exeter Book Riddles 21 and 38, for instance, testify to the use of the plough in the process of converting forested areas into farmland (88).

Bliss, Alan J. 'Single Half-Lines in Old English Poetry.' *Notes and Queries* 216, NS 18 (1971): 442–8.

Bliss takes as his cue the frequently made suggestion that the occurrence of short lines in the Old English *Maxims* is somehow connected with their systematic use in the Old Norse *ljóðaháttr* and *galdralag*. He points out that in Old English poetry as a whole short lines are much more frequent than editors have been accustomed to allow. He lists apparently hypermetric lines that should instead be printed as one regular long line followed by a short line. *Solomon and Saturn*, a partially gnomic poem, shares some of the metrical irregularities of *Maxims*: half-lines belonging to Sievers's Type F, with only three metrical elements, can be identified. The metrical Charms also contain many instances of short lines. Double alliteration is characteristic of *Maxims I*C, implying a closer connection with the Old Norse gnomic tradition than we see in *Maxims I*A and B and *Maxims II*.

273   **Cassidy, Frederic G., and Richard N. Ringler.** *Bright's Old English Grammar and Reader.* New York: Holt, 1971. xiv + 494 pp.

The editors present this as a thorough revision and updating of the *Reader* (190). Hulbert's 'Sketch of Anglo-Saxon Literature' is omitted, along with metrical Charms 1 and 4. The OEW poems now included are Exeter Book Riddles 7, 8, 26, 28, 29, 44, 47, and 57 (338–42) and *Maxims II* (372–5, along with a facsimile of MS Cotton Tiberius B.i, fol.115r). In their 'General Remarks' on Old English poetry (264–74) the editors comment on the extension of the Anglo-Saxon kenning into the sort of metaphor with which we are more familiar, citing *Rune Poem* line 66 'se brimhengest bridles ne gymeð' (268). By contrast the kenning 'fugles wyn' in Riddle 26 line 7, meaning 'goose-quill pen', clearly shows the affiliation of the kenning with the riddle. In their headnote to the Exeter Book Riddles the editors state that riddles have always been enormously popular among the 'folk'. In Anglo-Saxon England, as on the continent, this lowbrow form secured the extensive approval of intellectuals. 'In the variety of their subject-matter and treatment these enigmas appeal to all tastes: the "romantic" quality of 7 is Wordsworthian; Cowper would have been delighted by the fine mock-heroics of 47; the mysterious, semi-mythical 29 would have entranced Yeats; and Chaucer's monk, worn out by reading the object described in 26, would – while sipping 28 – have found instruction and delight in the manly strains of 44' (338–9). In Riddle 7 line 5 'wolcna strengu' is to be understood as a kenning for the wind. Riddle 8 should probably be solved as 'nightingale', though 'frog' also fits the available clues. This riddle may in fact be playing on a traditional association of these two night-time singers. The editors explain the conflict of moon and sun in Riddle 29. The insertion of *Maxims II* into a Chronicle manuscript, apparently as part of the prefatory material, strongly suggests that it struck Anglo-Saxons as a solemn, profound, and fittingly sententious prologue to a serious historical work. Lines 43b–5a amount to saying that 'girls who have secret lovers never get married'. This, the editors suggest, is rather naive: perhaps a moralizing scribe has juggled with folk wisdom, leaving us with 'nelle' where pragmatism wrote 'wille'.

274   **Göller, Karl Heinz.** *Geschichte der altenglischen Literatur.* Grundlagen der Anglistik und Amerikanistik 3. Berlin: Schmidt, 1971. 224 pp.

Göller assesses the various native and foreign traditions behind the metrical Charms. He sees the Exeter Book Riddles as being dominated by foreign influences and *Maxims II* as consisting of a mixture of heathen and Christian. He regards *Solomon and Saturn* as a comparatively tolerant correction of remnants of heathen belief current in contemporary England. He suggests connections between *Rune Poem* and Old English elegy and epic.

5 Schmitt, Ludwig Erich. *Kurzer Grundriss der germanischen Philologie bis 1500.* II. *Literaturgeschichte.* Berlin: De Gruyter, 1971. vi + 665 pp. 2 vols. to date. 1970–.

Frederick Norman, 'Altenglische Literatur', supplies brief introductions to the metrical Charms, *Maxims*, Exeter Book Riddles, *Rune Poem*, and *Solomon and Saturn* (117–63). Willy Krogmann, 'Friesische Spruchstrophe in altenglischer Übersetzung', restates his views on the 'Frisian wife' in *Maxims I* lines 94–9 **(561, 577)**, translating it into its putatively original Frisian form. He notes possibly parallel examples of poems translated from one Germanic dialect to another (165–7).

6 Stanley, Eric G. 'Studies in the Prosaic Vocabulary of Old English Verse.' *Neuphilologische Mitteilungen* 72 (1971): 385–418.

Stanley identifies prosaic vocabulary in *Homiletic Fragment II* line 5 (<a>*teorian*: cf. **524**), *Maxims I* line 183 (*æmetta*), *Maxims II* line 10 (*swicol*), and *Vainglory* line 75 (*ofermod*). The Exeter Book Riddles and *Solomon and Saturn* contain numerous similar items. He observes that the Riddles do not form a stylistically homogeneous unity. The high incidence of prosaic words in *Solomon and Saturn* seems to support the assumption of late West Saxon origin. Among specific points are his tentative arguments for 'æmedlan' ('frenzy') in *Maxims I* line 183 and against Holthausen's **(128)** emendation to 'geoguðmyrþe' in Riddle 38 line 2. Likewise, he dismisses Trautmann's **(751)** restoration 'receleas' in Riddle 63 line 15.

7 Wienold, Götz. *Formulierungstheorie – Poetik – Strukturelle Literaturgeschichte: am Beispiel der altenglischen Dichtung.* Frankfurt am Main: Athenäum, 1971. 200 pp.

Wienold investigates repetition and variation in Old English poetry, so as to arrive at a typology of poetic creativity. He argues against the derivation of *repetitio* (as used in *Wanderer*) from Latin rhetoric, instead contending that it is an established genre characteristic of such texts as *Maxims* and *Fortunes*. The heavy use of repetition to signal division into sections in *Fortunes* represents an extreme in Old English poetic composition. A contrastingly conservative use of the same generative principle is seen in *Order*.

8 Barley, Nigel F. 'Anglo-Saxon Magico-Medicine.' *Journal of the Anthropological Society of Oxford* 3 (1972): 67–76.

Barley attempts an anthropologist's corrective to Grattan and Singer **(423)**, who dismissed Anglo-Saxon medicine as a mass of folly and credulity. Barley emphasizes its international character, pointing out that the small self-contained world that we would ideally hope for in investigating a primitive people has already been shattered by contact with Romania when the Anglo-Saxons emerge as a distinct force. Barley refines on Singer by positing three basic causes of disease: (1) flying venoms, (2) *wyrmas* (a generic term including insects, reptiles, and dragons such as the 'weallende wulf' of *Solomon and Saturn* lines 212–24), and (3) lesser evil spirits (dwarves, elves, Christian devils). *Solomon and Saturn* makes the link between category 3 and the other two explicit. The basic concern of the leech is to de-structure the present state and either re-define or re-affirm boundaries. A structuralist analysis of metrical Charm 1 demonstrates that arguments concerning the possible survival of an ancient sun cult are beside the point. Although some remedies work on the basis of 'unlike negates unlike', there is also rich evidence of the most basic classificatory mechanism, 'like affects like', and this can be traced in metrical Charm 2. Barley's overall assessment is that Anglo-Saxon ethnomedicine is far from being the unstructured mass that some authors have implied. Rather, it constitutes a rich symbolic system in no way inferior to those treated by anthropologists in other parts of the world.

279 **Bliss, A.J.** 'The Origin and Structure of the Old English Hypermetric Line.' *Notes and Queries* 217, NS 19 (1972): 242–8.

Bliss argues that short lines in Old English poetry are found most abundantly in texts of an archaic type, such as the *Maxims* and the metrical Charms. In these works continued alliteration and double alliteration are about equally common. He notes that *Maxims* and *Solomon and Saturn* show, in contrast to the rest of Old English poetry, a high proportion of strong hypermetric types in the second half-line. This peculiarity may represent a survival of a characteristic metre eliminated elsewhere. The ancestral metre may have permitted an exceptionally weighty third section, so that there was a progressive increase in weight through the three sections of the line.

280 **Crane, John Kenny.** 'Simplifying the Complex and Complexifying the Simple: The Two Routes of Approach to Old English Literature.' *College English* 33 (1972): 830–9.

Crane's review article evaluates contributions by Isaacs (**264**) and Huppé (**270**). The title of Isaacs's book is misleading, in that the idea of narrative viewpoint is not included. His choice of poems is arbitrary. Isaacs's seeming disregard for previous analyses of *Order* is to be deplored (837). Nonetheless, 'one of Isaacs' greatest virtues is this lack of fear in taking a chance in an interpretation. By employing heavily Romantic analogues, he develops a fairly convincing case' for *Order* being 'primarily about the artistic selfconsciousness' (838). Crane notes a Robertsonian bias in Huppé's discussion of *Vainglory* and *Order*. In his discussion of *Vainglory* Huppé concentrates on 'the tying together of vocabulary patterns and the very process itself of poetic word-making', whereas with *Order* 'he pays more attention to formal and metaphorical structures' (836).

281 **Frank, Roberta.** 'Some Uses of Paronomasia in Old English Scriptural Verse.' *Speculum* 47 (1972): 207–26.

Frank distinguishes various forms and functions of paronomasia, using OEW poems among her examples. In a quasi-magical function, metrical Charm 8 addresses the bees as 'sigewif' in line 9 when it wishes them to 'settle' ('sigað'). In Charm 2 lines 14–15 invoke a herb called 'stune' which grows on 'stane' and can be used to 'stunan' ('repel') pain (209). In a more philosophical function, *Maxims I* line 120 contains an example of a widely prevalent systematic play on *god* 'god' and *god* 'good'. Similarly meaningful play on *man* 'sin' and *mann* 'man' occurs in *Solomon and Saturn* line 327 (220–1). Again, the play on *treo* and *treow* in *Maxims I* line 159 suggests a meditative exploration of language, to be contrasted with the purely phonological association attaching to the use of *ar* in lines 185–7 (224). Some forms of paronomasia act almost as an authorial signature: thus Cynewulf's distinctive play on *rod/rodor* 'cross/heaven' is otherwise found only in Exeter Book Riddle 55 line 5 (226).

2 **Greenfield, Stanley B.** *The Interpretation of Old English Poems.* London: Routledge, 1972. x + 188 pp.

Greenfield makes incidental comments on OEW poems in the course of tackling some major issues in the criticism and interpretation of Old English poetry. He resists Isaacs's **(264)** reflexive interpretation of *Order* as 'a poet talking to a prospective poet about poetry', on the grounds that it violates 'historical thematic probability' (6). In assessing the formulaic approach he notes that the uses of the 'recedes muð' formula in *Maxims II* line 37a and in *Beowulf* line 724 are very different: the formula gives a formal tightness to the passage in *Maxims*, but nothing further, whereas in *Beowulf* the kenning is 'peculiarly precise and metaphorically apt' (36–7). [This example is argued out in greater detail in **582**.] He cites some of the Exeter Book Riddles as instances of 'sound-sense play', notably 7 and 28 (86–8). In his discussion of the allegorical or exegetical approach to Old English poetry, Greenfield reviews the relationship between Riddle 60 and *The Husband's Message*. Kaske's **(852)** interpretation 'builds premise upon premise, including justifying Riddle 60 as part of the poem' (149). Yet the paragraphing divisions at two other points in the poem point to a scribe who thought the text consisted of several other riddles as well. Also, the lord–retainer relationship suggested in *The Husband's Message* has no counterpart in Riddle 60 (151–2). If the speaker in *The Husband's Message* is human, Riddle 60 cannot be part of it. Tupper's solution **(727)** 'reed pen' to Riddle 60 does not quite fit with the fact that the riddle-object is fashioned with the point ('ord') of a knife and not with the edge.

3 **Lee, Alvin A.** *The Guest-Hall of Eden: Four Essays on the Design of Old English Poetry.* New Haven: Yale UP, 1972. ix + 244 pp.

Order has been unfairly condemned for structural weakness. In fact, however, the description of the solar cycle in lines 59–81 is fully apposite, since the poem as a whole has as its theme the gaining of wisdom and the illumination of the mind of man by God's revelation of himself through created things. Lee also comments in passing on the treatment of the Cain story in *Maxims I* lines 192–8.

4 **Marckwardt, Albert H., and James L. Rosier.** *Old English Language and Literature.* New York: Norton, 1972. xviii + 394 pp.

This anthology of Old English poetry and prose is edited afresh from the manuscripts. Included are *Vainglory* and Exeter Book Riddles 29, 39, and 47 (197–201), along with detailed notes and glossary. *Vainglory* is compared to Hroðgar's 'homily' in *Beowulf*. The phrase 'þæs strangan staþol' in Riddle 47 line 5 is explained as 'the foundation of the strong' or 'of a strong man'.

285   **Doane, A.N.** ' "The Green Street of Paradise": A Note on Lexis and Meaning in Old English Poetry.' *Neuphilologische Mitteilungen* 74 (1973): 456–65.

Nearly all occurrences of the adjective *grene* in Old English poetry probably owe something of their usage and particular meaning to traditional Christian exegetical treatments of *viridis* and related Biblical words. Even so, their origin is to be traced to pre-Christian Germanic formulism. Very seldom is the adjective used with visual force, as in Exeter Book Riddle 15 line 6, or because of semantic necessity, as in *Maxims II* line 35 and *Solomon and Saturn* line 314. Normally, as in Riddle 66 line 5, the adjective alliterates and co-operates in meaning without determining it. Exceptional in this regard is Riddle 40, which contains two non-alliterating occurrences (lines 51 and 83).

286   **Grose, M.W., and Deirdre McKenna.** *Old English Literature in Perspective.* Totowa, NJ: Rowman, 1973. 160 pp.

OEW poetry is mentioned only in passing. Exeter Book Riddle 47 is cited as an example of Old English versification, *Fortunes* lines 80–4 in a discussion of the use of the Anglo-Saxon harp.

287   **Hacikyan, Agop.** 'The Runes of Old English Poetry.' *Revue de l'Université d'Ottawa* 43 (1973): 53–76.

Hacikyan reviews Trautmann's (**751**) theories on the poetic employment of runes. Trautmann posited three categories: the substitution of runes for their accepted names, the employment of groups of runes in the role of ordinary letters, and (more tentatively) the use of a rune as the initial letter of a missing word. Hacikyan deplores Trautmann's third category as a fertile source of error for subsequent scholars. He prefers to regard the name of each rune as lexically fixed but capable of semantic variation, thanks to the Old English love of wordplay. In *Rune Poem* 'rad' and 'sigel' are examples. Hacikyan makes passing mention of *Solomon and Saturn* and of the Exeter Book Riddles with runic letters.

288   **Kyte, E. Clemons.** 'On the Composition of Hypermetric Verses in Old English.' *Modern Philology* 71 (1973): 160–5.

Kyte discusses Bliss's extension (**279**) of his theory of hypermetric verses to posit a double hypermetric verse. Such verses result from the doubling of a process where the final syllables of the on-verse are replaced by a sequence equivalent to an ordinary verse. Kyte supplies a list of possible examples, thirteen in total, with nine from *Maxims I* and one from *Maxims II*. A second list comprises lines which Pope (**204**) scanned as hypermetric but which in Kyte's opinion are normal: included are lines from *Maxims I*, *Precepts*, and *Solomon and Saturn*. The general conclusion to be drawn is that the poet had at hand a storehouse of five basic types and their variations, such as the light, one-stress lines. This array could be combined into numerous varieties of hypermetric verses.

89 **Page, R.I.** *An Introduction to English Runes.* London: Methuen, 1973. xvi + 237 pp.

Page finds metrical Charm 2 and *Solomon and Saturn* an insecure basis for extrapolations to original rune names (or meanings for those names) in primitive Germanic. He criticizes as extreme the attempts of Schneider (**226, 594**) to build up pictures of the religious forces that influenced the formation of the rune-names. He suggests that in some cases the author of *Rune Poem* may have imposed his own interpretation upon a rare word. The 'rad' strophe is deliberately misleading, in the manner of an Exeter Book Riddle. The 'beorc' strophe may represent a learned revision of an older version that more unmistakably indicated a birch-tree. He characterizes the poet as apparently a simple and literal-minded man, who did not go in for the extensions of sense speculated on by some runic scholars but who was capable of directing his poem towards a dying fall with the 'ear' strophe.

90 **Rollinson, Philip B.** 'The Influence of Christian Doctrine and Exegesis on Old English Poetry: An Estimate of the Current State of Scholarship.' *Anglo-Saxon England* 2 (1973): 271–84.

Rollinson reacts favourably to Regan's (**1114**) description of *Vainglory* in terms of the 'patristic psychology of sin' (273). By contrast, he finds Kaske's (**852**) treatment of Exeter Book Riddle 60 and *The Husband's Message* not fully convincing (281).

91 **Schwab, Ute.** 'Eva reicht den Todesbecher. Zur Trinkmetaphorik in altenglischen Darstellungen des Sündenfalls.' *Atti dell'Accademia Peloritana, Classe di lettere, filosofia e belle arti* 51 (1973–4): 1–108.

Schwab briefly mentions *Maxims I* line 78 in connection with the concept of 'bitter death'. She suggests that the half-line 'æppel ond attor' in metrical Charm 2 line 34, where both nouns represent toxic substances, may be a folk reminiscence of the apple in the Adam and Eve story.

92 **Hieatt, Constance B.** 'Alliterative Patterns in the Hypermetric Lines of Old English Verse.' *Modern Philology* 71 (1974): 237–42.

Hieatt's analyses are designed to enhance our sense of the versificatory oddities of such poems as *Maxims I* and *II*, *Order*, *Rune Poem*, and *Solomon and Saturn*. She notes possible cases of triple alliteration in the on-verse, off-verses that begin with an alliterating lift, double alliteration in the off-verse, and crossed alliteration (sometimes confusable with single alliteration in the on-verse).

93 **Hume, Kathryn.** 'The Concept of the Hall in Old English Poetry.' *Anglo-Saxon England* 3 (1974): 63–74.

Hume argues for the existence of sharply divergent attitudes to the central concept of the hall in Old English poetry. In Exeter Book Riddle 3 storm-clouds are personified as battling horsemen striking terror into *burh*-dwellers. A similar motif occurs in Riddle 1. In Riddles 14 and 20 the rich variety of life is reduced to an elemental contrast between feast and field of battle. *Vainglory* and *Fortunes* lines 48–50 bring these two polarities together when they describe conflict within the hall. In *Maxims II* the essence of a king and his kingliness is distilled for us, as if he were a fly in amber.

294 **Schabram, H.** 'Altenglische "wlanc" und Ableitungen: Vorarbeiten zu einer wortgeschichtlichen Studie.' *Studien zur englischen und amerikanischen Sprache und Literatur: Festschrift für Helmut Papajewski.* Ed. Paul G. Buchloh, Inge Leimberg, and Herbert Rauter. Neumünster: Wachholtz, 1974. 70–88.

Schabram includes OEW poems in his survey of the incidence and uses of *wlanc*.

295 **Stanley, E.G.** 'The Oldest English Poetry now Extant.' *Poetica* (Tokyo) 2 (1974): 1–24. Repr. in Eric Gerald Stanley, ed. *A Collection of Papers with Emphasis on Old English Literature.* Toronto: Pontifical Institute of Mediaeval Studies, 1987. 115–38.

Stanley's discussion includes the *Winfrid Proverb* and the *Leiden Riddle*. He suggests that the *Proverb* may have been over a century old when the anonymous monastic correspondent, probably a member of St Boniface's circle of Anglo-Saxons at Mainz, used it in his letter (7). Preferable to Dobbie's translation (**203**) is 'The man slow in action generally puts off glory, puts off every victorious exploit; therefore he dies alone' (8) – with 'procrastinates' as an alternative for 'puts off'. The *Proverb* should be interpreted as a terse summary of the Germanic heroic ideal: the coward may live longer but he will die alone. This maxim concerning good fellowship in action is re-applied to missionary activity, with perhaps a special relevance to the circumstances of Boniface's martyrdom 'as one of twelve'. Stanley lists *Fortunes* and some of the Exeter Book Riddles, e.g. 2, 3, and 9, as poems starting with a light half-line: 'the effect of a light half-line to open the poem is to get into it with something of a swing' (15). The appearance of the *Leiden Riddle* in a northern French manuscript may be 'merely a capricious result of a delight . . . in deliberate obscurity' (21). The text is an exercise in translation, with an occasional clumsiness that emerges in line 11 (22). Although the *Leiden Riddle* cannot be judged in isolation from its Latin source, it is possible that the half-line 9b, 'uyrdi craeftum', contains an 'allusion to the skills of the weaving Fate' (24).

296 **Stanley, Eric G.** *The Search for Anglo-Saxon Paganism.* Cambridge: Brewer; Totowa, NJ: Rowman, 1975. x + 143 pp. Repr. in book form from the original articles in *Notes and Queries* 209–10 (1964–5).

In this survey and critique of the scholarly search for evidence of Anglo-Saxon paganism, Stanley argues that the hypothetical traces of paganism were systematically exaggerated. The certainty of being in contact with something very primitive caused Williams (**547**) and many other scholars to stigmatize all Christian elements in the *Maxims* as spurious. Williams shows the same tendency to praise the pagan and deprecate the Christian in her treatment of *Gifts, Homiletic Fragment I*, and *Vainglory* (65–6). In their discussions of *Solomon and Saturn* many early scholars, Kemble (**1047**) among them, were influenced by Jacob Grimm's (**363**) postulation of divine status for Saturn among the Germanic peoples (88). Bonser's **(432)** and Cockayne's **(365)** efforts to find references in the metrical Charms to Woden and Þunor (respectively) are part of the same trend (89–90). Menner's **(1073)** handling of *wyrd* in *Solomon and Saturn* is compromised by the failure to cite Boethius's *De Consolatione Philosophiae* IV.vii (120–1). The same passage could be applied to *Maxims II* lines 4–5, though Stanley concedes that perhaps those lines are ambiguous (114–15).

7 Ström, Åke V., and Haralds Biezais. *Germanische und baltische Religion.* Die Religionen der Menschheit 19.1. Stuttgart: Kohlhammer, 1975. 391 pp.

The chapter entitled 'Auf den britischen Inseln' (97–110) contains passing references to *Rune Poem* and metrical Charms 2 and 4 as sources for heathen mythology. The authors interpret 'os' in *Rune Poem* line 10 as equivalent in meaning to Old Norse *áss* 'heathen god'.

8 Allen, Michael J.B., and Daniel G. Calder. *Sources and Analogues of Old English Poetry: The Major Latin Texts in Translation.* Cambridge: Brewer; Totowa, NJ: Rowman, 1976. xviii + 235 pp.

Various OEW poems are included. In their brief discussion of previous work on *Gifts* (154–5) the editors differ from Cross **(240)** in attributing the sermon cited by Cross not to Haymo of Halberstadt but to Haymo of Auxerre. The section on the Exeter Book Riddles contains translated analogues, as follows: Pseudo-Symphosius 1 ('cuckoo'), Symphosius 56 ('soldier's boot'), Aldhelm 83 ('bullock'), and Eusebius 37 ('calf') are all compared with Riddles 12, 38, and, tentatively, 72. Eusebius 30 ('inkhorn') is compared to Riddles 14 and tentatively 80, 88, and 93. Symphosius 61 ('anchor') is compared to Riddle 16. Aldhelm 53 ('Arcturus') is compared to Riddle 22. Aldhelm 32 ('writing tablets'), Aldhelm 59 ('quill'), Tatwine 5 ('parchment'), Tatwine 6 ('quill'), Eusebius 32 ('parchment'), and Eusebius 35 ('quill') are all compared to Riddles 26 and, tentatively, 67. Symphosius 20 ('tortoise-lyre') is compared to Riddle 28. Aldhelm 33 ('lorica', 'breastplate') is compared to Riddle 35 and the *Leiden Riddle*. Aldhelm 84 ('pregnant sow') is compared to Riddle 36. Symphosius 73 ('bellows') is compared to Riddles 37 and 87. Aldhelm 100 ('creation') is compared to Riddles 40 and, tentatively, 41. Symphosius 16 ('bookworm') is compared to Riddle 47. Aldhelm 55 ('chrismal') is compared to Riddles 48 and 59. Aldhelm 89 ('bookcase') is compared to Riddle 49. Aldhelm 86 ('Aries/The Ram') is compared to Riddle 53. Symphosius 71 ('well') and Symphosius 72 ('wooden water-pipe') are compared to Riddle 58. Symphosius 2 ('reed') is compared to Riddle 60. Aldhelm 80 ('glass wine-cup') is compared to Riddles 63 and in part, tentatively, 14, 27, and 30. Symphosius 44 ('onion') is compared to Riddles 65 and in part, tentatively, 25. Symphosius 92 ('money') is compared to Riddle 83 as a remote analogue. Aldhelm 29 ('water') and 73 ('a spring') are compared to Riddle 84. Symphosius 12 ('river and fish') is compared to Riddle 85. Symphosius 95 ('one-eyed garlic seller') is compared to Riddle 86. Symphosius 4 ('key') is compared to Riddle 91. As to the metrical Charms, the editors find only remote analogues among the Latin charms. Three are cited as pertinent: *The Prayer of Mother Earth*, a pagan charm surviving in medieval manuscripts from the sixth century onwards, is compared to Charms 1 and 2. A bee charm is cited as an analogue to Charm 8. The *Lorica* is cited as of the same date and in the same spirit as Charm 11.

299 Hansen, Elaine Tuttle. 'From *freolicu folccwen* to *geomuru ides*: Women in Old English Poetry Reconsidered.' *Michigan Academician* 9 (1976): 109–18.

Hansen singles out *Maxims I* as containing the most thorough poetic enumeration of the virtues, privileges, and duties of Anglo-Saxon femininity. The worth of the ideal king and queen to each other is expressed not in words of love but rather in terms of the principle of reciprocity and its embodiment in their customary public behaviour (lines 81–92). Washing her homecoming man's clothes and offering him new ones, the wife of the Frisian sailor humbly adheres to the same general principle of duty as the queen (lines 94–9). As is often the case in gnomic verse, the poet goes on to explore the nature of right and good by contrasting it with its opposite, here juxtaposing the constant wife with the woman who strays and causes her name to be dishonoured (lines 100–2). Two further dicta in *Maxims I* underscore the poet's understanding of good women as honourable partners in the well-regulated institution of marriage, in which goods are exchanged for services and privileges. In *Fortunes* lines 13–14, by contrast, we are offered a brief reference to female suffering in the Germanic type of the woman mourner (111).

300 Shippey, T.A. *Poems of Wisdom and Learning in Old English.* Cambridge: Brewer; Totowa, NJ: Rowman, 1976. 152 pp.

Shippey supplies texts of *Precepts, Vainglory, Fortunes, Maxims I* and *II, Rune Poem*, and *Solomon and Saturn* II, with translations on facing pages and appended notes, textual variants, and bibliography. Sample translation (from *Fortunes* lines 1–6): 'It happens very often, through God's power, that a man and woman have children, bringing them into the world through birth and clothing them in fleshly form, coaxing and cherishing, until with the passing of many years the time comes that the young limbs, the members they gave life to, have grown to maturity.' In his Introduction, having noted the neglect of certain OEW poems in anthologies, Shippey identifies the purpose of this book as to enable some of Sweet's (**81**) and Bright's (**190**) rejects to reach a wider audience. Shippey notes that the poems covered here are homogeneous with *Gifts*, the *Homiletic Fragments, Order, Solomon and Saturn* I, and also some non-OEW poems such as *The Wanderer, The Seafarer*, and *The Rhyming Poem* in that most are around a hundred lines long, contain a thinly-characterized persona who speaks directly to the audience, embody gnomic generalizations or use the figure of an old man instructing his disciple, and exhibit pervasive minor similarities of tone or conclusion (1). To the Anglo-Saxon audience poetic forms were perhaps less important than the weight of meaning they were meant to carry. Even the meaning can seem either obfuscated or platitudinous to us nowadays, as in *Order* (3–4). The obscurities are particularly salient in *Precepts*, though mingled there with a sense of urgency (4–7). In *Vainglory*, too, vagueness was built into the poem: for instance, the poet does not discriminate between what the devil does to the sinner and what the sinner does to other people. The sinfulness of the sinner is almost comically exaggerated (7–10). In *Fortunes* we see the strength of feeling between one person and another, along with its total weakness when extended to the universe outside; recognition of God's power does not lead to any evident confidence that all is for the best (10–12). The term 'gnomic' is misleadingly comparative in relation to *Maxims I* and *II*, distracting attention from the question of whether the sayings are maxims or proverbs or straight (banal) statements of fact or (even in Anglo-Saxon times) invitations to read significance into cryptic remarks. It is impossible to tell now whether the sayings represent traditional received truths or personal discoveries on the part of the poet. Nor is it always possible to posit definite univocal logical links within the poems, especially when, as in the second section of *Maxims I*, the text indicates a taste for variety. Similarly in *Maxims II*, the links are suggestive rather than definite. The three sections of *Maxims I* are analysed as separate poems (12–19). *Rune Poem* cannot be simply a mnemonic poem, because the length of the strophes would impede memorization of the letters. Dismissing the theories of Schneider **(226)**, Shippey suggests that the persona of *Rune Poem* is that of the wise man and that the focus may be the opposition between human comfort and discomfort. Thus, in the 'rad' strophe, 'riding is pleasant in prospect but hard when one has to do it'. The 'nyd' strophe warns us to be aware of possible future adversity even as we live in prosperity (19–20). *Solomon and Saturn* can be seen as part of a tradition of proverbial literature in England at once widespread, durable, and distinctive. *Solomon and Saturn* I is characterized by meaningless exactness, whereas *Solomon and Saturn* II bears a closer resemblance, in seriousness, generality and a slight uncertainty in the answers, to the other wisdom poems surveyed. Nonetheless, the two poems come from a similar learned, cranky, impractical background. Both teach that a gloomy or grumbling person is either ill-instructed or perverse: one should cultivate hope, but without too much expectation. Literary merit can be seen in the 'weallende wulf' and 'Vasa Mortis' passages in *Solomon and Saturn* II (lines 212–24 and 253–81 respectively), where the poet may have been inventing freely, using the persona of the sage to give authority to his own opinions (20–8). In his general conclusion Shippey warns that source-studies, locating biblical or patristic 'sources' for particular motifs in these poems, may be misleading. The degree of overlap between poems and putative sources is quite limited, whereas much more far-flung analogues, such as the collections of anthropologists from Nigeria or [Papua] New Guinea, may be fully as revealing. The 'wise man's' suspicious and slightly cynical posture may arise directly from the experience of chronic uncertainty which is a Heroic Age characteristic, though tempered by an acknowledgement of Divine Providence (46–7). In his notes, Shippey compares translations of cruces, ambiguities, and other difficult passages. Textual uncertainties, e.g. Williams's **(131)** emendation in *Fortunes* line 43, are also discussed. Shippey follows Bliss **(272, 279)** in lineating with a preference for short lines over hypermetric ones.

1 **Tripp, Raymond P.** 'On the Continuity of English Poetry between Beowulf and Chaucer.' *Poetica* (Tokyo) 6 (1976): 1–21.

Tripp identifies the idea of mysteries beyond men's reach as a key element in English poetry. It is a paradox of much so-called Old English wisdom poetry that wisdom is presented as the recognition that there is no knowledge – beyond an empirical acknowledgement of the complexities and consistencies of experience. Experience is the only guide, and the best one (*Maxims II*). Such texts as

Fortunes, *Maxims*, and *Order*, along with the *Rhyming Poem*, might all be classed
in a genre of 'complexity poems', because they insist on the unattainability or
complexity of wisdom. The turmoil and tribulation of the world is a key theme in
Maxims I and *II*: the rush of the world is too complex for men to comprehend.
Nobody but God knows where the soul goes after death (*Maxims II* lines 61–6).
Gifts shows that no one person has a monopoly on wisdom: that would engender
sinful pride. *Maxims I* and *Vainglory* concede that the assertions in these poems
could be seen as lies. Old English wisdom poetry contains the awareness that 'tot
homines tot opiniones'.

302 **Mazzuoli Porru, Giulia.** *Manuale di inglese antico.* Orientamenti Linguistici 1.
Pisa: Giardini, 1977. 303 pp.

The texts in this student handbook are based on ASPR (**194, 203**) and include
metrical Charms 4, 7, and 12; Riddle 35; and *Leiden Riddle*, along with brief
introduction, notes, and glossary.

303 **Campbell, Jackson J.** 'Adaptation of Classical Rhetoric and Literature.'
Medieval Eloquence. Ed. James J. Murphy. Berkeley: U of California P, 1978.
173–97.

Campbell acknowledges that apparent rhetorical figures can arise from unstudied
'natural' use of language. Nonetheless, when a number of such figures appear in
the same poem, evidently used with conscious skill, the likelihood of the poet's
having had a background of Latin education is tremendously increased. The
examples cited include OEW poems. Anaphora on the word 'sum' provides a
structuring principle which develops into the very theme of the poem in both
Fortunes and *Gifts*. Anaphoric 'hwilum' is used in Exeter Book Riddle 1 to
indicate sections and shifts of idea in the poem, and then climactically toward its
end to summarize those sections. Campbell also comments briefly on
prosopopoeia in the Riddles.

304 **Fanagan, John M.** 'An Examination of Tense-Usage in Some of the Shorter
Poems of the *Exeter Book.*' *Neophilologus* 62 (1978): 290–3.

Fanagan argues that tense usage is a useful internal indicator of genre
demarcations. *Precepts* and *Vainglory* exhibit a similar present:past tense ratio to
The Wanderer and *The Seafarer*. Using the same criterion, he groups *Fortunes*
and *Gifts* with *Resignation* as either very largely or overwhelmingly
present-tense, as befits the part-religious, part-moral content.

305 **Grant, Raymond J.S.** *Cambridge Corpus Christi College 41: The Loricas and
the Missal.* Costerus NS 17. Amsterdam: Rodopi, 1978. 136 pp.

Grant calls into question Dobbie's (**203**) statement that twelve metrical Charms
are extant in Old English, pointing out the uncertainties about versification and
about demarcations in the manuscripts. To be deplored are heavy regularizations
of the Charms, such as those perpetrated on Charm 11 by Holthausen (**388, 397**).
Grant suggests that fragments of charms and incantations may well have been so
much interchangeable mumbo-jumbo and their ordering fortuitous rather than
significant. One of the Old English metrical charms for stolen cattle appears in

CCCC 41 side by side with two loricas. Citation in such a context radically alters a rather specific charm against theft of livestock into a general charm for the protection of the soul during and after life. Grant supplies a tentative stemma of this postulated compilation charm. He compares the versions of *Solomon and Saturn* in CCCC 41 and 422, noting that the scribe of 41 chose to transcribe only part of the text of *Solomon and Saturn* when more was available to him: this excerpt too should be treated as a lorica.

6 **Nelson, Marie.** 'Sound as Meaning in Old English Charms, Riddles, and Maxims.' *The Twenty-Seventh Annual Mountain Interstate Foreign Language Conference.* Ed. Eduardo Zayas-Bazán and M. Laurentino Suárez. Johnson City, TN, 1978. 122–8.

Nelson seeks to show some of the ways in which patterned use of sound contributes to meaning in the Exeter Book Riddles, metrical Charms, and *Maxims*. Imitation approximating to onomatopoeia is found mainly in the Riddles. Notable examples are Riddle 7 (where repeated *sw-* imitates the sound of the swan's wings) and Riddle 28. In Charm 2 the repetition of the consonant cluster *st-* in lines 14–16 and elsewhere carries associations with the narrations of victories in *The Battle of Maldon* and kindred battle poems. In Charm 12 the well-known translinguistic association between *-i-* and smallness reinforces the wished-for diminution of the wen. Symmetry of phrasing and rhythm strengthens the performative aspects of Charm 4 and the sense of assurance in the *Maxims*.

7 **Pope, John C.** 'Palaeography and Poetry: Some Solved and Unsolved Problems of the Exeter Book.' *Medieval Scribes, Manuscripts and Libraries: Essays Presented to N.R. Ker.* Ed. M.B. Parkes and Andrew G. Watson. London: Scolar, 1978. 25–65.

Pope takes a fresh look at the whole range of losses of material from the Exeter Book, demonstrable and possible, and considers some of the consequences for our understanding of the imperfect texts that survive. Appended is a revised table of contents, arranged according to the surviving quires and showing the position of known and possible losses. Losses from the Riddles include the endings of 20 and 40, the beginning of 41, and probably a few complete riddles of which we can know nothing. In quire xvi the gap occurs in the midst of what had passed for a six-line riddle (70) but is actually two unrelated fragments. The eighth leaf of the quire has disappeared and two or three riddles besides the missing portions of the two fragments may have been lost. There may also have been other riddles at the end, since no colophon or concluding formula exists to assure us that the book is complete. Pope agrees with those who believe that the seventeen-line passage immediately preceding *The Husband's Message* is actually the first paragraph of that poem, though printed as 'Riddle 60' in ASPR **(194)**. He argues that the speaker in *The Husband's Message* is a piece of yew-wood. The so-called 'Riddle 60' can be accepted as a description of the speaker's early existence as part of a yew-tree growing in a secluded spot near the sea (or a lake) until a man cut it down from its trunk, shaped it, and carved letters in it. Pope appends the conjecturally restored text and translation of the complete poem.

308 Rüden, Michael von. *'Wlanc' und Derivate im Alt- und Mittelenglischen: Eine wortgeschichtliche Studie.* Europäische Hochschulschriften. Reihe 14. Angelsächsische Sprache und Literatur 61. Frankfurt am Main: Lang, 1978. 324 pp.

Rüden includes numerous references to OEW poems in this word study, in the process of demonstrating that the word *wlanc* and its derivatives often have no clearly affirmative or pejorative sense in Old English. In Exeter Book Riddle 50 line 10 'wlonc-' means 'mighty', as befits the solution 'fire', rather than Baum's 'proud' **(837)** or Mackie's 'arrogan[t]' **(188)** (114). In *Maxims I* line 60 'wlencu' means 'wealth' (115) and in *Maxims II* line 27 'frætwum wlanc' means 'rich in treasures' (116). In *Solomon and Saturn* line 208 'goldwlonc-' similarly means 'rich in gold', not 'proud of gold', despite Kemble **(1047)** and others (121). Commentators such as Lindheim **(815)** tend to force pejorative connotations of the word into contexts such as Riddles 12, 25, 42, and 45, where it should be interpreted neutrally (143–5). On the other hand, a clearly pejorative use is seen in *Vainglory* line 40 (139). In Riddle 73 line 2 Grein's **(75)** emendation 'heofonwolcn' is to be rejected in favour of the manuscript reading 'heofonwlonc' (165).

309 Calder, Daniel G. 'The Study of Style in Old English Poetry: An Historical Introduction.' *Old English Poetry: Essays on Style.* Ed. Daniel G. Calder. Contributions of the UCLA Center for Medieval and Renaissance Studies 10. Berkeley: U of California P, 1979. vii + 174 pp.

This chapter includes passing references to older scholars' understandings of style in OEW poetry, e.g. *Maxims II* and *Precepts.*

310 Ritzke-Rutherford, Jean. *Light and Darkness in Anglo-Saxon Thought and Writing.* Sprache und Literatur: Regensburger Arbeiten zur Anglistik und Amerikanistik 17. Frankfurt am Main: Lang, 1979. 314 pp.

Ritzke-Rutherford argues that metrical Charm 1 cannot be regarded as evidence for sun-worship in early England, since it is overwhelmingly Christian in content (81–4). The names 'sigel' and 'tir' in *Rune Poem* might signify Christ, who would represent the 'Sun of salvation' for the Christian cast adrift in the sea of his life's voyage. Comparable is the treatment of runic *S* in *Solomon and Saturn* lines 111–17. Both *Rune Poem* and *Solomon and Saturn* are late, antiquarian efforts (181–2). Exeter Book Riddle 30 in both of its versions follows upon poems (Riddle 29 and *Homiletic Fragment II*) that contain the idea of light. This observation indicates 'Cross/Sun' as the solution to Riddle 30 (219–26).

311 Robinson, Fred C. 'Two Aspects of Variation in Old English Poetry.' *Old English Poetry: Essays on Style.* Ed. Daniel G. Calder. Contributions of the UCLA Center for Medieval and Renaissance Studies 10. Berkeley: U of California P, 1979. 127–45.

In his discussion of the definition and types of 'variation' Robinson notes the assumption that a major word may not be repeated within the two parts of a variation. He reviews attempts to emend away such repetitions, including those in Exeter Book Riddle 60 lines 12–13 ('ord') and metrical Charm 9 lines 14–15 ('mihta'). In no case is there warrant for emendation on other than stylistic grounds. Quite heavy lexical repetition may in fact have been acceptable, as is indicated by the surrounding lines in Charm 9.

2 **Foley, John Miles.** 'Epic and Charm in Old English and Serbo-Croatian Oral Tradition.' *Comparative Criticism* 2 (1980): 71–92.

Foley discusses the function of phonological patterning in Old English poetry, especially the metrical Charms. He argues that in *Maxims I* lines 22–6 alliteration maintains an aural bridge and a mnemonic route where no obvious semantic bridge exists. That the Charms to some extent depend for their magic on oral performance and sound patterns is evidenced by statements within Charm 3 and a Yugoslav spell. In Charm 9 'Garmund' can be identified as a heroic anthropomorphization of the spell's magic power. The significant name can be paralleled from the Yugoslav material. In Charm 1 lines 51–8 the prayer to the Earth-mother weaves its verbal magic round the word 'wæstm'. Conventional alliterative prosody is only partially constitutive of such patterns.

3 **Opland, Jeff.** *Anglo-Saxon Oral Poetry: A Study of the Traditions.* New Haven: Yale UP, 1980. xi + 289 pp.

In the course of this investigation Opland makes many references to OEW poetry. Terminology connected with poetry and related activities is analysed. The *Winfrid Proverb* and *Order* provide testimony to the memorization of poetry in a fixed form in Anglo-Saxon times (143–4, 160, and 228–9). 'Apparently it is necessary for the poet [of *Order*] to explain the use of poetry for didactic purposes' (228). The association of poetry, harp, music, laughter, and ring-giving is documented with reference to *Gifts*, *Vainglory*, and *Maxims I* lines 165–71. The lack of clarity in the *Maxims* passage is discussed (220–2). When *Gifts* (lines 35–6, 49–53) sharply distinguishes the various functions appertaining to poetry, its testimony may be misleading. The information on the harper in *Fortunes* lines 80–4 cannot be extrapolated to the *scop* (224–9). In Exeter Book Riddle 8 line 5 'æfenscop', possibly a nonce-compound, offers no reliable information about the activities of the human *scop* (234). Opland accepts Parkes's (**873**) finding that the manuscript neumes accompanying the *Leiden Riddle* are not integral to it (127). The reference to the *scop* in *Maxims I* lines 125–8 suggests someone who exhorted the war-band in battle (232–3). The word *woðbora* in *Gifts* line 35, Riddles 31 line 24 and 80 line 9, and *Order* line 2 might refer primarily to wisdom, not poetry (250). Likewise, the meaning of *wrixlan* in *Vainglory* line 16, *Maxims I* line 4, Riddle 8 line 2, and Riddle 60 line 10 is not necessarily confined to poetry (222–4).

4 **Osborn, Marijane.** 'Old English Ing and His *Wain*.' *Neuphilologische Mitteilungen* 81 (1980): 388–9.

Osborn proposes that the Ing of the *Rune Poem* is Boötes in his fiercer aspect. He would be sighted each night, first among the Danes in the east and then following his Wain (the constellation now called the 'Big Dipper') over the sea to the west. In Riddle 22, Osborn defends Dietrich's (**658**) theory that the sixty horsemen represent sixty days, on the grounds that this is the time that elapses between the winter solstice and the rising of the Wain. An agricultural society would be aware of this computation, even in the far North, where the Wain never goes beneath the horizon.

315 **Meaney, Audrey L.** *Anglo-Saxon Amulets and Curing Stones.* British Archaeological Reports, British Series 96. Oxford: British Archaeological Reports, 1981. xxxi + 364 pp.

Meaney places the metrical Charms that use amulets in the context of archaeological evidence. Comparative material suggests that the 'wiht' in Charm 3 line 9 is opposed to the dwarf, not identical with him. The use of spiders (if we accept the emendation) can be documented from known examples of spiders as amulets. Meaney argues against Dobbie's (203) view that the staff mentioned in Charm 11 could not be a rune-stave, citing the charm inscribed on the 'Magic Wand of Ribe'. The 'leaf' mentioned in Charm 12 line 5 might have been a vellum leaf or even the leaf of a tree, inscribed with the charm. Similarly, the wolf's foot and eagle's feather and claw (lines 6–7) might have made up a compound amulet. The elfshot countered in Charm 4 might have represented a traditional interpretation of the attack of the warble-fly, which leaves a characteristic hole in the animal's hide. In her discussion of keys as amulets Meaney cites Exeter Book Riddles 44 and 91, with comparative evidence for the key as phallic symbol.

316 **Stanley, E.G.** 'The Scholarly Recovery of the Significance of Anglo-Saxon Records in Prose and Verse: A New Bibliography.' *Anglo-Saxon England* 9 (1981): 223–62.

Noting that 'the new bibliography by Stanley B. Greenfield and Fred C. Robinson of the entire body of publications on Old English literature provides the occasion for reviewing not so much the bibliography itself as the subject it covers' (57) (223), Stanley briefly alludes to the history of Cynewulfian attributions (244–5). He characterizes scholarship on this writer as 'the extreme example of biographical folly' (245).

317 **Bradley, S.A.J.** *Anglo-Saxon Poetry: An Anthology of Old English Poems in Prose Translation with Introduction and Headnotes.* Everyman's Library. London: Dent, 1982. xxvi + 559 pp.

Bradley includes the following OEW poems: *Fortunes*; *Gifts*; *Maxims I* and *II*; metrical Charms 1 and 11; and Exeter Book Riddles 3, 5, 9, 25, 26, 29, 30a, 35, 38, 42–8, 53, 60, 61, 66, 69, 76, and 86. Brief introductions accompany each poem. Additionally, the commentary covers some poems (e.g. *Vainglory*) for which translations are not included. Sample translation, from Riddle 29 lines 1–4: 'I saw a creature wondrously carrying plunder between his horns, an airy lantern artfully adorned, plunder from a raiding foray, to his home. . .'

318 **Crossley-Holland, Kevin.** *The Anglo-Saxon World.* Woodbridge: Boydell, 1982. 278 pp.

This book of translations includes thirty-one of the Exeter Book Riddles; metrical Charms 8, 9, and 12; and *Fortunes*. A sample translation from *Fortunes* lines

21–6: 'One will drop, wingless, from the high tree/ in the wood; look how he flies still,/ dives through the air, until the tree's arms/ no longer surround him. Then sadly he slumps/ by the trunk, robbed of life; he falls/ to earth and his soul flies from him.' Brief introductions and bibliography are provided.

Hermann, John P. 'The Recurrent Motifs of Spiritual Warfare in Old English Poetry.' *Annuale Mediaevale* 22 (1982): 7–35.

Although it has long been recognized that Old English poetry reflects the influence of Christianity upon the native Germanic culture, the theme of spiritual warfare has never been systematically catalogued and discussed. Hermann documents the nexus of a pagan love of battle with a Christian push to transmute *machia* into *psychomachia*. The Pauline figure of spiritual armour is represented in metrical Charm 11, a work clearly influenced by the lorica genre. Hermann catalogues epithets for the Devil, with examples from OEW poems (10–11). In *Vainglory* the figure of the soul as a besieged fortress is combined with the recurrent motif of the arrows of the devil. The poet attempts to translate technical concepts of patristic psychology into Old English verse by employing a complex of military images which had become so pervasive as to seem a standard allegory. In *Solomon and Saturn* lines 22–9 the metaphor of the missiles of the devil is developed uniquely into the notion of a sling of the devil hurling iron balls. The catalogue of occurrences of the figure of the 'wounds of sin' includes OEW poems (18–19). The description of the good and evil angels contending for the soul of man in *Solomon and Saturn* lines 482–98 is unusually elaborate. It may refer specifically to the four Gregorian stages of sin. Anglo-Saxon belief in the historical reality behind the story of the war in heaven is manifested in the comparison of the haughty man to the rebel angels in *Vainglory* lines 50b–66. *Vainglory* also embodies and gains unity from a favourite irony in Old English poetry, where victory in literal battle leads to simultaneous spiritual defeat.

Calder, Daniel G., et al. *Sources and Analogues of Old English Poetry. II. The Major Germanic and Celtic Texts in Translation.* Cambridge: Brewer; Totowa, NJ: Barnes, 1983. xxiv + 222 pp.

The authors include analogues to the following: *Gifts* ('The Lay of Hyndla' [=*Hyndluljóð*]); *Maxims* (various wisdom and gnomic poems); Exeter Book Riddles ('Riddles of Gestumblindi' [from *Hervarar saga ok Heiðreks*] and the Middle Welsh 'The Song of the Wind'); *Rune Poem* (the Old Norse 'Rune Poem' and Old High German 'Abecedarium Nordmannicum'); *Solomon and Saturn* (the Old Norse 'Lay of Vafþrúðnir' [*Vafþrúðnismál*]); and the metrical Charms (*Skírnismál*, Old High German Charms, and the Old Irish 'St Patrick's Lorica').

Frantzen, Allen J. *The Literature of Penance in Anglo-Saxon England.* New Brunswick, NJ: Rutgers UP, 1983. xvi + 238 pp.

In his concluding pages (194–7), Frantzen briefly contrasts Anglo-Saxon wisdom poetry with penitential poetry. He finds the wisdom poetry characterized by a stoical determination to contain one's dissatisfaction and accept hardship as one's lot. In Frantzen's view, *Precepts* is an inept title for a most interesting poem. Like *The Wanderer*, it is exemplary in its caution against disclosing one's thoughts.

Homiletic Fragment II lines 3–4 is similar in showing that the wise man does not share the secrets of his heart, contrary to penitential practice, which demanded full disclosure.

322 **Hermann, John P.** 'Some Varieties of Psychomachia in Old English.' *American Benedictine Review* 34 (1983): 74–86 and 188–222.

In *Solomon and Saturn* Hermann sees a neglected body of work that adheres closely to the tradition of personification allegory established by Prudentius in his *Psychomachia*. Despite the popularity of this work in Anglo-Saxon England, its influence on *Solomon and Saturn* has hitherto gone unrecognized. The description of the T-rune (lines 94–5) has its unique parallel in the description of Fides as a tongue-piercer in *Psychomachia*. The S-rune passage (lines 111–17) is partially paralleled in the attack of Sobrietas upon Luxuria in *Psychomachia*. Metrical Charm 11 contains a version of the figure of spiritual armour. In *Solomon and Saturn* lines 25–8 the notion of a sling of the Devil hurling iron balls ('aplum') is a unique development of the missiles of the Devil as an allegorical system.

323 **Schneider, Karl.** 'The English Proverb: Definition – Determination of Age – Models.' *Poetica* (Tokyo) 15–16 (1983): 23–48.

Schneider attempts a definition of the proverb, as seen in English and other Germanic languages, so as to include *Maxims*. Among the features he lists are shortness, relative fixity, oral transmission, syntactic simplicity, antithesis or parallelism, fluctuation in formulation between concrete statement and abstract utterance, and 4/4 or 2/4 rhythmic structure. The proverb should contain a condensation of a truth or a received idea and may constitute a help in life or a criticism or a comment. As to rhythmical structure, the Old English proverbs, without exception, exhibit 4/4 measure. This measure is determined by the prevailing dynamic stress accent, which leads to a triple stress gradation of syllables (29). Some Old English proverbs are arranged in a four-line stanza resembling *ljóðaháttr*: thus *Maxims I* lines 22–5 and 66–70 (31). The Latin portion of the *Latin-English Proverbs* must be secondary, because it is not rhythmically well-formed according to these criteria of metrical shape (33). Using the same criteria Schneider attempts reconstructions of the Old English text of proverbs attested only at later stages of the English language. An original '*Ald wif witon þa wyrda' should be posited as the progenitor of 'she is an old wife that wats her weird'. This proverb achieved its formulation in a context where women (Old Norse *nornir*) were seen as shaping the fate of the individual (36).

324 **Elliott, Ralph W.V.** 'Runic Mythology: The Legacy of the Futhark.' *Medieval Studies Conference, Aachen 1983.* Ed. Wolf-Dietrich Bald and Horst Weinstock. Bamberger Beiträge zur englischen Sprachwissenschaft 15. Frankfurt am Main: Lang, 1984. 37–50.

Elliott cites runic material excavated at Bergen to support the 'yew-tree' solution to Exeter Book Riddle 60. Halsall's interpretation (**1033**) of *Rune Poem* as a Christian unity fails to reckon with the presence of 'aurochs' and 'Ing'.

Schneider's attempts **(594)** to find runic connotations in the *Maxims* are misguided.

5 **Fell, Christine, with Cecily Clark and Elizabeth Williams.** *Women in Anglo-Saxon England and the Impact of 1066.* London: British Museum, 1984. 208 pp.

Fell comments in passing on OEW poems for their possible value as documentation of Anglo-Saxon culture. *Fortunes* begins (lines 1–9) by presenting a 'charming picture of a close and loving family' (79). Neuter 'it' for the child is preferable to 'him'. The poem offers valuable documentation of the birth-gift (79). Problems in the *Maxims* are highlighted. For example, whereas it does not much matter whether 'sceal' in 'fisc sceal on wætere' (*Maxims II* line 27) is translated as 'ought to be' or 'by nature is', it does make a good deal of difference whether a woman 'ought' to be cheerful, or 'it is the nature' of a woman to be cheerful (*Maxims I* line 85b). Admittedly, this might be a difference without meaning in Anglo-Saxon culture (36). The male-centred but 'admiring' description of womanly behaviour in lines 81–92 of *Maxims I* is analysed in detail, with the suggestion that 'rune healdan' in line 86 means 'hand on knowledge' (36–7). *Maxims II* lines 43b–5a, where women are quite clearly urged to independence of action, should dispel the notion that women were viewed only as pawns in dynastic games (69). Among 'domestic glimpses' of the working woman, *Maxims I* lines 94–9 and the double entendre Riddles (Exeter Book 25, 45, 54, and the cluster of 61–3) suggest a 'rough good-humour in the attitude to ordinary domestic relationships' (70–1). Two or three texts imply that runes might be used to pass private messages between men and women. Significant here are Riddle 60 ('rune-stave'), Riddle 92 line 3 (where the piece of wood describes itself as 'wifes sond'), and perhaps *Maxims I*, with the phrase 'rune healdan'. Fell uses the Riddles, along with other evidence, to document further topics in social history. These include an ethnic class distinction (25 and 67), the improbability that jobs on the estate were rigidly allocated according to sex (48–9), the existence of women entertainers (54–5), and the maternal role (81).

6 **Oggins, Robin S.** 'Falconry in Anglo-Saxon England.' *Mediaevalia* 7 (1984 *for* 1981): 173–208.

Oggins draws on *Fortunes* lines 85–92, *Gifts* lines 80–1, *Maxims II* lines 17b–18a, and Exeter Book Riddles as evidence for the wide diffusion of the skills of falconry.

7 **Godden, M.R.** 'Anglo-Saxons on the Mind.' *Learning and Literature in Anglo-Saxon England: Studies presented to Peter Clemoes on the Occasion of his Sixty-Fifth Birthday.* Ed. Michael Lapidge and Helmut Gneuss. Cambridge: Cambridge UP, 1985. 271–98.

Godden discusses the relationship between psychological ideas and linguistic expression, e.g. the expression of emotion in Old English. Locutions such as we find in *Maxims I* line 121, 'hyge sceal gehealden, hond gewealden' and *Homiletic Fragment II* line 3, 'heald hordlocan, hyge fæste bind', invite us to see a distinction between the conscious self and some other, inner power. We might legitimately class that power as 'mind', though it could also be translated in particular contexts as 'passion, temper, mood'. Godden uses passages from the *Maxims*, *Order*, and *Precepts* to document localizations of the mind in the 'heort', 'breost-', or 'hreþer'. The word 'mod' signifies not a location or centre of consciousness but something more like an inner passion or wilfulness, an intensification of the self that can be dangerous (thus *Maxims I* line 50 and *Gifts* lines 70b–1a).

328   **Howe, Nicholas.** *The Old English Catalogue Poems.* Anglistica 23. Copenhagen: Rosenkilde, 1985. 208 pp.

Howe seeks to explain various Old English poems, including *Fortunes*, *Gifts*, *Precepts*, and the *Maxims*, by reference to late classical and medieval catalogues and encyclopaedias. He believes that although current criticism has disavowed organic form, it is still unconsciously influenced by it in its disregard for *Precepts*, *Fortunes*, *Gifts*, and similar poems. A more historically-oriented criticism would begin with the knowledge that Pliny and Isidore were central figures in the Latin intellectual tradition as it flourished in England. Their influence can be felt in the Exeter Book Riddles, among other places. The poet of *Gifts* sometimes presents the same occupation twice, once in a brief list and once in a more copious catalogue. In *Fortunes*, a formally superior poem, the catalogue form is governed by the experience of conversion. *Precepts* is to some degree organized on an 'ages of man' principle, although the emphasis falls upon the individual precepts. Attempts to find unity or coherent development in *Maxims I* and *II* are bound to be frustrated by the essential function of these texts as collections of sayings that could be free-standing. A length of about seventy lines seems to have been the norm for such collections. Howe canvasses the various translations of 'sceal', resisting the word 'typically' as conducing to platitude. The biblical Book of Proverbs should be read as the most important analogue, if not the source, for these latter three poems.

329   **Page, Raymond I.** *Anglo-Saxon Aptitudes.* An Inaugural Lecture delivered before the University of Cambridge on 6 March 1985. Cambridge: Cambridge UP, 1985. 30 pp.

Page discusses the translation of *Maxims I* line 81 'cyning sceal mid ceape cwene gebicgan', pointing out that propagandists can easily overlook differences in the semantic ranges of Old and Modern English words. The line is not to be literally translated by the notorious aphorism 'a king shall buy a queen with cash', but rather 'a king must pay for the privilege of a marriage contract with his queen', which puts Anglo-Saxon man in his proper place. Ample evidence exists that money paid for a wife was held on her behalf, to guarantee her financial security in marriage. Commenting on Exeter Book Riddle 77 line 5, Page notes that in all cases where *fretan* 'eat' is used of people, it implies behaviour that is bestial, unpleasant, evil, or improper.

330   **Roberts, Jane.** 'A Preliminary "Heaven" Index for Old English.' *Sources and Relations: Studies in Honour of J.E. Cross.* Ed. Marie Collins, Jocelyn Price, and Andrew Hamer. *Leeds Studies in English* NS 16 (1985): 208–19.

Roberts makes brief mention of *Order* and *Vainglory* in the course of her discussion of a thesaurus project on Roget number 971 'heaven'.

Anderson, James E. *Two Literary Riddles in the Exeter Book. Riddle 1 and the Easter Riddle: A Critical Edition with Full Translations.* Norman, OK: U of Oklahoma P, 1986. xxii + 282 pp.

Anderson considers that, like many other medieval collections, the Exeter Book was probably assembled on some more or less definite but unstated plan. He seeks to uncover two portions of that plan. The first group of poems borders on the Riddles and the second interrupts them. The latter group, which Anderson terms 'The Easter Riddle', consists of *The Wife's Lament, Judgement Day I, Resignation, Descent into Hell, Almsgiving, Pharaoh, Lord's Prayer I, Homiletic Fragment II*, Riddle 30b, *The Husband's Message*, and *The Ruin*. Although *Homiletic Fragment II* would deserve little notice for itself it gives to the 'Easter Riddle' a quiet moment of doctrinal preparation for the events at hand (136). A Trinitarian argument is concealed in the poem, which moves humankind from the last darkness of Easter exile to the 'ordfruma ealles leohtes' of line 20 (138). Both variants of Riddle 30 tell a great deal about the riddler's method of composition. In this case he has done almost wholesale borrowing, making deceptively few and minor changes in the text (138). The riddle is to be solved as 'fire' (i.e. 'Easter fire'): the kiss in the riddle is the 'Pax Domini'.

Bammesberger, Alfred. *Linguistic Notes on Old English Poetic Texts.* Anglistische Forschungen 189. Heidelberg: Winter, 1986. 124 pp.

Bammesberger agrees with Robinson (**617**) on 'soð bið swicolost' in *Maxims II* line 10 and on the need generally to defend manuscript readings. All the same, editors should reckon with a special category of easily-identified textual corruption, caused by glossatorial insertions. As to *Maxims I* lines 54–5, it is extremely unlikely that just these two half-lines would have been preserved, when generally the poem exhibits quite regular alliterating lines. Robinson (**580**) is therefore justified in taking lines 54–5 as one line and in proposing the emendation 'sund'. The translation should read 'as the sea is serene, when the ocean does not wake her up, so are the people agreeable when they have become reconciled' (72). Possibly 'some commentator thought the original reading *sund* needed some kind of explanation and added *wind* as an interlinear gloss roughly indicating one possible source of commotion on the sea' (72). In *Leiden Riddle* line 13, 'anoegun' must represent an original reading 'anoegu' ('dread').

Burrow, J.A. *The Ages of Man: A Study in Medieval Writing and Thought.* Oxford: Clarendon, 1986. xi + 211 pp.

Burrow cites *Maxims II* lines 10–12 as documentation of the Anglo-Saxon assumption that true wisdom will come only with advancing years (107). *Precepts*, like some other wisdom poems, is founded on a knowledge of transience and on a pattern of the old instructing the young (108).

334 Chance, Jane. *Woman as Hero in Old English Literature.* Syracuse, NY: Syracuse UP, 1986. xi + 156 pp.

Chance briefly surveys material on the *ides* in OEW poetry, emphasizing *Maxims I* and *II*, Exeter Book Riddles, and *Fortunes* (1–11). She also makes passing mentions of this genre elsewhere in the book.

335 Diller, Hans Jürgen. 'Wortbedeutung und literarische Gattung: Ein Versuch am Beispiel von ae. *wlanc.*' *Gattungsprobleme in der anglo-amerikanischen Literatur: Beiträge für Ulrich Suerbaum zu seinem 60. Geburtstag.* Ed. Raimund Borgmeier. Tübingen: Niemeyer, 1986. 1–11.

Diller investigates the possibility that different usages of the word *wlanc* point to differences of genre in the poems that contain this word. His specific comments include Exeter Book Riddles, *Rune Poem*, and *Vainglory* (8–9).

336 Duncan, Edwin. 'Chronological Testing and the Scansion of *frea* in Old English Poetry.' *Neuphilologische Mitteilungen* 87 (1986): 92–101.

Scansion of all the Old English verses containing *frea* demonstrates that the presence of disyllabic *frea* is neither a reliable chronological test nor an example of poetic licence. Rather, the word was apparently governed by its syntactic environment. It assumed monosyllabic form unless it occurred as the second element of a compound or as a separate word following a possessive pronoun. Thus the disyllabic appearance of the word in undatable poems such as *Maxims I* does not by itself give us any assurance of an early date of composition. Line 90b in this poem, 'to frean hond', is grammatically incorrect (dative/instrumental case is required after *to*) and should be emended to 'to frean honda'. In Exeter Book Riddle 91, line 6b is metrically deficient.

337 Kossick, S.G. 'Gnomic Verse and Old English Riddles.' *UNISA English Studies* 24.2 (1986): 1–6.

Kossick sees gnomic poems such as *Maxims II* as exhibiting some poetic qualities. Among them are a lively interest in the world around us and a refreshing wonder at the ways of nature. In *Maxims I* lines 39–45 she sees man's physical condition used to parallel his spiritual state. That chess was regarded as a game with the capacity to soothe frayed tempers is apparent from *Fortunes* line 70, *Gifts* line 73b, and *Maxims I* lines 181–3. Kossick proposes, however, that the primary significance of gnomic verse is as a source of traditional material for other poets. The poet of *The Seafarer*, for instance, re-uses *Maxims I* line 35 in such a way as to infuse it with new artistic vitality. In a separate section, Kossick emphasizes the lyric quality of the Exeter Book Riddles. Inherent in them is an impulse to know, explore, and wonder at the intrinsic and sometimes paradoxical attributes of natural and man-made phenomena. Such an impulse is surely the progenitor of all poetry.

338 Rissanen, Matti. ' "Sum" in Old English Poetry.' *Modes of Interpretation in Old English Literature: Essays in Honour of Stanley B. Greenfield.* Ed. P.R. Brown, G.R. Crampton, and Fred C. Robinson. Toronto: U of Toronto P, 1986. 197–228.

OEW poems, e.g. Exeter Book Riddle 47, are included among the illustrations of the use of *sum*. It probably carries stress in *Fortunes* line 10 and *Gifts* lines 106–7 (203). The structure of the lengthy passages built on *sum* in these two poems is compared with that of passages from *The Wanderer, Death of Alfred*, and other poems. Wherever this structure occurs, 'fortunes' and 'gifts' are staple themes (204–12). The use of *sum* in *Rune Poem* is also briefly discussed (217–18). Exceptional uses of *sum* in the Riddles and *Solomon and Saturn* are noted (224).

Schneider, Karl. 'On Camouflaged Paganism in Anglo-Saxon England.' *Sophia Lectures on Beowulf. . .* Ed. Shoichi Watanabe and Norio Tsuchiya. Tokyo: Taishukan for the Japan Science Society, 1986. 199–232.

By 'camouflaged paganism' Schneider means the survival of pagano-religious concepts under deliberate disguise in an intolerant Christian society. An instance of such obfuscation appears in Exeter Book Riddle 19: Schneider argues that the subject is speaking in line 1 and that the solution should therefore be 'the sun', since it is the sun that sees what is reported in the text. He explains the posited runic 'wegar' as 'woe spear', a spear used in a primitive Germanic sacrificial cult, to which the text of the Riddle as a whole covertly alludes. The poet of the Exeter Book Riddles must have been a pagan for part of his life. Later, as a Christian, he could only refer to the pagan cults and interpretations of the runes if he devised a harmless surface solution. Schneider adopts a similar approach to metrical Charm 9. He analyses *Maxims I* lines 71–80a as a multiply structured sequence of nine runes with the Primary God as focal point. Similarly, the opening of *Maxims II* (lines 1–13) reveals itself as a complete multiply structured special sequence of 24 runes. This latter sequence is not identical with the futhark but is rather a poetic transformation of an Old English runic calendar.

Wright, Charles D. ' "Insulae gentium": Biblical Influence on Old English Poetic Vocabulary.' *Magister Regis: Studies in Honor of Robert Earl Kaske.* Ed. Arthur Groos et al. New York: Fordham UP, 1986. 9–21.

Wright investigates occurrences of *ealand/igland* in the sense of 'land bordering on water' in *Solomon and Saturn* line 1 and *Maxims I* line 15. These passages are influenced by the use of Latin *insula* to translate a Hebrew word which covers the semantic range 'island, coastland, distant land'. The so-called 'Table of Nations', in which we find the reference to the 'insulae gentium' of Gen. 10: 5 embedded, has particular relevance to *Maxims I*. This same Biblical association of 'islands' with the unredeemed multitude of heathen nations helps to make sense of the geography of Saturn's opening speech in *Solomon and Saturn*. Solomon was famed in the 'islands' for his riddles and parables; meanwhile Saturn, having traversed the 'islands' in his own bookish way, wishes to match wits against Solomon.

Garavelli, Rossana. 'Il Lessico del Mare nella Poesia Anglo-Sassone.' *Annali Istituto Universitario Orientale di Napoli* Filologia germanica 30–1 (1987–8): 159–214.

This study of vocabulary relating to the sea, ships, sailors, navigation, and kindred topics includes scattered references to unusual lexical items and collocations in *Gifts* lines 53–8 (170 n. 16), Exeter Book Riddle 3 line 19 (167), and *Rune Poem* (189).

342 Hieatt, Constance. 'On Envelope Patterns (Ancient and – Relatively – Modern) and Nonce Formulas.' *Comparative Research on Oral Traditions.* Ed. John Miles Foley. Columbus, OH: Slavica, 1987. 245–58.

Hieatt argues that the useful formulaic unit for Old English verse is likely to be simply the repeated association of the same important lexical items in two or more lines or verses. She points to a remarkably common collocation of *wyrd* and *wendan*, seen for example in *Maxims I* line 9 and *Solomon and Saturn* line 437a (248).

343 Parks, Ward. 'The Traditional Narrator and the "I heard" Formulas in Old English Poetry.' *Anglo-Saxon England* 16 (1987): 45–66.

Parks cites the opening lines of *Vainglory* as a particularly unusual and interesting instance of a reference to the act of narration within the text (54). More generally, the 'I heard' formulas and the concept of the traditional narrator give one direct indication of how the narrative act was perceived by the Anglo-Saxons themselves. An appended table includes OEW poetry, notably Exeter Book Riddles 45, 48, and 67, in its documentation of the formulaic system.

344 Campbell, Jackson J. 'Ends and Meanings: Modes of Old English Poetry.' *Medievalia et Humanistica* NS 16 (1988): 1–49.

In Campbell's view, Old English poetry has developed a format for signalling closure that cuts across the arbitrary genre classifications imposed upon this body of literature by modern criticism. To judge from these typical endings, the preponderant reason for composing poetry in Old English was the salvation of souls. *Homiletic Fragment I* lines 43–7 exemplifies the salvation motif, in association with the 'X mid englum' formula (line 45a). Exhortation (exemplified in *Order*) is also common. *Gifts* is characterized by an envelope pattern, whose middle section could have been either expanded or contracted in other realizations of this poem. *Fortunes* follows a dual pattern. The Exeter Book Riddles have their own variety of terminal formula, though some end abruptly without formula, perhaps as a source of added puzzlement to the would-be solver. *Vainglory* is built on systematic contrasts, closing on a maxim. *Maxims II* exhibits a systematic shift from fact to faith. The final section in *Maxims I* is remarkable for lacking any of the closure motifs identified by Campbell, an indication that looking for unity in this text is futile.

345 Mitchell, Bruce. *On Old English: Selected Papers.* Oxford: Blackwell, 1988. xii + 363 pp.

Brief passing mentions of OEW poems are made in this collection of articles and reviews. Mitchell notes *Vainglory* lines 77–80 as an example of *þæt* being understood at the head of a noun clause (104). He finds it remarkable that the ASPR edition (194) punctuates *Maxims I* lines 184–5a so as to necessitate the translation 'The weary man seldom rows against the wind in a broad ship unless it is running under sail' (335). He instances Kaske's **(852)** allegorical interpretation of Exeter Book Riddle 60 as part of the critical tendency to allegorize everything (336–7).

Strauss, Jürgen. 'Metaphors and the Nominal(ized) Style of Old English Poetry.' *Essays on the English Language and Applied Linguistics on the Occasion of Gerhard Nickel's 60th Birthday.* Ed. Josef Klegraf and Dietrich Nehls. Studies in Descriptive Linguistics 18. Heidelberg: Gross, 1988. 199–205.

Strauss briefly compares Old English riddles and kennings as enigmatic creations enjoyed by the audience (203).

Halsall, Guy. 'Anthropology and the Study of Pre-Conquest Warfare and Society: The Ritual War in Anglo-Saxon England.' *Weapons and Warfare in Anglo-Saxon England.* Ed. Sonia Chadwick Hawkes. Oxford U Committee for Archaeology, Monograph 21. Oxford: Oxford U Committee for Archaeology, 1989. 155–77.

Using citations from metrical Charm 11, *Fortunes*, *Gifts*, and the *Maxims*, Halsall portrays Anglo-Saxon warfare as dominating the lives of the nobility. Some of the war-making he sees as ritual.

Meaney, Audrey L. 'Women, Witchcraft and Magic in Anglo-Saxon England.' *Superstition and Popular Medicine in Anglo-Saxon England.* Ed. Donald G. Scragg. Manchester: Manchester Centre for Anglo-Saxon Studies, 1989. 9–40.

Meaney posits a feminine culture passed on by individual mothers to their daughters. Supernatural powers must originally have been attributed to the 'hægtesse', seen in metrical Charm 4. The long tradition represented by that Charm is shown by its similarity to Babylonian charms. The word 'beræddon' in line 8 is explained as 'brought together by consultation'. A *hægtesse* was probably a local or tribal, perhaps tutelary, deity. Elemental in nature, she could be regarded as sometimes supportive, sometimes hostile. The significance of the actions in Charm 6 is discussed. In Charm 1 an eloquent woman ('cwidol wif', line 65) is envisaged as having the power to negate the charm. Meaney also discusses the thematic linking of women, witchcraft, and sexual promiscuity in *Maxims II* lines 43b–5a, proposing that 'dyrne cræfte' means 'by magic'.

Momma, Haruko. 'The "Gnomic Formula" and Some Additions to Bliss's Old English Metrical System.' *Notes and Queries* NS 36 (1989): 423–6.

Momma posits a new metrical category. Relevant here are lines composed of (1) a main clause with word order Adjective (or Interjection)–Copula–Pronoun and (2) a relative clause introduced by the particle *þe*. An appropriate term for this primarily gnomic category would be the 'Beatitude' formula. It occurs in *Maxims I* (e.g. line 37a: 'eadig bið se þe in his eþle geþihð'), in *Solomon and Saturn*, and elsewhere. *Maxims I* line 59a diverges from this category only in the omission of the copula *bið*, which however is understood from the previous line.

350 Nelson, Marie. *Structures of Opposition in Old English Poems.* Costerus NS 74. Amsterdam: Rodopi, 1989. 195 pp.

Nelson brings speech act theory to bear upon various OEW poems so as to establish 'structures of opposition'. Some of these, she notes, have been recognized under other rubrics by earlier critics. She acknowledges a major debt to Erich Fromm's research on aggressive behaviour (*The Anatomy of Human Destructiveness*, New York: Holt, 1973). His contributions have led to analysis of some of the ways in which Old English poets expressed their thoughts about what it meant to live in a world constituted as a complex structure of oppositions. *Maxims I* moves from J.R. Searle's 'brute fact' to his 'institutional fact' (*Expression and Meaning: Studies in the Theory of Speech Acts*, Cambridge: Cambridge UP, 1979), enabling the poet to demonstrate the desirability of the course of action he is advocating. In *Maxims II* the poet's exploration is based on an opposition between human and divine knowledge so as to move from a firm confidence about the way things should be through to a lesser certainty about the way they are. *Solomon and Saturn* presents riddles and gnomic observations in complementary opposition. *Order* is illuminated by Roy Leslie's distinction between 'explicit and implicit antitheses', supplemented by Nelson's 'apparent antitheses' ('Analysis of Stylistic Devices and Effects in Anglo-Saxon Literature', *Stil- und Formprobleme in der Literatur*, ed. Paul Böckmann, Heidelberg: Winter, 1959, 129–36). By contrast, Huppé's (**270**) notion of an 'ideal/real opposition' is less apposite. The antitheses in the three Old English riddles on the Creation have been enriched by the translator. Nelson also discusses a few of the other Exeter Book Riddles. The metrical Charms use words and specifically the actual sound of the words, along with paronomasia, to combat the causes of disease and death. The effects the performer might have achieved by varying the rhythm and volume of recitation are a matter for speculation.

351 Rowe, Elizabeth Ashman. 'Irony in the Old English and Old Norse Interrogative Situation.' *Neophilologus* 73 (1989): 477–9.

Rowe characterizes the Exeter Book Riddles and *Solomon and Saturn* as exhibiting a brief, to-the-point style of questioning. The blunt wording of Saturn's questions in *Solomon and Saturn* suggests his lowly status. It is a genre characteristic in the comparable Old Norse material (e.g. *Vafþrúðnismál* and *Alvíssmál*) that the controlling interlocutor speaks more politely. In some of the Riddles the riddler has the controlling role. This means that his addresses to the audience, especially when ceremonious, cannot be other than ironic.

352 Robinson, Fred C. 'Old English Poetry: The Question of Authorship.' *American Notes and Queries* NS 3 (1990): 59–64. Repr. in Fred C. Robinson. *The Tomb of Beowulf and other essays on Old English*. Oxford: Blackwell, 1993. 163–9.

The evidence surviving from Anglo-Saxon England and from the Germanic cultures in general suggests that women may have played as much of a role in Anglo-Saxon literary production as they have in the later periods of English literature. Particularly significant for possible female authorship are the Exeter Book Riddles that include references to kneading dough, churning butter, or weaving at a loom [Riddles 45, 54, and 56 respectively]. Similarly, where the *Maxims* are concerned, we might well envisage a woman composing a poem that transmits various kinds of folk wisdom to one's people, especially when that wisdom encompasses a sensitive comment on child-rearing and an account of a Frisian woman welcoming her husband home from the sea.

Sorrell, Paul. 'Oaks, Ships, Riddles and the Old English *Rune Poem.*' *Anglo-Saxon England* 19 (1990): 103–16.

Sorrell seeks to show that the author of *Rune Poem* was drawing on conventions of structure and language associated with the riddle genre in his explication of the runic letter-names. The riddle type termed the 'oak-ship' riddle provides the 'definition' of the *ac* rune (*Rune Poem* lines 77–80). It corresponds most closely, among the various analogues, to the solution of one of the Holme Riddles. The presence of a riddle in a catalogue poem like *Rune Poem* can be paralleled in *Fortunes*, where lines 21–4a read like an answer to a riddle-question, 'What flies without wings?' Sorrell points out a series of general commonalities between *Rune Poem* and the Exeter Book Riddles. He suggests that since the *iar*-rune is a late, non-epigraphic rune, an exotic referent such as 'hippopotamus' is thinkable. Eusebius 53 ('hippopotamus') would constitute a parallel.

Anderson, Earl R. 'The Uncarpentered World of Old English Poetry.' *Anglo-Saxon England* 20 (1991): 65–80.

In passing Anderson suggests that the homology of buildings and natural structures creates ambiguity in Exeter Book Riddle 29 ('moon and sun'). He also investigates architectural vocabulary in *Maxims II* and *Solomon and Saturn*.

Lendinara, Patrizia. 'The World of Anglo-Saxon Learning.' *The Cambridge Companion to Old English Literature.* Ed. Malcolm Godden and Michael Lapidge. Cambridge: Cambridge UP, 1991. 264–81.

Lendinara includes a general survey of OEW poems. She mentions *Fortunes* and *Gifts* as a source of information on Anglo-Saxon skills, crafts, and learning. She uses the example of Exeter Book Riddle 42 to make the general point that although there may be popular or even pagan elements in surviving Old English literature, we must never forget that it has all been transmitted to us through the filter of literate (which means, in effect, Latinate) Christianity. She identifies some elements in *Solomon and Saturn* as being of native, popular origin.

Lerer, Seth. *Literacy and Power in Anglo-Saxon Literature.* Regents studies in medieval culture. Lincoln, NE: U of Nebraska P, 1991. xii + 268 pp.

In his Chapter 3, 'The Riddle and the Book' (97–125), Lerer proposes that the controlling form behind the Exeter Book is the list or catalogue. 'To fit the wonders of Creation or the syllabus of learning on a single page is to construct a list, and the Exeter Book Riddles, read in tandem, make up such a list' (101). Within this list we find strange juxtapositions of the earthly and the imaginary, the sublime and the coarse. The written form is crucial to this endeavour to control Nature upon the page. The process becomes explicit in *Order, Homiletic Fragment II*, and *Solomon and Saturn*, whose metaphors allude to book production. The structures and methods of the Exeter Book Riddles and of other OEW poems, such as *Precepts* and *Vainglory*, employ the techniques of education. The Exeter Book is a vernacular counterpart to the eleventh-century Canterbury compilation known as the 'Cambridge Songs' manuscript, which possibly served as a 'classbook' for instruction in the school or a 'library book' for private reading in the monastery. Close correspondences in the detail of their contents can be observed between these two manuscripts. The annotations on Aldhelm's *Ænigmata* in the Canterbury manuscript shed light on the possible reception of the Exeter Book Riddles. The annotator himself 'becomes a riddler, as his remarks multiply the puzzles in the poem and announce his own skills at cryptography and interpretation' (110). This type of reception is apparent in Riddle 36 and its incorporated encrypted gloss. Allusions to books and reading in Riddle 42 invite the reader to appreciate its literary artistry rather than its mundane solution: interpretation, along with thought itself, is presented as a craft or skill comparable with the specialized technologies of book production.

357 Niles, John D. 'Pagan Survivals and Popular Belief.' *The Cambridge Companion to Old English Literature*. Ed. Malcolm Godden and Michael Lapidge. Cambridge: Cambridge UP, 1991. 126–41.

Niles points to the metrical Charms as evidence for animistic beliefs, not simple superstition. In Charm 12 lines 6–7 the 'wolf's paw, eagle's feather, and eagle's claw' probably allude to tokens of power that the shaman wears or brandishes. Another relict of animism may be present in *Maxims II*, where the wild boar is mentioned in company with two other creatures admired for their fierce independence, the hawk and the wolf. *Rune Poem* contains striking examples of Christian mediation of barbaric lore in the treatment of *tir, os*, and even *Ing*, who is not specifically identified as a god in the poem.

358 O'Keeffe, Katherine O'Brien. *Visible Song: Transitional Literacy in Old English Verse*. Cambridge Studies in Anglo-Saxon England 4. Cambridge: Cambridge UP, 1991. xiv + 204 pp.

In her investigation of the transitional state between orality and literacy, O'Keeffe finds the evidence of formatting, variants, and pointing in the manuscript texts of *Solomon and Saturn* indicative of a scribal reading process which avails itself of oral techniques of reception. The scholarly neglect of this interesting text is to be deplored. Of the diverse editorial policies pursued by Dobbie (**203**) and Menner (**1073**), Menner's is the more historically accurate, though his re-sequencing of the lines is to be resisted. As scribes read familiar formulas, they naturally and quite unconsciously substituted other alliterating words which were also metrically correct. Some of the lexical variants are true alternative readings. The result is a literate analogue of oral transmission by performers and poets. O'Keeffe argues that the runes in the Paternoster section were not intended to be pronounced. The scribe of CCCC 422 seems unperturbed by the generic distinction between verse and prose, treating the two as one text, and perhaps we should emulate him. Exeter Book Riddles 30a and 30b also testify to the scribal reading process. O'Keeffe's discussion of pointing in the Exeter and Vercelli Books includes many references to OEW poems: the differences between Latin and Old English pointing are demonstrated by an analysis of Riddle 40.

Pasternack, Carol Braun. 'Anonymous Polyphony and *The Wanderer*'s Textuality.' *Anglo-Saxon England* 20 (1991): 99–122.

Old English poems are composed of 'movements', which have no one primary context. There can be no fixed definition as to what movements a given text includes and how long or ornamented each movement should be. As examples of 'intertexts' for one movement, Pasternack adduces *Fortunes, Gifts, Christ, Elene* lines 130b–7, and *The Wanderer* lines 80b–4.

Trahern, Joseph B., Jr. 'Fatalism and the Millennium.' *The Cambridge Companion to Old English Literature*. Ed. Malcolm Godden and Michael Lapidge. Cambridge: Cambridge UP, 1991. 160–71.

Trahern discusses the significance of 'wyrd' in *Maxims II* line 5a, 'wyrd bið swiðost', suggesting that it belongs in the catalogue of superlatives which appear to expand upon the statement 'þrymmas syndan cristes myccle' in line 4b. He contrasts the depiction of a stable created world in *Order* with millenarian beliefs in the instability of the world.

The Metrical Charms

ORIENTATION TO RESEARCH

CORPUS OF MATERIAL FOR STUDY

The identification of a coherent corpus of related texts is problematic. The advisability of singling out the few charms that happen to be metrical from the wider collection of Anglo-Saxon medical texts, as done by Wülker (**6**), Leonhardi (**373**), and Dobbie (**203**), has been questioned by Singer (**396**), Storms (**418**), Wright (**427**), and Lendinara (**463**). Grant (**305**) pointed out definitional uncertainties concerning the metrical charms. Lendinara (**463**) alleged that Grendon (**381**) and Storms (**418**) tended to confuse medical recipes with true charms. Nöth (**458**) considered it a mistake to apply modern criteria of physiological or medical efficacy in devising such classifications.

MANUSCRIPTS AND EDITIONS

The manuscript provenances of the metrical charms are shown by Ker (**36**). For a list of editions, complete or partial, see the subject index.

DATING AND MILIEU

There has been widespread feeling that certain of the metrical charms embody early Germanic heathen material, even though in their extant form they show the signs of later Christian interpolation: thus Grimm (**363**), Earle (**88**), Wülker (**16**), Kögel (**106**), Helm (**420**), and Schröder (**422**) on Charm 1, Gummere (**103**) on Charms 1 and 4, Lambert (**410**) on Charm 2, Kennedy (**29**) on Charm 4, Kemble (**66**) on Charms 4 and 8, Zupitza (**367**) on Charm 8, and Ricci (**181**), Stürzl (**430**), Schneider (**431**), and Dolfini (**439**) on the metrical charms in general. Singer (**389**) posited four characteristic Germanic doctrines of medicine but was rebutted by Storms (**418**). Comparative Germanic analyses, e.g. of Charms 2 and 8, include those by Weinhold (**369**), Brie (**374**), Heusler (**166**), and Meissner (**386**). Stuart (**456**) and other scholars have used the charms as a source for the study of the elves and other pre-Christian cult figures. Other scholars, including Brooke (**109**), Payne (**372**), Grendon (**381**), Crawford (**433**), Duckert (**446**), Meaney (**262**), Howard (**462**), Jolly (**479**), Pearsall (**52**), Hill (**457**), and Furlani (**491**), have attempted to locate and explain the charms within the historical Anglo-Saxon period. Richter (**22**) suggested dating to the first half of the eighth century.

SOURCES AND ANALOGUES

Comparative studies have taken scholars in diverse directions. Heusler (**166**) and Bonser (**393**) have spoken for derivation from Finnish magic. Schröder (**422**) compared Charm 1 with Sanskrit, Greek, and Ukrainian analogues. Talbot (**437**) defended the claims of classical medicine, but Allen and Calder found clearer analogues in Germanic and Celtic texts (**320**) than in Latin (**298**). Sims-Williams (**495**) suggested influence from an 'indigenous British magic tradition'. Specific indebtednesses of the charms to Christian learning have been identified by Hill (**440, 461**), Boenig (**475**), and Keefer (**494**). Niles (**467**) linked Charm 1 with early modern English customs.

METRICS

Some scholars have posited genre-specific forms of versification. Malone (**30**) discerned a tradition independent of and freer than classical Old English poetry, but allied to legal verses and to pre-classical end-stopped linear verse. Various attempts have been made to align versification in the Charms with that seen in kindred genres in Old Norse poetry. Zupitza (**367**) divided the metrical portion of Charm 8 into two *fornyrðislag* strophes. Heusler (**170**) pointed out resemblances to *ljóðaháttr* and argued for a special closeness to traditional gnomic aphorisms. Lindquist (**390**) extended this so as to distinguish a special *galdr* verse-form from the more familiar *ljóðaháttr*. Holthausen (**404**) attempted to clarify the original *galdralag* by restoring the versification in Charm 2, with endorsement from Magoun (**405**) but disapproval from Storms (**418**).

STRUCTURE

Attempts have been made to define a generic structure for the charms. Ramat (**450**) proposed a formal definition of 'charm' as a text in which each of the two elements 'myth' and 'praxis' must be represented. Wardale (**26**) found a tripartite form to be standard. Van der Leeuw (**403**) focused upon the so-called 'epic introduction', motivating it by analysing the psychology of the process, but with rebuttal from Chickering (**444**). Considerable debate has also centred on the status of individual texts. Horn (**392**) and Kögel (**106**) doubted the integrity of Charm 4, though with dissension from Dobbie (**203**) and Hauer (**460**). Composite origins for Charms 6 and Charm 8 were suggested by Dobbie (**203**) and Fife (**436**) respectively. By contrast, the essential unity of Charm 8 was defended by Spamer (**464**) and Hamp (**470**), who laid emphasis on the discourse structure. Schneider (**441**) analysed Charm 12 as consisting of two strophes of six lines. As to Charm 2, Malone (**30**) suggested that it might always have been in a state of disorder, whereas Giraudi (**466**) proposed a restoration of the structure. Bloomfield (**435**) compared the form of *Deor* to that of a broadly comparative range of charms, notably Charm 4.

PERFORMANCE

Debate has persisted as to the identity of the performers and the mode of performance. As to possible performers, Ward and Waller (**20**) deduced from Charm 1 that the gift of song could extend to the 'plough-lad'. Similarly, Anderson (**32**) saw the charms as used by ignorant churls. Nelson (**480**) sought to demonstrate that Charm 6 might have been successfully used by a pregnant woman. Other scholars have opted for a more specialist type of performer. Kittredge (178) connected some charms with practices of witchcraft. Heusler (166) attributed Charm 2 to a female herbalist. Rathe (473) saw the *scop* of Charms 1 and 9 as a priest-poet who led sacral dances. Glosecki (492) connected the charms with shamanistic utterances. Niles (357) suggested that in Charm 12 the 'wolf's paw, eagle's feather, and eagle's claw' probably allude to tokens of power used by the shaman. The 'Garmund' mentioned in Charm 9 has attracted attention and varying explanations: Wyatt (153) saw him as a locally recognized magician, who invented the charm; Magoun (406) argued that the name 'Garmund' could be replaced with the name of the priest actually officiating at the time; and Kellermann (232) interpreted the description of Garmund as 'godes ðegen' as testifying to a primitive Germanic view of the gods. As to mode of performance, Brie (379) offered a general discussion of the ways in which the charms might have been delivered. According to Hälsig (382), they were mumbled or muttered, not sung, with actions and body language playing an important part. As to the instructions prefacing the charms, Charm 4 has attracted particular comment. Skemp (383) considered that the knife mentioned there was used to smear the salve on the patient, but according to Horn (392) the extant instructions deviate from the original practice of the healer.

EFFICACY

Considerable debate has persisted as to what ailments and evils particular charms were intended to combat. To mention one example, the Chadwicks (183) and Page (271) proposed that Charm 4 might have been directed against respectively sunstroke and rheumatism. Much work has gone into reconstructing the logic of the proposed remedies. Cockayne (365) emphasized superstition, although he conceded that the charms would have had a placebo effect. Singer (389), Storms (418), and other scholars likewise emphasized the irrational and magical elements. As to the specific magical processes, Barley (278) used Charm 2 to show that although some remedies work on the basis of 'unlike negates unlike', there is also evidence of 'like affects like'. Taylor (448) argued for the importance of 'fetter charms', designed as a defence against forces that debilitate natural processes. Other scholars have attempted to show that a rational element also exists. Hill (457) suggested that Charm 1 might have had some practical good effect in introducing 'uncuþ sæd' to the farmer's inventory. Cameron (486) argued for the efficacy of particular herbs and preparations. More generally, Robinson (7) believed that the charms would have been efficacious in their Anglo-Saxon cultural context. A good deal of comparatively recent work has focused on the power of the text itself. Magoun (407) located the powers of the exorcist in the words used. Foley (469) concentrated on the crucial importance of sound in comparing Old English and Yugoslav verbal magic. Nelson (478) accorded importance to both the constituent sounds of the words and the speech acts embodied in the text; cf. Nelson (306) and Foley (312). Frank (281) pointed to a quasi-magical function of paronomasia in Charm 8.

LITERARY CRITICISM

Because earlier scholars concentrated on the utilitarian aspects, purely formalist and aesthetic study of the metrical charms was uncommon until recent decades. The differences from other forms of Anglo-Saxon poetry received attention from Krackow (**118**), who found the charms closer than *Beowulf* to the vernacular, and Heusler (**166**), who noted that in style, as in prosody, Charm 1 is much closer to gnomic poetry than to epic. On the aesthetic front, Anderson (**31**) thought 'one should no doubt relegate such manifestations of the older order to the anthropologist', but conceded that 'the spirit which prompts these manifestations is also the spirit which produces Old English literature'. For Vaughan-Sterling (**476**) scholarly energy expended in anthropological approaches has diverted attention from the very close connection between the charms and other Anglo-Saxon poetry. Damico (**468**) used Charm 4 in an expressly literary study of the Valkyries. Some charms have been analysed as literary pieces. Jongeboer (**477**) argued that Charm 8 represents a literary adaptation of an earlier real charm and, similarly, Stuart (**471**) suggested that although Charm 11 belongs to the same genre as the Middle High German *Reisesegen* it contains elaborately and sensitively wrought images not to be expected in a merely functional charm. For Amies (**474**) Charm 11 may apply to allegorical journeys through life or even the journey of souls after death.

BIBLIOGRAPHY

1 Rask, Rasmus Kristian. *Angelsaksisk Sproglære tilligemed en Kort Læsebog.* Stockholm: Wiborg, 1817. 168. Trans. Benjamin Thorpe. *A Grammar of the Anglo-Saxon Tongue with a Praxis by Erasmus Rask.* . . Copenhagen: Möller, 1830. lx + 224 pp. Rev. edn. London: Trübner, 1865. vi + 191 pp.

The reader includes an annotated text of Charm 1, at 148 in the 1817 edition and at 189–92 in the 1830 (English) edition.

2 Thorpe, Benjamin. *Analecta Anglo-Saxonica: A selection, in prose and verse, from Anglo-Saxon authors of various ages: With a glossary. Designed chiefly as a first book for students.* London: John and Arthur Arch, 1834. xii + 268 pp. Rev. edn. London: John Russell Smith, 1868. xii + 303 pp.

In his Preface Thorpe advocates study of Anglo-Saxon as an aid to the study of English. Knowledge of Old English would help to improve the standard of writing and act as a corrective against an excessive emphasis on Greek and Latin in schools. Thorpe objects to Latin loanwords and hybrid words in English. In the Old English language he sees the strength of iron, with the sparkling and the beauty of burnished steel. His selected works include an edition of Charm 1 from the manuscript (116–19), without notes or introduction.

3 Grimm, Jacob L.K. *Deutsche Mythologie.* 2 vols. Göttingen: Dieterich, 1835. 4th rev. edn. Ed. Elard Hugo Meyer. 3 vols. Berlin: Dümmler, 1875–8. Graz: Akademische Druck- und Verlagsanstalt, 1953. Trans. James Stallybrass. *Teutonic Mythology.* 4 vols. London: Bell, 1880–4. New York: Dover, 1966.

The Stallybrass translation, to which references are keyed in the following abstract, comprises Grimm's second edition (1844) and appendix to the first edition (1835), together with a posthumous supplement compiled by E.H. Meyer. Included are texts and translations of Charm 1 (3.1236–40) and Charm 4 (3.1243–5), along with a text of Charm 7 (3.1245). Grimm interprets Charm 1 as designed to recuperate land that has been laid waste by magic. Even though Christian ceremonies have crept into this Charm, it appears to reach far back to the early times of heathen sacrifices and husbandry. Swedish and German partial analogues are cited (3.1238–9). The phrase 'eorþan modor' in line 51 refers not to the earth herself but to her mother. The word 'erce' (also line 51) should perhaps be linked with German proper names such as Herke or Harke, denoting a woman who flies through the country dispensing earthly goods in abundance (1.253–4). Restorations to the text of Charm 4 are suggested (3.1243–5). The conjunction of 'esa gescot' and 'ylfa gescot' in line 23 is compared with the combination 'æsir' and 'álfar' in the *Poetic Edda* (1.25). Charm 4 is also mentioned in connection with a discussion of 'elfshot' (2.460). Charm 8 is mentioned briefly, with explanation of 'sigewif' in line 9 as the general designation of all wise-women (1.431 and 3.1245). *Solomon and Saturn* is referred to in passing, as contributing to the evidence for Saturn as a Germanic god (1.247 n. 1)

364 Wright, Thomas, and Phillipps James Orchard Halliwell. *Reliquiae Antiquae: Scraps from ancient Manuscripts illustrating chiefly early English Literature and the English Language.* 2 vols. London: Pickering, 1841–3.

Volume 2 (237–8) contains an edition of Charm 4: text only is supplied, without translation or notes.

365 Cockayne, Oswald. *Leechdoms, Wortcunning and Starcraft of early England, being a Collection of Documents, for the most part never before printed, illustrating the History of Science in this Country before the Norman Conquest.* 3 vols. London: Longman, 1864–6. Rev. edn. with a new introduction by Charles Singer. London: Holland, 1961. New York: Kraus, 1965.

Cockayne supplies Old English texts and translations as follows:- Charm 11: 1.388–90; Charm 10: 1.390–2; Charm 1: 1.398–400; Charm 7: 2.350–2; Charm 2: 3.30–8; Charm 3: 3.42; Charm 4: 3.52–4; Charm 5: 3.60; Charm 6: 3.66–8. In his preface he emphasizes that the Charms were founded on superstition, although he concedes that they would have had a placebo effect. He places Anglo-Saxon medicine in a Classical context, noting that Greek medicine likewise embodied much irrationality. The Church in Anglo-Saxon England found itself unable to root out these superstitious and rarely beneficial ideas. Instead it tried to fling a garb of religion round them, invoking holy names to drive out devils by exorcisms. In his revised edition, Singer omits some of Cockayne's original material, in particular the index and the prefaces to each of the three volumes, as being misleading in the present state of knowledge. The new introduction contains a brief account of Cockayne's life and contributions to philology, along with an account of developments in the study of early English science and medicine since Cockayne's time. As to specific Charms, Singer discusses a separate *Lay of the Nine Darts of Woden*, which he sees as beginning with the words (in translation) 'These nine darts against nine venoms' (Charm 2 line 30) and ending 'against the crimson venom' (line 51).

66 Birch, Walter de Gray. 'On two Anglo-Saxon Manuscripts in the British Museum.' *Transactions of the Royal Society of Literature* 11 (1875): 463–512.

Birch prints Charm 12 for the first time, pointing out that it 'partakes more of the nature of a *charm* than of a medicine, and many such will be found in the appendix to my new edition of Kemble's "Saxons in England" volume 1' **(66)** (484–6).

67 Zupitza, Julius. 'Ein verkannter englischer und zwei bisher ungedruckte lateinische Bienensegen.' *Anglia* 1 (1878): 189–95.

Zupitza characterizes earlier scholarly treatments of Charm 8, except for Cockayne's **(365)**, as bedevilled by errors and misunderstandings. The metrical portion of the text divides into two *fornyrðislag* strophes. The Charm is intended to be spoken by the owner of a new swarm who fears that his bees may be stolen from him by supernatural means. The compound 'sigewif' appropriately describes the bees, whose belligerence is attested in one of the Latin analogues cited by Zupitza. The close similarity of Charm 8 to these analogues suggests that the Anglo-Saxons brought it to England from their continental homeland.

68 ———. 'Ein Zauberspruch.' *Zeitschrift für deutsches Altertum* 31 (1887): 45–52.

Zupitza corrects errors in the text and lineation of Birch's **(366)** edition of Charm 12. His text is accompanied by a German translation. The notes provide a detailed discussion of individual difficulties in the text. He catalogues other, non-metrical, charms against wens. A full linguistic analysis of the text is also included.

69 Weinhold, Karl. 'Die mystische Neunzahl bei den Deutschen.' *Abhandlungen der königlichen Akademie der Wissenschaften, Berlin, philologisch-historische Abhandlungen* 2 (1897): 1–61.

Weinhold deals with the metrical Charms in passing (20 and 34). He discusses traditions of a set of nine herbs that ensure protection and health, with documentation from different regions of Germany and further comparative material from Sweden and other countries. Included here is Charm 2. Other instances of the number 'nine', for instance in Charm 1, are also considered.

70 Ebermann, Oskar. *Blut- und Wundsegen in ihrer Entwickelung dargestellt.* Palaestra 24. Berlin: Mayer, 1903. x + 147 pp.

Ebermann surveys charms concerned with blood and wounds, from early Germanic texts down to the present day. In his opinion, Charm 7 is not indebted to Latin for its characteristically paired structure, which is better seen as conforming to the alliterative style of Germanic heroic poetry. He compares the women in Charm 4 with female figures in other charms.

371   **Bradley, Henry.** 'The Song of the Nine Magic Herbs (Neunkräutersegen).' *Archiv für das Studium der neueren Literaturen* 113 (1904): 144–5.

Bradley seeks to explain some obscurities in Charm 2, while admitting that the poem is probably, like most compositions of its type, not capable of being completely explained. He sees 'Regenmeld-' as a place-name, noting the occurrence of a Northumbrian personal name *Rægenmæld*, where *mæld-* = *mæðel*. He defends, though with a query, the explanation of 'wergulu' as 'nettle'. Cockayne (365) and Wülker (6) have, in his opinion, confused the order in which the nine herbs are named. The word 'onge/onga' should be identified with Old Norse *anga* 'shoot, sprout'. In other detailed explanations, he posits a compound 'færbregde' ('sudden stratagem') in line 43 and emends 'minra' in line 44 to 'manra'.

372   **Payne, Joseph F.** *English Medicine in the Anglo-Saxon Times.* Fitzpatrick Lectures for 1903. Oxford: Clarendon, 1904. vi + 162 pp.

In the course of expounding a seven-fold classification of the Anglo-Saxon charms, Payne discusses Charm 2 (138–41). He finds this text notable for its mingling of beliefs and different kinds of learning: paganism, Christianity, and classical botany. Such a blend is characteristic of Old English medicine. The form or contents of a charm do not always enable us to decide whether it originated in folklore or in borrowed learning. A great deal of so-called folk medicine is old-fashioned standard medicine which has sunk down to the level of the unlearned. Payne elaborates on the characteristics of folk medicine and on botanical references in the charms.

373   **Leonhardi, Günther.** *Kleinere angelsächsische Denkmäler I.* Bibliothek der angelsächsische Prosa 6. Hamburg: Grand, 1905.

This edition is based on a collation of Cockayne's text (365) with the manuscript. For comments on Charms 2 and 7 see 137 and 107 respectively. The entirety of Charm 7 but only the prose of Charm 2 is included. The notes are restricted to editorial and phonological questions. The introduction and promised glossary never appeared.

374   **Brie, Maria.** 'Der germanische, insbesondere der englische Zauberspruch.' *Mitteilungen der schlesischen Gesellschaft für Volkskunde* 16 (1906): 1–36.

In this broad discussion of the content and formal taxonomy of the Charms Brie compares the Old English material with other Germanic metrical charms. She finds the relationship of the Old English Charms with their German and Norwegian counterparts particularly close. The three traditions rest on a common base of superstitious beliefs, including a belief in the magic powers of the word, which may be written as well as spoken. She traces the history of charms in England, with reference to modern analogues, using Charm 8 as an example. The influence of the Christian liturgy on, for instance, Charm 2 is emphasized. The phrase 'wyrta modor' in this charm represents an Old English rendering of Latin 'mater herbarum'. The Charms exploit a wide variety of different tones and rhetorical approaches – flattering, wheedling, threatening, and so forth. Brie contrasts what she regards as the fully developed epic introduction in Charm 4 with the less elaborate introductions in the non-metrical charm [Grendon (**381**) B5] 'ic benne awrat'. The three lines (20–2) in Charm 4 on the pattern 'gif þu wære on X scoten' should be regarded as an interpolation. She discusses the power of earth in Charm 8, citing more recent parallels and analogues. Charm 11 exemplifies the difficulties inherent in reaching a classification of charms. Charm 12 is cited as evidence that the spirit of the disease was here envisaged as a small feathered being, suggesting a parallel with Charm 3. The other metrical Charms are mentioned in passing.

5   Schlutter, Otto B. 'Anglo-Saxonica.' *Anglia* 30 (1907): 123–34.

This continuing series of notes is intended as a contribution to Old English lexicography. Schlutter's collection of rare items and *hapax legomena* includes the hypothetical '*herse' ('millet'), which he arrives at via an emendation in Charm 1 line 55. This should read 'sceafta scira hersewæstma', where the last word would mean 'millet crop', or alternatively 'sceafta herses, scire wæstma' (125–8). Schlutter concedes that the cultivation of millet in England may not go back to Anglo-Saxon times.

6   ———. 'Anglo-Saxonica.' *Anglia* 30 (1907): 239–60.

These notes expand from a discussion of Old English *hama* in Charm 3 to an edition of the Charm (257–8). Schlutter conjecturally restores line 12. He understands 'geændade' in line 14 as 'ended [the healing process]'.

7   Holthausen, Ferdinand. 'Zur altenglischen literatur VI. 22. Ein frühmittelengl. zauberspruch.' *Anglia Beiblatt* 19 (1908): 213–15.

Holthausen attempts to refine on Zupitza's (**368**) publication of Charm 12. He emends 'ermig' to 'erming' in line 4, 'earnes' to 'earmes' in lines 6 and 7, and 'scesne' to 'scerne' (= Old English *scearn*) in line 9. He explains 'chichenne' as meaning 'child' and compares the diminutive *nessiklinon* in the Old High German charm 'contra vermes'. Like Zupitza, he sees the extant texts of Charm 12 as modernizations of an originally Old English text.

8   Schlutter, Otto B. 'Anglo-Saxonica.' *Anglia* 31 (1908): 55–71.

Beginning with a citation of *circian* 'circle' from Charm 11 line 36, Schlutter attempts to improve on Cockayne's (**365**) edition. He suggests construing 'sigere' in line 33 as an adverb, 'victoriously', and 'circian' as a by-form of the verb *cierran* 'turn'. He argues for the standard meaning of 'heofna rices' in line 41, as an obvious improvement on Cockayne's 'the mighty one of heaven'. He objects to the phrase 'swa swa ic gehyrde' (line 12) as an apparent qualification of the power of the Almighty verging on blasphemy. The article ends with a complete text (and translation) of the Charm, arranged as prose.

9   Brie, Maria. 'Über die ags. bezeichnung des wortes Zauberer.' *Englische Studien* 41 (1909): 20–7.

Brie discusses the term *gealdor* and the ways in which the charms might have been delivered (singing, declaiming, etc.). She suggests that a proposed derivation of *hægtesse* and its cognates from a word meaning 'derision', 'scorn' would appropriately account for the adjective 'hlude' in Charm 4 line 3.

380 Golther, Wolfgang. *Religion und Mythus der Germanen.* Leipzig: Deutsche Zukunft, 1909. 115 pp.

Golther quotes briefly from Charm 1 in the course of a discussion of Germanic cults (24).

381 Grendon, Felix. 'The Anglo-Saxon Charms.' *Journal of American Folklore* 22 (1909): 105–237. Repr. in book form. New York: Stechert, 1930.

This work comprises a text and translation of all the metrical charms and many of the prose charms, with full introduction, very detailed notes, and select bibliography. The text embodies various suggested emendations and restorations. After a review of the manuscripts and previous editions, translations, and scholarship, Grendon proceeds to identify and exemplify distinct characteristics which severally appear in a certain number of the charms: narrative introductions, an appeal to a superior spirit, the writing or pronouncing of potent names or letters, methods of dealing with disease demons, the exorcist's boast of power, ceremonial directions to patient and exorcist, the singing of incantations on parts of the body and on other objects, statement of time for the performance of rites, sympathy and the association of ideas, and minor superstitious practices (110). Parallels from Vedic, Old High German, and other literatures are cited and references are made to relevant examples from, *inter alia*, the Old English metrical Charms. A reference to Wayland the smith is suggested in Charm 4 (112). Invocations of the Seven Sleepers and other foreign names are 'permissible substitutes for the heathen appellations' (114). The 'water-elf' in Charm 7 can be related to Anglo-Saxon beliefs in spirits who 'haunted' brooks, rivers, and streams, and might be helpful or harmful (120). In Charm 8 the word 'sigewif' coaxingly addresses the evil spirits possessing the swarming insects (115). Grendon groups the charms (verse and prose) into five categories: (A) exorcisms of diseases or disease spirits, (B) herbal charms, (C) charms for transferring disease, (D) amulet charms, and (E) charm remedies. This grouping becomes the basis for an enumeration system, where A1 corresponds to the ASPR's (**203**) Charm 4, A2 to Charm 3, A3 to Charm 12, A4 to Charm 8, A13 to Charm 1, A14 to Charm 11, A16 to Charm 9, A21 to Charm 10, A22 to Charm 5, B4 to Charm 2, B5 to Charm 7, and E1 to Charm 6. Two charms lineated (as possessing some verse characteristics) but not included in ASPR are A9 'Neogone wæran Noðþæs sweoster' (170) and A15 (180). Herbal charms can be divided into those used while gathering herbs and those used preparatory to applying them medicinally, such as Charms 2 and 7 (128). Grendon seeks to locate the Charms in a context of Anglo-Saxon law and religion, arguing that their 'easy persistence' is attributable to the 'credulity of the clergy' (144), combined with the conciliatory policy of the missionaries (145). He traces the processes by which Christian elements came to be substituted for heathen in the Charms, for instance in the epic introductions, with special attention to Charm 1 (155–6). The introduction and notes mention many analogues in later folklore. [For reviews see Skemp, **384**; Binz, **385**; Klaeber, **401**.]

82 Hälsig, Friedrich. *Der Zauberspruch bei den Germanen bis um die Mitte des XVI Jahrhunderts.* Diss. U Leipzig. Leipzig: Seele, 1910. xi + 110 pp.

Hälsig organizes the material into three main chapters: (1) Types and formal characteristics of the charms (1–21); (2) Charms in Latin and various Germanic languages analysed according to content, with selected examples cited from printed sources and with a comprehensive list of these sources (22–74); (3) Special groups of charms (75–107). A bibliography is also included (vii–xi). A broadly comparative discussion in Chapter 1 is prefaced by the statement that charms can be distinguished depending on whether they ward off future harm (as with Charm 12), or counter present harm, or serve prophetic functions (2–3). Hälsig stresses the importance of action and body language in the performance of charms, citing the instructions in Charms 1 and 4. As examples of direct commands within charms, he cites passages from Charms 4 and 8. The 'epic introduction' is explained as a comparatively late development, influenced by oriental practices and a diminishing faith in demonic powers. The formula of command is the primary element and indeed was originally free-standing, despite Schröder (**104**), who postulated an original Indo-European format consisting of a prose core with accompanying metrical formula (10–15). The Charms were mumbled or muttered, not sung. Although the Church tried to eradicate demonic elements from the charms, it was not opposed to magic as such. Hälsig analyses the process of Christian censorship and reconstruction of charms. Old English metrical charms are cited in Chapter 2 as follows (from the text of Grein/Wülker (**6**) unless otherwise indicated): Charm 3 (25–6); Charm 12 (35), cited from Zupitza (**368**); Charm 6 (43); Charm 11 (49–50); Charm 8 (67); and Charm 2 (70–2). Although without annotation or textual analysis, these citations serve to place the Old English material in a comparative context of earlier and later charms. Chapter 3 includes motifs that occur in the Old English metrical Charms, e.g. the Seven Sleepers, but does not bring the Old English texts into the discussion.

83 Skemp, Arthur R. 'The Old English Charms.' *Modern Language Review* 6 (1911): 289–301.

Dissenting from Grendon (**381**), Skemp suggests that Charm 4 is a 'naming' charm: its first aim is to define the evil, and by identifying it to acquire power over it. The direction given at the end of the charm should in fact be applied with each iteration of 'ðis ðe to bote' in lines 25–6. The knife mentioned in the Charm would be used to stroke the salve on to the affected part. The smiths should be identified as elf-smiths, with a transposition of lines 13–15 and line 16. Charm 3 is intended to combat a dwarf in spider garb who engenders a fever-like disorder. Skemp attempts to bring metrical order to the text of Charm 11. The reading 'circinde' in Charm 11 line 36 should be emended to 'cercinde', meaning 'roaring'. In Charm 2 lines 21–2 the use of 'læss-' and 'mar-' can be accounted for on the basis that 'attorlaðe' is stronger than some poisons but weaker than others. The mention of the apple has its background in Tacitus's description of a *frugifera arbor* as a resource for Germanic magic. In line 34 'geændade' means 'accomplished' and 'and' means 'against'.

384 ———. Rev. of *Anglo-Saxon Charms*, by Felix Grendon **[381]**. *Modern Language Review* 6 (1911): 262–6.

Skemp comments on details in Charms 1, 4, 8, and 11, correcting translations and annotations in Grendon.

385 Binz, Gustav. Rev. of *Anglo-Saxon Charms*, by Felix Grendon **[381]**. *Anglia Beiblatt* 27 (1916): 161–3.

Pointing out that Grendon's contribution is not textual but chiefly folkloristic and concurring with Skemp's **(384)** criticisms, Binz adds notes and conjectures on Charms 1, 2, 3, 4, 5, 10, and 11.

386 Meissner, Rudolf. 'Die Zunge des grossen Mannes.' *Anglia* 40 (1916): 375–93.

In this explication of Charm 8 Meissner proposes linking 'micelan' with 'mannes' in line 6 and taking the phrase as a taboo term for 'bear'. The bear was very widely feared in early European communities; he was often given human or other tabu-names and bear-hunting was attended with special rituals. The word *micel* can only refer to physical size, not to greatness in any intangible sense, unless of God. The motif of binding the tongue through an oath or other supernatural means is illustrated by means of comparative material. Contrary to Grendon **(381)**, the word 'sigewif' refers to the bees, not to evil spirits possessing them. Bees kept near forests were apt to swarm out of reach of the bee-keeper and hence become lost. The throwing of earth protected the bees both in flight and in the hive and kept the honey safe from thieves.

387 ———. 'Zu alt- und mittelenglischen Denkmälern 2. Zum ae. Neunkräutersegen.' *Anglia Beiblatt* 29 (1918): 283–5.

In Charm 2 line 43a 'wið þæs hond' should be emended to 'wið fæcnan/fagan hond', preferably 'fæcnan'. The reading 'frea begde' in line 43b should be treated as a compound and emended to 'frea-bregde' ('great cunning'), with 'frea' to be understood as an intensive (283–4).

388 Holthausen, Ferdinand. 'Zu den altenglischen Zaubersprüchen und Segen.' *Anglia Beiblatt* 31 (1920): 116–20.

Holthausen contributes notes on Charms 1, 2, 4, 5, 6, and 11. In Charm 1 he suggests the restorations 'and þa soþan <mægð>' in line 30, 'sceafta <hehra> scirra wæstma' in line 55, and 'bærlicwæstma' for 'berewæstma' in line 56. In Charm 4 he emends for metre in line 14 and for alliteration in line 24, 'nu ic wille helpan ðin'. The restoration 'fleoh on fyrgenstream þær þu friðu hafast' is suggested for line 27. In Charm 2 line 30 Bradley's **(371)** 'onga' ('sprout') leaves the sentence without a verb: preferable is 'ðas viiii magon wið nygon attrum'. Holthausen understands 'geændade' in line 34 as 'spoke', comparing Exeter Book Riddle 48. Other lines are emended to regularize alliteration. Irregularities in the alliteration in Charm 3 point to corruption. Grendon's **(381)** explanation of 'þihtan' in Charm 6 fails to convince. In Charm 11 'Abrame <gedon>' should be read in line 13a, 'werod' (for 'rof') in line 24, and 'wælgar' in line 30b.

9 **Singer, Charles J.** 'Early English Magic and Medicine.' *Proceedings of the British Academy* 9 (1920): 341–74.

Singer observes that early English magic and medicine have been investigated mainly by philologists interested in Old English language and literature; the documents need to be studied as a whole, whether their language is Latin or Old English, if sources and affinities are to be correctly identified. He posits as one source 'native Teutonic magic and medicine', brought over by the Anglo-Saxons from their continental home. Charm 2 is the 'best specimen' from this source, in that it illustrates three of the four characteristic Germanic doctrines, 'specific venoms', 'the nines', and 'the worm' (the other being 'elf-shot'). He comments specifically on 'the nine twigs that Woden takes up', interpreting them as 'twigs of fate which are to bring a better lot to the sick man on recitation of the magic song'. He sees the custom of uttering a charm against disease to each of the four cardinal points in succession (evidenced by his restored version of Charm 2) as of 'Indo-Germanic origin'. Reminiscent of 'Nordic magic' is the action of blowing away the venom through the power of the incantation. Charm 7 is to be interpreted as a cure for dropsy and to be related to an Anglo-Saxon belief in malicious elves, some of whom may have been personifications of the deadly powers of marshes and water-logged land.

0 **Lindquist, Ivar.** *Galdrar: De gamla germanska trollsångernas stil undersökt i samband med en svensk runinskrift från folkvandringstiden.* Göteborgs Högskolas Årsskrift 29:1. Göteborg: Wettergren, 1923. viii + 193 pp.

Lindquist investigates the formal characteristics of Germanic *galdrar*. He distinguishes a special *galdr* verse-form from the more familiar *ljóðaháttr*. The criteria are alliteration, rhyme, and repetition of a concept. Examples of this *galdralag* are to be traced in Charm 1, where he reconstructs 'bidde ic þone mæran drihten,/ bidde ic þone miclan drihten,/ bidde ic þone haligan heofonrices weard' (27–8). The concluding curse in Charm 4 is also in *galdralag*. Lindquist excises certain half-lines in this charm, e.g. 'ic þin wille helpan', as later interpolations (25–6).

1 **Bonser, Wilfrid.** 'The Significance of Colour in Ancient and Mediaeval Magic, with some Modern Comparisons.' *Man* 25 (1925): 194–8.

Bonser engages in a very broad comparative treatment of, *inter alia*, specific-colour magic, citing Charm 2 as an outstanding example.

2 **Horn, Wilhelm.** 'Der altenglische Zauberspruch gegen den Hexenschuss.' *Probleme der englischen Sprache und Kultur: Festschrift Johannes Hoops zum 60. Geburtstag überreicht von Freunden und Kollegen.* Ed. Wolfgang Keller. Heidelberg: Winter, 1925. 88–104.

Horn regards Charm 4 as consisting of what would originally have been two charms. The break comes at the end of line 19; what follows is not composed in epic style and is therefore to be seen as a separate charm that has become appended to lines 1–19. Of the various weapons mentioned, only the arrow is to be used against the demons who are causing the disease; nevertheless, the knife and the spear would have been used similarly. The instructions have been added to the Charm and do not represent faithfully the original practice of the healer. The employment of the knife to spread the ointment could have occurred only after the original meaning of the Charm had become lost. Horn cites numerous parallels for motifs within the Charm, notably the powers of iron in traditional belief.

393 Bonser, Wilfrid. 'Magical Practices against Elves.' *Folklore* 37 (1926): 350–63.

Bonser uses Charms 3, 4, and 7, along with other evidence, to demonstrate that beliefs concerning the elves were varied and diffuse. He derives the notion of elf-shot from Finnish magic, rather than assuming native Teutonic origin as Singer **(389)** had done. Charm 4 has an analogue in a Finnish charm for stitch which presupposes that the ailment was produced by the agency of marsh-dwelling elves. Charm 3 is discussed in relation to an assortment of traditions on nightmare.

394 Grattan, John H.G. 'Three Anglo-Saxon Charms from the "Lacnunga".' *Modern Language Review* 22 (1927): 1–6.

Grattan suggests translating Charm 4 line 5 'Shield thou thee now; then mayest thou survive this onset.' He restores line 27 to read 'fle<ah> þær on fyrgen<holt>; <fyrst ne> hæfde', 'it hath fled there to the mountains; no respite hath it had.' In Charm 2 he makes various emendations and points out that what had hitherto been printed as eleven lines of prose following line 44 can be emended lightly to produce nineteen alliterative lines. Charm 3 he explains as 'the nightmare charm': he emends to 'inwriðen' in line 1, on the assumption that the incubus took the form of a corpse swathed in its grave-clothes. He explains the female divinity who grants the sufferer immunity as Eastre, the goddess of the dawn and (conjecturally) 'the sister of Ear'.

395 Ohrt, Ferdinand. 'Beiträge zur Segenforschung.' *Zeitschrift des Vereins für Volkskunde* 37 (1927): 1–9.

Ohrt discusses the mention of 'æppel and attor' in Charm 2 line 34b, arguing against Bradley's **(371)**, Wülker's **(6)**, and Grendon's **(381)** explanations of this phrase. He sees it as alluding to the book of Genesis: when God overcame the serpent, the effects of the apple of the Tree of Knowledge and the venom of the Devil came to an end. He also discusses the phrase 'gemyne þu' in line 1, placing it in a comparative context.

396 Singer, Charles J. *From Magic to Science: Essays on the Scientific Twilight.* London: Benn; New York: Boni, 1928. xix + 253 pp. Repr. with an autobiographical preface. New York: Dover, 1958. xxxiv + 253 pp.

The chapter entitled 'Early English Magic and Medicine' represents a somewhat abridged and restructured version of Singer's earlier paper **(389)**. Anglo-Saxon magic is interesting mainly for the evidence that it provides on the mingling of cultures at a very early date and in a simple state of society. Magic is essentially syncretic, passing easily and rapidly from people to people. The diversity of dates and languages to be detected in the texts must not distract us from studying the magic and medicine of early England as a whole. Among the diverse components 'native Teutonic magic and herb-lore' ranks as fourth in importance (on a scale of eight). It can be distinguished from other components by the presence of four characteristic elements: the doctrine of specific venoms, the doctrine of the nines, the doctrine of the worm (as a cause of disease), and the doctrine of elf-shot. Probably this material is ultimately of Indo-European origin and was brought by the Anglo-Saxons from their continental home. Singer illustrates the first three doctrines from Charm 2, adding a detailed explication of the text. He argues that the doctrine of elf-shot became confounded with the Christian idea of attacks from demons and devils.

7 **Holthausen, Ferdinand.** 'Der altenglische Reisesegen.' *Anglia Beiblatt* 40 (1929): 87–90.

Pointing out that the versions of Charm 11 in Wülker (**6**) and Grendon (**381**) are incomplete, Holthausen furnishes an improved edition with some explanatory notes. He restores older linguistic forms and makes some emendations. He withdraws his earlier emendations in lines 24b and 30b (**388**) in favour of (respectively) a new interpretation of manuscript 'rof' and the reading 'wegar', comparing Riddle 19 lines 5–6.

8 **Klaeber, Frederick.** '*Belucan* in dem altenglischen Reisesegen.' *Anglia Beiblatt* 40 (1929): 283–4.

Klaeber replies to Holthausen (**397**), explaining the construction 'Ic me beluce wiþ' at the start of Charm 11 as 'I shut myself off against, protect myself against'. The verb is used with a similar meaning at the end of the Charm (line 39), 'belocun wið þa<m> laþan', and a parallel exists in Psalm 34: 3. Unclear is 'gyrde': it might refer to a staff or stave, on which the sign of the Cross was made. Line 12 should be left unemended, as the end of the sentence, despite Holthausen (**388**).

9 **Holthausen, Ferdinand.** 'Nochmals der altenglische Reisesegen.' *Anglia Beiblatt* 41 (1930): 255.

This is a reply to Klaeber's reply (**398**). Holthausen now believes that 'on þisse gyrde' in Charm 11 line 1 refers to the traveller's staff, not to a cross or rune-stick. Despite Klaeber, the sense of line 12 is that God must assist the traveller, just as he assisted Abraham and others.

0 **Klaeber, Frederick.** Rev. of *Germanisches Heidentum bei den Angelsachsen*, by Ernst Philippson [**180**]. *Englische Studien* 65 (1931): 443–6.

Klaeber notes how little information about Germanic paganism can be derived from Old English poetry. He concedes that the metrical Charms, along with *Beowulf*, are a notable exception.

1 **Klaeber, Frederick.** Rev. of *Anglo-Saxon Charms*, by Felix Grendon [**381**]. *Anglia Beiblatt* 42 (1931): 6–7.

In Charm 1 Klaeber explains the expression 'toðum ontynan' in line 33 as 'remove the hedge/fence of the teeth', i.e. 'utter', comparing the Homeric 'hedge of the teeth'. Charms 2 and 3 are also mentioned.

402 **Naumann, Hans.** *Frühgermanisches Dichterbuch: Zeugnisse und Texte für Übungen und Vorlesungen über ältere germanische Poesie.* Berlin: De Gruyter, 1931. iv + 138 pp.

This reader contains only the Old English text of each of the selections, without notes or glossary. Charm 4 is included (119). The 'Zeugnisse' are Latin texts which shed light on early Germanic poetry.

403 **Van der Leeuw, Gerardus.** 'Die sogenannte "epische Einleitung" der Zauberformeln.' *Zeitschrift für Religionspsychologie* 6 (1933): 161–80.

Van der Leeuw seeks to motivate the so-called 'epic introduction' in the metrical Charms. These texts, whether for healing or (less commonly) for agricultural purposes, frequently include a narration of a relevant past event. He discusses the psychology of the process where such narrations cause the past to be seen as the present and enable the good effects of a spell, once used, to be repeated. In this way the myth comes to form part of the magic ritual. The effect is not simply to invoke an analogy. He documents this theory with analysis and interpretation of the narrative passages from a wide selection of charms, including Charm 4 but also material from a variety of other European countries.

404 **Holthausen, Ferdinand.** 'Die altenglischen Neunkräutersegen.' *Englische Studien* 69 (1934–5): 180–3.

Holthausen supplies a text of Charm 2, along with brief notes. The text is divided into four sections. He restores the versification in lines 5–6. The reading 'ondan' in line 29 is to be explained as an error for 'ondgan', from *ondig*.

405 **Magoun, Francis P., Jr.** 'Strophische Überreste in den altenglischen Zaubersprüchen.' *Englische Studien* 72 (1937–8): 1–6.

Magoun's article is conceived as a supplement to Lindquist (**390**), emphasizing the background of *galdralag* verse form in early Germanic. Magoun cites examples from Old English, among them Charm 1 lines 27–8 and Charm 4 lines 23–6. In the latter case line 22 lies outside the pattern and may represent a composer's afterthought. Other examples are cited from Charms 6, 8, 9, and 11. Holthausen's (**404**) restoration of the versification in Charm 2 lines 5–6 is to be endorsed as clarifying the original *galdralag*.

406 ———. 'Zu den ae. Zaubersprüchen.' *Archiv für das Studium der neueren Literaturen* 171 (1937): 17–35.

Magoun makes some additions and corrections to Grendon (**381**). In Charm 4 line 1 he discusses the phonological development of the word 'feferfuige'. In lines 1–2 he identifies 'reade netele' not with stinging nettle but with the red variant of white dead-nettle ('Taubnessel, der rote Biensaug'), which is often mentioned as a herbal remedy. If we accept that 'ærn' means not 'house' or 'building' but 'growing corn', the phrase as a whole can refer to a type of nettle that grows within the corn crop. In Charm 3 line 13 Grattan's (**394**) explanation of 'deores sweostor' is to be rejected. Charm 12 is preserved in too enigmatic a state for restoration or confident interpretation to be appropriate. The entire reading 'wen chichenne' in line 1 is suspect and perhaps to be restored as 'wende ic heone[ne]'. By 'handwurm' the itchmite is meant. Against Meissner (**386**), Magoun proposes that 'micelan mannes tungan' in Charm 8 line 6 should be understood as 'the powerful tongue of man', that is, a tongue capable of speaking charms and spells. Attempts to link 'erce' in Charm 1 with Irish 'acræ' are to be dismissed. In Charm 9 the name 'Garmund' could be replaced with the name of the priest actually officiating at the time. In Charm 2 'Regenmelde' is a place name, parallel to 'Alorford'; identification of its second element with 'melde' ('proclamation') is misguided. In Charm 7 the prose refers to a different disease from the verse.

7 ———. 'Zum heroischen Exorzismus des Beowulfepos.' *Arkiv för nordisk filologi* 54 (1939): 215–28.

Charms and spells in Old English and Old High German show that the powers of the exorcist lay in the words used, a typical example being 'ut, lytel spere' in Charm 4. The forces of evil were dealt with not by physical strength but by persuasion and by threats. These linguistic strategies were not in any way secret or ambiguous. The figures of Hero and Exorcist cannot be equated on the basis of the surviving texts.

8 **Beckers, W.J.** 'Urgermanisches Sprachdokument: Anruf des Flursegens.' *Sprachkunde* 1940, parts 3 and 4: 14–15.

Beckers supplies a text and German translation of Charm 1. He cites the rival explanations of 'erce' and speculates on connections between the Charm and the Nerthus cult and on the origins of this cult.

9 **Kammradt, Fr.** 'Zur Auswertung des ags Flursegens "Erce, Erce, Erce eorðan modor".' *Sprachkunde* 1940, part 6: 7–8.

Kammradt seeks to prove the existence of a benevolent field-goddess called Herke or Harke in Germanic religion. He documents the survival of her cult up until recent times and localizes it to the area between the lower Havel and the Elbe. This area may therefore be that from which at least some of the Anglo-Saxons migrated to the British Isles.

) **Lambert, Catherine.** 'The Old English Medical Vocabulary.' *Proceedings of the Royal Society of Medicine* 33 (1940): 137–45.

Charm 2 is a valuable relic of early Teutonic medicine and magic, as distinguished from the classical traditions or documents, for it is the latter that underlie most extant Old English medicine. The word 'onflyge' ('the on-flying things'), which occurs three times in the Charm, denoted an infectious disease.

I **Shook, Laurence K.** 'Notes on the Old-English Charms.' *Modern Language Notes* 55 (1940): 139–40.

Shook argues that the four liturgical prayers cited in Charm 1 lines 40–2 were chosen because they contained specific references to fertility or nourishment. The 'witega' ('prophet') in line 36 is David and the allusion is to the psalm 'Beatus Vir', which also contains appropriate sentiments. Shook compares Charm 2 line 6 with 1 Pet. 5: 8.

412 **Magoun, Francis P., Jr.** 'Old English Charm A 13: *butan heardan beaman.*' *Modern Language Notes* 58 (1943): 33–4.

Magoun notes that evergreenness is a salient characteristic of soft-wood trees, which are therefore readily associated with fertility. It is for this reason, he argues, that hard wood was excluded from the fertilizing ingredients listed in Charm 1.

413 **Meroney, Howard.** 'The Nine Herbs.' *Modern Language Notes* 59 (1944): 157–60.

Meroney brings to nine the number of herbs mentioned in the first part of Charm 2. He does so by proposing that *una* and *stune* are synonyms of *fille* and *finul* respectively and by distinguishing two varieties of *attorlaðe* (lesser and greater). The author of the charm did not consider apples as a herb. Meroney suggests that the scribe has ineptly pieced together several different charms to create Charm 2 and that the text beyond line 29 may be an excrescence.

414 **Bonser, Wilfrid.** 'The Seven Sleepers of Ephesus in Anglo-Saxon and later Recipes.' *Folklore* 56 (1945): 254–6.

Bonser cites Charm 3 and other comparable material in a discussion of the efficacy of the Seven Sleepers against nightmare, sleeplessness, and fever. He notes that the dwarf in Charm 3 relates to the belief that dwarves were the cause of bad dreams. The story of the Seven Sleepers was very widely diffused and could have reached Anglo-Saxon England from a variety of proximate sources, including the continental Germanic peoples.

415 **Meroney, Howard.** 'Irish in the Old English Charms.' *Speculum* 20 (1945): 172–82.

Meroney endorses Magoun (**406**) in his rejection of the apparent correspondence between 'erce erce erce' in Charm 1 and the Irish-derived 'acrae aercrae'.

416 **Bonser, Wilfrid.** 'Anglo-Saxon Laws and Charms relating to Theft.' *Folklore* 57 (1946): 7–11.

Bonser cites Charms 9 and 10 in discussing the mixture of practical and impractical expedients that underlie Anglo-Saxon laws and charms combatting cattle-theft. St Helen's skills as a discoverer encompass not merely the True Cross but also other sacred buildings and sites. The Cross is mentioned in Charm 10 as an object which had to be recovered after its loss.

417 **Magoun, Francis P., Jr.** 'On some Survivals of Pagan Belief in Anglo-Saxon England.' *Harvard Theological Review* 40 (1947): 33–46.

Magoun argues that the belief in *mana* as a force utterly distinct from mere physical power or strength was prevalent among the Germanic peoples and that it survived in Anglo-Saxon England. He identifies a series of allusions to this power in Charms 1, 2, 4, 7, and 9, ascribed to human beings and to plants. The key words are *cræft*, *mægen*, and *miht*, along with their derivatives and cognates. None of these words should be understood as relating solely to physical strength.

8 Storms, Godfrid. *Anglo-Saxon Magic.* The Hague: Nijhoff, 1948. xiii + 336 pp. New York: Gordon, 1974.

The material is organized as follows. Part 1 consists of a synthesizing study of Anglo-Saxon magic. Chapter 1 (1–11) deals with the general characteristics of Anglo-Saxon magic and its links with pre-Christian beliefs. Although the Icelandic sagas and eddaic poems refer to charms, it is Anglo-Saxon sources that supply actual texts. Storms argues that the use of crosses in Charm 1 is pre-Christian and comparable with rituals used by the rain-makers of the Lenni-Lenapi. Chapter 2 (12–26) examines the manuscript sources. Storms notes that 'with a few exceptions . . ., all the charm texts edited by me have been published before, and it has not been my primary aim to publish the texts but to analyse and, possibly, explain them' (26). Nonetheless, his edition is based on personal inspection of the manuscripts. [He was evidently unaware of the ASPR edition (**203**).] He expresses the view that, contrary to the practice of Wülker (**6**) and Leonhardi (**373**), the verse and prose components of the charms should be published together. Chapter 3 (27–48) investigates magic and magical practices. Chapter 4 (49–106) deals with the structure and atmosphere of the ritual. Chapter 5 (107–29) takes up the question of whether the texts are borrowing from classical sources or perpetuating ancient Germanic traditions. In Part 2 (132–318) Storms supplies texts and translations of all the Old English charms. The metrical Charms appear as follows. Charm 8: 132–40; Charm 4: 140–50; Charm 12: 154–8; Charm 7: 158–63; Charm 3: 166–72; Charm 1: 172–86; Charm 2: 186–96; Charm 6: 196–202; Charms 5, 9, and 10 (with analogues and commentary): 202–17; Charm 11: 216–23. All the charms, metrical and otherwise, are submitted to a detailed examination, with emphasis on magical elements. The links between magic and both Christian and pre-Christian religion are explored and made the basis of a classification. The 'hymn' beginning 'erce erce erce' is definitely pagan, with only very slight Christianization, and the word itself is possibly Celtic in origin. The magician who performed the practices of field-blessing described in Charm 1 was fairly certainly a pagan priest. In Charm 2 Storms interprets the 'wuldortanas' as 'nine twigs with the initial letters in runes of the plants representing the power inherent in them' (195). The characterization of the bees in Charm 8, one of the finest of the extant metrical Charms, is an instance of animism. Cockayne's (**365**) interpretation of 'funde' as 'I am trying' in line 3 detracts from the magician's necessary show of mastery. Storms, following Magoun (**406**), rejects Meissner's conclusions (**386**) concerning the 'mighty tongue' in line 6. The compound 'sigewif' is to be construed as a flattering address to the bees themselves. Specific charms are mentioned in relation to the use of iron, running water, and other materials. Comparisons with Sanskrit material in the Vedas open the possibility of tracing charms back to Indo-European origins. Singer's (**389**) identification of four doctrines as 'native Teutonic' is misleading because the same doctrines are to be found among all Indo-European peoples. Also included are a Glossary of plant names (319–28) and a Bibliography (329–333), which comprises editions, translations, and criticism of individual charms to 1948, along with general works on magic, medicine, and religion. [For a review see Jost **421**; Magoun, **425**.]

419 Stroh, Friedrich. *Kleines altgermanisches Lesebuch für Vorlesungen zusammengestellt.* Erlangen: Deutsches Seminar Erlangen 1949. 29 pp.

[Not sighted. According to Lendinara (**463**), he includes Charm 4 (4).]

420 Helm, Karl. 'Der angelsächsische Flursegen.' *Hessische Blätter für Volkskunde* 41 (1950): 34–44.

Helm identifies some vestiges of paganism in Charm 1. He sees the heavy repetition in lines 27 and 28 as reminiscent of *galdralag.* The etymological obscurity of 'erce' and the greeting formula 'hal wes þu . . .', complete with the obsolescent word *folde* 'land' (line 69), are further indications of pre-Christian origin. The phrase 'eastweard ic stande' (line 26) is in origin an element in sun-worship, only later Christianized. The use of 'ic' by the magician, here and elsewhere, is comparable with that seen in runic inscriptions and *Hávamál.* Helm notes the absence of any metrical distinction between heathen and Christian material, so that one of the appeals to the Christian God is couched in *ljóðaháttr.* If the Charm is printed with the remaining specifically Christian material excised, an ancient ritual hymn stands revealed. Originally the Charm was not intended for private use but as part of an official fertility cult.

421 Jost, Karl. Rev. of *Anglo-Saxon Magic,* by Godfrid Storms [**418**]. *English Studies* 31 (1950): 101–5.

Jost notes that Storms's book is not so much a study of Anglo-Saxon magic in general as of the Anglo-Saxon charms and the practices accompanying them. It therefore occupies similar territory to Grendon's edition (**381**), though representing a distinct improvement on it. Jost approves of Storms's conservative editing, especially his avoidance of *metri gratia* emendations. He adds specific notes on several charms. On Charm 8 he comments that 'funde' cannot be a form of *fundian,* as Storms argues, because that verb is intransitive. He suggests that the 'micelan mannes tungan' (line 6) would be that of a thief enticing bees out of somebody else's hive by means of a magic spell. In Charm 3 he reads 'ða liþa/u'. In Charm 7 he explains 'feologan' as 'join together'. He translates line 13 'May it ache you no more than it aches the earth in its ear.' In Charm 9 line 13 he takes 'gedige' (=*gedyge*) to be the optative of *gedugan* and suggests the interpretation 'may it never benefit him'.

422 Schröder, Franz Rolf. 'Erce und Fjørgyn.' *Erbe der Vergangenheit: Germanistische Beiträge. Festgabe für Karl Helm zum 80. Geburtstage 19. mai 1951.* Tübingen: Niemeyer, 1951. 25–36.

Schröder proposes that 'erce' represents a borrowing from a Celtic language, cognate with Gaulish **rica* (with metathesis), and means 'goddess of the furrow'. The name *rica* may indeed be preserved in an inscription associated with Hadrian's Wall. Etymologically similar would be Old Norse Fjørgyn, a divinity with the same attributes. Schröder discusses ploughing viewed as sexual penetration of the earth, adducing comparative material from the *Rigveda*, as well as from ancient Greece and the Ukraine.

Grattan, John H.G., and Charles J. Singer. *Anglo-Saxon Magic and Medicine: Illustrated specially from the Semi-pagan Text 'Lacnunga'.* Publications of the Wellcome Historical Medical Museum 3. London: Oxford UP, 1952. xii + 234 pp. + 5 plates.

Part 1 consists of a general survey of magico-medical practice in Anglo-Saxon England. Part 2 (*Lácnunga: a Magico-Medical Commonplace Book edited with Translation, Notes, Glossary,* ed. Grattan) contains text and translation of Charms 2, 3, 4, 5, and 6. The glossary announced in the title was later abandoned. The editors regard Charm 2 as not one charm but three, though they keep the conventional line numbering. Part I of this Charm, which they think may originally have followed the other two, is entitled 'Pagan Lay of the Nine Herbs'. Parts II and III bear the titles 'Lay of the Nine Twigs of Woden' and 'Pagan Lay of the Magic Blasts' respectively and are followed by a prose section entitled 'How to Use the Lays'. *Lacnunga* may have been of mixed authorship, the Teutonic pagan charms and lays being compiled by someone with some monastic training but not actually living in a monastery. It is unlikely that this almost pagan compiler was a professional leech or that he gave most of his time to attending the sick. Perhaps he occupied some office equivalent to that of bailiff to a monastic estate. Native Teutonic magic is distinguishable from imported Mediterranean elements by virtue of four characteristic doctrines on the causation of disease: the flying venoms, the evil nines, the worm as cause of disease, and the power of elves. [For a review see Magoun, **426**.]

4 Bonser, Wilfrid. 'General Medical Practice in Anglo-Saxon England'. *Science, Medicine and History: Essays on the Evolution of Scientific Thought and Medical Practice written in Honour of Charles Singer.* Ed. E. Ashworth Underwood. Vol. 1. London: Oxford UP, 1953. 154–63. 2 vols.

Bonser comments on 'elfshot', noting that it is also one of the chief characteristics of Finnish magic. He suggests that the word *stice* signifies the hole made in the victim by the elfshot. Thus 'færstice' (Charm 4) = 'sudden puncture'. The doctrine of elfshot as a cause of disease is akin to the classical theory that pestilence was occasioned by the arrows of irate gods, especially Apollo.

5 Magoun, Francis P., Jr. Rev. of *Anglo-Saxon Magic,* by Godfrid Storms **[418]**. *Speculum* 28 (1953): 203–12.

Magoun applies oral-formulaic theory to metrical charms, arguing that except for amulet charms and the like it is not plausible that they had a fixed text. Rather, each had some general purpose and thus, like an anecdote, had a central theme to be stated with varying amounts of embellishment and in phraseology varying with the singer of the moment. The specific reference to Garmund in Charm 9 is to be seen as due merely to the accident of the version recorded here. The extant versions of the metrical charms would seem to be the product of not very expert singers. Magoun supplies concordances of Grendon's **(381)** and Storms's numbering systems and adds notes on points of detail in various charms (4, 6, 8, 9, and 11). He suggests, *inter alia*, that in Charm 8 'sigewif' is merely a substitution for the taboo-word 'beon' ('bees') and therefore carries no allusion to valkyries. In Charm 6 line 17 'gebyrgen' may mean 'caul, amnion'.

426   ———. Rev. of *Anglo-Saxon Magic and Medicine*, by John H.G. Grattan and Charles J. Singer **[423]**. *Speculum* 29 (1954): 564–9.

Magoun adds detailed notes and corrections to the translations and points out the absence of the promised glossary.

427   **Wright, Cyril E.** *Bald's Leechbook: British Museum Royal Manuscript 12D xvii.* With an appendix by Randolph Quirk. Early English Manuscripts in Facsimile 5. London: Allen; Baltimore: Johns Hopkins UP; Copenhagen: Rosenkilde, 1955. 32 pp. + 256 collotypes.

This facsimile edition includes Charm 7 (ff.125a–125b). The editor seeks to show that Book 3, in which Charm 7 occurs, was originally a separate work, not part of Bald's *Leechbook*. He discusses palaeography, previous editions – notably Cockayne's **(365)** – , and other scholarly work on the charms. Wright stresses that the charms should not be studied in isolation but in their setting as part of the leech's practice, of which they formed an integral part. He calls for an edition of the *Leechbook* on the lines of that of the *Lacnunga* prepared by Grattan and Singer **(423)**.

428   **Davidson, Thomas.** 'Elf-shot Cattle.' *Antiquity* 30 (1956): 149–55.

Davidson traces the history of beliefs associated with elfshot and the influence these had on the treatment of cattle disease and on ploughing practices. His comparative material includes charms and folklore from Scotland (both English and Gaelic) and Shetland. One seventeenth-century Scottish recording of a charm contains a marked similarity to Charm 4 lines 25–6: 'I charm thé for arrow-schot,/ For dor-schot, for wondo-schot,/ For ey-schot, for tung-schot,/ For hert-schot. . .'

429   **Chaney, William A.** 'Paganism to Christianity in Anglo-Saxon England.' *Harvard Theological Review* 53 (1960): 197–217. Repr. in *Early Medieval Society*. Ed. Sylvia L. Thrupp. New York: Appleton, 1967. 67–83.

Chaney argues for the continued importance in Anglo-Saxon England of the pagan element in the Charms. An outstanding example of the assimilation of Christianity to the older paganism is seen in Charm 2, where Woden is equated with Christ. The Christian emendator of an originally pagan charm has added that the nine herbs were invented by Christ while he hung on the Cross: Christ's act here compares with Óðinn's in gaining knowledge of the runes.

430   **Stürzl, Erwin.** 'Die christlichen Elemente in den altenglischen Zaubersegen.' *Die Sprache* 6 (1960): 75–93.

The Anglo-Saxon Charms demonstrate that 'white' magic and religion were compatible. Hälsig's explanation **(382)**, invoking a prevalence of superstition among the Christian clergy, is to be rejected. Rather, the missionaries built on a traditional Germanic collaboration between magic and heathen religion. Such a collaboration is attested in the account of the 'wuldortanas' in Charm 2, corroborated in different respects by *Solomon and Saturn* and *Hávamál*. The Anglo-Saxon magician would have been encouraged in the assumption that magic and Christian religion were compatible by some detailed correspondences in ritual and sacred objects. Thus 'halig wæter' possessed a salvific function in both kinds of religion: not merely dew but spring water and other fresh, running water would have been 'holy' to the Germanic peoples, as testified by Charm 2 line 59. As a result the charms (e.g. 1, 3, and 4) came to incorporate numerous elements from Christian liturgy.

1 **Schneider, Karl.** 'Die strophischen Strukturen und heidnisch-religiösen Elemente der ae. Zauberspruchgruppe "wið þeofðe".' *Festschrift zum 75. Geburtstag von Theodor Spira.* Ed. H. Viebrock and W. Erzgräber. Heidelberg: Winter, 1961. 38–56.

After a brief review of scholarship on the charms, Schneider argues that three major problems have hitherto been virtually ignored: (1) the heathen-religious elements of the charms, (2) the Christianization of the charms, and (3) their strophic structure. Charms 5, 9, and 10 all contain allusions to the myths of Freyr and Baldr. Schneider attempts to reconstruct the pagan originals, positing narrative strophes in *fornyrðislag* verse-form and magical strophes in *ljóðaháttr*. By a process of eliminating Christian elements from Charm 9, he claims to have uncovered two original four-line strophes, followed by a six-line strophe, and concluded by a final four-line strophe. He explains 'Garmund' as the name of a Germanic god. The references to Christ and Bethlehem in Charms 5 and 10 are Christian substitutes for original references to Baldr and a postulated *Bradblic (Baldr's residence).

2 **Bonser, Wilfrid.** *The Medical Background of Anglo-Saxon England: A Study in History, Psychology, and Folklore.* London: Wellcome Historical Medical Library, 1963. xxxvi + 448 pp.

Bonser's monograph contains scattered references to the metrical Charms, with comparative material from Finland and Ireland. He notes how Christian elements, such as names, are gradually substituted for pagan ones: some references might be to either Woden or Christ. He points out traces of nature-worship in the Charms. The discussion also encompasses possible modes of recitation, along with comments on the elves and number magic. Good alliterative charms are of early date, whereas prose and gibberish ones are later. Bonser discusses Charm 2 in relation to Anglo-Saxon snake-lore, supplying a detailed account of the individual herbs. The significance of iron, especially its magnetic properties, in Charm 4 is pointed out. The monograph includes a bibliography (xvii–xxxv).

3 **Crawford, Jane.** 'Evidences for Witchcraft in Anglo-Saxon England.' *Medium Aevum* 32 (1963): 99–116.

Crawford comments that despite much scholarship little light has been shed on what the native magico-religious elements in poetic vocabulary meant to the poets who used them. The word 'sigewif' in Charm 8 relates to the bees, not to 'wise women', and the verb *galan* does not uniformly refer to incantation. To separate out genuinely pagan elements in the texts presents almost insuperable difficulties. Thus the poet of Charm 11 would probably be very surprised by all the meanings which modern scholars have read into the text. For him this was a special litany for travellers, closely related to earlier lorica poems and very likely to be said in the same spirit as the Creed or Paternoster (101). The list of supernatural beings in Charm 4 shows us a very early and rudimentary stage in the development of a Germanic mythology. The Charms suggest that as yet the Anglo-Saxons lacked the concept of especially evil women magicians (i.e. the witches of later times).

434 **Peters, R.A.** 'OE. Ælf, -Ælf, Ælfen, -Ælfen.' *Philological Quarterly* 42 (1963): 250–7.

Peters offers a systematic examination of the eleven 'elf' words in Old English. Passing references are made to the metrical Charms.

435 **Bloomfield, Morton W.** 'The Form of *Deor.*' *PMLA* 79 (1964): 534–41.

Bloomfield compares the form of *Deor* to that of a broadly comparative range of charms, concluding that it is either a sophisticated, Christianized charm or a poem influenced by the charm form and meant to suggest its prototype. He specifically mentions Charm 4 (540), noting that the speaker assumes a mysterious and hard-to-explain first person role which indicates that he is taking up the mask of a mythological or heroic character, comparably with *Deor*. Charm 4 and *Deor* are also compared in respect of their refrains.

436 **Fife, Austin E.** 'Christian Swarm Charms from the Ninth to the Nineteenth Centuries.' *Journal of American Folklore* 77 (1964): 154–9.

In this brief survey Fife classifies 97 swarm charms, among them Charm 8. He notes that the medieval examples are essentially ecclesiastical, used in the apiaries of monasteries, and traces the subsequent process of secularization. Fife argues that Charm 8 is in reality two separate charms, brought together in error by the displacement of the title in the manuscript. The prose introduction and the first four metrical lines do not conform with the other swarm charms known to us, and in reality represent a charm against witchcraft.

437 **Talbot, Charles H.** 'Some Notes on Anglo-Saxon Medicine.' *Medical History* 9 (1965): 156–69.

Talbot mentions the metrical Charms only in passing, in the course of a general contention that folklore and magic have been over-emphasized in studies of Anglo-Saxon medicine. England was in no way inferior to its continental neighbours in the ninth and tenth centuries in the assimilation of classical medicine.

438 **Rosenberg, Bruce A.** 'The Meaning of *Æcerbot.*' *Journal of American Folklore* 79 (1966): 428–36.

Rosenberg argues that 'cwicbeam' in Charm 1 line 18 refers to the rowan, not the aspen (or poplar), as thought by Grendon (**381**), Storms (**418**), and other scholars. In various traditions, the rowan could foster or save life, and hence may have had associations with fertility. In a society characterized by religious syncretism, a tree sacred to Thor, who as god of wind, rain, and weather in general was a patron god of agriculture, has been buried to induce growth. Charm 1 is designed to foster fertility at a set time of the year, not to counter evil spells worked against the land.

9 **Dolfini, Giorgio.** 'Sulle formule magiche e le benedizioni nella tradizione germanica.' *Rendiconti. Istituto Lombardo. Accademia di Scienze e Lettere. Classe di Lettere e Scienze Morali e Storiche* 101 (1967): 633–60.

Dolfini argues that there is a continuity of *Weltanschauung* from heathen charms onwards into Christian benedictions. He seeks to identify elements that survive from a primitive magical conception of the cosmos. The power attributed to the herbs in Charm 2 is founded on a mythic past. Charm 1 displays a faith not in the Christian God but in the language of magic. The 'cræftig man' of Charm 1 line 65 is to be compared with the 'micel mann' of Charm 8 line 6. Charm 11 demonstrates the Anglo-Saxon sense of an immediate kinship between word and action. Dolfini also cites Charm 3 line 13, reading 'dweorges sweostar': he characterizes her as a 'cwidol wif', after the fashion of Charm 1 line 65.

0 **Hill, Thomas D.** 'An Irish-Latin analogue for the Blessing of the Sods in the Old English Æcer-bot Charm.' *Notes and Queries* 213, NS 15 (1968): 362–3.

Hill discusses two details of the ritual described in the first part of Charm 1. The use of four different substances and the association of the fertility of the land with the four gospels are elucidated by comparison with an Irish-Latin tag phrase which associates Matthew with honey, Mark with milk, Luke with wine, and John with oil.

1 **Schneider, Karl.** 'Zu den ae. Zaubersprüchen *wið wennum* und *wið wæterælfadle.*' *Anglia* 87 (1969): 288–302.

Schneider furnishes a detailed analysis of Charms 7 and 12, to meet the need that he sees for a thorough investigation of heathen references and strophic form in the metrical Charms. He also examines the rhetorical and structural patterns of these two charms. Charm 12 emerges from his discussion as consisting of two strophes of six lines, parallel to the extended *fornyrðislag* strophe to be found in the Old Norse *Völuspá*, and hence as of great significance for the history of Old English poetics. He further identifies a pattern of allusions to the heathen god of death, represented in Scandinavian tradition by Heimdallr and by a corpse-eating giant who takes on the form of an eagle. The manuscript reading 'uolmes' is to be retained and interpreted as a reference to this eagle. Likewise the reading 'nihgan' means 'of the killer' and is cognate with various words meaning 'death'. The performer of the Charm calls on the god of death to destroy the force that has given rise to the wen. In Charm 7 line 7 the 'halig wæter' is to be explained not as Christian holy water but on pagan lines as the dew thought to be exuded by the god of death. The verb 'awrat' (line 8) is to be construed as a reference to the magical writing of runes to restore health. Magoun's suggestion (406) that the prose introduction constitutes a separate charm is to be resisted. The charm can be reconstructed as in *ljóðaháttr* form.

442 **Thun, Nils.** 'The Malignant Elves: Notes on Anglo-Saxon Magic and Germanic Myth.' *Studia Neophilologica* 41 (1969): 378–96.

Thun seeks to characterize the elves as they appear in Anglo-Saxon sources, including the metrical Charms. He finds that whereas *Beowulf* shows the elves adopted into Christian demonology, the Charms agree with other medical texts in showing them as belonging to the world of pagan witchcraft. They therefore form part of popular aetiology in the diagnosis of illnesses, though how far people literally thought of elves remains a question. Thun adduces comparative evidence for 'shooting elves', citing Charm 4 and emphasizing the pagan character of the incantation. In his opinion, it is a mistake to adduce the Old Saxon and Old High German worm charm variously titled 'Contra vermes' and 'Pro nessia' as a parallel to Charm 4. Discussing Charm 7, he notes that in continental and Scandinavian folklore skin eruptions are often attributed to elves.

443 **Pilch, Herbert.** *Altenglischer Lehrgang: Begleitband zur altenglischen Grammatik.* Commentationes Societatis Linguisticae Europaeae I.2. Munich: Hueber, 1970. 82 pp.

Charms 5 (38–42) and 6 (43–52) are used to illustrate points of Old English grammar. The text is conservative, with brief commentary and glossary.

444 **Chickering, Howell D.** 'The Literary Magic of "*Wið Faerstice*".' *Viator* 2 (1971): 83–104.

Charm 4 is typical of the methodological difficulties faced by literary scholars in dealing with an Anglo-Saxon anthropological document. The most fruitful means of analysing the text is perhaps the literary notion of the 'speaker' or 'voice' of the poem. Chickering argues against the notion of an epic introduction in this and other metrical charms. Both the wording of the charm and the choice of herbs suggest that the purpose was to cure a wide range of ailments.

445 **Breuer, Rolf, and Rainer Schöwerling.** *Altenglische Lyrik: Englisch und deutsch.* Stuttgart: Reclam, 1972. 180 pp.

[Not seen. According to Lendinara (463), Charms 3 (56) and 12 (56–7) are included amongst texts and German translations of some Old English 'lyrics'.]

446 **Duckert, Audrey R.** '*Erce* and Other Possibly Keltic Elements in the Old English Charm for Unfruitful Land.' *Names* 20 (1972): 83–90.

Duckert argues for an Irish element in the vocabulary of Charm 1. She annotates the Charm so as to identify specifically Irish motifs and reviews various Irish words reminiscent of 'erce'. The result is to posit a trilingual ritual, carefully constructed to satisfy pagan and Christian without offence to either and containing vestiges of Celtic traditions originating well before the *adventus Saxonum*.

Howe, G. Melvyn. *Man, Environment and Disease in Britain: A Medical Geography of Britain through the Ages.* Newton Abbot: David; New York: Barnes, 1972. xviii + 285 pp.

In his chapter 6, on pre-Norman times, Howe notes in passing that Bald's Leechbook provides an indication of the separation between spiritual and physical conceptions of disease healing.

Taylor, Paul Beekman. 'Charms of *Wynn* and Fetters of *Wyrd* in the *Wanderer.*' *Neuphilologische Mitteilungen* 73 (1972): 448–55.

Taylor contends that a good many of the metrical Charms can be described as 'fetter charms', designed as a defence against forces that debilitate natural processes. The prototypes of these charms would have been intended to loosen or dissolve literal fetters, as well as the metaphorical fetters of ice or winter. The motif of the melting of the iron fragment in Charm 4 has links to this prototype.

Reszkiewicz, Alfred. *An Old English Reader (Seventh–Eleventh Centuries): Texts Selected and Provided with Notes and Glossary.* Warszawa: Państwowe Wydawnictwo Naukowe, 1973. 146 pp.

[Not seen. Lendinara (**463**) lists this item as including Charm 9 lines 6–19 (47) and Charm 8 (47–8).]

Ramat, Paolo. 'Per una Tipologia degli Incantesimi Germanici.' *Strumenti Critici* 24 (1974): 179–97.

Ramat argues that approaches to the Germanic charms based on content analysis are not suitably rigorous. He proposes a formal definition of 'charm' as a text in which each of the two elements myth and praxis must be represented. Such a definition would distinguish Charm 4, which contains both myth and praxis, from, for example, 'Pro nessia', which contains praxis (since it conjures the worms to leave the horse) but lacks a mythological component.

Rubin, Stanley. *Medieval English Medicine.* Newton Abbot: David; New York: Barnes, 1974. 232 pp.

Rubin provides a brief, elementary introduction to the charms, emphasizing their medical function. There is no special discussion of the metrical Charms.

Swann, Brian. 'Anglo-Saxon Charms.' *Antaeus* 15 (1974): 117–18.

Swann translates Charms 3, 4, and 8. He sees the incantations as Christian-based, whereas the rituals are pagan. Sample translation from Charm 8: 'See, earth is strong against anything,/ and malice or forgetfulness,/ and against the tongue of a powerful man.'

Harris, Joseph. 'Cursing with the Thistle: *Skírnismál* 31, 6–8, and OE Metrical Charm 9, 16–17.' *Neuphilologische Mitteilungen* 76 (1975): 26–33.

Harris seeks to show that a disputed passage in the famous curse in *Skírnismál* can be clarified by comparison to a magical simile in the curse in Charm 9 line

17, 'swa breðel seo swa þystel'. The person so cursed must take on the aspect of a brittle autumn thistle about to burst with its load of seed. The two texts point to an ancient tradition of cursing with the thistle. Generally in folklore human life is associated with dying or waning natural objects.

454 Bierbaumer, Peter. *Der botanische Wortschatz des Altenglischen. I: Das Laeceboc, II: Lacnunga, Herbarium Apuleii, Peri Didaxeon.* Grazer Beiträge zur englischen Philologie 1 and 2. 2 vols. Munich: Lang, 1975–6.

This dissertation presents the complete botanical vocabulary of the Old English *Leechbook, Lacnunga, Herbarium Apuleii,* and *Peri Didaxeon.* The word studies include material from the metrical Charms, notably *attorlaþe, finul,* and *wegbrade* (Charm 2).

455 Doskow, Minna. 'Poetic Structure and the Problem of the Smiths in "Wið Færstice".' *Papers on Language and Literature* 12 (1976): 321–6.

Doskow argues that both the singular smith mentioned in Charm 4 line 13 and the plural smiths mentioned in line 16 partake of the same hostile nature. She characterizes as pure speculation the assumption that the single smith's knife would have been used beneficently, to smoothe a salve on the patient whose pain is being cured. The division of the smiths into two groups, one good and six bad, is also structurally inconsistent with other elements in the charm. Just as the work of the witches is exorcized in the second section of the Charm, so is the work of the smiths, now referred to as elves in line with the common tradition of elf-smiths.

456 Stuart, Heather. 'The Anglo-Saxon Elf.' *Studia Neophilologica* 48 (1976): 313–20.

Anglo-Saxon texts contain conflicting descriptions of the elves. From the metrical Charms, among other sources, it can be inferred that the elves were in Anglo-Saxon times absorbing the functions of the (night)mare and the dwarf. Charm 3 gives some indication of the older state of affairs. Charm 7 provides evidence that the elves could be associated with particular forces of nature, here water (in the form of rain). It is likely that the **wæterylfe* were the original elves, servants of Þunor and especially active during storms, and that the Anglo-Saxon leech had lost sight of this tradition. Charm 7 may have deployed sympathetic magic against a disease characterized by water-filled blisters. Charm 4 shows the leech's awareness that the disease is caused by 'mighty women': in his uncertainty as to which type of women are culpable he directs magic comprehensively against witches, goddesses, and elves. The association of these women with a hill suggests an identification as mountain elves.

457 Hill, Thomas D. 'The *æcerbot* Charm and its Christian User.' *Anglo-Saxon England* 6 (1977): 213–21.

This charm reflects the influence of pagan religion, not merely pagan magic, and hence has been extensively investigated. The fact that the charm required the participation of the local priest suggests that the ecclesiastical authorities were not hostile to such syncretism. Diachronic inquiry into the charms, attempting the separation of pagan from Christian, has its legitimacy, but interpretation and discussion inevitably suffer if this type of inquiry is not balanced by a concern for the meaning and significance of the charm in its present form. Hill offers an interpretation of the symbolism of Charm 1, along with a rationale for the actions and prayers which comprise it. The text invokes sympathetic magic through its allusions to the Judaeo-Christian creation story. Also, the cutting, blessing, and moistening of the four sods are reminiscent of the myth concerning the creation of Adam contained in *Enoch*. Hill further argues that the Charm may have had some practical efficacy, because the use of 'uncuþ sæd' would add crops or strains of crops to the farmer's inventory, helping him to find a more suitable variety for his hitherto recalcitrant land. If only a part or parts of it grew well, he might at least harvest enough seed for the following year and so solve his problem progressively.

Nöth, Winfried. 'Semiotics of the Old English Charm.' *Semiotica* 19 (1977): 59–83.

Nöth reacts against the notion that literary historians should only be concerned with magic in so far as it acquires a verbally aesthetic form. On the contrary, to disregard the dimensions 'sign and action' is to neglect the semiotic or the pragmatic dimension of the Old English charm. Nöth considers it a mistake to apply modern criteria of physiological or medical efficacy to the classification of the Old English material into respectively charms and herbal recipes. Instead, he urges a three-fold classification: (1) Charms which report not only a magic act but also a linguistic magic formula, (2) Charms that only report magic acts, (3) Simple recipes without magic features.

Stuart, Heather. ' "Spider" in Old English.' *Parergon* 18 (August 1977): 37–42.

Stuart criticizes the prevalent assumption that 'spider', not 'spiden', is to be read in Charm 3 line 9 as based in part upon folkloristic fantasies. In view of the oddity of the collocation 'inspidenwiht', emendation to 'unspedig wiht' ('wretched creature', analogous to 'ermig' in Charm 12 line 4) seems the best recourse. Grattan's emendation (**394**) to 'inwriðen wiht' has the weakness that no parallels are attested to his and Singer's idea (**423**) of an incubus in the form of a corpse swathed in grave-clothes.

Hauer, Stanley R. 'Structure and Unity in the Old English Charm *Wið Færstice*.' *English Language Notes* 15 (1978): 250–7.

Hauer defends the unity of the two parts of Charm 4, replying to Chickering (**444**) and earlier scholars. He argues that the seemingly disparate elements of the charm are actually bound together in a surprisingly well co-ordinated, balanced pattern of verbal and imagistic echoes. The three scenes describing the attacking spirits in the first part of the poem are echoed in the twice-intoned triplets of gods, elves, and witch in the second. These very parallels confer a common purpose, structure, and unity upon the two parts of the lyric. Hauer equates the group of horsemen with the Furious Host, the spear-hurling women with valkyries, and the smiths with the type of wizard-smith represented by Weland. These entities in turn equate, in the second part of the poem, with the *es-*, *hægtess-*, and *ylf-* (lines 23–6). Contrary to the opinion of Doskow (**455**) and others, the smiths belong in two categories: (1) the many malevolent smiths, (2) the one helpful smith.

461   Hill, Thomas D. 'The Theme of the Cosmological Cross in Two Old English Cattle Theft Charms.' *Notes and Queries* 223, NS 25 (1978): 488–90.

Charms 5 and 10 contain a conception, ultimately traceable to Eph. 3: 18–19, of the Cross as a centre which defines the spatial dimensions of the world. Just as Christ draws all humankind to himself as he 'embraces' east, west, north, and south, so the Charms attempt to draw back the cattle, regardless in which direction they have gone. These Charms demonstrate the dissemination of religious ideas to eminently popular forms of discourse.

462   Howard, Michael. *The Runes and Other Magical Alphabets.* Wellingborough: Thorsons, 1978. 95 pp.

Howard believes that the 'wise lord' in Charm 2 who wrought thyme and fennel while hanging on the cross is to be identified with Woden. He expresses the view that christianization of pagan rites and rhymes was sometimes encouraged by secret followers of the old religion, because it concealed their activities from prying eyes.

463   Lendinara, Patrizia. 'Gli incantesimi del periodo anglosassone: una ricerca bibliografica.' *Annali Istituto Universitario Orientale di Napoli* Filologia germanica 21 (1978): 299–362.

In this bibliography Lendinara furnishes a comprehensive list of studies of the charms, including both metrical and non-metrical texts. Both Old English and Latin-language charms are dealt with. She emphasizes the variety of techniques and content to be found in the charms and the difficulties of arriving at a classificatory system. Scholars such as Grendon (**381**) and Storms (**418**) tend to confuse medical recipes with true charms (i.e. incantations and conjurations). Scholarship has to some degree neglected the potentially significant descriptions of actions and gestures to be performed as part of some charms. In the ensuing bibliography data on manuscript provenance and printed editions are given concerning all texts that have been classified as charms by one or other previous scholar, regardless of the present compiler's views. Section I of the bibliography lists all texts according to their manuscript provenance (300–18). Other sections list facsimiles, editions, translations, and criticism. Lendinara includes here some items that make only incidental references to the charms. Items are briefly annotated, sometimes with indications of relevant pages. In a brief conclusion (361–2), summarizing the state of the scholarship, Lendinara comments that the metrical Charms have received an undue proportion of scholarly attention. Much work remains to be done, both in providing detailed analyses of the prose and Latin-language texts and in placing the entire production of charms in its wider cultural context.

464   Spamer, James B. 'The Old English Bee Charm: An Explication.' *Journal of Indo-European Studies* 6 (1978): 279–94.

Charm 8 is not designed to prevent the swarming of a hive. On the contrary, swarming was essential in the Anglo-Saxon state of hive technology if the bee-keeper was to extract the honey. Rather, the Charm ensures that the swarm will not be lost, either through theft or simply through the bees absconding. The first part of the Charm is a counter-charm against possible supernatural theft. The second part is an appeal directly to the bees, to remember their obligations to the bee-keeper. The ritualistic casts of earth associated with the Charm are parallel to rituals found in other charms and in Salic Law and are intended to confer power upon the bee-keeper. Thus the essential unity of the Charm, though doubted by Fife (**436**), is revealed by the single motive of the bee-keeper: to retain possession of his hive when it swarms. Spamer appends text and translation of Charm 8, the Lorsch Bee Charm, and relevant portions of Salic Law.

5 Braekman, Willy L. 'Notes on Old English Charms.' *Neophilologus* 64 (1980): 461–9.

Braekman draws attention to the old and widespread belief that the origin or the virtues of specific herbs were connected with an action of our Lord shortly before his death or his ascension. Accordingly, the word 'regenmelde' in Charm 2 would be the equivalent of Christ's 'great proclamation' of the virtues of herbs, though possibly blended with the story of Woden. The Latin word 'una', assigned to mugwort in the Charm (line 3), indicates that mugwort is first in the hierarchy of herbs.

6 Giraudi, Anna. 'La formula anglosassone delle 9 erbe.' *Aevum* 54 (1980): 283–6.

Giraudi notes previous solutions to the problem of harmonizing the two different lists of herbs in Charm 2 and of assigning them to specific herbs. The references to 'fille' and 'finule' (lines 36 and 65) represent interpolations: the identification of the herbs had already become obscure in Anglo-Saxon times, forcing the copyist to resort to more familiar items to make up the crucial number of nine. The excision of line 36, along with line 58, 'Crist stod ofer adle ængan cundes' (another obvious interpolation), reveals the original structure of the Charm clearly: (1) appeal to the herbs, (2) story of Woden's victory over the snake, (3) the idea that the nine herbs are powerful against nine poisons, (4) description of the nine herbs, (5) the magic formula. 'Apple' is mentioned not as a herb but because the 'wuldortanas' are cut from its branches. The first element in 'regenmelde', whatever the total meaning of the word, is to be related to *Rögnir*, one of the Old Norse names for Óðinn.

7 Niles, John D. 'The *Æcerbot* Ritual in Context.' *Old English Literature in Context: Ten Essays.* Ed. John D. Niles. Cambridge: Brewer; Totowa, NJ: Rowman, 1980. 44–56.

Niles believes that Charm 1 is the text of a solemn Christian communal rite, dating from the age of Cnut and intended to countervail black magic. The rite seeks to invoke the entire process of events by which God made man a tiller of the earth. Performances would have been ordered by the lord of the manor and officiated over by a priest in the service of a secular lord. The burial of the four crosses would be intended to guard the earth against the entry of malign influences. The object of accepting good seed from beggars is to dispose of one's own bad seed. Niles links Charm 1 with the early modern English customs associated with Plough Monday.

468 Damico, Helen. 'The Valkyrie Reflex in Old English Literature.' *Allegorica* 5.2 (1981 *for* 1980): 149–67.

Damico's objective is to write a literary (rather than religious) study of the Valkyries. As a metaphor for a sudden unexpected attack of physical pain, Charm 4 employs a horde of malevolent spear-throwing female riders advancing over a barrow and screaming out their battle cry as they attack. In Charm 8, the female squadron is a metaphor for swarming bees, suggesting a more benevolent and guardian-like aspect of the warrior maids. The Charms corroborate the glosses and prose documents in clearly depicting a figure which derived in essentials from the early war spirits of Germanic origin.

469 Foley, John Miles. '*Laecdom* and *Bajanje*: A Comparative Study of Old English and Serbo-Croatian Charms.' *Centerpoint* 4.3 (1981): 33–40.

Foley briefly compares some examples of Old English and Yugoslav verbal magic, concentrating on the crucial importance of sound as the source of their power. He discusses gibberish charms, demonstrating that their efficacy results from complying to certain basic rules of versification. In Charm 1 we should not be surprised that Dobbie's lineation (**203**) seems in places to be an approximate rather than an exact fit, since the prayer reveals phrase-structuring parameters unassociated with the conventional alliterative poetry. Foley also mentions Charms 3, 5, 9, and 10.

470 Hamp, Eric P. 'Notes on the Old English Bee Charm.' *Journal of Indo-European Studies* 9 (1981): 338–40.

Hamp, endorsing Spamer (**464**), lays emphasis on the discourse structure of Charm 8. The four sections, in which we see instruction followed by poetic text twice over, are linked by a reprise of key terms and ideas. Thus 'sigað to eorþan' (line 9) matches and partly explicates the earlier 'fo ic under fot' (line 3). Hamp interprets 'funde' as from the stem of Old Saxon *fundon*, Old English *fundian* 'go, go after', opening the possibility of a translation 'I go after it' or even 'I (speedily) travel on it'. The Lorsch bee-charm is a nearly exact Christianized transformation of Charm 8.

471 Stuart, Heather. ' "Ic me on þisse gyrde beluce": The Structure and Meaning of the Old English *Journey Charm*.' *Medium Aevum* 50 (1981): 259–73.

Stuart suggests that although Charm 11 belongs to the same genre as the Middle High German *Reisesegen* it contains elaborately and sensitively wrought images not to be expected in a charm and should therefore be viewed primarily as a work of literature. The true affinities of Charm 11 in Old English literature are with a specific type of poetic prayer, usually incorporated within a longer poem. It is also indebted to the 'lorica' tradition, though not necessarily to the Celtic elaboration of that tradition. The use of the verb 'belucan' in lines 1 and 39 gives a circular structure and confirms other vaguer references to the sphere of grace. The 'journey' in the Charm may be purely a metaphor for the journey through life, or similar.

2 **Nelson, Marie.** 'An Old English Charm against Nightmare.' *Germanic Notes* 13 (1982): 17–18.

Nelson suggests that sometimes reading a charm is a little like trying to solve a riddle. The text supplies us with the remedy, but may not clearly identify the problem which it is designed to cure. She endorses the conservative text of Charm 3 found in the ASPR edition (**203**), criticizing Grattan's emendations (**394**) and observing that they are not essential to the identification of 'nightmare' as the patient's problem. She notes the belief that dwarves had the weight of nightmares or incubi and that they could change to spider form.

3 **Rathe, Armin.** 'Tanzrunische Deutung altenglischer Strophenformen.' *Festschrift für Karl Schneider zum 70. Geburtstag am 18. April 1982.* Ed. Ernst S. Dick and Kurt R. Janowsky. Amsterdam: Benjamins, 1982. 405–15.

Rathe concludes from Charms 1 and 9 that originally the *scop* was a priest-poet who led sacral dances. The strophe-form in these two charms lent itself, by virtue of its syllable-count, to a dance where the shape of a relevant rune, *B* in Charm 1 lines 69–71 ('hal wes þu . . .') and *M* or *D* in Charm 9 lines 6–9 (the 'Garmund strophe'), was traced by the dancers. The three-line form in Charm 1 contributes toward creating the shape of the runic *B*.

4 **Amies, Marion.** 'The *Journey Charm*: A Lorica for Life's Journey.' *Neophilologus* 67 (1983): 448–62.

Amies argues that although Charm 11 has traditionally been understood as offering protection for travellers in their literal journeys, it may also apply to their allegorical journeys through life or even the journey of their souls after death. She discusses the relationship of Charm 11 to the Anglo-Saxon glosses of the *Lorica of Gildas* and suggests that despite a possibly pagan nucleus Charm 11 could more appropriately be classed as a prayer or a lorica. Storms's insistence (**418**) on a pagan interpretation for the verb 'belucan' lacks an evidential basis. The collocation of 'sygegealdor' and 'sigegyrde' in line 6 is reminiscent of the collocation of the Paternoster and the palm in *Solomon and Saturn*. The puzzling phrase 'wega Seraphin' (line 30b) is to be explained as 'those who were most burning with love of God and who recorded and taught the ways of eternal life'.

Boenig, Robert. '*Erce* and Dew.' *Names* 31 (1983): 130–1.

Boenig argues that 'erce' in Charm 1 represents a learned borrowing from Greek *herse* 'dew'. Greek uncial *c* (for sigma) could be taken over as Latin and subsequently Old English *c*. The presence of a word so incomprehensible to the laity in the Charm would have enhanced its magical value.

Vaughan-Sterling, Judith A. 'The Anglo-Saxon *Metrical Charms*: Poetry as Ritual.' *JEGP* 82 (1983): 186–200.

Vaughan-Sterling contends that scholarly energy expended in the anthropological study of the metrical Charms has diverted attention from their very close connection with Anglo-Saxon poetry. This connection is manifested by the presence of both in such manuscripts as CCCC 41. Also significant are commonalities in form, e.g. the oral formula, and content, e.g. the allusions to myths and legends. If the Garmund mentioned in Charm 9 is to be identified with St Germanus we could detect an allusion to a story where the saint restores a slaughtered calf to life. Some Charms point to the development of a specialized poetic lexicon, which includes such items as 'cwicbeam' (Charm 1) and 'beadowræda' (Charm 7). Charm 2, with its *hapax legomena*, evinces an effort to use rare names for herbs in preference to commonplace ones, in a ritual that requires differentiation from daily, non-magical discourse. In Charm 12 the word 'wenchichenne' may even have been created for the sake of a rhyme with 'wenne' (line 1).

477 **Jongeboer, Henk.** 'Der Lorscher Bienensegen und der ags. Charm *wiþ ymbe*.' *Amsterdamer Beiträge zur älteren Germanistik* 21 (1984): 63–70.

Jongeboer compares Charm 8 with the Lorsch Bee-charm in respect of content and manner of preservation, arguing that it represents a literary adaptation of an earlier real charm. Swarming was important to the total economics of bee-keeping. The throwing of sand in the Charm is a purely pragmatic (non-magical) act, to prevent the swarm from travelling too far. An escaped swarm would be accessible to persons who gathered wild honey, whereas the bee-keeper might be legally excluded from gathering honey in the woods. The word 'sigewif' should be interpreted as merely a respectful form of address, carrying no real overtones of 'victory'.

478 **Nelson, Marie.** ' "Wordsige and Worcsige": Speech Acts in Three Old English Charms.' *Language and Style* 17 (1984): 57–66.

Nelson argues that the metrical Charms can quite profitably be interpreted as directions for the performance of such speech acts as praying, commanding, and asserting power. Important for Charm 1 is the presence of a narrator who addresses a palpable audience, thus creating a context which lends shape to his recitations. The welfare of the social group depends upon the Charm. It provides its performer not just with a series of speech acts that enables him to show his confidence in his own power, but also with ways to demonstrate that he has control over the very sounds of which words are composed. Charms 8 and 11, similarly, could be used to achieve practical purposes like acquiring the confidence that one could journey in safety or secure useful food.

479 **Jolly, Karen Louise.** 'Anglo-Saxon Charms in the Context of a Christian World View.' *Journal of Medieval History* 11 (1985): 279–93.

According to Jolly, most previous criticism has tended to accentuate the pagan aspects of the Charms. There has been a tendency to assume that modern definitions of magic coincide with the attitudes to magic held by medieval Christianity. From Ælfric's *Homilies* and other works we see that in an Augustinian outlook God is the true leech, who controls life and death, sickness and health. The Charms are a Christian expression of belief in divine intervention, while the pagan rituals that sporadically occur in them represent no more than a subconscious remnant of paganism. In the elf-charms the process of on-going Christianization is especially evident.

0 **Nelson, Marie.** 'A Woman's Charm.' *Studia Neophilologica* 57 (1985): 3–8.

Charm 6 is unique among extant Old English charms in that it is to be spoken by a woman. By focusing on the physical and speech acts prescribed (a defiance of death and obstacles) and on the contribution of repeated sounds to the communication of this defiance, Nelson seeks to demonstrate that the Charm might have been successfully used by a pregnant woman to strengthen herself in the face of multiple uncertainties. The word 'maga' (line 26) should be translated 'son' and line 28 means 'then I wish to own myself [have control of my own body] and go home'.

1 **Stuart, Heather.** 'Utterance Instructions in the Anglo-Saxon Charms.' *Parergon* NS 3 (1985): 31–7.

Stuart argues that the verbs *cweþan* and *singan* are mutually exclusive in the instructions for utterances embodied in the metrical and other Charms. The former relates to short texts (five lines or fewer, such as those contained in Charm 6), the latter to longer ones (as in Charm 2). Exceptional are Charms 1, 5, 7, 9, and 10. In Charm 4 the utterance instruction is left implicit.

2 **Weston, L.M.C.** 'The Language of Magic in Two Old English Metrical Charms.' *Neuphilologische Mitteilungen* 86 (1985): 176–86.

Focusing on Charms 2 and 4, Weston seeks to show that it is in the nature of charms to enhance the healer's power and to effect his entrance into a healing state. The poem itself has efficacy as magic, in virtue of its rhythm, metre, paradigmatic repetition and manipulation of verb tense, fragmentation of action, and transformation of or shift in subject. Poetic and linguistic elements cohere to manifest and ultimately to produce a particular mode of magical thought. Ritual and poetry in these two charms combine to create and enforce an altered consciousness.

3 **Schneider, Karl.** 'The Old English *æcerbot* – an Analysis.' *Sophia Lectures on Beowulf*. . . Ed. Shoichi Watanabe and Norio Tsuchiya. Tokyo: Taishukan for the Japan Science Society, 1986. 276–98.

Schneider argues that the word 'haligwæter' in Charm 1 line 9 should be understood in the pagan sense, as 'dew', which was thought to fall down from the heavenly mountain and then to be collected by bees from the flowers and turned into honey. Later it would have been understood in the Christian sense. The word 'cwicbeam' (line 18) is probably to be identified with the birch, from which twigs are used to touch women to give them health. The leaves were thought to be charged with the energy of the Primary God. Schneider emends line 35 to read 'gefylle þas foldan mid fæste geleafe' (for manuscript 'geleafan') and translates 'to fill the fertile earth with strong leafage'. He understands lines 69–71 as alluding to a cosmogonical myth where the god embraces the earth to create fertility. By emending other lines he seeks to reconstruct the pagan form of the Charm.

484 Deegan, Marilyn. 'Pregnancy and Childbirth in the Anglo-Saxon Medical Texts: A Preliminary Survey.' *Medicine in Early Medieval England.* Ed. Marilyn Deegan and D.G. Scragg. Manchester: Manchester Centre for Anglo-Saxon Studies, 1987. Corrected re-issue 1989. 17–26.

Deegan briefly discusses Charm 6, on a comparative basis (21–2).

485 Elsakkers, Marianne. 'The Beekeeper's Magic: Taking a Closer Look at the Old Germanic Bee Charms.' *Mankind Quarterly* 27 (1987): 447–61.

Germanic bee charms were probably passed on by word of mouth for centuries. The main part of the audience for a bee charm consists of the bees themselves, since ancient customs testify to the treatment of bees as members of the family. In Charm 8 Storms's emendation (**418**) of 'wið on' in line 7 is unnecessary. The 'micelan mannes tungan' (line 6) refers to anyone who misuses the bee charms to secure a swarm he has no right to, while 'æminde' (line 5) refers to negligence on the part of the beekeeper. The first part of the Charm concerns itself with the beekeeper's duty to take good care of the livestock; the second part deals with the corresponding duties of the bees. The swarm is largely female (hence '-wif') and can be construed as winning a victory ('sige-') over the parent colony when it escapes from the hive.

486 Cameron, M.L. 'Anglo-Saxon Medicine and Magic.' *Anglo-Saxon England* 17 (1988): 191–215.

Cameron seeks to show that, despite Singer (**389**), Storms (**418**), and other scholars who emphasized the irrational and magical elements in the Charms, a rational element coexists with them. Thus the plantain stipulated by Charm 2 has an antibiotic efficacy, so long as freshly prepared. The recipe that forms part of Charm 4 consists of a quite rational salve for treating cramps and similar pains.

487 Gay, David E. 'Anglo-Saxon Metrical Charm 3 against a Dwarf: A Charm against Witch-Riding?' *Folklore* 99 (1988): 174–7.

Gay supports Kittredge's suggestion (**178**) that the dwarf in Charm 3 takes his victim on a wild witch-ride. Although the suggestion that the charm counters the nightmare is attractive, the description in lines 9–12 more closely matches the general pattern seen in accounts of witch-riding. In this pattern the witch bridles and mounts the victim and then proceeds to ride him, often into the air and with fatal results. The nightmare, by contrast, typically sits on a sleeper's chest and crushes him as he lies in bed. Gay points out that dwarves and spiders are often connected in folk tradition, so that Grattan's emendation (**394**) is unnecessary. He explains 'deores sweostar' (line 13) as 'the beast's sister'. One of the ways to get rid of the changeling is to threaten it, thus attracting one of its family to protect it by removing it.

488 Ogura, Michiko. 'Old English *wyrm, nædre*, and *draca.*' *Journal of English Linguistics* 21 (1988): 99–124.

In this study of a semantic field Charm 2 is among the texts briefly mentioned.

9 **Pàroli, Teresa.** 'Classico e germanico, due culture a contatto.' *Cultura classica e cultura germanica settentrionale. Atti del Convegno internazionale di studi, Università di Macerata. . .2–4 Maggio 1985.* Rome, 1988. 1–40.

[Not seen: annotation from 'The Year's Work in Old English Studies', *Old English Newsletter* 24.2 (1991): 5.] Pàroli studies the impact of Christian-Latin culture on Germanic literary tradition. She finds that traces of pagan mythology remain in certain texts, notably the metrical Charms, where invocations of pagan deities coexist with invocations of Christ and the saints and magical incantations of Christian texts such as the Paternoster.

0 **Bremmer, Rolf H., Jr.** 'Hermes-Mercury and Woden-Odin as Inventors of Alphabets: A Neglected Parallel.' *Amsterdamer Beiträge zur älteren Germanistik* 29 (1989): 39–48.
Bremmer argues for Mediterranean influence on the myth of Odin's discovery of runes. He is sceptical of the interpretation of 'wuldortanas' as runes or magical twigs in Charm 2, concluding from his survey of the meaning of *tan* and its cognates in other Germanic languages that the word refers to actual weapons, either rods or swords.

1 **Furlani, Fabio.** 'L'incantesimo anglosassone delle nove erbe: traduzione e ipotesi per un'analisi filologica ed antropologica.' *Studi Urbinati.* B. Scienze umane e sociali 62 (1989): 255–74.

Furlani's text and Italian translation of Charm 2 are based on the text and translation contained in Grattan and Singer (**423**). Furlani argues that the Woden episode can be accommodated to Ramat's definition (**450**) of 'myth' as a functional element in charms. The 'wyrm' should be regarded as the cause of the disease. Runes, incised and painted on the 'wuldortanas' with the different colours mentioned in the Charm, were originally used as the cure, but were later supplanted by herbs. Thus we see within the Charm a transition from Germanic, rune-based magic, centred on Woden, the arch-magician, to Mediterranean Christian herbal cures. The ninefold number of the 'wuldortanas' determines the number of herbs, which in turn determines the number of diseases.

2 **Glosecki, Stephen O.** *Shamanism and Old English Poetry.* New York: Garland, 1989. xv + 257 pp.

Glosecki sees the metrical Charms as close to the effective (i.e. not primarily aesthetic) utterance of tribal people, particularly of shamans. Some of the questions that puzzle the critics of Charm 4 disappear when the text is approached as a vestigially shamanic artifact. He offers a detailed reading of this Charm, arguing that strictly speaking it is a counter-charm, aimed at the figures held responsible for elf-shot, who use Odin's shamanic style of fighting. He sees little reason to limit the application of Charm 4 to rheumatic pain alone, since it could combat anything from a harmless stitch in the side through to a lethal ruptured appendix. A vision of apocalyptic riders confronts the persona, who then travels metempsychotically using the dissociative techniques of the shaman.

Glosecki suggests that the enemy roaming the land and shooting flying venom in Charm 2 may be the same furious host that rides loudly through the epic of Charm 4. A literal snake is probably not the primary referent in Charm 2, in spite of Storms (418). Rather the adder is a sympathetic image, another symbol for a magic shot. The Anglo-Saxon doctor uses exhalation to blow the flying venom out of his patient. In Charm 3 line 12 the verb 'colian' is explained as related to dreamtime flight, where the effect is felt as a rush of air chilling the sleeper's limbs. The transformation of the offending spirit, perhaps a sorcerer's companion, into a spider shape is distinctively shamanic. In Charm 8 the choosers of the slain ('sigewif'), with their unseen spears, are implicitly analogized to bees, with their stings.

493   **Molinari, Maria Vittoria.** 'Sull'*Æcerbot* anglosassone. Rituale per la benedizione dei campi MS Londra, B.L., Cotton Caligula A.VII.' *Romanobarbarica* 10 (1988–9): 293–308. = *Studi sulla cultura germanica dei secoli IV–XII in onore di Giulia Mazzuoli Porru.* Ed. M.A. D'Aronco et al. Rome: Herder, 1990. 293–308.

In this reassessment of the allegedly pagan and Christian elements in Charm 1, Molinari notes that the earth has a double function: (1) a power to be invoked, (2) the object on whose behalf the rite is performed. She interprets 'modor' in line 51 as a dative associated with 'þe' in line 52. The word 'erce' is a metathesis of *æcre*, from *æcer* 'field'. In her view the Charm relies not on paganism or syncreticism but on the magical use of typically Christian ritual and doctrinal elements.

494   **Keefer, Sarah Larratt.** 'A Monastic Echo in an Old English Charm.' *Leeds Studies in English* NS 21 (1990): 71–80.

Keefer analyses Charm 6 largely as sympathetic magic with a pagan background, but sees lines 12–15 as representing an echo of a monastic reference to scripture and liturgy. She attempts to explain line 15 without emendation as approximating to the meaning 'Through Christ I have spoken, this is made known', and suggests that it is influenced by the Magnificat.

495   **Sims-Williams, Patrick.** *Religion and Literature in Western England 600–800.* Cambridge Studies in Anglo-Saxon England 3. Cambridge: Cambridge UP, 1990. xv + 448 pp.

Brief comments are included on Charm 1 and relating to Charms 5, 9, and 10. As to Charm 1, Sims-Williams notes the existence of Old Irish *erc*, meaning a white cow, with red ears, considered to have magic properties in Celtic texts (292–3, n. 83). Likewise with the other Charms, influence from an 'indigenous British magic tradition' is a possibility to be considered (301).

The Fortunes of Men

ORIENTATION TO RESEARCH

DATING AND ATTRIBUTIONS

Fortunes is extant uniquely in the Exeter Book, dated by Ker (36) at the second half of the tenth century. Many early scholars, including Robinson (7), attributed *Fortunes* to Cynewulf, following the general direction established by Leo. Rieger (76) associated *Fortunes* specifically with a youthful Cynewulf's secular recitations in the mead-hall. Trautmann (17), Wülker (83), and Richter (22) rejected the attribution, arguing for a date between 700 and 740. Brandl (19) settled for a generally pre-Alfredian date.

STRUCTURE

Brandl (19) argued that the second part of the poem is a later continuation and reinterpretation of a heathen fragment: his arguments were supported by Sedgefield (164) but resisted by Dobbie (194). Kennedy (29) detected a thematic vacillation between crafts and fortunes. In Greenfield's opinion (40), these twin themes are drawn together at the conclusion. Resisting Greenfield, Dammers (502) posited a structure based on four sections: man's birth; evil fortunes; good fortunes; call for faith in Christ. Raw (54) identified the main theme as human helplessness and God's merciful care.

LITERARY CRITICISM

Brooke (13) and Wardale (26) considered *Fortunes* better than *Gifts,* a view shared by many subsequent critics. According to Greenfield and Calder (60), *Fortunes* is the more graphic and detailed of the two poems. According to Howe (328), it is formally superior. Campbell and Rosier (238) saw imagination and doctrine as effectively integrated in this text. Schücking (177) placed *Fortunes* and *Gifts* in the same relation to each other as Milton's 'Il Penseroso' and 'Il Allegro'. Similarly, Shippey (300) saw *Fortunes* as conveying the recognition of God's power, but without any evident confidence that all is for the best. Praise of specific passages can be found in the writings of such critics as Wyld (173). Pearsall (52) less charitably located *Fortunes*, along with *Gifts* and some other OEW poems in the Exeter Book, among the débris or spoil-heaps of the monastic tradition.

GENRE

Hotchner (199) identified a strong elegiac element in *Fortunes*. More specifically, Cross (239) traced the theme of the 'ways of death'. Perhaps hinting at a greater mixture of genres, Sorrell (353) pointed out that lines 21–4a read like an answer to a riddle-question.

RHETORICAL FEATURES

Patterns in the use of *sum* have attracted special interest, beginning with Bartlett (25). Cross (229) proposed that the Latin figure of *repetitio*, e.g. 'alii . . . alii', may underlie these patterns, though admittedly the poem does not otherwise demonstrate a close knowledge of Latin Christian writings. Similarly Campbell (303). Wienold (277) preferred to regard the figure of *repetitio* as an established native characteristic in *Fortunes* and other texts of this genre.

PLACE IN OLD ENGLISH LITERATURE

Some scholars have viewed *Fortunes* as a vestige of an archaic mode of poetry. Thorpe (65) compared it to *Maxims I* and *Hávamál* in this respect. Anderson (31) treated *Fortunes* as in essence gnomic verse. The Chadwicks (183) looked to ancient Greek texts for an analogue. Other scholars have attempted to locate *Fortunes* in the immediate context of Anglo-Saxon culture, with some characteristic differences of opinion about the role played by Christian doctrine in the text. Ten Brink (5) detected an interaction between secular and religious poetry. Schlauch (34) saw *Fortunes* as of Christian origin, though deriving from a pre-Christian genre. Schücking (177) saw it as a late, comparatively naturalistic poem. Though conceding that some of the deaths are made more realistic for Anglo-Saxon conditions, Cross (229) argued that the text is a tissue of Christian commonplaces. Cross subsequently (240) sought to place *Fortunes* against the background not merely of the Parable of the Talents but also of the commentaries upon it. Complementarily, Meaney (262) argued against contact with Germanic heathendom on the part of the poet and Weber (267) resisted any division of the text into Christian and heathen portions. Howe (328) sought to place *Fortunes* against the background of late classical and medieval catalogues and encyclopaedias. Pasternack (359) detected a general intertextuality in which *Fortunes* partakes.

SOCIAL OR HISTORICAL SIGNIFICANCE

Many scholars have attempted to situate this poem within a context of Anglo-Saxon society and material culture (thus Cross, 45). Rieger (76) saw the ending, with its emphasis on aristocratic gifts and virtues, as a compliment to the court. Merbot (87), Köhler (496), and Anderson (116) used *Fortunes* in their investigations of poetic performance, Roeder (114) for evidence concerning marriage customs, Budde (124) for the description of a drunkard's fate, Pfeilstücker (195) for information on gold-smithing, Whitelock (209) for sanctions against fighting in other people's houses, Wrenn (244) and Bessinger (261) for information on harp-playing, Hansen (299) for the Germanic type of the woman mourner, Fell (325) for the picture of a family and documentation of the birth-gift, and Oggins (326) for evidence on falconry. By contrast, Opland (313) warned against over-hasty extraction of data from the poem. Hansen (61) argued that the various endowments and fortunes should not be construed as mimetic descriptions of actual experience but as instances of the generic and the typical. The tree-climbing section (lines 21–6) has provoked controversy. Howard (**499**) saw a reference to falconry, Cross (**229**) to the gathering of green leaves for fodder, and Isaacs (**501**) to shamanistic ritual. Tripp (**503**) suggested an allusion to Óðinn's self-sacrifice.

BIBLIOGRAPHY

6   Köhler, Artur. 'Über den Stand berufsmässiger Sänger im nationalen Epos germanischer Völker.' *Germania* 15 (1870): 27–50.

Köhler discusses the profession of poet, drawing attention in passing to *Fortunes* lines 80–4, with their mention of the harp and the plectrum and of the performer's place 'æt his hlafordes fotum'. He compares the information in this source with that contained in *Widsith* and *Beowulf* (44).

7   Bradley, Henry. 'Two Corruptions in Old English Manuscripts.' *Academy* 43 (1893): 83.

Bradley explains *Fortunes* line 93 'weorod anes god' as a corruption of 'weoroda god'. The extra -*nes* stems from a supralinear or marginal correction of 'monna' in line 94 to 'monnes'. In line 94, therefore, 'monnes cræftas' should be read instead of 'monna cræftas'.

8   Swaen, A.E.H. 'Contributions to Anglo-Saxon Lexicography.' *Englische Studien* 37 (1907): 188–97.

[This is one in a series of vocabulary studies of the same title published in *Englische Studien* by Swaen.] Swaen discusses the hawking passage in *Fortunes* (lines 85–92), maintaining that it has been misunderstood by the lexicographers (195–7). He corrects Sweet 1897, Clark Hall 1894, and Bosworth-Toller 1882–98 on 'wyrplas', following the *NED*. The word 'feter' is to be explained contextually as the 'falconer's leash'. He sees 'lepeþ' as meaning 'feeds on small pieces of food' and related to the Modern English verb 'lap'. The noun 'wæd-' refers to the jesses. Once these misunderstandings have been cleared up, the passage can be recognized as an epitome of the falconer's craft.

9   Howard, Edwin J. 'Old English Tree Climbing: *Christ* vv.678–79.' *JEGP* 30 (1931): 152–4.

Howard deduces from *Fortunes* lines 21–6 that the climbing of trees played a considerable part in the lives of at least some Anglo-Saxons, since the other deaths listed in the poem do not seem to have been unusual ones. Tree-climbing might have been necessary to capture eyasses for falconry: the description of the one who falls as being 'fiþerleas' lends credence to this view.

10   Gatch, Milton McC. *Loyalties and Traditions: Man and his World in Old English Literature.* Pegasus Backgrounds in English Literature. New York: Bobbs, 1971. 180 pp.

Gatch notes the mention of performances on the harp in *Fortunes* lines 80–4 (48).

501   **Isaacs, Neil D.** 'Up a Tree: To See *The Fates of Men.' Anglo-Saxon Poetry: Essays in Appreciation. For John C. McGalliard.* Ed. Lewis E. Nicholson and Dolores Warwick Frese. Notre Dame: U of Notre Dame P, 1975. 363–75.

Isaacs notes that the tree-climbing activity in *Fortunes* lines 21–6 is paralleled in *Christ* lines 678b–9a, where it is treated as an occupation on the same basis as 'ship-driving' and 'sword-smithing'. The items in the list in *Fortunes* can all be related somehow to trials, tests, ordeals, or other activities appropriate to men of knowledge and power. Comparative ethnological evidence associates tree-climbing with shamanistic practices and rites of passage. The motif in *Fortunes* therefore probably has a ritual origin, though the poet may not have been aware of it.

502   **Dammers, Richard H.** 'Unity and Artistry in The Fortunes of Men.' *American Benedictine Review* 27 (1976): 461–9.

Fortunes, according to Dammers one of the most undervalued poems in Old English literature, has a thematic alliance with Samuel Johnson's 'The Vanity of Human Wishes'. Dammers places his discussion of *Fortunes* in the context of gnomic, didactic, Christian verse. The poem has four sections: man's birth; evil fortunes; good fortunes; call for faith in Christ. The ten E-type verses develop a refrain of the basic concepts in the poem. The inclusion of the repulsive scene of a raven picking out a man's eye (lines 36–7) can be related to the practice of requiring a repenting sinner to meditate upon a physical representation of human mortality. Greenfield's **(40)** criticism that the poet abruptly shifts gears at line 64 lacks justification. The poet's lesson is that all divinely given gifts, including drink, must be used correctly. The taming of the hawk epitomizes the Christianizing of human beings.

503   **Tripp, Raymond P., Jr.** 'Odin's Powers and the Old English Elegies.' *The Old English Elegies: New Essays in Criticism and Research.* Ed. Martin Green. Toronto: Associated University Presses, 1983. 57–68.

Tripp endorses Isaacs's **(501)** interpretation of *Fortunes* lines 21–6 as convincingly demonstrating the presence of shamanistic practices and therefore of northern influence. The fall of the man 'featherless' from a tree reflects Odin's sacrifice of himself to himself. The death-song and the confessional elegy are linked by the autobiographical perspective. Tripp sees a resemblance to the opening of *Maxims I*, in that the narrator here trades in secrets. Both shamanism and Christianity summoned up the dead to tell their stories in poetry.

The Gifts of Men

ORIENTATION TO RESEARCH

DATING AND ATTRIBUTIONS

Gifts is extant uniquely in the Exeter Book. Ker (36) dates this manuscript to the second half of the tenth century. Rieger (76), Robinson (7), and Grein (84) attributed *Gifts*, along with a great deal of other OEW poetry, to Cynewulf. Trautmann (17), Wülker (83), and Richter (22) rejected this attribution and argued for a date between 700 and 740. Brandl (19) settled for a generally pre-Alfredian date. Amos (56) observed that *Gifts*, along with *Cædmon's Hymn*, *Juliana*, and *Precepts*, is the only poetic text to contain exclusively long forms and seems likely to be earlier than those with a mixture of short and long forms.

SOURCES

Some scholars saw *Gifts* as a vestige of a very ancient type of poetry: Cook (504) and the Chadwicks (183) cited classical examples. For Abbey (102) *Gifts* seems like a Christian version of a Greek choral hymn. Calder et al. (320) identified the Old Norse *Hyndluljóð* as an analogue. There has been broad agreement as to specific Christian influences. Ward and Waller (20) cited the 29th homily of Pope Gregory's *Forty Homilies on the Gospels*, Cross (240) the Parable of the Talents, along with the commentaries upon it: Allen and Calder (298) refined on Cross's arguments. Raw (54) saw *Gifts* as combining the Parable of the Talents with Rom. 12: 3–8 so as to form a hymn. Short (509) detected an allusion to the Pauline analogy between the unity of divine gifts and the members of the body and (510) proposed an indebtedness to Gregory in the antithetical presentation of Christian doctrine. As to Old English vernacular influences, the specific similarities between the lists of occupations in *Gifts* and *Christ* were itemized by Cosijn (110). Krapp and Dobbie (194) suggested that the list in *Gifts* represents an elaboration on the list of gifts in *Christ*. Rieger (76) argued that Cynewulf, as author of *Gifts*, radically distorted the spirit of 1 Cor. 12: 8–10, under the influence of heathen poetry: similarly Brooke (109).

RHETORIC AND STRUCTURE

Cross (229) sought to show that repeated 'sum' is a figure of diction derived ultimately from pre-Christian Greek and Latin rhetorical teaching. Russom (512) opposed Cross, arguing that *Gifts* has close formal (and thematic) parallels in Old Norse. Campbell (303) saw anaphora on the word 'sum' as providing a structuring principle. In Campbell's opinion (344), *Gifts* is characterized by an envelope pattern, whose middle section could have been either expanded or contracted in other realizations.

LITERARY CRITICISM

Brooke (**13**) is typical of many critics in rating *Gifts* as inferior to *Fortunes*: see the introduction on that poem for comparisons and contrasts. Ebert (**79**) denied *Gifts* any poetic merit whatever. Wardale (**26**) criticized the repetitions and random juxtapositions: similarly Howe (**328**). Bartlett (**25**) found the use of the envelope pattern obvious and the handling of antithesis mechanical. For Sedgefield (**164**) *Gifts* is a mechanical compilation of pre-existing maxims, for Legouis and Cazamian (**168**) it is overly sententious.

PLACE IN OLD ENGLISH LITERATURE

Ten Brink (**5**) detected an interaction between secular and religious poetry in this text. Howe (**328**) placed it against the background of late classical and medieval catalogues and encyclopaedias. According to Diamond (**236**), the mentions of sea-voyaging in *Gifts* show a familiar theme being introduced in telescoped form. Similarly, Pasternack (**359**) saw *Gifts* as a component in Old English poetic intertextuality.

SOCIAL OR HISTORICAL SIGNIFICANCE

Cross (**45**), along with many other scholars, valued this text for its vignettes of Anglo-Saxon life. Grinda (**249**) and others have noted its implied admiration for crafts. Among specific discussions, Brooke (**13**) draws on *Gifts* to document armour and warfare, Budde (**124**) for drinking customs, Pfeilstücker (**195**) for metal-work, Whitelock (**209**) for the legal system, Opland (**313**) for poetic performance, Oggins (**326**) for falconry, and Garavelli (**341**) for navigation. Young (**211**) regarded the failure of *Gifts* to mention a chef as indicative of a culture that privileged drink. Not all scholars have been happy with the treatment of the material in *Gifts* as mimetic descriptions of actual experience: thus Wormald (**511**) and Hansen (**61**).

BIBLIOGRAPHY

504   **Cook, Albert S.** *The Christ of Cynewulf. A Poem in Three Parts: The Advent, The Ascension, and Last Judgment.* Boston: Ginn, 1900. ciii + 294 pp.

Cook cites classical examples attesting to the universality of the 'gifts of men' theme (136–7).

505   **Klaeber, Frederick.** 'Jottings on Old English Poems.' *Anglia* 53 (1929): 225–34.

Klaeber makes incidental references to *Gifts* in the course of a discussion of *Christ* lines 678–9 (231–3). He defends the notion that 'skill in gymnastic entertainment' (lines 82–4) could appear in this type of list (232). In *Gifts* 'the most diverse occupations are enumerated without any recognizable order' (233).

506   **Whitelock, Dorothy, ed.** *English Historical Documents c. 500–1042.* London:

Eyre, 1955. Vol. 1 of *English Historical Documents*. Ed. D.C. Douglas. 13 vols. to date. 1955–.

Whitelock includes a translation of *Gifts*, minus the introduction and conclusion (805). She suggests in a note that 'beorhyrde', translated as 'dispenser of beer' (line 75), may not be analogous in formation to *hlaford* but rather may mean 'cellarer'.

7   Clemoes, Peter. *Rhythm and Cosmic Order in Old English Christian Literature: An Inaugural Lecture.* Cambridge: Cambridge UP, 1970. 28 pp.

Clemoes makes a brief mention of *Gifts* (12–13).

8   Short, Douglas D. 'The Old English *Gifts of Men*, Line 13.' *Modern Philology* 71 (1974): 388–9.

In Short's opinion, line 13 of *Gifts* presents a serious crux not noted in ASPR **(194)**. It seems plausible that the 'oþþe' in line 13 is an unconscious reminiscence of 'oþþe' in line 12, substituting for original 'ond'. The line would then be translated as 'wise in intellect and in speech'.

9   ———. '*Leoðocræftas* and the Pauline Analogy of the Body in the Old English *Gifts of Men.*' *Neophilologus* 59 (1975): 463–5.

Short suggests that the word 'leoðocræftas' (line 29) does not mean 'bodily skills' or 'skills in the use of the limbs' but rather was devised as a deliberate allusion to the Pauline analogy between the unity of divine gifts (*cræftas*) and the members of the body (*leoþu*). The word would then be a 'metaphoric compound' perhaps best translated as 'member-crafts'. Each of the endowments of mankind is defined as individual members of a unified body – the metaphoric body of Christ, which is the Church.

———. 'The Old English *Gifts of Men* and the Pedagogic Theory of the *Pastoral Care.*' *English Studies* 57 (1976): 497–501.

Gifts lines 8–29 seems not to be based on the sources adduced for the poem as a whole by Cross **(240)**. In his *Pastoral Care* ch. 32, Gregory outlines methods of teaching Christian doctrine to opposed categories of people, e.g. rich versus poor, male versus female, young versus old, and humble versus proud. The poet of *Gifts* follows this lead by addressing part of the exordium to the humble and part to the proud. He encourages the humble and timid, assuring them that nobody is wholly deprived of God's gifts; conversely, he restrains the proud, warning them that nobody receives a superabundance of gifts. Only after preparing his audience with the appropriate exhortations does the poet begin illustrating his doctrine by enumerating the gifts. This antithetical technique for teaching Christian doctrine must be derived from Gregory, and specifically from the Alfredian translation.

Wormald, C.P. 'The Uses of Literacy in Anglo-Saxon England and its Neighbours.' *Transactions of the Royal Historical Society* 5th ser. 27 (1977): 95–114.

Wormald notes the references to individuals learned in poetry and/or the law in *Gifts* (lines 35–6 and 72–3) but argues that we can hardly use that poem as evidence of a class of secular English professionally learned people comparable with the Irish *filid*.

512   **Russom, Geoffrey.** 'A Germanic Concept of Nobility in *The Gifts of Men* and *Beowulf.' Speculum* 53 (1978): 1–15.

Russom opposes Cross's **(240)** suggestion that *Gifts* may have been inspired by patristic commentary on the parable of the talents. Cross's analogues all list ways of earning a living, whereas the Old English list is not restricted in this way. It consists entirely, in Russom's opinion, of endowments regarded as marks of aristocratic distinction. Both formally, in terms of a structure reliant on the lexical item *sum*, and thematically, in terms of the types of skills listed, *Gifts* has close parallels in Old Norse poetry and prose. Even such skills as horse-breaking (lines 69–70), carpentry (lines 44–8), and smithing (lines 58–60) can be shown from this material to have formed part of the Germanic aristocratic lifestyle. The essential distinction was that these activities were not used to earn a living. Skills involving mercantile or agrarian life are therefore absent from *Gifts* and other such lists.

513   **Orme, Nicholas.** *Early British Swimming 55 BC to AD 1719.* Exeter: U of Exeter, 1983. xi + 215 pp.

Orme notes the possible reference to swimming in *Gifts* line 58 (12).

Homiletic Fragment I

ORIENTATION TO RESEARCH

DATING AND ATTRIBUTION

Homiletic Fragment I appears uniquely in the Vercelli Book. Ker **(36)** dated this manuscript to the second half of the tenth century. Although the text is fragmentary, Förster **(519)** believed that only a small portion of the beginning of the poem has been lost. Raw **(54)** grouped *Homiletic Fragment I, Soul and Body I*, and *The Dream of the Rood* as items copied into the Vercelli Book from a single earlier manuscript. Kemble **(514)** argued for a late, tenth-century date of composition for all the Vercelli Book poems. *Homiletic Fragment I* was among those attributed to Cynewulf by some nineteenth-century scholars, e.g. Robinson **(7)**.

SOURCE STUDIES

This poem has widely been regarded as a homily based on Psalm 28 or even as a paraphrase of the entire psalm: so ASPR **(520)**. Other scholars have preferred to posit a freer relationship between the two texts. Förster **(518)**, for example, contended that the poem cannot have contained a treatment of the entire psalm and that the theme is only partially related. Magoun **(521)** described the poem as merely suggested by Psalm 28: 3: similarly Isaacs **(264)**. McKinnell **(1119)** characterized it as a religious meditation that happens to quote one verse of Psalm 28. Hill **(522)** found a patristic source for the poem's central metaphor of 'the bee with its honeyed mouth and poisoned tail'. Pulsiano **(523)** saw the link between Psalm 28: 3 and the poem's bee metaphor as arising from specific patristic interpretations of the Psalm.

LITERARY CRITICISM

Most surveys of Old English literature merely mention the poem without elaboration. Lies and falsehoods have consistently been identified as the central theme. Pearsall **(52)** argued that this text, like all the other poems in Vercelli Book, would have been overshadowed in the Anglo-Saxon scale of values by the volume's twenty-two prose homilies. Anderson **(31)** found *Homiletic Fragment I* more interesting than the thematically related *Vainglory*. According to Greenfield and Calder **(60)**, *Homiletic Fragment I* is intended as a work of consolation. Weber **(267)** compared it with *The Wanderer* in its deprecation of *tristitia*.

BIBLIOGRAPHY

514   **Kemble, J.M.** *The Poetry of the Codex Vercellensis, with an English translation.* Aelfric Society Publications 5 and 6. 2 vols. in one. London: Aelfric Society, 1843 and 1856.

Kemble describes *Homiletic Fragment I* as a religious fragment of 92 lines. He argues for a late, tenth-century date of composition for all the Vercelli Book poems. Vol. 2 contains a text and translation of *Homiletic Fragment I*, headed 'A Fragment, Moral and Religious' (79–82). There are no notes or glossary.

515   **Napier, Arthur S.** 'Collationen der altenglischen Gedichte im Vercellibuch.' *Zeitschrift für deutsches Altertum* 33 (1889): 66–73.

Napier notes where the Wülker (6) text of *Homiletic Fragment I* deviates from the manuscript (69). He also corrects Wülker's description of the manuscript.

516   **Holthausen, Ferdinand.** 'Zur Textkritik altenglischer Dichtungen.' *Beiträge zur Geschichte der deutschen Sprache und Literatur* 16 (1892): 549–52.

Holthausen discusses *Homiletic Fragment I* (551), referring to the poem as 'Predigt über ps.28' and also 'be manna lease'. He contributes textual notes on lines 12 and 40–1, with the aim of improving the versification.

517   **Wülker, Richard.** *Codex Vercellensis. Die angelsächsische Handschrift zu Vercelli in getreuer Nachbildung.* Leipzig: Veit, 1894. viii pp. + facsimile of manuscript.

The facsimile is reduced to half-size. The edition restricts itself to the poetic contents of the manuscript. Wülker entitles *Homiletic Fragment I* (Introduction, vii) 'Der Menschen Falschheit (Predigt über Psalm 28)' but adds no further commentary. In the facsimile, *Homiletic Fragment I* appears at 104a and b.

518   **Förster, Max.** 'Der Vercelli Codex CXVII nebst Abdruck einiger altenglischer Homilien der Handschrift.' *Festschrift für Lorenz Morsbach.* Ed. F. Holthausen and H. Spies. Studien zur englischen Philologie 50. Halle: Niemeyer, 1913. 20–179.

Förster describes *Homiletic Fragment I* (79–80), estimating that about half of the original text survives. He considers titles for the poem that imply a homily on Psalm 28 inappropriate, because the poem cannot have contained a treatment of the entire psalm and the theme is only partially related.

519   **Foerster, Massimiliano [i.e. Max Förster].** *Il Codice Vercellese con Omelie e Poesie in Lingua Anglosassone.* Rome: Danesi, 1913. 70 + 136 pp.

In the introduction to this reduced facsimile edition, Förster describes *Homiletic Fragment I* (63–4) as moralizing on the falsity of men and as alluding to Psalm 28: 3. He believes that only a small portion of the beginning of the poem has been lost. In the facsimile *Homiletic Fragment I* appears on folios 104a and b.

20	**Krapp, George Philip, ed.** *The Vercelli Book.* Vol. 2 of *The Anglo-Saxon Poetic Records: A Collective Edition.* New York: Columbia UP, 1932. xciv + 152 pp. 6 vols. 1931–53.

This volume contains text and notes for *Homiletic Fragment I.* In the Preface (v–vii) the editor points out that the poems of the Vercelli Book exhibit a certain degree of conformity, being legendary and homiletic in character. The present edition is based on the photographic reproductions of the manuscript by Wülker (**517**) and Förster (**518**). Emendations for metrical reasons are admitted only when metrical considerations seem to support other evidence that some accidental disturbance has taken place in the transmission of the text. In the Introduction (xi–lxxx) the editor describes the manuscript, with mentions of *Homiletic Fragment I* (xx, xxiii, xxvi, xxx, xxxvi, xxxix, xlvii, and li). That not much of this poem has been lost can be inferred from the fact that it is a loose amplification of Psalm 28, which itself contains only nine verses (xxxix). The Bibliography (lxxxi–xciv) includes studies of the complete manuscript and also of the separate poems up until *c.* 1927. The text of *Homiletic Fragment I* appears at 59–60. The notes (129–30) provide a very full account of conjectures and comments on the part of previous scholars.

21	**Magoun, Francis Peabody, Jr.** *The Vercelli Book Poems: Done in a Normalized Orthography.* Cambridge, MA: Department of English, Harvard U, 1960. vii + 118 pp.

Homiletic Fragment I is headed 'Reflections on back-biting two-faced people, suggested by Psalm 28.3' (62–3). Magoun provides a synopsis but no commentary or glossary.

22	**Hill, Thomas D.** 'The Hypocritical Bee in the Old English "Homiletic Fragment I", lines 18–30.' *Notes and Queries* 213, NS 15 (1968): 123.

Hill finds a patristic source for the poem's central metaphor of 'the bee with its honeyed mouth and poisoned tail' in Gregory's *Homiliae in Ezechielem.*

23	**Pulsiano, Phillip.** 'Bees and Backbiters in the Old English *Homiletic Fragment I.*' *English Language Notes* 25.2 (1987): 1–6.

Pulsiano analyses the links between the poem's bee metaphor (with its allusion to the Passion) and Psalm 28: 3 (the source for the opening lines of the poem). The basis for the linkage lies in Cassiodorus's interpretation of the Psalm as commemorating the Passion and Resurrection and Augustine's interpretation of it as spoken by 'the Mediator Himself'. The poet is not only speaking of slanderers, but, more importantly, is associating backbiters and hypocrites with the same people that persecuted Christ. In virtue of further allusions to Psalm 117, both Passion and Judgement Day are encompassed by the text.

Homiletic Fragment II

ORIENTATION TO RESEARCH

TEXT

This poem is uniquely extant in the Exeter Book, dated by Ker (**36**) to the second half of the tenth century. Whitbread (**263**) and Ritzke-Rutherford (**310**) commented on the manuscript context. The relevant section is severely damaged, leaving some words irrecoverable. Chambers and Flower (**185**) produced as complete a transcription as possible. Despite the editorial title, Greenfield (**40**) and Wittig (**525**) have disputed the poem's status as a fragment. Greenfield and Calder (**60**) pointed to thematic and verbal linking between beginning and end of the extant text as an indication of completeness.

SOURCE STUDIES

Wittig (**525**) saw the text as indebted to Eph. 4: 5–6 and possibly also Eph. 5: 17–20. Cross (**241**) found lines 6–7 reminiscent of the Christian idea of the declining world in its sixth age.

LITERARY CRITICISM

Anderson (**31**) found this poem quite negligible. Hotchner (**199**) detected a strong elegiac element and Frantzen (**321**) pointed out a thematic similarity to *The Wanderer*. Anderson (**331**) credited it with a Trinitarian argument and placed it amongst a series of Exeter Book texts which he termed 'The Easter Riddle'.

BIBLIOGRAPHY

524 **Cosijn, Peter J.** 'Anglosaxonica.' *Beiträge zur Geschichte der deutschen Sprache und Literatur* 19 (1894): 441–61.

Cosijn offers a series of brief textual notes based on a survey of Wülker's edition (**6**) and using Sievers's (**101**) analysis of Old English metre. Amongst the words and passages discussed is 'teoraŏ' in *Homiletic Fragment II* line 5, which he emends to 'ateoraŏ' on metrical grounds (442). Sievers (as editor of the journal) appends a footnote suggesting that the first syllable of *teoran* may have been scanned optionally either long or short to suit the various poetic contexts in which it is found.

525 **Wittig, Joseph S.** 'Homiletic Fragment II and the Epistle to the Ephesians.' *Traditio* 25 (1969): 358–62.

Wittig sees lines 8–10 of the text as certainly a close adaptation of Eph. 4: 5–6.

The Anglo-Saxon poet is merely adapting the scriptural verse to his metre, which calls in question Krapp and Dobbie's **(194)** conclusions about the style of this enumeration and its significance for dating the poem. Eph. 5: 17–20 may be relevant to the opening of the poem. The end of the poem contains a reference to the Incarnation. Altogether there seems to be no valid reason for calling the poem a fragment: structurally, two references to the tribulations of the world are enveloped within three passages emphasizing the Redemption.

26 Johnson, William C. '*Werig* and *Dreorig* in *The Wanderer*: The Semantics of Death.' *In Geardagum* 7 (1986): 45–69.

Johnson discusses in passing the idea of binding one's thoughts in *Homiletic Fragment II*.

Maxims I and *II*

ORIENTATION TO RESEARCH

MANUSCRIPTS, CONTEXTS, AND INTEGRITY OF THE TEXT

Maxims I is found uniquely in the Exeter Book, dated by Ker (**36**) at the second half of the tenth century. According to Dobbie (**194**), it is impossible to decide whether the three sectional divisions indicated in the manuscript for *Maxims I* were intended by the scribe to be taken as three parts of a single poem, or as three separate poems. *Maxims II* is found uniquely in Cotton Tiberius B.i, which Ker considered to be written in a mid-eleventh-century hand. Earle (**533**) sought to explain the inclusion of *Maxims II* in this manuscript, commenting that *Maxims II* and *Menologium* look as if they had been meant to stand as a sort of prelude to the *Anglo-Saxon Chronicle*. Dobbie (**203**) regarded the two poetic texts as originally separate from each other and from the *Chronicle*. Whitbread (**568**) presumed that the scribe gave *Maxims II* only a cursory examination before including it. Bollard (**595**) argued that *Maxims II* was prefaced to the *Chronicle* because the scribe correctly construed it as a description of the ordering of nature and society. Robinson (**614**) emphasized a common factor, the catenulate structure of each of these three texts. For editions and translations of *Maxims I* and *II* see the Subject Index.

DATING AND ATTRIBUTION

According to the methods used by Ricci (**181**), *Maxims I* and *II* emerge as amongst the earliest Old English poems. Williams (**547**) and Galinsky (**563**) placed *Maxims II* in the Conversion period. *Maxims I* was attributed to Cynewulf by Dietrich (**71**), Rieger (**72**), Sarrazin (**95**), and Strobl (**537**). Other scholars, including Brooke (**109**), Trautmann (**673**), and Williams (**547**), opted for a post-Cynewulf dating. Robinson (**352**) proposed that a woman might appropriately have composed a poem that transmits, besides other kinds of folk wisdom, a comment on child-rearing and an account of a Frisian woman welcoming her husband home. Other scholars have disavowed unitary authorship and analysed both texts as composite. According to Strobl (**537**), specific passages in *Maxims I* presuppose varying dates, either the Conversion period or the beginning of the eighth century. Krogmann (**576**) suggested that *Maxims I* lines 93–9 represents a translation from a Frisian original. Anderson and Williams (**189**) placed the compilation of *Maxims II* in Wessex, just after the Conversion. Brandl (**19**) saw both texts as having heathen, possibly ritual, origins; *Maxims II* represented a Conversion-period ritual poem adapted by a tenth-century Benedictine reformer (**559**). Brandl's views were, however, qualified by Timmer (**202**). Meaney (**262**) expressed doubt that the poet of *Maxims I* possessed substantial information about Woden. For Brooke (**13**), the two texts represented a literary collection made at York, during the time of Ecgberht or Æthelberht. Greenfield **(40)** saw the authors of both texts as clerics who fused heterogeneous aphorisms, some ancient and some more contemporaneous: similarly Sedgefield **(164)** in respect of *Maxims II*. According to Heusler **(166)**, the *Maxims* were perhaps designed for school use. In these discussions as to dating and authorship a crucial passage has been *Maxims II* lines 4–5. Galinsky **(563)** read the passage to mean that the powers of Christ rated lower than those of Fate, which would suggest composition early in the Conversion period; similarly Kellermann **(232)**. But Mittner **(222)** argued that the application of the adjective *swið* to *wyrd* indicates influence from Christianity. In Weber's opinion **(267)**, the statement 'wyrd bið swiðost' does not contradict Christian doctrine but rather expresses a heightened awareness of transience.

SOURCE STUDIES

Noting resemblances between *Maxims I, Hávamál,* the *Sentences* of Theognis, and the *Works and Days* of Hesiod, Thorpe **(65)** proposed that texts of this sort are characteristic of an archaic state of society. Strobl **(537)** argued that they transmit an inherited Germanic system of gnomes. Müller **(540)** traced the individual gnomes back to an early stage of cultural and cognitive evolution when human beings were beginning to make observations concerning themselves and their environment. Ettmüller **(68)** regarded the *Maxims* as a series of genuine proverbs which have been strung together by alliteration. To what extent the *Maxims* embody pagan material has been a point of dispute. Williams **(547)** and other scholars stigmatized Christian elements in the *Maxims* as spurious. But Grein **(3)** had already interpreted 'alwalda' in *Maxims I* as referring to the Christian God, not Woden. Timmer **(566)** believed that although the blending of heathen and Christian elements has been performed crudely, we cannot simply remove the Christian lines to disclose the 'original' text. Rankin **(550)** criticized Williams **(547)** for not taking Latin didactic prose and verse into account in her discussion of sources. Anderson **(31)** entertained the possibility that some lines in the *Maxims* are directly influenced by the Book of Proverbs, but concluded that they are more probably mere analogues. Hill **(588)** uncovered sources for parts of *Maxims I* and *II* in the Books of Proverbs and Ecclesiasticus respectively. Lendinara **(597)** postulated an Old Testament-inspired interpolation in *Maxims I*. Weber **(267)** pointed out parallels between *Maxims II* and certain passages in Boethius's *De Consolatione Philosophiae*, though without stipulating a direct literary connection.

ISSUES OF COHERENCE AND UNITY

A major source of dissension has been the degree of coherence exhibited by the two texts. A few scholars have tried to discern an organic unity but most have operated with assumptions of heterogeneity. Among the numerous contributions to this debate are the following. Wülker **(16)** and Ebert **(79)** suggested that the *Maxims* derived from drinking contests, where each participant had to contribute an aphorism in succession. Müller **(540)** tried to demonstrate instances of cohesion between the individual aphorisms, though admitting that the two poetic texts as a whole are not fully cohesive. According to Brooke (109), the *Maxims* are an unorganized collection that includes quotations from *Beowulf* and other poems. Williams likewise (547) found a general lack of cohesion. Malone (565), like many other scholars, posited expansions, contractions, or *ad hoc* compositions on the part of a monastic reviser-compiler. Wrenn (43) contended that *Maxims II* is marginally more organized than *I*. Barnes (582) argued that scholars' expectations about thorough-going order are misplaced. According to Howe (328), likewise, attempts to find unity or coherent development in *Maxims I* and *II* run counter to the function of these texts as collections of free-standing aphorisms. By contrast, Dawson (573) saw the two texts as built up by multiple associations so as to constitute a mnemonic arrangement. Lendinara (590) defended the thematic unity and cohesion of both texts. Greenfield and Evert (602) sought to correct what they saw as a virtually unanimous trend in previous criticism of *Maxims II* to deny the poem any aesthetic unity. Barley (607) sought to show that *Maxims II* establishes relationships of opposition and similarity between the parts of an overall orderly universe. Earl (618) described *Maxims IA* as characterized by learned and intelligible leaps of the imagination. Raw (54) believed that the control over logical progression is ceded to the audience, for them to construct as they please.

VERSE-FORM

Some scholars have attempted to define the format of the pre-existing aphorisms from which the extant texts were purportedly constructed. Kögel (106) explained the numerous irregular lines on the assumption that the material underlying *Maxims I* underwent careless conversion into a standard long-line scheme. Kock (155) argued that much early Germanic wisdom was expressed in short, pithy sentences that did not fit later systems of versification. Various scholars, among them Rieger (80), Sievers (101), Malone (206), and Williams (547), have sought to establish commonalities with Old Norse strophic patterns, notably those involving *ljóðaháttr*. Sievers (92) qualified this with the observation that in *Maxims I* certain lines, especially the three-syllable ones, do not fit any attested system. Holthausen (128) tried to extend the array of examples by emending divergent lines into a *ljóðaháttr* pattern. Robinson (579), followed by Bammesberger (332), advised against assuming isolated occurrences of *ljóðaháttr* metre until the possibility of textual corruption has been considered. The numerous hypermetric lines have also attracted a great deal of scholarly attention. Such investigators as Sievers (92), Schmitz (133), and Pope (204) have seen analysis of hypermetric lines in *Maxims I* as complicated by the need to reckon with irregular versification in the original text. Kock (163) defended hypermetric lines in *Maxims II* against emendation and similarly Heusler (170) argued that the mixture of different line types was an authentic feature, not an outcome of textual corruption. Bliss (227) saw *Maxims* as drawing on a different metrical tradition from the remainder of Old English poetry.

GENRE ISSUES

The 'epistemological' status of the aphorisms in these texts is open to dispute. Can some of them at least be seen as proverbs? Are they really maxims? (The title is of course purely editorial.) Taylor **(558)** noted the difficulty of distinguishing between a proverb and a maxim in these compositions. Barley **(592)** considered that as contrasted with the *Durham Proverbs* (a collection, which contains true proverbs and maxims) the sayings in *Maxims I* and *II* are unclear in status, though they have potential proverbial status. Schneider **(323)** attempted a definition of the proverb, as seen in English and other Germanic languages, so as to include the two texts. Pilch and Tristram **(55)** argued for an allegorical interpretation of many aphorisms. Tripp **(301)** suggested classing *Maxims* in a genre of 'complexity poems', because they insist on the unattainability or complexity of wisdom. Other suggestions have included Arend's **(530)**, that *Maxims II* embodies a prophecy or vaticination, perhaps designed to protect the kingdom, Strobl's **(537)**, that *Maxims II* consists of a set of mnemonic verses, and McGillivray's **(628)**, that the central subject of *Maxims IB* is the relationship between the sexes in marriage.

LEXIS

The exact senses of the verbs *sceal* and *bið* have been much scrutinized in a search for patterns and definitions. Taylor **(585)**, for example, contended that verses with the copula *bið* describe and define created entities, whereas the verses with *sceal* specify their functions. Henry **(259)** concluded that gnomic *sceal* typically expresses the notions of customary action or state, inherent quality and characteristic property, passing over on the one hand to ideal or hortatory action (state), and on the other to a sense of certainty. Fell **(325)** remarked that whereas it does not much matter whether 'sceal' in 'fisc sceal on wætere' is translated as 'ought to be' or 'by nature is', it does make a good deal of difference whether a woman 'ought' to be cheerful, or 'it is the nature' of a woman to be cheerful.

LITERARY CRITICISM

Most scholars would agree with Turner's **(527)** description of *Maxims II* as a 'very singular and curious composition'. Wardale **(26)** and Anderson **(32)** spoke for many in judging the *Maxims* as trite and commonplace, though interesting on account of their popular origin. To Cassidy and Ringler **(273)**, the insertion of *Maxims II* into a *Chronicle* manuscript suggests that it struck Anglo-Saxons as a solemn, profound, and fittingly sententious prologue to a serious historical work. As to more localized devices and effects, Anderson **(569)** contended that *Maxims I* lines 54–6 is to be regarded as an analogy, not a simile. Campbell **(572)** proposed that the phrase 'Frisian woman' in *Maxims I* might be an instance of metonymy.

COMPARATIVE LITERATURE APPROACHES

The legitimacy of comparison with other traditional literary forms is also in dispute. Do the *Maxims* really exist on the same footing as the *Works and Days* of Hesiod? Do they really point back to the origins of literature or should we see them as a functional literary form at the time of commitment to vellum? Among scholars who favour a placement in the origins of literature are Fox **(528)** and Arend **(530)**, who detected some resemblance to Pindar. The Chadwicks **(183)** incorporated *Maxims I* and *II* in a typology of gnomic poetry that covers a variety of 'heroic age' societies. But other scholars have looked for a more nearly contemporary context. Müller (**540**) posited literary analogues, notably *Fortunes*, *Gifts*, *Rune Poem*, and *Vainglory*, along with *Málsháttakvæði*. Martin (**584**) included *Maxims I* lines 71–7 in a discussion of the possible literary links between Old English poetry and Latin literature in their descriptions of winter. Jackson (**193**) observed that the characteristic Irish use of lists can be paralleled in *Maxims II* and *Solomon and Saturn*. Henry (**259**) entered into a detailed discussion of parallels between Old English and Welsh gnomic poetry.

MENTALITY

A related problem is the mentality which the *Maxims* represent. An anthropologist might analyse them on structuralist lines, arguing that they typify attempts in early societies to impose structure on the observed universe and that they signal early understandings of human nature and the environment. According to Gruber (**606**), *Maxims I* began as archaic 'initiatory utterances of an absolute, religious nature', whereas *Maxims II* represents a more drastic appropriation of older wisdom literature, revalorized into an instrument of an 'agnostic aestheticism'; cf. Gruber (**610**). Cherniss (**593**) cited the *Maxims* as testimony to traditional Germanic notions. Schneider (**594**) found references to runes and their meanings cryptically concealed in two passages and posited a heathen author who disguised an account of heathen cosmogony and cults in this seemingly harmless form (cf. **339**). Niles (**357**) proposed that a relict of animism may be present in *Maxims II*. Contrastingly Raw (**54**) envisaged the *Maxims* as depicting a world controlled by God. Lendinara (**590**) noted that gnomic poetry is among the few genres of Old English poetry whose essential Christianity has not been thoroughly acknowledged in the scholarly literature.

CULTURAL SETTING

The class perspective of the *Maxims* has been a topic of discussion. Hodgkin (**191**) believed that the *Maxims* encapsulate the viewpoint of the *ceorl*. According to Whitelock (**209**), they usefully correct the heroic emphases of much extant Old English poetry. Individual sentences from these texts have been used to illustrate aspects of early Anglo-Saxon culture: thus Heyne (**73**), on drinking customs; Mackie (**556**), Brown (**561**), Lendinara (**596**), and Russom (**627**), on funerary practices; Whitbread (**567**), on ceremonies of purification; Cross (**589**), on justifications of defensive war; Judd (**599**), on marriage settlements; Meaney (**613**), on women's role in love-magic; Busse (**626**), on the authority of books among late Anglo-Saxon aristocratic laypeople; and Opland (**313**), on the functions of the *scop*. Against these appeals to the *Maxims* as quasi-documentary sources, Schrader (**619**) observed that the comments on women do not necessarily provide pictures of actual behaviour. For his part, Robinson (**7**) rejoiced that the charge of unfaithfulness is levelled not at the Anglo-Saxon, but at the Frisian wife.

BIBLIOGRAPHY

Turner, Sharon. *The History of the Anglo-Saxons, from their first Appearance above the Elbe to the Death of Egvert.* . . 4 vols. London: Cadell, 1799–1805. 6th rev. edn. *The History of the Anglo-Saxons from the earliest Period to the Norman Conquest.* 3 vols. London: Longman, 1836.

Turner includes *Maxims II* in translation (3.330–2), describing it as a 'very singular and curious composition'. [Citation from the 6th edition.]

Fox, Samuel. *Menologium seu calendarium poeticum ex Hickesiano thesauro: or the poetical Calendar of the Anglo-Saxons with an English translation and notes.* London: Pickering, 1830. viii + 64 pp.

Fox includes a translation of *Maxims II* (44–55). In his opinion, the poem is wild, and exhibits the vagrant fancy of the ancient northern bards, which wandered through a variety of subjects, apparently unconnected. The classical reader will here see some resemblance to the luxuriant imagination of Pindar.

[Longfellow, Henry Wadsworth.] 'Anglo-Saxon Literature.' *North American Review* 47 (1838): 90–134. Repr. as 'Anglo-Saxon Language and Poetry' in Henry Longfellow. *The Poets and Poetry of Europe, with introductions and biographical notices.* Philadelphia: Carey, 1845. 1–29. New York: Francis, 1857.

Longfellow builds on Fox's discussion (**528**). He describes *Maxims II* in these terms: 'At the end [of the "Poetic Calendar", i.e. the *Menologium*] is a strange poem, consisting of a series of aphorisms, not unlike those that adorn a modern almanac' (1857, 6). In the appended selections from Old English poetry Longfellow has 'selected simple prose translations, as best calculated to convey a clear idea of the rhythmic but unrhymed originals' (7). These translations include Turner's (**527**) rendering of *Maxims II*, under the heading 'Poem from the Poetic Calendar' (21–2). A sample (lines 1–3, 28–31):- 'The king shall hold the Kingdom;/ Castles shall be seen afar,/ The work of the minds of giants,/ That are on this earth;/ The wonderful work of wallstones./. . . The king will in the hall/ Distribute bracelets./ The bear will be on the heath/ Old and terrible./ The water will from the hill/ Bring down the gray earth.'

Arend, Johannes Pieter. *Proeve eener Geschiedenis der Dichtkunst en Fraaije Letteren onder de Angel-Saksen.* Amsterdam: Schleijer, 1842. iv + 199 pp.

Arend translates *Maxims II* into Dutch (92–4) and points out a resemblance to the poetry of Pindar. He believes that the text embodies a prophecy or vaticination and that in some way it may have been designed to protect the kingdom.

Ebeling, Friedrich Wilhelm. *Angelsächsisches Lesebuch.* Leipzig: Romberg, 1847. ix + 138 pp.

Ebeling includes *Maxims II* (119–21), taking his text from the editions by Hickes (1705) and Fox (**528**). The reader includes a glossary but no substantive notes.

532 **Grimm, Jacob.** *Geschichte der deutschen Sprache.* 2 vols. Leipzig: Weidmann, 1848.

Grimm comments on *Maxims I* line 95, arguing that 'frysan' in this context means 'free, generous'. Had the meaning 'Frisian' been intended, the word used would have been *frysiscan* (2.668–71).

533 **Earle, John.** *Two of the Saxon Chronicles Parallel with Supplementary Extracts from the Others.* Oxford: Clarendon, 1865. lxxiv + 457 pp.

Maxims II appears at xxxiv–xxxvi: text only, with no translation or notes. Earle comments that *Maxims II* and *Menologium* look as if they had been meant to stand as a sort of prelude to the Chronicle. Although he concedes that the sentiment that 'truth is misleading' (line 10) has a strange Machiavellian look, he believes that the virtuous rendering of Hickes (1705), *verus facillime decipitur*, cannot be accepted. He understands 'clibbor' (line 13) as 'adhesive' and reads 'woe is wonderfully clinging'.

534 **March, Francis A.** *Introduction to Anglo-Saxon: An Anglo-Saxon Reader with Philological Notes, a Brief Grammar and a Vocabulary.* New York: Harper, 1870. viii + 148 pp.

March includes the text of *Maxims I*B, i.e. lines 71–137, with very brief notes and a glossary.

535 **Sievers, Eduard.** 'Collationen angelsächsischer Gedichte.' *Zeitschrift für deutsches Altertum* 15 (1872): 456–67.

Sievers notes where Grein's (2) text of *Maxims II* deviates from the manuscript (466).

536 **Cosijn, Peter J.** 'Anglosaxonica.' *Tijdschrift voor nederlandsche Taal- en Letterkunde* 1 (1881): 143–58.

Cosijn argues that in *Maxims II* line 13 'clibbor' should mean 'clinging' rather than 'burdensome'. If the manuscript readings are correct, the sense must be that sorrow does not speedily leave a person but rather clings to him. Such a thought is, however, uncharacteristic of the common-sense attitudes otherwise exhibited by the poet. Cosijn therefore tentatively proposes the emendation 'weax' ('wax'). In *Maxims I* line 152 he proposes 'wræd sceal wundum' to maintain parallelism, though acknowledging that the manuscript reading ('wunden') is linguistically acceptable. His discussion of *Maxims I* line 117 supports Kern (82).

537 **Strobl, Joseph.** 'Zur Spruchdichtung bei den Angelsachsen.' *Zeitschrift für deutsches Altertum* 31 (1887): 54–64.

Strobl seeks to clarify whether the *Maxims* transmit inherited Germanic wisdom. The opening of *Maxims I* (lines 1–3) misleadingly heralds a dialogue poem of the sort familiar from *Solomon and Saturn* and from Old Norse. It is comparable in form to the so-called Riddle 60. This latter text is in reality not a riddle: Dietrich's (658) solution 'reed' leaves details unaccounted for. Rather it should be seen as the opening section of *The Husband's Message*, with a rune stave as its central subject. The rest of *Maxims I* is analysed virtually line by line to demonstrate that despite its heterogeneity of content and form it consists of a series of gnomic utterances. Some gnomes can be seen as combining with others to form a cohesive strophe or verse paragraph. Lines 132–3 have their source in Psalm 95: 5, suggesting a context in the Conversion period. Lines 192–200 originate in the same cultural context as the *Beowulf* 'interpolation' on Cain and Abel and allude to the Oswald-Penda feud, which points to a dating of *Maxims I* around the beginning of the eighth century. *Maxims II* shows a preference for consonantal alliteration, rather than the less distinctive vocalic alliteration, which suggests that these are mnemonic verses, designed for use in schools.

8   Kauffmann,   Friedrich. 'Die   sogenannten   Schwellverse   der   alt-   und angelsächsischer Dichtung.' *Beiträge zur Geschichte der deutschen Sprache und Literatur* 15 (1891): 360–76.

Kauffmann cites lines from *Maxims I* as representing the Old English instances that most closely parallel the hypermetric lines in the *Heliand*, which he identifies as based on an expansion of the D-type.

9   Plummer, Charles. *Two of the Saxon Chronicles Parallel with Supplementary Extracts from the Others: A Revised Text with Introduction, Notes, Appendices and a Glossary on the Basis of an Edition by John Earle.* 2 vols. Oxford: Clarendon, 1892.

The text of *Maxims II* is included (1.280–2), along with the *Menologium*. Plummer concurs with Earle's (**533**) comment that the intimate association of *Maxims II* with the Chronicle justifies their incorporation in this edition. A very brief critical apparatus is subjoined.

)   Müller, Hugo. *Über die angelsächsischen Versus Gnomici.* Diss. U Jena. Jena, 1893. 55 pp.

Müller reconstructs the history of *Maxims I* and *II*, basing his argument on Grein's (**2**) edition. The individual gnomes within these poems go back to a time when people were beginning to make observations concerning themselves and their environment. These observations were embodied in short, pithy prose sentences, which were passed down in oral tradition, attracting other similar observations couched in the same mnemonic form. Strictly factual observations led naturally to moral and logical observations. Advances in observation and understanding were accompanied by a greater expansiveness in the expression of the individual gnomes. Further remodellings of the originally succinct prose sentences were brought about by the practice of agglomerating them into verse compilations. Müller classifies the gnomes according to their content, e.g. individual, general, or abstract (5–6). In Chapter 1 (6–25) Müller argues that *Maxims II* is an incoherent mass of material which divides into two main sections, as can be seen from a purely formal analysis: lines 1–49 consist of maxims of two lines or fewer, lines 50–66 of maxims of more than three lines. Further formal analysis yields a section (lines 16–40) where typically the b-verse enunciates the maxim and the a-verse merely elaborates on it. In this way the poet is not inconvenienced by the lack of two alliterating words within the original prose maxim. These original maxims are listed (12). The compilation can be credited, if that is the right word, to a monastic poet, who has embellished the original prose for didactic purposes. *Maxims I* is more skilfully adapted to a didactic purpose. Throughout section 1 of *Maxims I* (lines 1–70), which consists of a dialogue, we see a pattern where the simple traditional gnome is first enunciated and then amplified with didactic remarks. Thus 'god us ece bið' (line 8b) is amplified in lines 9a–12a. Similarly in section 2 of *Maxims I* (lines 71–137) gnomes about women undergo amplification: for example, lines 94b–5b ('leof wilcuma/ Frysan wife, þonne flota stondeð') are subjected to didactic elaboration in lines 96–9. This section is characterized by the pursuit of a coherent theme ('woman'). The themes in section 3 (lines 138–204) are consistent with a theory of composition and recitation on the part of a bard addressing the war-band in time of battle. Women are not mentioned here because they have no place within the overall topic of warfare. Müller tries to demonstrate instances of cohesion between the individual gnomes but also suggests that lack of cohesion in the manuscript form might have been compensated for in actual performance by gestures and other body language. In Chapter 2 (25–31) Müller investigates the changes that have been made to the putative original prose gnomes to adapt them to an extended work in poetic form. The gnomes are classified in respect of length and syntax (e.g. incidence of *bið* and *sceal*). The didactic passages that Müller interprets as later expansions are analysed in respect of content. He finds only a small proportion of genuine proverbs among the *Maxims*: these are listed (31), e.g. 'licgende beam læsest groweð' (*Maxims I* line 158). In Chapter 3 (31–9) Müller subjects the *Maxims* to stylistic analysis with respect to e.g. use of adjectives, ornamental epithets, and appositions. Chapter 4 (39–49) is devoted to metrical and prosodic analysis. Müller argues that some of Sievers's (92) supposed hypermetric lines are in reality prose. He documents a wide variety of types of rhyme and assonance, including *aðalhendingar* and *skothendingar* [types of line-internal rhyme in skaldic poetry] and alleged rhyme-links between lines and half-lines. In Chapter 5 (49–55) Müller identifies literary analogues, notably *Fortunes*, *Gifts*, *Rune Poem*, and *Vainglory*, along with *Málsháttakvæði* [the Old Icelandic versified compilation of proverbs].

541 Kock, Ernst A. 'Interpretations and Emendations of Early English Texts III.' *Anglia* 27 (1904): 218–37.

Kock's note 70, at 229–33, discusses the use of *stælan* in the context of *Maxims II* lines 51–4, and other poems: he argues that 'synne stælan' should be understood as 'call to account for injury, avenge (wrongful) hostility'.

542 Schlutter, Otto B. 'Ae. *lewesa* "inopia".' *Englische Studien* 41 (1910): 328–31.

Schlutter suggests two possible emendations for 'nefre' in *Maxims I* line 38 (328).

543 ———. 'Ae. *gamolian* "altern".' *Englische Studien* 41 (1910): 454–5.

Schlutter corrects his stricture on Sweet for omitting *gamolian* 'grow old' (cf. 'gomelað' in *Maxims I* line 11) from his Dictionary (1897), noting that the omission was actually perpetrated by Bosworth-Toller (1882–98). Sweet is nonetheless inconsistent in his policy of normalization. Schlutter speculates on the etymology of Old English *gamol* and its cognates and derivatives.

4 Holthausen, Ferdinand. 'Zur altenglischen Literatur X. 30. Zu den Gnomica Exoniensia.' *Anglia Beiblatt* 21 (1910): 154–6.

Holthausen rejects the postulated compound '*æradl' in *Maxims I* line 31 as a ghost-word and returns to Thorpe's (**65**) interpretation. In line 38 he rejects the postulated adjective '*nefre', here too returning to Thorpe. This becomes the occasion for an attack on Schlutter (**542**), for his discussion of this word and for his editorial methods in general, 'bei denen oft unwissenheit und methodelosigkeit um die palme streiten'. In line 161 'mon<na>', the weak form of the nominative singular, is to be restored.

5 Schlutter, Otto B. 'Zu "Anglia-Beiblatt" XXI, nr. 5, s.155–6.' *Anglia Beiblatt* 21 (1910): 317–9.

Schlutter polemicizes against Holthausen (**544**), with incidental mention of *Maxims I*. In line 38 'nefre' is to be explained as an error for 'wæfre'. In line 68 'gifstol' does not mean 'throne' but should be interpreted literally according to its etymology.

Holthausen, Ferdinand. 'Erwiderung.' *Anglia Beiblatt* 21 (1910): 319–20.

Against Schlutter (**545**), Holthausen declares continued confidence that 'gifstol' in *Maxims I* line 68 means 'throne'. In a short note appended to this reply, the editor, Max F. Mann, attempts to restore peace.

7 Williams, Blanche Colton. *Gnomic Poetry in Anglo-Saxon.* New York: Columbia UP, 1914. xiii + 171 pp. New York: AMS, 1966.

Williams provides a text, commentary, notes, and glossary of *Maxims I* and *II*. In the commentary she attempts a comprehensive description and definition of the types of *sententiae*, ranging widely outside the Germanic sphere. She discriminates between the heathen and Christian elements in *Maxims I* more minutely than her predecessors Strobl (**537**), Brandl (**19**), and Müller (**540**) – indeed virtually line by line. She detects resemblances to Old Norse poetry in both form (strophes in *fornyrðislag* and *ljóðaháttr*) and substance. She sees *Maxims I* line 144 as having a parallel in *Hávamál* and line 145 as containing an idiom which is probably a direct borrowing from Old Norse. The cohesion of *Maxims I* is negatively assessed. Frequently aphorisms separate in meaning are tied together by a primitive prosody, *Maxims I* lines 152–8 being an example. The realia documented in the individual gnomes (e.g. sexual fidelity among the Germanic peoples, games with dice, and fear of bears) are discussed in terms of analogues from other Old English poetry, Tacitus, Saxo, and elsewhere. She reviews attributions of *Maxims I* to Cynewulf on the part of Dietrich (**71**), Rieger (**72**), Sarrazin (**95**), and Strobl (**537**), but agrees with those scholars, including Brooke (**109**) and Trautmann (**673**), who regard them as postdating Cynewulf. To these scholars' metrical arguments she adds the consideration that Cynewulf's involution of runes into his signed poems is done with skill and subtlety, whereas the 'mortising' of these aphorisms has been performed, she thinks, by a 'prentice hand': 'weaving a literary fabric from odds and ends of sententious material is hardly worthy the name of authorship' (98). She finds evidence of West Saxon dialect in *Maxims I* such as to encourage an attribution to Aldhelm, or perhaps to Alfred, whose attested versifying is also crude (99). On *Maxims II* she makes similar comments concerning the indications of early origin, presence of internal divisions, the general lack of cohesion, and the possibility of distinguishing different compositional strata. Among her proposed sections is lines 1–16a, which are 'composed of sentences, almost the only connection between which is the bond of alliteration' (106). Lines 14–15, because of their regularity and polish, seem to represent a later distich inserted into this section. In the next section, lines 16b–41, 'the hand of the artificer is evident' (108) and the impression is of an exercise in verse technique. Less well-defined are lines 41–54. The remainder of the poem is shown by its reflective and religious qualities to be the addition of a Christian scribe. Strobl (537) is correct in maintaining that certain lines can be recognized as prose if severed from their verse context. The poem would be an early example of what became a popular practice in verse technique, to be compared with the Scandinavian rune poems and the *þulur*. The poem as a whole most likely represents an essentially ancient heathen work which has been lightly adapted for Christian consumption in a southern English setting. [For reviews see Klaeber, **548**; Haworth, **549**; Rankin, **550**.]

548   **Klaeber, Frederick.** Rev. of *Gnomic Poetry in Anglo-Saxon,* by Blanche Colton Williams [**547**]. *Englische Studien* 49 (1915–16): 428–30.

Klaeber appends detailed notes on the text of *Maxims I,* some correcting Williams's translation.

549   **Haworth, P.D.** Rev. of *Gnomic Poetry in Anglo-Saxon,* by Blanche Colton Williams [**547**]. *Modern Language Review* 11 (1916): 89–90.

In *Maxims I* line 107 Haworth suggests reading 'ceapeadig' and 'cyningwic' as compounds.

550   **Rankin, J.W.** Rev. of *Gnomic Poetry in Anglo-Saxon,* by Blanche Colton Williams [**547**]. *JEGP* 15 (1916): 163–5.

Rankin criticizes Williams for not taking Latin didactic prose and verse into account in the discussion of sources. Although the Germanic peoples might have developed a native 'gnomology', the maxims that survive do not necessarily belong to this native stock. He disapproves of Williams's attempts to separate heathen material from Christian and also doubts the attribution of the compilation to Alfred or Aldhelm.

551   **Sievers, Eduard.** *Metrische Studien IV: Die altschwedischen Upplandslagh nebst Proben formverwandter germanischer Sagdichtung.* Abhandlungen der philologisch-historischen Klasse der königlichen sächsischen Gesellschaft der Wissenschaften. 35.1–2. Leipzig: Teubner, 1918–19. vii + 262 pp.; 263–620.

In Part I Sievers supplies text and metrical scansion of *Maxims* (142–53). His

'Stimmanalyse' shows that the constituent maxims in *Maxims I* originate with a diversity of authors and have undergone revisions, certain of them on more than one occasion. *Maxims I* contains genuine examples of short lines (as in *ljóðaháttr*), though previously they have been mistakenly bunched together as hypermetric lines. Only the use of alliteration distinguishes them from the short lines found in the laws and other texts. Sievers lineates *Maxims II* line 42 as follows: 'Þeof sceal gangan/ in þystrum wederum./ Þyrs sceal on fenne gewunian.'

Holthausen, Ferdinand. 'Zur englischen Wortkunde III.' *Anglia Beiblatt* 32 (1921): 17–23.

In Note 60 Holthausen rebuts Schlutter **(542)** and Kock **(147)** on 'nefre' in *Maxims I* line 38 and reiterates his suggestion 'næfig' **(150)** without elaboration **(22)**.

Kock, Ernst A. 'Plain Points and Puzzles: 60 Notes on Old English Poetry.' *Lunds Universitets Årsskrift* NS 1, 17, no 7 (1922). Lund: Gleerup, 1922. 26 pp.

Kock discusses *Maxims I* lines 31–4, reading line 31 as an independent proverb 'the baby adds,/ when early sickness takes'. He explains 'nyde' in line 38 as 'fetter'. An emendation is proposed in lines 52–3. [For a review see Klaeber, **554**.]

Klaeber, Frederick. Rev. of *Plain Points and Puzzles*, by Ernst A. Kock **[553]**. *JEGP* 22 (1923): 313–15.

Klaeber approves of Kock's interpretation of *Maxims I* lines 31–2, but suggests emending 'þa ær' to 'þær'.

Krüger, Charlotte. *Beiträge zur gnomischen Dichtung der Angelsachsen.* Diss. U Halle. Halle, 1924.

Despite the title, much of this dissertation is not directly concerned with the *Maxims* or other OEW poems. Krüger examines the tradition of the gifts of God to mankind. These gifts, which are itemized in detail, come to human awareness through visions, such as Constantine's vision of the Cross and the various visions described in Old English literature. Krüger comments briefly on the tradition as it manifests itself in *Maxims II* (64–74).

Mackie, W.S. 'Notes on Old English Poetry.' *Modern Language Notes* 40 (1925): 91–3.

Note 1 deals with *Maxims I* lines 148–50, arguing that they provide evidence for a continuation into the Christian period of the custom where a band of horsemen rode round the memorial mound singing a funeral song.

Klaeber, Frederick. 'Altenglische wortkundliche Randglossen.' *Anglia Beiblatt* 40 (1929): 21–32.

In Note 11, on *aræd*, Klaeber finds the meaning of this word in *Maxims I* line 191 hard to determine and suggests emendation to 'æræd' ('lack of counsel', 'unreason'). The maxim would point to the hastiness of 'unreason'.

558 **Taylor, Archer.** 'The Proverbial Formula "Mann soll. . ."' *Zeitschrift für Volkskunde* 2 (1930): 152–6.

Taylor examines the evolution of formulas involving 'sceal' and its cognates in the other Germanic languages. His examples include citations from *Maxims I*. In such verses as 'styran sceal mon strongum mode' (line 50a), the word 'mon' should not be deleted, in spite of the metrical arguments urged by Kögel (106). The evidence from early Scandinavian texts shows that the old impersonal or passive 'shall' constructions were being replaced by the formula 'mon sceal' (and its cognates). So familiar was the formula that in Old English the dependent infinitive could be omitted, as in 'meotud sceal in wuldre' (line 7a), 'eorl sceal on eos boge' (line 62a), and other sentences in *Maxims I*. More generally, Taylor mentions the difficulty of distinguishing between a proverb and a maxim in a composition like *Maxims I*. We find the 'proverbial ring' in 'styran sceal mon strongum mode' (line 50a) and 'mægen mon sceal mid mete fedan' (line 114a), but usually the proverbial character of such remarks is difficult to establish in the absence of parallels in modern traditional proverbs (153).

559 **Brandl, Alois.** 'Vom kosmologischen Denken des heidnisch-christlichen Germanentums: der früh-ags. Schicksalsspruch der Handschrift Tiberius B 13 und seine Verwandtheit mit Boethius.' *Sitzungsberichte der preussischen Akademie der Wissenschaften. Philosophisch-historische Klasse* 14–16 (1937): 116–25.

Brandl reconstructs a history of *Maxims II* where a ritual poem originally composed at the time of the Anglo-Saxon conversion to Christianity came into the hands of one of the Benedictine reformers at the end of the tenth century. This reformer added a continuation, of a type consistent with learned poetry of the late Anglo-Saxon period in content and in form (e.g. the use of the definite article). The first thirteen lines, which are still half-heathen, give some idea of the form and content of the original poem. These initial lines supply a cosmology, invoking the king, the elements, the supernatural powers of Christ and Fate, and the seasons. The original sacral status and special powers of the king, in respect of cosmology, are implied by his mention at the head of the list. The meaning of 'wyrd' is discussed, with the observation that it was a common Germanic concept that lent itself to incorporation into a Christian world-picture seen in Aldhelm's *Ænigmata* and in Boethius. Brandl defends the maxim 'soð bið swicolost' (line 10) against modern emenders, relating it to Bede's statement that Coifi searched in vain for truth in the various heathen beliefs (120). Similarly, he defends the reading 'wea' (line 13) against the emendation 'weax' (120).

560 **Krogmann, Willy.** 'Altenglisches.' *Anglia* 61 (1937): 351–60.

Note 3 (355–6) deals with *Maxims I* line 106, explaining 'egsan' as the familiar word meaning 'fear' and rejecting suggestions, most recently in Mackie's edition (188), that it should be interpreted as 'possessor'. Krogmann also criticizes Mackie's handling of 'frysan' in line 95.

1 Brown, Carleton. 'Poculum Mortis in Old English.' *Speculum* 15 (1940): 389–99.

Brown seeks to clarify the problematic half-line *Maxims I* line 78a 'deop deada wæg' by explaining 'wæg' as 'cup' and 'deada' as an error for 'deaða', a *u*-declension form. He cites analogues for the 'cup of death' as a literary figure in Anglo-Saxon times – e.g. twice in *Guthlac B* – and posits a pre-Christian origin. Line 78b can be reconstructed as 'dyrne bið lengest holen' and line 79 as 'ad sceal inæled, yrfe gedæled': in translation, 'the deep cup of death is the secret longest hidden: the funeral pyre shall be kindled; the inheritance divided. . .' Thus lines 78–80 become a unit dealing with a single theme, mortality, in a pagan fashion.

2 Rositzke, Harry August. *The C-Text of the Old English Chronicles.* Beiträge zur englischen Philologie 34. Bochum-Langendreer: Pöppinghaus, 1940. 100 pp.

The text of *Maxims II* appears on 9–11, without notes, introduction, or glossary.

3 Galinsky, H. 'Sprachlicher Ausdruck und künstlerische Gestalt germanischer Schicksalsauffassung in der angelsächsischen Dichtung.' *Englische Studien* 74 (1941): 273–323.

Galinsky reads *Maxims II* lines 4–5 to suggest that the powers of Christ are being unfavourably contrasted with the powers of Fate. Since this is a sentiment which is incompatible with Christianity, an early date of composition is implied, perhaps at the onset of the Conversion period (279–83).

4 Holthausen, Ferdinand. 'Zu alt- und mittelenglischen Texten.' *Anglia Beiblatt* 54–5 (1943–4): 27–34.

Holthausen offers emendations in *Maxims I*. He suggests reading line 177 as 'a scylen þa rincas geræde lædan', where 'geræde' = 'armour'. He restores line 179 as 'næfre hi mon tomelde <on mædle>'.

5 Malone, Kemp. 'Notes on Gnomic Poem B of the Exeter Book.' *Medium Aevum* 12 (1943): 65–7.

Malone analyses *Maxims I*B (lines 71–137) as an independent poem. He sees lines 71–7 as made up of three sentences: the first on winter, the third on summer, and the second a link added by some cleric. In line 72 the growth of earth occurs as a consequence of the fall of snow. The word 'holen' in line 79 means 'prince', not 'holly'. Line 100a was originally a full line but has been reduced to half-line status by some clerical re-worker. Other lines too represent expansions, contractions, or *ad hoc* compositions on the part of a reviser-compiler.

6 Timmer, Benno J. 'Heathen and Christian Elements in Old English Poetry.' *Neophilologus* 29 (1944): 180–5.

Timmer believes that the blending of heathen and Christian elements has been performed more crudely in the *Maxims* than in *Wanderer* or *Seafarer*. Even here we cannot simply remove the Christian lines to disclose the 'original' text. He discusses the treatment of the theme of worldly glory before and after death in

Maxims. Maxims II shows an adaptation to Christianity, in that the word *dom* means 'glory' in line 21 but '(divine) judgement' in line 60. In *Maxims I lof* means 'praise' and *dom* means 'glory'.

567 Whitbread, Leslie. 'The Frisian Sailor Passage in the Old English Gnomic Verses.' *Review of English Studies* 22 (1946): 215–19.

Whitbread argues that *Maxims I* lines 94b–9 is based on realistic observation, adducing reports of modern folk customs, notably one from [Papua] New Guinea, as confirmation. These customs are characterized by special taboos and ceremonies of purification. Thus these lines in *Maxims I* should be seen as describing not one chance occurrence but a regularly repeated, traditional proceeding.

568 ———. 'Two Notes on Minor Old English Poems.' *Studia Neophilologica* 20 (1948): 192–8.

Whitbread seeks to explain the presence of *Maxims II* in Cotton Tiberius B.i, prefacing the *Anglo-Saxon Chronicle*. The scribe's first step was to include the *Menologium*, prompted by its strict chronological arrangement and computistic interests. Then because the *Menologium* was followed in his copy-text by *Maxims II* he concluded, after a cursory examination of the description of the seasons in the first lines, that it too was relevant.

569 Anderson, Orval J. 'Once more: the Old English Simile.' *West Virginia University Bulletin, Philological Papers* 8 (1951): 1–12.

Anderson surveys the use of similes in Old English poetry. He notes that the poetry of the Exeter Book seems to be particularly poor in similes. *Maxims I* lines 54–6 is to be regarded as an analogy, not a simile, though certainly it is picturesque and apt. As to the scarcity of similes, it is probably best to conclude that the poetic tradition of the time did not feel it expedient to use the simile extensively alongside the kenning, or to limit the use of the kenning in favour of the simile.

570 Whitelock, Dorothy. *The Audience of Beowulf.* Oxford: Clarendon, 1951. [v] + 111 pp.

In Whitelock's opinion, the evidence of place-names gives good support to the statements of *Maxims II* concerning the dragon and the *þyrs*. The latter maxim (lines 42b–3a) she translates as 'a *þyrs* shall inhabit the fens, alone in the depths of the country'. She points out that these statements are made in the same matter-of-fact tone as other parallel statements concerning the wolf or the stars (75).

571 Timmer, Benno J. 'A Note on Beowulf ll.2526b–2527a and l.2295.' *English Studies* 40 (1959): 49–52.

Timmer interprets *Maxims I* line 173b as 'he has his destiny appointed for himself', with a discussion of the syntax.

2 Campbell, Alistair. 'The Old English Epic Style.' *English and Medieval Studies Presented to J.R.R. Tolkien on the Occasion of his Seventieth Birthday.* Ed. Norman Davis and C.L. Wrenn. London: Allen, 1962. 13–26.

In the course of discussing possible examples of classical rhetorical figures in Old English poetry Campbell wonders if ingenuity is wisely expended in theorizing why a 'Frisian woman' appears in *Maxims I* line 95. He suggests that the epithet may be an instance of metonymy and hence immaterial to the substance of the text. In support of this suggestion, he cites Quintilian and Servius on the use of epithets (19).

3 Dawson, Robert MacGregor. 'The Structure of the Old English Gnomic Poems.' *JEGP* 61 (1962): 14–22.

Dawson assumes that there must have existed large collections of maxims which formed a corpus of general information. *Maxims I* and *II* could be regarded as representing different subsets of this corpus. As to their internal organization, the two poems are not simply lists but mnemonic arrangements in sequences built up by multiple phonetic and semantic associations. Dawson works his way through the two texts, recognizing a few definite breaks but mostly positing a continuous process of association. He finds *Maxims I* C less unified than A and B. The poetic methods in the two texts are in line with the general Old English poetic tendency to digression.

4 Nicholson, Lewis E. 'Oral Techniques in the Composition of Expanded Anglo-Saxon Verses.' *PMLA* 78 (1963): 287–92.

Nicholson includes *Maxims I* line 50a as one of only a handful of hypermetric verses to be repeated verbatim in the corpus of Old English poetry. Analysing the components of hypermetric verses, he instances *Maxims I* 46a as among the type where two normal formulas are juxtaposed. In *Maxims I* line 52a a word ('wægas') is omitted to avoid the full juxtaposition. Also mentioned are lines 41a, 52b, and 146a in *Maxims I.* In *Maxims II* line 4b unusual syntax suggests a lapse in the singer's art.

5 Kuhn, Hans. 'Der Name der Friesen.' *It Beaken* 25 (1963): 270–9.

Kuhn discusses 'frysan' in *Maxims I* line 95. The *-y-* must be intrinsic, not merely a spelling for *i*, because such spellings are very rare in the Exeter Book. The adjective is of unknown meaning. Kuhn relates it to the nickname *friesa*, which he argues cannot mean 'Frisian'. The root would be **frausja-* or **freusja-*, also of uncertain meaning.

Krogmann, Willy. 'Stabreimverse friesischer Herkunft.' *It Beaken* 26 (1964): 334–46.

Krogmann suggests that *Maxims I* lines 93–9 represent a translation from a Frisian original. The poem in general originated as a collage of pre-existing maxims, which are notorious for their migratory habits. Individual words in the 'Frisian wife' passage correspond to attested early Frisian words. The Old English 'warig' ('seaweed-covered') in line 98 represents a mistranslation of Old

Frisian *wasich* 'dirty'. With reference to a proposed new etymology of the word *Frisian* Krogmann argues that the phrase 'Frysan wife' should be interpreted as 'the Frisian's wife'.

577 **Mitchell, Bruce.** 'Pronouns in Old English Poetry: Some Syntactical Notes.' *Review of English Studies* NS 15 (1964): 129–41.

The discussion includes syntactical problems in *Maxims I*. Lines 37–8 exhibit possible examples of asyndetic parataxis, a vestige of a more primitive stage of Old English. Lines 99 and 104 contain examples of 'þæs' meaning 'what'. Line 169 exhibits 'þe' without an antecedent when the principal clause and adjective clause require different cases, comparable to Exeter Book Riddle 50 line 9. Re-punctuation is suggested for lines 183–4.

578 **Crossley-Holland, Kevin.** 'The Frisian Wife.' *Review of English Literature* 6.2 (April 1965): 101.

This is a rather free versified translation of *Maxims I* lines 71–7 and 94–106. Line 106 is translated 'the sea holds him in her hands'. A sample translation (lines 71–4): 'Frost will forge fetters, fire devour timber,/ Earth will quicken and ice build crystal bridges;/ Water will be strait-jacketed, will shackle/ Reeds and sprouting seeds.'

579 **Robinson, Fred C.** 'Notes and Emendations to Old English Poetic Texts.' *Neuphilologische Mitteilungen* 67 (1966): 356–64.

Note 2 (359–60) deals with *Maxims I* lines 54–6. Robinson advises against assuming an isolated occurrence of *ljóðaháttr* metre here until the possibility of textual corruption has been considered. Adoption of the conjecture 'sund', for manuscript 'wind', would improve the sense and restore a regularly alliterative long-line. Palaeographically the miscopying of 'sund' as 'wind' is highly plausible.

580 **Fry, D.K.** 'Old English Formulas and Systems.' *English Studies* 48 (1967): 193–204.

Fry expresses the view that 'feorhcynna fela' (*Maxims I* line 14a) and 'fela feorhcynna' (*Beowulf* line 2266a) probably originated from the one formulaic system, despite the reversal of word order (202).

581 **Greenfield, Stanley B.** 'The Canons of Old English Criticism.' *ELH* 34 (1967): 141–55.

Greenfield discusses the possible formularity of three apparently related phrases, 'rum recedes muþ' (*Maxims II* line 37a), 'recedes muþan' (*Beowulf* line 724), and 'merehuses muþ' (*Genesis A* line 1364a). He points out that major differences exist – metrically, alliteratively, syntactically, and lexically. What we seem to have is a conventional image expressed in three roughly similar phrases, which we can if we desire call a formulaic system. As shown by *Maxims II*, the image was habitually collocated with 'door'. There are sufficient semantic and syntactic differences to suggest that individual words and grammatical structures were elements involved in the choices of the poets. In context, the *Beowulf* phrase is unquestionably the most effective. What poetic quality inheres in the *Maxims II* phrase is as much rhythmical as anything: the swiftness of the first verse (an A-type) yields to the slower-paced D2 (150–2).

32   Barnes, Richard G. *From the Manuscript Cotton Tiberius Bi: An Anglo-Saxon Gnomic Poem.* San Francisco: Grabhorn-Hoyem, 1968. [Unpaginated. Limited edition.]

This book is devoted to a translation of *Maxims II*, with a brief introduction. Barnes argues that the lack of logical sequence in the poem has been over-emphasized in criticism, partly because in fact some order does exist, partly because the expectation of order is radically misplaced. We do not expect of a new poem any obvious order or continuity; we find in a list, a collage, a pile of things, order enough to conform to our deepest intuitions of nature. Sample translation (lines 1–4): 'A king keeps his realm. castra loom up afar, labor of giants when they lived on this earth, skilled rampart-masonry. in sky wind is swiftest, and loudest thunder. . .'

33   Fry, D.K. 'Some Aesthetic Implications of a New Definition of the Formula.' *Neuphilologische Mitteilungen* 69 (1968): 516–22.

Fry posits a formulaic system that includes *Maxims II* line 37a 'rum recedes muð'.

34   Martin, B.K. 'Aspects of Winter in Latin and Old English Poetry.' *JEGP* 68 (1969): 375–90.

Martin includes *Maxims I* lines 71–7 in this discussion of the possible links between Old English poetry and Latin literature in their descriptions of winter. Two distinctive and typical motifs found in the *Maxims I* passage are that land and water may be 'bound' by cold or ice and that ice may make 'bridges' over water. The emphasis on seasonal change finds its counterparts in *Beowulf* and *Menologium*. The same motifs occur frequently in Latin literature and may have been disseminated to Anglo-Saxon England via a tradition of formal literary exercises based on Virgil and Ovid. To assume a background for these motifs in Germanic antiquity is to risk the error of primitivism.

35   Taylor, Paul B. 'Heroic Ritual in the Old English Maxims.' *Neuphilologische Mitteilungen* 70 (1969): 387–407.

Taylor discusses lines 71–137 of *Maxims I*. Verses with the copula 'bið' describe and define created entities, whereas the verses with 'sceal' specify their functions. In distinct contrast with the 'bið' maxims, all of the 'sceal' maxims suggest a degree of choice. The 'sceal' maxims can therefore be seen as a sort of handbook on ritual. They comprise (1) the rituals of nature, which, being of God's provenance, are out of man's control, and (2) the rituals of men, which are heroic obligations. *Maxims I* serves as an inventory of poetic themes; some of the individual maxims echo important themes of heroic poetry and can be used to enhance our understanding of such poems as *The Battle of Brunanburh*.

586 Capek, M.J. 'A Note on Formula Development in Old Saxon.' *Modern Philology* 67 (1970): 357–63.

Capek argues that the type 'ymb ealra landa gehwylc' in *Maxims II* line 46 represents a late borrowing from the Old Saxon formula system.

587 Goldsmith, Margaret E. *The Mode and Meaning of 'Beowulf'.* London: Athlone, 1970. xi + 282 pp.

Goldsmith takes issue with Whitelock's **(571)** translation of 'ana innan lande' (*Maxims II* line 43a) as 'alone in the depths of the country', arguing that the last phrase is not as precise as this rendering suggests. The thief, the *þyrs*, and the woman with a secret lover juxtaposed associatively in *Maxims II* lines 42–5 are all evidently creatures of the night (97). The origins of the association of dragon and barrow-guardian seen in *Maxims II* lines 26b–7a are discussed (128–9) and the partial agreement with the depiction in *Beowulf* is noted (141). Goldsmith also argues that both the Latin *Ænigmata* and the English (Exeter Book) Riddles were more than *jeux d'esprit*. 'They flourished, I suppose, because of the belief that mundane objects, whether in the natural world or in art, could disclose to the enquiring mind some part of God's nature and purposes' (49).

588 Hill, Thomas D. 'Notes on the Old English "Maxims" I and II.' *Notes and Queries* 215, NS 17 (1970): 445–7.

Hill uncovers sources for parts of *Maxims I* and *II* in the biblical Books of Proverbs and Ecclesiasticus respectively. The latter discovery leads him to suggest that *Maxims II* can best be understood as a kind of playful juxtaposition of a whole variety of themes and images which the poet concludes by paraphrasing Ecclesiasticus on necessary conflict in a disordered world. An analogue to this thought-process is identified in Augustine's *De Civitate Dei*.

589 Cross, J.E. 'The Ethic of War in Old English.' *England before the Conquest: Studies in Primary Sources presented to Dorothy Whitelock.* Ed. Peter Clemoes and Kathleen Hughes. Cambridge: Cambridge UP, 1971. 269–82.

Cross cites *Maxims I* lines 127–8 to illustrate justifications of defensive war in Old English poetry and place them in a Christian theological context.

590 Lendinara, Patrizia. 'I *Versi Gnomici* anglosassoni.' *Annali Universitario Istituto Orientale di Napoli* 14 sezione germanica (1971): 117–38.

Lendinara notes that gnomic poetry is among the few genres of Old English poetry whose essential Christianity has not been thoroughly acknowledged in the scholarly literature. She briefly reviews the history of relevant scholarship, characterizing much of it as highly superficial. She compares the static impressions of life given in the *Maxims* with those of related poems, such as *Gifts* and *Fortunes*, arguing that the choice of topics (e.g. the poet and the sailor) within each text probably reflects the interests of the composer. *Maxims I* consists of a series of variations on the theme of the gifts of God. The focus is uniformly upon the member of society, not the individual as such. The poem is in no way primitive and presupposes a sense of the order of the universe. The individual maxims, such as the famous one on the Frisian wife (lines 94b–9), function in something approaching the manner of medieval exempla. Their non-proverbial character is indicated by their distinctive use of the word 'mann', the statements of Archer Taylor **(558)** notwithstanding. *Maxims II* should also be seen as a unity – a hymn to creation comparable as to content with *Order* and with Alfred's treatment of the *De Consolatione Philosophiae.*

1 **Remly, Lynn L.** 'The Anglo-Saxon Gnomes as Sacred Poetry.' *Folklore* 82 (1971): 147–58.

Remly argues that the *Maxims,* e.g. *Maxims I* lines 23b–9a, have their source in sacred experience. In studying them, we should conform to the methods of comparative religion if we wish to avoid reductive and anachronistic criticism. The speaker reveals a fascination with the central mystery of the world, namely the appearance of life. This fascination is expressed in a form which emphasizes the bare fact itself, the irreducible reality, not any active speculation on it. Other portions of the poem contrast in being further removed and abstracted from the sacred experience. One tell-tale sign of this distancing process is a more prolix style, where mythic images are replaced by discursive statements.

2 **Barley, Nigel.** 'A Structural Approach to the Proverb and Maxim with Special Reference to the Anglo-Saxon Corpus.' *Proverbium* 20 (1972): 737–50.

Barley argues for a more concerted study of paroemiology, pursued as part of semiotics and in association with linguistics and anthropology. He sees two primary questions: (1) What is a proverb? (2) What constitutes the ability of a member of a culture to use a proverb correctly? He distinguishes between a maxim (literal) and a proverb (metaphorical), using *Maxims II* line 18b 'the wolf shall live in the wood' as an example. If it is a maxim, the statement applies only to wolves, whereas if it is a proverb it is generally applicable, meaning 'there is a place for everything'. As contrasted with the *Durham Proverbs,* a collection which contains true proverbs and maxims, the sayings in *Maxims I* and *II* are unclear in status, though they are at the least potential proverbs. *Maxims II* constitutes a splendid example of *pensée sauvage,* where the world is split up into its due and proper order, relationships of hierarchy and opposition are established, and one structure is mapped on another. Barley elaborates a semiotic scheme in which the distinctions between proverbs, proverbial phrases, maxims, and riddles are clarified. The metrical Charms also work by metaphorical processes, sometimes suggested by words and sometimes by actions, such as the act of throwing the gravel on the ground in Charm 8.

3 **Cherniss, Michael D.** *Ingeld and Christ: Heroic Concepts and Values in Old English Christian Poetry.* Studies in English Literature 74. The Hague: Mouton, 1972. 267 pp.

In the course of his investigation into the use of pre-Christian elements in Old English Christian poetry, Cherniss cites the *Maxims* as testimony to traditional Germanic notions. Quoting *Maxims I* lines 144–51 he comments: 'The wolf is typical of the dangers to which the exile is exposed from the world of nature. It is perhaps fanciful, but nevertheless plausible, to read this [maxim] on a second, non-literal level as a metaphorical description of the treatment of the exile at the hands of wolfish men on alien lands among unknown tribes' (109). Cherniss quotes *Maxims I* lines 80 and 138–40 to demonstrate that 'the desire for personal glory is the motivating force in the life of a Germanic warrior, be he lord or thane' (35). He draws evidence for Germanic notions of loyalty from *Maxims I* line 37 (30), and makes other passing references to *Maxims I* and *II*.

594 **Schneider, Karl.** 'Dichterisch getarnte Begriffsrunen in der ae. Spruchdichtung (*Maxims I* and *Maxims II*).' *Annali Universitario Istituto Orientale di Napoli* 15 sezione germanica (1972): 89–126.

Schneider argues that references to runes and their meanings are cryptically concealed in two passages, *Maxims I* lines 71–80 and *II* lines 1–13. Thus, in *Maxims I*, the proposition 'forst sceal freosan' (line 1a) invokes the rune *ur*, in the senses 'fertile moisture', 'male semen'. The next phrase 'fyr [sceal] wudu meltan' (line 1b) invokes the rune *eoh*, in the sense 'world-yew' or 'world-tree'. More obvious is 'is [sceal] brycgian' (line 2b), with its mention of the rune *is*, and 'sumor swegle hat' (*sigel*). The total list of nine runes in *Maxims I* can be organized into various associative sequences: thus *haegel* (the primordial god) originated from *is* (the primordial material) through the agency of *sigel* (the sun). Similarly in *Maxims II* the proposition 'cyning sceal rice healdan' (line 1a) can be seen to contain the runes *Ing* and *lagu*. Likewise, after some adjustment of the text, 'þrymmas syndan Cristes myccle' (line 4b) contains *Tiw*. All twenty-four runes reappear in the passage from *Maxims II*. Here too they are arranged in a unique sequence, which can be organized meaningfully in various ways, despite some memorial errors on the part of the compiler. As author Schneider posits a heathen (possibly a priest) who survived the advent of Christianity in England and disguised an account of heathen cosmogony and cults in the seemingly harmless form of the *Maxims*.

595 **Bollard, J.K.** 'The Cotton Maxims.' *Neophilologus* 57 (1973): 179–87.

Bollard argues that *Maxims II* was prefaced to the *Anglo-Saxon Chronicle* because the scribe correctly construed it as a poem which describes the ordering of nature and society. In his opinion, the breakdown of the maxim format in the third section of the poem is to be ascribed to its subject-matter, not to any subsequent interpolation or scribal interference. Having defined all that he can about the existence and nature of the world and its inhabitants, the poet states that he cannot thus define the soul's relationship to God after death. Bollard appends a conservative text, translation, and bibliography of writings on the poem subsequent to 1942.

596 **Lendinara, Patrizia.** '*Maxims I* 146–151. A Hint of Funeral Lamentation.' *Neuphilologische Mitteilungen* 74 (1973): 214–16.

The reference in *Maxims I* lines 146–51 to a wolf who circles the grave must contain some veiled allusion to a hired mourner, whose grief is not felt but feigned. Such an allusion would not be unnatural in a poem that displays other instances of cynicism about human frailty. It should be seen as forming an ironic parallel to the unnamed woman's song of mourning in *Beowulf*.

7 ————. 'Un'allusione ai Giganti: Versi Gnomici Exoniensi 192–200.' *Annali Universitario Istituto Orientale di Napoli* 16 sezione germanica (1973): 85–98.

Lendinara develops her earlier contribution (591) to show that the giants are regarded as the descendants of Cain in *Maxims I* lines 192–200. She reviews earlier scholarship on this passage. The outcome is to demonstrate that the word 'atol-', posited for line 198, always attaches to beings that are superhumanly evil in some respect. This set of lines may conceivably represent an interpolation. Its author was familiar with the account of Cain in Genesis, as also with the apocryphal Book of Enoch, but presented it in an allusive and cryptic form. The use of the motif of Abel's blood shows a quality of imagination far superior to that of the poet of *Solomon and Saturn*, who alludes to the same biblical episode.

8 **Crépin, André.** 'Tradition et innovation: contexture de la poésie vieil-anglaise.' *Tradition et innovation: littérature et paralittérature. Actes du Congrès de Nancy 1972.* Société des anglicistes de l'enseignement supérieur. Études Anglaises 57. Paris: Didier, 1974. 25–31.

Crépin wonders whether the injunction contained in *Maxims I* lines 138–40 refers to the *scop* or to the perfect companion of the prince.

9 **Judd, Elizabeth.** 'Women before the Conquest: A Study of Women in Anglo-Saxon England.' *Papers in Women's Studies* (U of Michigan): 1.1 (1974): 127–49.

Judd cites *Maxims I* lines 81–2, 'cyning sceal mid ceape cwene gebicgan . . .', noting that although purchase of the wife may seem to be implied, what was sold was probably not the woman herself but the rights to her guardianship.

0 **Bollard, J.K.** 'A Note on the Cotton Maxims, Lines 43–5.' *Neophilologus* 59 (1975): 139–40.

Bollard mentions a possible parallel to *Maxims II* lines 43–5 in Ælfric's sermon 'De Auguriis', where the speaker denounces women who use charms or potions rather than the due process of social custom to secure a husband or lover.

1 **Fukuchi, Michael S.** 'Gnomic Statements in Old English Poetry.' *Neophilologus* 59 (1975): 610–13.

Fukuchi sees four categories of gnomic statements in Old English poetry: the self-contained gnome, the dependent gnome, the imperative gnome, and the gnome of direct address. He also notes the existence of statements that are not gnomes but have the potential to become gnomes in a different context. He considers these gnomes in the context of narrative poetry and hence makes only passing reference to *Maxims I* and *II*.

2 **Greenfield, Stanley B., and Richard Evert.** '*Maxims II*: Gnome and Poem.' *Anglo-Saxon Poetry: Essays in Appreciation: for John C. McGalliard.* Ed. Lewis E. Nicholson and Dolores Warwick Frese. Notre Dame: U of Notre Dame P, 1975. 337–54.

The authors seek to correct what they see as a virtually unanimous trend in previous criticism of *Maxims II* to deny the poem any aesthetic unity. Certainly the poem may consist of a series of aphorisms strung together, yet as a whole it subtly develops the idea that true wisdom ultimately reveals the limitations of human knowledge. Even on this earth the movements of thieves and young women (lines 42–5) contain an element of mystery; at the end of the poem (lines 57–66) life after death is shown as totally resisting our curiosity. The laconic collocation of 'wyrd' with Christ (lines 4b–5a) is best explained on the assumption that 'wyrd' is parallel to wind and thunder, being one of the glories of Christ. Taylor's (585) interpretation of 'sceal' is to be resisted: more probably it conveys the idea of 'typically'.

603 Gruber, Loren C. 'Old English Maxims and Narnian Gnomes.' *Man's 'Natural Powers': Essays for and about C.S. Lewis.* Ed. Raymond P. Tripp, Jr. Denver: Society for New Language Study, 1975. 59–63.

The platitudinous appearance of the *Maxims* may conceal a mode of access to the supernatural.

604 East, W.G. 'A Note on Maxims II.' *Neuphilologische Mitteilungen* 77 (1976): 205.

The distribution of hypermetric lines suggests that *Maxims II* consists of two strophes, one of 41 and the other of 25 lines. This proportion is a close approximation to the Golden Section. Consequently, critical impressions of this poem as not carefully structured need to be revised.

605 Florey, Kenneth. 'Stability and Chaos as Theme in Anglo-Saxon Poetry.' *Connecticut Review* 9.2 (1976): 82–9.

In Florey's opinion the Anglo-Saxons, though brave in battle, were terrified both by sudden change and by isolation from the community. He notes the utter simplicity of the gnomic phrases 'frost shall freeze, fire eat wood, earth shall bear, and ice shall bridge' in *Maxims I* lines 71–2. Poetry of this gnomic sort was intended not to educate but rather to re-affirm that what has been perennially true still holds. In a world subject to constant change, the idea that fire always burns wood must have been reassuring. Florey lays emphasis on the centrality of tradition in determining the themes of Old English poetry.

606 Gruber, Loren C. 'The Agnostic Anglo-Saxon Gnomes: *Maxims I* and *II*, *Germania* and the Boundaries of Northern Wisdom.' *Poetica* (Tokyo) 6 (1976): 22–47.

Gruber believes that 'criticism of *Maxims I* and *II* is possible only to the degree to which we are able to accommodate ourselves to the past world view' (22). We should not view such texts reductively as mere moral guides or reflective comments. Along with the Germanic gnome-like observations recorded by Tacitus, these texts represent what Edward Tylor (*Primitive Culture: Researches into the Development of Mythology, Philosophy, Religion, Language, Art, and Custom*, London: Murray, 1903) called 'survivals', whose original meanings have dwindled away as they 'carried on by force of habit into a new state of society' and lost their original context (24). *Maxims I* began as archaic 'initiatory utterances of an absolute, religious nature' and were weakened to their present form as mere assertions about the disposition of the universe (26). *Maxims II*, by contrast, is not an archaic poem at all but a more drastic appropriation of older wisdom literature, revalorized into an instrument of an 'agnostic aestheticism' (26). Gruber also discusses the distribution of 'bið' and 'sceal' in the *Maxims*, claiming that most 'bið' gnomes record the homological relationships between earthly and divine realms, whereas the 'sceal' gnomes either render assertive and largely ethical judgements or record the objective and consuetudinary features of universal phenomena (46). The revalorization of northern wisdom literature is observable as a movement from pagan certainty, through Christian faith, to rational agnosticism (47).

07 **Barley, Nigel F.** 'Structure in the Cotton Gnomes.' *Neuphilologische Mitteilungen* 78 (1977): 244–9.

Maxims II is probably to be viewed as a conscious literary work of a poet generating pseudo-maxims on the model of extant ones. The application of an ethnocentric and inappropriate concept of structure derived from modern Western literature has led to unnecessary theories of interpolation, dialogue form, and digression, here and elsewhere in Old English poetry. 'Modern Western literature spoon-feeds us. We have come to expect a single line of thought, a clear progression in time, treatment of a single subject throughout' (245). A line-by-line examination of linkages shows that *Maxims II* establishes relationships of opposition and similarity between the parts of an overall orderly universe, using such literary figures as parallelism, antithesis, and metaphor. Thus the idea of 'stone' can be followed by 'wind', one subsumed under 'structure', the other under 'process' (line 3). Whereas a dragon guards his hoard, a king should spend it freely (lines 26–9). Whereas grief clings, clouds scud past (line 13). Within its manuscript of provenance *Maxims II* earns its place as a synchronic justification for the current state of affairs.

08 **Gruber, Loren C.** 'The Rites of Passage: *Hávamál* Stanzas 1–5.' *Scandinavian Studies* 49 (1977): 330–40.

In Gruber's opinion, 'even the most careful translation of an old poem is likely to be dependent upon extensive commentary and epistemological enterprise, in which the reader discovers and formulates the life residing *in potentio* within dead metaphors' (330). He sees both Anglo-Saxon and [Old] Norse gnomic poems as revealing a 'correspondence between things in this world and those elsewhere and otherwise' (331). Wisdom poetry can be meaningful simultaneously at a practical and a metaphysical level. Although many maxims represent observations of mundane affairs, others seem to encode an ancient epistemology, allowing the audience 'to infer the operation of the invisible world from knowledge of the visible' (334). Thus the guest in *Hávamál* can be viewed both practically, as an ordinary traveller, and metaphysically, as a child entering this world.

09 **Lendinara, Patrizia.** 'I cosidetti "Versi Gnomici" del Codice Exoniense e del Ms. Cotton Tiberius B i: una ricerca bibliografica.' *Annali Istituto Universitario Orientale di Napoli* 20 sezione germanica, Filologia germanica (1977): 281–314.

In a brief survey (281–2) of the state of scholarship Lendinara criticizes a tendency to lump together the two sets of *Maxims* as if they were totally homogeneous as to origin, content, etc. She also deplores the tendency to isolate a postulated nucleus of original, pagan maxims and to characterize other material as the work of later interpolators. *Maxims I* should be seen as a series of variations on the theme of the gifts of God to humankind (with a few digressions), comparable to *Fortunes* and *Gifts* in the same manuscript. *Maxims II*, by contrast, is reminiscent of *Order*, describing all aspects of the created world. In the ensuing bibliography Lendinara furnishes a comprehensive list of editions, translations, and literary studies, including some that make only incidental reference to the *Maxims*. In a brief conclusion (313–14) the state of the scholarship is summarized. Lendinara notes the tendency of anthologies, readers, and literary histories to quote from the *Maxims* in a highly selective fashion (for instance, the hackneyed passage on the Frisian sailor). As a result the student and general reader gains a distorted impression of the true nature of these two texts. Critical attempts to construe these texts as raw material for incidental *sententiae* in such poems as *Beowulf* have aided and abetted a general tendency to see the *Maxims* as lacking coherence and unity. *Maxims I* in particular needs reassessment in this respect.

610 Gruber, Loren C. 'Of Holly, Vassalage, and *Oþþaet*: Three Notes on *Maxims I.*' *In Geardagum* 2 (1978 *for* 1977): 9–17.

Citing instances from *Maxims I*, Gruber contends that translation of Old English poetry must involve penetration to its 'informing epistemology' (9). One tangible survival of this epistemology is the phrase 'holen sceal inæled' (line 79). Originally it encapsulated a pre-Christian belief in the efficacy of holly to accompany the soul after its separation from the body. This meaning dwindled as the maxim was 'carried by force of habit into a new state of society' (10). Gruber interprets 'gifre' in line 69 as 'useful': the lord bestows favours upon the warrior because his bravery and fidelity are 'useful' to the comitatus. The key words 'oþþæt' and 'þæt' in lines 45b–50 should be seen as signalling a purely psychological, rather than spatial, movement.

611 Kirk, John M., Jr., ed. *A Critical Edition of the Old English Gnomic Poems in the Exeter Book and MS Cotton Tiberius B.I.* Middlebury, VT: Mrs Alison Kirk [privately distributed], 1978.

[Not seen.] This revision of Kirk's 1970 dissertation was distributed by Mrs Alison Kirk to a number of university libraries so that it could be consulted and copied. Kirk had intended to produce an edition of *Maxims I* and *II* for the Methuen's Old English Library series, but was prevented by a protracted illness and his death in 1976. His diplomatic text is the product of a fresh examination of the manuscripts and eschews emendations *metri gratia*. It is preceded by a long introduction in which the emphasis falls on the *Maxims* as two individual poems. [Information from Cinzia Melloni, review of Kirk's edition, *Schede Medievali* 1 (1981): 102–3.]

612 Gruber, Loren C. '*Hwaer cwom andgiet*: Translating the *Maxims.*' *In Geardagum* 3 (1979): 55–65.

Gruber considers that until very recently Old English studies have been deficient in any sustained awareness of psychological history. As a consequence, the subtle creative influence which editions exert has operated unchecked. He discusses the problem of 'biδ' versus 'sceal' in light of the belief that new absolutes and new settled purposes rearrange traditional categories. He provides a detailed analysis of *Maxims I* lines 7–12a and tries to capture the literal sense of lines 71–80. Defending the integrity of *Maxims II* he suggests that what we find is a worldly, aesthetic uncertainty concerning life's meaning.

3 **Meaney, Audrey L.** 'The *ides* of the Cotton Gnomic Poem.' *Medium Aevum* 48 (1979): 23–39.

Meaney sees some justification in taking *ides* in *Maxims II* line 43 to have been originally a word for 'woman' in her sacral and mysterious aspect. In Old English poetry it seems to carry the connotation 'noble'. The *Penitential* attributed to Theodore of Tarsus reflects a current belief that women were capable of working love-magic. Such beliefs may have persisted down to late Anglo-Saxon times. In *Maxims II* the phrase 'dyrne cræfte' might be interpreted as 'by magic'. The complete translation would then be: 'A lady, a young woman, must seek out for herself a lover by means of magic', followed by either (1) 'so that she may be married, if she is not of good reputation among the people' or (2) 'if she does not wish to bring it about among the people that she should be married'. In context a natural progression could be seen from two evildoing and outcast male creatures to this woman.

4 **Robinson, Fred C.** 'Old English Literature in its Most Immediate Context.' *Old English Literature in Context: Ten Essays.* Ed. John D. Niles. Cambridge: Brewer; Totowa, NJ: Rowman, 1980. 11–29.

Robinson argues that to study *Maxims II* in isolation is a mistake, leading to an exaggerated desire to discern unities and structures in the text. The outcome has been more diversity than congruence in the structures posited. To look at *Maxims II* in its manuscript context, with the *Menologium* on one side and the *Anglo-Saxon Chronicle* on the other, is to reveal that each of these texts embodies a listing (or catenulate) structure. This is an instance of a strong general tendency to anthologize lists. Similarly, in the Exeter Book we note that *Maxims I* is grouped with *Widsith* and *Fortunes*, two list-poems *par excellence*. Since the list-form suggested by the Latin encyclopaedia tradition conforms so well with the additive style of poetry inherited from the Germanic oral tradition, it is hardly surprising that listing should have become the structural principle of such poems as *Fortunes*, *Gifts*, *Precepts*, and *Rune Poem*. As to content, *Menologium* and *Maxims II* begin and end with Christ (envisaged as king or associated with royal powers), whereas the *Chronicle* begins with his incarnation. Thematically speaking, all three texts reveal a perspective on historical time where attention is called to the relation between antiquity and the present. The compiler may have adapted the end of *Menologium* and the beginning of *Maxims II* to create a verbal link between the two texts.

5 **Berkhout, Carl T.** 'Four Difficult Passages in the Exeter Book *Maxims*.' *English Language Notes* 18 (1981): 247–51.

In Berkhout's opinion each little passage of *Maxims I* encases its own peculiar puzzle, and a truly satisfactory reading of the whole must await persuasive solutions to many more of those puzzles than have been solved so far. Line 67a can be interpreted 'The head shall inform (or work within) the hand', i.e. action should be guided by thought: compare line 121 'hyge sceal gehealden, hond gewealden'. In line 106 Kock's (147) interpretation is strained, assuming as it does a three-member kenning and a non-obvious interpretation of the phrase 'dread of nations'. Accordingly we should emend to 'mægðes agen wyn' ('the maiden's own delight'): i.e. her sailor-lover. In line 191 'geara' is to be explained as 'formerly' or 'long ago'. In lines 196b–7a 'Cain, whom death spared' ('nerede') alludes to Gen. 4: 15, where God sets his mark on Cain so that he will not be killed.

616   Nitzsche, Jane Chance. 'The Anglo-Saxon Woman as Hero: The Chaste Queen and the Masculine Woman Saint.' *Allegorica* 5.2 (1981 *for* 1980): 139–48.

Maxims I is typical of Anglo-Saxon documents in introducing women in passive roles which underscore their subordinate relationships to men. The sexes are identified with complementary traits: masculine with reason and determination, feminine with passion and passivity. A dictum such as 'guð sceal in eorle' (line 83b) is in conformity with this principle.

617   Robinson, Fred C. 'Understanding an Old English Wisdom Verse: *Maxims II*, Lines 10ff.' *The Wisdom of Poetry: Essays in Early English Literature in Honor of Morton W. Bloomfield.* Ed. Larry D. Benson and Siegfried Wenzel. Kalamazoo, MI: Medieval Institute, 1982. 1–12. Repr. in Fred C. Robinson. *The Tomb of Beowulf and other essays on Old English.* Oxford: Blackwell, 1993. 87–97.

Robinson discusses the emendation from 'swicolost' to 'switolost' (or 'swutolost') in *Maxims II* line 10. Arbitrating between the claims of 'truth is most tricky' and 'truth is most evident', he prefers the former on the general grounds that wisdom literature is pessimistic and worldly-wise in tone. More specifically, the emendation from 'swicolost' to '*switolost' is not straightforward, because the vocalism with -*i*- would be highly unusual in this phonetic environment. Truth can be thought of as tricky or deceptive or perhaps elusive because it is difficult to recognize. The notion that the distinction between truth and falsehood is a subtle one for humankind, thanks to our inordinate love of money, was a current topic in Anglo-Saxon thought. It is hinted at in the text by the juxtaposition of a maxim about treasure and gold (lines 10b–11a) with one about truth.

618   Earl, James W. 'Maxims I, Part I.' *Neophilologus* 67 (1983): 277–83.

In this appreciation of *Maxims I*A, Earl describes the poem as characterized by learned and intelligible leaps of the imagination, even when they are not brilliant verse. He disagrees with Dawson's (573) notion of a stream of consciousness, but does seek to identify conceptual bridges, for instance the ambiguous application of line 23b 'tu beoð gemæccan'.

9 **Schrader, Richard J.** *God's Handiwork: Images of Women in Early Germanic Literature.* Contributions in Women's Studies 41. Westport, CT: Greenwood, 1983. x + 129 pp.

Schrader makes scattered references to OEW poems, especially the *Maxims,* whose content relates to women. He notes that the comments on women in the *Maxims* do not necessarily provide pictures of actual behaviour. They express the aristocratic conception of good, which involved the finding of a correct stance or posture to confront a given circumstance.

0 **Dane, Joseph A.** *'On folce geþeon*: Note on the Old English *Maxims II* Lines 43–5.' *Neuphilologische Mitteilungen* 85 (1984): 61–4.

Dane proposes the following translation for *Maxims II* lines 43–5: 'A woman must visit her friend with hidden craft (i.e. secretly), if she does not wish to bring it about among the people (i.e. if she does not want it to be rumoured) that she is bought with rings.' The reference in 'bought with rings' is not to marriage but to prostitution. The meaning of 'on folce geþeon' (line 44b) is discussed in relation to various possible parallels in other Old English texts.

1 **Nelson, Marie.** ' "Is" and "Ought" in the Exeter Book Maxims.' *Southern Folklore Quarterly* 45 (1984 *for* 1981): 109–21.

Nelson focuses on the cultural context of *Maxims I,* identifying 'binding and loosening' as two central themes that correlate with death and life respectively. Helped by the predictable structure of the gnomic sentence and by the multiple meanings of the auxiliary 'sceal', the poet could move between facts of which humankind can be certain and truths that we can only reach out to.

2 **Robinson, Fred C.** *Beowulf and the Appositive Style.* The Hodges Lectures. Knoxville: U of Tennessee P, 1985. 106 pp.

Robinson notes in passing that in *Maxims I,* as in some other Old English poems, words like *soð* and *sylf* are used where the poet is distinguishing between the pagan and Christian gods, as in line 134a. Equally, the Christian God may be specified by reference to his dwelling place in the heavens.

3 **Frank, Roberta.** ' "Mere" and "Sund": Two Sea-Changes in *Beowulf.*' *Modes of Interpretation in Old English Literature: Essays in Honour of Stanley B. Greenfield.* Ed. P.R. Brown, G.R. Crampton, and Fred C. Robinson. Toronto: U of Toronto P, 1986. 153–72.

Frank comments in passing (171 n. 60) on puns like that on *ar* ('oar' and 'honour') in *Maxims I* lines 185–6. 'Weary is the man who rows against the wind; very often he is accused of cowardice, of losing his valour; his oar (or honour) dries on board.' She compares the alliterative collocations 'ellen mid arum' in *Guthlac* line 450 and 'elne: are' in *The Wanderer* line 114.

4 **Earl, James W.** 'Transformation of Chaos: Immanence and Transcendence in *Beowulf* and Other Old English Poetry.' *Ultimate Reality and Meaning* 10 (1987): 164–85.

In Anglo-Saxon vernacular poetry we see the Anglo-Saxon conception of God in a striking way. Here is how educated and sophisticated Anglo-Saxons saw God, through the medium of their own poetic language and the unshakable bias of their native cultural heritage. In *Maxims I*A the storm is analysed by a Dark-Age Durkheim in purely psycho-sociological terms. The storm represents the world in which the complex of social controls is loosened. In the essentially realistic attitude of the poem, the kingship of God is imagined in strikingly materialistic terms. Earl comments on the word 'læne' in line 6 in this respect.

625 **Biggs, Frederick M., and Sandra McEntire.** 'Spiritual Blindness in the Old English *Maxims I*, Part 1.' *Notes and Queries* 233, NS 35 (1988): 11.

In *Maxims I*, lines 44b and 45a recall Christ's 'beati mundo corde quoniam ipsi Deum videbunt' (Matt. 5: 8) and 'non est opus valentibus medico sed male habentibus' (Matt. 9: 12) respectively. The entire passage in *Maxims I* gains in significance if we see it as chiefly concerned with spiritual, not physical, blindness.

626 **Busse, Wilhelm G.** 'Boceras. Written and Oral Traditions in the Late C10th.' *Mündlichkeit und Schriftlichkeit im englischen Mittelalter.* Ed. Willi Erzgräber and Sabine Volk. ScriptOralia 5. Tübingen: Narr, 1988. 27–38.

Busse infers from *Maxims I* lines 125–31 that in the world of late Anglo-Saxon aristocratic laypeople the authority of books did not yet count for much. What we find instead is that books as a typical feature are associated with the student, whereas treasure, courage, sword, and shield are expressly mentioned as class values of the aristocratic warrior (33).

627 **Russom, Geoffrey.** 'The Drink of Death in Old English and Germanic Literature.' *Germania: Comparative Studies in the Old Germanic Languages and Literatures.* Ed. Daniel G. Calder and T. Craig Christy. Cambridge: Brewer, 1988. 175–89.

Russom concurs with Carleton Brown's **(561)** emendation of 'deop deada wæg' in *Maxims I* line 78. He further suggests that a drinking cup ('wæg') that was deep in the literal sense would produce that deep slumber to which death is so often compared. The notion of 'mystery' might also be intended. Noting that the cup of *Maxims I* appears in a pre-Christian context, Russom resists Magennis's **(959)** postulation of a Christian origin for the 'poculum mortis' motif and goes back to Brown's suggestion that the figure was probably an inheritance from pre-Christian lore. Old English *deaðweg* corresponds to the last drink taken in early Germanic societies by suicides, human sacrifices, and those about to incur capital punishment. Attested to by Ibn Fadlan and Saxo Grammaticus, it served the humane or practical purpose of anaesthetizing the victim. As a literary figure, this cup could well come to represent the sentence of death eventually imposed on us all, or, from a theological point of view, the punishment for man's first disobedience.

628 **McGillivray, Murray.** 'The Exeter Book *Maxims I B*: An Anglo-Saxon Woman's View of Marriage.' *English Studies in Canada* 15 (1989): 383–97.

McGillivray emphasizes the danger of imposing our own cultural expectations on this difficult poetry. He proposes that *Maxims I*B possesses a central subject, the relations of the sexes in marriage. Although the topic is approached in a riddling and ironic fashion, it expresses a woman's opinion of these relations. The Frisian wife passage is an exemplum of marital fidelity. Similarly, the description of the duties of the king and queen emphasizes those of the queen.

The Order of the World

MANUSCRIPT AND INTEGRITY OF THE TEXT

Order occurs uniquely in the Exeter Book, which is dated by Ker (**36**) to the second half of the tenth century. Wülker (**8**) considered that the extant text might represent an abridgement of an originally fuller version and expressed doubts, followed by Brandl (**19**), as to the genuineness of the closing lines. But in Dobbie's opinion (**194**) *Order* is so loosely structured that these doubts lose their force.

THEME

The thematic focus of *Order* has been identified in a variety of ways. For Robinson (**7**) and Abbey (**102**), it is the wonders of Creation; for Pons (**172**) and Cross (**241**), it is the rigorous order of the universe; for Greenfield and Calder (**60**) it is the sun-symbol; for Trahern (**360**) it is a vision of stability, contrasting with millenarian beliefs in the instability of the world. In a new departure, Isaacs (**264**), endorsed by Crane (**280**) and to some degree by Jager (**633**), contended that *Order* primarily concerned the artistic self-consciousness. Rebutting these reflexive interpretations, Cross (**631**) focused on two non-Scriptural passages which embody Greek concepts of the world. Greenfield (**282**) also resisted reflexivity, characterizing it as anachronistic, but it has continued to exert influence in a series of new interpretations. Respectively, these centre on the illumination of the human mind by God's self-revelation through created things (Lee, **283**), the unattainability or complexity of wisdom (Tripp, **301**), the audience's involvement in the creative process, celebrating creation theology (Hansen, **61**), and the endeavour to control Nature upon the page (Lerer, **356**).

AFFILIATIONS

Fiocco (**632**) registered the resemblance between this poem and other Germanic wisdom poems, such as *Grímnismál*, but saw stronger connections with Alfredian didactic style.

LITERARY CRITICISM

Many scholars have felt that the structure of this poem is seriously flawed. Indeed Anderson (**31**) remarked scathingly that the poem is probably fragmentary, certainly incoherent, and less communicative on the topic of Creation than the much shorter *Caedmon's Hymn*. Kennedy (**29**) criticized a lack of balance in the treatment of Creation, whereby precisely half the passage is devoted to a glorification of light. Dobbie (**194**) faulted the autobiographical introduction for bearing no organic relationship to the rest of the poem. Wrenn **(43)**, on the other hand, characterized it as a homiletic device to personalize the exhortation. Shippey **(300)** complained of potential obfuscation or platitude, at least from the standpoint of a modern reader. Among the poem's defenders, Isaacs **(264)** pointed out the dramatic monologue frame. Huppé **(270)** also envisaged a tripartite structure, with an elaborate development of the image of light: cf. Fiocco **(632)**. Pearsall **(52)** saw potential in this structure for a richer poetic development. As to localized rhetorical features, Gummere **(629)** regarded the mixture of metaphors in line 19 as belonging to a stage prior to conscious attempts at figurative language. Pingel **(630)** pointed out the high incidence of asyndetic sentence construction and suggested that it arose from the poet's unsophisticated attempts at vividness.

BIBLIOGRAPHY

9 Gummere, Francis B. *The Anglo-Saxon Metaphor. . .* Diss. U Freiburg. Halle, 1881. 64 pp.

Gummere observes in passing that three different metaphors are crowded together in *Order* line 19, 'bewriten in gewitte wordhordes cræft'. He regards this style as belonging to a stage prior to conscious attempts at figurative language. It should hardly be described as metaphor, but rather as picturesque confusion.

0 Pingel, Ludwig. *Untersuchungen über die syntaktischen Erscheinungen in dem angelsächsischen Gedicht von den 'Wundern der Schöpfung': Ein Beitrag zu einer angelsächsischen Syntax.* Diss. U Rostock. Rostock, 1905. 95 pp.

This monograph is intended as a contribution to a complete investigation of Old English syntax. Pingel bases his text on Grein-Wülker **(6)** and provides notes. He points out the high incidence of asyndetic sentence construction in *Order* and suggests that it arises from the poet's attempt at vividness in presentation. A text so rich in parataxis as this one cannot be regarded as particularly polished or sophisticated.

1 Cross, J.E. 'The Literate Anglo-Saxon – On Sources and Disseminations.' Sir Israel Gollancz Memorial Lecture. *Proceedings of the British Academy* 58 (1972): 67–100.

In this discussion of the methods to be followed in source studies, Cross rebuts the interpretations of *Order* recently reached by Huppé **(270)** and Isaacs **(264)**. He focuses on two non-Scriptural passages in the poem which embody Greek concepts of the world. As to the first (lines 59–81), Huppé's interpretation of the journey of the sun as an allegory of human life is to be rejected. It should instead be related to ancient and medieval notions of a geocentric universe. *Contra* ASPR **(194)**, the word 'utgarsecg' (line 70b) can be explained as referring to the Ocean that surrounds this (flat) world. The sun comes over the waves of the Ocean each morning and departs over them each evening. The phrase 'on heape' is a reference to the number of fixed stars. In lines 80–1 the poet refers, perhaps heretically, to the possibility of peoples who inhabit the Antipodes. The second passage (lines 53b–4), referring to the tides, should be translated 'His power draws forth the heavenly candle(s), and the waters with them'. In a footnote (88 n. 4) Cross incidentally suggests that the meaning of 'scyldum bescyredne' in *Vainglory* line 8 is different from that of the apparent parallel 'scyldum biscyrede' in *Rhyming Poem* line 84.

632 **Fiocco, Teresa.** 'Osservazioni preliminari ad un commento su *Order of the World.*' *Atti dell'Accademia Peloritana, Classe di lettere, filosofia e belle arti* 52 (1974–5): 153–66.

In a review of the previous literature on *Order*, Fiocco remarks on the rediscovery of this poem in the previous few years, with the studies by Huppé **(270)** and Cross **(631)**. She provides a text and translation of *Order*, underlining (like Huppé) its formal division into three sections: an introduction, an account of the creation, and a brief moralizing conclusion. She differs from Huppé, however, concerning the precise demarcation of these sections. She registers the resemblance between this poem and other Germanic wisdom poems, such as *Grímnismál*, in respect of a dialogue format and the use of kennings, but sees stronger connections with Alfredian didactic style.

633 **Jager, Eric.** 'Speech and the Chest in Old English Poetry: Orality or Pectorality?' *Speculum* 65 (1990): 845–59.

Jager surveys attestations in Old English poetry to the notion that the chest is a source of thoughts and speech. He instances *Order* as a poem about the making of poetry. The text indicates that 'wordhordes cræft' (line 19) is lodged in the chest ('hreþre').

Precepts

ORIENTATION TO RESEARCH

MANUSCRIPT AND DATING

Precepts is uniquely extant in the Exeter Book, which is dated by Ker (**36**) to the second half of the tenth century. Grein (**84**) dated *Precepts* itself to the beginning of the eighth century. Amos (**56**) noted linguistic indications for a comparatively early date.

LITERARY AFFILIATIONS

Earlier opinion fluctuated as to whether *Precepts* has a heathen or a Christian basis. More or less in favour of the heathen hypothesis were Brandl (**19**) and Ward and Waller (**20**), who compared the form of *Precepts* to that of the Old Norse *Sigrdrífumál* and the last part of *Hávamál*. On the Christian side were ten Brink (**5**), who saw possible influence from the *Proverbia Salomonis*, Heusler (**166**), Kennedy (**29**), Anderson (**31**), who suggested that the poem was conceivably in use in church schools, and Dobbie (**194**). As to genre characteristics, Schücking (**177**) discerned an emphasis on self-control and resolution comparable with that seen in *The Wanderer*. Howe (**328**) posited an 'ages of man' structural principle. Burrow (**333**) pointed out a general conformity to wisdom poetry that is founded on a knowledge of transience and on a pattern of the old instructing the young. McEntire (**638**) invoked the tradition of the paternal religious figure to explain the dynamic of a wise father instructing his monastic son. As to later analogues, Robinson (**7**) pointed to Polonius in *Hamlet* and Alekseev (**635**) to the twelfth-century Russian poem *Instruction of Vladimir Monomakh*.

LITERARY CRITICISM

This poem has had a bad press. Anderson (**32**) thought it negligible, Ebert (**79**) repetitious, Shippey humdrum (**636**) and obscure (**300**), Greenfield and Calder (**60**) uninspired. Wrenn (**43**) found the opening a mere device to personalize the exhortation. Pearsall (**52**) lumped *Precepts* with various other OEW poems among the débris or spoil-heaps of the monastic tradition. But a few critics have found features to praise in *Precepts*. Abbey (**102**) appreciated its sound religious morality. Frantzen (**321**) saw it as a most interesting poem. Howe (**328**) blamed New Critical obsessions with organic form for its systematic neglect. Hansen (**61**, **637**) advocated an approach based on reflexivity. Lerer (**356**) noted that the structures and methods of *Precepts* employ the techniques of education.

SOCIAL DOCUMENTATION

Cross **(45)** saw *Precepts* as useful in shedding light on Anglo-Saxon manners. The poem figures in Budde's **(124)** study of drink and drunkenness and in Habicht's **(231)** study of the motif of noise.

BIBLIOGRAPHY

634 Bright, James W. 'Notes on *Faeder Larcwidas.*' *Modern Language Notes* 10 (1895): 68–9.

The author discusses lines 4, 5–7, 17, 23–6, 55, 62, 64, 67, 82, 85, and 93, correcting errors in Grein-Wülker **(6)** and proposing some new emendations.

635 Alekseev, M.P. 'Anglo-Saksonskaia parallel' k Poucheniiu Vladimira Monomakha.' *Trudy Otdela drevne-russkoi literatury.* IRLI 2 (1935): 39–80.

Alekseev notes parallels between *Precepts* and the twelfth-century Russian poem *Instruction of Vladimir Monomakh*, to be found in the Laurentian version of the Russian Primary Chronicle, under the year 1096. He speculates that Gytha, the daughter of King Harold Godwinson, had access to the Exeter Book (and therefore *Precepts*) while it was still in the possession of Bishop Leofric, possibly at the time of the siege of Exeter (AD 1068). Gytha subsequently married Vladimir Monomakh, Prince of Kiev from 1113–25. Her reading of *Precepts* might have suggested the idea of an analogous production in Russian when his sons began their schooling. Indeed, Vladimir himself may have been familiar with Old English and have acquired ideas for the poem via oral transmission. The result was the poem *Poucheniie Vladimira Monomakha*. Alekseev supports his argument with extensive documentation of the dynastic relations between England, Russia, Normandy, and Scandinavia. As to the literary aspects, Alekseev begins by providing a text and Russian translation of lines 1–14 of *Precepts* (62–3). He summarizes the contents of the poem (63) and gives a full review of previous literary analyses (63–5), with special attention to the *Disticha Catonis* and other analogues in a wide variety of languages, including Old Norse and Russian (65–70). This evidence leads him to the conclusion that with an eighth-century dating *Precepts* is older than most of the analogues, including those in Latin and Byzantine Greek. It might therefore have played a special role in determining the form and structure of the Russian poem (70). Having reviewed the Russian scholarly literature on *Poucheniie*, Alekseev identifies parallels as to form and content in the two texts, pointing out for instance that the first section in both poems speaks of one's obligations to God (78–9).

636 Shippey, T.A. 'Maxims in Old English Narrative: Literary Art or Traditional Wisdom?' *Oral Tradition: Literary Tradition. A Symposium.* Ed. Hans Bekker-Nielsen et al. Odense: Odense UP, 1977. 28–46.

Shippey mentions *Precepts* incidentally in the course of a discussion of gnomic indirection in *Beowulf*, noting that a component of the coastguard's maxim in *Beowulf* (lines 287–9) reappears in *Precepts* (line 46) in an imperative form. He finds *Precepts* indicative of a decidedly humdrum poet who shows no sign of having read *Beowulf* at all. Although Shippey's other remarks do not directly concern specific OEW poems, they have a general relevance to the discussion of the social function of this type of poetry, its status in terms of semantics and pragmatics, and kindred topics.

7   Hansen, Elaine Tuttle. 'Precepts: An Old English Instruction.' *Speculum* 56 (1981): 1–16.

Hansen resists the notion that *Precepts* belongs among the detritus of the monastic tradition, as contended by Pearsall (**52**). She instead seeks to situate this poem in an 'instruction genre' that has its analogues in ancient Near Eastern and Old Irish literatures, and which is characterized by address of father to son and a frequent use of the imperative mood. The poem is not designed, however, to simulate real advice given by an actual father. Rather, it reflects and celebrates the human capacity to structure reality and organize experience into an ethical and epistemological system based on relationships of similarity and opposition. What can seem like isolated misogyny is in actuality subsumed under this wider structural principle. Its assumptions about stability and order in the world are echoed metrically in a prevalence of C-type half-lines.

8   McEntire, Sandra. 'The Monastic Context of Old English "Precepts".' *Neuphilologische Mitteilungen* 91 (1990): 243–51.

McEntire contends, against Hansen (**637**), that the speaker in *Precepts* is not literally a father, in the strict sense of 'parent'. Rather, the tradition of the paternal religious figure who acts as a spiritual guide readily explains the dynamic in the poem of a wise father instructing his monastic son. McEntire's discussion includes a re-examination of the words 'þeodscype' (line 69), 'fyrngewritu' (line 67), and 'fremde meowlan' (line 39, where 'fremde' means not 'foreign' but 'outside our family').

The Metrical Proverbs

ORIENTATION TO RESEARCH

MANUSCRIPTS

Vienna, Nationalbibliothek 751, dated by Ker (36) to the ninth century, contains the *Winfrid Proverb*. Cotton Faustina A.x, dated by Ker (36) to the second half of the eleventh century, contains one version of the *Latin-English Proverbs*. Royal 2 B.v, dated by Ker (36) to the mid-tenth century, with Old English annotations from the eleventh century, contains a variant version of the *Latin-English Proverbs*. For editions see the subject index.

DATING AND PROVENANCE

The *Winfrid Proverb* was identified by Kemble (640) as one of the earliest pieces of Anglo-Saxon poetry on record. Stanley (295) concurred, suggesting that it considerably antedated the letter where it is cited. Sweet (91) posited either a West Saxon original or a West Saxon scribe. The Latin portion of the *Latin-English Proverbs* must be secondary, according to Schneider (323).

LITERARY AFFILIATIONS

Brandl (19) placed the *Proverbs* among early secular genres. Malone (30) classed the *Winfrid Proverb* with quasi-metrical passages from legal and other documents. Stanley (295) interpreted it as a summary of the Germanic heroic ideal. For Pilch and Tristram (55), it underlined the fragility of the distinction between texts that describe life as it should be and those that describe life as it is. Trahern (654) argued that the homily *De Descensu Christi ad Inferos* contains a hitherto unidentified metrical proverb.

LITERARY EVALUATION

The *Winfrid Proverb* was summarily dismissed by Anderson (31): 'Only the pedant would be interested in its discussion here.' Wülker (8) and Dobbie (203) suggested that it might have originated in a longer Anglo-Saxon poem, though Dobbie also contemplated free-standing status, comparable with *Bede's Death Song*. Levinson (651) put the citation of the *Winfrid Proverb* in a context of awakening national feeling. The *Latin-English Proverbs* interested Dobbie (203), as illustrating the informal use of the alliterative line, and Derolez (237), as constituting a rare example of homoeoteleuton in Old English.

BIBLIOGRAPHY

[Pertz, G.H.] 'Uebersicht des Briefwechsels: November und December 1820.' *Archiv der Gesellschaft für ältere deutsche Geschichtskunde* 3 (1821): 150–208. Pertz's letter from Vienna to the Secretary of the Gesellschaft reports on the manuscript of the Letters of Boniface and on errors in earlier editions and transcriptions. He comments on the palaeography, especially the confusability of certain letters, and gives a corrected transcription of the *Winfrid Proverb* (170–2).

Kemble, J.M. 'Anglo-Saxon Proverb.' *Gentleman's Magazine* NS 5 (1836): 611.

Kemble translates the *Winfrid Proverb* from its half-German half-Northumbrian dialect into West Saxon and Modern English. The latter reads 'Oft doth the dilatory man with justice lose by his delay, in every successful undertaking: therefore he dieth lonely.' As this was written down by St Boniface [= Winfrid], it is one of the earliest pieces of [Anglo-]Saxon poetry on record, evidently antedating Boniface himself and comparable with the Old English verses attributed to Bede.

Massmann, H.F. *Die deutschen Abschwörungs-, Glaubens-, Beicht- und Betformeln vom achten bis zum zwölften Jahrhundert.* Bibliothek der gesammten deutschen National-Literatur von der ältesten bis auf die neuere Zeit. VII. Die kleinen Sprachdenkmale des viii. bis xii. Jahrhunderts. Quedlinburg: Basse, 1839. x + 194 pp. + 6 plates. 47 vols. 1835–72.

Massmann prints a facsimile of the *Winfrid Proverb* text from Vienna Nationalbibliothek 751 (plate 1). His brief incidental discussion of the text is accompanied by translations into German and Gothic (25).

Giles, John Allen. *Sancti Bonifacii Archiepiscopi et martyris opera quæ extant omnia.* I. *Epistolae.* II. *Opuscula etc.* 2 vols. London: Nutt, 1844.

Giles supplies a text of the *Winfrid Proverb*. Although notes are provided for some of the *epistolae*, there are none for this one (1.274, no.141).

Migne, J.P. *Patrologiae cursus completus, series latina.* LXXXIX. *Maxima Pars Auctorum Octavi Sæculi.* Tomus Unicus. Paris: Migne, 1850. 221 vols. 1844–82.

The text of the *Winfrid Proverb* printed here reproduces Giles's **(642)** (column 798; letter no. 101). Notes and translation are not provided.

Jaffé, Philippus. *Bibliotheca Rerum Germanicarum.* III *Monumenta Moguntina.* Berlin: Weidmann, 1866. 6 vols. 1864–73.

Jaffé prints the text of the *Winfrid Proverb* as his no.147, along with a Latin translation provided by Karl Müllenhoff: 'Sæpe ignavus gloriam amittit,/ victoriam quamcunque; moriturus ideo solus' (311).

645 Zupitza, Julius. 'Lateinisch-englische Sprüche.' *Anglia* 1 (1878): 285–6.

Zupitza transcribes the *Latin-English Proverbs* to be found in Cotton Faustina A.x. In a series of notes he suggests emendations and analyses the versification.

646 Wülker, Richard P. 'Aus englischen Bibliotheken.' *Anglia* 2 (1879): 354–87.

Wülker prints the *Latin-English Proverbs* to be found in Royal 2 B.v. He points out that two of them correspond to two printed by Zupitza (**645**) from Cotton Faustina A.x. The two manuscripts may have drawn from an identical earlier collection.

647 Holthausen, Ferdinand. 'Der altenglische Spruch aus Winfrids Zeit.' *Archiv für das Studium der neueren Literaturen* 106 (1901): 347–8.

Holthausen corrects Wülker (**16**) on the manuscript provenance of the *Winfrid Proverb*. He reproduces Müllenhoff's (**644**) Latin translation.

648 Dewick, Edward Samuel. *Facsimiles of Horae de Beata Maria Virgine from English Manuscripts of the Eleventh Century.* Henry Bradshaw Society 21. London: Harrison, 1902. xix pp. + 72 columns.

Facsimile edn. of Royal 2 B.v and Cotton Tiberius A.iii. Each leaf of the facsimile is accompanied by a transcript on the opposite page. The manuscript text of the *Latin-English Proverbs* to be found in Royal 2 B.v is included.

649 Tangl, Michael. *Monumenta Germaniae historica. . . Epistolae selectae.* I. *S. Bonifatii et Lullii Epistolae.* Berlin: Weidmann, 1916. 4 vols. 1916–26. Trans. Ephraim Emerton. *The Letters of Saint Boniface.* Records of civilization, sources, and studies 31. New York: Columbia UP, 1940. 204 pp.

Tangl prints a text of the *Winfrid Proverb*, along with an apparatus but without discussion or commentary (283–4, no.146).

650 Holthausen, Ferdinand. 'Kleinere ae Dichtungen.' *Anglia* 41 (1917): 400–4.

Holthausen notes that the *Latin-English Proverbs* should be added to Grein's edition (**2, 6**). Referring to the two available manuscripts, he provides a brief edition of the *Proverbs*. It is substantially in agreement with previous scholarship.

651 Levison, Wilhelm. *England and the Continent in the Eighth Century.* Oxford: Clarendon, 1946. xii + 347 pp.

Levison discusses the *Winfrid Proverb* briefly (130), noting suggestions for an identification of the writer of the letter in which the *Proverb* occurs, but arguing against them. He puts the citation of the *Proverb*, in its native English, in a context of awakening national feeling.

652 Klaeber, Frederick. 'Eine kleine Nachlese zu altenglische Dichtungen.' *Beiträge zur Geschichte der deutschen Sprache und Literatur* 72 (1950): 126–30.

Klaeber suggests that 'foreldit' in the *Winfrid Proverb* governs the dative case, hence 'dome' and 'gahuem', rather than the accusative assumed by Dobbie **(203)**. It is true that *forildan* governs the accusative in *Solomon and Saturn* lines 362–3. Nevertheless, certain *for-* verbs exist that govern both dative and accusative and *forildan* might have been one of them.

Woolf, H.B. 'The Earliest Printing of Old English Poetry.' *English Studies* 34 (1953): 113–15.

The first Old English verse ever to be printed was the *Winfrid Proverb*. It was included in the edition by N. Serarius of the *Epistolae S. Bonifacii martyris*, Mainz 1605, at page 73 – as noted in the ASPR bibliography **(203)**. Woolf appends the text of the relevant letter. The *Proverb* thus substantially antedates other Old English poems to have been printed in the seventeenth century.

Trahern, Joseph B., Jr. 'An Old English Metrical Proverb in the Junius 121 *De Descensu Christi.*' *Anglia* 100 (1982): 419–21.

Trahern argues that the recently edited homily *De Descensu Christi ad Inferos* contains a hitherto unidentified metrical proverb, 'Se ðe on oðres mid unrihte geræsð/ se his agen þurh þæt oft forlyseð.' Except for the preposition 'mid' the alleged proverb scans as regular Old English verse. It represents a fairly literal rendering of the first line of the fourth fable of book one of the metrical fables of Phaedrus, or a prose paraphrase of this work. A much later translation of the same maxim is found in Caxton's Aesop, 1.5: 'He that desyreth to haue other mens goodes oft he loseth his owne good.'

The Exeter Book Riddles

ORIENTATION TO RESEARCH

MANUSCRIPT AND TEXTUAL ISSUES

The Exeter Book Riddles occur uniquely, except for Riddle 35, in the manuscript of that name, which Ker (36) dates at the second half of the tenth century. Robert Chambers's 1831–2 transcript of the Exeter Book (British Library Add. MS. 9067) has been used (first by Tupper, 727) in order to supplement now missing or illegible portions of the original. Because of manuscript lacunae, the total scope of the original riddle collection is unclear. Taylor (806) and other scholars suggested that the Exeter Book would originally have contained one hundred riddles, under the influence of hundred-fold collections by Symphosius and others. Trautmann (746) calculated the total of extant Riddles as 93. Other major studies of the manuscript have been contributed by Pope (307, 882). For editions, complete or partial, see the subject index. The Leiden Riddle presents highly intricate textual problems. In the opinion of Ker (36), Leiden Rijksuniversiteit Vossianus Lat. 4to as a whole dates to the earlier ninth century, with the Old English text as a contemporary addition. For editions and other manuscript investigations see the subject index.

AUTHORSHIP

Having solved *Wulf and Eadwacer* as 'Cynewulf' and detected a further allusion to him in Riddle 90, Leo (657) identified Cynewulf as author of the riddles containing runes and perhaps also of the other riddles in the Exeter Book. The theory of Cynewulfian authorship soon extended to the entire collection and came to pervade nineteenth-century studies. Fritzsche (668) was among the scholars whose specialist investigations into metre, lexis, and other aspects supported the theory. It encountered sharp opposition from Sievers (683), who argued that archaic linguistic forms preserved in the Riddles placed them earlier than the *floruit* of Cynewulf. Likewise, Barnouw (701) saw the collection as containing a variety of compositional strata, with most of the poems older than Cynewulf and datable to the period 680–700. Also central to the demolition of the Cynewulf hypothesis was Trautmann (17, 673). Nevertheless, it proved difficult to dispose of entirely. Tupper (727) countered by alleging that Sievers exaggerated the evidence for Northumbrian origin. Erlemann (709) and Tupper (728) were still discovering Cynewulfian signatures in the first decades of this century; Schneider (740) used linguistic criteria to demonstrate an affiliation with Cynewulf's juvenilia. Typical of more recent scholars, Spaeth (161) thought attributions to Cynewulf unjustified, though he was inclined to the belief that the collection shows the workmanship of a single poet. Against this, a prevalent twentieth-century view is that the collection represents the outcome of multiple authorship. This was already suggested by Dietrich (**658, 662**), who envisaged a compilation of works by different authors, including a youthful Cynewulf. Similarly, Wülker (**16**) had speculated that authorship might have been divided between Cynewulf and Aldhelm. Greenfield and Calder (**60**) urged a multiplicity of dates of composition, authors, themes, and types of source. Robinson (**352**) saw the riddles that include references to kneading dough, churning butter, or weaving at a loom as particularly significant for possible female authorship. More broadly, controversy has persisted over the relative homogeneity or heterogeneity of the collection. At one extreme, Wood (**738**) viewed it as purely a miscellany, but the notion of a compiler with some kind of plan has proved more generally attractive. Tupper (**727**) found the collection homogeneous in its artistry and detected a pattern where the constituent riddles are mutually explicatory.

SOURCES

Thorpe (**65**) believed that although the *Ænigmata* of Symphosius, Aldhelm, Bede, and others might occasionally have suggested themes and topics, the riddles were too essentially Anglo-Saxon to be viewed as other than original productions. But much nineteenth-century and later opinion has tended in the opposite direction. Earle (**88**) argued that most of the collection exhibits the influence of Symphosius and Aldhelm; Ebert (**666**) derived nearly all of it from one or other Latin-language collection. The culmination of this scholarly tendency is represented by Prehn (**672**), who found the overwhelming majority of the riddles to be directly influenced by Latin antecedents, with the remainder having undergone indirect influence. The Chadwicks (**183**) pointed out that riddles in the Old Norse form do not occur in the Exeter Book collection, which is more Latin and learned in its appearance; cf. Löwenthal (**744**). Similarly, Timmer (**202**) envisaged strong influence from Latin. Among particular instances, Herzfeld (**684**) saw Riddle 47 as a slavish imitation of Symphosius 16. In their compilation of sources and analogues, Allen and Calder (**298**) included many texts by (Pseudo-)Symphosius, Eusebius, Tatwine, and Aldhelm, some with query, whereas Old Norse and Middle Welsh texts found a more limited place in the companion compilation of Germanic and Celtic sources and analogues by Calder et al. (**320**). Kennedy (**29**) observed that learned input appears very strikingly in Riddles 1–3 and elsewhere. Erlemann (**704**) identified the ultimate source for the 'earthquake' section of Riddles 1–3 as Bede's *De natura rerum*. Schlauch (**782**) saw Riddle 72 as continuing a classical tradition of prosopopoeia. Brodeur and Taylor (**791**) identified Riddle 19 as a 'world-riddle' and therefore as a learned text designed to be read, not heard. Learned subject-matter has occasionally been linked with learned compositional technique: Magoun (**819**) saw the Riddles as a new genre which of necessity were composed word by word rather than formulaically. Countering this, Benson (**842**) observed that in Riddle 35 the Old English poet closely follows Aldhelm 33 ('lorica'), yet produces a version in which at least 50 per cent of the half-lines are formulas. The arguments of Prehn and other source-hunters have received more limited support or even outright rebuttal from many scholars. Tupper (**707**) and Trautmann (**745**) are typical in their view that cases of specific influence from the Latin riddles are quite isolated. Kennedy (29) believed that the collection as a whole reflects everyday experience in Anglo-Saxon England.

SOCIAL ISSUES

A closely related debate concerns the class affiliations of the collections. Although a monastic context of compilation is quite widely accepted, questions as to the nature of the tradition and the audience are more complex. Bülbring (685) and Lindheim (815) saw some riddles as being of folk origin; Hodgkin (191) believed that they reveal the viewpoint of the *ceorl*. Wyatt (737), by contrast, pointed out that the demarcation between learned and popular riddle types is not simple, in that some riddles contain elements of both. Similarly, although Tupper (706) detected some mechanisms of folk riddle transmission in the collection, he argued for their mutual dependence with literary riddles and indeed proposed (707) that most of the collection represents literary rather than folk productions. Wahrig (224) suggested that the Riddles would not have appealed to ordinary Anglo-Saxon humour, but rather to aristocratic and clerical taste.

GENRE

Genre demarcations have been exceedingly difficult to draw, for two principal reasons. The first is the apparently rather haphazard organization of contents in the Exeter Book, such that texts which from a modern standpoint are not clearly riddles fall next to or even within the main collection. Thus *Wulf and Eadwacer*, which immediately precedes the first section of the riddle collection, was integrated into it by many scholars following Leo (657). Even after Bradley (678) satisfied most scholars that *Wulf and Eadwacer* was no riddle, we find Patzig (766) supporting Tupper (728) in solving it as 'mill'. More ambitiously, Hicketier (682) tried to show that *The Wife's Lament*, *The Husband's Message*, and *The Ruin* are all riddles. Anderson (331, 950) proposed grand over-arching structures where, for example, *The Soul's Address*, *Deor*, and *Wulf and Eadwacer* are treated as comprising 'Riddle 1'. In addition, particular juxtapositions of texts have struck some scholars as significant. Ritzke-Rutherford (310) noted that Riddle 30 in both of its versions follows upon poems (Riddle 29 and *Homiletic Fragment II*) that contain the idea of light. Initiating an idea that has held continued appeal but never achieved consensus among scholars, Strobl (537) and Blackburn (698) grouped Riddle 60 together with *The Husband's Message* as a single poem. Influential on the positive side of this debate were Kaske (852), Elliott (219, 324), and Pope (307). Not convinced were Leslie (832, 858) and Greenfield (282, 844). The boundaries between riddles are not always certain, whether or not the manuscript seems to offer clear evidence, and this too has had implications for perceptions concerning genre. Riddles 1–3 have caused particular difficulties in this respect. Campbell (885) proposed that these riddles together comprise a unified poem which uses riddle conventions chiefly as structuring devices. Other scholars have attempted to link certain riddles into sequences and to argue for allegorical interpretations on this basis: thus Foley (910) in his discussion of Riddles 53, 54, and 55. Similarly, Anderson (949) invoked manuscript evidence to argue that Riddles 42 and 43, 47 and 48 should be treated as two paired riddles. A second complication for genre identifications is that even the acknowledged riddles in the Exeter Book have eluded definition in the abstract; indeed, certain of them have been denied true riddle status by modern scholars. If it is true that a riddle must mystify in order to deserve the name, then some particular riddles do pose real problems. Mitchell **(942)** disputed the conventional solution to Riddles 1–3 on this basis, maintaining that a one-to-one correspondence between the imagery of a riddle and the solution is contrary to a fundamental rule of most riddle-composition. Riddle 47 has often been blamed for obviousness: to redeem it from this accusation Robinson **(896)** pointed to its paronomasic complexity of meaning and Stewart **(898)** to its parody of Old English heroic poetry. Riddle 23, judged strangely transparent by Schlutter **(724)**, found defence from Wyatt **(737)**, who suggested that the author was subtly confusing the audience. Cherniss **(876)** disputed the solution of Riddle 55 as 'cross' on the grounds that a reference in the text gave the answer away. More generally, Wood **(738)** noted a tendency in the riddles to dwell on the pictorial or poetically suggestive possibilities of the theme, whereas the more typical genre characteristic in other collections is witty evasiveness. Other scholars have urged a more elastic understanding of the genre. The Chadwicks **(183)** argued that difficulty of solution is not necessarily a reliable genre characteristic. Tristram **(969)** extended this to the suggestion that partial identification of the solution was typical of the genre. Malone **(30)** saw paradox, not mystification, as possibly constituting the key feature. Many scholars would class these texts with lyric poetry rather than with true riddles.

MENTALITY ISSUES

Debate continues as to whether composers and audience of the riddles belonged to some kind of Alterity or participated in the Anglo-Saxon intellectual world or essentially shared our form of consciousness. On the side of Alterity, Brooke **(109)** and Moorman **(711)** saw in the riddles abundant evidence of a pre-Christian warrior ethos. Pons **(172)** found pagan attitudes to death in Riddle 7. Schneider **(339)** saw Riddle 19 as evidencing a surreptitious retention of pagano-religious concepts in an intolerant Christian society. Alexander **(257)** detected in the riddles a vestigial Anglo-Saxon consciousness that every created thing had its own personality. For Williams **(900)** the depiction of water as matriarch in Riddle 84 evoked early animism. A few recent scholars have contended that the words in our texts contain connotations that are radically alien to our mentality. Thus Jember **(911)** contended that the riddles are not themselves consistently rational but rather originate in what Eliade would term a 'boundary' situation. Tripp **(914)** urged us to avoid projecting our own commonplaces on to the Anglo-Saxon imagination. Against Alterity, Sedgefield **(164)** could see no trace of pre-Christian folklore in the riddles and Heusler **(166)** termed them learned and clerical. Meaney **(262)** argued that Riddles 1–3 cannot be used as a source for Woden cults. Some scholars follow a different logic again, positing a universal human imagination to which the Riddles belong: thus Cooper **(935)**. For Kranz **(828)**, Riddle 3 has the same appeal to us as Shelley's 'The Cloud' and the two poets can be imagined as extending hands to each other across eleven centuries.

Kennedy (888) advocated his solution 'cloud' to Riddle 39 with the argument that it must be a universal experience to be comforted by watching clouds form and reform.

SOLUTIONS

Conybeare (62) inaugurated research on solutions pessimistically, judging the Riddles to be 'so extremely obscure that they might well suffice to damp the ardour of a Saxon Oedipus'. Evidently undeterred, Dietrich (658) suggested a complete set of solutions. Trautmann subjected these solutions to a thorough review in separate articles (140, 691, 692, 712, 750) and in his edition (751). Another major solver was Tupper (707, 716, 727), with his emphasis on a comparative approach as a means of identifying typical solutions. Trautmann (735) countered by using Riddle 13 to demonstrate that comparative research could be misleading. Other notable or frequent contributors to the catalogue of would-be solutions include Doane (971), Erhardt-Siebold (768, 795, 796, 797, 802, 803, 805, 808, 809, 812, 817), Jember (904, 917, 965), Kiernan (889, 890), Lendinara (892, 906), Morley (74), Pinsker and Ziegler (961), Schneider (897, 913), Shook (255, 798, 826, 883), Swaen (757, 775, 785, 786, 788, 799, 804), Young (211, 789, 793), Whitman (859, 915), Williamson (916), and Wyatt (737). Numerous scholars have proposed solutions to particular riddles: a fairly complete list (to 1981) is given by Fry (936). In this bibliography I have attempted to note all new solutions, but have not registered all reiterations of pre-existing ones. Particular riddles, such as 8, 39, and 57, have given rise to prolonged and often inconclusive controversy. The obscene riddles have also occasioned much worry: for an instance, see Walz's turn-of-the-century Bostonian contribution (693). Jember (904), by contrast, in a less modest age, has greatly expanded their number, to the point where the monks of old might well have complained that predictability of solution spoiled the fun. Ultimately, conclusive solutions contain an irreducible element of serendipity, just as palmary emendations do. This, however, has not prevented some scholars from attempting to construct a more rigorous methodology. Specialists in Anglo-Saxon *realia* of various kinds, thus Whitman (694) on birds, Padelford (695) on music, and Shook (883) on scribes and scriptoria, have brought their knowledge to bear on problematic Riddles. Against this, Klaeber (752) pointed out that a riddle description of e.g. the badger would not necessarily possess the accuracy of a modern scientific description. Williamson (916), Bierbaumer and Wannagut (934), and Doane (971) used recent archaeological findings as an avenue to new solutions. More broadly, Trautmann (743) proposed that grammatical gender in some riddles indicated the solution. Recently a tendency to seek more than a single solution to each riddle has announced itself. To Gardner (886), the solution to Riddle 7 might be identified as either 'swan' or 'soul'. Nelson (881) saw possible allusions in Riddle 34 ('rake') to an anagogical harrowing of sinners and argued that we should not envisage solely one audience with one frame of reference. For Lendinara (892), Riddle 9 is only trivially solved as 'cuckoo': above and beyond that, it depicts human ingratitude. Jember (911) argued that in solving Riddle 21 exclusively as 'plough' we concentrate with undue empiricism on the physical object: instead, a 'generative' solution, 'phallus', ought to be seen as underlying the immediate physical solution.

LITERARY CRITICISM

Dietrich (658) set the tone and content for much later criticism when he judged the imaginative scope of the Riddles, rather than any intellectual depth, as their true achievement and suggested (662) that a primary objective was communication of the poet's experience of Nature. For Ker (121), the Riddles exhibit imaginative portrayal and projection and the power of a dramatic, literary game. Even scholars who accepted Prehn's identification of Latin sources, such as Moorman (711), conceded that the analogues only serve to show up the keen appreciation of natural phenomena and capacity for description in the Old English texts. Williams (28) found that, as distinct from those of Symphosius, they contain a dramatic insight into the human qualities of the object described. Treneer (772) saw them as enabling readers to transcend their individual selves, so as to feel and move in sympathy with other forces. Though disparaging them as riddles in the conventional sense, Legouis and Cazamian (168) noted their capacity to bypass the intellect and instead speak to the imagination. In a notable article essaying a New Critical approach, which has found many emulators, Adams (840) interpreted them as representing the lyric mode, otherwise sparsely evident in Old English poetry, and as exploring complex themes such as mutability (though not love). Shook (883) noted the power of the Riddles to generate that new intense awareness or epiphany that alone is the core of lyric poetry. On the exegetical front, Kaske (852) proposed that Riddle 60 is the first part of a poem on the Cross and therefore part of an allegorically conceived whole. Rollinson (868) proposed that Riddle 40, along with other long riddles, might exhibit a variety of the tropes subsumed under 'allegory' in the taxonomies of Bede and Isidore. At a more stylistic level, Robinson (867) observed that paronomasia and wordplay in the poetic language enhanced the riddling quality as well as generating humour. Whitman (869) took this emphasis further, conceiving the Riddles as primarily manifestations of verbal wit, though not altogether denying their artistic appeal. Marino (922) coined the term 'deceit' (in contrast to Donne's 'conceit') to denote their primary structural device. From an anthropological standpoint, Barley (879) saw them as performing a metalinguistic function in the discussion of categories. In a somewhat similar vein, Williamson (916) proposed that they mean that reality exists and is at the same time a mosaic of human perception. There has been a widespread feeling that the Riddles transcend routine Old English poetry. MacLean (689) saw anticipations of fable, allegory, and morality play in Riddle 15. Similarly, Burton (690) found, 'commingling with the feeling for the savagery of beast-kind', 'a certain spiritual good fellowship which foretokens Coleridge, Byron, and Wordsworth'. Anderson (32) saw the Riddles as prefiguring the allegorical literature so characteristic of the Middle Ages. Swann (874) suggested comparisons with the poetry of Góngora. Alexander (59) found resemblances to the Imagist poems of Ezra Pound in their 'pregnant brevity and enigmatic allusiveness'.

REALIA

The Riddles have been extensively quarried as evidence for aspects of Anglo-Saxon culture and technology. Just a few examples will be given here. Heyne (73) drew on them for information on Anglo-Saxon customs, along with specific artifacts such as the battering ram, hand-mill, and key; Hoops (98) for Anglo-Saxon plants and botanical knowledge; Bartels (138) for Anglo-Saxon law; Andrews (669) and Colgrave (780) for the plough; Hoops (730) for the crossbow; Wrenn (244) for the harp; Anderson (847) and Owen-Crocker (967) for looms and weaving; and Fell (325) for social history.

BIBLIOGRAPHY

655 Müller, Ludvig Christian. *Collectanea Anglo-Saxonica, maximam partem nunc primum edita et vocabulario illustrata.* Copenhagen: Wahl, 1835. viii + 141 pp.

This reader contains Old English text, with glossary but no notes. Included are two Exeter Book Riddles ('aenigmata anglosaxonica'), 5 and 26. Müller solves them as 'scutum' and 'liber' respectively (63–4).

656 Bethmann, L.C. 'Alte Glossen.' *Zeitschrift für deutsches Altertum* 5 (1845): 193–211.

Bethmann transcribes the text of the *Leiden Riddle*, with some lacunae and without comment (199). [His work is described by Smith (777) as a 'poor and careless transcript' (8). A detailed critique is provided by Dietrich (659).]

657 Leo, Heinrich. *Commentatio quae de se ipso Cynevulfus, sive Cenewulfus, sive Coenevulfus poeta Anglo-Saxonicus tradiderit.* Universitätsprogramm, U Halle. Halle: Hendel, 1857. 3–30.

Leo solves *Wulf and Eadwacer* as 'Cynewulf' and detects a further allusion to the same name in Riddle 90. Building on this evidence, he identifies Cynewulf as the author of the riddles containing runes and perhaps also of other riddles in the Exeter Book. Northumbria is identified as the place of composition.

658 Dietrich, [Franz E.C.]. 'Die Räthsel des Exeterbuchs: Würdigung, Lösung und Herstellung.' *Zeitschrift für deutsches Altertum* 11 (1859): 448–90.

In this article Dietrich suggests a complete set of solutions to the Exeter Book Riddles. The solutions, which take up the main part of the article (459–90), are based on the text of Grein (2) and therefore Thorpe (65). Riddles not included by Thorpe, as too fragmentary, are therefore not commented on by Dietrich. His solutions are as follows: Riddles 1–3 'storm'; 4 'millstone'; 5 'shield', following Müller (655); 6 'sun'; 7 'swan', 8 'pipe' or 'nightingale'; 9 'cuckoo'; 10 'ocean-furrow'; 11 'night'; 12 'leather'; 13 'the 22 letters of the alphabet'; 14 'horn'; 15 'badger'; 16 'anchor'; 17 'ballista'; 18 'leather bottle'; 20 'sword'; 21 'plough'; 22 'days of the month'; 23 'bow'; 24 'magpie, jay'; 25 'onion, leek'; 26 'book', following Müller (655); 27 'whip'; 28 'wine-cask'; 29 'sun and moon'; 30 'rain-water'; 31 'bagpipe'; 32 'ship'; 33 'iceberg'; 34 'rake'; 35 'mailcoat'; 36

'sow pregnant with five piglets' (the Riddle consists of two parts, each with this solution); 37 'wagon'; 38 'young bull'; 39 'day'; 40 'creation'; 41 'earth'; 42 'cock and hen'; 43 'soul and body'; 44 'key' or 'dagger-sheath'; 45 'bee?'; 46 'Lot with his two daughters and their sons', following Wright (64); 47 'bookmoth', following Grein (2); 48 'chrismal'; 49 'falcon-cage'; 50 'dog'; 51 'dragon'; 52 'two pails'; 53 'battering-ram'; 54 'baker's boy and oven'; 55 'shield'; 56 'weaver's loom'; 57 'swallows; gnats'; 58 'draw-well'; 59 'chalice'; 60 'reed-flute'; 61 'shirt'; 62 'gimlet'; 63 'beaker'; 64 'ring-tailed peacock', anagrammatizing the runes to read '*pea beah-swifeda'; 65 'onion'; 66 'power of God, creation'; 68–9 'ice'; 70 'shawm, shepherd's pipe'; 71 'cupping glass'; 72 'axle and wheel'; 73 'lance'; 74 'cuttlefish'; 76–7 'oyster'; 79–80 'falcon, hawk'; 81 'ship'; 83 'ore'; 84 'water'; 85 'fish and river'; 86 'organ'; 87 'cask and cooper'; 88 'staghorn, antler'; 90 uncertain, but the key feature is play upon various senses of 'lupus'; 91 'key'; 93 'inkwell fashioned from an antler'; 95 'wandering singer'. Dietrich offers these solutions in order that the imaginative scope of the Riddles may be better appreciated: this scope, rather than any intellectual depth, is their true achievement (449). The Riddles were probably not difficult for a contemporary to solve but are obscure now because of our limited knowledge of Old English language, perceptions, and material culture. The relationship between epic and riddles can be close, for instance when epic ventures into nature description or when the riddle subject speaks anthropomorphically of brothers and sisters, exile from his own country, or his feats and accomplishments, pleasures and sorrows (448). Dietrich sees the Exeter Book Riddles as the most successful and inspired examples of popular riddle composition. Dietrich agrees with Leo (657) that Cynewulf's signature is reasonably clear in *Wulf and Eadwacer* and Riddle 95 ('wandering singer'), treated by him as the first and last riddles respectively (459 and 488). Nevertheless, the Riddles represent a compilation of work by different authors. The repetitions in this collection point to multiple authorship, since a good poet does not indulge in repetition (488). We could possibly explain the collection as the product of Cynewulf's earlier years; he subsequently renounced them, perhaps on account of the obscene riddles (489). Dietrich challenges Thorpe's notion that the Riddles were purely native, without foreign sources. Influences from Symphosius can be traced, for example in the choice of 'anchor' (Riddle 16), 'bookworm' (Riddle 47), and 'river and fish' (Riddle 85) as themes. Yet even in clear cases of borrowing the Old English text shows an extensive reworking of the material (450). Where Aldhelm's riddles were used as source material, the Old English poets bypassed his learned allusions to ancient mythology and history, so that often his influence can be detected solely in the choice of riddle-object, as in the relation between his *Ænigma* 87 'clipeus' and Exeter Book Riddle 5 'shield' (453). Some of the observations underlying the Riddles, e.g. the notion of a singing swan in Riddle 7, can also be traced back to Greek or Latin sources. Although other (as yet unknown) written sources may underlie the Riddles, oral tradition should also be reckoned with. Indicative here are analogues in Middle High German to Dietrich's proposed solution of Riddle 51 as 'dragon' (457).

659 Dietrich, Franz. *Kynewulfi poetae aetas aenigmatum fragmento e codice Lugdunensi edito illustrata.* Universitätsprogramm. Marburg: Elwert, 1860. 27 pp.

In this investigation into the life and works of Cynewulf, Dietrich announces his concurrence with the Cynewulfian theories of Leo (**657**). He furthers these theories by pointing out resemblances between the signed poems and the Riddles in lexis and in a habit of repetition (3–4). He sees the *Leiden Riddle* as crucial evidence for the poet's *floruit* because of the early date of this text. He provides an edition of the Riddle (21), accompanied by a brief description of the manuscript (17), a recognition of at least two hands (24–5), a lithograph of the manuscript page (27), a transcription and discussion of the text, correcting errors by Bethmann (**656**) (18–20), an identification of the dialect as Northumbrian and of eighth-century date (23–6), and an analysis of the relationship between the *Leiden Riddle* and Exeter Book Riddle 35 (21–2). In Dietrich's opinion, the translations of Aldhelm seen in the two texts are so similar in technique and detail of wording that they must be one and the same. Moreover they contain characteristically Cynewulfian lexis and phraseology, eliminating any possibility that Cynewulf had merely incorporated another translator's work into his riddle collection. [According to Smith (**777**), Dietrich's transcript and lithographed facsimile of the Riddle were the last to be made before Pluygers's application of a reagent to the manuscript in 1864 and therefore possess primary importance in the establishment of the text.]

660 Müller, Eduard. *Über die angelsächsischen Räthsel des 'Exeterbuches': Programm der herzöglichen Hauptschule zu Cöthen.* Cöthen: Scheltser, 1861. 20 pp.

Müller includes Riddles 38, 12, 26 (excerpt), 14, 24 (excerpt), and 85, in that order. He suggests the solution 'jay' for Riddle 8 (noting the similarity with Riddle 24), 'horn' for Riddle 80, and 'bellows' for Riddle 87. The text is based on Grein (**2**) but also takes into account readings from Thorpe (**65**) and Ettmüller (**68**).

661 ———. 'Zwei angelsächsische Gedichte.' *Archiv für das Studium der neueren Literaturen* 29 (1861): 205–20.

Section 2 of this article (212–20) contains a fuller explication of Dietrich's (**658**) solution, 'soul and body', for Riddle 43. The full commentary includes a citation of German and Gothic cognates, wherever possible, for each word of the Riddle. The article as a whole is intended as a contribution to Old English pedagogy, which Müller discusses at length, stressing the needs of the beginner. He supports the attribution of Riddles 1–60 to Cynewulf, with the rest as a possible later addition by the same author. The theological subject-matter of Riddle 43 is one indication in that direction.

662 Dietrich, [Franz E.C.]. 'Die Räthsel des Exeterbuchs: Verfasser; Weitere Lösungen.' *Zeitschrift für deutsches Altertum* 12 (1865): 232–52.

The Riddles present us with a kind of poetry that goes far beyond simply demanding a solution to an enigma: communication of the poet's experience of

Nature becomes a goal in its own right (232). 'Riddle 1' [*Wulf and Eadwacer*], Cynewulf's introduction to the Riddles, should be seen as a structural parallel to Aldhelm's introduction to his *Ænigmata*. The fondness for Nature description in *Andreas* is an indication of Cynewulf's involvement in the composition of some at least of the Riddles. The occurrence of certain key ideas and rare lexical items and the use of runes are other features that point to him (233). On the other hand, the division of riddle material into three parts in the Exeter Book argues against single authorship. Also significant in this respect is the repetition of solutions – though admittedly the repetition is not always exact and the solutions can be regarded as merely related, not identical (234). We should therefore attribute Riddles 1–60 [this tally includes *Wulf and Eadwacer*] to Cynewulf: they are homogeneous in language and use of sources (235). The topics of these riddles centre upon Creation, along with human-produced objects. Riddle 43, on 'body and soul', would have represented a stepping stone in the development of the collection. The original generating principle would have been one of association of ideas. The order in which the Riddles now stand represents a later refinement, undertaken so that the task of solution would not be too easy (236). By contrast, the remaining Riddles form no such whole, but read like a series of amplifications or afterthoughts to the earlier collection. They make less use of non-native sources and are less elaborate in their introductions and conclusions (241–2). Nevertheless, it is not impossible that Cynewulf composed all the Riddles: in particular, Riddles 85–93 and 95 from the third group should be attributed to him. Riddle 95 would mark an appropriate farewell from the poet who had introduced himself in 'Riddle 1' [i.e. *Wulf and Eadwacer*]. Dietrich notes the general fondness for runes, repetition of phrases, similarities in ideas, and use of rare lexical items (244–7). Interpolation of non-Cynewulfian riddles remains a possibility, but the onus of proof rests with anyone positing interpolation (251). In footnotes Dietrich withdraws some solutions in favour of new ones: thus 'millstone' in Riddle 4, 'woodpigeon' in Riddle 8, 'bellows' in Riddle 37, 'bookcase' in Riddle 49, 'scabbard' in Riddle 55, 'lathe' in Riddle 56, 'starlings' in Riddle 57, 'one-eyed seller of garlic' in Riddle 86, and 'Cynewulf' in Riddle 90. Some of these alterations to his earlier account (658) are acknowledged as the contribution of his pupil Lange: thus the new solutions 'fortress' for Riddle 17, replacing 'ballista'; 'hemp' for Riddle 25, replacing 'onion'; 'mead' for Riddle 27, replacing 'whip'; and 'helmet with vizor' for Riddle 81, replacing 'ship'.

3 Dietrich, Franz Eduard Christoph. *(Disputatio) de cruce Ruthwellensi et de auctore versuum in illa inscriptorum qui ad passionem domini pertinent. Addita tabula lapide excusa. Index lectionum.* Marburg: Elwert, 1865. 19 pp. + illustration.

In passing, Dietrich notes resemblances between the Exeter Book Riddles and *The Dream of the Rood* (11). He argues that the Riddles were composed in Northumbria (19).

4 Grein, Christian W.M. 'Kleine Mittheilungen. 2: Zu den Rätseln des Exeterbuches.' *Germania* 10 (1865): 307–9.

Grein expresses appreciation of Dietrich's achievements in finding solutions to the Exeter Book Riddles (658), but offers a few dissenting suggestions. In Riddle 13 the number should be 10, not 22. The solution is 'looper caterpillar', its different types of legs being distinguished as 'brothers' (the six forward legs with claws) and 'sisters' (the four hinder legs). Riddle 52 involves a bucket descending into a well. Riddle 58 should be solved as 'well', the runic 'rad' indicating the mechanism responsible for raising the bucket. The runes in Riddle 64 can be construed to yield *aspide-uf* 'a snake-eating bird of prey' and *beah* 'the ring-shaped adder'. The complete picture is one of a bird flying over a lake carrying a snake in its beak.

665 **Zupitza, Julius.** *Altenglisches Übungsbuch zum Gebrauche bei Universitäts-Vorlesungen. Mit einem Wörterbuche.* Vienna: Braumüller, 1874. vi + 137 pp. 5th rev. edn. Julius Schipper, *Alt- und mittelenglisches Übungsbuch.* Vienna: Braumüller, 1897. 311 pp.

Riddle 15 is included, with critical apparatus but no other annotation.

666 **Ebert, Adolf.** 'Über die Räthselpoesie der Angelsachsen, insbesondere die Aenigmata des Tatwine und Eusebius.' *Berichte über die Verhandlungen der königlichen sächsischen Gesellschaft der Wissenschaften zu Leipzig, philologisch-historische Klasse* 29 (1877): 20–56.

The Exeter Book Riddles nearly all derive from one or other collection of Latin riddles. They are, however, most closely akin in style and presentation to the *Ænigmata* of Aldhelm. Ebert notes the tendency of the Exeter Book Riddles to focus on dramatic action, rather than simply listing a series of static characteristics.

667 **Körner, Karl.** *Einleitung in das Studium des Angelsächsischen.* I *Grammatik.* II *Text, Übersetzung, Anmerkungen, Glossar.* 2 vols. Heilbronn: Henninger, 1878 and 1880.

Included is Riddle 14 in Grein's edition (2), with German translation (2.166–7). The appended notes on the solution are largely taken from Dietrich (658).

668 **Fritzsche, Arthur.** 'Das angelsächsische Gedicht Andreas and der Dichter Cynewulf.' *Anglia* 2 (1879): 441–96.

Fritzsche considers versification and other features as criteria for Cynewulf's authorship. He finds that lines with three alliterative syllables are more common in the Exeter Book Riddles and *Christ* than in *Elene* and *Juliana*. Conversely, a pattern where the final stressed syllable in a line carries over into the alliteration of the following line is more common in *Elene* and *Juliana* than in the Riddles or *Christ*. All the Riddles are to be attributed to Cynewulf. Fritzsche also briefly considers rhymes (471) and vocabulary (488–92).

669 **Andrews, Charles McLean.** *The Old English Manor: A Study in English Economic History.* Johns Hopkins U Studies in historical and political science, extra vol. 12. Baltimore: Johns Hopkins, 1882. xi + 291 pp.

The Exeter Book Riddles are used in passing as sources of information on

Anglo-Saxon culture. In a substantive discussion of Riddle 21 ('plough'), Andrews argues that the description does not appear to be based on any Latin model and that the omission of the wheel is therefore significant. He also attributes significance to the information that the seed was cast immediately after the furrow was turned. Other Riddles mentioned are 4, 34, 35, 37, 40, and 56.

0 D'Ham, Otto. *Der gegenwärtige Stand der Cynewulf-Frage.* Diss. U Tübingen. Limburg, 1883. 46 pp.

[Not seen.] According to Lendinara (**905**), D'Ham comes to the conclusion that Cynewulf was the sole author of the Exeter Book Riddles. [For a review see Holthaus, **674**.]

1 Jansen, Gottfried. *Beiträge zur Synonymik und Poetik der allgemein als ächt anerkannten Dichtungen Cynevulf's.* Münster: Brunn, 1883. 147 pp.

Citations from the Exeter Book Riddles are included among the examples in a wide-ranging discussion of poetic synonyms, appositional phrases, pleonasm, tautology, parallelism, repetition, and other such devices. Alliteration and rhyme are also covered.

2 Prehn, A. *Komposition und Quellen der Rätsel des Exeterbuches.* Diss. U Paderborn. *Neuphilologische Studien* 3 (1883): 143–285.

Prehn finds the early English riddles composed in Latin impoverished and sterile compared to those composed in Old English. Nevertheless, a variation in quality can be discerned within the Latin riddles, such that Aldhelm is superior to Symphosius. Prehn endorses the attribution of the Exeter Book Riddles to Cynewulf. Influence from the Latin riddles can be posited in cases where there are parallel clues or a parallel solution. Parallelism in clues points to literary indebtedness even in cases where the actual solution differs. Cynewulf should be envisaged as sometimes using multiple sources, as in Riddle 30, which draws on Symphosius 9, Eusebius 15, and Aldhelm 3 for its various motifs. Using the solutions reached by Dietrich (**658, 662**), with the additional suggestion of 'stormclouds' for Riddle 57, Prehn attempts to identify Latin sources for each Exeter Book riddle. He finds that the overwhelming majority were directly influenced by Latin antecedents. Some twenty Riddles deviate from this trend in that they underwent only indirect influence, among them Riddles 7, 21, and 46. Here Cynewulf operated with somewhat greater freedom than customarily, re-working previously assimilated Latin material. As indications that the Exeter Book Riddles were recited to their audience, Prehn points to the epic amplifications, the invitations to offer solutions, and the repetition of a salient idea at beginning and end of the riddle. [For a review see Holthaus, **674**.]

3 Trautmann, Moritz. 'Cynewulf und die Rätsel.' *Anglia* 6 (1883): Anzeiger 158–69.

Trautmann rejects Leo's (**657**) and Dietrich's (**658**) interpretation of *Wulf and Eadwacer* as one of the Exeter Book Riddles and along with it their interpretation of Riddle 95, arguing that both should be solved as 'riddle'. The word 'gefea' should be supplied in Riddle 95 line 4. He also opposes the theory that Riddle 90 contains an allusion to Cynewulf. Leo's 'solution' of *Wulf and Eadwacer* presupposes a charade, a literary form which in reality does not occur in Old English or indeed anywhere in medieval English. Moreover, the solution depends on complicated lexical associations, e.g. between *cyne-* and *cen-*. Trautmann does not dismiss outright the theory that Cynewulf composed at least some of the riddles, but challenges Cynewulf's advocates to produce better proofs.

674 **Holthaus, E.** Rev. of *Komposition und Quellen der Rätsel des Exeterbuches*, by A. Prehn [672] and of *Der gegenwärtige Stand der Cynewulf-Frage*, by O. D'Ham [670]. *Anglia* 7 (1884): Anzeiger 120–9.

Holthaus rebuts many of Prehn's suggestions. He raises doubts about the attribution of the Exeter Book Riddles to Cynewulf, dissenting from D'Ham and agreeing with Trautmann (673).

675 **Trautmann, Moritz.** 'Zum 89. Rätsel.' *Anglia* 7 (1884): Anzeiger 210–11.

Following up on his solution (673) of Riddle 95 as 'riddle' but withdrawing his suggested restoration 'gefea' in line 4, Trautmann now suggests supplying the word 'fæðm' instead.

676 **Sarrazin, Gregor.** 'Beowulf and Kynewulf.' *Anglia* 9 (1886): 515–50.

Sarrazin ascribes the Exeter Book Riddles to Cynewulf and places them as the earliest among his compositions (544). His list of parallels between *Beowulf* and the Cynewulf attributions includes some from the Riddles, for instance the landscape descriptions in Riddle 3.

677 **Schröer, Arnold.** Rev. of *Das altenglische gedicht vom heiligen Andreas und der Dichter Cynewulf,* by Friedrich Ramhorst. Leipzig: Fock, 1886. *Englische Studien* 10 (1887): 118–22.

Schröer argues that, despite Trautmann (673), Cynewulf's authorship of the Exeter Book Riddles has not yet been finally disposed of. He notes in particular the play on the words *wulf* and *lupus* found in the Riddles (119).

678 **Bradley, Henry.** Rev. of *English Writers*, by Henry Morley [74]. *Academy* 33 (1888): 197–8.

Bradley inclines to the view that some, at least, of the Riddles should be ascribed to Cynewulf. Dissenting from Morley, he sees *Wulf and Eadwacer* as a dramatic soliloquy. He characterizes Morley's solution of Riddle 90 as ingenious but unconvincing.

679 **Wülker, Richard P.** 'Die Bedeutung einer neuen Entdeckung für die angelsächsische Literaturgeschichte.' *Berichte über die Verhandlungen der königlichen sächsischen Gesellschaft der Wissenschaften zu Leipzig, philologisch-historische Klasse* 40 (1888): 209–18.

Wülker agrees with earlier scholars that *Wulf and Eadwacer* is a riddle, to be solved as 'Cynewulf', and that Riddle 90 has the same solution. He rejects Trautmann's (675) solution to Riddle 95, without giving specific reasons.

0   Nuck, R. 'Zu Trautmanns Deutung des ersten und neunundachtzigsten Rätsels.' *Anglia* 10 (1888): 390–4.

Nuck defends Dietrich's (658) solution of Riddle 95 against Trautmann's (673) new suggestion, 'riddle', arguing that Trautmann's solution depends upon unjustifiable emendations, distortions in the translation, and inferences from the text.

1   Hicketier, Franz. 'Fünf Rätsel des Exeterbuches.' *Anglia* 10 (1888): 564–600.

Hicketier resists Dietrich's (658) solution, 'pike', for Riddle 90. Cynewulf, alluding to himself in the text, would not have understood the word 'lupus' in such a sense. Rather, 'hops' is the sense intended and the 'lamb' is to be imagined as eating them. He sees the discussions of Riddle 95 by Trautmann (673) and Nuck (680) as representing little advance over Dietrich's (658) solution, which can be vindicated by emendation in lines 5–6. Hicketier also suggests expansions of the runic abbreviations in Riddle 64, solving as 'horseman and hawk'. He proposes major emendations in Riddle 19 (solved as 'falconry') to fit his interpretation of the runes. The remainder of the article is devoted to *Wulf and Eadwacer.*

2   ———. 'Klage der frau, botschaft des gemahls und ruine.' *Anglia* 11 (1889): 363–8.

Hicketier opposes Strobl's (537) theory that *The Husband's Message* represents a versified solution to Riddle 60, arguing that its size would be disproportionate. He tries to show that all three of the poems mentioned in the title (*The Wife's Lament, The Husband's Message,* and *The Ruin*) are riddles and ponders the implications of this for the total grouping of poems in the Exeter Book. He notes variations in the handling of runes in the Riddles.

3   Sievers, Eduard. 'Zu Cynewulf.' *Anglia* 13 (1891): 1–25.

Sievers argues that archaic linguistic forms preserved in the Riddles demonstrate that they were composed prior to the *floruit* of Cynewulf. Examples are the reverse spelling in Riddle 23 ('agof' instead of '*agob') and the vocalism of the runes in Riddle 42 ('hæn', not 'hen'). The *Leiden Riddle* text contains parallel forms. The phonological/graphological forms indicated by the runes in Riddle 19 somewhat complicate the picture but can be reconciled with the theory of pre-Cynewulfian authorship. The only positive evidence so far adduced for a Cynewulfian ascription is Leo's (657) impossible interpretation of *Wulf and Eadwacer.* Anyone who wants to insist on the Cynewulfian hypothesis must suppose that in his youth Cynewulf spelt with medial -*i*- but in later life used medial -*e*- (as in his own name!). In Riddle 91 Sievers argues, against Dietrich (658) and Grein (664), for an expansion of runic *w* to *wynn*, comparing uses of this word elsewhere in Old English poetry. This argument is supported by an analysis of the workings of an Anglo-Saxon lock. Sievers argues against Dietrich's (658) solution of Riddle 64 on linguistic grounds. The language of other Old English wisdom texts (*Winfrid Proverb, Rune Poem*) is discussed in passing.

684 Herzfeld, Georg. 'Die Räthsel des Exeterbuches und ihr Verfasser.' *Acta Germanica* 2 (1891): 1–72.

Herzfeld argues that probably, though not provably, all the Riddles are of Cynewulf's authorship. He admits that stylistic and lexical correspondences would not in themselves be sufficient to enforce this conclusion, which derives rather from agreement in a great number of characteristic expressions and attitudes, similarities in methods of handling source-material, and in particular linguistic, rhetorical, and prosodic features shared by the Riddles and Cynewulf's signed works. Nonetheless, the Riddles do represent a special category and should be seen as belonging to Cynewulf's juvenilia. Herzfeld finds Leo's **(657)** hypothesis over-speculative and would exclude *Wulf and Eadwacer* from the collection. He tries to establish the homogeneity of the Riddle collection, drawing attention to similarities in solutions and in wording between the two main groups as arranged in the Exeter Book (1–60 and 61–95). The poet was not always successful in his work. Riddle 47 fails to elaborate in any way on Symphosius 16 ('bookworm'). Riddle 66 is to be explained as the poet's second attempt at reaching an audience for whom his first draft, preserved in the collection as Riddle 40, was too learned. Metrical analysis of the Riddles helps to reveal a high degree of manuscript corruption: suggestions on possible emendations (*metri causa*) and solutions are appended. The reading 'hilde to sæne' in Riddle 33 line 5 contradicts other motifs in the text and should be emended to 'hilde *tosæge' ('inclined to battle'). New suggestions for solutions are as follows: Riddle 45 'dough', 50 'fire'. Northumbrian characteristics of the language of the Riddles are listed. In an appendix Herzfeld responds to Sievers's **(683)** rejection of Cynewulfian authorship by arguing that the new linguistic datings do not pose any major obstacles to an ascription to a young Cynewulf, in the second quarter of the eighth century. This would have been precisely the time when the phonological changes described by Sievers were taking place. [For a review see Bülbring, **685**.]

685 Bülbring, Karl D. Rev. of 'Die Räthsel des Exeterbuches und ihr Verfasser', by Georg Herzfeld **[684]**. *Literaturblatt* 12 (1891): 155–8.

Bülbring argues against Herzfeld's notion of Cynewulfian authorship of the Riddles, or indeed single authorship on any poet's part. He points out that often the riddles in group 2, as arranged in the Exeter Book, are identical in solution to riddles in group 1. This twofold arrangement of the Riddles indicates separate transmission of the different groups prior to the compilation of the Exeter Book. The Riddles are to be attributed to more than one author; some are of folk origin. Bülbring appends a note on Riddle 3 and a restoration in Riddle 84 line 1.

686 Holthausen, Ferdinand. 'Zu alt- und mittelenglischen Dichtungen.' *Anglia* 13 (1891): 357–62.

In Note 4 Holthausen makes a metrical emendation in Riddle 3 line 3 (358).

687 Cook, Albert S. 'Recent Opinion concerning the Riddles of the Exeter Book.' *Modern Language Notes* 7 (1892): 10–11.

This note is not an independent contribution but is designed simply to call attention to recent opposed conclusions on the Cynewulfian authorship of the Exeter Book Riddles reached by Sievers (**683**) and Herzfeld (**684**). Cook also notes that both scholars have dismissed Leo's (**657**) interpretation of *Wulf and Eadwacer.*

88 Mather, Frank J. 'The Cynewulf Question from a Metrical Point of View.' *Modern Language Notes* 7 (1892): 193–213.

Mather accepts the results of non-metrical studies by previous scholars to the effect that the Riddles are not Cynewulf's work.

89 MacLean, George E. *An Old and Middle English Reader.* New York: Macmillan, 1893. lxxiv + 295 pp.

This reader includes introduction, texts, notes, and glossary. The account of Exeter Book Riddle 15 (4–5) contains a review of previous scholarship and advocacy of the solution 'badger'. In this Riddle MacLean sees anticipations of fable, allegory, and morality play. Analysis of the style, with attention to the large number of *hapax legomena*, leads to a cautious ruling in favour of Cynewulfian authorship.

90 Burton, Richard. 'Nature in Old English Poetry.' *Atlantic Monthly* 73 (April 1894): 476–87.

In this general appreciation of Old English poetry, Burton makes favourable mention of the Riddles as among Cynewulf's best productions: 'secular in subject, heathen in spirit, and full of the flavour of folk lore, myth, and northern melancholy' (485). The influence of Christianity may be traced in the 'lyrico-subjective position of the bard' vis-à-vis Nature. 'Commingling with the feeling for the savagery of beast-kind is a certain spiritual good fellowship which foretokens Coleridge, Byron, and Wordsworth' (485). Burton cites Riddles 7 'swan' and 8 'nightingale', with comments on the qualities of idyll, lyric, and imagination to be seen in the latter poem. Riddle 57 concerns 'a somewhat mysterious brown bird, the identification of which may perhaps be left most safely to Mr. Burroughs'. 'The hint in the final line [translated as 'their own names they sound'] suggests whip-poor-will, Bob White, and other songsters, but the analogy is not carried out' (486).

91 Trautmann, Moritz. 'Die Auflösungen der altenglischen Rätsel.' *Anglia Beiblatt* 5 (1894): 46–51.

Trautmann offers a preview of his solutions to the Exeter Book Riddles, to be fully discussed in his forthcoming edition. Among them are Riddle 8 'bell', 10 'bubble', 17 'oven', 25 'rosehip', 29 'swallow and sparrow', 30 'cornfield', 31 'fiddle', 34 'bee', 36 'ship' or 'man, woman, and horse', 41 'fire', 51 'horse and wagon', 52 'broom', 53 'spear', 54 'churn', 55 'harp', 57 'hailstones', 63 'flute', 70 'rye flute', 71 'iron helmet', 80 'spear', 81 'weathercock', 91 'sickle', and 92 'beech'. As preface he discusses problems in the numbering of the Riddles. He also outlines the history of attempts to solve the Riddles. A comprehensive list of previous would-be solvers, along with their solutions and a brief discussion of the runes in Riddles 19 and 64, is appended. Trautmann expresses gratitude to

Dietrich (**658**) for his pioneering efforts, but contends that only twenty-six of his solutions still command assent. Dietrich possessed a limited appreciation of the subtleties of the Riddles and of the Anglo-Saxon mind.

692 ———. 'Zu den altenglischen Rätseln.' *Anglia* 17 (1895): 396–400.

Trautmann seeks to withdraw two solutions advanced in his previous contribution (**691**). He now solves Riddles 52 and 57 as respectively 'flail' and 'raindrops'. He mentions further objections to Dietrich's (**658**) solution of Riddle 52 as 'buckets' and explains the fetters as the thongs that combine the two parts of the flail. He envisages the threshing as carried out by the slave mentioned in the text and inside a granary. The word 'ræced' in line 1 is explained as an inflectionless dative, a form chosen by the poet deliberately to obstruct attempts at a solution. The raindrops of Riddle 57 could legitimately be described as 'blace' (line 2) and as treading the ground. Trautmann construes Riddle 90, with a parallel from his schooldays, as an allusion to some now unknown person whose name contained the element *wulf*.

693 Walz, John A. 'Notes on the Anglo-Saxon Riddles.' *Harvard Studies and Notes in Philology and Literature* 5 (1896): 261–8.

Walz disagrees with Trautmann's (**691**) solution of Riddle 11 as 'wine'. Though conceding several correspondences between Riddle 11 and Riddle 27, the answer to which is undoubtedly 'wine', he points out that additional parallels occur elsewhere. These parallels make it very probable that the passages concerned were not the creation of any one poet, but belonged to the common stock of epic formulae. If 'gold' is the solution the adjective 'hasofag' (line 1) can be explained as describing its pernicious effects. Riddle 15 should be solved as 'porcupine', not 'badger', because the Old World porcupine is terrestrial and fossorial and shoots its quills, hence the appropriateness of 'hildepilum' in the text. Walz solves Riddle 25 as 'mustard', on the grounds that its pungency affects the eye. He discusses Riddle 45, noting Trautmann's solution (**691**) but without reaching a clear verdict. Other solutions: Riddle 29 'cloud and wind'; Riddle 52 'a yoke of oxen led into the barn or house by a female slave'; Riddle 74 'cuttlefish', supporting Dietrich's original solution (**658**); and Riddle 80 'sword'.

694 Whitman, Charles H. 'The Birds of Old English Literature.' *JEGP* 2 (1898): 149–98.

Whitman mentions some of the solutions to the Riddles in passing, as an endorsement of previous scholars' findings rather than a new contribution. He notes, following Dietrich (**658**), that 'nightingale' and 'pipe' both suggest themselves as solutions to Riddle 8. He opts for 'woodpecker' rather than 'jay' in Riddle 24, dissenting from Dietrich, because of the runic letters. He registers the difficulty, however, that the woodpecker is not generally considered a mimic, as the Riddle text would demand. The solution to Riddle 57 could be 'starlings' as well as Dietrich's 'swallows'.

695 Padelford, Frederick Morgan. 'Old English Musical Terms.' *Bonner Beiträge zur Anglistik* 4 (1899): 1–112.

[Padelford's article is so peppered with 'interjections' from Trautmann, the editor of *Bonner Beiträge,* as to take on virtually dialogue form.] Padelford itemizes musical forms current among the Anglo-Saxons as including choral hymns, enchantments against disease and evil spirits, and charms courting the favour of the Gods for the crops. He points to the existence of riddles where the solution is a musical instrument. Discussing Riddle 86, Padelford sides with Dietrich's (**658**) original solution as 'organ', suggesting that 'on mæðle' refers to a religious 'meeting' (46). Trautmann interjects in favour of 'one-eyed seller of garlic', endorsing Dietrich's revised solution (**662**). Padelford solves Riddle 31 as 'bagpipe', following Dietrich (**658**): Trautmann appends an objection. Riddles 8 and 60 are solved by Padelford as 'reed-pipe' and Riddle 70 as 'shawm', following Dietrich (**658**): Trautmann objects to all these and additionally argues that Riddles 28 and 55 have the solution 'harp'. Padelford adduces further evidence for Dietrich's (**658**) solution of Riddle 14 as 'horn'. He appends a glossary of musical terms, which includes *scearu* 'a plectrum'.

6 **B[utterfield], F.W.L.** *The Battle of Maldon and Other Renderings from the Anglo-Saxon; together with Original Verse.* Oxford: Parker, [1900]. xi + 59 pp.

The author states that in rendering the Old English pieces, which it is his aim to help to popularize, he has endeavoured to take as few liberties as possible. Included is a translation of Riddle 7, of which the following is a sample: 'Loudly my rustling pennons sigh,/ Gayly they sing, when, faring at last,/ No longer I rest on field or on flood' (25).

7 **Madert, Karl August.** *Die Sprache der altenglischen Rätsel des Exeterbuches und die Cynewulffrage.* Diss. U Marburg. Marburg: Bauer, 1900. 131 pp.

Madert reports on the results of a new investigation into the attribution of the Exeter Book Riddles to Cynewulf. Unlike Herzfeld (**684**), Madert bases his comparisons solely on the signed poems of Cynewulf. He places special emphasis on stylistic and linguistic criteria: lexis, phonology, morphology, and syntax. On these criteria the Riddles must be dated prior to Cynewulf and at the beginning of the eighth century. [For a review see Herzfeld, **699**.]

8 **Blackburn, F.A.** 'The *Husband's Message* and the Accompanying Riddles of the Exeter Book.' *JEGP* 3 (1901): 1–13.

Blackburn divides the manuscript material into four parts: (1) 'Piece 1' (= Riddle 30b), which is to be solved as 'beam', meaning 'tree, log, ship, and cross, also harp and cup', and which is fortuitously linked with the following three pieces by a similarity in subject matter. (2) 'Piece 2' (= Riddle 60), which, despite being customarily regarded as a riddle, declares plainly that its subject is 'beam', i.e. a slip of wood on which a message has been carved. (3) 'Piece 3' (= *The Husband's Message* lines 1–12), where the personified letter proclaims the good faith of the writer. (4) 'Piece 4' (= remainder of *The Husband's Message*), which constitutes the message proper, to be interpreted as from a wooer, not a husband. Pieces 2–4 constitute a single poem.

699 Herzfeld, Georg. Rev. of *Die Sprache der altenglischen Rätsel des Exeterbuches und die Cynewulffrage*, by Karl August Madert [697]. *Archiv für das Studium der neueren Literaturen* 106 (1901): 389–90.

Herzfeld reviews Madert's attempt to use close analysis of the language and syntax of the Riddles as a means of evaluating their ascription to Cynewulf. Herzfeld supports Madert's negative conclusions, proposing that many of the Riddles are of popular origin and that a variety of authors contributed to the collection in the Exeter Book. He points to linguistic evidence of multiple authorship. Herzfeld contends that Madert should have excluded *Wulf and Eadwacer* from his investigation, since its form and content show clearly that it is not a riddle.

700 Holthausen, Ferdinand. 'Zu alt- und mittelenglischen Dichtungen. XV. 63. Zu den ae. Rätseln.' *Anglia* 24 (1901): 264–7.

Holthausen supplements earlier notes (**105** and **112**) with some suggested restorations of lacunose passages. These suggestions are not founded on actual examination of the Exeter Book but nevertheless may help subsequent scholars. The restored passages occur in Riddle 67 lines 10–11; Riddle 71 line 8; Riddle 72 line 3; Riddle 73 lines 8–9, 11, 14–15, and 16–17; Riddle 77 lines 7–8; Riddle 78 lines 2–3 and 7 (with the suggestion that the solution was some water-dwelling creature); Riddle 82 lines 2 and 4; Riddle 83 lines 2–3; Riddle 84 lines 43, 47, and 52–6; Riddle 88 lines 1, 6, and 8; Riddle 93 lines 3–4, 6–7, and 32–3; and Riddle 94 lines 3 and 6.

701 Barnouw, Adriaan J. *Textkritische Untersuchungen nach dem Gebrauch des bestimmten Artikels und des schwachen Adjektivs in der altenglischen Poesie.* Diss. U Leiden. Leiden: Brill, 1902. vii + 236 pp.

Using criteria developed from the use of the definite article in combination with weak adjectives, Barnouw tries to establish a chronology of Old English poetry. In Chapter 19, on the Exeter Book Riddles (211–23), he points out that most of them do not lend themselves to his criteria because, by virtue of their subject-matter and style, they contain few instances of the definite article. The Riddle collection contains a variety of compositional strata, most of the poems being older than Cynewulf and datable to the period 680–700.

702 Hart, James M. 'Allotria II.' *Modern Language Notes* 17 (1902): 461–3.

In note 6 Hart argues that 'ord' in Riddle 60 line 13 should be emended to 'oroð', so as to avoid repetition from the previous line.

703 Lawrence, William Witherle. 'The First Riddle of Cynewulf.' *PMLA* 17 (1902): 247–61.

Lawrence supports Bradley's (**678**) contention that *Wulf and Eadwacer* is not a riddle at all, adding the suggestion that it represents a translation from Old Norse. He also argues against the attribution of the Exeter Book Riddles to Cynewulf.

4 **Erlemann, Edmund.** 'Zu den altenglischen Rätseln.' *Archiv für das Studium der neueren Literaturen* 111 (1903): 49–63.

Section 1 is an explication of Exeter Book Riddles 1–3, supplementing Dietrich **(658)** and proposing that in reality the three Riddles are one. Each occurrence of the word 'hwilum' ought to introduce a distinct aspect of the general idea of 'storm'. Riddle 1 describes storm in general, while complementarily Riddles 2 and 3 deal with particular facets of storm. Erlemann sees connections with *Andreas* but disputes Prehn's **(672)** identification of a source in Aldhelm and Eusebius. He relates the 'earthquake' section to Bede's *De natura rerum*, ch. 49, thinking particularly of submarine earthquakes, but doubts that the poet used Bede directly. More likely, the poet's teachers were acquainted with Bede's work and passed his ideas on. The author of the Riddles is therefore to be associated with Yarrow, Monkwearmouth, and the literary circle influenced by Bede: the period of composition is probably *c*. 732–40. The notion of God as ruler of the winds derives from the Old Testament. Erlemann argues that popular superstition, along with the poet's personal observation and inspiration, played the dominant part in the composition of these poems. Section 2 explains the first two lines of Riddle 90 on the basis of an allusion to Cynewulf. Nevertheless, because the authorship of each riddle needs to be considered separately, the allusion here is no guarantee that all the riddles were composed by Cynewulf. He may, however, have assembled pre-existing compositions into the collection we now have.

5 **Tupper, Frederick.** 'The Holme Riddles (Ms. Harl 1960).' *PMLA* 18 (1903): 211–72.

Tupper makes brief comparative comments on the Exeter Book Riddles. Riddle 19 is to be regarded as a 'world riddle'.

6 ———. 'The Comparative Study of Riddles.' *Modern Language Notes* 18 (1903): 1–8.

Tupper argues that the interdependence of literary and folk riddles has not received proper scholarly attention. The present article is to serve as a prolegomenon for such study. Tupper gives examples of the different possible processes, e.g. a folk riddle may receive literary treatment, or a literary riddle may become absorbed into a folk tradition, or a single riddle theme may pass through a succession of different treatments. Tupper notes many analogues. Among their uses is to demonstrate that the obscene riddles of the Exeter Book collection may not have had stable 'innocent' solutions. Any attempt whatever by a would-be solver to come up with a decorous solution would have the desired effect of adding to the joke. Source-hunting, where the Riddles are concerned, is bedevilled by the problem that certain subjects virtually demand a particular kind of treatment. Tupper also points out that similar solutions, such as 'salt' or 'ice', do not necessarily mean similar riddles. In folk tradition the solutions often become garbled or completely replaced. The diffusion of riddles follows geographical, not linguistic, lines.

707 ————. 'Originals and Analogues of the Exeter Book Riddles.' *Modern Language Notes* 18 (1903): 97–106.

Tupper argues that the Riddles of the Exeter Book are, in the main, literary rather than folk productions. This is apparent in those numerous riddles where concealment of solution has been forgotten in the joy of creation. The terseness or obscenity of a few exceptional riddles may, however, point to a folk origin. Resisting the arguments of Prehn (**672**), Tupper takes the view that only a tiny fraction of the Riddles is directly borrowed from the Latin. The importance of Tatwine and Eusebius in particular has been grossly over-rated in this respect. More than half of the Riddles are unrelated to the Latin riddles and there are eighteen others that only slightly resemble their Latin analogues. On the other hand, Blackburn's (**698**) attempt to deny the connection between Riddle 60 and Symphosius 2 ('reed') is too extreme in the other direction. Likewise, the solution 'siren' should be considered for Riddle 74. Here and in general, the proposer of any solution should consider the analogues. Trautmann (**691**) fails to do so in his suggestion for Riddle 13 and so misses the correct solution, 'ten fingers (with gloves)'. Analogues may also help in textual criticism, e.g. in revealing the fragmentary state of Riddles 19 and 64. Tupper emphasizes the importance of comparative study with other riddle collections from diverse periods and countries. Although the number of parallels to the Exeter Book Riddles among the modern folk riddles of England and Europe is not large, they may have exerted some influence on the later tradition.

708 ————. 'Riddles of the Bede Tradition. The "Flores" of Pseudo-Bede.' *Modern Philology* 2 (1904): 561–72.

Tupper discusses some of the Pseudo-Bede riddles as analogues to the Exeter Book Riddles, making particular mention of Riddles 13 and 29.

709 Erlemann, Fritz. 'Zum 90. angelsächsischen Rätsel.' *Archiv für das Studium der neueren Literaturen* 115 (1905): 391–2.

In a follow-up to the article by Edmund Erlemann (**704**) [evidently no relation], Erlemann argues that the name Cynwulf [sic] is concealed in Riddle 90. The phrase 'duo lupi' refers to the two letters which the word 'wulf' has in common with the word 'ewu'. The 'septem oculis' refers to the seven letters of 'Cynwulf'. The 'quattuor pedes' refers to the four letters of 'wulf'. We should bear in mind, in solving the riddle, the poor state of medieval Latinity.

710 Liebermann, Felix. 'Das angelsächsische Rätsel 56: "Galgen" als Waffenständer.' *Archiv für das Studium der neueren Literaturen* 114 (1905): 163–4.

Liebermann analyses Riddle 55 to show that the object intended is wooden, portable, and cruciform, appears at banquets, and serves the warrior by carrying his sword. Its name can also mean 'gallows', which would, in Liebermann's opinion, be natural enough for a sword-stand: he points to some partial parallels in Modern and Middle High German.

1 **Moorman, F.W.** *The Interpretation of Nature in English Poetry from Beowulf to Shakespeare.* Quellen und Forschungen zur Sprach- und Culturgeschichte der germanischen Völker 95. Strasbourg: Trübner, 1905. xiii + 244 pp.

Moorman accepts Prehn's **(672)** identification of sources for the Riddles, but argues that a comparison with their models only serves to show up the keenness of the Old English poet's capacity for description and appreciation of natural phenomena. The Riddles continue the primitive view of elemental forces, e.g. sea and wind, as conscious beings. This explains the prominent placing of Riddles 1–3, which describe the wind in time of storm. Moorman regards them collectively as the most imaginative piece of nature poetry in Old English literature. He suggests further that early mythological conceptions of the sun and moon might be embedded in Riddle 29. 'Nature' is to be preferred over 'Creation' as the solution of Riddle 40. Altogether, the Riddles furnish abundant evidence that the primitive attitude of the 'Teutonic mind' towards the external world, above all the sense of exultation felt at contemplating the stormier forces of Nature, did not die out with the Anglo-Saxon settlement.

2 **Trautmann, Moritz.** 'Alte und neue Antworten auf altenglische Rätsel.' *Bonner Beiträge zur Anglistik* 19 (1905): 167–215.

Trautmann withdraws some Riddle solutions proposed by him earlier **(691)** and adds some new ones. He disputes Stopford Brooke's barnacle goose solution for Riddle 10 **(13)**, arguing that the legend is not attested for the Anglo-Saxon period. He defends or further elaborates his previously-announced solutions of Riddles 11, 13, 17, 25, 74, and 95 against objections or rival solutions from such scholars as Nuck **(680)**, Hicketier **(681)**, Walz **(693)**, and Tupper **(707)**. Discussing Riddle 17, he contends that the grammatical gender of any proposed solution must be consistent with the gender of nouns and adjectives within the riddle text: 'fortress' **(662)** is therefore incorrect, because it presupposes Old English *burg*, which is feminine, whereas 'mundbora' in the text is masculine. New solutions are as follows: Riddle 10 'anchor' (cf. **714**); 11 'wine'; 29 'bird and wind', with the 'horns' referring to the two parts of the bird's beak; 49 'oven'; 51 'quill-pen' or 'pen and three fingers'; 52 'flail'; 57 'storm-clouds', with 'sanges rof' as a reference to thunder; 74 'water'; and 80 'horn', with 'heard is min tunge' referring to the sound of a horn. In Riddle 30 ('Old English *beam*') Trautmann is now in agreement with Blackburn **(698)**, except in preferring to restrict the meanings of *beam* to 'tree' and 'cross', because Blackburn's other suggested meanings do not inhere in *beam* as simplex. [For a review see Middendorff, **717.**]

3 ————. 'Hasu.' *Bonner Beiträge zur Anglistik* 19 (1905): 216–18.

Trautmann reviews previous opinions about the meaning of the word *hasu*, especially as used in the Riddles, and shows that it is applied to a multiplicity of different apparently incompatible objects in Old English poetry. He settles on a core meaning of 'shining' and explains 'hasofag' in Riddle 11 similarly, thus ruling out Dietrich's solution 'night' **(658)**. [For a review see Middendorff, **717.**]

714 ———. 'Die Auflösung des 11ten (9ten) Rätsels.' *Bonner Beiträge zur Anglistik* 17 (1905): 142.

Withdrawing his previously suggested solution to Riddle 10 (691), Trautmann now proposes 'anchor' (cf. 712). He translates 'awox' in line 3 as 'became, came', emends 'beames' in line 7 to 'bearmes', and similarly disposes with other indications in the text that the object described is a living creature, lifted by the wind.

715 **Klaeber, Friedrich.** 'Wanderer 44; Rätsel XII 3f.' *Anglia Beiblatt* 17 (1906): 300–1.

Klaeber supports Trautmann's (691, 713) solution of Riddle 11 as 'wine'. He offers corroboration from the Psalms for Trautmann's interpretation of 'dysge dwelle' and 'dole hwette' in line 3 as an antithesis. He supports Dietrich's (658) explanation of 'unrædsiþas' in line 4 as a genitive singular in -*as*, arguing that *hwettan* must be parallel to verbs of similar meaning in taking accusative of person and genitive of thing.

716 **Tupper, Frederick Jr.** 'Solutions of the Exeter Book Riddles.' *Modern Language Notes* 21 (1906): 97–105.

Tupper argues against many of the solutions put forward by Trautmann (691 and 712), though he does accept a few of them, notably 'pen and fingers' for Riddle 51. Tupper identifies problems of methodology in Trautmann's work, notably his disregard for the manuscript readings, for the importance of the historical method of riddle-study, and for the inherent instability of solutions in actual riddle traditions (as well as in scholarly discussion). Trautmann is also over-reliant upon emendation as a means of accommodating a previously envisaged solution. Tupper discusses in detail Riddles 10, 11, 13, 17, 25, 29, 57, 74, and 95. He solves Riddle 95 as 'moon' and further documents his proposed solution 'siren' for Riddle 74 (707). His arguments are supported by many analogues from other riddle collections.

717 **Middendorff, Hermann.** Rev. of *Bonner Beiträge zur Anglistik* 14 (1904), including 'Alte und neue Antworten auf altenglische Rätsel' and 'Hasu', by Moritz Trautmann. [712, 713.] *Anglia Beiblatt* 18 (1907): 109–10.

Middendorff resists the solutions to Riddle 10 proposed by Dietrich (658), Trautmann (712), and Holthausen (123) and defends the 'barnacle goose' solution, elaborating on points made by Stopford Brooke (13) and Tupper (712). He registers agreement with Trautmann's explanation of *hasu*.

718 **Sonke, Emma.** 'Zu dem 25. Rätsel des Exeterbuches.' *Englische Studien* 37 (1907): 313–18.

Sonke notes a certain arbitrariness in the assignment of Latin 'equivalents' to Old English animal and bird names. This affects Riddle 24, where 'higora' is variously explained as 'woodpecker' (694) and 'magpie' (658). Sonke argues that 'woodpecker' can be eliminated as a potential solution because this bird has no talent for mimicry. But ultimately the answer is probably not a bird at all, but an actor who specialized in animal and bird noises and was therefore called a *higora*.

9 **Jansen, Karl.** 'Die Cynewulf-forschung von ihrer Anfängen bis zur Gegenwart.' *Bonner Beiträge zur Anglistik* 24 (1908): 1–126.

Jansen opens his monograph with a bibliography of research into Cynewulf and the School of Cynewulf, arranged chronologically (3–53). Then (54–122) he charts the evolution of Cynewulf scholarship, covering the attributions and other major issues and listing the Riddles among the spurious and erroneous ascriptions. He traces the history of this attribution: from Leo (**657**), who 'decoded' 'Riddle 1' [*Wulf and Eadwacer*], to Dietrich (**658**), who solved Riddle 90, with its mention of 'lupus', and Riddle 95, to Ebert (**79**), who limited Cynewulf's contribution to Riddles 1–60, to ten Brink (**5**), who returned to Dietrich in explaining the Riddles as Cynewulf's juvenilia, to Trautmann (**673**), who rebutted all the foregoing arguments, to Ebert (**79**), who reasserted Cynewulf's authorship (93–9). Jansen's own belief (123) is that the Riddles cannot be attributed to Cynewulf.

0 **Schlutter, Otto B.** 'Das Leidener Rätsel nach der hs. Cod. Lat. Vossius 4 no.106. Fol.25 verso, Zeile 20–8.' *Anglia* 32 (1909): 384–8 and 516 (corrigenda).

Schlutter provides an account of the transcription of the *Leiden Riddle* by W.G. Pluygers, documenting his use of reagent to recover manuscript readings. Schlutter goes on to offer a new transcription, with interlinear Latin translation. He notes differences between his text and Sweet's (**91**).

1 **Swaen, A.E.H.** 'Contributions to Anglo-Saxon Lexicography. VI.' *Englische Studien* 40 (1909): 321–31.

Swaen comments on Riddle 91 line 3 (323). He suggests that in this context ('Oft ic begine þæt me ongean sticað') the word 'begine' should be translated as 'swallow'.

2 **Kern, J.H.** 'Das Leidener Rätsel.' *Anglia* 33 (1910): 452–6.

Kern offers corrections of Schlutter's (**720**) transcription of the *Leiden Riddle* from the manuscript.

3 **Schlutter, Otto B.** '*Afog* "Peruersus" im 24ten Rätsel, Die Balliste Bezeichnend.' *Englische Studien* 41 (1910): 453–4.

Schlutter prefers not to reverse the reading 'agof' (='agob') in Riddle 23 line 1, as done by Sievers (**683**). He explains it as a corruption of a postulated **afog*, which he would relate to Northumbrian *afulic* (=**afuhlic*) 'perversus'. In Riddle 21 line 15 he emends to '*hindeweardere', suggesting that this would have been a term for 'ploughman'.

4 ————. 'Berichtigung.' *Englische Studien* 42 (1910): 153.

Schlutter withdraws his suggestion about 'afog' (**723**) in Riddle 23 line 1, following personal communications from Trautmann and Kluge. He notes, however, that if 'bow' is the solution the riddle is strangely transparent.

725 ———. 'Zum Leidener Rätsel.' *Anglia* 33 (1910): 457–66.

Schlutter replies to Kern's (722) corrections, claiming that Kern was unduly influenced by the Exeter Book version of the *Leiden Riddle*.

726 **Trautmann, Moritz.** 'Beiträge zu einem künftigen "Sprachschatz der altenglischen Dichter".' *Anglia* 33 (1910): 276–82.

Item 1 of this collection of corrections to Grein (3) concerns the items *gedreag* and *gedrǽg*, which Trautmann wishes to treat as one and the same word. In Riddle 6 line 10, where the speaker is the sun, 'gedreag' must refer to the turmoil (i.e. waves) of the sea.

727 **Tupper, Frederick Jr.** *The Riddles of the Exeter Book.* The Albion series of Anglo-Saxon and Middle English poetry. Boston: Ginn, 1910. cxi + 292 pp. Darmstadt: Wissenschaftliche Buchgesellschaft, 1968.

In this, the first edition devoted entirely to the Exeter Book Riddles, Tupper provides a conservative text with a very full apparatus of previous emendations and conjectures. He is the first editor to use Robert Chambers's 1831–2 transcript of the Exeter Book (British Library Add. MS. 9067) in order to supplement now missing or illegible portions of the original. He argues against drastic emendation, especially attempts to 'improve' the versification, which fail to make sufficient allowance for poetic licence. The commentary, also very full, includes a discussion of proposed solutions. All solutions, whether accepted by Tupper or not, are indexed. Newly suggested solutions are as follows: Riddle 2 'submarine earthquake', 8 'jay', 12 'oxhide', 19 'man upon horseback with a hawk on his fist', 28 'beer', 39 'moon', 48 'paten', 60 'reed pen', 61 'kirtle', 62 'poker', 71 'sword, dagger', 78 'oyster', 88 'inkhorn', 89 'bellows or leather bottle', and 94 'creation'. A glossary is appended. The general discussion includes the following topics: the comparative study of riddles, originals and analogues, authorship, form and structure, manuscripts, and a very detailed review of previous scholarship. Tupper is sceptical of claims, especially Prehn's (672), for detailed indebtedness to early English riddles composed in Latin. He finds the Exeter Book Riddles homogeneous in their artistry, in that almost every potential obscurity can be clarified by reference elsewhere in the collection. At the same time, resisting Prehn, he emphasizes the eclecticism of the compilation in its selection of subjects and material. The Riddles range from pole to pole of contemporary English society, yet the line between high and low is not sufficiently distinct to indicate a different origin for riddles of different genres. Tupper argues for the oral transmission of the Riddles and for their continuity with medieval and postmedieval folklore. He agrees with Sievers's (683) eighth-century dating, prior to Cynewulf, but demurs at some details of Sievers's methods. In singling out forms in the *Leiden Riddle*, the runes in Riddles 19 and 42, and the spelling 'agof' in Riddle 23 Sievers relies overmuch on exceptional features and exaggerates the extent to which they are distinctively Northumbrian.

728 ———. 'The Cynewulfian Runes of the First Riddle.' *Modern Language Notes* 25 (1910): 235–41.

Tupper argues that his discovery of a 'cryptogram' for 'Cynwulf' in *Wulf and*

Eadwacer places the burden of proof on those who deny the attribution of the Exeter Book Riddles to Cynewulf. This is to recant his rejection of the attribution in his edition of the Riddles (**727**). His discussion includes documentation of the late medieval and early Renaissance Icelandic practice of embedding runic signatures in poetry. He believes that scholars have been over-hasty in taking *Wulf and Eadwacer*, a puzzling poem, out of the riddle category and in classing it with *The Husband's Message* and *The Wife's Lament*.

9 Bradley, Henry. 'Two Riddles of the Exeter Book.' *Modern Language Review* 6 (1911): 433–40.

In Riddle 4 line 7 Bradley reads 'wearm lim <onfehð>' (433–6). He tentatively suggests that the riddle relates to a particular story involving necromancy. The dead man, attentive to the call of his 'servant', the magician, comes forth from his grave bound in chains and wearing a magic collar. Bradley dismisses current attempts to link Riddle 90 with Cynewulf, arguing that there are no substantial reasons to link Cynewulf with the Riddles in general, *contra* Tupper (**728**). Instead he tentatively proposes (436–40) that Riddle 90 commemorates an occasion when a heathen named Wulfstan had accepted baptism: the Lamb of God had taken from him the stony and wolfish heart which his name suggests.

0 Hoops, Johannes. 'Die Armbrust im Frühmittelalter.' *Wörter und Sachen* 3 (1911): 65–8.

Hoops argues that Riddle 23 contains details that are not appropriate to the ordinary bow and therefore must describe the crossbow. The statement that the arrow is housed within the bow before being shot makes sense only in relation to the crossbow. Hoops regards this riddle as an important and rare piece of evidence that the crossbow was known among the Anglo-Saxons. He appends French illustrations from the tenth century.

1 Chambers, Raymond W. 'The British Museum Transcript of the Exeter Book.' *Anglia* 35 (1912): 393–400.

Chambers points out that although Thorpe's (**65**) edition of the Exeter Book was, in the main, accurate, he took very little trouble to record the exact readings of the manuscript in places where it was fragmentary, such as the Riddles, and occasionally omitted such passages entirely. Later scholars tried to fill these lacunae with a plethora of conjectures. Many of their conjectures can now be either corroborated or dismissed conclusively on the basis of evidence from the transcript. Having been executed at a time when the Exeter Book was in a better condition than currently, the transcript offers primary evidence concerning the original state of the text.

2 Kock, Ernst A. 'Två textförklaringar.' *Festskrift till K.F. Söderwall på hans sjuttioårsdag den 1 januari 1912.* Lund: Gleerup, 1912. 307–8.

The article includes a note on Riddle 26 line 17, explaining 'nales dol wite' as 'regard not what is foolish', with 'wite' as subjunctive from *witan* 'see to, care for'.

733 Trautmann, Moritz. 'Das sogenannte erste Rätsel.' *Anglia* 36 (1912): 133–8.

Repeating his own earlier opinion (**673**) and arguing against Tupper (**728**), Trautmann concurs with Bradley (**678**) that *Wulf and Eadwacer* cannot be a riddle.

734 ———. 'Zum altenglischen Versbau.' *Englische Studien* 44 (1912): 303–42.

Trautmann discusses possible metrical irregularities, mostly in the Exeter Book Riddles, with the objective of determining vowel length in such forms as *fea* and *cneo*. Two specific suggestions are a long vowel in 'wræce' in Riddle 1 line 4 and the emendation 'beaga-hroden' for manuscript 'beaghroden' in Riddle 14 line 9.

735 ———. 'Zum Streit um die altenglischen Rätsel.' *Anglia* 36 (1912): 127–33.

In this reply to Tupper's edition of the Riddles (**727**) and articles (**705, 707, 708, 716, 728**) on them, Trautmann deplores Tupper's polemical tone. Defending his own editorial practice, he contends that emendations are essential to understanding, since the manuscripts contain demonstrable errors. Riddle 13 is used to demonstrate that Tupper's comparative research is incomplete and therefore misleading. The idea of the glove hanging on the wall, which Tupper invokes as a step towards his solution of the riddle and to which he accords universal status, is distinctively German and motivated by the rhyme 'Hand:Wand', whose usefulness is of course restricted to that language. Similar hastiness can be detected in Tupper's comparative observations on other Riddles. Tupper also gives insufficient attention to the text and variant readings of the riddle collections he uses. Trautmann specifically disputes Tupper's solutions to Riddles 8, 13, 39, 41, 55, 74, and 95.

736 Tupper, Frederick Jr. 'The British Museum Transcript of the Exeter Book (Add. MS. 9067).' *Anglia* 35 (1912): 285–8.

Tupper concurs with Chambers (**731**) in his high valuation of the transcript. He regrets, however, that Chambers had not read the collation of the facsimile with its original that Tupper provided in his edition of the Riddles (**727**). He queries whether Wülker's (**8**) attribution of the transcript to Robert Chambers is correct.

737 Wyatt, Alfred John. *Old English Riddles.* Boston: Heath, 1912. xii + 193 pp. New York: AMS, 1972.

This edition was completed independently of Tupper's. In his general introduction Wyatt reflects on the editor's task: 'The Riddles are the most difficult Old English text I know, because the editor needs to combine the qualifications of an editor, a riddler, and an antiquary in about equal proportions' (v). The only secure strategy toward finding solutions is the comparative method, combined with investigations into material culture. He offers a brief history of scholarship on the Exeter Book Riddles. The shortcomings of Prehn's (**672**) methods are analysed in scathing terms: 'Abusing to the utmost the dangerous method of parallel passages he found evidence of borrowing everywhere. . . In effect – not in intention – Prehn was an impostor' (xv). Wyatt instead emphasizes the poet's eclecticism and inventiveness: 'a poet reads; here and there an idea, perhaps in itself a very trivial one, remains in his mind, and is unconsciously worked into something totally new. To try to trace its source is like asking where I bought the seeds for the poppies in my garden' (xv). As to sources and analogues, the conclusion is that Riddles 35 and 40 are direct translations from Aldhelm; that 47, 60, and 84 represent adaptations from Symphosius; that seventeen or eighteen other Riddles make free use of particular motifs from Aldhelm and Symphosius; and that no Riddles manifest influence from Eusebius or Tatwine (xx). As to solutions, it was unfortunate that Dietrich (**662**) let his pupil Lange induce him into discarding some good suggestions in favour of inferior ones. A table shows the various solutions and enumerations adopted by previous scholars. Wyatt claims to have produced the first edition in which *Wulf and Eadwacer* is not included as one of the Riddles. The demarcation between learned and popular riddle types is not simple, in that some Riddles contain elements of both. At each of the two extremes, the double entendre Riddles might be assigned to folk origin, whereas Riddles 1, 2, 3, 8, 15, 26, 40, 60, and 66 belong to another set which are poems rather than riddles and therefore presumably of learned origin (xxix–xxxi). As to dating, Sievers's arguments for pre-Cynewulfian composition are partly vitiated by the erroneous assumption that all the Riddles are of the same date. Nevertheless, for most of the Riddles, in their extant form, the most plausible dating is somewhere in the eighth century. As to authorship, Tupper's (**728**) attempt to revive the Cynewulfian attribution must be rejected. 'The most obvious conclusion is that the collection of Riddles partakes of the nature of the Exeter Book itself, and is a riddle-album, a riddle anthology' (xxxi). So miscellaneous does the collection appear that unity of authorship is precluded. Wyatt dissents from Trautmann's (**712**) contention that gender in the Riddles indicates the solution, finding that inconsistency was the rule (xxxv). In association with the ensuing texts, detailed notes and a full glossary are provided. As to Riddle 23, the alleged obviousness of the Riddle can be mitigated if we assume that the author was aware of the change of final *b* to *f* in 'agof' (line 1) and deliberately used it to confuse his audience. As to Riddle 36, 'this is one of the riddles one wishes at the bottom of the Bay of Portugal' (93). As to Riddle 60, an uninformed scribe started with a 'reed' riddle and, not recognizing it as such, 'attempted to weld it into one piece with the following lyric' (110). Newly proposed solutions are as follows: Riddle 1–3 'wind', 12 'hide or skin', 13 'ten chickens or pheasants', 32 'wheel', 43 'mind', 48 'chalice', 56 'flail', 57 'midges', 61 'helmet', 62 'borer', 68 'petrifaction', 71 'iron weapon or ore', 73 'spear', 76 'hen', 83 'metal or money', 92 'book', and 93 'antler or horn'.

8 Wood, George A. *The Anglo-Saxon Riddles. Aberystwyth Studies* 1–2 (1912–14): 9–64.

Wood's study of the Exeter Book Riddles includes lengthy summations of previous scholarly opinion. His discussion comprises the following topics: (1) The riddle as a literary genre: folk riddle and art riddle (the latter characterized variously by metaphor, paradox, and epigram), (2) The Exeter Book, (3) The emergence of the Riddle as a literary form (tracing genre connections with *Solomon and Saturn* and with Aldhelm's obscure Latinity), (4) How the Anglo-Saxon Riddles reflect early English life and character, (5) Problems: (a)

Did Cynewulf write the Riddles? (b) Do they form a preconceived whole? (c) Are they related to the Latin Riddles? (6) Individual Riddles, including solutions. Wood, following Prehn (672), considers the Exeter Book Riddles as influenced by the Latin riddles. He acknowledges that in contrast to the Latin riddles the Anglo-Saxon collection contains 'much poetry that is wonderfully vigorous and fresh, marked by emotional and imaginative qualities' (18). Yet, considered as imitations of the Latin, the Exeter Book Riddles 'lack brilliance, and sometimes are without definiteness and logical unity' (18). Riddle 23 is an instance here. Riddles ought to achieve witty evasiveness, whereas the Old English ones show a tendency to dwell on 'all that is pictorial or poetically suggestive in the theme' (18). 'New influence and changed conditions of life are reflected in the riddle poetry of a people whose instincts had hitherto been predatory and vagrant' (21). But 'both the Anglo-Saxon and the Latin riddles should be considered as independent "solos" on themes suggested by the common "chorus" of folk-riddle or by a widespread and common fund of learned material' (39): this explains the lack of conspicuous verbal correspondences between Latin and Old English. Wood resists the theory of Cynewulfian authorship and views the Exeter Book collection as purely a miscellany, not a homogeneous or unified whole. Among the instances of possible folk derivation are Riddles 4 and 20: Wood cites Renaissance English parallels.

739 Sarrazin, Gregor Ignatz. *Von Kädmon bis Kynewulf: Eine litterarhistorische Studie.* Berlin: Mayer, 1913. ii + 174 pp.

In his section on the Exeter Book Riddles (95–113), Sarrazin reacts favourably on the whole to Tupper's (727) edition. He nonetheless argues for closer indebtedness to Latin riddles (especially those of Eusebius) for a few of the Exeter Book Riddles. He believes that a chronological scheme can be deduced from these observations of influence. Siding with Tupper against Brandl (19), he argues for single authorship of the Riddles. Marked differences in tone, such as characterize the Riddle collection, also occur in such demonstrably single-author works as Chaucer's *Canterbury Tales* and Shakespeare's Sonnets. Agreeing with Madert (697) that the language of the Riddles is very early, he adds comparisons with *Beowulf*, which he sees as later (735–45) and influenced by the Riddles. He rejects the notion that shared phrases might represent epic formulas (110); rather they suggest that the author of the Riddles and *Beowulf* was one and the same person.

740 Schneider, Robert. *Satzbau und Wortschatz der altenglischen Rätsel der Exeterbuches: Ein Beitrag zur Lösung der Verfasserfrage.* Diss. U Breslau. Breslau: Schlesischen Friedrich-Wilhelms-Universität, 1913. viii + 85 pp.

Schneider contends that Trautmann's (673) and Sievers's (683) arguments against Cynewulf's authorship are not totally cogent. Testing vocabulary and sentence construction as indications of authorship, he considers conjunctions and adverbs, along with examples of asyndeton, and compares the patterns of usage in the Riddles with those seen in firm Cynewulf attributions. He concludes that the Riddles represent one group, attributable to one poet. Despite some linguistic counter-indications, they should be regarded as belonging to Cynewulf's juvenilia.

Holthausen, Ferdinand. 'Nochmals die altenglischen Rätsel.' *Anglia* 38 (1914): 77–82.

In a series of textual notes, referring specifically to Tupper's edition (727), Holthausen suggests emendations in some of the Riddles, mostly to improve the metre and alliteration. He also attempts to restore readings in damaged parts of the manuscript.

Kern, J.H. 'Noch einmal zum Leidener Rätsel.' *Anglia* 38 (1914): 261–5.

Kern defends his editorial procedures with the Leiden Riddle against Schlutter's (725) criticisms. He finds himself unable to recognize Schlutter's new 'readings' in the manuscript and disputes them in detail.

Trautmann, Moritz. 'Das Geschlecht in den altenglischen Rätseln.' *Anglia Beiblatt* 25 (1914): 324–7.

Trautmann argues that the grammatical gender of nouns, pronouns, and adjectives in certain Exeter Book Riddles served to guide the contemporary audience towards the solution. Similarly, gender indications can help scholars nowadays to check the correctness of proposed solutions. Thus in Riddle 3 line 67 the masculine gender of 'þeow' guides us to the solution 'wind'. Similarly in Riddle 21 the words 'gongendre' (line 9) and 'hindeweardre' (line 15) point to a feminine-gender word meaning 'plough'. Although this rule has exceptions, solvers such as Tupper (727), whose linguistic assumptions are based on modern English, show insufficient awareness of the importance of gender in languages such as Old English and German.

Löwenthal, Fritz. *Studien zum germanischen Rätsel.* Germanistische Arbeiten 1. Heidelberg: Winter, 1914. 150 pp.

[The author's name is also variously spelt as Lowenthal and Loewenthal.] Löwenthal notes the lack of a close affinity between the Old English Exeter Book Riddles and the Old Norse *Heiðreksgátur* – aside from such shared features as the introductory formulas 'ic seah'/'ek sá' and the sense of wonder. Likewise, an examination of Middle High German riddles reveals an almost total lack of correspondence with the Old English material. *Wulf and Eadwacer* and Riddle 40 should not be regarded as riddles. Reviewing the solutions reached by previous scholars, Löwenthal suggests that Riddle 39 should be solved as 'time' and Riddle 74 as 'hyena'. The hyena was thought to be hermaphroditic and to possess both aquatic and terrestrial forms. He dissents from Trautmann's (743) theory that the grammatical gender of nouns within the riddle indicates the solution. He discusses the subject-matter of the Exeter Book Riddles, their feeling for Nature, and their style.

Trautmann, Moritz. 'Die Quellen der altenglischen Rätsel.' *Anglia* 38 (1914): 349–54.

Trautmann lists the Riddles which he thinks owe something to the Anglo-Latin riddles. Since these total only eighteen, it seems that the composers of English-language riddles worked very independently. Brandl (19) was right to argue that the Riddles belong to the court rather than to the Church. Nonetheless, the Anglo-Latin riddles, notably those of Symphosius, Aldhelm, Tatwine, and Hwætberht [identified with Eusebius], remain the ultimate inspiration of the Exeter Book Riddles and we can see how the English-language poet improved on this source.

746 ———. 'Die Zahl der altenglischen Rätsel.' *Anglia Beiblatt* 25 (1914): 272–3.

Trautmann discusses the numbering of the Riddles. He calculates that the total is 93, basing this conclusion on a different logic from that used by Wyatt (**737**). Riddles 1–3 so transparently form a single unified poem that they should not be numbered and printed separately.

747 ———. 'Berechtigungen zu Anglia Beiblatt XXV september-nummer s.272ff.' *Anglia Beiblatt* 25 (1914): 327.

Trautmann corrects errata in his article 'Die Zahl' (**746**).

748 ———. 'Sprache und Versbau der altenglischen Rätsel.' *Anglia* 38 (1914): 355–64.

Trautmann briefly describes the phonology, orthography, morphology, and syntax of the Exeter Book Riddles. What appear to be rare metrical types (e.g. shortened A-types) should really be ascribed to manuscript corruptions. The same observation applies when the alliterating syllable is abnormally placed. Data from versification can be used to determine vowel length and syllable count in certain problematic words.

749 ———. 'Zeit, Heimat und Verfasser der altenglischen Rätsel.' *Anglia* 38 (1914): 365–73.

Trautmann places the composition of the Riddles in the period 700–50, but with the possibility that a few are of later date. He adds other linguistic criteria to those noted by Sievers (**683**) and defends the reading 'haofoc' against Sievers's attempt to excise the first *-o-*. Barnouw's (**701**) arguments for distinguishing earlier and later Riddles on the basis of the use of the definite article are dismissed as inconclusive. The Riddles appear to originate in Northumbria. The attribution to Cynewulf, along with all theories of single authorship, is to be rejected. Similarities in composition could be explained by positing a school of writers, of which Hwætberht [identified with Eusebius] could conceivably have been a member.

750 ———. 'Zu den Lösungen der Rätsel des Exeterbuchs.' *Anglia Beiblatt* 25 (1914): 273–9.

Adding items overlooked in his earlier article on this topic (**691**), Trautmann lists aspiring solvers and solutions of the Exeter Book Riddles in chronological order. He suggests the solution 'iron shield' for Riddle 71.

751 ———. *Die altenglischen Rätsel. (Die Rätsel des Exeterbuchs.)* Alt- und mittelenglische Texte 8. Heidelberg: Winter; New York: Stechert, 1915. xix + 201 pp. + 3 unnumbered pages + 16 plates.

In his Preface (v–vi) Trautmann outlines the history of this much-interrupted project and indicates some differences of opinion on the glossary and the text between him and Holthausen, one of the two general editors of the text series in which this volume appears. A list of works cited is given (vii–xvii), followed by the text of the Riddles (1–55) and of the former 'First Riddle' [i.e. *Wulf and Eadwacer*] (56). Riddles 1–3 are printed as one poem. Both the West Saxon and the Northumbrian forms of Riddle 35 (the *Leiden Riddle*) are printed (20–1). Riddle 40 is accompanied by Aldhelm 100 (23–8). Riddle 60 is printed separately from *The Husband's Message* (35–6). A brief account of scholarship on the Riddles is given (57–64). Trautmann agrees with Tupper (**727, 736**), against Wülker (**8**), on the value of the Chambers transcript. He asserts the independence of the Riddles from Latin sources, though ascribing Dietrich's (**658**) fecundity with solutions to his knowledge of Symphosius and Aldhelm. He admits that Cynewulf might have composed a small number of the Riddles but insists that in the mass they are of varied authorship and perhaps even periods. The Riddles should be seen as learned poetry, regardless of their subject matter. Weak points in the versification are to be ascribed to scribal transmission, not to authorial blundering. A very full commentary section follows (65–142). It includes a history of solutions and an often polemical discussion of textual and metrical problems. The following new (or newly justified) solutions are proposed: Riddle 4 'flail'; 5 'chopping block'; 18 'cask'; 19 'horseman, servant, and hawk'; 20 'hawk, falcon'; 22 'bridge'; 23 'crossbow'; 26 'hide' (but he also follows Müller (**655**) in 'book' and Grein (**2**) in 'Bible'); 28 'harp'; 30 'cross' or 'wood', though he also follows Blackburn (**698**); 31 'musical instrument'; 57 'swifts'; 61 'mailshirt'; 62 'burning arrow'; 63 'can or flask'; 64 'horseman, hawk, and servant'; 65 'chive, leek' (though Dietrich's solution (**658**) is also possible); 70 'harp'; 71 'bronze shield'; 73 'battering ram'; 92 'beechwood shield'; and 95 'soul, spirit'. A few conjectures supplied by Holthausen, e.g. 'unstrong spræce' in Riddle 27 line 13b, are included (89). Trautmann disapproves of readings that give away the solution, as appears from his discussion of Riddle 39. Nevertheless he defends Riddle 47 on the grounds that the mention of the moth, not the larva, would disguise the solution. The differences between Riddle 60 and Symphosius 2 ('reed') are emphasized (119). A full glossary concludes the work. A few additions (incorporating more suggestions from Holthausen) and corrections are registered on the final pages [unnumbered]. The sixteen plates illustrate folios from the Exeter Book. [For reviews see Klaeber, **752**; Barnouw, **753**; Binz, **755**.]

Klaeber, Frederick. Rev. of *Die altenglischen Rätsel*, by Moritz Trautmann [**751**]. *Modern Language Notes* 31 (1916): 426–30.

Klaeber points out that we should not necessarily expect a riddle description of e.g. the badger, as posited for Riddle 15, to possess the strict accuracy of a modern scientific description. He adds brief discussions of some specific passages, rejecting, for instance, the emendation 'unstrong spræce' in Riddle 27 line 13b (**751**): he argues that 'strong on spræce' is not inappropriate with reference to an intoxicated person.

753 Barnouw, Adriaan J. Rev. of *Die altenglischen Rätsel*, by Moritz Trautmann [**751**]. *Neophilologus* 3 (1918): 77–8.

Barnouw defends the manuscript readings against several of Trautmann's emendations, notably Riddle 27 line 13. He makes suggestions of his own in relation to Riddle 3 line 34 ('yrnan' for 'hyran'), Riddle 8 line 3, Riddle 9 line 9, Riddle 15 line 21, Riddle 33 lines 2 and 5, and Riddle 49 line 3.

754 Trautmann, Moritz. 'Zu meiner Ausgabe der altenglischen Rätsel.' *Anglia* 42 (1918): 125–41.

Trautmann makes some corrections and additions to his edition (**751**) of the Riddles, along with replies to comments by Klaeber (**752**) and Barnouw (**753**). He accepts a few of Barnouw's and Klaeber's suggested emendations and revivals of older conjectures. Most of them, however, he rejects. Barnouw's attempts at conjectural emendation are too drastic and do not adequately account for the manuscript readings. Holthausen's metrical improvements (**686, 741**) are also usually rejected, because they are excessively conditioned by Sievers's theories (**101**) and needlessly tamper with the manuscript readings. Discussed are Riddles 3; 4 (with remarks on the meaning of 'þragbysig' in line 1); 5 (accepting Holthausen's transposition (**144**) of 'ecgum werig' in line 3 and attributing the manuscript order to a failure of memory on the part of a compiler); 6 (defending his emendation of 'hwilum' in line 7 to 'willum' on the grounds that the postulated error could have been aural); 9 ('friðe' in line 9 as a separate word); 11 (supporting his solution as 'wine'); 15; 16 (metrical); 20; 23 (arguing that if such manuscript readings as 'ond' in line 3 are correct they point to a lack of clarity on the part of the poet); 27; 30 (modifying Blackburn's solution (**698**) to 'wooden cross'); 33; 37; 39; 46 (material omitted from his edition); 49; 53; 54; 64 (reading runic 's' and 'p' in line 6 as 'splot'); 67 (restoration); 72 (metrical, and counselling caution in attempting to restore extensive lacunae); 85; 89; and 94. He appends some alterations to the Glossary in his edition.

755 Binz, Gustav. Rev. of *Die altenglischen Rätsel*, by Moritz Trautmann [**751**]. *Literaturblatt* 40 (1919): 29–31.

Binz traces the history of Trautmann's work on the Riddles, commenting on the enormous problems that beset Riddle scholarship. He describes Trautmann's low opinion of Tupper's edition (**727**) as unjustified. He rejects a few of Trautmann's emendations and solutions, sometimes in favour of solutions proposed by Tupper, and reaches different conclusions from Trautmann concerning the process of translation in Riddle 40.

756 Holthausen, Ferdinand. 'Zu den altenglischen Rätseln.' *Anglia Beiblatt* 30 (1919): 50–5.

Holthausen replies to Trautmann (**754**) with some brief notes. In Riddle 5 he defends the solution 'shield' (**655, 658**). It calls itself an 'anhaga' because each warrior carries only one. Trautmann's 'chopping block' (**751**) does not fit with the idea of 'at night', whereas battles can be fought at night. The text of certain Riddles should be defended against Trautmann's emendations. In Riddle 23 Holthausen proposes emending 'geap' in line 9 to 'gegrap'. Riddle 30 refers to a wooden drinking vessel, passed from hand to hand. Riddles 31 and 70 should be solved as 'organistrum', by which Holthausen seems to intend some kind of hurdygurdy, Riddle 82 as 'crab'. In Riddle 33 line 5 his new suggestion is 'næs to sæne'. The *Leiden Riddle* and Riddle 40 line 73 are also discussed.

7 Swaen, A.E.H. 'Het 18e oudengelsche raadsel.' *Neophilologus* 4 (1919): 258–62.

Swaen attempts to show that 'sword' is a more appropriate solution to Riddle 20 than 'falcon', adducing detailed information from falconry. He argues against Trautmann's **(751)** emendation of 'wir' (line 4) to 'wirn', partly on the grounds that the technology envisaged by Trautmann did not exist in Anglo-Saxon England. The adjective 'radwerigne' (line 14) could apply to the sword.

8 Trautmann, Moritz. 'Weiteres zu den altenglischen Rätseln und Metrisches.' *Anglia* 43 (1919): 245–60.

Trautmann here comments on particular points in numerous Riddles, in reply to Holthausen **(756)** and Binz **(755)**. In general he finds their remarks insufficiently supported by argument and evidence. He dismisses their criticisms of his solutions to various Riddles, along with most of their suggested emendations, but modifies his explanations of Riddles 53, 55, and 92. He elaborates on Holthausen's discussion of Riddle 40 line 73. He suggests the new solution 'beechwood battering ram' for Riddle 92. In a final section on metrics, he sums up the principal differences between himself and Holthausen, whom he sees as a disciple of Sievers **(101)**. In Trautmann's view, an application of Sievers's metrics emphasizes syllable count at the expense of rhythm and leads to bad textual criticism.

9 Holthausen, Ferdinand. 'Zu altenglischen Dichtungen.' *Anglia* 44 (1920): 346–56.

Numerous points of detail in the Riddles are discussed in these notes. Holthausen rejects various emendations by Trautmann **(751)**, e.g. in order to return to Cosijn's **(110)** conjecture 'hæste' in Riddle 3 line 5. Some of Trautmann's emendations and restorations are conditioned by his hypothesis concerning the solution, e.g. in Riddle 71 line 7. Trautmann's metrical analyses fail to satisfy because they entail many consequential emendations. Holthausen goes on to propose numerous emendations on metrical grounds. He advocates a reversal of pairs of words so as to improve the alliteration or stress patterns, e.g. 'rideð on bæce' replaces 'on bæce rideð' in Riddle 3 line 36. The words 'wealde' and 'woþe' are mooted as replacements for manuscript 'healde' and 'hleoþre' in Riddle 8 line 4 to bring the alliteration into a regular pattern. Similar considerations lead to an alteration in the order of the runes in Riddle 19 line 6. Missing words are restored in Riddle 23 line 14 ('fullwered'), in Riddle 71 line 7, and elsewhere. Holthausen proposes the solution 'handmill' for Riddle 4, without elaboration.

10 Klaeber, Frederick. Rev. of *Jubilee Jaunts and Jottings*, by Ernst A. Kock **[147]**. *JEGP* 19 (1920): 409–13.

Klaeber praises Kock's comparative approach. Although he approves of Kock's resistance to supposed laws of metre, Klaeber notes that the laws of style, to which Kock appeals, are not universal either. As an instance of Kock's cavalier attitude to earlier scholars, he shows that Kock's explanation of *frið-* in Riddle 22 line 4 had been anticipated by Grein (3).

761   **Kock, Ernst A.** 'Interpretations and Emendations of Early English Texts VII.' *Anglia* 44 (1920): 245–60.

Note 202 (256–7) deals with Riddle 27 line 13b, arguing for the reading 'strongan spræce binumen' on the grounds that the speech of an intoxicated man, at least at a certain stage of his inebriation, is faltering and weak. He further defends the half-line 13a 'strengo bistolen' against metrical emendations: 'Holthausen juggles, Trautmann struggles.' Note 203 (258) deals with Riddle 51 line 4, emending 'frumra fleotgan' to 'framra fleag on' on the grounds that an adjective **fleotig* is without formal parallel. [The reading 'frumra' was subsequently corrected to 'framra' in ASPR (**194**), as an error of transcription on the part of previous editors.]

762   **Patch, Howard R.** 'Anglo-Saxon Riddle 56.' *Modern Language Notes* 35 (1920): 181–2.

Patch detects an allusion in Riddle 55 line 6 to the medieval allegorization of the ladder as a cross, citing parallels from Latin hymns. The ultimate origin of the motif is to be found in the apocryphal *Acta Philippi*.

763   **Holthausen, Ferdinand.** 'Zu den Leidener Denkmälern.' *Englische Studien* 55 (1921): 312.

In Note 1 Holthausen reports on his personal inspection of the manuscript of the *Leiden Riddle* under a magnifying glass. He supports the observations of Kern (**742**) and offers some comments on individual readings.

764   **Kock, Ernst A.** 'Interpretations and Emendations of Early English Texts VIII.' *Anglia* 45 (1921): 105–31.

Note 232 (124–5) deals with Riddle 27, arguing that the correct explanation of 'burg' in 'burghleoþu' (line 2) is not 'fortress' but 'high point', 'mountain terrace'. Note 241 (129–30) deals with Riddle 40, defending the manuscript reading 'þonne' in line 59 against Trautmann's (**751**) emendation (to 'þon þon'). Trautmann had failed to recognize that single conjunctions meaning 'as' or 'than' were frequently employed in the sense of 'as if' or 'than if'. In support of this argument, Kock cites parallels from Swedish and Middle High German.

765   ———. 'Interpretations and Emendations of Early English Texts IX.' *Anglia* 46 (1922): 63–96.

Note 245 (64) deals with 'gedreag' in Riddle 6 line 10, discountenancing the identification of *gedræg* and *gedreag* and the respective translations 'assembly' and 'wide extent'. In the Riddle he translates 'ofer deop gedreag' as 'over deep commotion', i.e. 'over the tossing sea'.

6 Patzig, H. 'Zum ersten Rätsel des Exeterbuchs.' *Archiv für das Studium der neueren Literaturen* 145 (1923): 204–7.

Patzig here rebuts Tupper's **(728)** theory that *Wulf and Eadwacer* is a charade on the name Cynewulf. Nevertheless, Tupper was right in regarding the poem as a riddle where the passionate monologue cunningly steers the hearer away from a trivial solution. If the solution is 'mill', the two islands mentioned in the poem can be recognized as the two stones of the mill. We should envisage the stones as having been left standing in the rain or sprinkled with salt water, as described by Pliny. Patzig compares Aldhelm 66.

7 Klaeber, Frederick. Rev. of *An Anglo-Saxon Verse Book*, by W.J. Sedgefield **[164]**. *JEGP* 23 (1924): 121–4.

Klaeber agrees with Sedgefield's emendation in Riddle 15 line 16b, from 'nele' to 'ne ic', but points out that Kock **(147)** had independently arrived at the same solution.

8 Erhardt-Siebold, Erika von. *Die lateinischen Rätsel der Angelsachsen: Ein Beitrag zur Kulturgeschichte Altenglands.* Anglistische Forschungen 61. Heidelberg: Winter, 1925. xvi + 276 pp.

In the course of an organization of the Latin riddles into lists of objects described (inanimate, animate, abstract), the author makes passing references to the Exeter Book Riddles. Riddle 55 refers to the Cross. Riddle 8 should be solved as 'nightingale', on the basis of its alleged analogue, Aldhelm 22.

9 Pitman, James Hall. *The Riddles of Aldhelm: Text and Verse Translation with Notes.* Yale Studies in English 67. New Haven: Yale UP, 1925. vii + 85 pp. Hamden, CT: Archon, 1970.

Pitman comments in passing that the Exeter Book Riddles have a close connection with Aldhelm's *Ænigmata*. Since, however, the exact nature of the relationship is controversial, he refrains from exploring it in his notes. He refers the reader to Tupper's **(727)** and Wyatt's **(737)** editions for further information on this topic. This edition includes the Latin text and a translation of the source poems of Exeter Book Riddles 35 and 40.

10 Crotch, W.J. Blyth. 'An Old English Riddle.' *Times Literary Supplement* 17 June 1926: 414.

Crotch praises the faithfulness of Riddle 29 to observed nature. The initial lines describe phenomena pertaining to the early hours of the morning. Dissenting from Stopford Brooke **(109)**, Crotch argues that the end of the Riddle refers to the apparent disappearance of the moon: 'progressing in its orbit, the waning crescent had been swallowed up in the blaze close to the sun, until, having passed the phase of new moon, it would reappear more than a week later to begin its cycle anew.'

771   Mackie, W.S. 'Notes on Old English Poetry.' *Modern Language Review* 21 (1926): 300–1.

In Riddle 26 line 17 Mackie suggests translating 'dol' as 'the foolish unbeliever' and 'wite' as the verb 'find fault'.

772   Treneer, Anne. *The Sea in English Literature from Beowulf to Donne.* London: Hodder, 1926. xvii + 299.

Relevant is the chapter on 'The Sea in Old English literature' (1–44). Treneer singles out a few of the Riddles on sea-related themes (2 and 3 on 'storm', 10 on 'barnacle-goose', 16 on 'anchor', and 33 on 'iceberg') as lyric poems of power and beauty, comparing them with recent English poetry, notably Masefield's. She sees these Riddles as poetry fulfilling its function of lifting us out of our individual selves, to which, save for imagination, we should be bound, to feel and move in sympathy with other forces (18–26).

773   Brett, Cyril. 'Notes on Old and Middle English.' *Modern Language Review* 22 (1927): 257–64.

Brett argues that solutions to animal or bird riddles have greater plausibility if they represent species native to the British Isles. He eliminates other suggested solutions to Riddle 57 so as to leave the possibilities 'swifts' (following Trautmann, **751**) and 'jackdaws'. Of these two, the latter are more strongly indicated, since the phrase 'they name themselves' suggests a bird with an onomatopoeic name, such as *ceo*. In Riddle 15 the solution 'fox' fits best, though some of the habits mentioned are more reminiscent of the badger.

774   Holthausen, Ferdinand. 'Ein altenglisches Rätsel.' *Germanisch-romanische Monatsschrift* 15 (1927): 453–4.

Following up from Brett's **(773)** suggestion, Holthausen proposes 'rooks' or, more precisely, 'crows', the northern English name, as the solution of Riddle 57. The bird says its own name, since the verb *crawan* 'crow' is used not just of poultry but also of crows and rooks. Also congruent with the Riddle is the fact that rooks are sociable birds which seek shelter round human settlements in snow and other inclement weather.

775   Swaen, A.E.H. 'Het angelsaksische raadsel 58.' *Neophilologus* 13 (1928): 293–6.

Swaen defends the manuscript reading 'rop' in Riddle 57 line 3, comparing the gloss *roopnis* 'liberality', and opts for Wyatt's **(737)** suggested solution 'midges' with some new arguments. Line 6 would refer to their humming or buzzing.

776   Abercrombie, Lascelles. *Poems.* London: Oxford UP, 1930. x + 550 pp.

Abercrombie writes a free imitation of Riddle 8 in modern English alliterative verse (16). Sample translation: 'I through my throat the thronging melodies/ delicately devising in divers moods,/ Let my little breath lavishly chime.'

7 **Smith, Albert Hugh.** *Three Northumbrian Poems: Caedmon's Hymn, Bede's Death Song, and The Leiden Riddle.* London: Methuen, 1933. Rev. edn. 1968. x + 54 pp.

Smith supplies an edition of the *Leiden Riddle* ('Northumbrian version') alongside Exeter Book Riddle 35 (44–7), with introduction, critical apparatus, and glossary. In the Introduction he describes the manuscript context of the *Leiden Riddle* (*Ænigmata* by Symphosius and Aldhelm) and the condition of the Riddle text. He advocates greater editorial attention to Dietrich's **(659)** edition and facsimile, since this was the last to be made before Pluygers's application of a reagent to the manuscript. He describes his own text, derived from independent investigation of the manuscript under ultraviolet light, as closer to those of Sweet **(91)** and Kern **(722, 742)** than to either of Schlutter's **(720, 725)** (7–10). He regards the differences between the Leiden and Exeter Book versions as the result of a long oral tradition. The inclusion of the *Leiden Riddle* at the end of the manuscript suggests that it should be seen as a literary exercise (17). Aldhelm himself may have been the translator, if we assume an almost immediate and very careful revision into Northumbrian dialect (18). The date, localization, orthography, and language of the Riddle text are also discussed (26–37). [For a review see Ekwall, **778**.]

8 **Ekwall, Eilert.** Rev. of *Three Northumbrian Poems*, by Albert Hugh Smith [**777**]. *Modern Language Review* 29 (1934): 78–82.

Ekwall suggests that *þreat*, as used in the *Leiden Riddle* line 6a, means 'loom-weight'. The phrase 'þurh þreata geþræcu' would mean 'owing to the pressure of the weights'.

9 **Colgrave, Bertram, and B.M. Griffiths.** 'A Suggested Solution of Riddle 61.' *Modern Language Review* 31 (1936): 545–7.

The reed, often suggested as the solution to Riddle 60, does not grow in the sea. Preferable would be 'kelp-weed' (*laminaria digitata*), which has a thick, firm stem. A runic message could be incised on this stem while it was still wet. Experiments conducted by Colgrave and Griffiths showed that in a few days the stem dries up but that renewed soaking in water renders the inscription easily decipherable. Symphosius 2 ('reed') would nevertheless have been an influence on this Riddle.

10 **Colgrave, Bertram.** 'Some Notes on Riddle 21.' *Modern Language Review* 32 (1937): 281–3.

Colgrave argues, with detailed reference to the text, that Riddle 21 describes a plough of the heavy type represented in the Anglo-Saxon Calendar in Cotton Tiberius B.v. This type is described by Virgil in the *Georgics*. The verb 'wegeð' in line 5 may imply that the ploughman lifts the handles of the plough slightly, in order to position the share at the correct angle for cutting.

11 **Konick, Marcus.** 'Exeter Book Riddle 41 as a Continuation of Riddle 40.' *Modern Language Notes* 54 (1939): 259–62.

Konick explains lines 1–5 of Riddle 41 as a summary of Riddle 40. He argues that the translator of Aldhelm 100 has shown progressively greater freedom as Riddle 40 goes on but reverts to a stricter method in lines 6–9 of Riddle 41. The two fragments make up one relatively complete riddle, with a regular beginning and a formal conclusion, the latter of which clearly translates Aldhelm's conclusion. Only a brief lacuna need be posited.

782 **Schlauch, Margaret.** 'The "Dream of the Rood" as Prosopopoeia.' *Essays and Studies in Honor of Carleton Brown.* New York: New York UP, 1940. 23–34.

Schlauch briefly discusses Riddle 72. This poem shows a similarity of phraseology with *The Dream of the Rood*. It continues a classical tradition of prosopopoeia exemplified by the pseudo-Ovidian 'De Nuce', where a nut-tree laments the harsh treatment it receives from human beings (30).

783 **Holthausen, Ferdinand.** 'Zu altenglischen Dichtungen.' *Englische Studien* 74 (1941): 324–8.

Holthausen contributes a series of textual notes, some of which propose minor emendations, often to improve the versification. In Riddle 49 line 3 he traces 'gopes' to *gapian* and accordingly explains the 'gop' as identical to the 'wonna þegn' in line 4. He argues that Riddle 31 should be solved as '(portative) organ', the 'niþerweard . . . neb' of line 6 being the tip of the pipes. In Riddle 64 the names of the runes do not yield sense in context and must be treated as approximations to phonologically similar words, e.g. 'ear' for 'eardas'. Corruption may have occurred in Riddle 19, another rune riddle. Other notes concern Riddle 1 line 32, Riddle 23 line 14, Riddle 25 line 6, Riddle 38 line 6, Riddle 40 lines 16 and 72, Riddle 56 line 5, Riddle 60 line 16, Riddle 63 lines 1–2, Riddle 73 line 19, Riddle 74 line 4, Riddle 88 line 23, and Riddle 92 line 4.

784 **Swaen, A.E.H.** 'The Anglo-Saxon Horn Riddles.' *Neophilologus* 26 (1941): 298–302.

Swaen defends the reading 'wæpen wigan' in Riddle 14 line 1, following Rieger (**72**) and Trautmann (**751**). He supports Stopford Brooke's (**109**) interpretation of 'bordum' (line 9) as ornamental borders. In Riddle 80 he supports Müller's solution 'horn' (**660**), rejecting Dietrich's 'hawk' (**658**). In Riddles 88 and 93 he opts for for the specific identification 'ink-horn', supporting Tupper (**727**) and Trautmann (**751**) in the former case and Dietrich (**658**) in the latter.

785 ———. 'Riddle XIII (XVI).' *Neophilologus* 26 (1941): 228–31.

Swaen discusses Trautmann's (**751**) drastic emendations in Riddle 15. He points out that Trautmann, following Walz (**693**), misinterprets 'heals' to mean the throat only, rather than neck, nape, and throat. The word 'fealu' must in context mean dusky or swarthy. He cites zoological descriptions of the badger. The word 'swift' can be explained if we remember that although badgers normally move rather slowly they can work a new passage in their earths with amazing rapidity. Line 5b fits well with the fact that badgers often walk on the toes of their hind feet. The word 'hlifiað' in line 4 can be explained as a poetic hyperbole, since although the badger's ears are not long they are clearly visible, even at a distance, on account of their white rims.

6 ———. 'Riddle 9 (6,8). Facts and Fancies.' *Studia Neophilologica* 14 (1941–2): 67–70.

Swaen describes this paper as merely negative, a refutation, trying to show that no acceptable solution has yet been offered to Riddle 8. The solution 'nightingale' (658) is hardly acceptable, because this bird does not visit towns, is not a mimic, and does not announce welcome things. Also, the verbs *cirman* and *styrman*, as used in lines 3 and 7 respectively, are inappropriate for this bird and there is no evident reason why it should be called 'eald' (line 5). On the other hand, the solutions *ceo* and 'jay' (660 and 727) are inappropriate because of 'eald æfensceop'. The suggestion *sangpipe* (658) does not fit the clues after 'wisan' (line 4). This leaves 'bell' (691) as the least objectionable solution, yet how can a bell imitate a jesting-song? The word 'sceawendwisan' (line 9) is a crux regardless of the solution preferred.

7 Das, Satyendra Kumar. *Cynewulf and the Cynewulf Canon.* Calcutta: Calcutta UP, 1942. xx + 260 pp.

Das aims to ascertain whether any of the ascriptions of unsigned texts to Cynewulf can be validated in the light of metrical and stylistic tests derived from a study of the signed ones. He concludes that none of these attributions, including the Exeter Book Riddles, can be upheld.

8 Swaen, A.E.H. 'Riddle 63 (60, 62).' *Neophilologus* 27 (1942): 220.

Swaen suggests that if the solution to Riddle 62 is not an obscene one it might be 'poker', following Tupper (727), or 'oven-rake'. The words 'suþerne secg' (line 9) evidently refer to the non-Anglo-Saxon baker's man.

9 Young, Jean I. 'Riddle 8 of the *Exeter Book*.' *Review of English Studies* 18 (1942): 308–12.

Young argues that the solution 'jay' (660) loses much of its motivation once the supposed 'rune' inscribed above the riddle is disallowed as a clue. She proposes as a superior alternative solution 'song-thrush' or 'blackbird', preferably the former. The thrush corresponds well to the clues in the Riddle in that it has a main melody ('heafodwoþ' in line 3) which it often varies, lives to the comparatively advanced age of fifteen years, is among the last birds to sing in the evening, and is an effective mimic. Such close observation of a particular bird is matched visually by the naturalism of Anglo-Saxon animal ornament.

Mincoff, Marco. 'Zur angelsächsischen Dichtersprache.' *Godishnik na Sofiiskiya Universitet, Istoriko-filologicheski Fakultet* 39.2 (1942–3): 52.

Mincoff discusses the lexical item *frið*- in Riddle 9 line 9 and Riddle 22 line 4.

Brodeur, Arthur G., and Archer Taylor. 'The Man, the Horse, and the Canary.' *California Folklore Quarterly* 2 (1943): 271–8.

The authors place Riddle 19 in a broad comparative context, showing that integral features of a given riddle type can be omitted in actual realizations, regardless of their date. It is a 'world-riddle' with three 'terms', man, horse, and hawk. Attempts to bring in a fourth term, such as Tupper's (727) 'spear', are to be resisted. In the Old English version any real mystery as to the solution is eliminated. Riddle 19 thereby reveals itself as a learned riddle designed to be read, not heard. The runic reverse spellings and metrical irregularities corroborate this theory. Riddle 64 is a variation on the same type. The authors offer a new interpretation of the runic letters.

792 **Klaeber, Friedrich.** 'Das 9. altenglische Rätsel.' *Archiv für das Studium der neueren Literaturen* 182 (1943): 107–8.

In an answer to Swaen (786), Klaeber argues that lines 9–10 of Riddle 8 point to the solution 'higera/higere' ('jay'), as proposed by Müller and Tupper (660 and 727). He explains motifs in the Riddle by reference to Priscus's account of an entertainer at Attila's court who amused his audience by composing in a mixture of the Gothic and the Hunnish languages. The adjective 'eald' (line 5) compares with Old Norse *gamall* in 'inn gamli þulr', suggesting that age was a professional characteristic of the *scop*.

793 **Young, Jean I.** 'Riddle 15 of the *Exeter Book*.' *Review of English Studies* 20 (1944): 304–6.

A robust faith in the author's powers of observation may lead to a more satisfactory solution of Riddle 15 than those hitherto proposed. Though 'vixen' (773) is superior to other suggestions, 'weasel' is better yet, since this creature invariably displays the utmost bravery when called upon to defend its offspring. It fits other clues in the Riddle in that it walks on its toes, has needle-like teeth and towering ears, and is preyed upon by an enemy that travels on its belly. The enemy concerned is the adder: the compound 'wælhwelp' (line 23) should not be interpreted as a literal description of the adder.

794 **White, Beatrice.** 'Whale-hunting, the Barnacle Goose, and the Date of the "Ancrene Riwle": Three Notes on Old and Middle English.' *Modern Language Review* 40 (1945): 205–7.

White mentions Riddle 10 purely in passing, as the earliest English reference to the barnacle goose legend.

795 **Erhardt-Siebold, Erika von.** 'Old English Riddle No. 4: Handmill.' *PMLA* 61 (1946): 620–3.

Noting that the principal problem with Dietrich's (658) solution 'handmill' to Riddle 4 is the clue 'ring' (or 'rings'), Erhardt-Siebold suggests that this ring is the socket in which the crank turning the mill would pivot. The clue 'bed' refers to the 'sheet' of grain being ground. The type of handmill posited lacks archaeological parallels. The poem may have celebrated it as a wonderful new invention.

6 ———. 'The Anglo-Saxon Riddle 74 and Empedokles' Fragment 117.' *Medium Aevum* 15 (1946): 48–54.

The Empedocles fragment reads, in translation: 'Once I was young man, maiden,/ plant, bird, and mute fish cast ashore.' Erhardt-Siebold argues for its detailed correspondence with Riddle 74, which therefore should be recognized as concerned with metempsychosis. Parallels to an Anglo-Saxon interest in this topic can be located among the Celts.

7 ———. 'Old English Riddle No. 39: Creature Death.' *PMLA* 61 (1946): 910–15.

Erhardt-Siebold suggests that Riddle 39 draws on theological speculation, countered by Alcuin but nonetheless current in Anglo-Saxon England, that death possesses reality. Death's eternal life is mentioned in the Riddle as governed by God's law and the workings of *wyrd*. Riddle 39 can be grouped with Riddle 74, as interpreted by Erhardt-Siebold (**796**), and Aldhelm 100 ('creation'). All three texts are reflexes of a putative thesaurus of knowledge originating in the Italy of the post-Plotinian, Neoplatonic-Christian era and mediated by Celtic writers.

8 **Shook, Laurence K.** 'Old-English Riddle 1: "Fire".' *Mediaeval Studies* 8 (1946): 316–18.

Shook argues that Riddle 1 has been almost completely misunderstood. The true solution is 'fire'. The riddle consists of two clearly defined episodes, lines 2–9, a forest fire, and lines 10–14, a human sacrifice. The latter section depicts a boiling cauldron containing the flesh of human victims, suspended over a fire. It is well established that Germanic peoples sometimes sacrificed their prisoners of war to the victory god.

9 **Swaen, A.E.H.** 'Riddle 9 (12). Riddle 8 (10, 11).' *Neophilologus* 30 (1946): 126–7.

Swaen supports Dietrich's solution of Riddle 11 as 'night' (**658**), arguing against Trautmann's (**713**) interpretation of 'hasofag' and also his punctuation of line 4. In discussing Riddle 10 he tries to eliminate confusion between two nearly-allied species of geese.

0 **Whitbread, Leslie.** 'The Latin Riddle in the Exeter Book.' *Notes and Queries* 190 (1946): 156–8.

Whitbread opposes a strict classical scansion of the verses of Riddle 90. An alternative possibility is simply lines with six main stresses in the style of the so-called hypermetrical lines found in batches in Old English verse. Building on Morley (**74**), Whitbread explains the Riddle as an allusion to the Crucifixion.

1 **Zanco, Aurelio.** *Storia della Letteratura Inglese.* Vol. 1. *Dalle origini alla Restaurazione 650–1660.* Turin: Chiantore, 1946. 2 vols. 1946–7. Rev. edn. 1958.

Zanco briefly discusses the Riddles, expressing the view that sometimes they attain the status of true poetry. Riddle 7 is translated into Italian verse (10).

802   Erhardt-Siebold, E. von. 'Old English Riddle No. 57: OE *Cā* "Jackdaw".'
PMLA 62 (1947): 1–8.

Erhardt-Siebold notes that although the earlier motifs in Riddle 57 fail to identify
one uniquely appropriate solution, the final line points to a play on
onomatopoeia, so long as we read it 'they name themselves' (and not 'name
them!'). Analogously, Pseudo-Symphosius 1 'cuckoo' relies on onomatopoeia
for the identification of the solution. An Old English *cā* 'jackdaw' can be
posited as the solution, partly on the basis of place-name evidence.

803   ————. 'Old English Riddle No. 95.' *Modern Language Notes* 62 (1947): 558–9.

The solution to Riddle 95 is 'quill'. The kenning 'hiðendra hyht' in line 5 refers
to the ink which the quill takes pleasure in plundering. Analogues contain
references to the paradox of silent letters that speak, whereas the present riddle
substitutes the motif of the wise men who remain silent when reading.

804   Swaen, A.E.H. 'Notes on Anglo-Saxon Riddles.' *Neophilologus* 31 (1947):
145–8.

Swaen opts for the solution 'books' for Riddle 49. He solves Riddle 61 as 'shirt',
on the assumption that the word 'sticade' (line 5) is graphic and that each of us
must at one time or other have got entangled in our shirts, like Hercules. He
understands the double entendre as applying only to the latter part of the poem. In
Riddle 25 line 4 he argues against Trautmann's **(751)** change of 'staþol' to
'stapol'. He also briefly discusses 'wincel' and 'weax' in Riddle 45 line 1 and
'efnelang' in Riddle 44 line 7.

805   Erhardt-Siebold, E. von. 'The Old English Hunt Riddles.' *PMLA* 63 (1948):
3–6.

Erhardt-Siebold proposes the solution 'water-fowl hunt' for Riddle 36. Described
in the Riddle, in a scene still familiar in Europe, are hunters, game-birds, and a
punt, with dogs sometimes inside and sometimes outside the punt. This punt is
conceived of as a larger bird with the smaller (dead) birds in its womb. Female
participation in the scene is unlikely, since the Anglo-Saxon woman would be
busy at home. Riddles 19 and 64 can be solved as 'falconry': they depict a man, a
horse, and a hawk. In Riddle 64 lines 5–6 'the falcon (*FÆlcen*) rejoiced; it flew
over the arrows (*EArwe*) and spears (*SPere*) of that company'.

806   Taylor, Archer. *The Literary Riddle before 1600.* Berkeley: U of California P,
1948. 131 pp.

This broad comparative treatment, with bibliography, contains only passing
references to the Exeter Book Riddles. The Exeter Book would originally have
contained one hundred riddles, under the long-enduring influence of
Symphosius. Despite this influence, however, the Exeter Book Riddles possess a
distinctly English flavour, some themes being taken from native folksong and
saga. The Riddles are distinctly atavistic in presenting the powers of nature as
objects of worship.

7 Eliason, Norman E. 'Riddle 68 of the *Exeter Book.' Philologica: the Malone anniversary studies.* Ed. Thomas A. Kirby and Henry Bosley Woolf. Baltimore: Johns Hopkins UP, 1949. 18–19.

Riddles 68 and 69 should be read as one riddle consisting of three lines, where 'wege' in line 3 refers back to 'weg' in line 1. The solutions so far suggested for Riddle 69, 'winter', 'ice' (**658**), or 'something in the nature of petrifaction' (**737**), apply to and derive from line 3 alone. Eliason therefore proposes a solution 'Christ walking on the sea'.

8 Erhardt-Siebold, Erika von. 'The Old English Loom Riddles.' *Philologica: the Malone anniversary studies.* Ed. Thomas A. Kirby and Henry Bosley Woolf. Baltimore: Johns Hopkins UP, 1949. 9–17.

Erhardt-Siebold describes the process of weaving on the vertical (warp-weighted) loom. In relation to Riddle 35 she discusses the humming sound produced by the shuttle being passed rapidly between the warp threads. She compares 'wundene me ne beoð wefle' (line 5) with Old Norse *vinda vef*. Riddle 56 is to be solved as 'web in the loom'. The 'treow' which is 'getenge' (line 9) is a 'distaff with the flax or wool on it'. The 'feet' are the two rows of warp weights. The solution to Riddle 70 is 'shuttle': it 'sings through its sides' because it produces sounds through the lateral warp threads.

9 ———. 'The Old English Storm Riddles.' *PMLA* 64 (1949): 884–8.

Erhardt-Siebold suggests the solution 'the atmosphere' for Riddles 1–3. The conventional solution 'storm/wind' leads to inconsistencies and Shook's solution (**798**) 'fire' is far-fetched. She concurs with Kennedy (**29, 233**) in treating 2 and 3 as a single poem. These riddles draw on Graeco-Roman cosmology, which conceived of the atmosphere as a mixture of the four elements. It was capable of producing lightning, meteors, and submarine storms (the latter a notion due to Pliny or Lucretius).

0 Whitbread, Leslie. 'The Latin Riddle in the Exeter Book.' *Notes and Queries* 194 (1949): 80–2.

Whitbread considers the ornamentation of the Sutton Hoo jewelled purse-lid in relation to the content of Riddle 90. Possibly the composer of the Riddle had in mind some striking jewelled object on which were depicted the two animal scenes alluded to in the text.

1 Zandvoort, R.W. 'The Leiden Riddle.' *English and Germanic Studies* 3 (1949–50): 42–56. Repr. in R.W. Zandvoort. *Collected Papers: A Selection of Notes and Articles originally published in English Studies and other Journals.* Groningen: Wolters, 1954. 1–16.

Zandvoort briefly surveys the development of the riddle genre, from Symphosius onwards. In his discussion of the differences between Aldhelm 33 ('lorica') and the *Leiden Riddle*, he notes how the Old English version clusters related material together and omits the give-away clue at the conclusion. He reviews the history of scholarship on the *Leiden Riddle*, including the contributions of Kern (**722,**

742), Schlutter (**720, 725**), Smith (**777**), and the ASPR (**194, 203**), along with the various attempts to interpret 'þreata giþræc' (**778**).

812 **Erhardt-Siebold, Erika von.** 'Old English Riddle 13.' *Modern Language Notes* 65 (1950): 97–100.

Erhardt-Siebold accepts Trautmann's solution of Riddle 13 (**751**), 'ten chickens', but attempts to refine it by presenting the answer in a hypothetical Old English form, '*ten ciccenu'. Of the ten letters here, six are consonants and four are vowels, explaining the number puzzle in the riddle. This type of puzzle can be compared with Aldhelm 30.

813 ———. 'Old English Riddle 23: Bow, OE *Boga*.' *Modern Language Notes* 65 (1950): 93–6.

Erhardt-Siebold proposes three emendations in Riddle 23. In line 2 'gesceapen' should *metri causa* replace 'sceapen'. In line 11 'sprice' should be emended to 'spirce', from *spircan* 'to sparkle'. In line 14 'wer' should read 'wege', 'cup', with an allusion to the *poculum mortis* motif. Erhardt-Siebold regrets that the riddle is not more informative on the technology of Old English archery.

814 **Girvan, Ritchie.** 'The Medieval Poet and his Audience.' *English Studies Today: Papers Read at the International Conference of University Professors of English.* . . Ed. C.L. Wrenn and G. Bullough. Oxford: Oxford UP, 1951. 85–97.

Girvan argues that written Old English poetry was of monastic origin, definitely for a religious purpose, and addressed to a more or less instructed class for their edification or amusement. As written texts, the Exeter Book Riddles were frankly intended for the entertainment of the company. Many of these riddles must have been as unintelligible to the vulgar as the Latin riddles of Tatwine and his confrères.

815 **Lindheim, Bogislav von.** 'Traces of Colloquial Speech in Old English.' *Anglia* 70 (1951): 22–42.

Lindheim operates on the assumption that the Riddles are to a large extent of popular origin. It is intrinsically probable that traces of colloquial speech, so strikingly absent in Old English poetry, had a chance to take refuge in them (26). Characteristically, the verb *swætan* in the sense of 'to sweat' is instanced only in Riddle 3 line 43 and nowhere else in Old English verse (27). Here, and nowhere else, we find *wamb* used of inanimate objects and *hrycg* meaning 'back' as part of the body. Similarly, the controversial word *wlonc* is used with overtones of 'lustful, lascivious, desirous for sexual intercourse' in three of the Riddles. Contextual analysis of the remaining instances of *wlonc* in the Riddles confirms that the meaning 'lustful, greedy' was undoubtedly part of the original semantic nucleus of the word (34–5). Such usages may have been resorted to consciously on the part of the Riddle authors, so as to impart a particular colloquial tone to their compositions.

816 **Eliason, Norman E.** 'Four Old English Cryptographic Riddles.' *Studies in Philology* 49 (1952): 553–65.

Eliason suggests that the cryptogram in Riddle 75 involves substitution of the following vowel for the preceding consonant. Thus DNLH should be read EOLH. He takes the next line 'ic ane geseah idese sittan' as referring to the female elk. Thus the 'ic' of the riddle is an elk hunter. He argues that Riddles 19 and 64 cannot be solved as simply 'horse-man-hawk' but rather as 'writing': the 'ic', i.e. the speaker, is the person doing the writing. In Riddle 36 the cryptographic line 5 should be rejected, as breaking the flow of lines 4 to 6. Moreover, the first eight lines and the final six should be treated as separate riddles. The last six are obscure, but the first eight should be solved as 'a pregnant horse with two pregnant women on its back', on the basis of analogies in other riddle traditions.

17 Erhardt-Siebold, Erika von. 'Note on Anglo-Saxon Riddle 74.' *Medium Aevum* 21 (1952): 36–7.

In a supplement to her article on Riddle 74 (**796**), Erhardt-Siebold notes that an entry for 'metempsychosis' is included in the *Leiden Glossary*. She believes that Riddle 74 stems directly from a Greek text that faithfully reproduced Empedocles's thought.

18 Slay, Desmond. 'Some Aspects of the Technique of Composition of Old English Verse.' *Transactions of the Philological Society* 1952: 1–14.

Slay suggests that although metrically irregular lines like 'hæfde fela ribba' (Riddle 32 line 8b) and 'hafað fela toþa' (Riddle 34 line 2b) may be due to a late date of composition, it is just possible that they are phrases descending from an early period when the rules of versification were not so strict. A number of the Riddles may retain some of the former looseness of Germanic alliterative verse.

19 Magoun, Francis P., Jr. 'Oral-formulaic Character of Anglo-Saxon Narrative Poetry.' *Speculum* 28 (1953): 446–67. Repr. in *Essential Articles for the Study of Old English Poetry*. Ed. J.B. Bessinger and S.J. Kahrl. Hamden, CT: Archon, 1968. 319–51.

Magoun believes that at least some of the language of the Riddles is traditional, since verses in them can be paralleled elsewhere. It may turn out, however, that many riddles, often very short compositions, were composed word by word rather than formulaically. Such a technique would have been necessary because the literary riddles of the Exeter Book were a new genre to the Anglo-Saxons, a direct imitation of Latin enigmas.

20 Sisam, Kenneth. 'The Exeter Book' and '*Note C to p. 97*: The Arrangement of the Exeter Book.' *Studies in the History of Old English Literature*. Oxford: Clarendon, 1953. 97–109 and 291–2.

In this analysis and appraisal of the Exeter Book Sisam notes the haphazard order of contents which leaves the Riddles divided into three groups, with Riddle 30 repeated (97). He sees *Pharaoh* as a kind of riddle. There is no indication that the Riddles and the elegies were drawn from different manuscript sources (291). 'In the only place where the Exeter Book can be compared with a much older copy, the *Leiden Riddle*, it comes fairly well out of the test' (98).

821 Gerritsen, Johan. 'Þurh þreata geþræcu.' *English Studies* 35 (1954): 259–62.

Gerritsen investigates the weaving terminology in the *Leiden Riddle*. He discusses the allusion to the shedding operation in Aldhelm 33, translating 'no leashes draw, nor do noisy threads spring back'. He points out that the fall of the loom-weights would set up a vibration in the attached section of the warp when the natural shed is restored. The Old English translation of this line seems not to be a close one. Ekwall's suggestion (**778**) that *þreat*, as used in line 6, = 'loom-weight' is counter-indicated by the recorded meanings of *þreat* which are either abstract or collective. Alternatively, therefore, Gerritsen suggests that 'þurh þreata geþræcu' = 'by means of the system of leashes'.

822 Malone, Kemp. 'Epithet and Eponym.' *Names* 2 (1954): 109–12. Repr. in *Studies in Heroic Legend and in Current Speech*. Ed. Stefán Einarsson and Norman E. Eliason. Copenhagen: Rosenkilde, 1959. 189–92.

In the course of an investigation of the eponym *Angle*, Malone interprets the lexical item *anga* 'point' in Exeter Book Riddle 23 line 4 as meaning 'point (of an arrow)'. The poet had an arrow in mind but avoided the word *earh* because its use would have revealed at once that 'bow' was the solution.

823 Bessinger, J.B. 'Oral to Written: Some Implications of the Anglo-Saxon Transition.' *Explorations* 8 (1957): 11–15.

In the course of a general discussion of 'the invasion of bookish culture into an oral tradition' in Anglo-Saxon England, Bessinger cites the 'joking' Riddle 47 as an occasion when 'the best traditions of the old verse and a delight in literacy fuse' (14).

824 Tucker, S.I. 'The Anglo-Saxon Poet Considers the Heavens.' *Neophilologus* 41 (1957): 270–5.

Tucker refers in passing to Riddle 29, contesting the allegation that the poet has become confused between the Latin and Germanic genders of the words for 'moon' and 'sun'.

825 Blakeley, L. 'Riddles 22 and 58 of the Exeter Book.' *Review of English Studies* NS 9 (1958): 241–52.

Solutions to Riddle 13 and 22 have been bedevilled by hasty identifications of analogues. The wagon of Riddle 22 is in fact the Plough, or Charles's Wain. Once every twenty-four hours this constellation leaves the horizon and travels round the Pole Star until it comes down again toward the land – this being the journey referred to in the Riddle. A stimulus toward the composition of the Riddle was provided by Aldhelm 53 ('Arcturus'). Tupper's (**727**) theory of a popular origin is to be rejected. Riddle 58 is to be solved as 'well sweep', a piece of apparatus for drawing water. Runic names concealed in the Riddle enable us to fix the Old English word as **rad-lim*, 'moving beam'. The use of homonymy in this runic code alerts us to fresh possibilities of interpretation of the problematic 'ear' in *Rune Poem*.

26 **Shook, Laurence K.** 'Old-English Riddle 28 – Testudo (Tortoise-Lyre).' *Mediaeval Studies* 20 (1958): 93–7.

Shook expands on Trautmann's (751) idea that Riddle 28 alludes to Symphosius 20 ('testudo', 'tortoise'), arguing that 'tortoise' is indeed the solution. The first section of the riddle describes the tortoise shell, the second the preparation of the shell to serve as a sounding-board for a stringed instrument, and the third the making of music. Shook notes that the solution is better in the Latin analogues than in Old English, since in Latin the word *testudo* can mean both 'tortoise' and 'musical instrument'.

27 **Huppé, B.F.** *Doctrine and Poetry: Augustine's Influence on Old English Poetry.* New York: State U of New York P, 1959. vi + 248 pp.

Huppé's discussion of Aldhelm's work includes reference to Enigma 33, as translated in the *Leiden Riddle*. This riddle illustrates the close attention to detail which characterizes early Christian poetry in English. Texts like these demanded active comprehension on the part of the audience. The etymology of the word *lorica* in the *Etymologiae* of Isidore of Seville provided a hint for the verbal structure of the Riddle. The spiritual implication of 'lorica' may well have been intended by Aldhelm, given that the image of the spiritual lorica is so commonplace. The Riddle therefore seems to belong in the tradition of Christian poetry and theory.

28 **Kranz, Gisbert.** 'Lyrik der Angelsachsen.' *Antaios* 1 (1959): 153–69.

This general appreciation of Anglo-Saxon lyricism contains many translations into German. Kranz attributes a marked degree of elegiac tone and a strong feeling for Nature to poems of the Cynewulf school. Included in this category are Riddles 1 and 2, with their description of the storm. Riddle 3, on the hurricane, has the same appeal to us as Shelley's 'The Cloud'. The two poets can be imagined as extending hands to each other across eleven centuries. Kranz also notes the anthropomorphization of Nature in Riddle 9.

9 **Tucker, S.I.** 'Laughter in Old English Literature.' *Neophilologus* 43 (1959): 222–6.

Tucker cites Riddles 28 ('John Barleycorn') and 47 ('bookworm') as places in Old English literature where laughter glimmers gently. In Riddle 33 the terrible laughter of the crashing iceberg implies a personification of an uninhibited warrior like Holofernes.

0 **Barnes, Richard.** 'Horse Colors in Anglo-Saxon Poetry.' *Philological Quarterly* 39 (1960): 510–12.

Barnes argues that the common quality among things described as *fealu* in the poetry is paleness, not brightness: here he includes the badger's head, citing Riddle 15 line 1.

1 **Raffel, Burton.** 'Six Anglo-Saxon Riddles.' *Antioch Review* 20 (1960): 52–4.

Raffel translates Riddles 8, 11, 14, 29, 32, and 60 into English verse, using the text and notes of the ASPR edition (**194**). He solves Riddle 8 as the 'jay'. Sample translation from Riddle 8 lines 8b–11: 'Who can I be,/ Aping a singing buffoon with a shining,/ Brassy voice that bellows happiness,/ The welcome sound of my strident cry?' Riddle 60 is probably a love message carved into a reed.

832 **Leslie, Roy F.** *Three Old English Elegies.* New York: Barnes; Manchester: Manchester UP, 1961. Rev. edn. 1966. xii + 86 pp. Rev. edn. Exeter: Exeter UP, 1988.

Leslie considers that, despite Strobl (**537**), Riddle 60 should be kept separate from *The Husband's Message*. There are a number of references in the text which appear to militate against the speaker being a rune-stave personified and which support his identification as a human messenger.

833 **Bouman, A.C.** *Patterns in Old English and Old Icelandic Literature.* Leiden: UP, 1962. viii + 159 pp.

Bouman includes a brief discussion of Riddle 60, considered as part of *The Husband's Message*. He endorses Blackburn's (**698**) view and argues against Tupper's claims (**707**) for a relation between Riddle 60 lines 1–17 and Symphosius 2 ('reed'). Although the similarity in phrases cannot be denied, it is not sufficient to make the solution 'reed' acceptable. Likewise, a solution 'musical instrument' is counter-indicated by certain details in the text.

834 **Crossley-Holland, Kevin.** 'Thirteen Riddles.' *Listener* 20 Dec. 1962: 1046–7.

A transcript of a Third Programme talk, this article offers translations of Exeter Book Riddles 9, 16, 27, 29, 32, 34, 37, 53, 57, 77, 81, and 85. Crossley-Holland points out the element of contest in many of them: mead against man, shield against spear, anchor against wind and wave. Sample translation from Riddle 77 lines 1–4: 'The deep sea suckled me, the waves sounded over me;/ Rollers were my coverlet as I rested on my bed./ I have no feet, and frequently open my mouth/ To the flood.'

835 ———. 'Two Old English Riddles for Xmas.' *Spectator* 21 Dec. 1962: 968.

Crossley-Holland translates Riddles 30a and 40. A sample translation from Riddle 30 lines 1–4: 'I am supple of body and sport with the wind,/ I am clothed with finery, and the storm's great friends,/ Ready to travel, but troubled by fire. . .' A note explains the different connotations of the word *beam* in Old English.

836 **Hacikyan, Agop.** 'The Exeter Book: the Anglo-Saxon Riddles.' *La Revue de l'Université de Sherbrooke* 4 (1962): 243–7.

Hacikyan tries to explain the inclusion of the Riddles in the Exeter Book. We should note that riddles were popular even in ecclesiastical circles. Because of the learned nature of some of these enigmas, the scribe perhaps felt the necessity of including them for the sake of pastime and recreation. The Riddles were composed by diverse unknown authors and at diverse periods, though mostly during the first half of the eighth century.

57   Baum, Paull F. *Anglo-Saxon Riddles of the Exeter Book.* Durham, NC: Duke UP, 1963. xx + 70 pp.

This aims to be a complete but non-scholarly translation of the Exeter Book Riddles, with a brief commentary. The order of the Riddles diverges from that found in the Exeter Book in order to bring together related themes or subjects. Baum classifies the fragmentary Riddle 87 with the acknowledged obscene or double entendre Riddles (57–60). He defends Strobl's theory (**537**) that Riddle 60 and *The Husband's Message* form a single poem on the grounds that 'it is unusual for a riddle to carry a secret message "for us two alone" '. The speaker is a reed staff (34). Riddle 28 should be solved as 'malt liquor', 68 as 'running water', 74 possibly as 'rain'. In his brief introduction, Baum discusses the problems of translation. A sample translation from Riddle 7 lines 1–6a : 'Silent is my garment when I tread the earth/ or dwell in the towns or stir the waters./ Sometimes my trappings lift me up over/ the habitations of heroes and this high air,/ and the might of the welkin bears me afar/ above mankind.'

58   Raffel, Burton. 'Two Old English Riddles.' *Arizona Quarterly* 19 (1963): 270.

Raffel translates Riddles 7 and 66 into verse. Sample translation from Riddle 7 lines 5–6a: 'Sometimes that which/ Makes me beautiful raises me high/ Above men's heads. . .'

59   Århammar, Nils. 'Altsächsische skion m. "Wolke" und altenglische sceo (?): mit einem Beitrag zur Textkritik von Genesis 16ff und des altenglischen Rätsels vom Gewittersturm.' *Jahrbuch des Vereins für niederdeutsche Sprachforschung* 87 (1964): 24–8.

The occurrence of 'sceo' in Riddle 3 line 41 is the sole evidence for this Old English cognate of Old Saxon *skion* and Old Norse *ský* 'cloud'.

60   Adams, John F. 'The Anglo-Saxon Riddle as Lyric Mode.' *Criticism* 7 (1965): 335–48.

Adams remarks that it has not been common to offer a literary evaluation of the Exeter Book Riddles. These riddles embody the lyric mode that would otherwise have been unrepresented in Old English poetry. They afforded the poet an excuse to examine an object minutely in verse. The insistent paradoxes are not simply transcended by the discovery of the solution, but linger to expand our knowledge of the object described. Themes as complex as mutability (though not love) may be explored. Thus in Riddle 47 humankind's intellectual pretensions to immortality are consumed by worms, in a novel twist of an old topos. In Riddle 85 the solution ('fish in river') has metaphysical implications concerning human limitations. In Riddle 16 the 'anchor' symbolizes the human struggle for survival in an alien world. Riddle 7 communicates the awe and admiration which the swan has always inspired. The poem 'called "The Wind" ' [Riddles 1–3] resembles Shelley's 'Ode to the West Wind' in structure and in other respects. Through inevitable identification of God with Wyrd there emerges the pagan sense of dread, almost an existential hopelessness.

841   Hacikyan, Agop. 'The Exeter Manuscript: Riddle 19.' *English Language Notes* 3 (1965): 86–8.

Hacikyan discusses the third rune-group in Riddle 19 (line 6). He rejects Mackie's **(188)** explanation, 'wega'. The poets of the Exeter Book Riddles usually used runes to represent the major characters or the theme of the riddle, and not for ordinary content words such as 'ways'. He suggests that the word actually intended was 'wiga', used as an apposition to 'mon'. The *-e-* for *-i-* would represent the scribe's attempt to enhance the difficulty of the Riddle.

842   Benson, Larry. 'The Literary Character of Anglo-Saxon Formulaic Poetry.' *PMLA* 81 (1966): 334–41.

In Riddle 35 the Old English poet closely follows Aldhelm 33, yet produces a version in which at least 50 per cent of the half-lines are formulas. The final two lines of Riddle 35 were either missing or corrupt in the Exeter Book scribe's copy-text. The scribe therefore used two formulaic lines to supply a new conclusion. These two phenomena contribute to demonstrate that literate poets (and scribes), contrary to the oral-formulaic hypothesis, can write formulaic verse pen in hand, in the same way that any writer observes a literary tradition.

843   Garvin, Katharine. 'Nemnað hy sylfe: a Note on Riddle 57, Exeter Book.' *Classica et Mediaevalia* 27 (1966): 294–5.

Garvin suggests solving Riddle 57 as 'bees'. The phrase 'nemnað hy sylfe' (line 6), translated as 'they name themselves', fits with the onomatopoeic properties of Old English *beon* 'bees'.

844   Greenfield, Stanley B. 'The Old English Elegies.' *Continuations and Beginnings: Studies in Old English Literature.* Ed. E.G. Stanley. London: Nelson, 1966. 142–75.

Greenfield comments in passing on Riddle 60, noting that its connection with *The Husband's Message* becomes very tenuous once we recognize that the speaker in the latter poem is human rather than a message-bearing piece of wood. A piece of wood is not likely to have travelled repeatedly aboard ship or to refer to itself as 'þisne beam' or to say that his lord told him something (169–70).

845   Hacikyan, Agop. *A Linguistic and Literary Analysis of Old English Riddles.* Montreal: Casalini, 1966. viii + 94 pp.

Hacikyan reviews previous scholarship on the Exeter Book, the age of composition of the Riddles, and their literary and social aspects. Defending the literary merits of the Riddles, he suggests that it is perhaps possible to establish a certain rapport between the enigmatist and the modern symbolist poet. He notes a closeness to nature perhaps not recorded elsewhere in any other literature with so much enthusiasm and vividness of description. He also points out instances of dramatic intensity, irony, wit, humour, and paradox.

846   ———. 'The Literary and the Social Aspects of the Old English Riddles.' *Revue de l'Université d'Ottawa* 36 (1966): 107–20.

Hacikyan follows up on Ker's (121) emphasis on the imaginative qualities of the Exeter Book Riddles by suggesting that it might be possible to establish a certain rapport between the enigmatist and the modern symbolist poet. Kennings become original reflections of a state of mind, offering as they do a means of evading literary commonplaces. Hacikyan supports this contention by an analysis of the kennings used in the Riddles. Admittedly a few of the Riddles are mere *jeux d'esprit* but more generally they are of value not only for the philologist but also for the social historian and the literary scholar. Through them we sense the freshness of the early world as well as the temper and the philosophy of a young, virile race.

7 **Anderson, George K.** 'Aldhelm and the Leiden Riddle.' *Old English Poetry: Fifteen Essays.* Ed. Robert P. Creed. Providence: Brown UP, 1967. 167–76.

Anderson supports Smith's (777) conjecture that Aldhelm himself translated the *Leiden Riddle* into Old English. His original Wessex dialect would have been converted into Northumbrian perhaps a century later. Anderson agrees with other scholars that the Exeter Book version was written later than the Leiden version. The Exeter Book copyist might have omitted material in order to cram the text into the bottom of the folio. Though the Old English translation is on the whole more verbose and repetitious than the Latin, it does improve the organization of the references to weaving equipment. Anderson disagrees with Dietrich's (659) notion that here the Old English translator was working from a superior lost Latin version. The *Leiden Riddle* and Exeter Book Riddles 35 and 40 are the only extant examples of a Latin hexameter being rendered into two lines of Old English verse. As to the poem's testimony on Anglo-Saxon weaving, Anderson suggests that the paucity of weaving vocabulary, here and in other texts, implies that the Anglo-Saxon weaver produced good results with a fairly low level of technology.

8 **Blauner, D.G.** 'The Early Literary Riddle.' *Folklore* 78 (1967): 49–58.

In the course of a brief history of the literary riddle, Blauner mentions the Exeter Book Riddles as inspired by Symphosius.

9 **Böðvarsson, Haukur.** 'Understatement in Old English and Old Icelandic.' *Tímarit Þjóðræknisfélags Íslendinga* 49 (1967): 48–58.

Haukur points out that understatement does not necessarily result in a strong rhetorical effect, instancing Riddle 60 line 7b 'lyt ic wende' and noting some parallels (50).

Campbell, Jackson J. 'Knowledge of Rhetorical Figures in Anglo-Saxon England.' *JEGP* 66 (1967): 1–20.

In passing, Campbell suggests the influence of Lucretius on Riddles 2 and 3 (16).

Hacikyan, Agop. 'Emendations for Codex Exoniensis, Folios 101a–15a; 122b–3a; 124b–30b.' *Revue de l'Université d'Ottawa* 37 (1967): 46–66 and 344–58.

Hacikyan lists some of the emendations previously suggested in the text of the Exeter Book Riddles and proposes some new ones.

852   **Kaske, R.E.** 'A Poem of the Cross in The Exeter Book: "Riddle 60" and "The Husband's Message".' *Traditio* 23 (1967): 41–71.

Riddle 60 is the first part of a poem on the Cross, which should be interpreted allegorically. Christ's love for the Church or the human soul is reflected by the literally developed message of a lover to his lady. This message, exhorting the soul to seek its heavenly union with Christ, is delivered by the Cross, similarly reflected by a rune-staff or other wooden object. Kaske points out partial parallels with *The Dream of the Rood*. He also correlates the sea-side or lake-side location of the object in Riddle 60 with certain early accounts of the Creation where the Tree of Life is associated with a sea or ocean, rather than the customary river. The total poem might represent either an allegorization of the Conversion of England or a celebration of the arrival of a fragment of the True Cross in England.

853   **Vermeer, P.M.** Rev. of *An Old English Anthology*, by W.F. Bolton [246]. *English Studies* 48 (1967): 431–3.

In his comments on Bolton's handling of the *Leiden Riddle*, Vermeer seeks to correct some longstanding and persistent errors in the naming and transcription of Leiden Rijksuniversiteit Vossianus Lat. 4to 106.

854   **Abbott, H.H.** *The Riddles of the Exeter Book.* Cambridge: Golden Head, 1968. v + 57 pp.

This set of translations was completed in 1925, following the editions of Tupper (**727**) and Wyatt (**737**), and some extracts were published in the collection *An Essex Harvest and Other Poems*, London: Chatto, 1925. Abbott supplies a brief introduction and notes. Sample translation (from Riddle 7 lines 1–4): 'My garment is still when I go on the earth/ Both inhabited dwelling and on heaving of waters./ At times my adornment in the air on high/ Raises me over the roofs of men.'

855   **Crossley-Holland, Kevin.** 'Five Old English Riddles.' *Encounter* 30.6 (June 1968): 45.

Crossley-Holland offers verse translations of Riddles 8 ('jay'), 12, 14, 35, and 45. A sample translation from Riddle 12 lines 1–5: 'I travel by foot, trample the ground,/ the green fields, for as long as I live./ Lifeless, I fetter dark Welshmen,/ sometimes their betters too. At times/ I give a warrior liquor from within me. . .'

856   **Kay, Donald.** 'Riddle 20: a Revaluation.' *Tennessee Studies in Literature* 13 (1968): 133–9.

The solution is 'phallus' but the riddle-setter misleads his audience into the commonly accepted but too obvious solution 'sword'. Guidance to the true solution is provided by sexual imagery in lines 20–35.

7 **Kossick, Shirley G.** 'Old English Riddles.' *UNISA English Studies* 4 (1968): 42–6.

Kossick sees the Exeter Book Riddles as lyrical comments on aspects of Anglo-Saxon life, making the audience look at and consider afresh the objects described. The element of deception is nominal. Once the solution has been found, in fact, this element is generally replaced by recognition of the paradoxes which inform so much of creation. Riddle 7 is typical, in that it reads as a lyric once the solution 'swan' is known. This poem, like Riddle 60, reflects evocatively the Anglo-Saxon love and awareness of Nature.

8 **Leslie, Roy F.** 'The Integrity of Riddle 60.' *JEGP* 67 (1968): 451–7.

Leslie argues that the last four lines of Riddle 60 seem to preclude the attachment of that text to *The Husband's Message*. Its stylistic affinities with acknowledged riddles justify its inclusion among them. The most likely habitat for the subject of the riddle is the brackish water of a coastal marsh, which is consistent with solution as a 'reed from which pens were cut'. Symphosius 2 ('reed') is much less developed and vivid than the Old English riddle and can at best only have provided a starting-point. The person addressed in line 14 is the writer using the pen.

9 **Whitman, Frank H.** 'Old English Riddle 74.' *English Language Notes* 6 (1968): 1–5.

Whitman argues that the solution to this riddle is 'pen'. He points out a number of parallels to other riddles that seem to deal with the subject of writing. The phrase 'dead mid fiscum' (line 4) is best explained as a component of the 'living dead' theme that is almost always associated with quill-pen riddles. Line 3 describes the 'living' phase, before the quill was plucked.

0 ———. 'The Origin of Old English "Riddle LXV".' *Notes and Queries* 213, NS 15 (1968): 203–4.

Although Riddle 65 might seem to have its source in Symphosius 44 ('onion'), the length of line 1 and the syntactic uniqueness of the half-lines may indicate a different origin. These features are likely to represent a rather clumsy expansion of some Latin line, probably hexameter. This and the balanced antitheses suggest an adaptation of a lost three-line Latin riddle.

1 **Gerritsen, Johan.** 'The Text of the Leiden Riddle.' *English Studies* 50 (1969): 529–44.

Gerritsen notes that no close study of Leiden Rijksuniversiteit Vossianus Lat. 4to 106 as a whole has been made in connexion with the *Leiden Riddle*. He furnishes a detailed codicological investigation, showing that the *Leiden Riddle* was copied along with Aldhelm's *Ænigmata* from an insular exemplar. The copyist, accustomed to Continental letter-forms, failed to recognize certain insular letter-forms; additionally, he knew no Old English. In copying the riddle, he imitated insular letter-forms that he did not understand. Gerritsen concludes that a native inscription in Old Northumbrian is immediately behind our text. He offers a new transcription.

862   **Hacikyan, Agop.** 'The Modern English Renditions of Codex Exoniensis, Folios 101a–115a; 122b–123a; 124b–130b.' *Revue de l'Université d'Ottawa* 39 (1969): 249–73, 442–95.

Hacikyan provides a brief review of previous translations of the Riddles. This review is followed by his own parallel-text translation, which is literal in terms of word correspondence and intended to help the novice follow the Old English text word by word.

863   **Whitman, Frank H.** 'The Christian Background to Two Riddle Motifs.' *Studia Neophilologica* 41 (1969): 93–8.

Whitman endorses Tupper's **(707)** rejection of any close indebtedness of Riddle 29 to Eusebius 11 ('moon'). In the Eusebius *Ænigma* the sun and moon are allies, seeking to defeat darkness, whereas in Riddle 29 they are enemies. Both motifs are explicable as part of a Christian exegetical tradition. Darkness, night, and the West align with sin and Satan, whereas light, day, and the East symbolize Christ's presence, often figured as the sun. Within this scheme the moon can be either the ally of the forces of light or their opponent. Given that the motif in Riddle 29 is much the rarer of the two, it is possible that it stems not from a riddle tradition but, at least proximately, from early Christian typology.

864   **Crossley-Holland, K.** *Storm and other Old English Riddles.* Illustrated by Miles Thistlethwaite. London: Macmillan, 1970. 76 pp.

The introduction to this set of translations relates the Riddles to the kennings in Old English poetry. The illustrations indicate the solution to each riddle. Sample translation (from Riddle 27 lines 1–5): 'Favoured by men, I am found far and wide,/ taken from woods and the heights of the town,/ from high and from low. During each day/ corbiculas' wings brought me through the bright sky/ skilfully home to a safe shelter.'

865   **Lendinara, Patrizia.** 'L'enigma n. 8 del Codice Exoniense.' *Annali Istituto Universitario Orientale di Napoli* 13 sezione germanica (1970): 225–34.

Lendinara defends the solution 'nightingale' for Riddle 8. The supposed 'cen' rune in the margin had undue influence on Dietrich **(662)**, who allowed it to dissuade him from this solution. Similarly influenced has been a succession of more recent solvers who have sought Old English bird-names beginning with *c-*, despite Förster's negative verdict **(185)** on the 'rune'. An emphasis on line 9, with its apparent suggestion of mimicry, has favoured the solution 'jay', but the reading 'scirenige' is unreliable. Riddles 8 and 24 are too dissimilar to have the solution 'jay' in common. Decisive is Riddle 8's emphasis on the bird's singing, where the likeliest source is the description in Pliny's *Natural History* (X.xliii.81–4).

6 Reisner, T.A. 'Riddle 75 (Exeter Book).' *Explicator* 28 (1970): 78–9.

Reisner suggests the application of Julius Caesar's substitution cipher *ad tertiam literam* to the runes in Riddle 75. This yields the reading GROM, i.e. *grom* 'groom, boy, servant', which Reisner regards as a plausible solution.

7 Robinson, Fred C. 'Lexicography and Literary Criticism: a Caveat.' *Philological Essays: Studies in Old and Middle English language and literature in honour of Herbert Dean Meritt*. Ed. James L. Rosier. The Hague: Mouton, 1970. 99–110. Repr. in Fred C. Robinson. *The Tomb of Beowulf and other essays on Old English*. Oxford: Blackwell, 1993. 140–52.

Robinson briefly discusses puns remarked on by Tupper (**727**) in the Exeter Book Riddles, demonstrating that the standard dictionaries do not adequately gloss these words in their double significations. Examples are 'wonge' ('field' or 'cheek' in Riddle 31 line 14), 'blæd' ('breath' or 'prosperity' in Riddle 37 line 7), and 'hæfte' ('handle' or 'confinement' in Riddle 73 line 22). In Riddle 20 the double sense of the poetic language creates the riddling quality as well as the light humour of the poem. The fine equivocation between sword as comrade and as inanimate instrument is brought to perfect balance in line 23, where the sword speaks of its relationship to a 'healdende' ('ruler', but also 'holder') who gave it rings ('hringas' in this context meaning both 'finger-ring' and 'sword-ring').

8 Rollinson, Philip. 'Some Kinds of Meaning in Old English Poetry.' *Annuale Mediaevale* 11 (1970): 5–21.

In his survey of varieties of allegory in Old English poetry, Rollinson notes in passing that the Exeter Book Riddles offer 'examples of literary allegory of a general descriptive nature' (12). A long riddle, such as Riddle 40, might exhibit a variety of the tropes subsumed under 'allegory' in the taxonomies of Bede and Isidore (9–10).

9 Whitman, Frank H. 'Medieval Riddling. Factors Underlying its Development.' *Neuphilologische Mitteilungen* 71 (1970): 177–85.

Whitman considers the Exeter Book Riddles as manifestations of verbal wit. He concedes that a few of them are exceptional among medieval riddles for their artistic appeal. In Riddles 1–3 ('storm'), 33 ('iceberg'), and 60 ('reed') artistic suggestiveness has prevailed over the ingenuity characteristic of the oral riddle. Nonetheless, many of the Riddles are undistinguished efforts designed chiefly to trick the reader about an object that anyone should recognize. Such verbal wit appears to have enjoyed a period of unusual popularity in the early Middle Ages. This popularity can be attributed partly to a decadence in the composers of Latin verse, from the third century onwards, and partly to the widespread use of poetic texts as a means of teaching grammar and rhetoric in the Middle Ages. Latin riddles are quite commonly associated with grammatical tracts, for use at an elementary pedagogical level. Riddles also belonged naturally in the encyclopaedic tradition. Everything in the world, regardless of how trivial, bore the marks of the Creator and therefore deserved study. This may account for the frequent evocation of 'wonder' in the Exeter Book Riddles.

870   **Kispert, Robert J.** *Old English: An Introduction.* New York: Holt, 1971. x + 275 pp.

Kispert's selection of texts includes three riddles (7, 50, and 66). He supplies a brief introduction and annotations.

871   **Whitman, Frank H.** 'Riddle 60 and its Source.' *Philological Quarterly* 50 (1971): 108–15.

Symphosius 2 ('reed') provides the most reliable clue as to the solution of Riddle 60. Scholars who favour 'runic message' over 'reed (pen)' have neglected to ensure objectivity by comparing the Riddle's motifs with analogues in other texts. Envisaged is a reed growing in a marshy area around the mouth of a tidal river. Being a poor Latinist, the Anglo-Saxon adaptor of Symphosius misunderstood motifs that relate to the flute as relating to the pen. As to line 17, two speakers are intended: one the writing process and the other the reader (who could be a scribe reading the text aloud while writing).

872   **Bridier, Yvonne.** 'La Fonction Sociale du Horn chez les Anglo-Saxons.' *Études Anglaises* 25 (1972): 74–7.

Bridier briefly refers to the 'horn' riddles (14 and 80), suggesting that the beverage envisaged here might be a decoction of wine and mulberry juice.

873   **Parkes, M.B.** 'The Manuscript of the Leiden Riddle.' *Anglo-Saxon England* 1 (1972): 207–17.

Parkes reports on the results of a re-examination of the manuscript. The conditions chosen were such as to minimize the effects of the reagent used by Pluygers. Parkes offers his own transcription, with various new readings and notes on the more difficult passages. He interprets the evidence of the pen trials on the manuscript page differently from Gerritsen (**861**). He concludes that the text of the Riddle was almost certainly added to the manuscript at Fleury in the tenth century.

874   **Swann, Brian.** 'Anglo-Saxon Riddles.' *Antaeus* 7 (1972): 12–17.

In his introduction to a set of translations Swann urges the literary claims of the Exeter Book Riddles. Adams (**840**) is the only scholar to have perceived that these riddles are the lyrics of Anglo-Saxon poetry. Riddle 27 'has a secular vigour and inventiveness which leaves any didactic purpose somewhere in its wake' (12). Swann suggests comparisons with the poetry of Góngora. 'A crossword-puzzle has no value outside its solution. Not so these riddles' (12). The Riddles can be sinister (Riddles 4, 9, and 28), gentle (Riddle 8), flamboyant (Riddle 14), or sacramental (Riddle 38). 'And always there is a sense of something beyond, something defying solution' (13).

875   **Anderson, Earl R.** 'Voices in the "Husband's Message".' *Neuphilologische Mitteilungen* 74 (1973): 238–46.

Anderson includes Riddle 35 among instances of Old English prosopopoeia in which the personified object refers to itself in the third person. He points out that the paradox of speaking without a mouth, as in Riddle 60, or without a tongue, as in Riddle 48, is conventionally associated with written messages in Old English personification and prosopopoeia. In his opinion Riddle 60 should be kept separate from *The Husband's Message*.

'6 Cherniss, Michael D. 'The Cross as Christ's Weapon: the Influence of Heroic Literary Tradition on *The Dream of the Rood.*' *Anglo-Saxon England* 2 (1973): 241–52.

In passing, Cherniss disputes the solution of Riddle 55 as 'cross' **(768)**. He argues that the reference within the Riddle to 'rode tacn' would 'destroy the enigmatic quality desired in a riddle' (247). Other Exeter Book Riddles are also mentioned.

'7 Pinsker, Hans. 'Neue Deutungen für zwei altenglische Rätsel (Krapp-Dobbie 17 und 30).' *Anglia* 91 (1973): 11–17.

Pinsker regrets that much scholarly publishing on the Riddles concerns itself with isolated points of the text rather than with translation and interpretation of the text as a whole. As to Riddle 17, he points out errors in Baum's translation **(837)**, dismisses the runic annotations as possible clues to the solution, urges that 'eodor' and 'wirum' (line 2) be treated as separate words, proposes the restoration 'hwilum ic sweartum <nihtum>' (line 7), notes the weaknesses in existing suggestions about the solution, and suggests the new solution 'forge' (11–14). Riddle 30 is to be solved as 'snowflakes'. Certainly snow is not hot (as required by the clue in line 4b), but hands chilled in a blizzard burn as if in fire. Emendations (e.g. 'lyftbysig' for 'leg/ligbysig' in line 1, 'ycan' for 'ywan' in line 9, and 'upcymes' for 'upcyme', also in line 9) are tentatively suggested. They are needed to eliminate manuscript readings that represent mere conjectures on the part of scribes in pursuit of a mistaken solution (15–17).

'8 Whitman, F.H. 'A Major Compositional Technique in Old English Verse.' *English Language Notes* 11 (1973): 81–6.

Whitman argues that translators into Old English verse had recourse to a technique where a word or phrase was added to the literal translation of a unit for the purpose of meeting the alliterative and metrical requirements. Examples are seen in Riddles 35 and 40. In neither case are the additions semantically important. Riddle 1, though not demonstrably a translation, shows the same mode of composition: the number of redundancies is astonishing. In Riddles 2 and 6 the technique has taken on a more flexible form.

'9 Barley, Nigel F. 'Structural Aspects of the Anglo-Saxon Riddle.' *Semiotica* 10 (1974): 143–75.

Barley argues that riddles and jokes are both essentially parasitic on other systems of classification. The riddle questions established systems, whereas the joke turns them on their heads. The riddle performs a metalinguistic function in the discussion of categories. It links the unlike, denies conventional similarities, and generally dissolves barriers between categories. The result is to make us realize that the grid we impose upon the world is far from a perfect fit and not the only one available. Barley distinguishes four basic types among the Exeter Book

Riddles: (1) the metaphoric riddle (Riddles 4 and 13), (2) the joke riddle (Riddle 86), (3) the riddle of generalization (Riddles 39 and 58), and (4) the riddle of negation (Riddle 40).

880   **Joyce, John H.** 'Natural Process in Exeter Book Riddle 29: "Sun and Moon".' *Annuale Mediaevale* 14 (1974): 5–8.

In Joyce's opinion Riddle 29 offers a view of Nature as destroyer and preserver. The sense is one of perpetual activity and of self-sustained natural process. The poet offers no solution to the workings of this process, only awe at its mystery and inscrutability. Among the subtleties of the text is the word 'huðe' ('plunder') in line 4. In context it should be identified as 'light' but it also has the secondary meaning 'home'. The poet knows that the dwelling place of the moon is night or darkness, but ironically the booty she attempts to conceal there is light itself.

881   **Nelson, Marie.** 'The Rhetoric of the Exeter Book Riddles.' *Speculum* 49 (1974): 421–40.

In Nelson's opinion, study of the Riddles militates against the mistaken notion that a patristic orientation applies to all Old English poetry. A comparable error would be to see Freudian interpretation as the only 'correct' approach to modern literature. The Riddles were not performed solely for one audience with one frame of reference. For example, Riddle 34 ('rake') may refer to an anagogical harrowing of sinners but it nonetheless has its basis in a literal raking up of weeds. The composers of the Exeter Book Riddles attempted to produce enigmatic definitions. Many of the poetic devices used in this task, such as prosopopoeia, anaphora, antithesis, and paronomasia, may be derived from Classical rhetoric. Nelson discusses in detail Riddles 7, 11, 12, 24, 28, 39, 47, and 83.

882   **Pope, John C.** 'An Unsuspected Lacuna in the Exeter Book: Divorce Proceedings for an Ill-matched Couple in the Old English Riddles.' *Speculum* 49 (1974): 615–22.

Pope observes that the text printed in ASPR (**194**) as Riddle 70 seems to fall into two mismatched halves. He therefore posits a lacuna after line 4. Decisive is the failure of lines 5 and 6 to make any normal connection with what precedes. Additionally Pope adduces new observations and supporting evidence from the codicology of the Exeter Book. Taking the first four lines as a fragment of Riddle 70a he suggests the solution 'lighthouse' and points to possible influence from Aldhelm 92. Trautmann's (**751**) 'harp' remains the best solution for the fragmentary Riddle 70b.

883   **Shook, Laurence K.** 'Riddles Relating to the Anglo-Saxon Scriptorium.' *Essays in Honour of Anton Charles Pegis.* Ed. J. Reginald O'Donnell. Toronto: Pontifical Institute of Mediaeval Studies, 1974. 215–36.

Shook offers solutions to Exeter Book Riddles 4 ('quill'), 17 ('inkwell'), 18 ('inkwell'), 49 ('pen and ink'), and 57 ('musical notes as notated in a manuscript'). All are related to the activities of the scriptorium. Shook suggests that whereas the Latin riddles were composed for pedagogical purposes, the composition of the Exeter Book Riddles is more likely to represent a diversion on the part of the scribes. One of the serious obstacles to fully satisfactory scholarship on the Exeter Book Riddles over the years has been the determination of scholars to identify the poems of Symphosius, Aldhelm, and the other composers of Latin riddles in their Anglo-Saxon dressing. In reality, the Anglo-Saxon riddles, like most Anglo-Saxon poems, display minimal dependence upon Latin models. In a brief appreciation of the riddle genre in Old English Shook suggests that when the riddling question has been asked, and the surprising senses of its nature grasped, there follows that new intense awareness or epiphany that alone is the core of lyric poetry.

4 Swanton, M.J. *Pages from the Exeter Book.* Exeter: Exeter U Department of English Occasional Papers, 1974. [32 pp.].

The editor explains that the recent discovery of batches of unbound sheets of certain of the collotype plates has made possible the issue of these few folios from the facsimile edition of the Exeter Book (185). Seven folios in all are included, containing *inter alia* the twelve Riddles 84–95. Each manuscript page is accompanied by a typed transcript. [The latter contains evident errors: 'þeohtigra' for 'þreohtigra' in Riddle 85 and 'iii' for 'iiii' in Riddle 90.]

5 Campbell, Jackson J. 'A Certain Power.' *Neophilologus* 59 (1975): 128–38.

Campbell proposes that the so-called 'Storm Riddles' form parts of a unified poem conceived on a largish scale, using the traditional riddle conventions almost incidentally as structuring devices. The speaker (and therefore the solution) is not 'wind' but 'the power of Nature', whose *frea* is God. Campbell doubts that any pervasive allegory is at work in a neat and consistent way throughout the poem. Nevertheless, the internal human violence termed *tempestas spiritus* in Psalm 54 is suggested at various points. The text furnished by Campbell is based on the ASPR edition (194) but with some reinstatement of manuscript readings.

6 Gardner, John. *The Construction of Christian Poetry in Old English.* Carbondale: Southern Illinois UP, 1975. xii + 147 pp.

In Chapter 2 'From the Riddle to the Christian Elegy' (40–53) Gardner analyses an allegorical technique where the image presented is simultaneously literal and iconographic. This technique has its logical beginning in the riddle, whose necessary obfuscation produces a rich or ambiguous verbal texture, seen for example in Riddle 25 ('onion'). Riddles 1–3 exhibit the same rich ambiguity, directed towards producing a sense of awe comparable to that seen in Blake's 'Tyger, Tyger'. Riddle 1, though not specifically referring to the biblical flood, as Baum had asserted (837), has 'overtone solutions' built into it suggesting savagery, exile, and hell. The same nexus of ideas is found in *Beowulf* and in several Cynewulfian poems. Through the storm the poet calls up the whole idea of evil. In Riddles 2–3 (actually one poem and here with line-numbering to reflect that fact) the poet supports his similar characterization of God as chieftain over natural forces by consistently selecting verbal contexts that anthropomorphize Nature. His understanding of cosmology is drawn from Isidore and Pliny, mediated through Bede. A metaphorical identification of the storm and Satan is achieved by the connotations of vocabulary in Riddle 3 lines 1–16. The poem as a consequence dramatizes our human weakness before the power of the devil and our need for God's protection. This type of vertical allegory relied on the reader's sensitivity to the connotations and metaphorical possibilities of vocabulary. Its recognition, where the Anglo-Saxon audience was concerned, remained to some degree optional. Riddle 7 is an instance, since the solution might be identified as either 'swan' or 'soul', depending on how one weighs the connotations of the lexical items used in the text. In Riddle 30 the connection between the tree, the ship, and the cross, all aspects of Blackburn's suggested solution (**698**), functions emblematically. We see an equation of Noah's ship (adumbrative of the Church) and the cross.

887 Goldsmith, Margaret. 'The Enigmas of *The Husband's Message.' Anglo-Saxon Poetry: Essays in Appreciation: for John C. McGalliard.* Ed. Lewis E. Nicholson and Dolores Warwick Frese. Notre Dame: U of Notre Dame P, 1975. 242–63.

Against Blackburn (**698**), Goldsmith argues that Riddle 30b belongs with Riddle 30a and is independent of Riddle 60 and *The Husband's Message.* The mixture of edifying and obscene riddles to be found in the Exeter Book suggests that the principle of signifying one thing by another could be 'stood on its head by waggish spirits' (243). The poet of Riddle 60 seems to have modelled his work on Riddles 53 and 73. In reality, however, Riddle 60 forms the introduction to *The Husband's Message.* Moreover, it constitutes the finest part of the total work, which in its latter part becomes increasingly cerebral. The speaker throughout this work is not a wooden object but a reed pen, symbolizing primarily Holy Writ. In this context, the manuscript reading 'ofer meodu' (line 9) should be reinstated and be understood as meaning both 'in the meadhall' and 'surpassing mead'.

888 Kennedy, Christopher B. 'Old English Riddle No. 39.' *English Language Notes* 13 (1975): 81–5.

Rejecting previous attempts at a solution to Riddle 39 (**658, 751, 727,** and **797**), Kennedy suggests 'cloud'. The word 'sundorcræft' in line 3 would then refer to the cloud's ability to make rain. The ability to comfort human beings mentioned in lines 18–19 is easily explained, for surely it is a universal experience to lie on the grass and to be soothed and comforted by watching clouds form and reform. The Exeter Book Riddles appeal to a perennial element in human nature.

889 Kiernan, K.S. 'Cwene: The Old Profession of Exeter Riddle 95.' *Modern Philology* 72 (1975): 384–90.

Kiernan maintains that earlier recourses to emendation to solve Riddle 95 are unnecessary. The text can be solved as it stands if proper attention is paid to systematic ambiguities in the lexis of the riddle. Thus 'swaþe' in line 12 can be interpreted as 'bandage', 'lastas' in line 11 as 'observances', and 'hiþendra hyht' in line 5 as 'the joy of ravagers'. The latter phrase may possibly represent a kenning for 'sexual gratification'. These interpretations lead to the solution 'prostitute'. Riddle 95 is complementary to *Maxims I* and *II*, which tell women how to act so that they will not be considered prostitutes. A double solution should perhaps be envisaged, since the demonstrably obscene riddles have a second, innocent solution.

0 ————. 'The Mysteries of the Sea-Eagle in Exeter Riddle 74.' *Philological Quarterly* 54 (1975): 518–22.

Kiernan suggests that the creature described in Riddle 74 is a diving bird, probably a white sea-eagle. Using Ambrose's *Hexameron* and the *Physiologus*, he demonstrates that diving birds, such as the eagle, were associated with the Resurrection. Similarly, vultures were associated with parthenogenesis. Tupper's solution (707), 'siren', can be rejected because the Riddle says that the creature is male and female simultaneously.

1 **Lendinara, Patrizia.** 'Poculum mortis: una nota.' *Annali Istituto Universitario Orientale di Napoli* 18 sezione germanica, Filologia germanica (1975): 131–4.

Lendinara emends 'wer' in Riddle 23 line 14 to 'weg' ('cup'), on the analogy of *Guthlac B* lines 987–91b. Since the Exeter Book Riddles are for the most part purely literary productions, emanating from a monastic milieu, the source for the use of a *poculum mortis* topos in this Riddle may lie in the Gospel of St Matthew. The verb 'togangan' ('by-pass, avoid') in line 10 seems to be a recollection of Matt. 26: 39 'Pater, si possibile est, transeat a me calix iste', where *calix* corresponds to 'weg' in the Riddle.

2 ————. 'E se B stesse per "bana"? Una nuova interpretazione dell'enigma n. 17 del Codice Exoniense.' *Annali Istituto Universitario Orientale di Napoli* 18 sezione germanica, Filologia germanica (1975): 161–81. [*B* in the title is printed as runic *B*.]

According to Lendinara, Riddle 17 describes in allegorical terms the daily struggle of humankind against temptation. It uses standard patristic images which recur frequently in other Old English poems and in works, e.g. Gregory's, that were familiar in Anglo-Saxon England. Lendinara posits a double solution, one easy ('fortress') and one hard ('soul'). She compares Hroðgar's 'homily' in *Beowulf*, where we learn that the proud man or soul that does not maintain vigilance will be struck down. Lendinara believes that the Riddles have not been sufficiently read in a biblical or patristic context by previous solvers and that much of their significance has therefore been missed. Thus Riddle 9 is only trivially solved as 'cuckoo': it should preferably be seen as depicting human ingratitude. Equally, the rival solutions 'ballista' and 'fortress' are too obvious in Riddle 17 and it should rather be read on two levels, (1) the assault of the enemy upon a fortress, and (2) the assault of the devil upon the soul (comparable with *Vainglory*). In allusion to the devil, the runic *b* in the manuscript marginalia should be understood as standing for 'bana' ('killer').

3 **Nelson, Marie.** 'Old English Riddle No 15: the "Badger": an Early Example of the Mock Heroic.' *Neophilologus* 59 (1975): 447–50.

Nelson suggests a parallel between this riddle and Chaucer's creation of Chaunticleer. The use of mock heroic includes a suggestion of epic fatedness. In one of a series of reminiscences of heroic poetry, the badger must defend a narrow place. His 'beorg' ('hill') in line 18 is his 'burg' ('fortress').

894 ———. 'Time in the Exeter Book Riddles.' *Philological Quarterly* 54 (1975): 511–18.

Nelson seeks to show that one of the features distinguishing the Exeter Book Riddles (e.g. Riddles 1–3, 5, and 72) from their Latin counterparts is a greater consciousness of time. Poetic devices, among them anaphora, variation, and the 'envelope' patterns commented on by Bartlett (25), could be used to provide a sense of duration or futurity or of arrested time. Nelson adds Riddle 1 to Bartlett's list of riddles exhibiting the envelope pattern.

895 **Quirk, Randolph, Valerie Adams, and Derek Davy.** *Old English Literature: A Practical Introduction.* London: Arnold, 1975. 79 pp.

Included in this student reader are Riddles 10, 61, and 86, with notes and a facing-page vocabulary list (62–3). A general glossary and brief introduction to the entire volume are also provided. Riddle 86 is shown in both Old English orthography and a reconstructed IPA transcription (11).

896 **Robinson, Fred C.** 'Artful Ambiguities in the Old English "Book-Moth" Riddle.' *Anglo-Saxon Poetry: Essays in Appreciation: for John C. McGalliard.* Ed. Lewis E. Nicholson and Dolores Warwick Frese. Notre Dame: U of Notre Dame P, 1975. 355–62. Repr. in Fred C. Robinson. *The Tomb of Beowulf and other essays on Old English.* Oxford: Blackwell, 1993. 98–104.

Robinson suggests that in Riddle 47 the poet has used a series of related and highly functional verbal ambiguities to develop a specific theme, the simultaneous reality and insubstantiality of language. Thus 'swealg' can mean not only 'swallowed' but also 'assimilated' (e.g. of wisdom). If we accept this interpretation the final clause of the riddle becomes a genuine paradox. The word 'staþol', similarly, can suggest 'intellectual basis' as well as 'page'; furthermore, 'wyrd' can mean 'speech' as well as 'fate'. Associative processes might have led the audience from 'cwide' ('utterance') to 'cwidu' ('thing chewed'). A postulated play on the idea of darkness is compared with Aldhelm 89 ('bookcase'). Robinson cites *Solomon and Saturn* as a repository of standard wisdom on books. This complexity of meaning offsets the otherwise embarrassing straightforwardness of the Riddle.

897 **Schneider, Karl.** 'Zu vier ae. Rätseln.' *Gedenkschrift für Jost Trier.* Ed. Hartmut Beckers and Hans Schwarz. Cologne: Böhlau, 1975. 330–54.

Schneider lists the Exeter Book Riddles that in his opinion have so far been convincingly solved (30 out of a total of 95). He blames this relative lack of success on what he sees as current weaknesses in interpretive method, along with excessive obscurity on the part of the poet. Some riddles appear difficult to us because they refer to objects or behaviours that had their currency in older, now forgotten, stages of the culture. Thus in Riddle 30a 'legbysig' is to be interpreted as a metaphor for 'producing/growing twigs'. Other phrases involving fire and burning in the Riddle likewise point to a solution 'birch'. We should envisage this birch as passed from hand to hand in an originally heathen May ceremony. Riddle 92 can be solved as 'yew', with reference to the Old Norse Yggdrasill: the phrase 'gold on geardum' in line 4 refers to the characteristic golden-yellow blossoms on this tree. Riddle 70 is to be solved as 'harp' but with the understanding that a pun on a farming implement of the same name is intended. Riddle 50 alludes to the production of fire by friction between two pieces of wood, to combat evil spirits.

Stewart, Ann Harleman. 'Old English Riddle 47 as Stylistic Parody.' *Papers on Language and Literature* 11 (1975): 227–41.

Stewart suggests that the Old English poet regarded the riddle form as no more than a vehicle for various kinds of poetry, among them parody. The anomalies of Riddle 47, as contrasted with Symphosius 16 ('bookworm'), can be explained if we assume that the poet observed the letter but not the spirit of the riddle genre. The real purpose was not to mystify but to construct a parody of Old English heroic poetry. In general the Old English riddle, as a genre, resists precise formulation. The device of paradox, for example, may be used both to obscure the subject of the riddle and to place it in a new perspective.

Whitman, Frank H. 'The Meaning of "Formulaic" in Old English Verse Composition.' *Neuphilologische Mitteilungen* 76 (1975): 529–37.

Whitman argues that an examination of Old English poetic texts based on Latin sources discloses a twofold compositional process: first, literal translation of a Latin unit, and second, the addition of words that either are semantically empty or do not advance the meaning significantly, in the key alliterative slots. This observation can be generalized across other Old English poetic texts. The outcome is to suggest that the notion of formulaic composition should be restricted to a recurrent use of words and phrases. These components, although functional from a metrical standpoint, add nothing to the meaning of a verse. Whitman identifies the fillers to be found in Riddle 40 lines 6–15, noting the use of doublets to fill the alliterative slots. Thus 'ærest' in line 2, repeating the idea in 'æt frymþe' in line 1, carries alliteration. Whitman dissents from Benson's **(842)** analysis of formularity in Riddle 35 lines 1 and 2. The doublets in Riddle 42 lines 1–8a are also tentatively identified, with the comment that the word 'wlanc' (line 4) is 'in some ways inappropriate because it inverts the traditional motif of the cock's pride' (537).

Williams, Edith Whitehurst. 'The Relation between Pagan Survivals and Diction in Two Old English Riddles.' *Philological Quarterly* 54 (1975): 664–70.

The Riddles often display a powerful personification. Formative here was a pre-Christian belief in animism which had not been uprooted or even very much diluted in Anglo-Saxon England. In Riddles 1–3 a Christian interpretation is not mandatory, since certain key words, such as 'frea' (Riddle 3 lines 1 and 66) and 'latteow' (Riddle 1 line 11), can be seen as secular. The word 'meotud' in Riddle 3 line 54 points to Fate, a relentless, even malevolent, spirit, who cannot be reconciled with a beneficent God. Riddle 84 shows a lack of integration between Christian and non-Christian: the depiction of water as matriarch evokes the old animism. Although line 39 describes a ritual cleansing, it need not be the Christian baptism. Respect for etymology, Williams thinks, is the key to success with this type of investigation.

901 ———. 'What's so New about the Sexual Revolution? Some Comments on Anglo-Saxon Attitudes towards Sexuality in Women Based on Four Exeter Book Riddles.' *Texas Quarterly* 18 (1975): 46–55.

Williams argues from some double-entendre riddles (25, 45, 61, and 91) that sexual pleasure clearly lay in the province of women in Anglo-Saxon England and that they are not portrayed as degraded or exploited in this context. The dark-haired woman of Riddle 12 is only an apparent exception; she is degraded because she is Welsh, not because she is female. In Riddle 25 the woman is portrayed as a lively participant: the alliterating verbs 'ræseð' and 'reafað' (line 8) imply not only willingness but aggressiveness. Williams proposes solving Riddle 91 as 'key-hole', not 'key'. Here she interprets 'begine' (line 3) as meaning 'open wide' and as alluding to the vagina within the double entendre scheme. This riddle, offering the strongest argument of all for the mutuality of the sex experience, was perhaps composed by a woman.

902 **Foley, John Miles.** ' "Riddle 1" of the Exeter Book: The Apocalyptic Storm.' *Neuphilologische Mitteilungen* 77 (1976): 347–57.

In Foley's view, Riddles 1–3 are a unit. Dietrich's solution (**658**), 'storm', needs to be enlarged to the hyperbolical scale of the archetypal storm of the Apocalypse. In amplifying the pagan Storm-giant motif, the poet concurs with the millennial sentiment observable in the Riddles and elsewhere in Old English verse. The winds were thought of as originating in caves, as is evident in the writings of Pliny and Lucretius. The manuscript reading 'heanu<m> meahtum' in Riddle 1 line 10 is therefore to be defended. The three answers requested by the speaker are: God the Father, Christ, and the Cross. Riddle-making as we see it in the Exeter Book is undergoing an epistemological change from Wyrd to God.

903 **Hume, Kathryn.** 'The "Ruin Motif" in Old English Poetry.' *Anglia* 94 (1976): 339–60.

Hume makes incidental references to the 'storm' motif seen in Riddles 1–3.

904 **Jember, Gregory K.** *The Old English Riddles: A New Translation.* Denver: Society for New Language Study, 1976.

[Not seen. Fry (**936**) lists the following suggested new solutions: Riddle 1 'raiding party', 2 'anchor' (following Grein, **2**), 3 'revenant', 4 'phallus', 5 'guilt', 6 'guilt and conscience', 7 'soul', 8 'crying baby', 9 'conception and birth/revenant/soul', 10 'alchemy/baptism', 11 'phallus', 14 'man', 17 'phallus', 18 'phallus?', 20 and 21 'phallus', 22 'rite of passage', 23 and 25 'phallus', 27 'sleep?', 28 'trial of soul', 30 'phallus', 31 'harp', 33 'archetypal feminine', 34 and 37 'phallus', 38 'man', 39 'revenant', 44 and 45 'phallus', 47 'demon', 48 'bell/sacramental vessel', 49 'barrow, sacrificial altar', 50 'phallus?', 51 'alchemy', 53 'phallus', 54 'phallus/intercourse', 55 'tetraktys', 56 'execution', 57 'damned souls', 58 'phallus', 60 'revenant', 61 'vagina', 62 'phallus', 65 'revenant, spirit', 71 'revenant', 72 'slave?', 73 'revenant, spirit', 77 'female genitalia', 80 'phallus', 81 'man', 83 'revenant, spirit', 85 'body and soul', 87 'phallus', 88 'body and soul', 89 and 91 'phallus'. For the method and philosophy underlying these solutions see **911**.]

5 **Lendinara, Patrizia.** 'Gli enigmi del Codice Exoniense: una ricerca bibliografica.' *Annali Istituto Universitario Orientale di Napoli* 19 sezione germanica, Filologia germanica (1976): 231–329.

Lendinara acknowledges the bibliography to the Exeter Book Riddles in the ASPR edition **(194)** but registers some problems with its use (231 n. 2). She expresses the hope that the ensuing bibliography will act as a corrective to the paralysing scholarly tendency to study the Riddles en bloc or solely in quest of an author or a series of solutions (232). Rather, each Riddle should be subjected to a literary analysis in its own right as a separate short poem. There is no reason to deny the individual Riddles the detailed attention that has been accorded to the other shorter poems in the Exeter Book. Another adverse influence has been the type of romantic criticism that credits the Riddles with a popular, non-monastic origin (233). In the remainder of the article Lendinara furnishes a comprehensive list of studies, including some that make only incidental references to the Riddles. Some entries are very briefly annotated.

6 ———. 'Ags. wlanc: alcune annotazioni.' *Annali Istituto Universitario Orientale di Napoli* 19 sezione germanica, Filologia germanica (1976): 53–81.

Lendinara extends her investigation of the adjective 'wlanc' **(892)** to argue that the authors of the Exeter Book Riddles availed themselves of the potential ambiguity of this word in riddles that were designed to be read on two different levels. Lendinara resists the emendation of '-wlonc' to '-wolcn' in Riddle 73 line 2 but accepts it in Riddle 84 line 26. In Riddle 25 the innocent solution ('onion') and the not-so-innocent solution co-exist. To accommodate them both '-wlonc' (line 7) must be understood as both 'proud' and 'dedicated to sensual pleasures'. In some other texts, such as Riddles 12 and 45, the same slippage of meaning may be observed. But further meanings are possible too, e.g. 'ardent in faith' in Riddle 30 line 6. Lendinara solves Riddle 19 as descriptive of a hand writing on a manuscript sheet with a pen.

7 **Meyvaert, Paul.** 'The Solution to Old English Riddle 39.' *Speculum* 51 (1976): 195–201.

Meyvaert points out that nearly all the elements of Aldhelm 3 ('cloud') are also found in Riddle 39. The Old English poet may have adopted additional motifs from Aldhelm 71 ('fish'). An important clue in the Riddle is that its subject appears on great occasions. The Bible furnishes numerous possible sources for this idea, the most obvious being the cloud that took Christ to heaven at his ascension. Meyvaert notes that his article was written independently of Kennedy **(888)**, who reached the same solution on different grounds.

8 **Dauenhauer, Richard, Marijane Osborn, and Roni Keller.** 'From the Anglo-Saxon Riddles; from the Old English, the Exeter Book, #7 and #10; from

the Old English Riddle #47; from the Old English, the Exeter Book, #31 and #61.' *Hyperion* (1976): 72–4.

In this volume of *Hyperion*, which draws together translations from a variety of sources, the desideratum is 'fine versions of some classic poems' (iii). Riddle 7 is given in two translations, one by Dauenhauer and one by Osborn. Osborn also translates Riddles 10, 31, and 61 and follows Jember (**904**) in solving the latter two as 'harp' and 'vagina' respectively. Keller translates Riddle 47, of which lines 1–4 are as follows: 'This moth swallowed down someone's song,/ a person's poetry, that poacher after nightfall;/ took an immortal motto and made off with the pulp,/ very substance of its power. He made a voice mute' (73).

909 Crossley-Holland, Kevin. 'Seven Questionable Riddles.' *Ambit* 71 (1977): 26–34.

This set of translations comprises Riddles 25, 44, 45, 54, 61, 62, and 37. Crossley-Holland alleges that scholars have been eager to postulate alternative, safe solutions for this group of obscene riddles. The safe solutions are: (1) Onion; (2) Key; (3) Dough; (4) Churn; (5) Helmet or Coat of Mail; (6) Gimlet or Poker; (7) Bellows. Ralph Steadman contributes illustrations. Sample translation from Riddle 62 (lines 1–4): 'I'm strong and pointed. Shuddering I die,/ a violent release. For my reputable master/ I'll plunge below the plimpsoll line,/ well and truly engineer an opening.'

910 Foley, John Miles. 'Riddles 53, 54, and 55: an Archetypal Symphony in Three Movements.' *Studies in Medieval Culture* 11 (1977): 25–31.

Foley contends that Riddles 53, 54, and 55 use three distinctly different metaphors to describe precisely one archetypal process – the act of entry and impregnation. He endorses the standard solutions, respectively, 'battering-ram', 'butter-churn', and 'cross/gallows', but suggests that in Riddle 54 the poet intended to correlate the act of procreation with that of churning butter, not to subordinate the former to the latter. The cross of Riddle 55 fits the 'entry and impregnation' archetype because it is by means of the cross that souls are saved and therefore brought into heaven. Christ on the cross is seen as undergoing the punishment of an outlaw, hence the word 'wulfheafedtreo' (line 12). Such a meaningful collocation of three riddles should be seen as constituting a new genre that over-arches the old dichotomy between popular riddle and literary riddle (*Volksrätsel* and *Kunsträtsel*).

911 Jember, Gregory K. 'A Generative Method for the Study of Anglo-Saxon Riddles.' *Studies in Medieval Culture* 11 (1977): 33–9.

Jember argues that traditional rational-empirical approaches to riddles cannot provide verifiable exclusive solutions because riddles are not themselves consistently rational or empirical. Would-be solvers of riddles must stand outside their own consciousness and history. The fact that the composition of the Riddles took place during the transition from pagandom to Christianity puts them in what Eliade would term a 'boundary' situation. The meanings of specific lexical items are in flux and systematic punning is always a possibility. To exemplify his contentions, Jember explores the possible multiple meanings of 'goman' in

Riddle 49 line 6. In solving Riddle 21 exclusively as 'plough' we concentrate with undue empiricism on the physical object. Instead, a 'generative' solution, 'phallus', ought to be seen as underlying the immediate physical solution. Similarly, Riddle 60 should be seen as possessing the 'generative' solution 'revenant/spirit'. This solution underlies the physical solutions, such as 'reed pen', that are customarily suggested. On the basis of these ideas, Jember proposes a new system of classification for the Exeter Book Riddles.

2 **Russom, Geoffrey.** 'Exeter Riddle 47: a Moth Laid Waste to Fame.' *Philological Quarterly* 56 (1977): 129–36.

Russom considers that too much attention has been paid to the Riddle genre at the expense of the individual Riddles, which should be analysed carefully as separate works of art. Riddle 47 follows its model, Symphosius 16 ('bookworm'), in punning on verbs to do with eating. The Old English version is distinctive, however, because the audience's problem is to divine that written words are intended. They were apt to be distracted by the fact that 'cwide', 'gied', and the other terms employed in the Riddle normally refer to the spoken word. By directing a grim irony on the Germanic ideal of immortality through poetry, this Riddle instructs its audience to seek true immortality and glory in Heaven. In such a teaching it is comparable to *Homiletic Fragment I* and other similar poems.

3 **Schneider, Karl.** 'Zu den altenglischen Runenrätseln des Exeter Book.' *Commentationes linguisticae et philologicae Ernesto Dickenmann lustrum claudenti quintum decimum.* Ed. Friedrich Scholz, Wilma Woesler, and Peter Gerlinghoff. Heidelberg: Winter, 1977. 345–82.

Schneider differentiates between one group of poems where runic characters are used consistently (Riddles 19, 24, 64, and 75) and another group where transliteration into the Roman alphabet has occurred (Riddles 42 and 58). Schneider also excludes Riddle 75 from his set of genuine runic riddles. Against Eliason (**816**), careful inspection of the manuscript shows that 'hund' (not 'hlnd') is the sequence of letters intended. Probably this word originated as a marginal indication of the solution. Riddle 58 is tentatively solved as **ridrod* 'moving pole'. Riddle 42 alludes to the primitive significance of the rune-names. Thus *nyd* 'fire-drill' bears the metaphorical meaning 'membrum virile', consistent with the theme of copulation in the Riddle.

4 **Tripp, Raymond P., Jr.** 'The Effect of the Occult and the Supernatural upon the Way we read Old English Poetry.' *Literature and the Occult: Essays in Comparative Literature.* Ed. Luanne Frank. U of Texas at Arlington Publications in Literature, Department of English. Arlington, Texas: U of Texas at Arlington, 1977. 255–63.

Tripp urges us to avoid projecting our own commonplaces on to the Anglo-Saxon imagination and to approach Old English poems as epistemological riddles. Many of the locative expressions in the shorter poems of the Exeter Book ('among the people', 'in houses' etc.) seem to involve the idea of here and alive as opposed to elsewhere and dead. The admission of the supernatural as a viable possibility in readings of Riddle 49 reveals 'altar' (perhaps one for human sacrifice) as a candidate solution. Similarly, Riddle 7 can be solved as both 'swan' and 'soul' (261–3).

915 **Whitman, Frank H.** 'Significant Motifs in Riddle 53.' *Medium Aevum* 46 (1977): 1–11.

The generally accepted solution, 'battering ram', is, in Whitman's opinion, superficial and does not suit the word 'fæcnum' ('deceitfully') in line 8. This word should be read as an adverb, not construed adjectivally with 'hildegieste' (line 9). A medieval audience would have solved the Riddle as 'Cross', since all the motifs are to be found associated with the subject in the writings of the period. Significant are 'the joyous tree', 'the mutilated tree', 'the clearing of a way', 'deceit', and 'plundering the hoard'. Who the 'hildegieste' is cannot be established positively, because many different interpretations are possible, among them Christ, the Church Militant, and the Good Thief. Riddle 55 is definitely also on the subject of the Cross, and Riddle 73 may be as well.

916 **Williamson, Craig.** *The Old English Riddles of the Exeter Book.* Chapel Hill: U of North Carolina P, 1977. xx + 484 pp + 23 plates.

In the Introduction to this edition of the Exeter Book Riddles (3–62), Williamson gives notice that his system of enumeration differs from ASPR **(194)**. This reflects his decision to combine several riddles or riddle fragments (Riddles 1, 66, 73, and 76) hitherto printed separately (3). In his discussion of the date, authorship, and general provenance of the Riddles Williamson argues that Sievers **(683)** exaggerated the reliability of linguistic criteria and underestimated the extent to which the poet might have taken liberties with the traditional norms of Old English metre. It is not impossible that the bulk of the Old English riddles came to be written as the result of literary communication between the circles of Aldhelm in Wessex and King Aldfrith of Northumbria. Hypotheses that riddling was a well-established aspect of early English oral poetry have no evidential basis. The authors of the Riddles were, in addition to their other attributes, learned men with access to medieval writings on philosophy and natural history (5–12). Williamson's text is based on direct consultation of the Exeter Book and the 1831–2 Robert Chambers transcript. The editorial policy is conservative, especially in respect of emendations *metri causa*. Modern punctuation is used to clarify the editor's interpretation of syntactic relationships. After a full discussion of manuscript punctuation Williamson concludes that points may carry metrical, rhetorical, syntactic, or palaeographical significance. The scribe tends to point where a point might be indicated by more than one category of significance (12–19). Modern scholarship on the Riddles is briefly reviewed, with some criticism of Tupper's **(727)** comparative and folkloristic leanings (19–23). In his discussion of the form and substance of the Riddles (24–8) Williamson agrees with Ker **(121)** that they assumed distinct Old English qualities of imaginative portrayal and projection and the power of a dramatic, literary game. This was so even though they derived from a Latin literary tradition of riddling. Differing from Kennedy's **(29)** emphasis on realism in the Riddles, Williamson proposes that what they mean is that reality exists and is at the same time a mosaic of human perception. The poets of the Riddles were imbued with a native strain of negative capability which allowed them to celebrate in human, poetic terms the nonhuman world about them. In appendices to the Introduction (31–62), the use of accents, capitals, and points is minutely documented; twenty-three plates illustrate the runic annotations, offset blotting, and other features of the manuscript. For the most part, the marginalia seem not to have been penned by the scribe of the main text. Williamson's text (63–121) is followed by a very full section of notes and commentary, with emphasis on the history of attempts to solve the Riddles and with some suggestions concerning the contribution to be made in this direction by recent archaeological findings (123–402). The following comments and new solutions are especially notable: Williamson defends the interpretation of Riddles 1–3 as one riddle with the solution 'wind' (**188**). The decision on the part of many editors to print three 'storm' riddles with five or six different 'storm' solutions reflects the modern scientific inability to see the wind in rain-storms, thunder, lightning, earthquakes, submarine quakes, sea storms, and the like. Riddle 6 draws upon the tradition of the Christ-like sun, acting as both a blessing and a scourge to human beings, after the fashion described in Isidore's *De Natura Rerum*. Riddle 7, despite Dietrich (**658**), may be derived from contemporary Anglo-Saxon observation of swans rather than a Mediterranean source. Williamson argues against Young's (**793**) suggestion of 'weasel' for Riddle 15 and against Pinsker's (**877**) suggestion of 'forge' for Riddle 17. Riddle 18 is solved as 'jug (amphora)', using archaeological evidence, and Riddle 19 as 'ship'. In runic passages like those contained in Riddle 19 the poet sometimes took metrical liberties not seen elsewhere. Riddle 28 is solved, with query, as 'yew-horn', i.e. a horn made of yew, a suggestion based on a recent archaeological find in Northern Ireland. Riddle 39 is solved as 'speech': 'I believe that the key to this riddle lies in the deliberate ambiguity of lines 24b–25a . . . which may be translated either as "That is a marvellous thing to be told" or as "Speaking is a marvellous thing" ' (259). In Riddle 41 'water' Williamson argues against Konick (**781**), who has misread 'the trial strokes in the lower margin of folio 111b as part of the text' (276). In Riddle 47 the poet is concerned 'with the mutability of songs as they pass from the traditional wordhord of the scop into the newer and strangely susceptible form of literate memoria' (285). Williamson points out the difficulties in Shook's (**883**) solution of Riddle 49. Although noting Kaske's (**852**) deployment of a 'symphony of patrological learning' (315) in examining Riddle 60, Williamson expresses some sympathy with his and Goldsmith's (**887**) views. Some other solutions: Riddle 64: 'ship', with the runic clue 'EASP' interpreted as 'easpor' ('water-track'). Riddle 68: 'iceberg'. Riddle 74: 'ship's figurehead' (comparable to the human figure-heads to be seen in the Bayeux Tapestry). Riddles 75–6: 'piss'. Riddle 78: 'lamprey' (with query). Riddles 79–80: 'horn'. Riddle 82: 'harrow' (comparable with the one shown in the Bayeux Tapestry). Riddle 90: 'web and loom' (with wordplay on Old English *wulflys* 'fleece of wool' and with an explanation of the phrase 'septem oculis' as loomweights). Riddle 95: 'book with gilding'. In the latter case Williamson argues against Kiernan's (**889**) solution 'prostitute'. A glossary, bibliography, and index of solutions are also included.

Jember, Gregory K. 'Riddle 57: A New Proposal.' *In Geardagum* 2 (1978 *for* 1977): 68–73.

In Jember's opinion the solution of Riddle 57 would appear to be not birds, insects, or natural phenomena, but rather a swarm of demons or souls of the damned. Similar characterizations are seen in Anglo-Saxon hagiographic, homiletic, historical, and poetic texts. The word *cirm-* has sinister and demonic connotations. Similarly, the correct solution to Riddle 8 would appear to be 'the devil as buffoon'.

918 Crossley-Holland, Kevin. *The Exeter Riddle Book.* London: Folio Society, 1978. 139 pp. Repr. as *The Exeter Book Riddles.* Harmondsworth: Penguin, 1979.

Crossley-Holland includes a general introduction to the Exeter Book Riddles. The notes evaluate the different solutions. A new solution is 'house-martins' for Riddle 57. He follows Jember (**904**) in the solution 'phallus' for Riddle 62. A few literary-critical comments are also offered. The Anglo-Saxon cast of mind and literary mode seems ideally suited to the metaphorical riddle when one considers that the entire body of Old English poetry is packed out with mini-riddles. These mini-riddles are known as kennings, and are in fact condensed metaphors. All except five textually lacunose riddles are translated. Sample translation from Riddle 7 (lines 1–4): 'Silent is my dress when I step across the earth,/ reside in my house, or ruffle the waters./ Sometimes my adornments and this high windy air/ lift me over the livings of men/. . .' [For a review see Cooper, **935**.]

919 ———. 'Riddle 40: Creation.' *Tablet* 2 Sept. 1978: 848.

A sample of this translation of Riddle 40 (lines 1–4): 'Enduring the Creator, He who now guides/ this earth on its foundations and governs this world./ Powerful is the Ruler, and properly King/ and Sovereign over all. . .'

920 ———. 'Riddles from the Exeter Book.' *Tablet* 11 Feb. 1978: 130.

Crossley-Holland translates Riddles 22, 46, 67, and 94. The following (Riddle 46 lines 1–4) is a sample: 'A man got sozzled with his two wives,/ his two sons and his two daughters,/ darling sisters, and with their two sons,/ favoured first-born. . .'

921 Göbel, Heidi and Rüdiger. 'The Solution of an Old English Riddle.' *Studia Neophilologica* 50 (1978): 185–91.

The authors propose a new solution for Riddle 28, 'pattern-welded sword'. The details of the Riddle text are correlated with the steps in the process of pattern-welding. In line 4 the iron is shown as cut to form rods ('corfen'), smoothed ('sworfen'), twisted ('cyrred'), and alternately cooled and heated ('þyrred'). Being springy, the iron blade could be called resilient ('wæced' in line 5). In lines 9–12 the point of view changes from that of a proud owner to that of a victim.

922 Marino, Matthew. 'The Literariness of the Exeter Book Riddles.' *Neuphilologische Mitteilungen* 79 (1978): 258–65.

Marino maintains that the Exeter Book Riddles have been excluded from serious literary consideration and seeks to rescue them. He coins the term 'deceit' (in contrast to Donne's 'conceit') to denote their primary structural device.

Characteristically, the paradox of apparently contradictory referents is sustained by the yoking of disparate elements until the misapprehension engendered in the audience yields to significance at the solution. Noteworthy among the examples cited are Riddle 50, which Marino uses as a case study in the elaboration of a single 'deceit', and Riddles 4 and 27. Riddles 40 and 66 are briefly compared with other Old English poems on 'creation'.

3 **Nelson, Marie.** 'The Paradox of Silent Speech in the Exeter Book Riddles.' *Neophilologus* 62 (1978): 609–15.

In such Exeter Book Riddles as 85 ('fish and river'), 48 ('chalice'), and 60 ('reed pen') the speaker claims to communicate meaning without sound. This is part of a pattern where some Riddles avoid a requirement to choose between certain routine binary oppositions that is normally entailed within the language and culture. The double subject of Riddle 85 is another form taken by this evasion of binary choices. Riddles 48 and 60 are, according to Nelson, the riddles that exploit the paradox of silent speech to the fullest degree, the latter through a supplementation of the Symphosius 2 ('reed'), which does not contain this paradox.

4 **Ryan, William M.** 'Let the Riddles Be Your Key.' *New Letters: A Magazine of Fine Writing* 45.1 (1978): 107–12.

Ryan suggests the Exeter Book Riddles as a way of wooing students into the study of Old English. They have the advantages of brevity and also, as in the case of Riddle 47, of conscious design and aesthetic effects. Moreover, the Riddles must contain attractions for non-specialists of the sort who thrive on enigmatists like Joyce and Nabokov. Williamson's **(916)** edition, despite blemishes, offers the best access to the Riddles.

5 **Walters, Frank.** 'Language Structure and the Meanings of the Exeter Book Riddles.' *Ball State University Forum* 19.3 (1978): 42–55.

Walters believes that no significant body of scholarship attempts to equate the language structures of the Exeter Book Riddles with their moral statements. A reader's decision to select one solution over another (key, not penis, for example, or vice versa) is evidence of the riddle-master's neat semantic trap. Tension between the two possibilities makes it impossible for the reader to arrive at a final solution; the alternative solution will always suggest itself. A language which purports to adhere to the paradigm is in tension with one which departs from the paradigm to criticize the riddling mode. Riddle 47 ('bookmoth') involves its reader in this tension.

Wells, Richard. 'The Old English Riddles and their Ornithological Content.' *Lore and Language* 2.9 (1978): 57–67.

Wells lists references to birds in the Riddles as they contribute to an understanding of the 'impact of birds' (57) upon Anglo-Saxon society. He supposes that whereas Riddle 9 ('cuckoo') represents material derived from the experience of others, the natural beauty of Riddle 7 ('swan') could only be attained through the poet's personal experience, observation, and appreciation of the bird itself. Among the specific solutions he recommends is 'nightingale' for Riddle 8, since the nightingale can appear to imitate other birds. For Riddle 24 it is difficult to choose between 'jay' and 'green woodpecker'. He suggests solving Riddle 57 as 'blackbirds' (*turdus merula*): the words 'tredað bearonæssas' (line 5) describe the sight and sound of blackbirds rummaging among dead leaves.

927 Haarder, Andreas. *Det episke liv.* Copenhagen: Berlingske Forlag, 1979. 153 pp.

Haarder discusses Riddle 27 in the context of a general thesis that all Old English poetry bears the impress of heroic poetry. He traces allusions to battle poetry in the Riddle. Additionally, he offers a broad account of the riddle genre in its Old English literary context. A prose translation into Danish is supplied.

928 Jember, Gregory K. 'Proposed Restorations in Riddle 48.' *In Geardagum* 3 (1979): 91–3.

Jember suggests reading 'ic gefrægn for hæleþum hringende an torht/ ne butan tungan' in Riddle 48 lines 1–2, incorporating 'torht' into line 1 from ASPR (**194**) line 2 and combining this word with 'an' to form a semi-adverbial phrase, translatable as 'clearly'. This reading would be in conformity with the Exeter Book, which contains an elevated period after 'an' and after 'torht'.

929 Stewart, Ann Harleman. 'Kenning and Riddle in Old English.' *Papers on Language and Literature* 15 (1979): 115–36.

Stewart contends that whereas the ostensible likeness between the kenning and the riddle lies in mystification, there is an ultimately truer and more important (but less recognized) likeness that lies in recognition. She cites Riddles 23 and 47 as instances where mystification is not even attempted. But even if the individual riddle is utterly obscure, the literary outcome is similar: an enhanced perception of the world. The impossibility of finding a single correct solution to Riddle 28 (including Stewart's own new suggestion, 'woman') should be our cue towards considering the poem not as a puzzle but as a 'lovely lyric' characterized by play with images and sounds and by a delight in the intricacy and variousness of the world (135).

930 Alexander, Michael. *Old English Riddles from the Exeter Book.* Poetica 11. London: Anvil P Poetry, 1980. 71 pp.

A very brief general introduction is followed by translations of fifty-four Exeter Book Riddles. Excluded are those that involve runic characters, duplicate other Riddles, or are obscure, unsolved, or textually incomplete. Twenty of the riddles included previously appeared in **257**. The translations are poetic in intention, although they are faithful and as accurate as is possible while following the Old English versification. Sample translation (from Riddle 7 lines 1–4): 'When it is earth I tread, make tracks upon water/ Or keep the houses, hushed is my clothing,/ Clothing that can hoist me above house-ridges,/ at times toss me into the tall heaven.' [For a review see Cooper, **935**.]

1 **Göbel, Helga.** *Studien zu den altenglischen Schriftwesenrätseln.* Epistemata. Würzburger wissenschaftliche Schriften. Reihe Literaturwissenschaft 7. Würzburg: Königshausen, 1980. xiv + 638 pp.

Göbel discusses the Exeter Book Riddles that have to do with books and book production. She provides lengthy expositions of previous scholarship on the Riddles and on Anglo-Saxon book production. A text and German translation of Riddles 26, 47, 49, 51, 60, 67, 74, 88, 92, 93, and 95 is followed by a very full commentary and attempts at interpretation.

2 **Greenfield, Stanley B.** 'Old English Riddle 39 Clear and Visible.' *Anglia* 98 (1980): 95–100.

Greenfield tentatively suggests 'dream' as the solution to Riddle 39. The solution 'cloud' independently suggested by Meyvaert (**907**) and Kennedy (**888**) must be discarded, since clouds do not seek out individual people or fail to return a second night, as the clues in the Riddle dictate. Nor can 'cloud' account for the central paradox in the Riddle, that the creature has no form or soul yet lives. By contrast dreams visit a specific person and were considered to wander when they leave that dreamer. The dream figures in *The Wanderer* testify to this belief.

3 **Orton, Peter.** 'The Technique of Object-Personification in *The Dream of the Rood* and a Comparison with the Old English Riddles.' *Leeds Studies in English* NS 11 (1980): 1–18.

Orton finds that the poets of *The Dream of the Rood* and the Exeter Book Riddles followed similar procedures. For instance, in the Riddles the investment of animism in a material object was often the method used to veil its identity. Similarities in detailed motifs also occur. One instance is the idea that builders or makers of the subject are enemies to its original, natural state. The evidence suggests either that the composition of the *Dream* provided a stimulus toward the development of a more sophisticated form in the riddle genre, or (more probably) that the *Dream* poet was familiar with the conventions of vernacular riddles.

4 **Bierbaumer, Peter, and Elke Wannagut.** 'Ein neuer Lösungsvorschlag für ein altenglisches Rätsel (Krapp-Dobbie 17).' *Anglia* 99 (1981): 379–82.

The authors propose the solution 'plaited bee-hive' for Riddle 17, citing evidence for the actual existence of such hives. Rival solutions, such as Pinsker's (**877**) 'forge', do not account for all the clues in the text. The 'frea' in line 5 is the bee-keeper. The word 'eodorwir-' in line 2 might refer either to the plaiting of the individual hive or to the enclosure around the hives. Here the authors dissent from the glosses in Bosworth-Toller (1882–98) and Clark Hall (1894).

5 **Cooper, Arthur.** Rev. of *Old English Riddles from the Exeter Book,* by Michael Alexander **[930]**, and *The Exeter Book Riddles,* by Kevin Crossley-Holland **[918]**. *Agenda* 18.4 and 19.1 (two issues in one) (1981): 170–3.

Cooper posits a universal human imagination to which the Riddles belong. He contends that this type of imagination must supplement academic scholarship when modern critics engage with the Riddles. As an instance, he suggests 'snow' as a solution for Riddle 74, arguing that the gender of 'rinc' in line 2 should act as a clue.

936 Fry, Donald K. 'Exeter Book Riddle Solutions.' *Old English Newsletter* 15.1 (1981): 22–33.

Fry attempts a collection of all solutions so far proposed for the individual Exeter Book Riddles. His reference guide provides ready access to scholarship in which solutions are proposed or discussed. Part 1 displays the solutions to the individual Riddles. Part 2 supplies a chronological bibliography of works in which solutions have been proposed. Part 3 indexes the solutions alphabetically.

937 Lendinara, Patrizia. 'Gli *Aenigmata* Laureshamensia.' *PAN: Studi dell' Istituto di Filologia Latina* 7 (1981 *for* 1979): 73–90.

Lendinara comments on possible parallels for the Lorsch enigmas, which she assigns to the same cultural context as the Exeter Book Riddles. As a parallel for Lorsch 8 ('egg'), Lendinara cites Exeter Book Riddle 13, along with Eusebius 38 ('chicken') and others. Although the Lorsch enigma and Exeter Book Riddle 13 are based on the same traditional material, evidently Riddle 13 represents a free and highly complex treatment of it. The handling of the motif of latent life, with its potential for paradox, can be further compared with that seen in Riddle 9 ('cuckoo'). Lorsch 11 ('cow'), along with 69 ('soldier's boot'), contains parallels with Exeter Book Riddles 12 ('leather'), 38 ('young bull'), and 72 ('ox').

938 Pinsker, Hans. 'Ein verschollenes altenglisches Rätsel?' *A Yearbook of Studies in English Language and Literature.* Ed. Siegfried Korninger. Wiener Beiträge zur englischen Philologie 78. Vienna: Braumüller, 1981. 53–9.

According to Pinsker, Riddle 86 is a cheat, because it would have proved insoluble had not Symphosius 95, with its title ('luscus vendens allium', 'one-eyed seller of garlic'), existed to provide the clue. The Old English version is different in detail from Symphosius and lacks the key detail of a 'vendor'. A common source, rather than direct indebtedness to Symphosius, may be the explanation. More generally, Pinsker disputes the notion that Old English riddle composers were closely dependent on older works. The exception is where clear indications exist in the shape of a motif shared in common with more than one Latin riddle. Thus the motif of the leather straps used to fetter captives also crops up in Riddle 36, Aldhelm 83 ('bullock'), and Eusebius 37 ('calf'). In Riddle 86 Pinsker resists Williamson's **(916)** emendation of 'ic' (line 7) to 'hio', arguing that the anacoluthon, where the subject of the riddle itself addresses the reader, is perfectly natural.

939 ———. 'Bemerkungen zum ae. Sturmrätsel.' *Arbeiten aus Anglistik und Amerikanistik* 6 (1981): 221–6.

Pinsker argues that the three so-called 'storm riddles' (1–3) are in reality a single poem. This poem, a didactic hymn, glorifies the power of the Creator by depicting various aspects and activities of the storm. The subject is too obvious to be explicable as an exercise in the riddle genre. Riddles 15 and 20 are not true riddles either, but elegiac self-portraits. Pinsker offers new explanations of words in Riddle 3 lines 24–5: 'brimgiest' = 'sea-yeast', i.e. 'foam', and 'wudu' is an error for '*þudu', an unrecorded cognate of Old English *þyddan* and Modern English 'thud'.

0 Stewart, Ann Harleman. 'The Solution to Old English Riddle 4.' *Eight Anglo-Saxon Studies.* Ed. Joseph Wittig. *Studies in Philology* (Texts and Studies) 78.5 (1981): 52–61.

Stewart suggests the solution 'bucket of water' for Riddle 4. The bucket has been left standing overnight, probably outdoors during the winter, so that a skin of ice has formed. Bound with rings, i.e. with the iron hoops of the bucket, the water must break its bed, i.e. the ice. The notion of the 'neck-wreath' having been given by the creature's lord echoes the notion found elsewhere in the Riddles that meteorological phenomena and their results are gifts of the Creator. Stewart notes elegiac echoes in the Riddle.

1 Talentino, Arnold. 'Riddle 30: the Vehicle of the Cross.' *Neophilologus* 65 (1981): 129–36.

According to Talentino, Riddle 30 appears to have a more or less well-defined solution, which seems so far to have precluded the close study that the riddle deserves. He elaborates on Blackburn **(698)** by arguing that we have a cross with a difference. In addition to projecting the symbol, the poem reveals its significance as a vehicle of salvation. The references to fire would have reminded the Anglo-Saxon audience of the biblical significance of fire as purification. The phrase 'byrnende gled' (line 4b) represents a possible reference to incense. The words 'winde' (line 1b), 'wedre' (line 2b), and 'blowende' (line 4a) would have invoked the presence of the Holy Spirit. Talentino sees Riddle 30 as standing in a special relationship to *The Phoenix*, for both its detailed motifs and its overall meaning. The cross is also depicted as a spiritual vehicle in *The Dream of the Rood*.

2 Mitchell, Stephen A. 'Ambiguity and Germanic Imagery in OE Riddle 1: "Army".' *Studia Neophilologica* 54 (1982): 39–52.

According to Mitchell, all past interpretations of Riddle 1 have accepted at face value statements that it 'shakes the woods' and 'fells the trees'. But such a one-to-one correspondence between the Riddle's imagery and the solution is contrary to a fundamental rule of most riddle-composition. Within a riddle the solution should be described in terms of an entirely different object. Mitchell therefore suggests that 'army' is the solution. Old Norse kennings point to a common metaphoric tradition throughout the Germanic world which linked 'battle' and 'storm'. In lines 8b–11b two clashing armies can be envisaged, with emendation of 'holme' (line 10a) to 'helme'. In lines 12–14a the reference is to a ship, used first for transport and later for burial.

3 Nelson, Marie. 'Old English Riddle 18 (20): a Description of Ambivalence.' *Neophilologus* 66 (1982): 291–300.

Nelson points out that the Exeter Book Riddles are capable of both embodying and describing human experience. She disagrees with Kay's **(856)** solution of

Riddle 20 as 'phallus' and follows Shook (255) in opting for 'sword-swallow'. Dissenting from Williamson's (916) division of the Riddle into two unrelated parts, she interprets it as a unified presentation of ambivalence. The Riddle describes both the confident feelings necessary for a performance of the sexual act and the associated fears of loss of strength. The author may have been a warrior turned monk.

944 **Oda, Takuji.** *A Concordance to the Riddles of the Exeter Book.* Tokyo: Gaku Shobo, 1982. vii + 293 pp.

Oda's concordance is based on the ASPR edition (194), with two minor emendations. The desired word is concorded along with the sentence in which it appears. Every word and all forms of each word are concorded. Frequencies are indicated. Where a headword is homographic, its sense is indicated. A table of the various numbering systems for the Riddles is appended.

945 **Partridge, Astley Cooper.** *A Companion to Old and Middle English Studies.* London: Deutsch; Totowa, NJ: Barnes, 1982. xi + 462 pp.

Partridge sees Riddle 7 as containing the Celtic aspect of Old English poetry. This aspect is marked by a certain romantic tenderness in natural description.

946 **Whitman, Frank H.** *Old English Riddles.* Canadian Federation for the Humanities Monograph Series 3. Port Credit, ON: Canadian Federation for the Humanities, 1982. xii + 236 pp.

In his introduction Whitman explains that this book is designed to complement the past individual editions of the Riddles, which are now all sixty or more years old. [Evidently he was unaware of Williamson's edition (916).] He notes that the appendix omits the usual explanatory and textual notes and regrets his scant use of scholarly material from the last decade. He discusses the function of riddles in various societies, also the structure of riddles. The Exeter Book Riddles should be seen, in the absence of conclusive evidence to the contrary, as literary riddles. Attempts to fix their origin in a folk tradition are purely speculative. A scribe may have brought together originally heterogeneous riddles from diverse sources for incorporation in one collection. Not all of them possess literary merit. They would have appealed to a mindset accustomed to allegory. In his Chapter 4, 'Exegesis and the Old English Riddles', Whitman looks closely at Riddles 29 and 53 (the latter solved as 'cross'). Riddle 60 should definitely be linked with Symphosius 2 and hence solved as 'reed flute or reed pen'. Riddle 73 should be solved as 'writing'/'pen'. Both these Riddles are discussed in detail. Riddle solving should be approached through comparative analysis as well as antiquarian investigations. Whitman appends texts and translations of the Riddles and an Index of Solutions.

947 **Williamson, Craig.** *A Feast of Creatures: Anglo-Saxon Riddle-Songs Translated with Introduction, Notes and Commentary.* Philadelphia: U of Pennsylvania P, 1982. xii + 231 pp.

Williamson's translations are based on his edition (916). The verse-form he chooses for the translations is a cross between the traditional Anglo-Saxon metre and the looser form used by Ælfric. A sample translation, from Riddle 7 (lines 1–4): 'My gown is silent as I thread the seas,/ Haunt old buildings or tread the land./ Sometimes my song-coat and the supple wind/ Cradle me high over the homes of men.' He also includes a collection of translations of Riddle 47 by various hands. Detailed notes are appended to each riddle. Mostly they are based on the notes to his edition but they also incorporate comparisons with modern poetry, including his own. In his introduction he offers a general comparative appraisal of the Exeter Book Riddles, with terminology and insights from anthropology, e.g. in the comparison of the poet and the shaman. He notes that *Solomon and Saturn* is akin to a series of riddles.

8 Ziegler, Waltraud. 'Ein neuer Lösungsversuch für das altenglische Rätsel Nr 28.' *Arbeiten aus Anglistik und Amerikanistik* 7 (1982): 185–90.

Taking his inspiration from three Latin riddles with the solution 'parchment', Ziegler seeks to explain Riddle 28 similarly. He sees allusions to a process where the skin is shaved with a knife and dyed purple. Parallels to Riddle 26 are noted and the cultural-historical background of medieval parchment production is briefly discussed.

9 Anderson, James E. 'Two Spliced Riddles in the Exeter Book.' *In Geardagum* 5 (1983): 57–75.

Anderson argues that when Riddles 42, 43, 47, and 48 are viewed as four separate riddles, as is conventional, their solutions seem inadequate. In the latter pair, 'bookworm' seems too obvious and 'chalice, chrismal' too obscure. We need to note that the links of punctuation and graphology between Riddles 47 and 48 in Exeter Book seem intentionally dubious and small. Likewise, the texts of Riddles 42 and 43 form one text in the manuscript. Examination of these two palaeographically spliced riddles shows that through intricate wordplay the solver is challenged to find the divinity hidden in earthly things (57). In 42–3 the cock symbolizes the soul, the hen the folly of the flesh. The double enclosure of souls within the body and within earth is symbolized by the visual appearance of the runic letters of Riddle 42 when they are laid out in a straight line. A transparent thematic link exists between Riddle 47 (on the bookworm) and Riddle 48 (on a book, perhaps a decorated gospel book or book of offices). Riddles 47 and 48 represent two originally longer separate riddles which the 'Exeter Book Riddler' (60) conflated. Anderson argues against Brooks's **(1076)** contention that *hring*, as seen in Riddle 48 line 1, cannot mean 'ringing sound' (60). [He does not take account of Jember's **(928)** discussion of this line.]

0 ———. '*Deor, Wulf and Eadwacer* and *The Soul's Address*: How and Where the Old English Exeter Book Riddles Begin.' *The Old English Elegies: New Essays in Criticism and Research.* Ed. Martin Green. Rutherford: Associated U Presses, 1983. 204–30.

In his search for patterns and design behind the compilation of the Exeter Book Anderson suggests that the Exeter Book Riddles really begin at *The Soul's Address* on fol. 98a. Taken in combination, *The Soul's Address, Deor,* and *Wulf and Eadwacer* seem to make up a riddlic pilgrimage of their own, through the *visibilia* of wasted lives in this world to the *invisibilia* of eternal grief in the next. They lead down a remarkable hidden path of contemplative discovery and could be said to comprise 'Riddle 1'. Anderson argues that the refrains of *Deor* and *Wulf and Eadwacer* display the same deceptive habit of mind that contrived more obvious double riddles elsewhere in the Exeter Book. He cites Riddles 42–3 and 75–6 as examples of allegedly double or twinned riddles. Although the lack of a break between 42 and 43 has been dismissed as a mere scribal error, it can also be defended as a scribal response to the *orponcbendum,* or secret word linkages, in the two texts. In only thirty-two lines this double riddle transforms the farmyard cock and hen into the body and soul, as travelling companions through mortal life. The solution to 75–6 is probably identical to that of Riddle 42, namely 'cock and hen'. The cock pecking his way through scattered corn is a frequent symbol of Christ, who (as 'hælend') is referred to by the runes in Riddle 75. Riddle 76 presents the image of a 'setting hen', perhaps symbolizing the brooding Church on earth. These tandem riddles of the Exeter Book, with their slight division in mid-line, show tantalizing signs of the scribe's complicity, or at least faithfulness to, their game. The existence of fairly certain paired riddles provides a good reason for approaching *Deor* and *Wulf and Eadwacer* with a riddler's care.

951 Blake, N.F. 'Reflections on Old English Scholarship'. *In Geardagum* 5 (1983): 77–83.

In an answer to Anderson **(949)**, Blake counsels caution in positing two diverse levels of meaning for individual riddles. It would be asking a lot of the audience's sophistication to expect them to form a mental picture of the runes. To consider the punctuation and graphology of four Riddles in isolation from the rest of the Exeter Book is not an adequate approach.

952 Fiocco, Teresa. 'Cinque enigmi dall'Exeter Book (Krapp-Dobbie 30, 53, 55, 67, e 73).' *Atti dell'Accademia Peloritana dei Pericolanti: Classe di Lettere, Filosofia e Belle Arti* 59 (1983): 145–228.

Fiocco provides a very full review and critique of previous scholarship on Riddles 30, 53, 55, 67, and 73, from Dietrich **(658)** up to the present. The solution 'cross' proposed for each of the five by various scholars at various times is accepted by the author only for Riddle 30. Holthausen's **(756)** solution, 'wooden cup', is counter-indicated by the fact that both men and women (not just men, as in the parallels he cites) kiss the riddle object (166). Discussing Jember's **(904, 911)** solution 'phallus', she points out that Riddle 30 has little in common, beyond a few verbal parallels, with the acknowledged 'obscene' Riddles (153). She argues that the opening description of the tree in pleasant weather anticipates its later conversion into the 'tree of glory', i.e. the cross (158–9). In Riddle 53 (168–84) she argues against Whitman **(915)** in order to confirm the solution 'battering-ram', pointing to the parallel in Aldhelm 86. Riddle 55 (185–202) alludes to three approximately cruciform objects, the cross, the gallows, and some type of weapon-holder, the last of these constituting the actual solution. She argues against Williamson's **(916)** 'sword-box'. Riddle 67 (203–13) is solved as 'bible', *contra* Mackie **(188)**, who proposed the solution 'cross'. Riddle 73 (214–28) is solved as 'lance' or 'javelin', with parallels for the depiction of the 'suffering' of the raw material that gets manufactured into the riddle object.

Fiocco argues against Whitman's 'cross' **(915)** and Jember's 'revenant' **(904, 911)**.

53 O'Keeffe, Katherine O'B. 'Exeter Riddle 40: the Art of an Old English Translator.' *Proceedings of the PMR Conference* 5 (1983 *for* 1980): 107–17.

O'Keeffe summarizes the evidence for the popularity of Aldhelm's *Ænigmata*. Riddle 35, the Exeter Book version of his *Ænigma* 33 ('lorica'), is demonstrably early, whereas Riddle 40, the Exeter Book version of his *Ænigma* 100 ('creation'), dates to the tenth century. It represents not merely a translation but also a re-creation and interpretation of Aldhelm's Latin. The Anglo-Saxon poet-translator was demonstrably aware of Aldhelm's figures of diction, matching them with a native English technique where possible but also modifying it. Wordplay on 'rice' and 'ryht' imitates Aldhelm's paronomasia on 'rector' and 'regnorum'. Unlike the Latin, the Old English version is highly repetitive in its vocabulary. Here the translator was making a deliberate stylistic choice, in an adaptation of the Old English poetic practice of generative composition. This term signifies a habit of contiguous lexical recurrence where forms reappear, often with varied lexical and syntactic shapes, within a few lines. The length of Aldhelm's clauses forces the Old English translator into an abandonment of the usual technique of development by accretion and synonymy. The half-line, though preserved as a metrical unit, loses its force as a discrete unit of meaning.

54 Stewart, Ann Harleman. 'The Diachronic Study of Communicative Competence.' *Current Topics in English Historical Linguistics.* Ed. Michael Davenport, Erik Hansen, and Hans Frede Nielsen. Proceedings of the Second International Conference on English Historical Linguistics held at Odense University, 13–15 April, 1981. Odense U Studies in English 4. Odense: Odense UP, 1983. 123–36.

Stewart considers the literary riddle in general, showing how its form and function can be explained in terms of Grice's Cooperative Principle and his maxims concerning conversational exchanges (H. Paul Grice, 'Logic and Conversation', in Peter Cole and Jerry L. Morgan, eds., *Syntax and Semantics III: Speech Acts*, New York: Academic, 1975, 41–58). As to the Exeter Book Riddles in particular, she notes that they involve a principled exchange between speaker and hearer, and thus are more amenable than poems in most other early genres to an analysis in terms of pragmatics. She suggests that hearers of a riddle are more alert to the possibility of implicature than they would be in an ordinary speech act. Riddle 28 flouts Grice's first maxim of quantity by furnishing so little detail that the riddle resists solution. By contrast, Riddle 92 violates the second maxim of quantity by furnishing too much detail. Riddle 25 violates the first maxim of quality, 'do not say that which you believe to be false'. Riddle 47, on the other hand, would exemplify a maxim of consistency not propounded by Grice: 'Do not contradict yourself without explanation.' Stewart explains the words 'wifes sond' in Riddle 92 line 3 as 'woman's meal', in this context beech-nuts.

5 ———. 'Double Entendre in the Old English Riddles.' *Lore and Language* 3.8 (1983): 39–52.

Stewart provides an overview of the nine double entendre riddles (25, 37, 87, 42, 44, 45, 54, 61, and 62). Typologically, they belong with riddles where 'details are provided that lead to an ability to discern a referent, and thus call for an answer, but the answer is wrong' (39). The presence of such riddles seems strange in the context of the Exeter Book, a collection of otherwise largely serious poetry presented by a bishop to his cathedral. Presumably the fact that the 'real' solutions are innocent made these poems safe. Comparison with a nineteenth-century 'onion' riddle illustrates that the poet avoided falling into outright coarseness. These riddles are characterized by a special lexicon, with such key words as *eage* and *heafod*. The protagonists are described largely in upper-class terms, such as *ides*, *þeodnes dohtor*, and *frea*. Riddle 44 ('key') is analysed in detail, to highlight the systematic wordplay and the contrasts with Riddle 91 (also 'key', but not double entendre).

956 **Gerritsen, Johan.** 'Leiden Revisited: Further Thoughts on the Text of the Leiden Riddle.' *Medieval Studies Conference, Aachen 1983.* Ed. Wolf-Dietrich Bald and Horst Weinstock. Bamberger Beiträge zur englischen Sprachwissenschaft 15. Frankfurt am Main: Lang, 1984. 51–9.

In this reply to Parkes (**873**), Gerritsen argues that the *Leiden Riddle* was copied contemporaneously with the Latin text of the manuscript and by one of its two scribes, i.e. that it was not a later addition. This copying (*contra* Parkes) preceded the pen trials on the page and may have been as early as the ninth century. Gerritsen provides a detailed discussion of the manuscript readings, as revealed by renewed investigation. He observes that the neumes appear to have been positioned in such a way as to avoid the writing space. In one crucial reading, Gerritsen opts for 'uaat' (line 3), with a postulated scribal misreading of '*uuat', whereas Parkes had opted for 'uuat'.

957 **Gleissner, Reinhard.** *Die 'zweideutigen' altenglischen Rätsel des 'Exeter Book' in ihrem zeitgenössischen Kontext.* Sprache und Literatur, Regensburger Arbeiten zur Anglistik und Amerikanistik 23. Frankfurt am Main: Lang, 1984. xxiv + 450 pp.

Gleissner reviews the history of scholarship on the obscene riddles, arguing that both their obscenity and their humour have been played down. He places these riddles against the background of the Benedictine Revival in England, taking as his cue the fact that the manuscript originated during this period. He contends that Riddle 46, on Lot and his children, does not derive directly from the Bible but rather from rabbinical or other medieval Latin versions of the riddle. The discussion also includes 'superne secg' in Riddle 62 line 9.

958 **Fiocco, Teresa.** 'Il viaggio della nave nell'enigma 32 dell'Exeter Book.' *Blue Guitar* 7–8 (1984–7): 80–9.

Fiocco analyses the poetic effects in Riddle 32, in particular the poet's precise articulation of the different types of motion of the merchant ship. She disputes the identification of the 'muð' (line 9) with a hatch, pointing out that archaeological investigations have not so far demonstrated the presence of hatches on Anglo-Saxon ships. She also resists the notion that the word 'feldas' (line 8) refers directly to the sea: rather, it means any kind of flat surface.

9   **Magennis, Hugh.** 'The Cup as Symbol and Metaphor in Old English Literature.' *Speculum* 60 (1985): 517–36.

Magennis incidentally mentions Riddle 30a as containing one of the most attractive of the many images of drinking cups in Old English poetry and creating a charming vignette of hall life.

0   **O'Keeffe, Katherine O'Brien.** 'The Text of Aldhelm's *Enigma* No. c in Oxford, Bodleian Library, Rawlinson C. 697 and Exeter Riddle 40.' *Anglo-Saxon England* 14 (1985): 61–73.

Dissenting from Tupper (**727**), O'Keeffe argues that Riddle 40, in its Old English form, was a much later poem than the *Leiden Riddle*. The translator of Aldhelm 100 used as his source Oxford Bodleian Rawlinson C.697, a ninth-century continental manuscript with tenth-century English corrections. This manuscript came to England as early as the first quarter of the tenth century but not later than the middle of that century, and therefore some decades before the compilation of the Exeter Book. Tupper's theory of two translators, with the inferior one recognizable through translation errors and technical weaknesses that set in after line 81, is not viable in view of the incidence of similar features throughout Riddle 40. In fact, the changes wrought on the Latin source are uniformly indicative of generative composition. The sequence of lines in Riddle 40 agrees exactly with Rawlinson and the poet of Riddle 40 has altered the text in precisely the places where Rawlinson contains peculiar emendations.

1   **Pinsker, Hans, and Waltraud Ziegler.** *Die altenglischen Rätsel des Exeterbuchs.* Anglistische Forschungen 183. Heidelberg: Winter, 1985. 422 pp.

This edition of the Exeter Book Riddles is accompanied by a German translation and commentary. In a brief introduction, issues concerning the manuscript, previous editions, and editorial principles are sketched out. The editors advocate a liberal approach to emendation, positing both visual and aural errors in the transmission of the manuscript text. A bibliography is supplied. Fourteen wholly or partly new solutions are included, including Riddle 8 'flute', Riddle 13 'twelve chickens', Riddle 22 'ice bridge', Riddle 29 'abduction of Venus', Riddle 30 'snow-flakes', Riddle 32 'wheelbarrow', Riddle 40 'primordial matter: water', Riddle 61 'hood', Riddle 70 'bell', and Riddle 73 'bow and incendiary arrow'.

2   **Shaw, Patricia.** 'Elementos humoristicos en la literatura medieval inglesa, 800–1400.' *Estudios literarios ingleses: edad media.* Ed. J.F. Galván Reula. Critica y estudios literarios. Madrid: Cátedra, 1985. 85–106.

Shaw makes passing mention of double entendre in the Exeter Book Riddles.

3   **Stewart, Ann Harleman.** 'Inference in Socio-historical Linguistics: the Example of Old English Wordplay.' *Folia Linguistica Historica* 6 (1985): 63–85.

Stewart uses wordplay in the Exeter Book Riddles as a good place to begin exploring the role of participants in historical texts. She discusses examples of puns, lexical play, and play with formulas. Among the puns she includes 'wiht' in Riddle 4 line 11 and Riddle 58 line 10. Lexical play is exemplified by 'stiþ' ('stiff') in Riddle 44 line 3 and Riddle 54 line 5, where there is reliance on the possibility of two applications of a single meaning. Play with formulas is exemplified by Riddle 20, where the formulas, e.g. 'since ond seolfre' in line 10, summon up heroic and religious associations.

964 Fanger, Claire. 'A Suggestion for a Solution to Exeter Book Riddle 55.' *Scintilla* 2–3 (1985–6): 19–28.

The solution of Riddle 55 as 'cross' is suspect because of the explicit reference to 'rode tacn' within the text (line 5). Preferable is the solution 'reliquary (containing a splinter of the True Cross)'. Fanger reads lines 12a–13b to mean 'that [i.e. the wolfheadtree or gallows] often asked/prayed for a weapon for its man-lord'. Comparably with *The Dream of the Rood*, the cross wishes to smite Christ's enemies. The 'healle' in line 1 is the Church; 'druncon' alludes to the Eucharist.

965 Jember, Gregory K. 'Some Hints on Ambiguity and Meaning in Riddle 39.' *Hiroshima Studies in English Language and Literature* 31 (1986): 26–38.

Discussing approaches to solving the Exeter Book Riddles, Jember notes that the postulation of Latin analogues is unhelpful, since there is no way of determining the direction of any influence that might exist. He also resists the itemization and paraphrasing of 'clues', on the grounds that this practice can lead to the neglect of the metaphorical subtlety of individual statements and the shifting relationships between them. The language of Riddle 39 is analysed on the assumption of complex word-play: the word 'sundorcræft' (line 3), for instance, might be construed as 'special power', 'distant power', or (reading 'sund-orcræft') 'great power over the sea'. The outcome is to vindicate Tupper's **(727)** solution 'moon'.

966 Magennis, Hugh. '*Monig oft gesæt*: Some Images of Sitting in Old English Poetry.' *Neophilologus* 70 (1986): 442–52.

Magennis makes the incidental suggestion that the act of sitting in Riddle 76 has an 'elegiac aspect' (452 n. 39).

967 Owen-Crocker, Gale R. *Dress in Anglo-Saxon England.* Manchester: Manchester UP, 1986. xi + 241 pp.

Owen-Crocker comments on the *Leiden Riddle* and Exeter Book Riddle 35, stressing that it is uncertain that the warp-weighted type of loom is referred to there. The references to looms that have been claimed for Riddles 56 and 70 also strike her as uncertain (176).

968 Rissanen, Matti. '*Nathwæt* in the Exeter Book Riddles.' *American Notes and Queries* 24 (1986): 116–20.

Rissanen observes that *nathwæt* and *nathwær* occur only in the Riddles of the

Exeter Book. Moreover, five of the total of six occurrences are found in the 'so-called obscene riddles' (Riddle 93 is an apparent exception). The referent is the sexual organ or its location. In Riddle 93 the symbols for the sexual act appear in rapid succession: knife penetrating horn, horn swallowing liquid, pen intruding into the womb of the horn. With the use of *nathwæt*, the clash between the denotational meaning of the elements of the compound and the structural meaning of the indefinite pronoun is cleverly exploited to appeal to an alert audience.

9 Tristram, Hildegard L.C. 'In Support of Tupper's Solution of the Exeter Book Riddle (Krapp-Dobbie) 55.' *Germanic Dialects: Linguistic and Philological Investigations.* Ed. Bela Brogyanyi and Thomas Krömmelbein. Amsterdam Studies in the Theory and History of Linguistic Science. Series 4, Current Issues in Linguistic Theory 38. Amsterdam: Benjamins, 1986. 585–98.

The solution to Riddle 55 is a wooden liturgical cross as used in various social occasions in Anglo-Saxon England. It might be carried into the hall on the occasion of a feast. The interpretation of the four woods mentioned in the Riddle as the four woods of the Holy Cross is permissible, despite Williamson (**916**), because the list of trees was variously adapted to local contexts. Both the personification of the cross (naming its noble ancestors) and its identification as 'wulfheafedtreo' (i.e. gallows) in line 12 can be paralleled from *The Dream of the Rood*. The reference to the sword is explained by the idea of the cross as a spiritual weapon. The partial identification of the solution within the Riddle should be recognized as a genre characteristic.

0 Couch, Christopher L. 'From Under Mountains to Beyond Stars: the Process of Riddling in Leofric's *The Exeter Book* and *The Hobbit*.' *Mythlore* 14.1 (1987): 9–13 and 55.

Couch compares the Exeter Book Riddles to those of Tolkien in terms of their power to edify the audience. The riddles that Leofric compiled were for the advantage and entertainment of learning Christians.

1 Doane, A.N. 'Three Old English Implement Riddles: Reconsiderations of Numbers 4, 49, and 73.' *Modern Philology* 84 (1987): 243–57.

The two key elements in solving the Exeter Book Riddles are familiarity with recent archaeological findings and attention to the obfuscatory and other techniques in the texts themselves. Doane considers Williamson's (**916**) solution of Riddle 28 as 'yew-horn' a success in these respects. Riddle 4 is to be solved as 'bucket on a chain or rope in a cistern or well'. The clue concerning rings can be explained as alluding to the iron hoops on a stave bucket. Likewise, the clue concerning breaking alludes to the early morning ice broken by the disgruntled servant who fills the bucket. [Doane was evidently unaware of Stewart's (**940**) similar solution.] Riddle 49, a riddle-within-a-riddle, can be solved as 'millpond and its sluice'. The precious thing mentioned in the Riddle is water and the 'sweart ond saloneb' object in line 5 is the sluice gate, with its blackened wood. Riddle 73 cannot be a 'spear' or 'battering ram' but rather the 'bow', the weapon actually used to penetrate a fortress, as specified in the text.

972 **Machan, Tim William, and Robyn G. Peterson.** 'The Crux of Riddle 55.'
     English Language Notes 24.3 (1987): 7–14.

The authors suggest that the solution of Riddle 55 is 'cross reliquary', in the form
of a cross-shaped receptacle housing a fragment of the True Cross. Evidence of
such a reliquary is to be found in both literature and archaeology. The Riddle
evokes the tradition of the cross as a weapon (especially a sword) for the faithful
Christian. This consideration helps to account for earlier solutions of the Riddle
as 'weapon-holder'.

973 **Nelson, Marie.** 'Plus Animate: Two Possible Transformations of Riddles by
     Symphosius.' *Germanic Notes* 18 (1987): 46–8.

According to Nelson, the Anglo-Saxon riddler's art means his ability to give
animate, even human, life to his subject through his power of language. Thus
whereas [Pseudo-]Symphosius 1 ('cuckoo') and Exeter Book Riddle 9 are both
on the subject of the cuckoo, the Old English riddle makes a marked
improvement by focusing on the offspring, which received only one line in the
Latin. Similarly, although Symphosius 73 ('bellows') and Exeter Book Riddle 37
agree in their use of the oppositions life/death, full/empty, the subject of the Old
English version is more animate, being not merely 'bellows' but also 'phallus'.

974 **Osborn, Marijane.** 'Riddle Eighty-One of the *Exeter Book* (translated from the
     Anglo-Saxon for Stella).' *Giant Steps poetry magazine* 7 (Spring 1987): 48.

A sample translation from Riddle 81 lines 1–3: 'Puff-breasted, bulgy-naped,/
holding on high my head and tail,/ I've ears too and eyes, and one foot to stand on
. . .' (48).

975 **Alexander, Michael.** 'Old English Literature.' *The Cambridge Guide to the Arts
     in Britain.* Ed. Boris Ford. 1. *Prehistoric, Roman, and Early Medieval.*
     Cambridge: Cambridge UP, 1988. 179–93.

Alexander briefly discusses Riddle 26, expressing the view that riddling is at the
root of the Anglo-Saxon poetic reading and representation of the world.

976 **Jacobs, Nicolas.** 'The Old English "Book-moth" Riddle Reconsidered.' *Notes
     and Queries* 233, NS 35 (1988): 290–2.

Jacobs considers Robinson's (**896**) analysis of wordplay in Riddle 47 as strained.
The Riddle can only *be* a riddle, needing a solution, if we take it as asking what
form words must assume in order to be devoured by a worm or a moth. Thus the
solution should be 'writing on vellum' or similar. Alexander's (**257**) translation,
'I heard of a wonder, of words moth-eaten', is therefore to be endorsed. In a
society where writing was a specialized accomplishment the idea of a literary
product which, viewed materialistically, is nothing but food for moths and
maggots would not necessarily be obvious.

977 **Jember, Gregory K.** 'Literal and Metaphorical: Clues to Reading the Old
     English Riddles.' *Studies in English Literature* (Tokyo) 65 (1988): 47–56.

Jember presents the Exeter Book Riddles, in common with other riddles, as a special case of the essential quality of language: a vital capacity for polysemy. The bulk of scholarship on the Riddles has not considered them as literature. Instead, the principal concern has been to find literal, concrete solutions. The composers of the Riddles are consciously distinguishing between two levels of language, between true or *literal* language on the one hand and twisted or *metaphorical* language on the other. The reader is intended to enter into participative and metaphysical truths, where the anchor of Riddle 16 can be seen as embodying in a metaphysical or theological sense not only the trials of a faith, but also the trials of an individual soul, anchored in faith.

8 Liuzza, Roy Michael. 'The Texts of the Old English *Riddle 30*.' *JEGP* 87 (1988): 1–15.

Liuzza offers a detailed comparison of the variant readings in the two different Exeter Book versions of Riddle 30. He ascribes the divergences to scribal correction and corruption rather than to authorial revision or memorial transmission. As an instance of the scribe needing further correction, he recommends the excision of 'ond' in Riddle 23 line 3. He suggests that the Exeter Book Riddles may owe their relative homogeneity to alterations made after they were collected as a group in a manuscript. The scribe of the Exeter Book may have found the text of Riddle 30b among a group of brief religious works in one of his copy-texts. Its second appearance in the Exeter Book is explicable on the assumption that it could be read for its devotional content as well for its appeal as an enigma.

9 Stanley, E.G. 'Parody in Early English Literature.' *Poetica* (Tokyo) 27 (1988): 1–69.

Stanley points out that the riddle is the only distinctive literary genre which the Anglo-Saxons themselves demonstrably recognized as such. The 'elegy', by contrast, is 'a term so loose as to admit a wide range of compositions' (6). He identifies Riddles 75 and 76 as possible candidates for classification as parody, commenting that Williamson **(916)** is probably correct in taking these two texts as a single riddle (5). By contrast, although the obscurity of Riddle 74 mocks the reader this does not make it a parody (6).

0 Davis, Patricia, and Mary Schlueter. 'The Latin Riddle of the Exeter Book.' *Archiv für das Studium der neueren Literaturen* 226 (1989): 92–9.

The word *morti*, not *rupi*, should be inserted in line 2 of Riddle 90. If the first half of the Riddle is read as a sophisticated letter game and charade, it is possible to arrive at the solution 'Augustine and Tertullian'. Medieval anagrams were not necessarily exact. Along with acrostics, they occur frequently in (Anglo-)Latin writers. The notion of seeing with seven eyes can be traced to Zech. 4: 10, where the eyes of the Lord, which run to and fro through the whole earth, are seven in number.

4 Lerer, Seth. 'The Riddle and the Book: Exeter Book Riddle 42 in its Contexts.' *Papers on Language and Literature* 25 (1989): 3–18.

Riddle 42 is securely based on the inheritances of Anglo-Saxon education, with its idioms drawn from wisdom literature, from learned exegesis, from contemporary book-production, and from the Latin *ænigmata*. The reader's attention is diverted from the ostensible solution to the real topic, which is interpretation itself. By transforming a metaphor for spiritual or religious understanding into a claim for farmyard knowledge, Riddle 42 succinctly juxtaposes the learned and the lewd. The word 'orþoncbendum' (line 15) embodies a specific reference to the technology of book-binding. Lerer also considers attitudes to the power of language in *Homiletic Fragment II*, *Maxims I*, and *Order*.

982 Stanley, E.G. 'Notes on OE Poetry.' *Leeds Studies in English* NS 20 (1989): 319–44.

Stanley detects a tendency in many poems, including Exeter Book Riddles 42, 56, and 60, to start with a light verse. The pattern is associated with the verbs *wæs* and *seah* in the Riddles.

983 Kelly, Susan. 'Anglo-Saxon Lay Society and the Written Word.' *The Uses of Literacy in Early Medieval Europe*. Ed. Rosamund McKitterick. Cambridge: Cambridge UP, 1990. 36–62.

In passing, Kelly mentions the use of runes in the Exeter Book Riddles as evidence for familiarity with the runic alphabet among the educated classes of society (37).

984 Reifegerste, E. Matthia. 'Die altnordischen Rätsel.' *Skandinavistik* 20 (1990): 20–3.

Reifegerste notes in the course of a comparison between the Exeter Book Riddles and the Old Norse *Heiðreks gátur* (the only sets of riddles in an early Germanic vernacular) that the interest shown in contemporary technology in the Old English riddles has no Old Norse counterpart.

985 Rodrigues, Louis J. *Anglo-Saxon Riddles*. Lampeter: Llanerch Enterprises, 1990. 118 pp.

This collection contains a selection of sixty riddles, translated with facing original text. [The Old English text is taken from the edition of Wyatt (**737**). On this point see the comments in 'The Year's Work in Old English Studies,' *Old English Newsletter* 25.2 (1992): 34.] The translation deliberately uses an approximation to Old English lexis where possible. A brief general introduction is also supplied. A sample translation, from Riddle 29 lines 1–4: 'A wight in wondrous wise saw I/ hale booty 'tween her horns,/ a radiant air-vat, artfully adorned,/ forage homewards from the fray.'

986 Welsh, Andrew. 'Swallows Name Themselves: Exeter Book Riddle 57.' *American Notes and Queries* NS 3 (1990): 90–3.

Accepting the solution 'swallows' for Riddle 57, Welsh suggests paronomasic punning on *swealwe* 'swallows' (noun) and *swelgan/swealg* 'swallow(ed)' (verb). Paronomasia turns on the repetition of similar (rather than identical) sounds in words of different meaning. The swallow 'swallows', as every living creature does, but it is the only creature that names itself when it swallows.

7 **Wilcox, Jonathan.** 'New Solutions to Old English Riddles: Riddles 17 and 53.' *Philological Quarterly* 69 (1990): 393–408.

Wilcox solves Riddle 17 as 'quiver', partly by comparison with Riddle 23 'bow'. He opposes Dietrich's **(658)** solution, 'ballista', on the grounds of the probable absence of any Anglo-Saxon war machine more complicated than the sling. He resists the solution 'bee-hive' **(934)** because there is no mention of honey. The clues in Riddle 53 indicate that the object described is manufactured from wood and rope, has something that can be seen as a head, and is used to clear the way for a wicked man. The solution is a gallows, with a plunderer or a thief hanging from it.

8 **Blockley, Mary.** 'Perfecting the Old English Past: *Beowulf* 2 and Limits on the Equivalence of the Old English Simple Past and Present Perfect.' *Philological Quarterly* 70 (1991): 123–40.

Blockley suggests that we should understand *we* and *ic* at the opening of some poems, such as Riddles 45, 48, and 67, as the voice of the text, declaring in the manner of a title-page what its contents are.

9 **Brown, Ray.** 'The Exeter Book's *Riddle 2*: A Better Solution.' *English Language Notes* 29.2 (1991): 1–4.

The suggested solution for Riddle 4 is 'watchdog'. Fitting clues to this solution, Brown notes that dogs dig up gardens: the sense of 'brecan' in this context (line 3) can be compared to that in which the bull of Riddle 38 'duna briceð'. Lines 11–12 should be translated 'if I guard (*wite*) things, and can, with words (i.e. barks) successfully say my piece'. [Brown does not cite Stewart **(939)** or Doane **(970)**].

) **Lester, G.A.** '*Sindrum Begrunden* in Exeter Book Riddle No. 26.' *Notes and Queries* 236, NS 38 (1991): 13–14.

Lester queries the translation of this phrase in Riddle 26 line 6 as 'with all impurities ground off' and suggests instead 'ground away with cinders'. He cites the well-known process of smoothing vellum surfaces with pumice, arguing that the word *sinder* can be interpreted as equivalent to pumice.

4 **Nelson, Marie.** 'Four Social Functions of the Exeter Book Riddles.' *Neophilologus* 75 (1991): 445–50.

Three of the social functions of the Exeter Book Riddles were to provide an arena for the competitive exercise of verbal skills, to permit the playing out of aggressive roles, and to respond to the destructive forces of Nature. The Riddles provided a number of safe equivalents for roles men were often required to play in war. In a fourth function, the Riddles respond to human destructiveness. Thus, although the primary answer to Riddle 50 is 'fire' **(684)**, a secondary solution, 'anger', can also be posited. Similarly in Riddle 33, the primary and secondary solutions would have been respectively 'iceberg' (658) and 'hatred'. These Riddles seem to correlate destructive natural and human forces.

992 **Stanley, E.G.** 'Stanley B. Greenfield's Solution of Riddle (ASPR) 39: "Dream".' *Notes and Queries* 236, NS 38 (1991): 148–9.

Stanley supports Greenfield's (932) solution and accordingly emends line 12b to read 'ne muð hafaþ se wiþ monnum spræc', comparing other Riddles (including 60) that use the paradox of mouthless speech.

993 **Wilson, John.** 'Old English Riddle No. 39: "Comet".' *Notes and Queries* 236, NS 38 (1991): 442–3.

Wilson argues that 'comet' fits the clues provided in the Riddle 39, for instance in presaging dire or momentous events and in moving to a new point in the skies each night, unlike the fixed stars. He emends 'earmost' in line 14 to 'earwost' ('swiftest') to accommodate this solution.

994 **Walker-Pelkey, Faye.** ' "*Frige hwæt ic hatte*": "The Wife's Lament" as Riddle.' *Papers on Language and Literature* 28 (1992): 242–66.

Walker-Pelkey compares *The Wife's Lament* with some of the acknowledged Riddles of the Exeter Book, noting such commonalities as elegiac tone, psychological penetration, and apparent disunity. To minimize these qualities in the Riddles is tacitly to consign literary riddles to the category of folk riddles. Detailed examples are adduced from Riddles 20, 71, and 88. Problems of genre classification can be detected in Riddle 20. Riddle 88 contains powerful references to anxieties of separation and uncertainty.

The *Rune Poem*

ORIENTATION TO RESEARCH

EDITIONS

Rune Poem is uniquely extant in Hickes's print (1705) of a single leaf, now lost, from Cotton Otho B.x. Derolez (**216**) described Hickes's print as not a very trustworthy substitute for the manuscript evidence. For other editions see the subject index.

DATING AND LOCALIZATION

Scholars have diverged considerably concerning date. Among those opting for the seventh century or earlier are Grimm (**995**), Grein (**84**), Brandl (**19**), and Wardale (**26**). Among those who envisage a mixture of archaic and later composition are ten Brink (**5**) and Earle (**88**). In favour of an eighth- or ninth-century date are Kemble (**63**), Brooke (**109**), Dickins (**1004**), Dobbie (**203**), Anderson (**31**), Musset (**1025**), and Ritzke-Rutherford (**310**). As to localization, Breeze (**1045**) speculated concerning a Mercian origin.

VALUE AS RUNOLOGICAL EVIDENCE

Many attempts have been made to use this text as one means of reconstructing the posited original Germanic rune names. Major uncertainties exist, however, concerning the quality of the *editio princeps* as a witness. Hempl (**1002**), followed by Ker (**36**), cast doubt on the integrity of Hickes's text, though with a rebuttal from Page (**1027**). How far the poem itself offers reliable testimony is also a matter of controversy. More or less on the side of reliability are Grienberger (**1000**), Keller (**1013**), Elliott (**219, 230, 324**), Schneider (**226**), Wrenn (**245**), Page (**289, 1022**), Ström and Biezais (**297**), and Jones (**1026**). On the side of unreliability are Botkine (**996**), Arntz (**1011**), Blomfield (**1017**), Derolez (**216**), and Schwab (**1028**). Other scholars, notably Redbond (**1014**), Osborn and Longland (**1032**), and Nicholson (**1035**), have argued that the names are of mixed origin. The god Ing has been a natural focus of enquiry, with contributions from Hoffory (**998**), Kossinna (**999**), Malone (**1007**), and Krause (**1019**).

LITERARY AFFILIATIONS

Much interest has centred on the possibility of reconstructing an original Germanic rune poem from the surviving Old English, Norwegian, and Icelandic rune poems: generally in favour were Meyer (**1003**) and Arntz (**1011**). More sceptical were Heusler (**166**), Dobbie (**203**), Jungandreas (**1012**), Halsall (**1033**), and Clunies Ross (**1044**). Among attempts at a looser contextualization, Grimm (**995**) connected *Rune Poem* with Old Norse and Old High German poetry, Rydberg (**997**) with lost Scandinavian epic poetry, the Chadwicks (**183**) with gnomic poetry, Jackson (**193**) and Hanscom (**120**) with nature poetry, Malone (**30**), Wrenn (**43**), and Sorrell (**353**) with the Exeter Book Riddles, Schubel (**41**) with heathen poetry, Göller (**274**) with Old English elegy and epic, Pilch and Tristram (**55**) with proverb, maxim, and riddle, Halsall (**1033**) with Old English gnomic poetry and Latin analogues, and Osborn (**1034**) with divinatory poetry. As to a possible heathen or magical component in *Rune Poem*, Derolez (**1038**) and Halsall (**1041**) favoured Christian interpretations. On the folkloristic side, Elliott (**1021**) noted a custom of using yew sticks to protect the house. Divergently from all other scholarship, Bradley (**1040**) proposed that some strophes are derived from Chinese radical sequences.

LITERARY CRITICISM

Some scholars have dismissed any claims for literary value. Among those who privilege a mnemonic purpose are Dickins (**1004**), Heusler (**166**), Kennedy (**29**), and Musset (**1025**); this viewpoint was rebutted by Shippey (**300**). Hamp (**1030**) and Jungandreas (**1012**) saw wordplay and riddling as the poem's dominant literary aspects. Many scholars, including Heusler (**166**), Bolton (**246**), Ritzke-Rutherford (**310**), Botkine (**996**), Hall (**1031**), and Halsall (**1033**), have detected some Christian didacticism on the themes of earthly prosperity and mortality. Other qualities of the poem, such as its circular structure and occasional humour, have been commented on by Greenfield (**40**) and by Greenfield and Calder (**60**). Osborn and Longland (**1036**) saw *Rune Poem* as potentially providing today's readers with a fresh approach to the problems of individuality and existence.

BIBLIOGRAPHY

995 Grimm, Wilhelm Karl. *Über deutsche Runen.* Göttingen: Dieterich, 1821. iv + 326 pp. Repr. with an introduction by Wolfgang Morgenroth and Arwed Spreu. Vienna: Böhlau, 1988.

Grimm includes an emended text and German translation of the *Rune Poem*, entitled 'Angelsächsisches Gedicht über die Runen-Namen' (217–45). In his detailed commentary he describes *Rune Poem* as among the oldest and most valuable of Old English poems. Its kinship with eddaic poetry is demonstrated by periphrases such as 'hyrde fyres' (line 36), which are quite in the spirit of the skaldic kenning. *Rune Poem* is characterized by a vividness and feeling for Nature, seen in the 'is', 'lagu', and 'dæg' strophes. In the 'þorn' strophe the influence of stories about the 'sleep-thorn' ('Schlafdorn') is to be discerned. A definite borrowing from Old Norse is 'yr'. Either 'evil spirit' or 'body' can be suggested as possible meanings for 'ear'. The word 'eoh' ['yew'] is a borrowing from Old High German *eih* 'oak'.

6 **Botkine, Léon.** *La chanson des runes: Texte anglo-saxon. Traduction et Notes.* Le Havre: Lepelletier, 1879. 23 pp.

[The present work originated as a paper read before the Société Havraise d'Études diverses, as appears from a letter by Botkine bound into the copy of this work held by the University of Illinois Library.] Botkine provides a general introduction to runology, derivative from previous scholarship. His text and translation are based on Grein (2). In the translation some rune names are left unidentified, thus 'ur', 'os', 'rad', 'peorð', 'tir', 'ior', and 'ear'. Possible meanings are discussed in the detailed notes that follow. The word 'rad' is used in two senses, 'harmony' and 'riding' (18). He interprets the contentious *w*-rune as 'wen' ('hope') and the *s*-rune as 'sigel' ('sail') with query. Both words represent deviations from the original names, either because of a natural confusion between similar words or because of an actual difference in the value of the runic characters in Old English and Old Norse (19). The name 'tir' may refer to a circumpolar constellation used as a navigational guide. For 'ior' Botkine tentatively suggests the interpretation 'eel' on the basis of a Slavonic form *ougor* (22). He finds the end of *Rune Poem* comparable with *The Wanderer* and *The Rhyming Poem* and typical of Old English poetry in general in its melancholy (23).

7 **Rydberg, Viktor.** *Undersökningar i germansk mytology.* 2 vols. Stockholm: Bonnier, 1886–9. Trans. Rasmus B. Anderson. *Teutonic Mythology: Gods and Goddesses of the Northland.* London: Sonnenschein, 1889. xii + 706 pp.

Among the 'investigations' in this book is a discussion of Ing with reference to the 'Ing' strophe in *Rune Poem*. The strophe is explained as an episode from a lost Scandinavian epic poem. The 'wæn' mentioned in the strophe (line 69) is to be construed as a proper name, cognate with the Danish name Vagn. This Vagn would be the foster-father of Hadding, the eponymous founder of the 'Heardingas' mentioned in *Rune Poem* (English edn., 180).

8 **Hoffory, Julius.** 'Der germanische Himmelsgott.' *Nachrichten von der königlichen Gesellschaft der Wissenschaften und der Georg-Augusts-Universität zu Göttingen.* Göttingen: Dieterich, 1888. 426–43.

Hoffory argues for an identification of Ing with *Tiwaz, using *Rune Poem* as a key piece of evidence (434–6).

9 **Kossinna, Gustav.** 'Die ethnologische Stellung der Ostgermanen.' *Indogermanische Forschungen* 7 (1897): 276–312.

Kossinna notes in passing (309) that *Rune Poem* stresses the North-Germanic affinities of the Ingvaeones. He suggests that we should interpret 'mid Eastdenum' (line 67) as 'in Skåne'. This reasoning leads him to resist the idea that the Ingvaeones were a purely West Germanic, English/Frisian group.

10 **Grienberger, Theodor von.** 'Die ags runenreihen und die s.g. Hrabanischen alphabete.' *Arkiv för nordisk filologi* 15 (1899): 1–40.

Grienberger discusses the meaning of the different rune names, including *Rune*

Poem in his investigation. The word *wynn* ('joy') makes sense in context, whereas *wen* 'hope' does not, therefore the *wen* version of the name must be a Kenticism, added in a later hand than that of the main scribe. He notes evidence from *Rune Poem* that the actual name of *x* was the full compound *eolxsecg* 'elchsegge' and that the form in the futhark is an abbreviation, lacking appellative value. But he himself prefers to regard the rune-name as *eolhx* 'elk', with analogical *-x* from *fox* etc. The word *sigel* in *Rune Poem* must mean 'sun', not 'sail', on grounds of phonology and sense, since the sailor is thought of as steering by or towards the sun. In considering the problem of *yr* in *Rune Poem*, Grienberger rejects the hypothesis of a borrowing from Old Norse and suggests as a possibility Old English **yrh* < **ierh* = *earh* 'arrow'. In his opinion, these words were not written by the main scribe of the manuscript.

1001 Hempl, George. 'The Runic Words, Hickes 135.' *Englische Studien* 32 (1903): 317–18.

Hempl notes that nobody thus far has successfully explained the series of runes reproduced by Hickes at the end of his edition of the *Rune Poem* (1705). Hempl conjectures that it represents 'eald, ungefog' ('old, intemperate'). He discusses the circumstances in which the semi-vowels can be represented by runes. Hickes may have found these runes in association with his text of *Rune Poem* or he may have introduced them from another source because he had sufficient room for them in the lithographic plate.

1002 ———. 'Hickes's Additions to the Runic Poem.' *Modern Philology* 1 (1904): 135–41.

Hempl discusses Hickes's (1705) text, pointing out the ways in which Hickes's arrangement on the page must have differed from that of the lost manuscript. He also notes the various additions made by Hickes and argues that most of them must have been taken from the manuscript Cotton Domitian A.ix. Hempl analyses the procedures of the scribe of this manuscript, along with Hickes's procedures in copying it, and concludes that many errors must have crept in. In his view, *wen* arose from *wyn* via the influence of *cen* and should therefore be treated as a ghost form. *Rune Poem* can be appealed to as evidence on runic matters only in regard to the right-hand forms (and perhaps most of the names) of those runes that have corresponding strophes in the poem.

1003 Meyer, Richard M. 'Runenstudien. II. Die altgermanischen Runengedichte.' *Beiträge zur Geschichte der deutschen Sprache und Literatur* 32 (1907): 67–84.

Meyer posits an early Germanic counterpart to *Rune Poem* and the Norwegian and Icelandic rune poems. This poem would have been composed for mnemonic purposes shortly after the invention of the runic alphabet. Traces of such a composition can be seen in the fourth-century *Technopaegnion* of Ausonius (on the Greek alphabet), in *Rune Poem* and *The Wanderer*, and in *Hávamál*, among other works. It may have survived in oral tradition in Iceland down to the late eighteenth century. *Rune Poem* and the Norwegian and Icelandic rune poems are connected only in so far as they all descend, with various remodellings, from this archetype. Especially significant is the handling of the themes of 'mann' and 'feoh'. The Old English poem is truer than the Icelandic to the original format of the Germanic poem because it preserves with greater fidelity the gnomic and moralizing utterances that accompanied each rune name.

4 **Dickins, Bruce.** *Runic and Heroic Poems of the Old Teutonic Peoples.* Cambridge: Cambridge UP, 1915. x + 92 pp.

In his Preface (v–vii) the editor describes his aims as to supply a conservative text, to make use of 'the archaeological method which Professor Ridgeway has applied so brilliantly to the study of the Homeric poems' (cf. William Ridgeway, *The Origin of Tragedy, with Special Reference to the Greek Tragedians,* Cambridge: Cambridge UP, 1910) and to emphasize the 'essential unity of the old Teutonic languages in "matter" as in poetic diction'. The literary value of *Rune Poem* is assessed negatively, as comparable with the old nursery rhyme 'A was an Archer who shot at a frog;/ B was a Butcher who had a big dog.' The edition includes a text and translation of *Rune Poem* (12–23), in company with the Norwegian and Icelandic rune poems (24–33) and the *Abecedarium Nordmannicum* (34). In his introduction to *Rune Poem* (6), Dickins briefly reviews its editorial history, beginning with Hickes (1705). He accepts the conclusions of Hempl **(1002)** on the derivation of variant runes from Cotton Domitian A.ix, commenting that 'some such theory is needed to account for the frequent discrepancy between the strophes and the names which they describe.' 'Hickes, following the ignorant scribe of Dom. A. ix., inserts *m, mann,* above the correct value *d*' (21, note to line 74). But Dickins seems to regard the gap in date between the manuscript (scarcely earlier than the eleventh century) and the text ('far earlier, pre-Alfredian at least') as also contributing to the discrepancies. Early date is indicated by the absence of occurrences of the definite article and the correctness of versification. *Rune Poem* perhaps exhibits traces of an original from which the Scandinavian poems are likewise derived. A selective bibliography is provided (9–11). In the text and notes some important matters of detail are discussed. Dickins suggests that the poet, who is hardly likely to have seen an aurochs in the flesh, may have used an aurochs drinking horn brought to England from the continent. It is not very plausible that the origin of human speech would be attributed to a heathen divinity, and on the whole it is preferable to assume that the subject of the 'os' strophe is the Latin *os,* 'mouth', which would be equally appropriate. The rune-name *rad* is best taken as 'riding', though the editor reports a personal communication from Henry Chadwick suggesting that a word meaning 'tackle', hence a double sense 'furniture' and 'harness', might have been intended. The *w*-rune is 'wynn' ('joy') not 'wen' ('hope'). The rune name 'tir' is attributed to a misreading of 'tiw', in Botkine's **(996)** suggested sense of a 'circumpolar constellation'. Possibly the poet had in his mind a word different from the original name of the letter (comparing a supposed Old Norse *týri* 'lumen'). The 'beorc' strophe, with its indication of an unusual reproductive system, better describes the grey poplar than the birch and reflects a common Anglo-Saxon confusion between these two trees. The 'Ing' strophe is compared to the Roman and Scandinavian witnesses as to this deity. The word 'heardingas' is to be spelt with an initial capital and related to the Old Norse *Haddingjar* and to the *Asdingi,* a sub-group of the Vandals. A 'General Bibliography' is supplied (86–91) but no glossary.

1005 Grienberger, T. von. 'Das ags. Runengedicht.' *Anglia* 45 (1921): 201–20.

Using Kluge's 1902 edition (**94**), Grienberger analyses the poem in fine detail with respect to phonology, graphology, lexis, morphology, and syntax. He cites parallels from Gothic, Middle High German, and other languages. A series of notes deals with problematic readings in Hickes's print (1705). Grienberger attempts to define the genre of most of the strophes, using the categories 'proverbial', 'descriptive', 'epic', and 'riddle'. He sees these genre characteristics as very unevenly distributed through the poem, with some strophes severely factual but others ambiguous and riddle-like. As to specifically runological issues, he explains 'os' as equivalent to Old Norse *áss*, in this context Óðinn. The 'tir' rune is a spelling for *ti* (which is also attested), under the influence of the Old Norse form of the god's name (*Týr*), and is not to be connected with the Old English word 'tir' ('glory'). This strophe is especially riddle-like in the shifting meanings that its vocabulary can bear. The word 'heardingas' in the 'Ing' strophe (line 70) is to be explained as a proper name, related to 'Hasdingi' and also Old Norse *haddr* 'hair'.

1006 Klaeber, Friedrich. 'Die Ing-Verse im angelsächsischen Runengedicht.' *Archiv für das Studium der neueren Literaturen* 142 (1921): 250–3.

Klaeber finds it difficult to understand how Ing's 'wæn' (line 69) can be said to run 'over the waves'. He suggests that the wagon formed a standard part of the mental image of the hero or god held by the primitive Germanic peoples. A sea-going Ing was therefore envisaged as occupying a miraculous type of vehicle that could serve now as a wagon and now as a ship. Additionally Klaeber argues that the word 'heardingas' (line 70) is not to be construed as a national name but rather in some such general significance as 'heroes', 'the brave'.

1007 Malone, Kemp. *The Literary History of Hamlet.* I. *The Early Tradition.* Anglistische Forschungen 59. Heidelberg: Winter, 1923. New York: Haskell, 1964. xii + 268 pp.

Malone uses *Rune Poem* to help in the reconstruction of the Germanic North during the Migration Period (26–33). He notes that Ing has usurped the place of Nerthus in *Rune Poem*. A consequence is the addition of the myth concerning the vegetation daemon or eponymous ancestor who comes to Denmark by sea out of the unknown. The departure certainly symbolizes the death of the god. This most peculiar finale may well equate with the lavation of goddess and wain told of in the *Germania*. Malone further argues, using the *t*-strophe, that Týr was sometimes associated with stars. The word 'ear' is nothing more or less than a *heiti* [poetic alternative name] for Tiw. We can deduce that the poet of *Rune Poem* misinterpreted the meaning of *Ear* and that the verses which he attached to the T-rune more properly go with the EA-rune.

1008 Wrenn, Charles. 'Late Old English Rune Names.' *Medium Aevum* 1 (1932): 24–34.

Wrenn analyses the description given by Wanley (1705) of the manuscript leaf containing *Rune Poem*. He also discusses Hickes's account (1705) of his procedure in preparing the text of *Rune Poem* for the printer. The supposed rune-name *wen*, for *wynn*, can be explained as a Kenticism in Cotton Domitian A.ix. Kemble **(63)** originated the error by paying insufficient attention to Wanley's and Hickes's descriptions.

Krappe, Alexander Haggerty. 'Le char d'Ing.' *Revue Germanique* 24 (1933): 23–5.

Krappe sets out to explain why the god precedes the chariot, rather than sitting in it, and why it crosses the sea, not the land. He rejects Klaeber's **(1006)** suggestion of a boat with wheels, since such a vehicle would be called a boat, not a wagon. Preferable is to suppose that the reference is to the constellation Charles's Wain. The separate star Boötes, outside the constellation, would be the wagon-driver in front of the wain. Stars obviously can 'cross the sea'. Krappe argues the necessity of a knowledge and a mythology of the stars to a navigating people, whether the coastal and insular Germanic nations or the Polynesians. Although the passage in *Rune Poem* is based upon an astral myth, this is not to presuppose an Anglo-Saxon cult or worship of the stars.

Jungandreas, Wolfgang. 'Die germanische Runenreihe und ihre Bedeutung.' *Zeitschrift für deutsche Philologie* 60 (1935): 105–21.

Jungandreas argues that the 'þorn' strophe in *Rune Poem* could equally well be read as a verse about the *þurs*. He defends Leo's **(4)** interpretation of 'peorð' as 'vulva', but suggests that 'penis' would be more appropriate iconographically and etymologically.

Arntz, Helmut. *Handbuch der Runenkunde.* Sammlung kurzer Grammatiken germanischer Dialekte. B. Ergänzungsreihe 3. Halle: Niemeyer, 1935. Rev. edn. 1944. xv + 314 pp. + 16 plates.

In the first edition Arntz supplies a text and translation of *Rune Poem* (114–19), along with the Norwegian and Icelandic rune poems. Among his interpretations are 'mouth' for strophe 4, 'riding' for strophe 5, 'dance' (with query) for strophe 14, 'sun' for strophe 16, 'Tyr' for strophe 17, and 'grave' (with query) for strophe 29. The subject of strophe 28 remains unidentified. He refers to Dickins **(1004)** for further explanations. In the second edition this material was deleted but a few corrections to the translation are given in the footnotes to 174. In his Chapter 10 in the second edition, on the rune-names and their significance (167–233), Arntz expresses the view that the three rune poems are not independent of each other, though they have undergone a lengthy process of separate development. Reviewing previous scholarship (177–83), Arntz warns against placing too much reliance on the rune poems in reconstructing original meanings for the rune names. The original cultic content of the names tends to be effaced or disguised in these sources. In his discussion of the names Arntz makes scattered references to *Rune Poem* (188–229). The 'ur' strophe in *Rune Poem* suggests that the word was already coming to be understood symbolically in the sense of 'virility, strength'; its presence in an Old English poem clearly indicates a survival of an ancient Germanic rune cult. The 'þorn' strophe perhaps contains underlying allusions to the older name, *þurs*, consistent with the frequent use of double meanings in *Rune Poem*. Comparable is the substitution of Latin *os* 'mouth' for 'os' (meaning 'god'). The 'rad' strophe represents a toning down of the original cultic sense of 'riding' (in a funeral procession). The treatment of *gyfu, wynn,* and the pair *hægl* and *is* is similar. The original significance of this pair lay in the suffering brought by hail and ice. By contrast, the content appropriate to *gear* ('fecundity, harvest') has been maintained in *Rune Poem* under Scandinavian influence. *Rune Poem* uses *ger* side by side with *iar* and *eoh* ('yew') side by side with *yr* without apparent awareness that these names were originally identical. Different possible names of the *c-* rune can be accommodated to the 'cen' strophe: 'torch', 'bold', and 'ship'. The descriptions of the yew and the birch form a nice contrast, but are not necessarily based on traditional material. The attempts of Jungandreas to explain *peorð* as 'vulva' or 'penis' (**1010**) fail to reckon with Old English prudery. The form *eolhx* represents 'eolh' plus 'x', i.e. name plus sound value. The word 'eolhsecg' ('reed') is introduced solely to supply the appropriate sound value, and most of this strophe describes the elk. The *s*-strophe should be interpreted as referring to the sail, not the sun, an explanation unique to *Rune Poem*. The substitution of 'tir' for 'Tiw' must have occurred under influence from early Scandinavian *Týr*. The word 'heardingas' (line 70) should be interpreted as 'die *Hazdingen'.

1012 Jungandreas, Wolfgang. 'Zur Runenreihe.' *Zeitschrift für deutsche Philologie* 61 (1936): 227–32.

Jungandreas reviews the reception of his earlier (**1010**) article, registering Schücking's opinion (personal communication) that the interpretation of *peorð* as 'penis' is dubious in view of the prevailing Anglo-Saxon prudery. His interpretation of the *k*-rune as 'boat' (**1010**) is corroborated by *Rune Poem*. The rune-names in this poem would originally have had to be supplied by the reader, in a riddle-solving process which was made all the more difficult by the poet's penchant for ambiguity and wordplay. The *s*-strophe can refer equally well to the sun or to the sail. The *x*-strophe can point to either 'elk' or 'spear fashioned from a reed'. Similarly, the *c*-strophe would have referred to funerary rites where the deceased prince was launched into the sea in a burning ship. Jungandreas reports a suggestion of Holthausen (personal communication) that 'fyre' in this strophe (line 16) be emended to 'fyrre', yielding the appropriate sense of 'in the distance'. He dissents from the view that the English, Norwegian, and Icelandic rune poems stem from a common source, arguing that the differences are too great.

1013 Keller, Wolfgang. 'Zum altenglischen Runengedicht.' *Anglia* 60 (1936): 141–9.

Although prompted by the appearance of Arntz's (**1011**) edition and translation, which Keller regards as inferior to that of Dickins (**1004**), this article is primarily a discussion of the origin of the names of runes in *Rune Poem*. Keller considers the Icelandic and Norwegian rune poems, arguing that all three need to be studied together if we wish to arrive at an understanding of the genre and the common source of these poems and their mutual influence. This applies despite the differences in date and cultural context. The presence of obscure and hard-to-parallel lexical items suggests an ancient tradition. The sources of some rune-names are to be sought in Germany, others in Scandinavia. The word 'cen' can perhaps be linked to German *Kien*, whereas 'yr' and 'iar' are erroneous duplications of 'eoh' ('yew') and 'ger' ('year'). Keller notes that the English version of the postulated original rune poem suppresses reference to the god Tiw. The name *tir*, with its characteristic final *-r*, betrays Scandinavian influence. English and Scandinavian mnemonic verses on the rune names influenced each other, but the basic series of names in *Rune Poem* is a heritage from continental times.

4 **Redbond, William J.** 'Notes on the Word Eolhx.' *Modern Language Review* 31 (1936): 55–7.

The word, as compounded with *secg* in *Rune Poem*, cannot be connected with *eolh* 'elk'. Some foreign source is more probable and of these the Latin *helix* 'willow herb, epilobium' is the most convincing.

5 **Wright, C.E.** 'A Postscript to "Late Old English Rune-Names".' *Medium Aevum* 5 (1936): 149–51.

Wright corrects Wrenn's (**1008**) account of the codicology and palaeography of the leaf containing the *fuþark* in Cotton Domitian A.ix.

6 **Keller, Wolfgang.** 'Zur Chronologie der altenglischen Runen.' *Anglia* 62 (1938): 24–32.

In passing Keller mentions that the poet of *Rune Poem* knew the Bewcastle supplementary runes but not those of the Ruthwell Cross.

7 **Blomfield, Joan.** 'Runes and the Gothic Alphabet.' *Saga-Book of the Viking Society* 12 (1941–2): 177–94 and 209–31.

Blomfield notes (212) that some of the rune-names in the three rune poems have been altered in accordance with the vocabulary and sound-systems of the various languages. In England further changes were engendered by punning and etymological fancies. These poems are better preservers of tradition than Cynewulf and the compilers of manuscript futharks, 'but here again we owe the recording of such matter to lovers of the curious' (213). In the 'os' strophe of *Rune Poem* there is evidently a pun on the two senses 'god' and 'mouth'. The two Scandinavian poems are the most reliable witnesses, because the 'northern tradition remained much longer immune from the interference of Latin scholarship' (213). The Old English name 'cen' may represent an adaptation from Old Norse *kaun* 'swelling, ulcer'; its meaning in *Rune Poem* 'may well be derived from a different source' (218). None of the vowel names in the English extension to the futhark has any known meaning, 'apart from that devised by the inscrutable etymological methods of the author of *Rune Poem*' (220). The rune *ear* corresponds to the letter *z* in being the last character of the series. 'The word *ear* in *Rune Poem* has never been explained; but if it means "the end" the description given is entirely appropriate' (225).

8 **Klaeber, Frederick.** 'Zur Texterklärung altenglischer Dichtungen.' *Anglia Beiblatt* 54–5 (1943–4): 170–6.

In note 2 (171–2) Klaeber deals with *Rune Poem* lines 41–3. He calls in question

Rieger's explanation (72) of 'eolh-secg' as 'sedge as food or resting place for the elk' and supports Redbond's explanation (1014), where the word is connected to Latin *helix*. In line 43 'breneð' may be explained as a form of *brynan* 'to turn red/brown'. In note 3 (172–3) Klaeber argues for an *apo koinou* construction in line 59 and an interpretation of 'swican' in line 60 as 'give him the slip' (through death).

1019   Krause, Wolfgang. *Ing. Nachrichten von der Akademie der Wissenschaften in Göttingen, philologisch-historische Klasse,* 1944 no. 10. 229–54.

The 'Ing' strophe in *Rune Poem* can be better understood if we conceive of Ing as a fertility god associated with the sun. The word 'wæn' (line 69) refers to the chariot of the sun. Krause also discusses the reference to the 'Heardingas' (line 70), arguing that the cult of Ing had already established itself prior to the Danish conquest of Vendsyssel.

1020   Brooks, K.R. 'Old English *EA* and Related Words.' *English and Germanic Studies* 5 (1952–3): 15–66.

In the course of this article Brooks discusses Old English *ear* in the two possible senses 'water/sea' and 'earth'. He confirms the sense 'water', citing Riddle 3 line 22 and other texts (43). This *ear* cannot, on semantic grounds, be connected with the Old Norse *aurr* 'gravel, mud, clay'. He notes that the putative second Old English *ear* ('earth') has been seen as occurring in *Rune Poem* and as cognate with *aurr* by many scholars. He points out, however, that the etymological methods of the author of *Rune Poem* are often obscure. He therefore endorses Blomfield's (1017) suggestion that since the equivalent rune in most other futharks corresponds to *z*, the meaning of 'ear' in this context may be simply 'the end'. If 'end' were taken in the sense 'death', this interpretation would suit the strophe in *Rune Poem* admirably (47).

1021   Elliott, Ralph W.V. 'Runes, Yews, and Magic.' *Speculum* 32 (1957): 250–61.

Elliott mentions in passing (259) a custom of using yew sticks to protect the house and suggests that the expression 'hyrde fyres' in *Rune Poem* line 36 should be taken in the sense of 'guardian against fire', not 'guardian of fire'.

1022   Page, Raymond I. 'The Old English Rune *ear.*' *Medium Aevum* 30 (1961): 65–79.

Page defends the interpretation of 'ear' in *Rune Poem* as 'grave, earth', cognate with Old Norse *aurr*. Within the poem, 'os' is a parallel for the presumed survival of a word not exemplified elsewhere in the Anglo-Saxon corpus. Arntz's theory (1011) that this and other runes were assigned purely arbitrary names is counter-indicated by the likelihood that *Rune Poem*, as a mnemonic poem, would use commonly recognized names for the runes.

1023   Wrenn, C.L. *Anglo-Saxon Poetry and the Amateur Archaeologist.* The Chambers Memorial Lecture 12 March 1962. London: Lewis, for University College, London, 1962. 24 pp.

Wrenn discusses the meaning of 'rad' in *Rune Poem* (11). He agrees with Grein-Köhler (**3**) on 'modulatio' for the first occurrence. The translation is therefore 'Rhythmical music (*rad*) is a pleasant thing to every man in a hall: but riding (understanding *rad* again in its ordinary sense) is a mighty hard thing for one who sits on a powerful horse going over the miles of road.' Schneider's (**226**) interpretation of *rad* in *Rune Poem* as 'flute' or 'clarionet' is too speculative. In passing Wrenn makes additional comments on *Rune Poem* and also refers to *Solomon and Saturn* (14) and the 'harp' passage in *Fortunes* lines 80–4 (12).

4 **Ross, Alan S.C.** 'Three Lexicographic Notes. . .: III "Ac byð . . . flaesces fodor" '. *English Philological Studies* 8 (1963): 30–5.

The word 'flæsc' is used in the rare sense of 'pig-meat' in *Rune Poem* line 78 (34–5).

5 **Musset, Lucien.** *Introduction à la Runologie.* En partie d'après les notes de Fernand Mossé. Bibliothèque de Philologie Germanique 20. Paris: Aubier-Montaigne, 1965. xxi + 468 pp. + 20 ill.

Rune Poem is discussed alongside its Old Norse and Old Icelandic counterparts (114–27). Musset sees tenuous connections in tradition between the overall scheme of this poem and the arrangement of the alphabetical psalms in the Bible, mediated by alphabetical poems by Augustine and hymns by Fortunatus, but cannot locate any precise parallel (115–16). The poet may have reversed the order of the last two runes, in order to reach a suitably moralistic conclusion on the significant word 'ear' (121). Musset suggests a ninth-century date on unstated stylistic and metrical grounds. He notes the absence of the supplementary runes found in the Ruthwell Cross inscription. He describes the poem as an assemblage of clichés from heroic poetry and Christian doctrine, possessing only limited literary value. Beyond attempting to produce a mnemonic formula, the poet's main concern was to demonstrate erudition and virtuosity (122). More generally, Musset regards the form of the rune names as possessing greater permanence than the sense, which could be manipulated or altered to suit the convenience of the individual poet (136).

6 **Jones, Frederick G.** 'The Hypermetric Lines of the *Rune Poem*.' *Neuphilologische Mitteilungen* 74 (1973): 224–31.

Noting that there are only two hypermetric strophes in *Rune Poem*, those on 'hægl' and 'nyd', Jones speculates on the possible reasons for the poet's using expanded lines for his treatment of these two particular runes. Both strophes deal with processes of transformation. This thematic parallel may be given a further dimension through the association of the 'nyd' rune with the mystery of the Cross. The poem as a whole may be seen as cross-shaped, with the 'hægl' and 'nyd' strophes forming the cross bar. An allusion to the self-sacrifice of Woden, as the discoverer of the runes, may also be involved.

Page, Raymond I. 'Anglo-Saxon Texts in Early Modern Transcripts. 1. The Anglo-Saxon Runic Poem.' *Transactions of the Cambridge Bibliographical Society* 6 (1973): 69–85.

Page discusses the date and condition of the lost manuscript of *Rune Poem*. He reassesses Hempl's examination (1002) of the integrity of Hickes's *Thesaurus* material (1705). Hempl's theory that Hickes (or Wanley) added material from Cotton Domitian A.ix to the text of *Rune Poem* found in Cotton Otho B.x cannot be sustained. In Page's opinion Otho B.x already contained marginalia derived from Domitian A.ix before Wanley saw it. These marginalia were perhaps added by the early Tudor antiquary Robert Talbot. Page adds the caveat that imprecisions in Wanley's and Hickes's descriptions of the *Rune Poem* text make this reconstruction of events merely probable, rather than certain (69–75).

1028 **Schwab, Ute.** *Die Sternrune im Wessobrunner Gebet: Beobachtungen zur Lokalisierung des clm 22053, zu Hs. BM Arundel 393 und zu Rune Poem v. 86–89.* Amsterdamer Publikationen zur Sprache und Literatur 1. Amsterdam: Rodopi, 1973. 147 pp.

Schwab identifies christianizing and censoring tendencies on the part of the redactor of our extant version of *Rune Poem*. A variety of traditions, both Nordic and Anglo-Saxon, must be posited to explain the complexities of the poem. The choice of the rune names *ear* and *ior* may have been conditioned by the existence of other names ending in -*r*, such as *ur*. Lines 55–8 depend on the name *eoh* 'horse': both the standard meaning and the half-kenning 'horse [of the waves], i.e. ship' would be involved. Schwab accepts Marquardt's (198) theory that Cynewulf revived the kenning-type 'sea-horse' (= 'ship'), working from an antecedent of the extant *Rune Poem*.

1029 **Jungandreas, Wolfgang.** 'Die Namen der Runen: Futhark und Kosmologie.' *Onoma* 18 (1974): 365–90.

Jungandreas postulates that the runes derive from the Roman alphabet. The letters are of course ordered very differently, but the changes can be explained in relation to the meaning of the rune names. In his discussion of the meanings of these names Jungandreas makes reference to *Rune Poem*, emphasizing ambiguities in their use there. He argues that *cen* 'torch' was homonymous with an Old English **cen* 'boat', with a resultant ambiguity in the relevant strophe in *Rune Poem*. He explains 'peorð' as 'sinew, gut' and relates the strophe in *Rune Poem* to a custom of target-shooting with bow and arrow in the Anglo-Saxon beer-hall.

1030 **Hamp, Eric P.** 'On the Importance of *os* in the Structure of the Runic Poem.' *Studia Germanica Gandensia* 17 (1976): 143–51.

In Hamp's opinion, one function of *Rune Poem* should be seen as associating or cataloguing or even explicating homophonous words. One example is 'rad', another is 'os'. In the treatment of 'os' we find the poet referring to the glosses 'mouth', 'god', and even 'prop'. This word was instrumental in a breakaway from the older function of the poem, which was to supply a single gloss, as with 'cen'. Sometimes we see polysemy being restrained, so that 'tir' in the poem refers solely to a constellation. A factor here would be assimilation in meaning to the preceding 'sigel'. The version of *Rune Poem* that we have is a single token of a traditional rune-song which had a history of re-shapings. These transformations would have led to the failures in homogeneity and occasional obscurities which we see.

Hall, J.R. 'Perspective and Wordplay in the Old English *Rune Poem.*' *Neophilologus* 61 (1977): 453–60.

Hall argues that antithesis between different aspects of the same concept or object is fundamental to the thought in *Rune Poem*. The poem is designed to induce the audience to perceive the complexity of creation and the multiple aspects of realities within it. Thus, in the 'ur' strophe, the poet would have operated with two senses of 'oferhyrned' (line 4), a word which was probably his own coinage. This strophe, which makes such play with horns, is juxtaposed with deliberate humorous intent with the 'þorn' strophe. The ash is envisaged by the poet throughout the 'æsc' strophe as both tree and spear. In the 'ac' strophe the word 'treowe' (line 80), though signifying primarily 'good faith', carries the connotation of 'wood'.

Osborn, Marijane, and Stella Longland. 'A Celtic Intruder in the Old English *Rune Poem.*' *Neuphilologische Mitteilungen* 81 (1980): 385–7.

The poet of *Rune Poem* undertook to compose a poem specifically about the meanings of the rune-names. It was therefore essential to find meaningful words that came close to matching the established names, even those in the expanded section of the futhorc. In seeking to pair each rune with a meaningful word the poet was sometimes obliged to borrow from another language, as in the cases of *os* and *iar*. The common-Celtic word *iar* 'small brown animal of the rodent family', corresponding to Irish *íaru* 'stoat, squirrel, weasel, etc.' and Gaelic *iarag* 'any little creature of brownish hue', was taken over in the specific sense of 'beaver'. The beaver is referred to as a 'river-fish' in *Rune Poem* line 87 because, with its scaly tail, it was classed with fish for Lenten dietary purposes.

Halsall, Maureen. *The Old English Rune Poem: A Critical Edition.* McMaster Old English Studies and Texts 2. Toronto: U of Toronto P, 1981. x + 197 pp.

Halsall's edition outlines the origin, development, and uses of runes, before proceeding to an examination of text, language, literary sources, style, and themes in *Rune Poem*. Following the text and translation, explanatory notes give special attention to the background of each individual rune and rune name. Text and translation of the two Scandinavian rune poems, glossary, and bibliography are also provided. In Chapter 1 'Runes and their Use' (4–20) Halsall attempts to determine what rune lore the author of *Rune Poem* possessed. *Rune Poem* conforms to the traditional order of the *fuþorc*, its forms, and the rune names. Possibly also it reflects an awareness of the threefold division of the *fuþorc*. Like Ælfric, the poet was probably aware that runes once were used for magical purposes. In Chapter 2 'The Textual Background of the *Rune Poem*' (21–32) Halsall takes the view that the Wanley transcript which served as Hickes's copy-text (1705) is likely to have been painstakingly accurate. The addition of rune names to the text, which spoils the intellectual game between poet and audience, perhaps antedates Hickes and Wanley by centuries. The manuscript leaf is of late tenth-century date and the language of the poem and the rune names alike is late West Saxon, with a few possible Kenticisms. In Chapter 3 'Source and Genre of the *Rune Poem*' (33–45) Halsall rules against the hypothesis of a Germanic 'ur-poem'. *Rune Poem* shows formal similarities with gnomes centred on the verb *bið*, which attempt to record stable realities in the flux of existence. Formal similarities with riddles, both Exeter Book and Latin, include a delight in verbal ingenuity. Among the alphabetic poems in Latin is a remarkably close analogue, the *Versus Cuiusdam Scoti de Alphabeto*, where, as in *Rune Poem*, a short strophe is devoted to the description of each letter. In Chapter 4 'Style and Themes of the Old English *Rune Poem*' (47–60) Halsall argues for a 'bookish' poem on the basis that the riddling effect of the twenty-nine strophes of the *Rune Poem* surely would be wasted if the rune names were uttered aloud. As part of the poet's metrical virtuosity, the hypermetric verses are associated with the idea of change. Moreover, the irregularities of strophe length coincide with the ancient threefold grouping of the *fuþorc*, which was still used contemporaneously with the poet of *Rune Poem* for cryptic communication. Contrary to the adverse literary assessment reached by Musset (**1025**) and others, the poet has succeeded in forging a mass of inherited rune lore into a Christian unity, where the good things of the created world are put into their proper perspective, especially by the final strophe. In Chapter 5 'The Literary Achievement of the *Rune Poem*' (61–3) Halsall urges the reader of *Rune Poem* to cultivate a readiness to perceive loose and subtle structuring methods. Following a facsimile reproduction of Hickes's print (84) the text and facing-page translation of *Rune Poem* are given (86–93). Sample translation (lines 67–70): 'Ing among the East-Danes was first/ beheld by men, until that later time when to the east/ he made his departure over the wave, followed by his chariot;/ that was the name those stern warriors gave the hero.' In her notes on the poem Halsall points to the strength of traditions regarding the rune name *ur*. The reason should be sought in the veneration for family heirlooms, which may have included drinking horns fashioned from the aurochs. By contrast, the original meaning of 'feoh' would have been eclipsed and even 'os' would have been unfamiliar in the sense 'pagan god'. The preservation of the name 'Ing' can be attributed to the early anthropomorphization of a fertility deity into the legendary ancestor of the Swedes. The *w*-rune should not be interpreted as 'wen' ('hope'). At various points, e.g. in discussing the rune names 'hægl' and 'ac', Halsall argues that *Rune Poem* offers no evidential support for the theories of Schneider (**226**). Similarly, the unease about the sea voiced in the 'lagu' strophe relates to a perfectly natural fear and has nothing to do with ship burial.

1034 Osborn, Marijane. *'Hleotan* and the Purpose of the Old English *Rune Poem.'* *Folklore* 92 (1981): 168–73.

Osborn contends that the purpose of *Rune Poem* is in some sense divinatory, but not necessarily pagan. Compared with the two Scandinavian rune poems, *Rune Poem* innovates in respect of its ethical stance and overall design, moving from the good life in the hall to the burial of the corpse. Osborn proposes to translate the first strophe (lines 1–3) as follows: '(Wealth) is a comfort for everyone; but every man must share it generously if he wishes to cast the lots of judgement before his lord.' Here and elsewhere in the poem secular and Christian traditions are fused. Although it is entirely possible that the poet used a genuine tradition of runic oracles, it is also possible that the system is of his own devising.

Nicholson, Peter. 'The Old English Rune for *S.' JEGP* 81 (1982): 313–19.

Nicholson argues that 'sigel' ('sun') does not fit the context in *Rune Poem*: 'segl' ('sail') would make better sense. It would allow the pronoun 'hine' in line 46 to refer back to the previous clause, as is normal, rather than forward to 'brimhengest' in the next clause, as construed by Grienberger **(1005)** and Page **(289)**. Although certainly there is some external evidence that the *s*-rune was called 'sigel', *Rune Poem* is also an important source of information on the meanings that the runes could have, and it is difficult to ignore both the grammar and the sense. Cynewulf's use of variant rune-names 'suggests both that two different meanings could have been current for a single rune and that a traditional name could be abandoned for a phonetic doublet if the context were clear' (316). The interpretation 'segl' would also make sense in the runic passage in *The Husband's Message.* The word 'sigel' was evidently obsolescent in Old English.

Osborn, Marijane, and Stella Longland. *Rune Games.* London: Routledge, 1982. xi + 299 pp.

The authors believe that *Rune Poem* has the potential to provide us with a fresh approach to the problems of individuality and existence. A text, after Dickins **(1004)**, and translation are supplied. The authors argue that the runes were thought of as more than an archaic 'alphabet'. In *Rune Poem* an old system of the wise found refuge with the new, having been censored so as not to offend the morals of the new order. The appearance of the keyword 'hleotan' ('to cast lots') in the first strophe of *Rune Poem* (line 3) seems designed to alert the reader to the oracular nature of the poem as a whole. But typical of the poem is an ambivalence such that a Christian interpretation is equally plausible. The authors relate 'peorð' to a Celtic word *port*, meaning a tune played on bagpipes. They relate 'iar' to 'beaver', again on the basis of a postulated Celtic etymon. They suggest that 'sigel' refers to the sun-stone, a navigational instrument. They explain 'ear', the final rune, as meaning 'dust'. The 'tir' rune is to be identified with the Pole Star, in keeping with the indication that it 'næfre swiceþ' (line 50).

Stanley, Eric G. 'Notes on the Text of *Christ and Satan*; and on *The Rhyming Poem* and *The Rune Poem*; chiefly on *wynn, wen* and *wenne.' Notes and Queries* 229, NS 31 (1984): 443–53.

Stanley advocates reading 'wen ne', not 'wynne', as the opening word in the *w*-strophe of *Rune Poem* (line 22). Strophes in *Rune Poem* normally open with the nominative of the rune name. An uninflected accusative 'wen', possible even though governed by *brucan*, is therefore preferable to a genitive 'wynne'. The idea is that the prosperous person has no occasion for Hope.

Derolez, René. 'Runes and Magic.' *American Notes and Queries* 24 (1986): 96–102.

Derolez reviews evidence for rune magic in Old English inscriptions. As to *Rune Poem*, he finds that even the complete set of explanatory strophes contained there gives very little indication of applications in magic.

1039 Ellis Davidson, Hilda. *Myths and Symbols in Pagan Europe: Early Scandinavian and Celtic Religions.* Manchester: Manchester UP, 1988. xii + 268 pp.

Ellis Davidson discusses the 'Ing' strophe in *Rune Poem* (119–20). She points out the key problems: Did Ing travel to the east ('est') or return back ('eft')? Is the wagon a symbol for travel to the Other World? The wagon graves of the Celts in the late Halstatt and early La Tène periods might indicate the adoption of such a symbol, later replaced in Scandinavia by a ship.

1040 Bradley, Daniel J. 'The Old English *Rune Poem*: Elements of Mnemonics and Psychoneurological Beliefs.' *Perceptual and Motor Skills* 69 (1989): 3–8.

Bradley proposes that the runes evolved from Near and Far Eastern protoalphabets. Hence the Chinese radical R.38 'Woman', 'Nu', is the phonetic and graphic eidolon of *Ing*, which in turn means 'inglenook'. Likewise, some strophes in *Rune Poem* are derived from Chinese radical sequences and afford us insights into ancient mnemonic techniques. The Sanskrit letters are, in Hindu belief, gravid with sound-energy if placed systematically and meditatively as mnemonics on critical points of the nervous system. The thirty-three runes are mnemonically valenced in a similar fashion.

1041 Halsall, Maureen. 'Runes and the Mortal Condition in Old English Poetry.' *JEGP* 88 (1989): 477–86.

Halsall contends that runic symbols were employed by both Cynewulf and the anonymous author of *Rune Poem* in order to emphasize the theme of human mortality. Such emphasis accorded with an Anglo-Saxon tradition that ultimately derived from the pre-Christian practice of incising runes on Continental Germanic memorial stones. This tradition accounts for the emphasis on mortality in the 'ear' strophe that closes *Rune Poem*.

1042 Solari, Roberto. 'Eoh.' *Romanobarbarica* 10 (1988–9): 329–39 = *Studi sulla cultura germanica dei secoli IV–XII in onore di Giulia Mazzuoli Porru.* Ed. M.A. D'Aronco et al. Rome: Herder, 1990. 329–39.

Solari discusses the etymology of the rune-name *eoh* 'yew', opposing Schneider's reconstruction (**226**) of the relevant strophe in *Rune Poem*. He argues that *Rune Poem* seems to avoid references to the mythical or legendary associations of the yew tree. Nor do its curative and toxic properties come into the picture. Instead the text focuses upon the resistance of yew to fire and slowness to burn away. These properties arise because it does not possess channels for the sap to flow through.

1043 Stanley, E.G. '*The Rune Poem* 34: *beornum.*' *Notes and Queries* 235, NS 37 (1990): 143–4.

Dissenting from previous interpretations of 'beornum and ðearfum' in line 34, Stanley argues that *beorn* means not 'rich man' but 'vigorous man'. Hence the antithesis is between 'men of vigour' and poor men, 'perhaps men debilitated by indigence'.

44 Clunies Ross, Margaret. 'The Anglo-Saxon and Norse *Rune Poems*, a Comparative Study.' *Anglo-Saxon England* 19 (1990): 23–39.

Clunies Ross points out that much previous discussion of *Rune Poem* has proceeded on the assumption that it and the Icelandic and Norwegian counterparts reflect a shared cultural prototype. At the same time, however, an exaggerated attention to the pagan allusions, misunderstandings concerning skaldic diction, and general neglect of wisdom poetry have all impeded comparative scholarship on these poems. She argues that the three rune poems used a human cultural instrument, the runic alphabet and its attendant lore, as a means of ordering nature. Comparison of the verse-forms and diction of the three poems reveals how each displays an indigenous development of a probably prototypical short definitional strophe type. Examination of the 'feoh' material in each poem shows adaptations to different cultures of traditional ideas about wealth and its use. Similarly, gnomic texts in Old English and Old Norse agree in revealing a tension between the advantages and the risks of horse-riding. Consequently, there is no need to postulate punning on the word *rad* in *Rune Poem*. Where the 'tir' strophe is concerned, *Rune Poem* participates in an encyclopaedic tradition of setting pagan star names alongside those of the Christian-classical tradition, thus attesting to general human knowledge of the heavens.

45 Breeze, Andrew. '*Exodus, Elene*, and *The Rune Poem*: milþæþ 'Army Road, Highway.' *Notes and Queries* 236, NS 38 (1991): 436–8.

Breeze suggests that *mil-* may be a loan element from Welsh *mil* 'army'. In *Rune Poem* line 15 the sense of 'roads taken by an army' for 'milpaþas' fits the senses suggested for 'rad' by Dobbie (**203**), i.e. 'riding, a raid'. The poet is playing with contrasting perceptions of war. One perception is that of officers back in the mess or HQ ('recyde': line 13), the other is that of a combatant on an army horse making his way to the front. This interpretation may help improve critical opinions of *Rune Poem*, transforming a banal observation into a terse and perennial comment on war. Breeze suggests some literary connection between the three rather similar passages contained in the three poems of his title. The borrowing from Welsh might indicate a Mercian origin for *Rune Poem*.

Solomon and Saturn

ORIENTATION TO RESEARCH

MANUSCRIPTS AND EDITIONS

The three *Solomon and Saturn* fragments, two poetic with a third middle section in prose, are contained in CCCC 422 and (part only) in CCCC 41. Ker (**36**) dated 422 as mid-tenth-century and 41 at the first half of the eleventh century. Sisam (**208**), followed by Jabbour (**266**) but qualified by O'Keeffe (**358**), identified traces of oral transmission in the text. Harris (**1102**) regarded the three fragments as components in a Solomon and Saturn anthology. For editions and other textual commentary see the subject index.

DATING, LOCALIZATION, AND AUTHORSHIP

Opinions on dating and localization have varied greatly. Suggested datings include Grein (**84**), to the beginning of the eighth century; Anderson (**31**), to the first half of the ninth century; Schipper (**1051**), to the time of King Alfred; Menner (**1073**), to the ninth or possibly tenth century; and Brandl (**19**) and Richter (**22**), to the late tenth century. Other datings, attached to localizations, have been as follows: Vincenti (**1061**), Northumbrian verse and West Saxon prose, written between 868 and 1000; Menner (**1073**), West Saxon copy of an originally Anglian version; and Stanley (**276**), late West Saxon. Menner's views were rebutted by Sisam (**215, 1075**). Sarrazin (**95**) postulated Cynewulfian influence upon the text. Opinion has also fluctuated on the relationship between the three parts of the text, but with a decided tendency to assume separate authorship. Schmitz (**134**) believed that the two poetic sections are too diverse to have originated with the same author. Wülker (**18**) reversed his earlier opinion (**8**) in identifying *Solomon and Saturn* II as the older of the two verse sections, and most scholars, for example ten Brink (**5**), Brooke (**109**), and Dobbie (**203**), have concurred with the latter view. Pilch and Tristram (**55**) believed that the prose section is probably a continuation of *Solomon and Saturn* I.

SIGNIFICANCE FOR MYTHOLOGY

Some scholars have identified vestiges of Germanic heathendom in these fragments. Grimm (**363**) and Kemble (**66, 1047**) used them as evidence for Saturn's place in the Germanic pantheon. Wrenn (**43**) saw Saturn as ultimately related to Woden. Vogt (**1053**), supported by Vincenti (**1061**), preferred an oriental affiliation. Deering (**1055**) posited some residual heathen conceptions of Judgement, hell, and heaven. Weber (**267**) saw the attitude to Fate as not native Germanic but a blend of Stoic and Christian.

METRICAL STUDIES

Metrically, the two poetic fragments are highly irregular, so much so that Sievers **(92)** largely excluded them from his investigation of hypermetric lines. Dissenters from Sievers include Kaluza **(15)**, Holthausen **(132)**, and Schmitz **(133, 134)**. The importance of hypermetric lines is documented by Schmitz **(133, 134)** and Pope **(204)**. Bliss **(227)** concluded that *Solomon and Saturn* and other gnomic poetry belonged to a distinct tradition, a view supported by evidence adduced by Momma **(349)**.

FUNCTION OF THE RUNIC LETTERS IN *SOLOMON AND SATURN* I

Dissent continues as to the status of the runes which in the manuscript accompany most of the Roman versions of the constituent letters of the Paternoster. In the opinion of Kemble **(63, 1046)**, Derolez **(216)**, O'Keeffe **(358)**, and Sweet **(1075)**, it is the Roman letters that are integral to the text, whereas the runes represent later additions of some kind. But many scholars, including Kittredge **(178)**, Elliott **(230)**, Schneider **(226, 1100)**, Menner **(1073)**, Zolla **(1083)**, Sharpe **(1093)**, Kellermann and Haas **(1100)**, and Nelson **(1108)**, have read deeper significance into the runes, usually as an intrinsic part of the text.

LITERARY AFFILIATIONS

The relationship between *Solomon and Saturn* and other texts with similar protagonists has proved difficult to unravel. Förster **(1057)** demonstrated correspondences between the prose section of *Solomon and Saturn* and *Adrian and Ritheus*. Kemble **(1047)** distinguished the content of *Solomon and Saturn* from that of the dialogues of the same (editorial) name preserved in Cotton Vitellius A.xv, as also from that of the Salomon and Marcolf dialogues in German, French, Russian, and other languages. Wright **(64)** compared *Solomon and Saturn* to the Latin *Disputatio inter Pippinum et Alcuinum*. Some scholars, including Kemble **(1047)**, Sweet **(77)**, Menner **(1073)**, Dane **(1096)**, and Hammerich **(1049)**, agreed that *Solomon and Saturn* shows a mixture of Germanic question-and-answer dialogue, familiar from *Vafþrúðnismál*, and of oriental mysticism, mediated by Greek and Latin sources. Schaumberg **(1050)**, Ker **(121)**, O'Keeffe **(1110)**, and Hansen **(61)** preferred to privilege the European element, whereas Morley **(74)**, followed by Ebert **(79)**, highlighted oriental hyperbole, humour, and other allegedly non-Anglo-Saxon qualities. Some scholars, including Robinson **(7)**, Förster **(1059)**, Merrill **(1064)**, and James **(1068)** have given prominence to Old Testament analogues and sources, both canonical and apocryphal. Vincenti **(1061)** and Menner **(1070, 1071)** posited proximate but so far untraced Latin sources. Specific affiliations to Germanic literature and culture have been adduced by Ellis Davidson **(242)** and Taylor **(1088)**. Specific allusions to Latin analogues have been detected by Hill **(1086)**, Cilluffo **(1097)**, and Hermann **(319, 322, 1090, 1106)**. Pearsall **(52)** saw influence from Hisperic tradition in *Solomon and Saturn* I.

LITERARY CRITICISM

A consensual characterization of the dominant tone to be found in these fragments has proved elusive. Greenfield (40) and Shippey (47, 300) compared *Solomon and Saturn* II with elegiac poetry. Tripp (1094) preferred to see both poetic sections as conveying the momentum of Christian optimism. Harris (1102) found the tone of *Solomon and Saturn* II harsher than that of Boethius in that it emphasizes irreconcilable oppositions. As to genre, Grant (305) proposed that the part of the text transcribed in CCCC 41 should be treated as a lorica. Uncertainty has also reigned as to the respective merits of the various sections. Shippey (300) saw both poetic sections as emanating from a learned, cranky, impractical background. Greenfield and Calder (60) preferred the second poetic section to the first on formal grounds.

BIBLIOGRAPHY

1046 **Kemble, John M.** *Salomon and Saturn.* Page-proofs without title page. [London]: privately printed, 1845 or earlier.

[According to the British Library catalogue, 'the Anglo-Saxon text to which this is an introduction was afterwards published by Mr Kemble for the Aelfric Society'. On the first page Vincenti (1061) found the following comment: 'This Edition of Salomon and Saturn, (with the exception of twenty copies), was cancelled by Mr Kemble when he undertook to bring out the Edition printed for the Aelfric Society.' According to Larsen (1069), the book was privately distributed (e.g. copies were provided for consultation at the Bodleian, Cambridge University Library, and the British Museum) but never formally published.] The book contains an account of the origins and dissemination of the Solomon and Saturn/Marcolf story, without text or the other materials to be found in the 1848 edition (1047).

1047 **Kemble, John Mitchell.** *The Dialogue of Salomon and Saturnus, with an Historical Introduction.* London: Aelfric Society, 1845–8. viii + 326 pp.

Included are an edition and translation of *Solomon and Saturn* (verse and prose), with notes (132–77). This is the first scholarly edition of *Solomon and Saturn*, edited from the manuscripts. Noting that the scribe of CCCC 422 has modernized many earlier forms, Kemble further normalizes in accordance with late West Saxon orthography. Manuscript forms thus altered are not signalled in the apparatus. Appended is the first complete translation into any language. In his discussion of the text Kemble argues that *Solomon and Saturn* I bears no relation whatever, save in name, to the tradition of dialogues between Solomon and an interlocutor, e.g. Hyram. *Solomon and Saturn* II, by contrast, represents a closer approach to the main tradition, consisting as it does of a series of riddling questions proposed by the two interlocutors. Even so, it bears little resemblance to the Cotton Vitellius A.xv *Solomon and Saturn* texts. Although the subjects are similar, none of the questions found in the poetic *Solomon and Saturn* are repeated either in the prose version or in the *Adrian and Ritheus*. There is no resemblance whatever to the other versions of the Salomon and Marcolf material.

The subjects of *Solomon and Saturn* II are theological and moral. Allowing for difference in religion, they might best be compared to *Vafþrúðnismál*. The poetic *Solomon and Saturn* is partly of Scandinavian origin, an echo from the days of Germanic heathenism. Kemble proposes to restore Saturnus or Marcolfus to his place in the pagan Germanic Pantheon. The oriental part of the legend can be traced back to Jewish traditions, notably the Old Testament. Kemble collects allusions to serious dialogues between Solomon and Marcolf in the Middle Ages, prior to the degeneration of the genre into coarse comedy. A detailed examination of German, Latin, French, and other versions shows the extreme popularity and wide dissemination of this dialogue in European tradition. Kemble compares Marcolfus with characters in early Germanic wisdom dialogues, such as *Vafþrúðnismál*. Other collections of wisdom, e.g. 'Proverbs of Alfred' and 'Proverbs of Hendyng', are appended for comparison.

48 **Hofmann, C.** 'Über Jourdain de Blaivies, Apollonius von Tyrus, Salomon und Marcolf.' *Sitzungsberichten der Münchener Akademie, phil.-hist. Kl.* 1871, 1: 415–33.

Hofmann regards *Solomon and Saturn* as stemming from an oriental tradition. On the topic of Solomon's interlocutor he suggests that patristic writers equated Saturn with Malcol, i.e. Moloch, on the grounds that both were considered as eaters of children (431).

49 **Hammerich, Friedrich.** *De episke-kristelige Oldkvad hos de gotiske Folk.* Copenhagen: Schultz, 1873. 207. Trans. A. Michelsen. *Älteste christliche Epik der Angelsachsen, Deutschen und Nordländer: Ein Beitrag zur Kirchengeschichte.* Gütersloh: Bertelsmann, 1874. viii + 280 pp.

The Old English material is covered on pages 17–132. Hammerich characterizes *Solomon and Saturn* as half Germanic, half oriental. The descriptions which it contains deserve credit for maintaining the attention of the reader. In the account of the battle between the Paternoster and the devil in *Solomon and Saturn* I, the personified prayer is described in terms reminiscent of Thor. In the prose section Hammerich, following Kemble (**1047**), envisages Thor with the fire-axe in single combat with the devil. The riddles in *Solomon and Saturn* II are compared with the riddles of ancient Scandinavia (111–13).

50 **Schaumberg, W.** 'Untersuchungen über das deutsche Spruchgedicht Salomo und Morolf.' *Beiträge zur Geschichte der deutschen Sprache und Literatur* 2 (1876): 1–63.

Where studies of the 'Salomon and Marcolf' tradition are concerned, Schaumberg notes that the redactions in the various vernaculars, such as German, French, and Old English, can only be compared in their general outlines, since they differ completely as to detail. *Solomon and Saturn* is important chiefly for the light it can shed on the name Marcolf. The serious tone of *Solomon and Saturn* contrasts with the flippancy of the bulk of extant redactions, and is an indication that the hypothetical composition from which the tradition took its origin would itself have been serious. This composition originates in Europe and not, as usually argued, in the Orient. *Solomon and Saturn* II is a very one-sided dialogue and lacks a narrative frame. The lack of a frame is also apparent in the French version but not in the others. The choice of Saturn as one of the interlocutors in the Old English version can be attributed to the primacy that Roman mythology continued to accord to the pagan god Saturn and the Golden Age. In terms of this centrality, Saturn formed a natural counterpart to Solomon in Judaic tradition (31).

1051 **Schipper, Julius.** 'Salomo und Saturn.' *Germania* 22 (1877): 50–70.

Schipper produces the results of a new textual investigation, where CCCC 422 is collated against CCCC 41 and published in a diplomatic transcription. Kemble's edition (**1047**) is revealed as showing the same editorial weaknesses as Thorpe's edition of the Exeter Book (**65**). Schipper's text includes the prose as well as both verse sections. Some restorations are suggested. Schipper argues that a series of early West Saxon forms dates *Solomon and Saturn* to the time of King Alfred, the first classical period of Anglo-Saxon literature. The later spellings that appear in the manuscripts ought therefore to be normalized in conformity with early West Saxon dialect, in a reversal of Kemble's procedure.

1052 **Sweet, Henry.** 'Collation of the Poetical Salomon and Saturn with the MS.' *Anglia* 1 (1878): 150–4.

Sweet gives the results of a collation of Kemble's edition (**1047**) against CCCC 422. He notes that the manuscript seems to have been more legible in Kemble's time. Some of Kemble's textual alterations can be justified as corrections of obvious errors in the manuscript. Many others, however, lack justification, being prompted purely by ignorance or carelessness. The alterations have the effect of effacing archaisms, in particular spellings with *ie*. These spellings have potential importance as pointing to a ninth-century West Saxon origin for the text. Sweet adds explanations of various passages that were not understood by Kemble.

1053 **Vogt, Friedrich.** *Die deutschen Dichtungen von Salomon und Markolf.* I. *Salman und Morolf.* Halle: Niemeyer, 1880. clx + 218 pp.

In a brief discussion of *Solomon and Saturn* (liii–lv), Vogt identifies this work as the oldest Solomon dialogue preserved in Western vernacular literature. Since the speaker named Saturn has nothing more in common with the god Saturn than his name, it is incorrect to explain the interlocutors as representing divine and secular wisdom respectively. Vogt notes Saturn's affiliation with the Orient, as the leader of the Chaldeans. The traditional magic worked by Solomon against demons has been thoroughly Christianized in *Solomon and Saturn. Solomon and Saturn* I has the specific objective of purging superstitious elements from the tradition. *Solomon and Saturn* II is designed to extol Christian wisdom at the expense of learning in secular magic.

1054 **Zupitza, Julius.** 'Zu Salomon und Saturn.' *Anglia* 3 (1880): 527–31.

Zupitza observes that although Sweet (**1052**) and Schipper (**1051**) both aim to correct Kemble (**1047**) and therefore Grein (**2**), they disagree with each other on a significant number of points. He presents a series of corrections to Schipper's edition and to Sweet's corrections of Kemble and Grein, based on fresh inspection of the manuscript evidence. Sweet's main error is the omission of manuscript accents.

55 **Deering, Robert Waller.** *The Anglo-Saxon Poets on the Judgment Day.* Diss. U Leipzig. Halle: Karras, 1890. 85 pp.

Deering compares conceptions of the Last Judgement in Old English poetry with doctrine in Scripture and current Christian or heathen tradition. He sees references to the Last Judgement in *Solomon and Saturn* as largely accidental. Certain motifs, such as the 'din' of Doomsday (lines 273 and 326), are to be viewed as stereotypical (cf. 2 Pet. 3: 10). *Solomon and Saturn* also participates in the Anglo-Saxon idea that after the Last Judgement the doors of hell are locked (line 173) and the wicked are cut off forever from the presence of God. This motif represents an elaboration in true Anglo-Saxon detail on the simple Biblical doctrine (Matt. 25: 46, and elsewhere) that the evil shall go away into everlasting punishment and the righteous into life eternal. On the other hand, the typical three hundred years of waiting are greatly augmented (lines 272 and 291). *Solomon and Saturn* is also singular in mentioning water as among the torments of hell (line 470). This, along with other discrepant features, may point to derivation from pagan Germanic conceptions of Hel or Hel-like places. Deering envisages a gradual assimilation of Christian and heathen conceptions of Judgement, hell or heaven.

56 **Duff, Edward Gordon.** *The Dialogue or Communing between the Wise King Salomon and Marcolphus.* London: Lawrence, 1892. xxvi + facsimile (unpaginated) + 46 pp.

In his introduction Duff gives an account of the growth of the Solomon and Marcolf tradition, preparatory to the main purpose of the book, which is a facsimile of Gerard Leeu's edition of *The Dialogue or Communing between the Wise King Salomon and Marcolphus.* Duff notes that the name of Marcolphus has never been satisfactorily explained. He objects to Kemble's **(1047)** 'Mearc-wulf' on the grounds that no explanation can be accepted which does not supply the original source of the name. He documents the connections between the personages and names Saturnus, Morcholom, Markolis, and Mercurius, suggesting that these tend to show that Marcolphus was originally conceived as a superhuman personage (xii). In Duff's opinion, the earliest form of the story was a serious dialogue on theological and mystical questions between two persons of equal learning but with very different attitudes. If we accept Asmodeus, the prince of demons, as a prototype of the early Marcolf, or, as he was called in England, Saturn, the contest becomes one between inspired and infernal wisdom. *Solomon and Saturn* I consists of Solomon's elaborate explanation of the Paternoster. It expounds the power and value of the individual letters in a manner which, to a modern reader, would seem to require wisdom even greater than Solomon's to understand (xiii).

57 **Förster, Max.** 'Zu *Adrian und Ritheus.*' *Englische Studien* 23 (1897): 431–6.

In the course of his discussion of *Adrian and Ritheus*, Förster evaluates Kemble's edition of *Solomon and Saturn* **(1047)** and criticizes his deviations from the manuscript in respect of orthography, punctuation, and morphology. Förster compares the detached items of information found in *Adrian and Ritheus* (e.g. on the length of Noah's ark) with some pieces of information in the prose portion of *Solomon and Saturn*. The similarity in themes and form points to a common (Latin) source. Copyists may have been in the habit of condensing dialogues into simple summaries to save space. An appended table shows the detailed correspondences between the prose section of *Solomon and Saturn* and *Adrian and Ritheus*.

1058 Holthausen, Ferdinand. 'Zu alt- und mittelenglischen Dichtungen. XII. 60. Salomo und Saturn.' *Anglia* 23 (1901): 123–5.

Holthausen responds to the new Assmann edition (**6**) of *Solomon and Saturn* with some emendations and exegetical comments. He suggests emendations in lines 11, 34, 107, 108, 167, 180, 214, 236, 252, 277, 287, 311, 339, 341, 396, 465, and 478–9 (most of these *metri gratia*), points out errors in the editor's line division in lines 163–4 and 482–3, and notes failures to adopt emendations made by previous scholars, e.g. in line 16.

1059 Förster, Max. 'Das lateinisch-altenglische Fragment der Apokryphe von Jamnes und Mambres.' *Archiv für das Studium der neueren Literaturen* 108 (1902): 15–28.

Förster refers briefly to *Solomon and Saturn* as exemplifying the characteristic Anglo-Saxon and early Irish interest in the more arcane apocryphal books of the Old Testament. Familiarity with these otherwise almost forgotten materials can be attributed to distance from the central authority of Rome. Förster notes instances of indebtedness to the apocrypha in Old English and Old Irish literature (27–8).

1060 Abbetmeyer, Charles. *Old English Poetical Motives Derived from the Doctrine of Sin.* Minneapolis: Wilson, 1903. 42 pp.

Abbetmeyer discusses the meaning of *wyrd* in *Solomon and Saturn*, arguing that the pagan hypostatis of Wyrd is discredited by being identified with Satan.

1061 Vincenti, A.R. von. *Die altenglischen Dialoge von Salomon und Saturn mit historische Einleitung, Kommentar und Glossar.* Münchener Beiträge zur romanischen und englischen Philologie 31. Leipzig: Deichert, 1904. xxi + 125 pp.

Despite the promise of the title, all that was actually completed of this project is contained in the present volume: the historical introduction, with bibliography (ix–xxi) but without text, commentary, or glossary. Evidently the edited text would have differed from Assmann's (**6**) in line numbering (cf. 27 n. 2). A discussion of the phonology was also promised (vii) but never appeared. Vincenti's main findings are that the text breaks up into three independent sections, a prose section by a West Saxon author and two poetic sections by Northumbrian authors. The second poetic section deserves recognition as a pearl of Old English poetry. The principal sections of the Introduction are on the general history of Solomon narratives – biblical, Talmudic, Semitic, and

'Indogermanic' – and their relation to the Old English version (1–25). Vincenti
shows how the narratives associated with Solomon in the oriental traditions have
been shorn away in the Old English versions. What remains is a pure dialogue
format and a conception of Solomon as a defender of Christendom against Satan.
This role reflects Solomon's combats against demons in the older stories. The
giant Paternoster in the prose section is reminiscent of Asmodeus. The inquiry
about Wyrd is one genuinely Germanic element in *Solomon and Saturn* II.
Despite Vogt's suggestion (**1053**), Saturn is not to be regarded as Solomon's
brother. The motifs of palms and pilgrimage provide a link, albeit a weak one,
between the Old English and the German versions (24–5). Vincenti reviews
previous editions of *Solomon and Saturn*, noting confusions of the different
Solomon and Saturn dialogues in Conybeare (**62**) and anticipating a few
corrections of his own to Assmann (**6**), e.g. concerning the manuscript accents.
He also gives a very full review of previous literary-critical discussions of
Solomon and Saturn (26–44). The manuscripts and their relationships to each
other are described (44–8). The incidence of accents in the manuscripts is
documented (49–51). Vincenti notes Kemble's conjecture (**1047**) that the writing
is in a female hand. He reports on readable portions of page 1 of CCCC 422 and
observes that little from the end of *Solomon and Saturn* II has been lost. He prints
a collation of the two manuscripts (47–9), with the comment that it is difficult to
give one preference over the other. The authors of the texts have Northumbrian
affiliations. In his analysis of *Solomon and Saturn* (51–85) Vincenti points out
that the poet of *Solomon and Saturn* I must be using the St Matthew text of the
Paternoster, not the St Luke one, and shows that, along with the Creed, this
prayer enjoyed primacy in the conversion effort. The notion of using the
individual letters of the prayer can be traced back to Psalm 118. *Solomon and
Saturn* I is to be seen as countering Germanic heathendom and not, with Vogt, as
a Christian purging of oriental traditions. Close analysis reveals the prose portion
of *Solomon and Saturn* to be the product of insanity. A dialogue between a devil
and a hermit in Cotton Tiberius A.iii is cited from Kemble (**84**) as a close
analogue to this section. The lost page after the prose did not contain the
remainder of the prose text, for which there would not have been room, but rather
the conclusion of *Solomon and Saturn* II. Lines 170–8, which appear
immediately following the prose dialogue, form part of this conclusion. *Solomon
and Saturn* II is analysed in great detail, with summary in tabular form (80–2).
The core of the poem is located in the dialogues concerning Fate, Old Age,
Death, and the Last Judgement. The poet is trying to warn heathen Anglo-Saxons
about the transitory nature of life. All three texts are to be referred to a period
when Christianity had not yet conclusively won the battle against Viking
heathendom in England. This would indicate a time-span from 868 up until 1000.
The texts have no close parallels elsewhere in Old English poetry, but
Scandinavian and French analogues deserve special mention. In his discussion of
the characterization of Solomon and Saturn (86–106), Vincenti notes that few of
the sayings attributed to Solomon in the Bible appear in *Solomon and Saturn* and
that to put other wise sayings in his mouth is common in medieval literature (cf.
Chaucer's *Tale of Melibee*). Saturn may be a Prince of the East but the knowledge
he possesses is Germanic. In spite of Vogt, he should not be identified with the
'weallende wulf'. Vogt's identification of the oriental sources for *Solomon and
Saturn* is to be disputed, likewise his description of Solomon and Saturn as

brothers. Vincenti investigates other occurrences of the name Saturn in Old English literature, dissenting from Kemble's speculation (66) that Saturn was a Germanic deity. A Saturn of the Chaldeans would naturally share in that nation's general reputation for astrology and soothsaying. On the topic of sources (122–5), Vincenti questions the authenticity of the Gelasian decree prohibiting a *Contradictio Salomonis*. The decree is summarized (122–3). The *Contradictio*, whatever its contents, is unlikely to have included a contest between Christian and Germanic wisdom, as *Solomon and Saturn* does, and therefore is probably not the source of *Solomon and Saturn*. In fact no Latin texts resembling either dialogue in content have as yet been discovered.

1062 Emerson, Oliver F. 'Legends of Cain, Especially in Old and Middle English.' *PMLA* 21 (1906): 831–929.

Emerson refers to *Solomon and Saturn* in passing (853 and 909). When Solomon reminds Saturn of his connection with an evil race which strove against God (lines 451–76), the Christian poet no doubt had in mind the common medieval interpretation of the war of the giants on Jove. This interpretation connected them with the giants of Genesis. Mercury is also treated as a giant in *Solomon and Saturn*, illustrating how the divinities of the heathen were associated with the giants by early English commentators.

1063 Liebermann, Felix. 'Zu Salomo und Saturn.' *Archiv für das Studium der neueren Literaturen* 120 (1908): 156.

Liebermann argues that 'burg-' in line 307 means 'palace', 'aristocratic residence'. He takes the entire phrase 'burga geatu', with 'geatu' for manuscript 'geat' following Kemble (1047), as a pars pro toto for 'house'. Parallels in various Germanic laws are adduced.

1064 Merrill, Elizabeth. *The Dialogue in English Literature.* Yale Studies in English 42. New York: Holt, 1911. iv + 131 pp.

In her discussion of *Solomon and Saturn*, Merrill argues that the biblical mention of the visit of the Queen of Sheba to Solomon and the questions interchanged during that interview probably formed a starting-point for a story which soon assumed Teutonic rather than oriental colouring. The love of gnomic wisdom, associated in the Bible and in medieval tradition with the name of Solomon, joined forces in the dialogues with the Teutonic love of verbal contest. Some of the dialogue consists of question and answer, some of a competition where each interlocutor tries to outdo the other. Merrill compares the contests in wit found in the Eddaic poems. *Solomon and Saturn* exhibits practically no interplay or interaction between speakers. Where medieval English literature is concerned, the didactic tendencies manifested in *Solomon and Saturn* I worked themselves out in popular and learned catechisms.

1065 Holthausen, Ferdinand. 'Zu Salomo und Saturn.' *Anglia Beiblatt* 27 (1916): 351–7.

Holthausen proposes numerous restorations and minor emendations, often in order to regularize the versification. He comments on the problem of the 'twins of the church' (line 107), suggesting that 'n' and 'o' are so called because they are adjacent letters both in the Paternoster and in the alphabet. The letter 'n', being pronounced /en/, shares in the alliteration in line 108. Similarly, 'h' carries vocalic alliteration in line 138. The 'lifgetwinnan' of lines 141–5 must be 'b' and 'h', since they stand adjacent to each other in the Paternoster. In line 339 'niðes' should be substituted for the puzzling 'niehtes'. Identifications of some of the proper nouns in lines 186–201 and 277–8 are attempted.

6 **Hüttenbrenner, F.** Rev. of *Die gelehrten lateinischen Lehn- und Fremdwörter in der altenglischen Literatur,* by Otto Funke **[141]**. *Anglia Beiblatt* 28 (1917): 33–61.

Hüttenbrenner analyses the occurrences of 'Filistinas' in *Solomon and Saturn.* He adds 'fruma' to fill out line 214a (52–3).

7 **Holthausen, Ferdinand.** 'Zu alt- und mittelenglischen Texten. 1. Zum ae. Salomo und Saturn.' *Anglia Beiblatt* 31 (1920): 190–207.

Holthausen proposes emending 'cirican' in line 107 to 'cirlican' ('male'). He also attempts restoration in line 479 (190–1).

8 **James, M.R.** *The Lost Apocrypha of the Old Testament, Their Titles and Fragments.* Translations of Early Documents, series 1: Palestinian Jewish Texts (Pre-Rabbinic). London: SPCK, 1920. xiv + 111 pp.

James argues that the information concerning 'weallende wulf' in *Solomon and Saturn* lines 212–24 is a reminiscence of an episode in a lost apocryphal 'Book of Og the Giant'. Og was said by heretics, possibly the Manicheans, to have fought with a dragon after the Flood. James links *Solomon and Saturn* with the text referred to as the *Interdictio* or *Contradictio Salomonis* in the Gelasian decree, a Latin list of books 'to be received and not to be received'. He regards the motif of a combat between the devil and a personified Paternoster as unique. He compares *Solomon and Saturn* with an Irish book called *The Evernew Tongue,* where a Latin original has been thickly overlaid with Celtic imagery.

9 **Larsen, Henning.** 'Kemble's *Salomon and Saturn.*' *Modern Philology* 26 (1929): 445–52.

Larsen describes the edition **(1046)** which Kemble evidently abandoned at page-proof stage without full revision and lacking the Old English text. It was bound for the convenience of a few inquirers until the 1848 edition **(1047)** appeared. Subsequently it was called in, but twenty copies were preserved. The introduction to this edition was apparently very different in content from the 1848 one, containing much more comparative and illustrative material from the Solomon and Marcolf tradition. Some of this material was omitted from the 1848 edition for reasons of delicacy. Kemble also toned down hostile references to French literature.

10 **Menner, Robert J.** 'The *Vasa Mortis* Passage in the Old English *Salomon and Saturn.*' *Studies in English Philology: A Miscellany in Honor of Frederick*

Klaeber. Ed. Kemp Malone and Martin B. Ruud. Minneapolis: U of Minnesota P, 1929. 240–53.

Menner notes how the early Christian church's condemnation of all apocryphal material savouring of magic and demonology resulted in the disappearance of a vast body of writings in Latin. As a consequence, it is unlikely that the immediate sources of *Solomon and Saturn* will ever be discovered. Solomon's physical mastery of demons, as recounted in oriental lore, has become a spiritual dominance in the Christian poem. Menner rejects Kock's emendations **(147)** of 'hwælen' and 'geowes' (lines 264–5). He explains the origin of the Vasa Mortis story, along with the motifs of the Philistines, the two hundred guards, and the demon's waiting for Doomsday. The name 'vasa mortis' derives from the Vulgate text of Psalm 7: 14. The poet of *Solomon and Saturn* must have been familiar with some commentary in which 'vasa mortis' was applied to orders of demons. In *Solomon and Saturn* the phrase is attached to Asmodeus, who in turn is identified with Dagon, the Philistine god.

1071 ———. 'Nimrod and the Wolf in the Old English *Solomon and Saturn.' JEGP* 37 (1938): 332–54.

According to Menner, the reference to Nimrod in *Solomon and Saturn* line 214 needs to be understood in light of the Hebrew and medieval traditions that he was the builder of the Tower of Babel. According to Hebrew tradition Nimrod became the first mortal to hold universal sway and tried to convert men away from faith in God and into a trust in their own powers and abilities. But ultimately he and the other rebels against God destroyed each other. Here lies the germ of the dragon-combat described in *Solomon and Saturn*, in which the slayer, the raging Wolf, himself is slain. Other rebels are scattered over the earth, producing a poisonous brood of monsters. The author of *Solomon and Saturn* must have learnt the Hebrew traditions through some so far undiscovered Latin intermediary. Menner suggests reading line 213 as containing an identification of Wulf with Bel. He points to contacts in the tradition between Bel and respectively Nimrod and Saturn.

1072 **Dickins, Bruce.** 'John Mitchell Kemble and Old English Scholarship.' *Proceedings of the British Academy* 25 (1939): 51–84.

Dickins makes passing reference to Kemble's editions **(1046, 1047)**. He assigns the unissued edition to the year 1844. The actual research may have been done as much as ten years earlier. Dickins describes the 1848 edition as a wide-ranging study in comparative literature and a contribution to the history of fiction.

1073 **Menner, Robert James.** *The Poetical Dialogues of Solomon and Saturn.* Modern Language Association of America, monograph series 13. New York: Modern Language Association of America, 1941. ix + 176 pp.

Menner's edition of *Solomon and Saturn* encompasses both the verse texts, with the prose section included as an appendix. It is based on photostats, supplemented in the case of CCCC 422 by partial transcripts by John C. Pope. The lengthy introduction comprises discussion of the manuscripts, the differences between the two poems, the prose dialogue, the date (ninth or possibly tenth century), the language (early West Saxon copy of an originally Anglian text), the legend of Solomon, the use of the Paternoster and the Palm Tree, the Christian use of oriental and Germanic sources, and the dialogue and riddle forms. In his account of the manuscripts Menner argues that neither was copied from the other or directly from the original. He corrects Vincenti (**1061**) concerning the loss of conjugate leaves in quire 2 of CCCC 422. In support of the arguments for separate poems, he finds Poem I characterized by fantastic superstition and childish literalism. By contrast Poem II possesses greater sophistication, with its intermittent vivid description and writing in a dark, riddling vein. Possibly the author of Poem I or his source merely used the familiar form of the Solomon and Saturn dialogue in order to give instruction in the value of the Paternoster. Stylistic and metrical differences between the two poems also exist. The prose dialogue is of distinct origin again and may have been added to the text because of references in Poem I to the shape-shifting of the devil. The immediate sources of *Solomon and Saturn* must have been written in Latin (possibly with Irish affiliations) and adapted from Greek originals. The later Latin dialogues of Solomon and Marcolf have little in common with *Solomon and Saturn* but probably both types go back to the same original. *Solomon and Saturn* preserves elements of the Talmudic and Cabbalistic depiction of Solomon as a great magician. The use of the runic letters of the Paternoster in Poem I is simply a transformation of the inherited power of Solomon's magical ring and magical prayers. As displayed in the poem, the letters do not follow the strict order of the Paternoster. The use of the prayer in *Solomon and Saturn* can be compared with its widespread use as a protection against the devil throughout Christianity. The personification of the letters, while vaguely reminiscent of Prudentius, derives from a blend of rune magic and ancient Greek and Hebrew alphabetical mysticism. Possibly the motif of the palm tree was used to adorn the Paternoster in early Christian art. The dialogue form derives not only from the classical dialogue, with contributions from Boethius, but also from Germanic verbal contests, as seen in the *Poetic Edda*. Riddle contests, both classical and Germanic, and gnomic poetry also contribute. Poem II is full of details to which an oriental origin must be ascribed: the Philistines and their demon-god Vasa Mortis, the Tower of Babel and Nimrod, and perhaps even a dim reflection of the Babylonian myth of creation. Wyrd is to be seen as still embodying elements of the heathen conception even though greatly influenced by both classical and Christian views of Fate. Menner comments that it will be obvious from his commentary that many difficult allusions are only partially or tentatively explained. It is his hope that other medievalists will now be able to throw light on them. A bibliography, very full notes (suggesting sources and analogues for detailed motifs), and glossary are appended. In the notes Menner partially retracts (123–4) the conclusions concerning 'weallende wulf' reached in his separate article (**1071**). [For a review see Sisam, **1075**.]

Timmer, Benno J. 'The Elegiac Mood in Old English Poetry.' *English Studies* 24 (1942): 33–44.

Timmer notes that the word *wyrd* is used to denote the heathen goddess of Fate in

Solomon and Saturn lines 437–49, but regards this as exceptional when the tendency was otherwise towards a weakening of the meaning of the word (43).

1075 Sisam, Kenneth. Review of *The Poetical Dialogues of Solomon and Saturn*, ed. Robert James Menner **[1073]**. *Medium Aevum* 13 (1944): 28–36.

Sisam suggests lacunae at lines 389 and 478. Menner's arguments for Northumbrian origin fail to convince and the rationale of the compiler of the manuscript (CCCC 422) needs further consideration. The manuscript runes have nothing to do with the original poem but were added beside the Roman capitals in one branch of the manuscript tradition at a time when the heathen associations of the runes were forgotten or harmless. If the poem is referring to letter-shapes, it must be the descender of Roman *p*, rather than any part of runic *p*, that is envisaged as a goad in lines 90–1.

1076 Brooks, K.R. 'Old English "wopes hring".' *English and Germanic Studies* 2 (1948–9): 68–74.

In passing Brooks discusses the meaning of the verb *hringan*, as used in *Solomon and Saturn* line 267 to describe the sound made by the trappings of the Vasa Mortis.

1077 Woolf, Rosemary E. 'The Devil in Old English Poetry.' *Review of English Studies* NS 4 (1953): 1–12. Repr. in *Essential Articles for the Study of Old English Poetry.* Ed. J.B. Bessinger and S.J. Kahrl. Hamden, CT: Archon, 1968. 164–79.

Woolf shows how the devil, as characterized by the Church Fathers, possessed natural affinities with characters in both northern mythology and northern literature. Thus in *Solomon and Saturn* he is a shape-shifter, parallel in this and other respects to Loki in Scandinavian mythology (165). The identification of the devil with *wyrd* found in *Solomon and Saturn* derives not primarily from theology but from the 'literary point of view', which sees Satan as 'simply one who has the power to bring misfortune to mankind' (173).

1078 Hopkins, R.H. 'A Note on Solomon and Saturn II, 449 (Menner edition).' *Notes and Queries* 204 (1959): 226–7.

Hopkins points to the possibility of alliterative formulas where the same three words are found together in different patterns within different contexts, suggesting that these alliterative triads are primarily conventions of sound rather than of meaning. This leads him to defend Menner's lineation of lines 459–60 **(1073)**, following Holthausen **(132)**, against that in ASPR **(203)**.

1079 Wild, Friedrich. *Salomon und Saturn. Sitzungsberichte der österreichischen Akademie der Wissenschaften, philosophisch-historische Klasse* 243, no. 2 (1964). 44 pp.

Wild reproduces Menner **(1073)**, along with facing-page German verse translation, introduction, and detailed notes. This is the first complete translation into German. In his opinion, the use of the Roman alphabetical order and pronunciation of the letters in the Paternoster passage presupposes strong Church-Latin influence.

Clark, George. 'The Traveler Recognizes his Goal: a Theme in Anglo-Saxon Poetry.' *JEGP* 64 (1965): 645–59.

Clark identifies lines 232–7a of *Solomon and Saturn* as an instance of a traditional poetic theme where the traveller stands within sight of his goal. Relevant elements of the theme are contained in the collocation 'weallas blican' (line 236a). The traditional image of the shining destination exactly fits the recurring Christian conception of a paradise bathed in light. This indicates, in Clark's opinion, a poet who is capable of manipulating inherited materials and fusing them with new materials for consciously artistic ends.

Page, R.I. 'A Note on the Text of Ms CCCC 422 (*Solomon and Saturn*).' *Medium Aevum* 34 (1965): 36–9.

Page offers a new investigation of manuscript pages 1 and 14, using ultraviolet light. He discovers a few new readings on page 1. He confirms several of the readings made by Pope as a contribution to Menner's edition (**1073**), but is unable to confirm others by Pope and Vincenti (**1061**). Nothing new resulted from the examination of page 14. Page adds minor additions and emendations to other parts of Menner's text. An error in the common original of the two manuscripts of *Solomon and Saturn* (CCCC 422 and 41) shows that this cannot have been the author's holograph.

Hill, Thomas D. 'The Tropological Context of Heat and Cold Imagery in Anglo-Saxon Poetry.' *Neuphilologische Mitteilungen* 69 (1968): 522–32.

Hill draws attention to the figurative conception that heat represents charity and cold its opposite, sin. This conception enters into metaphors throughout patristic and early medieval exegetical and homiletic works. Its clearest expression in Old English poetry occurs in *Solomon and Saturn*, at lines 353–8, where Solomon indirectly expresses the idea that sin and charity are as ineluctably and absolutely opposed to each other as are opposite forces within the natural order. The idea may also be hinted at in lines 462–9. Hell is there described as murderously cold and wintry because it lacks the warmth of charity.

Zolla, Elémire. 'Le metafore bellicose nella poesia anglosassone ed il dialogo fra Salomone e Saturno.' *Strumenti Critici* 2 (1968): 364–77.

Solomon and Saturn is the esoteric jewel of Anglo-Saxon literature. It constitutes the most significant treatment of the life of the mystic as warfare. The Paternoster takes on the militant function of Saint Michael, who in the northern countries supplanted Odin in this role. Each word or phrase in the prayer is assigned a rune with an appropriate meaning. Zolla deduces these meanings from *Rune Poem* and from pagan rune magic, but dissents from the interpretations of Schneider (**226**). Thus the phrase 'qui es in coelis' is represented by *ac* (line 93), signifying the oak as pillar of the cosmos and as source of nutriment. The word 'sanctificetur' is represented by *tir* (line 94), a word which possesses associations with Thor and Tiw. The runes *nyd* and *os* were avoided (cf. line 108) because of their unpropitious and heathen associations. The mention of *dæg* (lines 135–6) contains an allusion to the five wounds of Christ. The rune name *hægl* (cf. line 138) signifies the cosmic egg from which the universe took its birth. *Solomon and Saturn* II can be seen as focusing on the temptations of Satan, which the runic Paternoster is designed to counter.

1084   **Gardner, Thomas J.** 'Þreaniedla and Þreamedla: Notes on two Old English Abstracts in -la(n).' *Neuphilologische Mitteilungen* 70 (1969): 255–61.

Gardner notes that the ASPR (**203**) reading 'þreamedla' in *Solomon and Saturn* lines 242 and 430 represents a revival of Schipper's (**1052**) old tentative explanation 'Drohmittel' ('means of threatening'). Yet this suggestion had been rejected by all editors and lexicographers except Assmann (**6**) and Holthausen, the latter in his *Berichtigungen und Nachträge* to the revised edition of Grein's *Sprachschatz* (**3**). Gardner reviews other occurrences of the two candidate readings, along with the array of weak masculine abstracta in **-ilan*, to show that the form *þreamedla* (with short -*e*-) does not meet all the criteria he has evolved. A form with long -*ē*- (derived from *mod* and meaning 'mental oppression') would suit the context in *Solomon and Saturn* lines 241–2. Also, it would be as appropriate to line 430 as the rival reading 'þreaniedlan'. Gardner cites *ofermedla* and *modþrea* as possible parallels.

1085   **Hill, Thomas D.** 'The Falling Leaf and Buried Treasure: Two Notes on the Imagery of *Solomon and Saturn* 314–22.' *Neuphilologische Mitteilungen* 71 (1970): 571–6.

In the 'falling leaf' passage of *Solomon and Saturn* II (lines 314–22) the poet is dealing with the idea of death as entailed by sin, rather than with the inevitable physical death that awaits all men. The comparison is a moral one: just as leaves fall, so must those who have done evil for a long time. Hidden treasure in the poem is emblematic of *avaritia* taken in its largest sense as the over-estimation of all earthly goods.

1086   ———. 'Two Notes on *Solomon and Saturn*.' *Medium Aevum* 40 (1971): 217–21.

Hill argues that in line 47 the 'xii fyra tydernessum' is an allusion to a widespread numerical topos, the *duodecim abusivis sæculi* 'twelve abuses of the world'. In lines 487–502 the allusion is almost certainly to Gregory's famous definition of the four sequential stages of the process of sin. The references in the same passage to the 'day' ('dæglongne fyrst': line 501b) in which the sinner ignores the angel and yields to the devil derive from the figurative use of 'day' in John 9: 4. There Christ tells the Pharisees that he must work 'donec dies est: venit nox quando nemo potest operari'.

1087   **Laurini, Anna Camilla.** *I passi runici della poesia anglosassone: 'Salomone e Saturno'*. Genoa: Università di Genova, 1971. 100 pp.

In spite of the title, Laurini provides a complete text and Italian translation of *Solomon and Saturn*, along with a review of previous scholarship. A brief introduction traces the history of the 'Solomon and Marcolf' genre, drawing on previous scholarship.

88   Taylor, Paul B. 'The Old Icelandic *Völuspá* as Eschatology.' *For W.H. Auden, February 21, 1972.* Ed. Peter H. Salus and Paul B. Taylor. New York: Random, 1972. 133–46. (Limited edn.)

Taylor compares the binding of the cosmic fiend Loki in *Völuspá* to the binding of the devil in chains for a thousand years in Rev. 20.1–3. The paraphrase of this scriptural account in *Solomon and Saturn* transforms Satan into a Germanic chieftain who betrays the heroic code of his society. The 'insceaft' ('incest') mentioned in *Solomon and Saturn* line 457 is pertinent to the patristic picture of Lucifer coupling with Sin. It also however reflects the mythological tradition of Loki's monstrous begetting of Fenrir and other monstrous progeny. The flying dragon Niðhöggr in *Völuspá* has no scriptural parallels, but can be compared with the monstrous bird Vasa Mortis in *Solomon and Saturn* (137–8).

89   Whitbread, Leslie. 'Adam's Pound of Flesh: a Note on Old English Verse *Solomon and Saturn* (II): 336–9.' *Neophilologus* 59 (1975): 622–6.

Whitbread suggests replacing the very obscure 'of niehtes wunde' in *Solomon and Saturn* line 339a with the emendation 'of eahta pundum' ('from eight pounds'). This would constitute an allusion to the early Christian Latin tradition where the ingredients from which Adam was created were sometimes itemized as a series of eight separate weights or 'pounds'. An analogue is the *Durham Ritual*, which contains a list 'de octo pondera de quibus factus est Adam'.

90   Hermann, John P. 'The Pater Noster Battle Sequence in Solomon and Saturn and the Psychomachia of Prudentius.' *Neuphilologische Mitteilungen* 77 (1976): 206–10.

The letters of the Lord's Prayer are personified as powerful warriors, some of whom behave in a manner that suggests the influence of the Christian allegorical epic of Prudentius. Menner (**1073**) had found only a vague reminiscence of *Psychomachia*. By contrast, Hermann argues that the description of T in lines 94–5 is derived from the encounters between Fides and Discordia and between Operatio and Avaritia in Prudentius. An otherwise unparalleled common motif is that of the pierced tongue. The treatment of the letter S in lines 111–17 suggests artistic manipulation of the conflict between Sobrietas and Luxuria described by Prudentius. Illustrated manuscripts of the *Psychomachia* may have suggested the motif of the placing of fire on the fiend's hair in lines 129–30. Artistic creation in the Middle Ages did not always involve exact duplication of a verbal source.

91   Meling, Kjell. 'A Proposed Reconstruction of Runic Line 108a of *Solomon and Saturn.*' *Neuphilologische Mitteilungen* 77 (1976): 358–9.

Meling argues against the restoration of 'O' in line 108a, pointing out that O is not the only letter omitted from the poem, as extant. Preferable would be a reconstruction of the line with the roman *n* preceding the runic one, although admittedly this runs counter to the normal order in the poem. The posited irregularity might have been the poet's way of drawing attention to letters which he terms 'twins of the church' (line 107b). This phrase could have been devised because the Roman 'n' is dome-shaped and the Runic 'n' is cross-shaped.

Hermann, John P. '*Solomon and Saturn* (II), 339a: *niehtes wunde*.' *English Language Notes* 14 (1977): 161–4.

Hermann defends the manuscript reading against the various proposed emendations. In particular, he finds Whitbread's suggestion (**1089**) ingenious and well-documented but improbable. Line 339a is in reality based on the frequent metaphorical association of both night and wounds with sin. The wound of darkness is a figure of speech which means, simply, sin.

1093   Sharpe, Eric J. 'The Old English Runic Paternoster.' *Symbols of Power*. Ed. H.R. Ellis Davidson. Papers given at a joint conference held by the Folklore Society and the Department of Religious Studies at the University of Lancaster, 1973. Cambridge: Brewer, for the Folklore Society; Totowa, NJ: Rowman, 1977. 41–60 and 162–5 (notes).

Sharpe regards Saturn in *Solomon and Saturn* as representing Time, perhaps even Father Time. He notes the absence of direct quotations or paraphrases of the Paternoster in *Solomon and Saturn*. He dissents from Kemble's (**1047**) and Menner's (**1073**) depreciation of this poem, arguing that it was meant as a most serious piece of practical theology. He finds the ethos of the dialogue Germanic through and through. Accordingly, the Paternoster should be seen primarily as an incantation, not as a religious affirmation or intellectual statement. Saturn's self-proclaimed search for books is really a search for 'power-words', oral as well as written. *Solomon and Saturn* represents a tenacious tradition which ascribed to each of the runes a particular power. This power was brought to bear upon a text (the Paternoster) which was in itself a source of divine protection. The poem typifies in its formation the syncretic processes which gave rise to northern medieval Christianity: 'new impulses from the Christian tradition combined in subtle and infinitely varied and variable ways with ancient impulses from the Germanic and Celtic heritages to form northern medieval Christianity' (51).

1094   Tripp, Raymond P., Jr. 'The Dialectics of Debate and the Continuity of English Poetry.' *Massachusetts Studies in English* 7.1 (1978): 41–51.

Tripp compares *Solomon and Saturn* and Chaucer's 'The Book of the Duchess' as two medieval debate poems. Whether we call them dialogues, elegies, or *contentiones*, they exhibit the same dialectical structure. These common features of structure and progression constitute one strand of continuity between Old and Middle English literature, and beyond. Both are big debates, in the sense that they exhibit a collision of worlds rather than a discussion of truths. Tripp differs from Shippey (**300**) in seeing *Solomon and Saturn* not as inculcating awareness of the sad state of this world and appealing to our innate strength of mind, but as conveying the momentum of Christian optimism. Saturn wants to know why he should not be sad; Solomon answers with an attitude rather than with a reason, leaving Saturn delighted and satisfied.

1095   Cilluffo, Gilda. 'Il dialogo in prosa *Salomone e Saturno* del ms. CCCC 422.' *Annali Istituto Universitario Orientale di Napoli* Filologia germanica 23 (1980): 121–46.

Comparison of the CCCC 422 prose *Solomon and Saturn* with the two verse dialogues in the same manuscript demonstrates that these works, despite their commonalities of theme, cannot be ascribed to the same author or even milieu. They were intended for different audiences.

6 Dane, Joseph A. 'The Structure of the Old English *Solomon and Saturn II.*' *Neophilologus* 64 (1980): 592–603.

Dane contends that previous scholarship has focused on detail to the exclusion of broader questions such as the structure of this poem. He distinguishes two main sections, lines 179–301 and 302–506 respectively. Within the first, three of the riddle subjects are associated with a specific element, sea ('Weallende Wulf'), land (books), and air ('Vasa Mortis'). The Vasa Mortis should be interpreted not literally but allegorically, as associated with undue curiosity and therefore spiritual danger. In the second section Saturn's worldly-physical view is opposed to Solomon's spiritual-abstract view, which sometimes offers a higher synthesis to Saturn's dichotomous imagery. Possibly the poem has its roots in early Christian-Manichean debate literature.

7 Cilluffo, Gilda. '*Mirabilia* ags.: il *Vasa Mortis* nel *Salomone e Saturno.*' *Annali Istituto Universitario Orientale di Napoli* Filologia germanica 24 (1981): 211–26.

Cilluffo traces monster depiction, as a hypostasization of human fears, back to the ancient Greeks. She argues that the poet of *Solomon and Saturn* conforms to the topoi of 'fantasy literature' as defined by Jacques Le Goff. The same topoi recur in the *Letter of Alexander to Aristotle*, the *Marvels of the East*, and the *Liber Monstrorum*. The Saturn of *Solomon and Saturn* can be compared with the Alexander of the *Letter*. The Vasa Mortis has no counterpart among the monsters in the *Letter* but rather with the griffin in *Marvels* and (more closely) with the Monstrum Nocturnum in *Liber*. The description of the Vasa Mortis also draws on Virgil's description of Fame (*Æneid* 4.173–88), though the author of *Solomon and Saturn* has of course Christianized Virgil's monster by adding the idea that it suffers. Cilluffo criticizes Menner (**1073**) for postulating derivation from Hebrew without specifying the proximate sources.

8 ———. 'Il Salomone e Saturno in Prosa del ms. CCCC 422.' *Quaderni di Filologia Germanica* 2 (1981). Palermo: Facoltà di Lettere e Filosofia Università di Palermo, 1981. 125.

In her prefatory remarks Patrizia Lendinara deplores the neglect of the prose section of *Solomon and Saturn*. Cilluffo attributes this neglect in part to confusion with the Cotton Vitellius A.xv prose *Solomon and Saturn*. The Cotton Vitellius text is a true dialogue on a variety of topics and therefore in the mainstream of the dialogue tradition. By contrast, the CCCC text forms a virtual monologue and concerns itself entirely with the Paternoster. The CCCC prose *Solomon and Saturn* should not be connected with *Solomon and Saturn* I, despite the similarity of topic. The prose treatment derives from the redaction of the Paternoster contained in the Gospel of St Luke, whereas the verse is to be associated with St Matthew. In a literary analysis of the text Cilluffo emphasizes the part played by hyperbole in constructing the hypostasization of the Paternoster as a giant. The text is accompanied by a [faint] photocopy of the manuscript original, translation, glossary, bibliography, discussion of *hapax legomena*, and an appendix (contributed by Lendinara) on technological terms, in which the text is very rich.

1099   Cross, James E., and Thomas D. Hill. *The Prose Solomon and Saturn and Adrian and Ritheus.* McMaster Old English Studies and Texts 1. Toronto: U of Toronto P, 1982. xi + 186 pp.

This book takes the form of an edition of the relevant British Library manuscripts, with commentary. In their discussion of a dialogue genre, based upon question and answer, the editors note that the interlocutors in the Cotton Vitellius A.xv prose *Solomon and Saturn* are almost certainly the same as the interlocutors in the other Old English dialogues between Solomon and Saturn contained in CCCC 422 and 41. This, however, is the only contact, since the CCCC texts are concerned with altercations between Christian and pagan, whereas the Cotton Vitellius text contains a series of questions and answers concerning the Scriptures – canonical, apocryphal, and rabbinical (12–13).

1100   Kellermann, Günter, and Renate Haas. 'Magie und Mythos als Argumentationsmittel in den ae. Dialoggedichten *Salomon u. Saturn.*' *Festschrift für Karl Schneider zum 70. Geburtstag am 18. April 1982.* Ed. Ernst S. Dick and Kurt R. Janowsky. Amsterdam: Benjamins, 1982. 387–404.

Solomon and Saturn is to be read as an embodiment of both pagan and Christian lore in a poem with an evangelistic purpose. The concept of a natural knowledge of God among the heathen is ascribed to Saturn. Although the immediate sources of *Solomon and Saturn* are unknown, it is possible to base attempts at interpretation on medieval Latin works, principally the *Missale Romanum*, Isidore's *Etymologiae*, *Synonyma*, and *De Natura Rerum*, works by Gregory the Great, and the *De Civitate Dei* of Augustine. Kellermann and Haas interpret the runes following Schneider (226), arguing that some of them have taken on a Christian significance and represent concepts traceable to Augustine, e.g. *De Civitate Dei* 7.30. Thus *ræda* correlates with Christ; *os*, *beorc*, and *hegel* [sic] correlate with *virtutes Dei*; and *tiw*, *sigel*, and *dæg* correlate with Gabriel, Michael, and Raphael respectively. Since *nyd* stands for eternal light and *os* for the Word of God, emendation of 'cirican getuinnas' in line 107b is not necessary. The rune *hegel*, Schneider's 'primordial god/giver of life', is to be explained in the context of *Solomon and Saturn* line 138 as 'Spring'. The rune *peorð* in line 89 equates with 'Fortuna', in keeping with Schneider's interpretation as 'dice-box'). The emendation 'sunde' is proposed for 'wunde' (line 339a).

1101   Donoghue, Daniel. *Style in Old English Poetry: The Test of the Auxiliary.* Yale Studies in English 196. New Haven: Yale UP, 1987. xii + 234 pp.

Solomon and Saturn is among the poems analysed. Appendix 1 supplies statistical information on auxiliaries in each poem. The incidence of auxiliaries in *Solomon and Saturn* I and *Solomon and Saturn* II, along with the patterns of word order in the verbal phrase, is demonstrated to be identical. Appendix 2 lists three textual clarifications or emendations in *Solomon and Saturn.*

2   **Harris, Joseph.** 'Deor and its Refrain: Preliminaries to an Interpretation.' *Traditio* 43 (1987): 23–53.

In section 3 of his article (45–51) Harris suggests that the strange mortal consolation found in *Deor* is in harmony with the Solomonic mood found elsewhere in Old English. This type of consolation emphasizes hardship and conveys the idea that human misery subsumes the individual under a general law. It can be linked to *Solomon and Saturn,* which possibly represents a small Solomon anthology, and in particular to *Solomon and Saturn* II. Harris finds the tone of *Solomon and Saturn* II harsher than that of Boethius in that it emphasizes irreconcilable oppositions. Dissenting from Shippey **(300)**, he does not see the poem as qualifying the notion that Old English poetry is inherently melancholic (45–6).

3   **Hill, Thomas D.** 'Saturn's Time Riddle: An Insular Latin Analogue for *Solomon and Saturn II* lines 282–91.' *Review of English Studies* NS 39 (1988): 273–6.

Hill focuses on the fourth of the exchanges between Saturn and Solomon, concerning the destructive power of time in its passing. A hitherto uncited riddle from the *Collectanea Bedae* should be seen as an analogue. More broadly, both *Solomon and Saturn* II (to be viewed as a separate work from *Solomon and Saturn* I) and the *Collectanea Bedae* are early medieval insular texts in which wisdom literature, riddles, and scientific and biblical lore are inextricably mixed together.

4   **Jonassen, Frederick B.** 'The Pater Noster Letters in the Poetic *Solomon and Saturn.' Modern Language Review* 83 (1988): 1–9.

Jonassen examines the cultural context of the personified warrior-letters in *Solomon and Saturn* I. To the medieval Christian mind, correctly ordered letters reflect the meaning and order of God's universe. This is especially apparent in the *Institutiones* of Cassiodorus. Also mentioned are the Cynewulfian runic signatures and two riddles of Eusebius whose subjects are letters of the alphabet. Historiated initials in human form, as seen in the Book of Kells and elsewhere, may also have contributed to the poet's notion of warrior letters. Some other OEW poems appear among the partial parallels adduced. In *Rune Poem,* some of the letters represent human (or divine) beings or activities: similarly in Exeter Book Riddle 19.

5   **Stanley, E.G.** 'Rhymes in English Medieval Verse: from Old English to Middle English.' *Medieval English Studies Presented to George Kane.* Ed. Edward Donald Kennedy et al. Cambridge: Brewer, 1988. 19–54.

Stanley mentions internal rhyming combined with end-rhyme in *Solomon and Saturn.*

6   **Hermann, John P.** *Allegories of War: Language and Violence in Old English Poetry.* Ann Arbor, MI: U of Michigan P, 1989. ix + 226 pp.

Hermann argues that *Solomon and Saturn* I represents a survival in Old English literature of the psychomachia tradition. Specifically, the battle descriptions in *Solomon and Saturn* contain several parallels to the *Psychomachia* of Prudentius. What Menner (1073) considers vague reminiscences can better be interpreted as artistic transformations of the source material. Comparable imagery cannot be located in any other works that might conceivably have influenced the Anglo-Saxon poet. The letters and runes T and S become Prudentian characters. The similarity of the *t*-rune to the Cross may have caused the poet of *Solomon and Saturn* I to recall the commonplace of the bait of Christ's humanity and the hook of his divinity catching Leviathan at the crucifixion. Both runes conduce to an association of violence with the mouth, the locus of speech. Such an association would be consistent with the general pattern in *Solomon and Saturn* that true wisdom lies in the destruction of all that resides outside the margins of true speech. By contrast, the motifs associated with other letters and runes in *Solomon and Saturn* cannot be traced to any specific tradition (32–7).

1107 **Cronan, Dennis.** 'Old English Waterlands.' *English Language Notes* 27 (1990): 6–9.

Cronan surveys the occurrences of *ea/igland* in the putative sense 'land bordering water, coast'. He believes that the sense 'land reached by water' would suit *Solomon and Saturn* line 1. Nevertheless, the poem is not a geographic treatise, and indeed may have rested on only a vague knowledge of geography. The poet may even have regarded 'Libia and Greca,. . . Indea rices' (lines 3–4) as islands in the conventional sense. [Cronan does not refer to Wright (340).]

1108 **Nelson, Marie.** 'King Solomon's Magic: the Power of a Written Text.' *Oral Tradition* 5 (1990): 20–36.

Having established that the Paternoster passage occurs in a manuscript context of charms, Nelson argues that this passage can be analysed in terms of Sebeok's observations concerning the structure of Cheremis charms. It represents an oral performance in which Solomon draws his power from the Paternoster to counter loss of reason, which was attributed to the devil. By speaking the Paternoster, Solomon the magician gives individual life to each of its runic and Roman letters. The instruction to 'sing' the Paternoster is consistent with the performance of a charm. *Solomon and Saturn*, as a written composition, conforms to Ong's observation that the dialogue form was one of the means by which early writers enabled readers to place themselves in relationship to written texts. Nelson also makes reference to metrical Charms 2 and 11.

1109 **Davis, Steven.** 'Salomon and Saturn 235: *winrod*.' *Notes and Queries* 236, NS 38 (1991): 443–4.

[The line number in the title appears to be an error for 236.] Davis suggests that 'winrod' in line 236b is a compound derived from *wynn* 'joy' and *rad* 'riding', and therefore neuter in gender. The use of 'eorod' in *Exodus* line 157 is closely similar. The meaning would be 'joyous band' or 'joyous procession'. Thus -*rod* has nothing to do with *rod* 'cross' and emendation is unnecessary.

) **O'Keeffe, Katherine O'Brien.** 'The Geographic List of *Solomon and Saturn* II.' *Anglo-Saxon England* 20 (1991): 123–42.

O'Keeffe notes that Menner's edition **(1073)** has influenced modern reception by presenting the work in a predominantly oriental context. A close study of the list of places visited by Saturn in *Solomon and Saturn* II lines 179–201 suggests that actually it was compiled by recourse to English recensions of geographical texts such as the *Cosmographia* of Æthicus Ister, Bede's *Nomina locorum*, and Isidore's *Etymologiae*. Æthicus's work provided the author of *Solomon and Saturn* with the motif of a travelling wise man who engages in learned disputations. The simple listing of places in *Solomon and Saturn* II one after the other, as contrasted with the mode of presentation in *Widsith*, makes original oral composition unlikely.

Murphy, G. Ronald. 'Magic in the *Heliand.*' *Monatshefte* 83 (1991): 386–97.

The Paternoster in *Solomon and Saturn* is treated as a precedent for and influence on a posited magical treatment of the Paternoster in the *Heliand*. The phrase 'ða cirican getuinnas' in line 107 is to be understood as 'the twin churches', i.e. the Irish and Roman churches at about the time of the Synod of Whitby.

Wilcox, Jonathan. 'Eating Books: . . . *Solomon and Saturn.*' *American Notes and Queries* NS 4 (1991): 115–18.

The words 'boca onbyrged' in line 2 refer to a literal though ineffectual ingestion of books.

Vainglory

ORIENTATION TO RESEARCH

MANUSCRIPT, ATTRIBUTIONS, AND DATINGS

The poem is uniquely extant in the Exeter Book, dated by Ker (36) at the second half of the tenth century. Critics influenced by Leo and Dietrich, e.g. Robinson (7), sought to include it in the Cynewulf canon. Wülker (83), Trautmann (17), and others dissented. In turn, Grein (84), Sarrazin (95), and others defended the attribution. Trautmann placed *Vainglory* between AD 700 and 740, Richter (22) specifically in the period before Cynewulf, and Brandl (19) more agnostically at a pre-Alfredian period.

EDITIONS AND TEXTUAL STUDIES

For editions see the subject index. As to textual criticism, Grein (2), Cosijn (110), Klaeber (122), and Holthausen (112) tried to eliminate aberrant lexis as representing scribal error. Other scholars defended the anomalous readings: noteworthy are Kock (147), Sedgefield (160), Marquardt (198), Del Pezzo (1118), Huppé (270), and Pickford (1115).

SOURCES

Dobbie (194) could identify no single source for *Vainglory*. Several scholars have nonetheless posited specific patristic influences. Doubleday (1113) pointed to Gregory the Great, Regan (1114) to Augustine, Trahern (1116) to Caesarius of Arles, and McKinnell (1119) to 1 John 3, possibly supplemented by Bede. On a broader front, Hermann (319) argued that the poet translated patristic psychology by employing a complex of military images.

GENRE AFFILIATIONS

Vainglory has been classed with *The Wanderer* and *The Seafarer* by Wrenn (43), on the basis of similarities in tone, and by Fanagan (304), on the basis of tense usage. McKinnell (1119) preferred an affiliation with the Exeter Book Riddles. Hill (1117) placed *Vainglory* among the Old English poems that ascribe Lucifer's rebellion to pride. Pickford (1115) saw the poem as a homily designed for mealtime recitation.

STRUCTURE

Structural analyses have been assayed by Bartlett (25), Huppé (270), Campbell (344), Pickford (1115), and Lerer (356). Dobbie (194) criticized the autobiographical introduction as extraneous **(194)**. Parks **(343)** cited the opening lines as a rare instance of reflexivity in Old English poetry.

LITERARY CRITICISM

Though seldom the object of praise, *Vainglory* has attracted a modest amount of critical attention. Schücking **(177)** pointed to the digressive realism, Anderson **(31)** to the poem's inferiority as compared with *Homiletic Fragment I*, Cross **(45)** to the 'effective fulmination', Shippey **(300)** to vagueness and almost comical exaggeration, Tripp **(301)** to the idea of mysteries, Pearsall **(52)** to the schematic doctrinal commentary, and Hansen **(61)** to the audience's involvement in the creative process. Huppé **(270)** took a Robertsonian approach, resisted by Crane **(280)**.

SOCIAL CONTEXT

Citations from *Vainglory* are used by Budde **(124)** to document Anglo-Saxon drinking customs and by Habicht **(231)** in his study of the motif of noise in medieval English poetry.

BIBLIOGRAPHY

Doubleday, James F. 'The Allegory of the Soul as Fortress in Old English Poetry.' *Anglia* 88 (1970): 503–8.

Doubleday points out that in two Old English poems, *Vainglory* and *Juliana*, the soul is depicted as a fortress, attacked and destroyed by the devil and his arrows of sin. In *Vainglory* the description comes as part of the progress of corruption in a proud man. The military metaphor has patristic origins, in the common Christian image of the battle against sin, seen notably in Prudentius's *Psychomachia*. The principal elaborator of the allegorical figure is Gregory the Great, in his *Moralia in Job*.

Regan, C.A. 'Patristic Psychology in the Old English *Vainglory*.' *Traditio* 26 (1970): 324–35.

Regan believes that in both its content and its form *Vainglory* bears a striking resemblance to specific teachings of the Church Fathers. Lines 1–8 bear an organic relationship to the portraits that follow. The poet is alerting his readers to the purpose of the portraits in the same way that Pomerius and Cassian did. Flying weapons as a type of imagery of pride also have precedents in patristic writings. Augustine's definition of the dual penalty of sin as *ignorantia* and *difficultas* underlies the poem. Against Grein **(2)** and Krapp and Dobbie **(194)**, who emend to 'feond', Regan would retain the manuscript reading 'freond' in line 70b, comparing 1 John 3: 10–24.

Pickford, T.E. 'An Edition of *Vainglory*.' *Parergon* 10 (1974): 1–40.

Pickford supplies introduction, text, commentary, glossary, and bibliography for this neglected but cleverly conceived poem. He dissents somewhat from Huppé's (**270**) analysis of the structure, preferring an eight-part scheme. Although *Vainglory* has a psalmic ring about it and some resemblance to Psalm 9 it cannot yet be shown to depend upon any single source. Huppé's ideas on systematic ambiguity are accepted and expanded, e.g. where 'winburg-' and 'wigsmiþas' are concerned (line 14), but his theory of an ambiguity in 'læteþ' (line 10) is rejected. Some manuscript readings are defended against long-accepted emendations: thus 'hine' (line 10), 'mæþelhergendra' (line 13), 'þrymme' (line 24), and 'feoh' (line 36). The word 'mæþelhergendra' may mean the innocuous habit of holding assemblies or speeches but it may also turn out to be 'assemblies for self-praising or boasting'. In line 33 the deliberate choice of verbs that rhyme rather than alliterate is most effective in conveying the disorder in the proud man's behaviour: not only does he break the accepted code, but he is also repetitiously boring. The incidence of small capitals, points, and accents in the manuscript is documented. The poem, with its emphasis on feasts, its parallels with descriptions of feasting in *Judith* and *Daniel*, and its mention of 'mæla gehwylcum' in line 83 (understood by Pickford as 'every mealtime'), appears to be a homily designed for mealtime recitation. The feast is a symbol of unity, love, and peace, yet the tragedy is that this same feast can so soon degenerate into a battlefield.

1116 **Trahern, Joseph B., Jr.** 'Caesarius, Chrodegang and the Old English *Vainglory*.' *Gesellschaft, Kultur, Literatur: Rezeption und Originalität im Wachsen einer europäischen Literatur und Geistigkeit: Beiträge Liutpold Wallach gewidmet.* Ed. Karl Bosl. Stuttgart: Hiersemann, 1975. 167–78.

Trahern investigates Caesarius of Arles as a source for *Vainglory*. He points out that the theme of the children of God and of the devil is found in paragraph 4 of Caesarius's *Sermo* 233. Paragraphs 3 and 5 of this sermon can be used to explain lines 9–12 and 28–9 of *Vainglory* respectively. The phrase 'on gescead witan' in line 8 is paralleled by Caesarius's 'discernere'. In lines 52–6, which describe how the wicked will be punished, the poet may be indebted to Chapter 1 of Chrodegang of Metz's *Regula Canonicorum*, which itself draws on Caesarius. The figure of the scholar in the poem is to be identified with Caesarius. The speech of the *witega* is to be taken as ending at line 56.

1117 **Hill, Joyce M.** 'Figures of Evil in Old English Poetry.' *Leeds Studies in English* NS 8 (1976 *for* 1975): 5–19.

Hill briefly mentions *Vainglory* as among the Old English poems that ascribe Lucifer's rebellion to pride.

1118 **Del Pezzo, Raffaella.** 'Ags *Winburg*, "città del convivio".' *Romanobarbarica* 10 (1988–9): 103–14. = *Studi sulla cultura germanica dei secoli IV–XII in onore di Giulia Mazzuoli Porru.* Ed. M.A. D'Aronco et al. Rome: Herder, 1990. 103–14.

The occurrences of *winburg* are listed, to include *Vainglory* line 14. Marquardt's (**198**) interpretation of '-burg-' in this context as 'hall' is rejected. Del Pezzo likewise rejects Huppé's (**270**) interpretation of the first element in the compound ('city of wine'), preferring 'fortified city'.

McKinnell, John. 'A Farewell to Old English Elegy: the Case of *Vainglory.*' *Parergon* NS 9.2 (1991): 67–89.

McKinnell seeks to demonstrate that *Vainglory* is a poetic meditation based on parts of 1 John 3. Additionally it shows the influence of the ideas and occasionally the phraseology of a patristic source, which was probably either Bede's *In Epistolas Septem Catholicas* or some related text. Correspondences of thought between Bede and the poem are noted at eight points. By contrast, Trahern's **(1116)** identification of Caesarius as the source accounts for little of the poem except its opening statement of theme. The clear structural organization of *Vainglory*, with its 'frame' at beginning, middle, and end, is shared by a number of other meditational religious poems that appear in the same section of the Exeter Book. These are *Order, Fortunes, The Wanderer,* and *The Seafarer.* Although fragmentarily, *Homiletic Fragment I* in the Vercelli Book exhibits the same structure. The latter poem should be seen as a religious meditation that happens to quote one verse of Psalm 28, not, *contra* ASPR **(520)**, as a paraphrase of the entire psalm. It would be incorrect to link these poems with the shorter secular dramatic monologues which appear in a group later in the Exeter Book. As enigmatic puzzle poems, they are better associated with the Riddles that appear round them. The central theme of *Vainglory* is how to distinguish between God's child and his opposite, the child of the devil. The speech of the *witega* (St John, perhaps so called because of his authorship of the Book of Revelation) ends at line 77a, as in the ASPR edition **(194)**.

Works Cited

Bosworth, Joseph, and T. Northcote Toller. *An Anglo-Saxon Dictionary* based on the manuscript collections of the late Joseph Bosworth . . . edited and enlarged by T.N. Toller. Oxford: Clarendon, 1882–98.

Hall, John R. Clark. *A Concise Anglo-Saxon Dictionary for the Use of Students.* London: Sonnenschein; New York: Macmillan, 1894.

Hickes, George. *Linguarum Veterum Septentrionalium Thesaurus.* 3 vols. Oxford: Clarendon, 1705.

Smith, Thomas. *Catalogus Librorum Manuscriptorum Bibliothecæ Cottonianæ.* Oxford: Clarendon, 1696.

Sweet, Henry. *The Student's Dictionary of Anglo-Saxon.* Oxford: Clarendon; New York: Macmillan, 1897.

Wanley, Humphrey. *Librorum Veterum Septentrionalium, qui in Angliae Bibliothecis extant, nec non multorum Veterum Codicum Septentrionalium alibi extantium Catalogus Historico-Criticus, cum totius Thesauri Linguarum Septentrionalium sex Indicibus.* Vol. 2 of George Hickes's *Linguarum Veterum.* 3 vols. Oxford: Clarendon, 1705.

Index of Scholars

This index refers to entries in the General Bibliography. It includes the authors of works listed, those who have made a significant contribution to them (e.g. by a preface, glossary, or bibliography), translators, and reviewers (indicated by a lower-case *r* after the entry number). For the authors of works mentioned but not annotated, see the *List of Works Cited*. Authors who appear under more than one name in the General Bibliography have been entered under the more usual name, with a cross-reference from the alternative name. Icelandic names are entered under the patronymic.

Århammar, Nils **839**
Abbetmeyer, Charles **1060**
Abbey, C.J. **102**
Abbott, H.H. **854**
Abercrombie, Lascelles **776**
Adams, John F. **840**
Adams, Valerie **895**
Alekseev, M.P. **635**
Alexander, Michael J. **59, 257, 930, 975**
Allen, Michael J.B. **298**
Amies, Marion **474**
Amos, Ashley Crandell **56**
Anderson, Earl R. **354, 875**
Anderson, George K. **31, 32, 847**
Anderson, James E. **331, 949, 950**
Anderson, L.F. **116**
Anderson, Marjorie **189**
Anderson, Orval J. **569**
Andrews, Charles McLean **669**
Arend, Johannes Pieter **530**
Arntz, Helmut **1011**
Assmann, Bruno **6**

Bammesberger, Alfred **332**
Barley, Nigel F. **49, 278, 592, 607, 879**
Barnes, Richard G. **582, 830**
Barnouw, Adriaan J. **701, 753r**
Bartels, Arthur **138**
Bartlett, Adeline Courtney **25**
Bashe, Edwin J. **24**
Baugh, Albert C. **30**
Baum, Paull F. **837**
Beale, Walter H. **51**
Becker, Ernest J. **111**
Beckers, W.J. **408**

Benson, Larry **842**
Berkhout, Carl T. **615**
Bessinger, Jess B., Jr. **261, 823**
Bethmann, L.C. **656**
Bierbaumer, Peter **454, 934**
Biezais, Haralds **297**
Biggs, Frederick M. **625**
Binz, Gustav **385r, 755r**
Birch, Walter de Gray **366**
Blackburn, F.A. **698**
Blake, N.F. **951**
Blakeley, L. **825**
Blauner, D.G. **848**
Bliss, Alan J. **227, 272, 279**
Blockley, Mary **988**
Blomfield, Joan **1017**
Bloomfield, Morton W. **44, 435**
Böðvarsson, Haukur **849**
Boenig, Robert **475**
Bollard, J.K. **595, 600**
Bolton, W.F. **246**
Bone, Gavin David **205**
Bonser, Wilfrid **35, 391, 393, 414, 416, 424, 432**
Botkine, Léon **996**
Bouman, A.C. **833**
Bouterwek, Karl W. **69**
Bracher, Frederick **196**
Bradley, Daniel J. **1040**
Bradley, Henry **371, 497, 678r, 729**
Bradley, S.A.J. **317**
Brady, Caroline **214**
Braekman, Willy L. **465**
Brandl, Alois **19, 156, 559**
Breeze, Andrew **1045**

Bremmer, Rolf H., Jr. **490**
Brett, Cyril **773**
Breuer, Rolf **445**
Bridier, Yvonne **872**
Brie, Maria **374, 379**
Bright, James Wilson **190, 634**
Brink, Bernhardt A.K. ten **5**
Brodeur, Arthur G. **791**
Brooke, Stopford A. **13, 109**
Brooks, K.R. **1020, 1076**
Brown, Carleton **561**
Brown, Ray **989**
Budde, Erich **124**
Bülbring, Karl D. **685r**
Burrow, J.A. **333**
Burton, Richard **690**
Busse, Wilhelm G. **626**
B[utterfield], F.W.L. **696**

Calder, Daniel G. **58, 60, 298, 309, 320**
Cameron, Angus **48**
Cameron, M.L. **486**
Campbell, Alistair **572**
Campbell, Jackson J. **238, 258, 303, 344, 850, 885**
Capek, M.J. **586**
Cassidy, Frederic G. **273**
Cazamian, Louis **168**
Chadwick, H. Munro **183**
Chadwick, Nora Kershaw **183, 228**
Chambers, Raymond W. **185, 731**
Chance, Jane **334**
Chaney, William A. **429**
Cherniss, Michael D. **593, 876**
Chickering, Howell D. **444**
Cilluffo, Gilda **1095, 1097, 1098**
Clark, George **1080**
Clemoes, Peter **507**
Clunies Ross, Margaret **1044**
Cockayne, Oswald **365**
Colgrave, Bertram **779, 780**
Conybeare, John Josias **62**
Conybeare, William Daniel **62**
Cook, Albert S. **96, 115, 504, 687**
Cooper, Arthur **935r**
Cortelyou, J. Van Zandt **125**
Cosijn, Peter J. **99, 110, 536**
Couch, Christopher L. **970**
Craigie, William A. **165**
Crane, John Kenny **280**
Crawford, Jane **433**
Crawford, Samuel J. **167r**

Crépin, André **598**
Cronan, Dennis **1107**
Cross, James E. **45, 229, 239, 240, 241, 589, 631, 1099**
Crossley-Holland, Kevin **250, 318, 578, 834, 835, 855, 864, 909, 918, 919, 920**
Crotch, W.J. Blyth **770**

Damico, Helen **468**
Dammers, Richard H. **502**
Dane, Joseph A. **620, 1096**
Das, Satyendra Kumar **787**
Dauenhauer, Richard **908**
Davidson, Thomas **428**
Davis, Patricia **980**
Davis, Steven **1109**
Davy, Derek **895**
Dawson, Robert MacGregor **573**
Deegan, Marilyn **484**
Deering, Robert Waller **1055**
Del Pezzo, Raffaella **1118**
Derolez, René **216, 237, 1038**
Dewick, Edward Samuel **648**
D'Ham, Otto **670**
Diamond, R.E. **236**
Dickins, Bruce **1004, 1072**
Dietrich, Franz **71, 658, 659, 662, 663**
Diller, Hans Jürgen **335**
Doane, A.N. **285, 971**
Dobbie, Elliott Van Kirk **194, 203**
Dolfini, Giorgio **439**
Donoghue, Daniel **1101**
Doskow, Minna **455**
Doubleday, James F. **1113**
Dubois, Marguerite Marie **39**
Duckert, Audrey R. **446**
Duff, Edward Gordon **1056**
Duncan, Edwin **336**

Earl, James W. **618, 624**
Earle, John **88, 533**
East, W.G. **604**
Ebeling, Friedrich Wilhelm **531**
Ebermann, Oskar **370**
Ebert, Adolf **79, 666**
Ekwall, Eilert **778r**
Eliason, Norman E. **807, 816**
Elliott, Ralph W.V. **219, 230, 324, 1021**
Ellis Davidson, Hilda R. **242, 1039**
Elsakkers, Marianne **485**
Emerson, Oliver F. **1062**

Erhardt-Siebold, Erika von **768, 795, 796, 797, 802, 803, 805, 808, 809, 812, 813, 817**
Erlemann, Edmund **704**
Erlemann, Fritz **709**
Ettmüller, Ernst Moritz Ludwig **1, 68**
Evert, Richard **602**

Fanagan, John M. **304**
Fanger, Claire **964**
Faust, Cosette **146**
Fell, Christine **325**
Fife, Austin E. **436**
Fiocco, Teresa **632, 952, 958**
Flom, George Tobias **182**
Florey, Kenneth **605**
Flower, Robin **185**
Förster, Max **185, 518, 519, 1057, 1059**
Foerster, Massimiliano. *See* Förster, Max.
Foley, John Miles **312, 469, 902, 910**
Fox, Samuel **528**
Frank, Roberta **281, 623**
Frantzen, Allen J. **321**
Fritzsche, Arthur **668**
Fry, Donald K. **580, 583, 936**
Fukuchi, Michael S. **601**
Funke, Otto **141**
Furlani, Fabio **491**

Galinsky, H. **563**
Garavelli, Rossana **341**
Gardner, John **886**
Gardner, Thomas J. **1084**
Garvin, Katharine **843**
Gatch, Milton McC. **500**
Gay, David E. **487**
Geldner, Johann **126**
Gerritsen, Johan **821, 861, 956**
Giles, John Allen **642**
Gillam, Doreen M.E. **243, 248**
Giraudi, Anna **466**
Girvan, Ritchie **814**
Gleissner, Reinhard **957**
Glosecki, Stephen O. **492**
Godden, M.R. **327**
Göbel, Heidi **921**
Göbel, Helga **931**
Göbel, Rüdiger **921**
Göller, Karl Heinz **274**
Golding, G.F. **184**
Goldsmith, Margaret E. **587, 887**
Gollancz, Israel **107**

Golther, Wolfgang **380**
Gordon, Robert K. **174**
Grant, Raymond J.S. **305**
Grattan, John H.G. **394, 423**
Greenfield, Stanley B. **40, 57, 60, 220, 282, 581, 602, 844, 932**
Grein, Christian W.M. **2, 3, 70, 75, 84, 664**
Grendon, Felix **381**
Grienberger, Theodor von **1000, 1005**
Griffiths, B.M. **779**
Grimm, Jacob L.K. **363, 532**
Grimm, Wilhelm Karl **995**
Grinda, Klaus R. **249**
Grose, M.W. **286**
Gross, Erika **201**
Gruber, Loren C. **603, 606, 608, 610, 612**
Gummere, Francis B. **97, 103, 629**

Haarder, Andreas **927**
Haas, Renate **1100**
Habicht, Werner **231**
Hacikyan, Agop **287, 836, 841, 845, 846, 851, 862**
Hälsig, Friedrich **382**
Hall, J.R. **1031**
Halliwell, Phillipps James Orchard **364**
Halsall, Guy **347**
Halsall, Maureen **1033, 1041**
Hamer, Richard **269**
Hammerich, Friedrich **1049**
Hamp, Eric P. **470, 1030**
Hanscom, Elizabeth D. **120**
Hansen, Elaine Tuttle **61, 299, 637**
Harris, Joseph **453, 1102**
Hart, James M. **702**
Hauer, Stanley R. **460**
Haworth, P.D. **549r**
Helm, Karl **139, 420**
Hempl, George **1001, 1002**
Henry, Patrick L. **259**
Hermann, John P. **319, 322, 1090, 1092, 1106**
Herzfeld, Georg **684, 699r**
Heusinkveld, Arthur H. **24**
Heusler, Andreas **166, 170**
Heyne, Moritz **73**
Hicketier, Franz **681, 682**
Hieatt, Constance B. **292, 342**
Hill, Joyce M. **1117**
Hill, Thomas D. **440, 457, 461, 522, 588, 1082, 1085, 1086, 1099, 1103**
Hodgkin, Robert H. **191**

Hoffory, Julius **998**
Hofmann, C. **1048**
Holthaus, E. **674r**
Holthausen, Ferdinand **105, 112r, 123,
    128, 132, 135, 144, 150r, 154, 157,
    162, 171, 192r, 212, 377, 387, 388,
    397, 399, 404, 516, 544, 546, 552, 564,
    647, 650, 686, 700, 741, 756, 759, 763,
    774, 783, 1058, 1065, 1067**
Hoops, Johannes **98, 730**
Hopkins, R.H. **1078**
Horn, Wilhelm **392**
Hotchner, Cecilia Audrey **199**
Howard, Edwin J. **499**
Howard, Michael **462**
Howe, G. Melvyn **447**
Howe, Nicholas **328**
Hüttenbrenner, F. **1066r**
Hume, Kathryn **293, 903**
Huppé, Bernard F. **270, 827**

Isaacs, Neil D. **264, 501**

Jabbour, Alan **266**
Jackson, Kenneth **193**
Jacobs, Nicolas **976**
Jaffé, Philippus **644**
Jager, Eric **633**
James, M.R. **1068**
Jansen, Gottfried **671**
Jansen, Karl **719**
Jember, Gregory K. **904, 911, 917, 928,
    965, 977**
Jente, Richard **158**
Johnson, William C. **526**
Jolly, Karen Louise **479**
Jonassen, Frederick B. **1104**
Jones, Frederick G. **1026**
Jongeboer, Henk **477**
Jordan, Richard **117**
Jost, Karl **130, 421r**
Joyce, John H. **880**
Judd, Elizabeth **599**
Jungandreas, Wolfgang **1010, 1012, 1029**
Juzi, Gertrud **200**

Kail, J. **10**
Kaiser, Rolf **217**
Kaluza, Max **15**
Kammradt, Fr. **409**
Kaske, R.E. **852**
Kauffmann, Friedrich **538**

Kay, Donald **856**
Keefer, Sarah Larratt **494**
Keiser, Albert **151**
Keller, Roni **908**
Keller, Wolfgang **1013, 1016**
Kellermann, Günther **232, 1100**
Kellner, Leon **108**
Kelly, Susan **983**
Kemble, John Mitchell **63, 66, 514, 640,
    1046, 1047**
Kennedy, Arthur G. **179**
Kennedy, Charles W. **29, 233**
Kennedy, Christopher B. **888**
Ker, Neil R. **36**
Ker, William P. **121, 136**
Kern, H. **82**
Kern, J.H. **722, 742**
Kiernan, K.S. **889, 890**
Kirk, John M., Jr. **611**
Kispert, Robert J. **870**
Kissack, R.A. **175**
Kittredge, George Lyman **178**
Klaeber, Frederick **122, 159, 398, 400r,
    401r, 505, 548r, 554r, 557, 652, 715,
    752r, 760r, 767, 792, 1006, 1018**
Klaeber, Friedrich. *See* Klaeber, Frederick.
Klipstein, Louis F. **67**
Kluge, Friedrich **94**
Kock, Ernst A. **147, 148, 149, 152, 155,
    163, 541, 553, 732, 761, 764, 765**
Kögel, Rudolf **106**
Köhler, Artur **496**
Körner, Karl **667**
Körting, Gustav **9**
Konick, Marcus **781**
Kossick, Shirley G. **337, 857**
Kossinna, Gustav **999**
Krackow, Otto **118**
Kranz, Gisbert **828**
Krapp, George Philip **179, 194, 520**
Krappe, Alexander Haggerty **1009**
Krause, Wolfgang **1019**
Krogmann, Willy **560, 576**
Krüger, Charlotte **555**
Kuhn, Hans **575**
Kyte, E. Clemons **288**

Lambert, Catherine **410**
Lange (pupil of Dietrich) **662**
Larsen, Henning **1069**
Laurini, Anna Camilla **1087**
Lawrence, William Witherle **703**

Lee, Alvin A. 283
Lefèvre, P. 86
Legouis, Émile 168
Lehnert, Martin 221
Lendinara, Patrizia 355, 463, 590, 596,
    597, 609, 865, 891, 892, 905, 906, 937
Leo, Heinrich 4, 657
Leonhardi, Günther 373
Lerer, Seth 356, 981
Leslie, Roy F. 832, 858
Lester, G.A. 990
Levison, Wilhelm 651
Liebermann, Felix 710, 1063
Lindheim, Bogislav von 815
Lindquist, Ivar 390
Liuzza, Roy Michael 978
Löwenthal, Fritz 744
Longfellow, Henry Wadsworth 529
Longland, Stella 1032, 1036
Lüning, Otto 11

MacLean, George E. 689
Machan, Tim William 972
Mackie, W.S. 186, 188, 556, 771
Madert, Karl August 697
Magennis, Hugh 959, 966
Magoun, Francis Peabody, Jr. 33, 210, 225,
    234, 405, 406, 407, 412, 417, 425r,
    426r, 521, 819
Malone, Kemp 30, 206, 565, 822, 1007
Manganella, G. 251
March, Francis A. 534
Marckwardt, Albert H. 284
Marino, Matthew 922
Marquardt, Hertha 198
Martin, B.K. 584
Massmann, H.F. 641
Mather, Frank J. 688
Mazzuoli Porru, Giulia 302
McEntire, Sandra 625, 638
McGillivray, Murray 628
McKenna, Deirdre 286
McKinnell, John 1119
Mead, William E. 113
Meaney, Audrey L. 262, 315, 348, 613
Meissner, Rudolf 386
Meling, Kjell 1091
Menner, Robert James 1070, 1071, 1073
Merbach, Hans Johann 89
Merbot, Reinhold 87
Meroney, Howard 413, 415
Merrill, Elizabeth 1064

Mertner, Edgar 42
Meyer, Elard Hugo 100, 363
Meyer, Richard Moritz 12, 1003
Meyvaert, Paul 907
Middendorff, Hermann 717r
Migne, J.P. 643
Mincoff, Marco 790
Mitchell, Bruce 250, 252, 253, 345, 577
Mitchell, Stephen A. 942
Mittner, Ladislaus 222
Molinari, Maria Vittoria 493
Momma, Haruko 349
Moorman, F.W. 711
Morley, Henry 74
Mossé, Fernand 207
Müller, Eduard 660, 661
Müller, Hugo 540
Müller, Ludvig 655
Murphy, G. Ronald 1111
Musset, Lucien 1025

Napier, Arthur S. 515
Naumann, Hans 402
Nelson, Marie 306, 350, 472, 478, 480,
    621, 881, 893, 894, 923, 943, 973, 991,
    1108
Newton, Cosette. *See* Faust, Cosette.
Nicholson, Lewis E. 574
Nicholson, Peter 1035
Niles, John D. 357, 467
Nitzsche, Jane Chance 616
Nöth, Winfried 53, 458
Nuck, R. 680

O'Keeffe, Katherine O'Brien 358, 953,
    960, 1110
Oda, Takuji 944
Oggins, Robin S. 326
Ogura, Michiko 488
Ohrt, Ferdinand 395
Olivero, Federico 142
Opland, Jeff 313
Orme, Nicholas 513
Orton, Harold 27
Orton, Peter 933
Osborn, Marijane 314, 908, 974, 1032,
    1034, 1036
Owen-Crocker, Gale R. 967

Padelford, Frederick Morgan 695
Paetzel, Walther 23

Page, Raymond I. **271, 289, 329, 1022, 1027, 1081**
Parkes, M.B. **873**
Parks, Ward **343**
Pàroli, Teresa **489**
Partridge, Astley Cooper **945**
Pasternack, Carol Braun **359**
Patch, Howard R. **762**
Patzig, H. **766**
Payne, Joseph F. **372**
Pearsall, Derek **52**
Peltola, Niilo **46**
Pertz, G.H. **639**
Peters, R.A. **434**
Peterson, Robyn G. **972**
Pfeilstücker, Suse **195**
Philippson, Ernst **180**
Pickford, T.E. **1115**
Pilch, Herbert **55, 443**
Pingel, Ludwig **630**
Pinsker, Hans **877, 938, 939, 961**
Pitman, James Hall **769**
Plummer, Charles **539**
Pons, Émile **172**
Pontán, Runar **145**
Pope, John C. **204, 307, 882**
Prehn, A. **672**
Pulsiano, Phillip **523**

Quirk, Randolph **218, 247, 895**

Raffel, Burton **235, 831, 838**
Ramat, Paolo **450**
Rankin, J.W. **21, 550r**
Rask, Rasmus Kristian **361**
Rathe, Armin **473**
Raw, Barbara **54**
Redbond, William J. **1014**
Regan, C.A. **1114**
Reifegerste, E. Matthia **984**
Reisner, T.A. **866**
Remly, Lynn L. **591**
Renwick, W.L. **27**
Reszkiewicz, Alfred **449**
Ricci, Aldo **181**
Richter, Carl **22**
Rieger, Max **72, 76, 80**
Ringler, Richard N. **273**
Rissanen, Matti **338, 968**
Ritzke-Rutherford, Jean **310**
Roberts, Jane **330**

Robinson, Fred C. **57, 311, 352, 579, 614, 617, 622, 867, 896**
Robinson, William Clarke **7**
Rodrigues, Louis J. **985**
Roeder, Fritz **114**
Rollinson, Philip B. **290, 868**
Rosenberg, Bruce A. **438**
Rosier, James L. **238, 284**
Rositzke, Harry August **562**
Ross, Alan S.C. **1024**
Rowe, Elizabeth Ashman **351**
Rubin, Stanley **451**
Rüden, Michael von **308**
Russom, Geoffrey **512, 627, 912**
Ryan, William M. **924**
Rydberg, Viktor **997**

Sanesi, Roberto **260**
Sarrazin, Gregor Ignatz **14, 95, 676, 739**
Schabram, Hans **254, 268, 294**
Schaumberg, W. **1050**
Schipper, Julius **78, 1051**
Schlauch, Margaret **34, 782**
Schlueter, Mary **980**
Schlutter, Otto B. **375, 376, 378, 542, 543, 545, 720, 723, 724, 725**
Schmitt, Ludwig Erich **275**
Schmitz, Theodor **133, 134**
Schneider, Karl **226, 323, 339, 431, 441, 483, 594, 897, 913**
Schneider, Robert **740**
Schöwerling, Rainer **445**
Schrader, Richard J. **619**
Schröder, Eduard **104**
Schröder, Franz Rolf **422**
Schröer, Arnold **677**
Schubel, Friedrich **41**
Schücking, Levin Ludwig **143, 177**
Schwab, Ute **291, 1028**
Sedgefield, Walter J. **160, 164, 767**
Sharpe, Eric J. **1093**
Shaw, Patricia **962**
Shippey, T.A. **47, 300, 636**
Shook, Laurence K. **255, 411, 798, 826, 883**
Short, Douglas D. **508, 509, 510**
Sievers, Eduard **90, 92, 101, 535, 551, 683**
Sims-Williams, Patrick **495**
Singer, Charles J. **365, 389, 396, 423**
Singer, S. **169**
Sisam, Kenneth **208, 215, 820, 1075r**
Skemp, Arthur R. **383, 384r**

Slay, Desmond 818
Smith, Albert Hugh 777
Solari, Roberto 1042
Sonke, Emma 718
Sorrell, Paul 353
Spaeth, John Duncan 161
Spamer, James B. 464
Stallybrass, James 363
Standop, Ewald 42
Stanley, Eric G. 223, 276, 295, 296, 316, 979, 982, 992, 1037, 1043, 1105
Stern, Gustav 187
Stewart, Ann Harleman 898, 929, 940, 954, 955, 963
Storms, Godfrid 418
Strauss, Jürgen 346
Strobl, Joseph 537
Ström, Åke V. 297
Stroh, Friedrich 419
Strunk, William 119
Stuart, Heather 456, 459, 471, 481
Stürzl, Erwin 430
Swaen, A.E.H. 498, 721, 757, 775, 784, 785, 786, 788, 799, 804
Swann, Brian 452, 874
Swanton, M.J. 884
Sweet, Henry 77, 81, 91, 93, 1052

Talbot, Charles H. 437
Talentino, Arnold 941
Tangl, Michael 649
Taylor, Archer 558, 791, 806
Taylor, Paul Beekman 448, 585, 1088
Thompson, Stith 146
Thorpe, Benjamin 65, 362
Thun, Nils 442
Timmer, Benno J. 202, 213, 566, 571, 1074
Tinker, Chauncey B. 115
Trahern, Joseph B., Jr. 360, 654, 1116
Trautmann, Moritz 17, 140r, 673, 675, 691, 692, 712, 713, 714, 726, 733, 734, 735, 743, 745, 746, 747, 748, 749, 750, 751, 754, 758
Treneer, Anne 772
Tripp, Raymond P., Jr. 301, 503, 914, 1094
Tristram, Hildegard L.C. 55, 969
Tucker, S.I. 824, 829
Tupper, Frederick Jr. 137, 705, 706, 707, 708, 716, 727, 728, 736
Turner, Sharon 527

Van der Leeuw, Gerardus 1403
Vaughan-Sterling, Judith A. 476
Vermeer, P.M. 853r
Vincenti, A.R. von 1061
Vogt, Friedrich 1053
Von der Leyen, Friedrich 197

Wahrig, G. 224
Walker, J.A. 210
Walker-Pelkey, Faye 994
Waller, A.R. 20
Walters, Frank 925
Walz, John A. 693
Wannagut, Elke 934
Ward, A.W. 20
Wardale, Edith E. 26
Warren, Kate M. 127
Warton, Thomas 77
Watson, George 50
Weber, Gerd Wolfgang 267
Weinhold, Karl 369
Wells, Richard 926
Welsh, Andrew 986
Weston, L.M.C. 482
Whitbread, Leslie 263, 567, 568, 800, 810, 1089
White, Beatrice 794
Whitelock, Dorothy 209, 506, 570
Whiting, Bartlett Jere 265
Whiting, Helen Wescott 265
Whitman, Charles H. 129, 694
Whitman, Frank H. 859, 860, 863, 869, 871, 878, 899, 915, 946
Wienold, Götz 277
Wilcox, Jonathan 987, 1112
Wild, Friedrich 1079
Williams, Blanche Colton 189, 547
Williams, Edith Whitehurst 900, 901
Williams, Margaret 28
Williams, Owen Thomas 131
Williamson, Craig 916, 947
Wilson, John 993
Wittig, Joseph S. 505
Wood, George A. 738
Woolf, H.B. 653
Woolf, Rosemary E. 1077
Wormald, C.P. 511
Wrenn, Charles L. 37, 43, 244, 245, 256, 1008, 1023
Wright, Charles D. 340
Wright, Cyril E. 427, 1015
Wright, Thomas 64, 364

Wülker, Richard Paul **6, 8, 16, 18r, 83, 85,
517, 646, 679**
Wyatt, Alfred John **153, 176, 737**
Wyld, H.C. **173**

Young, Jean I. **211, 789, 793**

Zanco, Aurelio **801**
Zandvoort, R.W. **811**
Zesmer, David M. **38**
Ziegler, Waltraud **948, 961**
Zolla, Elémire **1083**
Zupitza, Julius **367, 368, 645, 665, 1054**

Subject Index

This index covers the General Bibliography. References are by entry-number, in bold type.

acorns: as foodstuff for human consumption **98**

aðalhendingar: in *Maxims* **540**

Ælfric: views on Wyrd **52**

—— *De Auguriis*: possible parallel to *Maxims II* **600**

Æthicus Ister, *Cosmographia*: as source for *Solomon and Saturn* **1110**

Ages of Man **333**; in *Precepts* **328**

Ages of World **241**

Alcuin: authorship of Latin riddles **121**

Aldhelm

—— authorship of Riddles **16**; dialect **203**; influence on Riddles **20, 65, 79, 298, 658, 662, 666**; Latin riddles of **121, 356, 559**; literary merit in relation to Symphosius **672**

—— Enigma 3: as analogue to Riddle 30 **672**; as analogue to Riddle 39 **907**

—— Enigma 29: as analogue to Riddle 84 **298**

—— Enigma 30: as analogue to Riddle 13 **812**

—— Enigma 32: as analogue to Riddles **298**

—— Enigma 33: as source for Riddle 35 **842**; as source for Leiden Riddle and Riddle 35 **298**; edition and translation into English **769**

—— Enigma 53: as analogue to Riddles **298**; as analogue to Riddle 22 **825**

—— Enigma 55: as analogue to Riddles **298**

—— Enigma 59: as analogue to Riddles **298**

—— Enigma 71: as analogue to Riddle 39 **907**

—— Enigma 73: as analogue to Riddle 84 **298**

—— Enigma 80: as analogue to Riddles **298**

—— Enigma 83: as analogue to Riddles **298**

—— Enigma 84: as analogue to Riddle 36 **298**

—— Enigma 86: as analogue to Riddle 53 **298, 952**

—— Enigma 89: as analogue to Riddle 47 **896**; as analogue to Riddle 49 **298**

—— Enigma 92: as analogue to Riddle 70a **882**

—— Enigma 100: as source for Riddle 40 **953, 960**; as source for Riddles 40 and 41 **298**; edition and translation into English **769**

Alfred: translation of Boethius, *De Consolatione Philosophiae* **177**; views on Wyrd **52**

allegorical interpretations **282, 345**

allegorical techniques **886**

allegory: as defined by Bede and Isidore **868**; in relation to Riddles **31**. *See also* Riddle 16, theme; Riddle 17, theme; Riddle 25, literary qualities; Riddle 30, literary qualities; Riddle 55, literary qualities; Riddle 60, literary qualities; Riddle sequences, Riddles 42–3; Riddles 1–3, literary qualities; Riddles, literary qualities; Riddle 15, literary qualities.

alliteration: irregularities **80, 162**; mnemonic function **161, 312**

ambiguity. *See entries for individual texts, under literary qualities.*

Ambrose: influence on *Vainglory* **270**

amulet charms **381, 425**

anagrams: in Riddles **658, 980**

anaphora **25**; in Riddle 35 **258**; on *hwilum* **303**; on *sum* **303**

Andreas: Nature description **662**

animals: in Riddles **251**; in *Solomon and Saturn* **147**

animism **357**; in Charm 8 **418**

anthropological approach to OEW poems
300
anthropomorphism: in *Maxims* **55**; in
Riddles **658**
anthropomorphization: in Charm 9 **312**
antiquarian learning **43**
antiquarian poetry **183**
antithesis **25**; explicit and implicit **350**; in
Rune Poem **1031**
antler: as architectural feature **73**
apocope of *-u*: as criterion for dating **56**
apple: in Charm 2 **291, 395, 413, 466**
archery. *See* Riddle 23.
architectural vocabulary: in *Maxims II* and
Solomon and Saturn **354**
aristocratic attributes: as evidenced in *Gifts*
512
Aristotle: classification of gnomic
utterances **183**
armour, spiritual **319, 322**. *See also* lorica.
art, Anglo-Saxon: as illustrated by OEW
poems **195**
artifacts: as described in OEW poems **73**
Augustine: influence on *Vainglory* **270**; *De
Civitate Dei*, as analogue to *Maxims II*
588; in relation to *Solomon and Saturn*
1100
Ausonius, *Technopaegnion*: compared with
Rune Poem **1003**
authority: on part of poet **54**
authorship **352**. *See also entries under
individual poems.*
autobiographical introductions: *Vainglory*
and *Order* **194**

Babylonian charms: in relation to Charm 4
348
Baldr: alluded to in Charms **431**
The Battle of Maldon: compared with
Vainglory **52**
bears: in relation to Charm 8 **386**
beautiful: concept of in OEW poems **200**
Bede: as source for the Riddles **65**; *De
natura rerum*, in relation to Riddle 1
704; *Death Song*, in relation to *Winfrid
Proverb* **203**; *In Epistolas Septem
Catholicas*, as source for *Vainglory*
1119; *Nomina locorum*, as source for
Solomon and Saturn **1110**
bees. *See* Charm **8**.
Benedictine Reform: in relation to
Solomon and Saturn **19**
beon and *wesan*: use in OEW texts **130**

Beowulf: compared with *Precepts* **636**;
Fate in **156**; influence from Riddles
739; influence on *Maxims* **13**
Biblical apocrypha: as source for *Solomon
and Saturn* **1059, 1068**
bibliographies: OEW poetry **24, 27, 35, 50,
51, 57**; Charms **463**; *Maxims* **609**;
Riddles **905, 936**
birth-gift: as evidenced in *Fortunes* **325**
blindness, spiritual: in *Maxims I* **625**
blood: in Charms **370**
Boethius, *De Consolatione Philosophiae*:
audience for Alfred's translation **177**;
in relation to Anglo-Saxon views on
Wyrd **52**; in relation to *Solomon and
Saturn* **296**; parallels to *Maxims II* **267**
Book of Enoch: as source for *Maxims I* **597**
Book of Proverbs: as analogue to OEW
poems **328**; influence on *Maxims* **31,
588**
books: authority of **626**
British Library Add. MS. 9067 **727**
brun: definition of colour **113**

CCCC 41 **36, 305, 476, 1051**
CCCC 422 **36, 358, 1047, 1051, 1052,
1061, 1073, 1075, 1081**
Caedmon's Hymn: compared with *Order*
31
Caesarius of Arles: as source for *Vainglory*
1116, 1119
Cassiodorus: influence on *Vainglory* **270**;
Institutiones: as source for *Solomon
and Saturn* **1104**
catalogue: as structural principle **356**;
catalogue poetry: Riddles and *Order* as
instances **116**
catenulate structure **614**. *See also*
catalogue, lists.
ceorl: in *Maxims* and Riddles **191**
Chambers, Robert: transcript of Exeter
Book. *See* Exeter Book.
charade riddles **246**
Charms **361–495**
Charm 1
———— comparative discussions: Irish
motifs **446**; Irish-Latin analogues **440**;
Skírnismál **106**; Swedish and German
analogues **363**
———— dating **16**
———— editions **66, 67, 68, 72, 85, 94,
153, 164, 165, 190, 217, 225, 361, 362,
363, 408**; excerpts **221**

―――― efficacy **457**; fertility **438**; fertilizing ingredients **412**

―――― language: *cwicbeam* **476, 483**; *erce* **106, 153, 158, 406, 408, 409, 415, 418, 420, 422, 446, 475, 493**; Old Irish *erc* **495**

―――― literary qualities: structuralist analysis **278**; symbolism **457**

―――― metrics: versification **469**

―――― origins: as Germanic ploughman's lay **109**; reconstruction of pagan form **483**; ritual poetry **166**

―――― passages discussed in detail: lines 9 **483**; 18 **438**; 26 **420**; 27–8 **405**; 30 **388**; 33 **401**; 35 **483**; 36 **411**; 40–2 **411**; 51 **363**; 51–2 **493**; 51–8 **312**; 55 **154, 375, 388**; 56 **388**; 65 **348, 439**; 69–70 **109**; 69–71 **483**

―――― performance **74, 418, 467**; on part of narrator **478**

―――― religion: Christian ritual **493**; Germanic cults **380**; heathen religion **180**; Nature worship **103**

―――― text: Christian revisions **109**; possible interpolation **106**

―――― title, meaning of **438**

―――― translations: into English **103, 115, 146, 184, 210, 233, 317, 365**; excerpts **28, 40, 161, 191, 221, 235**; into German **408**; into German, retranslated into English **363**

Charm 2

―――― authorship on part of female herbalist **166**

―――― comparative discussion: *Solomon and Saturn* **1108**

―――― doctrines: medical **396**; principle of 'like affects like' **278**; snake-lore **432**

―――― editions **85, 98, 164, 165, 189, 373, 394, 404, 423, 491**

―――― efficacy **486**; of apple **383**; of colour magic **391**; of early Germanic magic and medicine **109, 389, 410**; of herbs **8, 203, 413, 439, 466**; identity of enemy **492**

―――― influence from Christian liturgy **374**

―――― language: lexis **488**; *onflyge* **410**; *regenmelde* **371, 406, 465, 466**; sound as meaning **306**; *wergulu* **371**; *wuldortanas* **418, 430, 490, 491**

―――― literary qualities: structure **30, 466**

―――― passages discussed in detail: lines 1 **395**; 5–6 **404, 405**; 6 **411**; 14–15 **281**; 21–2 **383**; 24a **159**; 29 **404**; 30 **371, 388**; 34 **159, 291, 383, 388**; 34b **395**; 36 **466**; 43 **387**; 48 **123**; 50 **123**; 58 **466**; 59 **430**

―――― religion: Christian belief **31**; mixture of beliefs **372**; Woden equated with Christ **429**

―――― text: as composite **413, 423**; *Lay of the Nine Darts of Woden* **365**

―――― translations: into English **115, 365, 423**; into German **98**; into Italian **491**

Charm 3

―――― comparative discussion: Yugoslav spells **312**

―――― editions **164, 179, 376, 423, 445**

―――― editorial policy **472**

―――― efficacy **31**; against swelling **125**; against dwarf **315**; against dwarf in spider garb **383**; against nightmare **472**; against witch-riding **487**; role of Seven Sleepers **381 382, 414**; role of dwarf **31**

―――― passages discussed in detail: lines 1 **394**; 9 **125, 171, 315, 459**; 11 **212**; 12 **492**; 13 **406, 439, 487**

―――― title **125**

―――― translations: into English **365, 423, 452**; into German **445**

Charm 4

―――― comparative discussion: Finnish analogues **166, 393**; 'Contra vermes' and 'Pro nessia' **442**; 'Pro nessia' **450**

―――― cultural significance **444**

―――― editions **66, 68, 69, 72, 81, 85, 94, 164, 165, 182, 190, 221, 225, 302, 363, 364, 402, 419, 423**

―――― efficacy **492**; against headaches **166**; against rheumatism **271**; magnetic properties of iron **432**; naming function **383**; role of smiths **383**

―――― language: *færstice* **424**

―――― literary qualities: epic introduction **374**; literary merit **30**

―――― passages discussed in detail: lines 1 **406**; 5 **394**; 8 **228, 348**; 13 **455**; 13–14 **212**; 13–15 **383**; 14 **388**; 16 **383**; 19 **154, 228**; 20–2 **374**; 20–6 **106**; 22 **405**; 23–6 **405**; 24 **388**; 25–6 **170, 383, 428**; 27 **212, 388, 394**

―――― performance: practice of healer **392**; shamanism **166, 492**

—————— religion: Christian tolerance **5**;
Christian uses **457**; cult of 'mighty
women' or *dísir* **103**; valkyries **468**
—————— text: as composite **392**; as unity
460; interpolation **374**
—————— translations: into English **103, 115,
146, 161, 184, 205, 210, 233, 365, 423,
452**; excerpts **28, 40, 191**; into German
106; into German, re-translated into
English **363**
Charm 5
—————— editions **179, 423, 443**
—————— efficacy: role of cross **461**
—————— translations: into English **115, 184,
365, 423**
Charm 6
—————— comparative discussion **484**
—————— editions **66, 423, 443**
—————— efficacy **480**; in pregnancy and
childbirth **484**
—————— passages discussed in detail: lines
15 **494**; 17 **425**; 26 **480**; 28 **480**
—————— performance: woman as speaker
480
—————— religion: monastic references **494**
—————— source: Magnificat **494**
—————— text: status of **203**
—————— translations: into English **365, 423**
Charm 7
—————— editions **164, 302, 363, 373**
—————— efficacy: against dropsy **389**;
against water-elf **381**
—————— literary qualities: structure **370**
—————— passages discussed in detail: line
13 **421**
—————— text: facsimile **427**
—————— translation: into English **365**
Charm 8
—————— audience **485**
—————— cultural significance: Christian
tolerance **5**
—————— editions **72, 81, 85, 94, 127, 164,
165, 179, 182, 189, 207, 221, 449, 464**
—————— efficacy **464, 477, 478**; against
swarms **436**; against bees **386**
—————— language: *sigewif* **109, 182, 367,
381, 386, 418, 425, 433, 477, 485, 492**
—————— literary qualities: structure **367,
470**
—————— origins: Continental origins **367**
—————— passages discussed in detail: lines

3 **418, 470**; 6 **386, 406, 418, 421, 439,
485**; 7 **485**; 9 **281, 363, 470**
—————— religion: valkyries **468**
—————— scholarship **367**
—————— text: as two separate charms **436**;
as unity **464**
—————— translations: into English **28, 115,
127, 184, 221, 250, 271, 318, 452, 464**;
excerpts **40**
Charm 9
—————— editions **153, 176, 207**
—————— efficacy: significance of thistle **453**
—————— passages discussed in detail: lines
13 **421**; 14–15 **311**; 17 **98, 453**
—————— performance: identity of Garmund
30, 153, 232, 312, 406, 425, 431, 476
—————— translations: into English **250, 318**
Charm 10
—————— efficacy: role of cross **416, 461,
416, 461**
—————— translation: into English **365**
Charm 11
—————— comparative discussion: with
lorica genre **298, 305, 319, 433, 471,
474**; with Middle High German
Reisesegen **471**; with Old Irish 'St
Patrick's Lorica' **320**; with *Solomon
and Saturn* **1108**; with *þulur* **30**
—————— editions **39, 68, 378, 383**
—————— efficacy **478**; role of rune-stave
315
—————— language: *hand ofer heafod* **68,
137**
—————— literary qualities: structure **471**
—————— passages discussed in detail: lines
1 **398, 399**; 6 **474**; 12 **398, 399**; 13a
388; 24 **68, 388**; 24a **137**; 24b **397**; 27
68; 30b **388, 397, 474**; 36 **383**; 36–7
154; 39 **3**
—————— translations: into English **317, 365**;
into German **378**
Charm 12
—————— editions **217, 269, 302, 366, 368,
377, 445**
—————— language: *wenchichenne* **476**
—————— literary qualities: sound as
meaning **306**
—————— passages discussed in detail: lines
1 **406**; 3 **97**; 5 **315**; 6–7 **315, 357**
—————— religion: pagan elements **441**
—————— translations: into English **250, 269,
318**; into German **368, 445**

Charms
———— comparative discussion **183, 382**; with Classical medicine **437**; with *Deor* **435**; with Finnish material **432**; with Germanic metrical charms **106, 374**; with Icelandic material **418**; with Indian material **166**; with Irish material **432**; with *Solomon and Saturn*, Paternoster section **1108**; withVedas **418**
———— cultural significance: context in Anglo-Saxon law and religion **381**
———— dating **16, 22, 181**
———— definition **450**; classificatory system **38, 463**
———— editions **6, 7, 203, 381**; edition excluding 8, 9, and 12 **365**. *See also entries under individual Charms.*
———— efficacy **7, 458, 482**; against theft **416**; fetter motif **448**; in relation to leech's practice **427**; medical function **451**; powers **407**; prophetic functions **382**; rational element **486**; use of amulets **315**
———— language: botanical vocabulary **454**; commands in **139**; sound as source of power **469**; speech acts **47**
———— literary qualities: context in Anglo-Saxon poetry **476**; epic introduction **382, 403, 444**; formulas **10**; literary merit **30, 40**; metaphorical processes **592**; narrative introductions **381**
———— metrics **43, 170, 305**; strophic form **26**
———— origins: common European **55**; native and foreign traditions **274**; oral transmission **181**
———— performance **20, 180, 379, 381, 382, 383, 463, 473, 478, 1108**; connection with witchcraft **178**; shamanism **492**; speaker's powers **139**; utterance instructions **481**
———— religion: animistic beliefs **357**; Christian censorship **382**; Christian elements **30, 166, 381, 431, 479**; Germanic paganism **34, 166, 297, 400, 429, 431, 489**; mixture of heathen and Christian material **203**; superstition **365**
———— scholarship **8**
———— sources and affinities **389**; British tradition **495**; Christian sources **411**

———— text: as compilation **305**; manuscript contexts **271, 305**; manuscripts **381, 418**
———— translations: into English **7, 174, 381, 418**; excerpts **2**; into Italian (selection) **260**. *See also entries under individual Charms.*
Chaucer, 'The Book of the Duchess': compared with *Solomon and Saturn* **1094**
chess: as depicted in OEW poems **337**
childlike qualities in Old English poetry **31**
Christian doctrine: on Hell **111**; influence on Old English poetry **25, 290**
Christian elements. *See relevant entries under individual texts.*
Christianity: regarded as continuation of charm tradition **191**
Chrodegang of Metz, *Regula Canonicorum*: as source for *Vainglory* **1116**
Church, Anglo-Saxon: attitude to Charms **190, 365**. *See also entries under individual charms.*
closing formulas: in Riddles **25**
closure: in Old English poetry **344**
Collectanea Bedae: as source for *Solomon and Saturn* **1103**
colour: Anglo-Saxon perceptions of **120**
colour: in magic **391**. *See also entries under* Charm 2.
colour words: in OEW poetry **113**. *See also* brun, grene, hasofag.
commendation ritual **137**
common people: as documented in OEW texts **32**
communicative process: in OEW poetry **61**
comparative religion, methods of: in relation to *Maxims* **591**
complexity poems **301**
compounds: incidence in poetic works **118**
consolation genre **54, 1102**
Contradictio Salomonis: as source for *Solomon and Saturn* **74, 1061, 1068**
cosmology: in *Maxims I* **232**
Cotton Caligula A.vii **36**
Cotton Domitian A.ix **1002, 1008, 1014, 1027**
Cotton Faustina A.x **36**
Cotton Otho B.x **36, 1027**
Cotton Tiberius A.iii **1061**
Cotton Tiberius B.i **36**; fol.115r: facsimile **273**

Cotton Vitellius A.xv **1047**
crafts: as evidenced in OEW poems **249, 355**; in Riddles **249**
creation: as theme in Riddles **662**
cross: as possible solution in Riddles. *See entries under* Riddles 30, 53, 55, 67, *and* 73.
cross: as motif in Charms. *See entries under* Charms 5 *and* 10.
cup of death **561, 813**; in *Maxims I* **627**; in relation to Riddle 23 **891**
Cynewulf: authorship **316**; of *Fortunes* **76**; of *Gifts* **76, 109**; of *Maxims* **134**; of *Maxims I* **76**; of OEW poems **7, 10, 17, 83, 86, 95**; of Riddles **5, 8, 13, 16, 22, 26, 71, 72, 74, 77, 79, 83, 84, 96, 99, 109, 161, 657, 658, 659, 661, 662, 668, 670, 672, 673, 674, 676, 677, 678, 681, 683, 684, 685, 687, 688, 689, 690, 697, 699, 701, 703, 719, 728, 729, 737, 738, 740, 749, 751, 787**; of *Wulf and Eadwacer* **99**
—— in relation to *Rune Poem* **1028, 1041**
—— runic signatures **63**
—— school of **194**

dædlata: in *Winfrid Proverb* **91**
Dafydd ap Gwilym, riddle on wind: compared with Riddles 1–3 **259**
dating: linguistic criteria **17, 22, 56, 181**; metrical criteria **52, 181, 206**; of OEW poems **19, 56, 84**. *See also entries under individual texts.*
debate format: in gnomic poetry **177**
definite article: as dating criterion **22**
Deor: compared with *Solomon and Saturn* **1102**
descriptive poetry **201**. *See also entries under* Riddles, literary qualities.
Devil: epithets for **319**; missiles of **322**
dialect: scribal alterations **181**
dialogue form: in OEW poems **632**. *See also* Solomon and Saturn, literary qualities.
Dialogues of Solomon and Saturn: as distinct from *Solomon and Saturn* **31**
didacticism **136, 207**
disease: causation **278**. *See also* doctrines *and entries under individual charms.*
Disputatio inter Pippinum et Alcuinum: compared with *Solomon and Saturn* **64**

Disticha Catonis: compared with *Precepts* **5, 635**
divination **158**
doctrines: in Anglo-Saxon medicine **396, 418, 423**
dom: in *Maxims I* **148**
Doomsday. *See* Last Judgement.
double alliteration **272, 279, 292**
dragon: in *Maxims II* **570, 587**
The Dream of the Rood: compared with Riddle 55 **964, 969**; compared with Riddle 60 **852**; compared with Riddle 72 **782**; compared with Riddles containing prosopopoeia **663, 933**
drink: drinking customs, as evidenced by OEW texts **73, 124**
—— drunkenness, in *Fortunes* lines 51–7 **124**; in *Precepts* line 34 **124**; in Riddle 12 **124**; in Riddle 60 **124**
—— popular attitudes to drinking in Riddle 27 **124**
Duodecim abusivis sæculi: in relation to *Solomon and Saturn* **1086**
Durham Proverbs: in relation to *Maxims* **592**
Durham Ritual: in relation to *Solomon and Saturn* **1089**
dwarf: in Charm 3. *See* Charm 3.

earth: as possessing double function in Charm 1 **493**; power of ritualistic casts of earth in Charm 8 **374, 464**; worship of, as evidenced in Charm 1 **158**
Eastern Christianity: influence of **169**
Eastre, goddess of dawn: in Charm 3 **394**
Ecclesiasticus: as source for *Maxims II* **588**
Edward the Confessor, Latin laws: in relation to *Winfrid Proverb* **30**
elegy: elegiac tone **267**; in relation to wisdom literature **47**. *See also* Vainglory.
elf-shot **389, 396, 428**; as derived from Finnish magic **393**; as derived from native Teutonic origin **389**; in Charm 4 **178, 315, 363**; in relation to Finnish magic **424**
elves **389, 393, 423, 432, 434, 442, 455, 456**. *See also* elf-shot.
emendations: opposed, in cases of irregular metrics, especially in Charms **90, 133, 162, 163, 305, 421, 472**; in cases of lexical repetition **311**; in Charms **485, 487, 494**; in general **107, 188**; in

Maxims 617; in Exeter Book Riddles 276, 308, 680, 716, 752, 753, 889, 916; in *Solomon and Saturn* 1070, 1092, 1100, 1109; in *Vainglory* 270, 1114, 1115
——— proposed, in Charms 98, 123, 125, 154, 176, 375, 377, 381, 383, 387, 388, 394, 404, 405, 406, 459, 483; in *Fortunes* 131, 497; in *Homiletic Fragment I* 520; in *Homiletic Fragment II* 105; in *Maxims* 82, 150, 152, 332, 336, 536, 552, 553, 554, 557, 559, 561, 564, 579, 615, 627; in *Order* 92, 252; in *Precepts* 92, 154; in *Proverbs* 645; in Exeter Book Riddles 105, 117, 135, 144, 148, 150, 152, 157, 171, 252, 267, 681, 684, 686, 702, 714, 723, 727, 734, 735, 741, 751, 754, 755, 756, 758, 759, 761, 764, 767, 783, 813, 851, 877, 891, 906, 942, 961, 978, 992, 993; in *Rune Poem* 94, 226, 1012; in *Solomon and Saturn* 144, 154, 157, 226, 1052, 1058, 1065, 1067, 1081, 1089, 1091, 1100, 1101; in various texts 75, 110, 112, 119, 122, 128, 132, 133, 147, 160, 163, 186, 192, 204, 212

emotions 327
encyclopaedia tradition 328, 614
end-stopped lines 30; in Charm 1 166; significance for dating 52, 20
entertainment in the hall: as evidenced in OEW poems 76
envelope pattern 25, 34; in *Gifts* 25, 344; in *Order* 52; in Riddles 25
eoh, 'horse': in *Rune Poem. See entries under* Rune Poem.
eolh(x)secg: in *Rune Poem. See entries under* Rune Poem.
eorod 'band of horsemen' 214
epic introduction. *See entries under* Charms, literary qualities.
epic poetry: in relation to Riddles 658; metrics of 5
erce. See entries under Charms, language.
ethnocentrism: in modern scholarship 49
Eusebius, Enigma 11: as analogue to Riddle 29 863; Enigma 15: as analogue to Riddle 30 672; Enigma 30: as analogue to Riddles 298; Enigma 32: as analogue to Riddles 298; Enigma 35: as analogue to Riddles 298; Enigma 37: as analogue to Riddles 298

——— in relation to Riddles 353; in relation to *Solomon and Saturn* 1104; influence on Riddles 73, 298, 707, 737
Exeter Book 27, 194, 307, 635, 738
——— binding 188
——— British Museum transcript 727, 731, 736, 751
——— compiler's rationale 52, 331; compared to 'Cambridge Songs' manuscript 356; inclusion of the Riddles 836; list or catalogue basis 356; order of contents 820; selection of poems 47
——— condition: damaged passages 188; lacunae 882; mutilated passages 185
——— dating 36
——— editions 112; partial edition (excluding Riddles 67, 78, 82, 89, 92, and 94) 65; partial edition 107
——— facsimile 185; facsimile of page 125a 188
——— scholarship 845; inaccessibility to Grein 2; textual criticism 78
——— scribal methods: accuracy 820; cryptic script 185; errors 135; spellings 575
exile: theme of 220, 658
expanded lines. *See* hypermetric lines.
experience: as represented in OEW poems 301

fæge 243
falconry 326, 497, 499, 757
Fall of the Angels: as theme in Old English poetry 47; in relation to *Solomon and Saturn* 47, 165
fatalism: Germanic 139; in relation to the Millennium 360
fate: as shaped by Norns 323; as subordinated to Divine Providence 202; heathen belief in 202; in relation to death 158. *See also entries under* Maxims, Solomon and Saturn, *and* Wyrd.
feast: as theme in *Vainglory* 1115
female authorship: *Maxims*, Riddles 45, 54, and 56 352. *See also* Charm 2 *and* Riddle 92.
female beauty: Anglo-Saxon criteria of 114
female demons: in Charm 4 271
female suffering: as mourner 299

feminine influence: on Anglo-Saxon
culture **177**
femininity, Anglo-Saxon **299**
fetters: in relation to Charms **448**
folk poetry: distinguished from OEW
poems **166**
folk wisdom: as transmitted by women **352**
folk-riddle. *See* popular riddle.
folklore elements: in Charms **13**; in
Solomon and Saturn **43**
formulas, poetic. *See* poetic formulas.
fornyrðislag: in Charms **367, 431, 441**
Fortunes **496–503**
———— comparative discussion: with
Beowulf **177, 496, 229**; with Johnson's
'The Vanity of Human Wishes' **502**;
with Latin and Greek texts **239**; with
Widsith **496**
———— cultural significance **177**; fowler
passage **255**; shamanism **501, 503**
———— dating **5, 17**
———— editions **2, 6, 65, 67, 68, 164, 165,
188, 194, 217, 221, 238, 300**; excerpt
131
———— genre: elegiac element **199**
———— language: formulas **10**; *sceacol*
'plectrum' **186**; *sum . . . sum* **229**; tense
usage **304**
———— literary qualities: catalogue form
328; dichotomy of feeling **243**; literary
merit **79, 109, 238, 502**; movements
359; naturalism and secularism **177**;
structure **29, 40, 194, 502**
———— passages discussed in detail: lines
1–9 **325**; 10 **338**; 13–14 **299**; 15–17
133, 213; 21–6 **229, 353, 499, 501,
503**; 33 **214**; 33–42 **173, 209, 262**; 39
248; 41 **267**; 43 **131, 300**; 43–4 **186**;
48–50 **209, 293**; 52–3 **167**; 70 **337**; 73
192; 80–4 **244, 313, 496, 500, 1023**; 83
160, 186, 261; 84 **3, 4, 261**; 85–92 **255,
326, 497**; 86 **255**; 93 **160, 497**; 94 **497**
———— sources: Christian commonplaces
229
———— text: compilation **19**; facsimile
185; interpolation **164**
———— theme **54, 300**
———— translations: into English **62, 65,
74, 146, 161, 174, 188, 205, 221, 300,
317, 318**; excerpts **7, 29, 40, 102, 233**;
into German **2, 70**
frea: scansion of **336**

Freyr: alluded to in Charms **431**
Frisian reference in *Maxims I* line 95. *See*
Maxims I line 95.
Frisians **7**; as typical sailors **191**
Fromm, Erich: research on aggressive
behaviour **350**
funerary customs: as evidenced by *Maxims
I* **556, 561, 596**
Furious Host: in Charm 4 **460**

galdralag: in Charms **390, 405, 420**; in
Maxims **272**
Garmund. *See* Charm 9.
gealdor: definition of **49**; in relation to
Charms **104**
generative composition: in relation to
Riddle 40 **953, 960**
giants **156, 597**
Gifts **504–13**
———— comparative discussion: analogues
240; *Christ* **76, 110, 194, 505**; Classical
analogues **504**; *Fortunes* **177**; Greek
choral hymns **102**; *Hyndluljóð* **320**;
Pastoral Care **510**; Pauline Analogy of
the Body **509**
———— cultural significance **511**;
emphasis on drink **211**; social role of
poetry **313**
———— dating **5, 17, 56**
———— editions **2, 6, 65, 67, 107, 127,
164, 165, 194, 221**; excerpt **131**
———— genre: as Christian gnomic poem
29
———— language: formulas **10**; *sum . . .
sum* **229, 512**; tense usage **304**
———— literary qualities: literary merit **79**;
movements as compositional unit **359**;
structure **26, 54, 328**
———— passages discussed in detail: lines
2 **122**; 13 **508**; 35 **313**; 44–8 **512**;
49–50 **247, 261**; 50 **234**; 53–8 **341**; 54
214; 58 **513**; 58–60 **512**; 69–70 **512**;
70b–1a **327**; 73b **337**; 75 **506**; 80–1
326; 106–7 **338**
———— sources **240**; 1 Cor. 12: 8–10 **76**;
29th homily of Pope Gregory **20**;
Parable of the Talents **54**; Rom. 12: 3–8
54
———— text: facsimile **185**; textual history,
as Christian revision of heathen poem
109
———— themes: Christian doctrine **510**;

concept of nobility 512; concept of *cræft* 87; voyage theme 236
—— translations: into English 65, 107, 174, 205, 221, 317, 506; excerpts 7, 28, 29, 40, 102, 127; into German 2
glory: as motivating force for Germanic warrior 593
gnomes. *See* gnomic statements.
gnomic poetry 259; as beginning of science 193; as source of poetic material 337; Germanic origin of 106, 183; Icelandic examples of 259; Irish and Greek traditions 183. *See also entries under* Maxims *and other relevant individual poems.*
gnomic statements: concerning action and conduct 183; definition of 193, 601; observations 183
Greek loanwords 475
Gregory the Great, *Forty Homilies on the Gospels*: Homily 9, as source for *Fortunes* and *Gifts* 240; Homily 29 194
—— *Homiliae in Ezechielem* 522
—— in relation to *Solomon and Saturn* 319, 1100; in relation to psychomachia 1113; methods of teaching 510; policies on use of pagan material 29; stages of sin 1086
grene: as colour word in OEW poetry 113, 285
Grímnismál: compared with *Order* 632
Guthlac B: in relation to *Maxims I* 561

hægtesse: in Charm 4 348, 379, 460
Hakenstil. See run-on style.
hall: in Old English poetry 293
Hamlet: speeches of Polonius, compared with *Precepts* 7, 31
hanging. *See* Fortunes, passages: lines 33–42.
Harley 585 36
harps and harp-playing 244, 261, 286, 313, 496, 500. *See also* Fortunes, passages, lines 80–4.
haso: definition of 113. *See also* Riddle 11.
Hávamál: compared to *Maxims* 77; compared with Old English gnomic poetry 183; source for *Precepts* 20
hawking. *See* falconry.
Haymo of Auxerre: influence on *Gifts* 298
Haymo of Halberstadt: influence on *Gifts* 240
heathen religion: cosmogony 594; cults 20,

69, 158, 594; literature 31, 41, 59, 146; in relation to Charm 1 88, 153; vestiges in *Solomon and Saturn* 77
Heaven: as depicted in *Order* and *Vainglory* 330
Hell: as depicted in Riddle 40 and *Solomon and Saturn* 111
Henryson, *Fables*: as contrasted with Riddles 13
herbs 381, 486; in relation to Christ 465; herbal charms 381, 406; herbal remedies 491. *See also* Charm 2, efficacy: herbs.
heroic age societies: gnomic poetry in 183
heroic ideal, Germanic: in *Winfrid Proverb* 295
Hesiod, *Works and Days*: as compared with *Maxims* 65, 183
Hickes: methods in assembling *Rune Poem* materials; use of Cotton Domitian A.ix, fol.10a 203. *See* Rune Poem, text: Hickes.
Hisperic tradition: as source for *Solomon and Saturn* 52
Holme Riddles 353, 705
Homiletic Fragment I 514–23
—— comparative discussion: with Riddle 47 912; with *The Wanderer* 267
—— editions 2, 6, 131, 514, 520, 521
—— influence of Gregory the Great 522
—— literary qualities: bee metaphor 522, 523; structure 264
—— passages discussed in detail: lines 9–15a 264; 12 516; 28 128; 40–1 516; 43 128; 43–7 344
—— scholarship 7
—— sources: Psalm 28 31, 264, 516, 518, 519, 520, 523, 1119; Psalm 117 523
—— text: collation 515; facsimile 517, 519; manuscript context 52
—— theme: antifeminism 7
—— translations: into English 514; excerpts 7; into German 2
Homiletic Fragment II 524–6
—— dating 194
—— editions 2, 6, 65, 188, 194, 331
—— genre: consolation 60, 194; elegiac element 199
—— literary qualities: argument 331; literary merit 331; structure 525
—— passages discussed in detail: lines 3 327; 3–4 321; 5 276, 524; 6–7 241

—————— source: Epistle to the Ephesians
525
—————— text: facsimile 185; manuscript
context 263, 331; status as complete
poem 40; status as fragment 60, 194;
textual notes 105; transcription 185
—————— themes 526; power of language
981
—————— translations: into English 65, 188,
331; into German 2
homiletic passages 25; in *Maxims* 30. *See
also* Homiletic Fragments I *and* II.
homoeoteleuton: in *Latin-English Proverbs*
237
The Husband's Message. *See* Riddle 60.
hydrometridae (pond skaters): in Riddle 40
125
hypermetric lines 15, 92, 133, 134, 163,
204, 227, 272, 279, 288; groupings of
25; in *Maxims II* 604; in off-verse 279;
rhetorical function of 133, 213. *See
also* Maxims I.

Icelandic rune poem: compared with *Rune
Poem*. *See* Rune Poem, comparative
discussion.
ides 334. *See also* female, women.
Ing: in *Rune Poem*: *See* Rune Poem,
passages: Ing.
insects: 125. *See also* Riddle 40.
Instruction of Vladimir Monomakh:
compared with *Precepts* 635
intensifying words 46
interrogation: in Riddles and *Solomon and
Saturn* 351
introductory formulas 25; in Riddles 25
Irish: in Old English charms 415. *See also*
Charm 1, language.
iron: as element in fetter charms 44; in
Charms 418; magnetic properties in
Charm 4 432; properties in traditional
belief 392
irony 319
Isidore, *Etymologiae*: as source for
Solomon and Saturn 1110
—————— influence on Riddles 328

Juliana lines 468–505: as analogue to
Fortunes 183
Kalevala 234
kennings 21, 198; for human beings and
activities 21; for the Deity 21; for the
natural world 21; in *Solomon and*

Saturn 211; in relation to Riddles 121,
346, 846; in relation to metaphor 273;
in relation to simile 569; Latin
influence 21
keys: as amulets 315
king: connections with the heathen gods
156; sacral status 559

Last Judgement 263
Latin vocabulary: in OEW poetry 25, 141
Latin-English Proverbs
—————— comparative discussion: *Rhyming
Poem* 203
—————— editions 179, 203, 645, 646, 650
—————— literary qualities: Latin portion 323
—————— text: facsimile 648; transcription
645
laughter 224
learned rhetoric 258
leech: role in Charms 278
legal documents: metrics in 30
legal terms 138
Legends of Cain: as source for *Solomon
and Saturn* 1062
Leiden Riddle
—————— comparative discussion: analogues
298; lorica genre 827
—————— cultural significance: Anglo-Saxon
weaving 847; weaving terminology 821
—————— dating 56
—————— dialect 659
—————— editions 6, 72, 91, 93, 203, 207,
217, 246, 302, 659, 777
—————— localization 91, 777; Northumbria
203, 659, 861; Wessex 847
—————— metrics: end-stopped lines 206
—————— passages discussed in detail: lines
3 956; 6 821; 6a 778; 9b 295; 13 332
—————— scholarship 811
—————— source: Aldhelm, Enigma 33 811,
821. *See also* Aldhelm, Enigma 33.
—————— text: facsimile 659; manuscript
853; manuscript context 295, 777, 861,
873, 956; manuscript neumes 313;
scribal accuracy 208; transcription 656,
720, 722, 725, 742, 763, 777, 861, 873;
transcription by W.G. Pluygers 720;
versions of 181
—————— translations (medieval) 17, 295,
659; by Aldhelm himself 777, 847; in
relation to Riddle 35 659, 777
—————— *See also* Riddle 35.

Leiden Rijksuniversiteit Vossianus Lat. 4 to 106 **36, 853, 861**. *See also* Leiden Riddle, text.

Letter of Alexander to Aristotle, as source for *Solomon and Saturn* **1097**

lexical collocations **247**; as formulaic principle in poetry **342**

Liber Monstrorum: as source for *Solomon and Saturn* **1097**

light half-lines **295**

linguistic criteria for dating. *See* dating: linguistic criteria *and also entries under individual poems.*

lists: as structural principle in OEW poems **614**; parallels in Irish texts **193**

liturgy, Christian: in Charms **430**. *See also* Charm 1.

ljóðaháttr: in relation to Charms **170, 431**; *Maxims* **80, 92, 101, 106, 155, 272, 323, 579**; *Maxims I* **147**; *Maxims II* **170**; *Wulf and Eadwacer* **101**

localizations of the mind **327**

lorica genre: in relation to *Solomon and Saturn* fragment in CCCC 41 **305**. *See also* Charm 11, Riddle 35, *and* Leiden Riddle, comparative discussion: lorica genre.

Lorsch Bee Charm: in relation to Charm 8 **464, 470, 477**

Lorsch Enigma 8: as analogue to Riddle 13 **937**

Lorsch Enigma 11: as analogue to Riddles **937**

Lorsch Enigma 69: as analogue to Riddles **937**

love poetry **43**

loyalty: Germanic notions of **593**

Lucretius: influence on Riddles 1–3 **29**

magic **158, 348, 396, 403, 418, 423, 439, 457, 458, 479, 482, 485**
—— black magic **467**
—— colour magic **391**. *See also* Charm 2.
—— origins: continental **180**; Germanic **423**
—— in *Maxims II* **613**
—— in relation to religion **430**
—— number magic **432**. *See also* nine.
—— verbal magic **469**

Magic Wand of Ribe: compared to Charm 11 **315**

Málsháttakvæði: as analogue to *Maxims* **540**

mammals: in OEW poetry **117**

mana: as element in Germanic culture **256**; in Anglo-Saxon England **417**

manuscripts: named. *See entries under individual names or abbreviations.*
—— survey of **36**

marriage **43**
—— marriage contract **114, 329**
—— marriage customs **114, 620**; in *Maxims I* **299, 599, 628**

Marvels of the East: as source for *Solomon and Saturn* **1097**

maxim: definition of **592**

Maxims I and *II* **527–628**. *See also* Maxims.

Maxims. Entries under this heading comprise both *Maxims I* and *Maxims II*.
—— audience: schools **166**
—— classification of gnomic statements **540**
—— comparative discussion: analogues **320, 540**; *Gifts* and *Fortunes* **590**; Heroic Age literatures **183**; *Hávamál* **65**; Latin didactic literature **550**; Riddles **183, 246**; Welsh analogues **193**
—— cultural significance: as containing peasant experience **34**; as encoding ancient epistemology **608**; as evidencing history of human cognition **540**; as mode of access to the supernatural **603**; as poetic game **79**; as testimony to traditional Germanic notions **593**; as transmitting inherited Germanic wisdom **537**; role of Christianity in **547**; heathen and Christian elements **566**; popular origin **68**; source in sacred experience **591**
—— dating **181**
—— definitional problems **300**
—— editions **2, 6, 85, 165, 300, 547, 551, 611**
—— function: mnemonic **573**
—— genre: elegy **193**
—— influence on *Beowulf* **609**
—— language: *dom* **566**; *sceal* **540**; style **540, 591**
—— literary qualities: as proverbs **323**; design **61**; logical cohesion **5, 54, 259, 267, 300, 328**; literary merit **32**; origin of format **16**; structure **223, 573**

——— localization of redaction 109
——— metrics 5, 155, 272, 279, 551;
end-stopped lines 206; hypermetric
lines 15, 133, 227, 288
——— scholarship 8, 590, 609
——— text: Christian redactor 202;
compilation 13, 19, 40, 43, 109; unity
29
——— theme: antifeminism 7
——— translations: into English 174, 300,
317; excerpts 7, 28, 29, 40, 43, 109;
into German 2
Maxims I
——— authorship 547, 551; attribution to
Aldhelm 547; attribution to Alfred 547
——— comparative discussion: with Old
Norse poetry 547; with *The Seafarer* 76
——— cultural significance: as reflecting
ancient epistemology 610; heathen
elements 606; vestiges of ritual usage
in 257
——— dating 336, 537
——— editions 62, 65, 69, 188, 194, 221;
excerpts 68, 72, 153, 217, 238
——— language: dialect 547
——— literary qualities: as inventory of
poetic themes 585; coherence 54;
cohesion 547; didactic purpose 540;
envelope pattern 60; structure 194, 540;
unity 344, 537
——— metrics 227; hypermetric lines
133, 134, 538, 551, 574; irregularities
106; *ljóðaháttr* 551; short lines 551;
strophe-like pattern 101
——— passages discussed in detail: lines
1–3 537; 4 313; 7–12a 612; 7a 558; 8–9
267; 9 202, 342; 11 543; 14a 580; 15
340; 22–5 323; 22–6 312; 23b 618; 27
187; 31 126, 544; 31–2 554; 31–4 553;
35 337; 35a 227; 37 349, 593; 37–8
128, 577; 38 150, 542, 544, 545, 552,
553; 39–45 337; 41a 15, 574; 44b–5a
625; 45b–50 610; 46 132; 46a 574; 50
327, 558, 574; 50b–5 259; 52–3 553;
52a 574; 52b 574; 54–5 155, 332; 54–6
569, 579; 59a 349; 60 308; 62 214; 62a
558; 66–70 323; 67–8 137; 67a 615; 68
545, 546; 69 610; 71–2 605; 71–7 578,
584; 71–80 232, 594, 612, 339; 73 232;
78 147, 238, 291, 561; 78b–9 561; 79
128, 610; 80 593; 81 329; 81–2 599;
81–92 325; 85b 325; 86 325; 90b 336;

94b–106 578; 94b–9 74, 325, 567; 95
532, 560, 572, 575; 95: Frisian
reference 7, 43, 114, 152, 299, 352,
567, 590, 609, 628; 96 138; 98 89; 99
577; 100a 565; 104 253, 577; 106 3,
147, 198, 560, 615; 107 549; 108 152;
111a 227; 113a 227; 114a 558; 117
128, 150, 536; 120 281; 121 327; 124a
227; 125–31 626; 125–8 313; 127–8
589; 132 3, 262; 134a 622; 138–40
593, 598; 144 547; 144–51 593;
146–51 596; 146a 574; 148–50 556;
150–1 196; 152 536; 158 540; 159 281;
161 544; 161–3 155; 164 128; 165–6
128; 165–71 313; 166 234; 169 577;
169–70 211; 169–71 234; 170–1 247;
172–3 247; 173 156, 571; 174–5 128;
175a 15; 176 145, 186; 177 564;
177–80 147, 155; 179 128, 150, 186,
564; 181–3 337; 183 128, 276; 183–4
577; 184–5a 345; 185 265; 185–6 623;
187–90 155; 191 557, 615; 192–200
537, 597; 192–8 283; 196b–7a 615;
198a 227
——— performance 540
——— source: Psalm 95 537
——— text: as compilation 565; facsimile
185; manuscript context 614
——— themes 605, 621; depiction of God
232; gifts of God 590, 609; *lof* 566
——— translation (medieval) 275, 576
——— translations: into English 59, 65,
188; excerpts 62, 115, 146, 161, 191,
221, 233, 250, 257, 578; into German
(excerpts) 5, 69; into Old Frisian
(excerpts) 275
*Maxims I*A
——— literary qualities: structure 618
——— theme: storm 624
*Maxims I*B
——— edition 534
——— literary qualities: as independent
poem 565
Maxims II. See also Maxims.
——— authorship 95, 594
——— comparative discussion: with
Alfred's treatment of Boethius, *De
Consolatione Philosophiae* 590; with
Boethius 267; with *Menologium* 614;
with *Menologium* and *Anglo-Saxon
Chronicle* 203; with *Order* 590, 609;
with Pindar 528, 530; with

Scandinavian rune poems 547; with *þulur* 547; with *The Ruin* 199
────── cultural significance: as example of *pensée sauvage* 592; as reflecting early Germanic tradition 201; heathen and Christian elements 203
────── dating 189, 563
────── editions 2, 62, 68, 81, 94, 164, 203, 221, 225, 269, 273, 531, 533, 539, 547, 562, 595; excerpts 176, 179, 182, 189, 190, 217
────── function 530; mnemonic function 537
────── literary qualities 273, 607; aesthetic unity 602; catalogue structure 360; coherence 540; cohesion 582; literary merit 337, 527, 528; structure 350, 595, 604
────── localization of redaction 189
────── passages discussed in detail: lines 1–13 339, 594; 1–5 139, 156; 1a 204; 4–5 202, 232, 296, 563; 4b 574; 4b–5a 602; 5 267; 5–9 193; 5a 360; 10 147, 150, 276, 332, 533, 559, 617; 10–12 333; 13 536, 559; 14–15 183, 547; 17b–18a 326; 18b 592; 19a 220; 26b 228; 26b–7a 587; 27 308, 325; 33–4 201; 35 285; 37a 282, 581, 583; 42 551; 42a 15; 42b 228; 42b–3a 570; 43 613; 43a 587; 43–5 114, 167, 259, 273, 325, 348, 600, 620; 46 586; 51–4 541; 61–6 301
────── text: collation 535; compilation 540, 559; facsimile 273; manuscript context 273, 533, 568, 595, 607, 614
────── themes: gifts of God 555; hymn to creation 590; kingliness 293; missionary ethos 156; natural description 11
────── translations: into Dutch 530; into English 161, 205, 210, 233, 269, 527, 528, 529, 582, 595; excerpts 62, 115, 221
*Maxims II*B: edition 246
medicine, Anglo-Saxon 278, 365, 372, 424
melancholy in Old English poetry 1102
memorial transmission 266, 313
Menologium: in relation to *Maxims II* 568
Mercury: compared with Saturn in *Solomon and Saturn* 43
Merseburger Spruch: compared to Charm 4 197

metal-work: as evidenced in *Gifts* 195
metaphors: in *Order* 629; alluding to book production 356
Metres of Boethius: compared with *Maxims* 201; contrasted with *Solomon and Saturn* II 5
metrical proverb: in *De Descensu Christi ad Inferos* 654
metrics 30, 80, 90; Beatitude formula 349; metrics in legal documents 30; metrical irregularities 292; Type F line 272. *See also* double alliteration, hypermetric lines, light half-line, *along with entries under* metrics *for individual poems.*
Miðgarðsormr 226
millet 375
minor deities: in Charm 4 271
missionary activity: reflected in *Winfrid Proverb* 295
mnemonics 43. *See also* Maxims II, function *and* Rune Poem, function.
mod: definition of 327
monasticism: in relation to Charm 6 494; monastic origins of Old English poetry 814; monastic schools 52, 356; monastic tradition 52
moralizing 32, 37; in early Germanic verse 25; in *Precepts* 102; scribal moralizing 273
movements: as components of Old English poems 359
musical forms 695
myth: as functional element in Charms 491; in relation to Charms 450
mythology, early English: as evidenced in OEW poetry 158

Nature: Anglo-Saxon perspective on 120
────── as solution to Riddles. *See entries under* Riddles 40, 41, *and* 66.
────── Nature description: in OEW poetry 120, 175, 193; in early Germanic poetry 11; influence of classical literature 98
────── Nature description in Riddles 43, 84, 172, 690. *See also entries under relevant Riddles.*
────── Nature description in *Rune Poem* 120. *See also entries under* Rune Poem.
────── Nature poetry: comparative study 193
────── Nature worship 20; in Charms 432
nettle: in Charm 4 406

nightmare **393, 394, 456, 472, 487**
nine: in number magic **369, 389, 396, 423**
noise: motif of **231**
Northumbria: as localization for poetic
   composition **83, 199**
———— as localization of Leiden Riddle.
   See Leiden Riddle, localization.
———— as localization of Riddles. *See*
   Riddles, localization.
———— as localization of *Solomon and
   Saturn. See* Solomon and Saturn,
   localization.
———— as localization of *Winfrid Proverb.
   See* Winfrid Proverb, localization.
Norwegian rune poem: compared with
   Rune Poem. See Rune Poem.
numbers: in magic **432**. *See also* nine.

oak-ship riddle: parallel in *Rune Poem* **353**
obscenity in Riddles. *See* Riddles, theme,
   obscenity.
obscurity in Riddles. *See* Riddles,
   solutions, obscurity.
oferhygd and *ofermod*: definitions of **254**
Old Irish literature: instruction genre **637**
Old Norse gnomic tradition: compared
   with *Maxims* **272**
Old Norse legal formulas: compared to
   Old English gnomic poetry **183**
old man instructing his disciple **300**
onomatopoeia: in Riddles **306**. *See also
   entries under* Riddles 7 *and* 28.
oral tradition **33**; in Riddles **5, 658**; in
   relation to *Maxims* and *Hávamál* **65**
oral transmission **208, 358**; as criterion for
   proverb **323**; in relation to Charms **56**
oral-formulaic theory **842**; in relation to
   Charms **425**
orality and literacy: transitional stage **358**
Order **629–33**
———— comparative discussion: with
   Psalms **264**
———— editions **2, 65, 188, 194, 270, 630,
   632**
———— influence of Cynewulf **194**
———— language: syntax **218**
———— literary qualities: dramatic
   monologue in **264**; metaphor of journey
   270; structure **31, 194, 270, 632**
———— metrics: hypermetric lines **133**
———— passages discussed in detail: lines
   1 **252**; 2 **270, 313**; 11–12 **234**; 19 **629,
   633**; 37 **270**; 41 **186**; 53b–4 **631**; 70b

631; 80–1 **631**; 89 **192, 252**; 102 **204**;
   102a **227**
———— source: Greek concepts **631**
———— text: facsimile **185**; state of text **8**
———— themes **7**; beauty of created things
   102; description of sun **173**; exegetical
   interpretation **280**; fixed order of world
   241; gaining of wisdom **283**;
   glorification of light **29**; interpretation
   631; millenarian beliefs **360**; natural
   description **11**; power of language **981**;
   reflexive interpretations **280, 282, 633**;
   treatment of Creation **29**
———— translations: into English **62, 65,
   188, 270, 632**; excerpts **7, 28, 29, 59,
   102**; into German **2**
ordinary people: as shown in OEW texts
   209
organic form: as criterion in literary
   criticism **328**
Ovid: as source of literary exercises **584**;
   influence on Old English elegy **199**
Oxford Bodleian Rawlinson C.697 **960**

pagan literature. *See* heathen literature.
pagan mythology: traces of in Charms **489**
paganism: camouflaged **339**; scholarship
   on **296**
Parable of the Talents: as source for
   Fortunes and *Gifts* **240**
parallelism: in Riddles **25**
Parcae: glossed as 'wyccan' **156**
paroemiology: in relation to *Maxims* and
   Proverbs **592**
paronomasia **281**; in Charms **350**
paten in Riddles 48 and 59 **151**
Pater Noster: in *Solomon and Saturn. See*
   Solomon and Saturn, Paternoster.
penitential poetry **321**
performance of OEW poetry **166**. *See also
   relevant entries under individual
   poems.*
persona **300**
personification: in Riddle 19 **1104**; in *Rune
   Poem* **1104**; in *Solomon and Saturn*
   1104
The Phoenix: compared with Riddle 30
   941
phonological patterning **312**
Physiologus: compared with *Solomon and
   Saturn* **34**
plants **98**

Pliny: influence on Riddles **29, 328**
——— *Natural History*, as source for
Riddle 8 **865**
plough: in Riddles 21 and 38 **271**
Plough Monday: in relation to Charm 1
467
ploughing **428**; as sexual penetration of the
earth **422**
Pluygers, W.G. *See* Leiden Riddle, text:
transcription.
poet. *See* scop.
poetic formulas **10, 12, 14, 236, 282, 285,
580, 581, 583, 586, 739, 842, 899,
1078**; in Riddle 11 **693**; in Riddle 20
963; in Riddles **819**
poetic performance **87**
poetic synonyms **200**
poetry: association with wisdom **116**
pointing in manuscripts **358**
polysyndeton: in Riddle 35 **258**
popular composition: in Riddles **153, 658**
popular tradition: in versification **52**
Pound, Ezra: in relation to Riddles **59**
praxis: as component of Charms **450**
The Prayer of Mother Earth: as analogue
to Charms 1 and 2 **298**
Precepts **634–8**
——— audience: use in church schools **31**
——— comparative discussion: with
Beowulf **636**; with Book of Proverbs
29; with *Disticha Catonis* **5**; with
Hamlet, speeches of Polonius **7, 31**;
with *Instruction of Vladimir Monomakh*
635; with *Maxims* **55**; with *Proverbs of
Alfred* **31**; with *The Wanderer* **177**
——— cultural significance: monastic
context **638**
——— dating **56, 635**
——— editions **2, 6, 65, 67, 68, 85, 107,
164, 165, 194, 300**
——— genre: instruction poem **637**
——— language: formulas **10**; tense usage
304
——— literary merit **60, 79, 321**
——— metrics: hypermetric lines **133**
——— passages discussed in detail: lines
4 **634**; 4–7 **167**; 5–7 **634**; 5–8 **147**; 12
200; 17 **634**; 23–6 **634**; 39 **638**; 46 **636**;
55 **154, 634**; 62 **634**; 64 **634**; 67 **634,
638**; 69 **638**; 82 **634**; 85 **634**; 87 **128**;
93 **634**
——— scholarship **8**

——— sources: influence of *Proverbia
Salomonis* **5**; influence of traditional
elements **61**
——— text: facsimile **185**
——— theme **637**; ages of man **328**;
Christian spirit **74**; Christian doctrine
194; human need for order **61**;
knowledge of transience **333**;
localizations of the mind **327**
——— translations: into English **65, 107,
300**; excerpts **7, 29, 102**; into German **2**
pregnancy and childbirth. *See* Charm 6,
efficacy.
prologues in OEW poems **43**
prophecy **158**
prosaic vocabulary: in *Maxims I* **276**; in
Old English verse **276, 313**
prosopopoeia: in Riddles **43, 293, 303, 782**
proverb: definition of **49, 323, 592**
Proverbia Salomonis: influence on
Precepts **5**
proverbial material: in OEW poems **265**
Proverbs of Alfred: compared with
Precepts **31**; in relation to *Solomon and
Saturn* **1047**
Proverbs of Hendyng: in relation to
Solomon and Saturn **1047**
proverbs, metrical **639–54**. *See*
Latin-English Proverbs *and* Winfrid
Proverb.
proverbs: in Old English poetry **19**;
relation to *Maxims I* **540, 558**; semiotic
analysis of **49**
Prudentius, *Psychomachia*: as source for
Solomon and Saturn **322, 1090, 1106**;
as source for *Vainglory* **1113**. *See also*
Solomon and Saturn, sources *and*
Vainglory, sources.
Psalm 18: 1: influence on *Order* **270**
Psalm 28: as interpreted by Augustine and
Cassiodorus **523**. *See also* Homiletic
Fragment I, source.
Pseudo-Bede riddles: as analogues to
Riddles **708**
Pseudo-Symphosius, Enigma 1: as
analogue to Riddle 9 **298, 973**
psychological history: in Old English
studies **612**
psychomachia **319, 322**. *See also*
Prudentius.
puns. *See* wordplay.

questioning **351**. *See also* interrogation.

Quintilian: on epithets **572**

religious awe: as feature of Old English
poetry **59**
repetitio **229, 240, 277**; in *Fortunes* **277**; in
Order **277**
repetition: lexical **311**
rhetoric: adaptations of Classical rhetoric
in OEW poems **303**; rhetorical figures
in Old English poetry **572**; rhetorical
patterns: in *Fortunes* **45**; in *Gifts* **45**.
See also anaphora, envelope pattern,
repetitio.
rhyming: in *Rune Poem* **101**; in *Vainglory*
101, 1115
Riddles. *See after entries under individual
Riddles.*
Riddle 1
———— editions **164, 189, 217**
———— literary qualities: composition **878**;
envelope pattern **894**
———— passages discussed in detail: lines
4 **734**; 10 **160, 902**; 10a **942**; 32 **783**
———— solved as 'army' **942**; 'fire' **798**;
'raiding party' **904**
———— translations: into English **184, 235**
Riddles 1–2
———— edition **127**
———— theme: Nature description **828**
———— translations: into English **115, 127**
Riddles 1–3
———— cultural significance: animism **900**
———— edition **885**
———— literary qualities: allegory **885**;
imagery of storm **177**; imaginative
qualities **711**
———— solved as 'apocalyptic storm' **902**;
'atmosphere' **809**; 'power of Nature'
885; 'storm' **658**; 'wind' **737, 916**
———— source: Graeco-Roman cosmology
809
———— text: as single poem **704, 746, 751,
754, 885, 902, 916, 939**
———— translations: into English **109, 146**
Riddles 2–3
———— solved as 'sun' **62**
———— sources: cosmology derived from
Isidore and Pliny **886**; influence of
Lucretius **850**
———— text: as single poem **886**
———— translations: into English **233**;
excerpts **62**; into Italian **142**
Riddle 2

———— editions **68, 72, 189, 221**
———— literary qualities: composition **878**
———— solved as 'anchor' **2, 904**;
'submarine earthquake' **727**
———— translations: into English **221, 235**
Riddle 3
———— comparative discussion: *Christ* 3
201
———— editions **68, 164**; excerpt **217**
———— literary qualities: personification
293; structure **188**
———— passages discussed in detail: lines
1–16 **886**; 3 **686**; 5 **759**; 17 **144**; 19
113, 265, 341; 22 **1020**; 24 **160**; 24–5
939; 31–2 **122**; 34 **753**; 36 **759**; 37 **143**;
41 **839**; 43 **815**; 45 **128**; 49 **214**; 67 **743**
———— solved as 'hurricane' **2**; 'revenant'
904
———— theme: Nature description **828**
———— translations: into English **235, 250**
Riddle 4
———— literary qualities: metaphoric
riddle **879**; structural devices **922**
———— passages discussed in detail: lines
7 **729**; 11 **963**
———— solved as 'bucket of water' **940**;
'bucket on chain or rope in cistern or
well' **971**; 'flail' **751**; 'handmill' **759,
795**; 'lock' **144**; 'millstone' **658, 662**;
'phallus' **904**; 'quill' **883**; 'watchdog'
989
———— theme: necromancy **729**
Riddle 5
———— editions **68, 72, 127, 179, 221,
269, 655**
———— passages discussed in detail, line 3
144, 754
———— solved as 'chopping block' **751**;
'guilt' **904**; 'shield' **655, 658, 756**
———— translations: into English **127, 146,
161, 221, 233, 250, 269**
Riddle 6
———— edition **246**
———— literary qualities: mode of
composition **878**
———— passages discussed in detail: lines
7 **754**; 10 **140, 726, 765**
———— solved as 'guilt and conscience'
904; 'sun' **658**
———— theme **916**
Riddle 7
———— editions **68, 81, 127, 179, 182,
190, 217, 221, 225, 257, 269, 273, 870**

────── literary qualities: anticipation of modern poetry **13**; onomatopoeia **282, 306**; realism **172**; Wordsworthian features **273**

────── passages discussed in detail: line 5 **273**

────── solved as 'soul' **904**; 'swan' **658**; both 'swan' and 'soul' **914**; either 'swan' or 'soul' **886**

────── theme: natural description **945**

────── translations: into English **115, 127, 146, 161, 184, 210, 221, 233, 235, 250, 257, 269, 696, 838, 908**; into Italian **142, 801**

Riddle 8

────── comparative discussion: Aldhelm, Enigma 22 **768**

────── editions **68, 190, 221, 225, 273**

────── language: *scirenige* **1, 2**

────── passages discussed in detail: lines 1–3 **54**; 2 **313**; 3 **753**; 4 **759**; 5 **313**; 9 **1, 2, 3, 4, 29, 786, 865**

────── solutions: undecidable **786**; 'bell' **691**; '*ceo*', 'chough or jackdaw' **186**; 'crying baby' **904**; 'devil as buffoon' **917**; 'flute' **961**; 'jay' **660, 727, 792**; 'nightingale' **658, 768, 865**; 'pipe' **658**; 'reed-pipe' **695**; 'song-thrush' **211**; 'song-thrush' or 'blackbird' **789**; 'woodpigeon' **662**; both 'nightingale' and 'pipe' **694**; either 'nightIngale' or 'frog' **273**

────── source: Pliny, *Natural History* **865**

────── text: runic annotation **789, 865**

────── translations: into English **146, 210, 221, 235, 776, 831, 855**

Riddle 9

────── comparative discussion: [Pseudo-]Symphosius, Enigma 1 **973**

────── editions **81, 153, 217, 257, 269**

────── passages discussed in detail: lines 1 **128**; 9 **753, 754, 790**; 10 **128**

────── solved as 'conception and birth/revenant/soul' **904**; 'cuckoo' **658**

────── themes: anthropomorphization of Nature **828**; human ingratitude **892**

────── translations: into English **184, 233, 250, 257, 269, 834**

Riddle 10

────── editions **68, 153, 895**

────── passages discussed in detail: lines 3 **714**; 7 **714**

────── solved as 'alchemy/baptism' **904**;

'anchor' **712, 714**; 'barnacle goose' **13, 712, 717, 794, 799**; 'bubble' **691**; 'ocean-furrow' **658**; 'water-lily' **123**

────── translations: into English **161, 908**

Riddle 11

────── edition **269**

────── language: *hasofag* **693, 713**

────── passages discussed in detail: lines 1 **693**; 3 **715**; 4 **118, 715**; 9 **144**

────── solved as 'night' **658, 713, 799**; 'phallus' **904**; 'wine' **693, 712, 715, 754**

────── translations: into English **235, 269, 831**

Riddle 12

────── comparative discussion: analogues **298**

────── cultural significance: mention of Welsh woman **901**

────── editions **68, 164, 257, 269, 660**

────── passages discussed in detail: line 4 **138**

────── solved as 'hide or skin' **737**; 'leather' **658**; 'oxhide' **727**

────── translations: into English **257, 269, 855**

Riddle 13

────── comparative discussion: Aldhelm, Enigma 30 **812**; analogues **708**; Lorsch Enigma 8 **937**

────── edition **67**

────── literary qualIties: metaphoric riddle **879**

────── solved as 'aurelia of the butterfly, and its transformations' **64**; 'letters of the alphabet' **658**; 'looper caterpillar' **664**; 'ten chickens or pheasants' **737**; '*ten ciccenu*', 'ten chickens' **812**; 'ten fingers (with gloves)' **707**; 'twelve chickens' **961**

Riddle 14

────── comparative discussion: analogues **298**

────── editions **5, 7, 68, 72, 81, 189, 207, 269, 660, 667**

────── passages discussed in detail: lines 1 **784**; 1–3 **249**; 9 **734, 784**; 14 **135**

────── solved as 'horn' **658, 695**; 'man' **904**

────── translations: into English **7, 115, 146, 184, 233, 235, 269, 831, 855**; into German **5, 667**

Riddle 15
—— editions **68, 164, 665, 689**
—— literary qualities: anticipations of fable and allegory **689**; mock heroic **893**
—— passages discussed in detail: lines 1 **830**; 2 **135**; 6 **285**; 15–16 **160**; 16b **767**; 21 **753**
—— solved as 'badger' **658, 689, 785**; 'fox' **773**; 'hedgehog' **128, 235**; 'porcupine' **128, 693**; 'weasel' **211, 793**
—— translations: into English **146, 184, 235, 250**
Riddle 16
—— comparative discussion: analogues **298**
—— edition **153**
—— solved as 'anchor' **658**
—— theme: allegorical interpretations **977**
—— translations: into English **161, 233, 250, 834**; into Italian **142**
Riddle 17
—— passages discussed in detail: line 11 **135**
—— solutions: role of grammatical gender in determining the solution **712**; 'ballista' **658**; 'forge' **877**; 'fortress' **662**; 'fortress' and 'soul' **892**; 'inkwell' **883**; 'oven' **691, 712**; 'phallus' **904**; 'plaited bee-hive' **934**; 'quiver' **987**
—— text: runic annotation **892**
—— theme: allegory **892**; temptation **892**
Riddle 18
—— solved as 'cask' **751**; 'inkwell' **883**; 'jug (amphora)' **916**; 'leather bottle' **658**; 'phallus?' **904**
—— theme: ambivalence **943**
Riddle 19
—— comparative discussion: as 'world riddle' **705, 791**
—— edition **68**
—— passages discussed in detail: lines 1–2 **212**; 5 **214**; 5–6 **397**; 5b–6a **163**; 6 **759, 841**
—— solution, as overly obvious **791**; 'falconry' **681, 805**; 'hand writing on manuscript sheet with pen' **906**; 'horse, man, wagon, and hawk' **67**; 'horseman, servant, and hawk' **751**; 'man upon horseback with a hawk on his fist' **727**; 'ship' **916**; 'sun' **339**; 'writing' **816**

—— text: as fragment **707**; runes **216, 683, 783, 791**
—— translation: into English **250**
Riddle 20
—— literary qualities: double sense **867**
—— passages discussed in detail: lines 4 **757**; 10 **963**; 11 **145**; 14 **214, 248, 757**; 16–17 **144**; 20–1 **144**; 23 **867**; 29 **144**
—— solved as 'hawk' and 'sword' **242**; 'hawk, falcon' **751**; '*heoruswealwe*', 'sword-swallow' **255**; 'phallus' **856, 904**; 'sword' **658, 757**
Riddle 21
—— cultural significance: description of plough **669, 780**
—— editions **153, 269**
—— passages discussed in detail: lines 5 **780**; 9 **743**; 15 **723, 743**
—— solved as 'phallus' **904, 911**; 'plough' **658**
—— translations: into English **161, 233, 269**
Riddle 22
—— comparative discussion: Aldhelm, Enigma 53 **825**; analogues **298**; popular origin **825**
—— cultural significance: knowledge of constellations **825**
—— editions **68, 164**
—— passages discussed in detail: lines 3 **214**; 4 **117, 200, 760, 790**
—— solution **314**; solved as 'bridge' **751**; 'days of the month' **658**; 'ice bridge' **961**; 'rite of passage' **904**
—— translation: into English **920**
Riddle 23
—— language: *agof* **683**
—— passages discussed in detail: lines 1 **723, 724**; 2 **813**; 3 **144, 754, 978**; 4 **822**; 8 **144**; 9 **756**; 11 **813**; 14 **144, 759, 783, 813, 891**
—— solutions: obviousness **929**; 'bow' **658, 724**; 'crossbow' **730, 751**; 'phallus' **904**
—— translations: into English **115, 146**; into Italian **142**
Riddle 24
—— edition (excerpt) **660**
—— passages discussed in detail: lines 2 **128**; 7–9 **140**
—— solved as 'jay' **658**; 'actor specializing in animal and bird noises'

718; 'jay' or 'green woodpecker' **926**; 'magpie' **658**; 'woodpecker' **694**

Riddle 25

—— comparative discussion: analogues **298**

—— edition **257**

—— literary qualities: anticipation of allegorical technique **886**

—— passages discussed in detail: lines 1–3 **59**; 4 **804**; 6 **138, 783**; 7 **906**; 8 **901**

—— solved as 'hemp' **69, 662**; 'leek' **658**; 'mustard' **693**; 'onion' **658**; 'phallus' **904**; 'rosehip' **691**

—— translations: into English **257, 909**

Riddle 26

—— comparative discussion: analogues **298**

—— editions **68, 72, 81, 190, 225, 238, 257, 269, 273, 655, 931**; excerpt **660**

—— passages discussed in detail: lines 6 **990**; 7 **273**; 17 **238, 732, 771**

—— solved as 'book' **655, 658**; 'hide' **751**

—— translations: into English **115, 146, 184, 210, 235, 250, 257, 269**; into German **931**; into Italian **142**

Riddle 27

—— comparative discussion: analogues **298**; influence of heroic poetry **927**

—— editions **68, 153, 189, 238**

—— literary qualities: structural devices **922**

—— passages discussed in detail: lines 2 **764**; 7–8 **128**; 13 **753, 761**; 13–14 **163**; 13b **751, 752**

—— solved as 'mead' **662**; 'sleep?' **904**; 'whip' **658**

—— translations: into Danish **927**; into English **115, 161, 233, 250, 834**

Riddle 28

—— comparative discussion: analogues **298**; Symphosius, Enigma 20 **826**

—— cultural significance: methods of book production **195**

—— editions **67, 68, 190, 217, 221, 225, 273**

—— language: onomatopoeia **282, 306**

—— literary qualities: humour **829**; literary merit **929**

—— metrics: internal rhymes **147, 237**

—— passages discussed in detail: line 11 **148, 149**

—— solved as 'beer' **727**; 'harp' **43**,

695, 751; 'John Barleycorn' **64**; 'malt liquor' **837**; 'parchment' **948**; 'pattern-welded sword' **921**; 'stringed instrument' **186**; 'tortoise' **826**; 'trial of soul' **904**; 'wine-cask' **658**; 'woman' **929**; 'yew-horn?' **916**

—— translations: into English **210, 221**

Riddle 29

—— comparative discussion: analogues **708**; Eusebius, Enigma 11 **863**

—— cultural significance: mythological conceptions of sun and moon **711**

—— editions **68, 72, 81, 127, 182, 257, 273, 284**

—— language: genders **824**

—— literary qualities: ambiguity **354**; Yeatsian features **273**

—— passages discussed in detail: lines 1–3 **13**; 4 **880**; 5 **128**; 7b **73, 182**

—— solved as 'abduction of Venus' **961**; 'bird and wind' **712**; 'cloud and wind' **693**; 'sun and moon' **658**; 'swallow and sparrow' **691**

—— theme: Christian doctrine **863**; conflict of moon and sun **273**; Nature description **193, 770, 880**

—— translations: into English **127, 205, 235, 250, 257, 831, 834**; into Italian **142**

Riddle 30

—— comparative discussion: Aldhelm, Enigma 3 **672**; analogues **298**; Eusebius, Enigma 15 **672**; Symphosius, Enigma 9 **672**; *The Phoenix* **941**

—— edition **257**

—— literary qualities: allegorical interpretation **886**

—— passages discussed in detail: lines 1 **877**; 3 **187**; 3a **257**; 5 **257**; 6 **268, 906**; 9 **877**

—— solved as 'cornfield' **691**; 'cross as vehicle of salvation' **941**; 'cross' or 'wood' **751**; 'cross/sun' **310**; 'fire' (i.e. 'Easter fire') **331**; 'phallus' **904**; 'rain-water' **658**; 'snow-flakes' **877, 961**; 'tree' and 'cross' **712**; 'wooden cross' **754**

—— text: manuscript contexts **310**; oral transmission **266**; repetition in Exeter Book **820**; variants **208, 978**

—— translations: into English **250, 257**

Riddle 30a
——— literary qualities: description **959**
——— solved as 'birch' **897**
——— translation: into English **835**
Riddle 30b
——— comparative discussion: *The Husband's Message* **698**
——— edition **331**
——— solved as '*beam*' **698**
——— text: manuscript context **331**, **887**, **978**
——— translation: into English **331**
Riddle 31
——— edition **68**
——— passages discussed in detail: lines 4 **163**; 4–6 **157**; 4–7 **155**; 13 **253**; 14 **867**; 24 **313**
——— solved as 'bagpipe' **658**, **695**; 'fiddle' **691**; 'harp' **904**; 'musical instrument' **751**; 'organistrum' **756**; 'portative organ' **783**
——— translation: into English **908**
Riddle 32
——— editions **68**, **164**
——— literary merit **958**
——— passages discussed in detail: lines 8–9 **958**; 8b **818**
——— solved as 'millstone' **69**; 'ship' **658**; 'wagon' **62**; 'wheel' **737**; 'wheelbarrow' **961**
——— translations: into English **62**, **235**, **831**, **834**
Riddle 33
——— edition **68**
——— literary qualities: personification as warrior **829**
——— passages discussed in detail: lines 2 **753**; 5 **122**, **128**, **684**, **753**, **756**
——— solved as 'archetypal feminine' **904**; 'iceberg' **658**; 'iceberg' and 'hatred' **991**
——— translations: into English **235**, **250**; into Italian **142**
Riddle 34
——— editions **221**, **269**
——— passages discussed in detail: line 2b **818**
——— solved as 'bee' **691**; 'phallus' **904**; 'rake' **658**
——— theme: harrowing of sinners **881**
——— translations: into English **221**, **250**, **269**

Riddle 35
——— comparative discussion: analogues **298**
——— cultural significance: communication within learned circle **215**; weaving process **808**
——— editions **68**, **72**, **91**, **164**, **207**, **217**, **221**, **246**, **257**, **302**, **777**
——— literary qualities: anaphora and polysyndeton **258**; formularity **899**; prosopopoeia **875**
——— passages discussed in detail: lines 1–2 **899**; 8 **128**; 9 **267**; 9b **257**
——— solved as 'mailcoat' **658**
——— source. *See* Aldhelm, Enigma 33.
——— text: memorial transmission **266**; scholarship on **91**
——— translation (medieval) **258**, **878**
——— translations: into English **221**, **257**, **855**
——— *See also* Leiden Riddle.
Riddle 36
——— comparative discussion: analogues **298**
——— passages discussed in detail: lines 4–5 **128**, **737**; 5 **816**
——— solved as 'pregnant horse with two pregnant women on its back' (lines 1–8 only) **816**; 'pregnant sow' **658**; 'ship' or 'man, woman, and horse' **691**; 'two men, woman, horses, dog, bird on ship' **188**; 'water-fowl hunt' **805**
——— text: encrypted gloss **216**, **356**, **737**
Riddle 37
——— comparative discussion: Symphosius, Enigma 73 **973**
——— edition **68**
——— passages discussed in detail: line 7 **867**
——— solved as 'bellows' **662**; 'phallus' **904**; 'wagon' **658**
——— translations: into English **250**, **834**, **909**
Riddle 38
——— comparative discussion: analogues **298**
——— edition **257**, **660**
——— passages discussed in detail: lines 2 **128**, **276**; 5–7 **128**; 6 **783**; 12b **992**
——— solved as 'man' **904**; 'young bull' **658**
——— translation: into English **257**

Riddle 39
———— comparative discussion: Aldhelm,
Enigma 3 **907**; Aldhelm, Enigma 71
907; riddle of generalization **879**
———— editions **164, 284**
———— literary qualities: ambiguity **965**
———— passages discussed in detail: lines
3 **965**; 10 **163**; 14 **993**; 18–19 **888**; 26
128
———— solved as 'cloud' **888, 907**; 'comet'
993; 'Creature Death' **797**; 'day' **658**;
'dream' **932**; 'moon' **727**; 'revenant'
904; 'speech' **916**; 'time' **744**
———— theme: exile **220**
Riddle 40
———— comparative discussion **922**;
analogues **298**; riddle of negation **879**
———— cultural significance: mention of
lily and rose **120**
———— dating **960**
———— edition (excerpt) **153**
———— passages discussed in detail: lines
5b **133, 204**; 16 **783**; 59 **764**; 65 **144**;
68 **141**; 71 **129**; 72 **783**; 72–3 **125**; 73
756, 758; 78 **265**; 84 **128**
———— solutions: obviousness **744**;
'creation' **658**; 'nature' **711**;
'primordial matter: water' **961**
———— source. *See* Aldhelm, Enigma 100.
———— text: pointing **358**
———— translation (medieval) **755, 781,
878, 899**
———— translations: into English **835, 919**
Riddle 41
———— comparative discussion: analogues
298; with Riddle 40 **781**
———— passages discussed in detail: line 7
144
———— solved as 'earth' **658**; 'fire' **691**
———— translation (medieval):
compositional process **781**
Riddle 42
———— edition **257**
———— language: *hæn* **683**; significance of
rune-names **913**
———— literary qualities: compositional
process **899**
———— passages discussed in detail: lines
2 **135**; 11 **135**
———— solved as 'cock and hen' **658**
———— theme: interpretation **981**
———— translation: into English **257**

Riddle 43
———— solved as 'mind' **737**; 'soul and
body' **658, 661, 662**
Riddle 44
———— edition **257, 273**
———— literary qualities: wordplay **955**
———— passages discussed in detail: lines
3 **963**; 7 **804**
———— solved as 'dagger-sheath' **658**;
'key' **658**; 'phallus' **904**
———— translations: into English **257, 909**
Riddle 45
———— passages discussed in detail: line 1
804
———— solved as 'bee' **658**; 'dough' **684**;
'phallus' **904**
———— translations: into English **146, 855,
909**
Riddle 46
———— editions **67, 68**
———— passages discussed in detail: line 6
135
———— solved as 'Adam and Eve with two
sons and a daughter' **62**; 'Lot and his
two daughters and their two sons' **64,
658**
———— sources: Rabbinical or other
medieval versions **957**
———— translations: into English **62, 920**
Riddle 47
———— comparative discussion: Aldhelm,
Enigma 89 **896**; analogues **298**;
Symphosius, Enigma 16 **684, 898, 912**
———— editions **72, 81, 153, 179, 190,
217, 221, 225, 257, 273, 284, 931**
———— language: *moppe* **125**
———— literary qualities: as anticipating
Cowper **273**; as parody of Old English
heroic poetry **898**; as stimulus to
laughter **829**; literary merit **924**; verbal
ambiguities **896**; wordplay **976**
———— passages discussed in detail: lines
2 **162**; 5 **284**
———— solutions: obviousness **30, 929**;
'bookmoth' **2, 658**; 'demon' **904**;
'writing on vellum' **976**
———— theme **823, 912, 916**
———— translations: into English **146, 161,
184, 205, 210, 221, 233, 235, 250, 257,
908**; into German **931**
Riddle 48
———— comparative discussion: analogues
298

—————— language: *hring* **151**
—————— passages discussed in detail: lines
1 **122, 159, 949**; 1–2 **928**; 2 **218**; 2a
133
—————— solved as 'bell/sacramental vessel'
904; 'chalice' **737**; 'chrismal' **658**;
'gospel book or book of offices?' **949**;
'paten' **727**
—————— translation into Italian **142**
Riddle 49
—————— comparative discussion: analogues
298
—————— edition **931**
—————— literary qualities: as
riddle-within-a-riddle **971**
—————— passages discussed in detail: lines
3 **753, 783**; 6 **911**
—————— solved as 'altar' **914**; 'barrow,
sacrificial altar' **904**; 'bookcase' **662**;
'books' **804**; 'falcon-cage' **658**;
'millpond and its sluice' **971**; 'oven'
712
—————— translation: into German **931**
Riddle 50
—————— cultural significance: production of
fire **897**
—————— edition **870**
—————— literary qualities: structural devices
922
—————— passages discussed in detail: lines
9 **577**; 10 **308**
—————— solved as 'dog' **658**; 'fire' **684**;
'fire' and 'anger' **991**; 'phallus?' **904**
—————— translation: into English **250**
Riddle 51
—————— edition **931**
—————— passages discussed in detail: line 4
761
—————— solved as 'alchemy' **904**; 'dragon'
658; 'horse and wagon' **691**; 'quill-pen'
or 'pen and three fingers' **712**
—————— translations: into English **250**; into
German **931**
Riddle 52
—————— passages discussed in detail: line 1
692
—————— solved as 'broom' **691**; 'bucket in
well' **664**; 'buckets' **692**; 'flail' **692,
712**; 'pails' **658**; 'yoke of oxen led into
barn or house by female slave' **693**
Riddle 53
—————— comparative discussion: Aldhelm,
Enigma 86 **952**; analogues **298**

—————— passages discussed in detail: lines
2 **128**; 10 **122, 152**
—————— solved as 'battering-ram' **658**;
'cross' **915**; 'gallows' **987**; 'phallus'
904; 'spear' **691**
—————— translations: into English **250, 834**;
into Italian **142**
Riddle 54
—————— passages discussed in detail: lines
2 **128**; 5 **963**
—————— solved as 'baker's boy and oven'
658; 'churn' **691**; 'phallus/intercourse'
904
—————— translation: into English **909**
Riddle 55
—————— comparative discussion: *The
Dream of the Rood* **969**
—————— edition **164**
—————— literary qualities: allegory **762**;
figure of *digressio* **55**
—————— passages discussed in detail: lines
5 **281**; 6 **762**; 9 **167**; 12 **117**; 12a–13b
964; 14 **144**; 14–16 **128**; 15 **160**
—————— solved as 'cross reliquary' **972**;
'cross' **768, 876**; 'harp' **691, 695**;
'reliquary (containing a splinter of the
True Cross)' **964**; 'scabbard' **662**;
'shield' **658**; 'sword-stand' **710**;
'tetraktys' **904**; 'wooden liturgical
cross' **969**
—————— theme: cross **910**; four woods **98**
—————— translations: into English **250**; into
Italian **142**
Riddle 56
—————— passages discussed in detail: lines
5 **783**; 12 **171**
—————— solved as 'execution' **904**; 'flail'
737; 'lathe' **662**; 'loom' **658**; 'web in
the loom' **808**
Riddle 57
—————— editions **67, 81, 153, 190, 225,
257, 273**
—————— literary qualities: paronomasia **986**
—————— passages discussed in detail: lines
2 **692**; 3 **775**; 6 **690, 775**
—————— solved as 'a somewhat mysterious
brown bird' **690**; 'bees' **843**;
'blackbirds' **926**; '*cā', 'jackdaw' **802**;
'damned souls' **904**; 'gnats' **658**;
'hailstones' **691**; 'martins' **13**; 'midges'
737, 775; 'musical notes as notated in
manuscript' **883**; 'raindrops' **692**;

'rooks' or 'crows' **774**; 'starlings' **662, 694**; 'storm-clouds' **672, 712** ; 'swallows' **658**; 'swarm of demons or souls of damned' **917**; 'swifts' **751**; 'swifts' or 'jackdaws' **773**
—— translations: into English **161, 210, 250, 257, 834**

Riddle 58
—— comparative discussion: analogues **298**; as riddle of generalization **879**
—— passages discussed in detail: line 10 **963**
—— solved as 'phallus' **904**; '*ridrod', 'moving pole' **913**; 'well sweep' **105, 825**; 'well' **658, 664**
—— text: runes **825**

Riddle 59
—— comparative discussion: analogues **298**
—— language: *hring* **151**
—— solved as 'chalice' **658**

Riddle 60
—— comparative discussion: analogues **298**; Symphosius, Enigma 2 **59, 779, 833, 858, 871, 923, 946**
—— editions **68, 153, 164, 221, 246, 269, 307, 931**
—— literary qualities: allegorical interpretation **345, 852, 916**
—— passages discussed in detail: lines 7b **849**; 9 **887**; 10 **313**; 12–13 **311**; 13 **702**; 14 **858**; 16 **783**
—— solved as 'kelp-weed' **779**; 'letter beam cut from stump of old jetty' **74**; 'reed ' **13, 537**; 'reed flute' **658**; 'reed pen' **282, 727**; 'reed pipe' **695**; 'revenant' **904**; 'revenant/spirit' **911**; 'yew-tree' **324**
—— text: in relation to *The Husband's Message* **30, 43, 115, 217, 219, 282, 290, 307, 537, 682, 698, 707, 737, 751, 832, 833, 837, 844, 852, 858, 875, 887**
—— translations: into English **74, 146, 221, 235, 269, 307, 831**; into German **931**

Riddle 61
—— edition **67, 895**
—— solved as 'helmet' **737**; 'hood' **961**; 'kirtle' **727**; 'mailshirt' **751**; 'shirt' **658, 804**; 'vagina' **904**
—— translations: into English **908, 909**

Riddle 62
—— cultural significance: reference to slaves **135**
—— passages discussed in detail: line 9 **143, 957**
—— solved as 'borer' **737**; 'burning arrow' **751**; 'gimlet' **658**; 'oven-rake' **788**; 'phallus' **904**; 'poker' **727**
—— theme: obscenity **788**
—— translation: into English **909**

Riddle 63
—— comparative discussion: analogues **298**
—— passages discussed in detail: lines 1–2 **783**, 15 **276**
—— solved as 'beaker' **658**; 'can or flask' **751**; 'flute' **691**
—— theme: sexuality **114**

Riddle 64
—— passages discussed in detail: lines 5–6 **805**; 6 **754**
—— solved as 'falconry' **805**; 'horseman and hawk' **681**; 'horseman, hawk, and servant' **751**; 'ring-tailed peacock' **658, 683**; 'ship' **916**; 'snake-eating bird of prey and ring-shaped adder' **664**; 'writing' **816**
—— text: as fragment **707**; runes **144, 162, 216, 783, 791**

Riddle 65
—— comparative discussion: analogues **298**; Symphosius, Enigma 44 **860**
—— solved as 'chive, leek' **751**; 'onion' **658**; 'revenant, spirit' **904**
—— source: lost Latin riddle **860**

Riddle 66
—— comparative discussion: other Old English poems on 'creation' **922**; Riddle 40 **684**
—— editions **68, 246, 870**
—— passages discussed in detail: line 5 **285**
—— solved as 'creation' **658**; 'divine power' **62**; 'nature' **188**; 'power of God' **658**
—— translations: into English **62, 235, 250, 838**

Riddle 67
—— comparative discussion: analogues **298**
—— edition **931**
—— passages discussed in detail: lines 2–3 **144**; 10–11 **700**

—— solved as 'cross' **188**
—— translation: into English **920**; into German **931**
Riddles 68–9
—— solved as 'Christ walking on the sea' **807**; 'ice' **658**; 'winter' **2**
—— translation: into English **250**
Riddle 68
—— edition **257**
—— solved as 'iceberg' **916**; 'petrifaction' **737**; 'running water' **837**
—— translation: into English **257**
Riddle 70
—— edition **257**
—— literary qualities: wordplay **897**
—— passages discussed in detail: lines 4 **252**; 4–6 **882**
—— solved as 'bell' **961**; 'harp' **244, 751, 897**; 'organistrum' **756**; 'rye flute' **691**; 'shawm' **695**; 'shawm, shepherd's pipe' **658**; 'shepherd's pipe' **257**; 'shuttle' **808**
—— text: as two fragments **307**
—— translation: into English **257**
Riddle 70a
—— comparative discussion: Aldhelm, Enigma 92 **882**
—— solved as 'lighthouse' **882**
Riddle 70b
—— solved as 'harp' **882**
Riddle 71
—— passages discussed in detail: lines 6 **128**; 7 **759**; 8 **700**
—— solved as 'bronze shield' **751**; 'cupping glass' **658**; 'iron helmet' **691**; 'iron shield' **750**; 'iron weapon or ore' **737**; 'revenant' **904**; 'sword, dagger' **727**
Riddle 72
—— comparative discussion: analogues **298**; *The Dream of the Rood* **782**
—— passages discussed in detail: lines 3 **700**; 4 **144**; 6–7 **3**; 12 **144**; 18 **218**
—— solved as 'axle and wheel' **658**; 'ox' **13**; 'slave?' **904**
Riddle 73
—— passages discussed in detail: lines 2 **308, 906**; 8–9 **700**; 10 **148**; 11 **700**; 14–15 **700**; 16–17 **700**; 19 **783**; 22 **867**
—— solved as 'battering ram' **751**; 'bow and incendiary arrow' **961**; 'bow' **971**; 'cross' **915**; 'lance' **658**; 'lance' or

'javelin' **952**; 'revenant, spirit' **904**; 'spear' **737**; 'writing'/'pen' **946**
Riddle 74
—— editions **67, 257, 931**
—— passages discussed in detail: line 4 **171, 783**
—— solutions: obscurity **979**; 'cuttlefish' **658, 693**; 'diving bird' **890**; 'hyena' **744**; 'nature' or 'life' **257**; 'pen' **859**; 'rain' **837**; 'ship's figurehead' **916**; 'siren' **707, 716**; 'snow' **935**; 'swan' **171**; 'water' **712**
—— theme: metempsychosis **796, 817**
—— translations: into English **257**; into German **931**
Riddles 75–6
—— solved as 'cock and hen' **950**; 'piss' **916**
Riddle 75
—— solved as 'dog' **2**; 'elk hunter' **816**; '*hælend*', 'saviour' **186**
—— text: cryptogram **816, 866**; runes **186, 216, 866, 913**
Riddles 76–7
—— solved as 'oyster' **658**
Riddle 76
—— genre: elegiac elements **966**
—— solved as 'hen' **737**
Riddle 77
—— passages discussed in detail: lines 5 **329**; 7–8 **128, 700**
—— solved as 'female genitalia' **904**
—— translations: into English **250, 834**
Riddle 78
—— passages discussed in detail: lines 2–3 **700**; 7 **700**
—— solved as 'lamprey' **916**; 'oyster' **727**; 'water-dwelling creature' **700**
Riddles 79–80
—— solved as 'falcon' **658**; 'hawk' **658**; 'horn' **916**; 'sword in its scabbard' **242**
Riddle 80
—— comparative discussion: analogues **298**
—— editions **68, 189, 257**
—— passages discussed in detail: lines 4 **114**; 9 **313**
—— solved as 'horn' **660, 712, 784**; 'phallus' **904**; 'spear' **691**; 'sword' **693**
—— translations: into English **115, 250, 257**

Riddle 81
——— edition **257**
——— passages discussed in detail: lines
5 **150**; 11–12 **144**
——— solved as 'helmet with vizor' **662**;
'man' **904**; 'ship' **658**; 'weathercock'
691
——— translations: into English **250, 257,
834, 974**
Riddle 82
——— passages discussed in detail: lines
2 **144, 700**; 4 **700**
——— solved as 'crab' **756**; 'harrow' **916**
Riddle 83
——— comparative discussion: analogues
298
——— passages discussed in detail: lines
2–3 **700**
——— solved as 'gold' **188**; 'metal or
money' **737**; 'ore' **658**; 'revenant, spirit'
904
Riddle 84
——— comparative discussion: analogues
298
——— cultural significance: animism **900**
——— passages discussed in detail: lines
1 **685**; 22–3 **128**; 26 **906**; 33a **171**; 43
700; 45 **144**; 47 **70**; 52–6 **700**
——— solved as 'water' **658**
——— text: facsimile **884**
Riddle 85
——— comparative discussion: analogues
298
——— edition **660**
——— passages discussed in detail: lines
1–2 **144**
——— solved as 'body and soul' **904**;
'fish and river' **658**
——— text: facsimile **884**
——— translations: into English **233, 250,
834**
Riddle 86
——— comparative discussion:
Symphosius, Enigma 95 **298, 938**
——— editions **68, 257, 895**
——— genre: joke riddle **879**
——— passages discussed in detail: line 7
938
——— solved as 'one-eyed seller of
garlic' **662**; 'organ' **658, 695**
——— text: facsimile **884**; phonetic
transcription **895**

——— translations: into English **250, 257**
Riddle 87
——— passages discussed in detail: lines
4–5 **128**
——— solved as 'bellows' **660**; 'cask and
cooper' **2, 658**; 'phallus' **904**
——— text: facsimile **884**
——— theme: obscenity **837**
Riddle 88
——— comparative discussion: analogues
298
——— edition **931**
——— passages discussed in detail: lines
1 **700**; 5 **128**; 6 **700**; 8 **700**; 23 **783**
——— solved as 'antler' **658**; 'body and
soul' **904**; 'horn' **188**; 'ink-horn' **727,
784**; 'stag-horn' **658**
——— text: facsimile **884**
——— translation: into German **931**
Riddle 89
——— passages discussed in detail: line 3
144
——— solved as 'bellows or leather
bottle' **727**; 'phallus' **904**
——— text: facsimile **884**
Riddle 90
——— cultural significance: in relation to
Sutton Hoo jewelled purse-lid **810**
——— metrics: Latin verses as
counterpart to hypermetrical lines **800**
——— passages discussed in detail: line 2
980
——— solved as 'Augustine and
Tertullian' **980**; 'Cynewulf' **662, 679,
729**; 'Cynwulf' [sic] **709**; 'Lamb of
God who overcame the Devil' **74, 678**;
'lupus' **658**; 'pike' **681**; 'web and loom'
916; as allusion to some person whose
name contained element *wulf* **692**
——— source: reference to Matt. 16: 18
186
——— text: facsimile **884**; new readings
188; restoration of Latin verses **128**
——— theme: as allusion to Crucifixion
800; commemorating acceptance of
baptism **729**; Cynewulf allusion **657,
673, 704**
——— translation: into English **62**
Riddle 91
——— comparative discussion: analogues
298

——— passages discussed in detail: lines
3 **721**; 6b **336**; 7 **216**; 8 **128**; 8a **171**
——— solved as 'key' **658**; 'key-hole'
901; 'phallus' **904**; 'sickle' **691**
——— text: facsimile **884**; runes **683**
Riddle 92
——— authorship, female **901**
——— edition **931**
——— passages discussed in detail: lines
1 **128**; 3 **128, 325, 954**; 4 **783**
——— solved as 'ashtree' **128**; 'beech'
691; 'beechwood battering ram' **758**;
'beechwood shield' **751**; 'book' **737**;
'yew' **897**
——— text: facsimile **884**
——— translation: into German **931**
Riddle 93
——— comparative discussion: analogues
298
——— edition **931**
——— literary qualities: sexual
symbolism **968**
——— passages discussed in detail: lines
3–4 **700**; 4 **144**; 6–7 **700**; 12 **135**; 13
248; 32–3 **700**
——— solved as 'antler or horn' **737**;
'ink-horn' **784**; 'inkwell fashioned from
an antler' **658**
——— text: facsimile **884**
——— translation: into German **931**
Riddle 94
——— passages discussed in detail: lines
3 **128, 700**; 6 **700**
——— solved as 'creation' **727**; 'nature'
186
——— text: facsimile **884**
——— translation: into English **920**
Riddle 95
——— authorship: Cynewulf **662**
——— edition **931**
——— passages discussed in detail: lines
4 **673, 675**; 5–6 **681**
——— solved as 'book with gilding' **916**;
'moon' **716**; 'prostitute' **889**; 'quill'
803; 'riddle' **673, 675, 679, 680**; 'soul,
spirit' **751**; 'thought' **171**; 'wandering
singer' **658**; 'word of God' **74**
——— text: facsimile **884**
——— translation: into German **931**
Riddle sequences
——— Riddles 42–3: allegory in **949**; text

of, as single poem **949**; text of, as
twinned riddles **950**
——— Riddles 47–8: text of, as single
poem **949**
——— Riddles 53–5: thematic unity **910**
——— Riddles 75–6: parodic element
979; text of, as single poem **979**; text
of, as twinned riddles **194, 950**
Riddle, Leiden. *See* Leiden Riddle.
Riddles **655–994**
——— audience **881**; aristocratic and
clerical taste **224**; court audience **745**;
dichotomy between popular and literary
910; modern audience, pedagogical
value for **661, 924**; modern audience,
perennial appeal with **888**; popularity
among the 'folk' **273**
——— authorship **17, 662, 727, 739, 916**;
attribution to Cynewulf: *see* Cynewulf,
authorship of Riddles; multiple
authorship **9, 31, 60, 194, 658, 685,
699, 749, 751, 836**
——— bibliography **905, 936**
——— classification **879**
——— comparative discussion **707, 735,
947**; Aldhelm **916**; analogues **716, 727**;
encyclopaedic tradition **869**; epic **658**;
folk riddles **706**; Góngora **874**;
Heiðreks gátur **169, 183, 320, 744,
984**; kennings **31, 346, 864, 918, 929**;
Lorsch enigmas **937**; Middle High
German analogues **658**; Middle High
German riddles **744**; Renaissance
English parallels **738**; *Solomon and
Saturn* **738**; *The Dream of the Rood*
933; *The Wife's Lament* **994**; Tolkien
riddles **970**
——— concordance **944**
——— cultural significance **669**;
anthropomorphism **658**; descriptions of
birds **926**; in relation to modern
scientific description **752**; mentality
911, 914; observation **211, 789, 926**;
references to dark hair and complexion
97; social conflict **61**; social functions
991; weaving terminology **967**
——— dating **17, 22, 43, 71, 697, 701,
704, 727, 737, 739, 749, 751, 845, 916**;
linguistic criteria for **683, 684**
——— double entendre. *See* theme:
obscenity
——— editions **6, 188, 194, 727, 737**,

751, 946, 961; excluding Riddles 67, 78, 82, 89, 92, and 94 **65**; excluding Riddles 67, 78, 82, 92, and 94 **2**; selection of sixty riddles **985**
—— enumeration **691, 746, 747, 916, 944**
—— genre: elegiac elements **939, 940, 994**
—— language: colloquial speech **815**; Grice's Cooperative Principle **954**; linguistic features **748**; onomatopoeia **802**; prosaic vocabulary **276**; syntax **697**; use of first person singular **223**; use of first-person pronouns **988**; use of *nathwæt* and *nathwær* **968**; vocabulary **96, 668**
—— literary qualities **707, 891, 994**; allegorical interpretations **868, 951**; ambiguity **906, 911, 925**; analysis **905, 912**; as antecedent to allegory **32**; as lyric poetry **857, 874, 883**; dislocation of perspective **257**; dramatic insight **28**; entertainment value **814**; formulas **343**; humour **224**; imaginative qualities **121, 168, 658, 690, 738, 772, 846, 935**; in relation to modern symbolist poetry **846**; introductory formulas **744**; jokes **879**; literary merit **109, 121, 168, 172, 189, 337, 587, 840, 845, 869, 916, 922, 946**; paradox **337, 840, 875, 896, 898, 922, 932, 992**; paradox of silent speech **923**; prosopopoeia **109, 933**; rhyming **668**; sexual imagery **856**; typology **955**; verbal wit **869**; wordplay **867, 963**
—— localization **71, 109**; affiliation with Aldfrith **916**; affiliation with Aldhelm **71**; affiliation with Bede **704**; Northumbria **71, 657, 663, 684, 723, 727, 749, 777**; Northumbrian affiliations **657, 663, 684, 749**; Wessex and Northumbria **916**
—— metrics **748, 751, 754, 758, 759, 818, 982**; irregularities **734**
—— origins **199**
—— performance **672**
—— scholarship **8, 737, 755, 916**
—— solutions **41, 194, 691, 727, 737, 750, 936**; double solutions **889, 892**; list of **188**; methodology in finding solutions **74, 712, 716, 737, 743, 744, 897, 911, 916, 946, 971**; obscurity **62, 65, 300, 658, 814, 897**; obviousness

183, 724, 737, 738, 751, 876, 896, 939, 969, 976; scribal solutions **877**. *See also individual Riddles.*
—— sources: adaptations from Latin originals **183**; Aldhelm's *Ænigmata* **769**; as original productions **65**; Classical rhetoric **881**; folk origin **685**; folk tradition **946**; folklore elements **727, 737**; foreign influences **274, 662**; Germanic sources **55**; influence of Aldhelm **88** (*See also* Aldhelm); influence of Celtic nature poetry **109**; influence of Latin riddles **166, 194, 666, 672, 674, 707, 727, 737, 738, 739, 745, 751, 819, 883, 938, 965**; influence of Latin works **5, 13, 55, 202, 711, 916**; influence of Virgil **109**; list of sources and analogues **298**; methodological problems in source-hunting **706**; native origin **183, 806**; patristic orientation **881**; popular composition **658**; popular origin **699, 738, 815, 905**; Symphosius **88, 848, 973**
—— text: compilation policies in Exeter Book **190**; cryptography **816**; facsimile **185**; losses from Exeter Book **307**; manuscript context **74, 682, 950, 955**; manuscript punctuation **916**; marginalia **916**; oral transmission **727**; runes **216, 841, 916, 983**; transcription by Chambers **916**
—— themes: animal descriptions **13**; books and book production **931**; contest **834**; exile **658**; learned conception of Nature **34**; limits of human knowledge **59**; multiple interpretations **977**; Nature **109, 662, 711, 744, 806, 828, 845, 857, 991**; obscenity **325, 658, 706, 707, 901, 909, 925, 952, 955, 957, 962, 968**; ordinary experience **29**; psychological penetration **994**; purpose of composition **883**; representation of the world **975**; scribes and scriptoria **883**; theology **661**; time **894**
—— translations (medieval) **199**
—— translations: into English **188, 837, 854, 862, 864, 918, 946, 947**; excluding Riddles 67, 78, 82, 89, 92, and 94 **65**; selections **13, 28, 40, 59, 174, 317, 318, 874, 930, 985**; into German **70, 961**;

excluding Riddles 67, 78, 82, 92, and
94 **2**; into Italian (selection) **260**
rowan: in relation to Charm 1 **438**
Royal 2 B.v **36**
Royal 4 A.xiv **36**
Royal 12 D.xvii **36**
run-on style **30**
Rune Poem **995–1045**
———— comparative discussion: analogues
1025, 1033; Ausonius, *Technopaegnion*
1003; Chinese radical sequences **1040**;
Cynewulfian runes **1017**; Norwegian
'Rune Poem' and Old High German
Abecedarium Nordmannicum **183, 320**;
Norwegian and Icelandic rune poems
**1003, 1004, 1011, 1012, 1013, 1017,
1025, 1034, 1044**
———— cultural significance: applications
in magic **1038**; as evidence for early
Germanic heathendom **226**; as source
for runology **1002**; Christian mediation
of barbaric lore **357**; cult origins **1011**;
divinatory function **1034**; heathen
mythology **297**; origin of names of
runes **1013**; original meanings of rune
names **1011**; T-rune **256**
———— dating **5, 31, 63, 88, 109, 203,
1004, 1025, 1033**
———— editions **2, 6, 7, 63, 68, 72, 85, 94,
127, 165, 203, 221, 246, 300, 995,
1004, 1011, 1033, 1036**; excerpts **217**
———— functions: mnemonic function **26,
29, 30, 31, 166, 300, 1003, 1022, 1025,
1040**; oracular function **1036**
———— genre **55, 1005, 1013, 1033**;
affiliation with wisdom poetry **1044**;
elegiac and epic elements **274**; elegiac
elements **996**; gnomic and moralizing
elements **1003**; riddle elements **30,
1012**; similarities with gnomes **1033**;
similarity to Riddles **43, 353, 1033**
———— language **683**; *biþ*-maxims **246**;
coverage of supplementary runes **1016,
1025**; etymologies **1017, 1020**;
linguistic analysis **1005**
———— literary qualities **289, 1033, 1045**;
ambiguity **1029, 1030**; ambiguity and
wordplay **1012**; humour **40, 60**;
kennings **995, 1028**; literary merit **221,
1004, 1025**; persona **300**; structure **60**;
wordplay **1017, 1031**
———— localization: Mercian origin **1045**

———— metrics: hypermetric lines **134,
203, 1026, 1033**; strophe type **101,
1044**
———— passages discussed in detail: lines
10 **297**; 15 **1045**; 16 **1012**; 19–21 **152**;
22 **1037**; 27–8 **28**; 34 **1043**; 36 **198,
1021**; 37 **129**; 41–3 **1018**; 46 **1034**; 56
268; 59–60 **1018**; 66 **173, 273**; 77–80
353; 78 **1024**; 84 **99**; 87 **129, 1032**; *ac*
strophe **1031**; *æsc* strophe **1031**; *beorc*
strophe **289, 1004**; *cen* strophe **226,
1011, 1017, 1029, 1030**; *dæg* strophe
219; *ear* strophe **66, 825, 995, 1007,
1011, 1017, 1020, 1022, 1028, 1036,
1041**; *eh* 'horse' strophe **117, 226,
1028**; *eoh* 'yew' strophe **226, 995,
1021, 1042**; *eolhx* strophe **98, 117,
1000, 1011, 1014, 1018**; *feoh* strophe
1003, 1033, 1044; *gear* strophe **1011**;
hægl strophe **1026**; *iar* strophe **219,
226, 230, 353, 996, 1013, 1028, 1032,
1036**; *Ing* strophe **197, 314, 997, 998,
999, 1004, 1006, 1007, 1009, 1019,
1033, 1039**; *Ing* strophe: *Heardingas*
997, 1004, 1005, 1006, 1011, 1019; *Ing*
strophe: *wæn* **997, 1006, 1009, 1019**;
ior strophe: *See* iar strophe; *lagu*
strophe **1033**; *mann* strophe **1003**; *nyd*
strophe **300, 1026**; *os* strophe **26, 158,
245, 256, 1004, 1005, 1011, 1017,
1022, 1030, 1033**; *peorð* strophe **1010,
1011, 1012, 1029, 1036**; *rad* strophe
**214, 244, 289, 300, 996, 1004, 1011,
1023, 1030**; *sigel* strophe **996, 1000,
1011, 1030, 1035, 1036**; *Tir* strophe
**996, 1004, 1005, 1007, 1011, 1013,
1030, 1036, 1044**; *þorn* strophe **226,
995, 1010, 1011**; *þorn* strophe:
thunder-god **226**; *ur* strophe **117, 1004,
1011, 1031, 1033**; *wen* strophe **996,
1037**; **1000, 1002, 1004, 1033**; *yr*
strophe **135, 995, 1000, 1013**
———— scholarship **8, 1011**
———— sources: background in tradition
1028, 1030, 1033, 1034, 1041, 1044;
Celtic elements **1032**; common
Germanic antecedent **166, 203, 1003**;
Latin analogue **1033**; Scandinavian
influence **1011**
———— text: appended series of runes
1001; compilation **203**; facsimile **1033**;
Hickes's account of his procedure **36**,

216, 1008, 1027; Hickes's text in relation to that of the lost manuscript 1002; manuscript 1027; runes 216; variant runes from Cotton Domitian A.ix 1004; Wanley transcription 1033; Wanley's description of manuscript leaf 1008
———— themes 1031, 1033, 1041; Christian interpretation 310, 324, 1033, 1036; explicatory function 1030; moralizing 1025; Nature description 11, 995; Nature poetry 193
———— translations: into English 63, 221, 300, 1004, 1033, 1036; excerpts 7, 28, 29, 40, 127; into German 2, 995, 1011
runes: as cult script 256; associated with Riddles 112; cryptography 71; in Cynewulf's signed poems 547; in *Maxims* 594; in OEW poems 25, 64, 74, 310, 324, 339; in Riddles 63, 140, 152, 216, 230, 657, 662, 664, 681, 682, 683, 691, 913; in *Solomon and Saturn* 63; in poetry 287, 728; in private messages 325; in relation to Charm 2 491; in relation to Charms 473; incised on kelp-weed 779; rune magic 178; rune magic, in Charms 106, 441, 490; rune magic, in relation to *Solomon and Saturn. See* Solomon and Saturn, Paternoster section, manuscript 216; rune names, evidence from OEW poems 289. *See also* Rune Poem; Riddles, text: runes; *and* Solomon and Saturn, Paternoster runes.
runic sorcery. *See* rune magic.

sacrifices, human 798
sage: as typical speaker of wisdom poetry 47
Salic Law: in relation to Charm 8 464
salvation of souls: as motive for poetic composition 344
Saturn: as leader of the Chaldeans in *Solomon and Saturn* 79; as pagan Germanic deity 296, 363, 1047, 1061; as speaker in *Solomon and Saturn* 43, 340, 351
Saxo Grammaticus: in relation to *Maxims* 547
sceacan 248
sceal: connection with Germanic notion of Fate 267; in *Maxims* 60, 183, 259, 325, 328, 558, 585, 602, 606, 612, 621

scholarly attitudes to Christian elements in OEW poetry 296
scholarship on OEW poetry 55, 296. *See also entries on* scholarship *under individual OEW poems.*
scop: as depicted in *Fortunes* 116; as depicted in Riddle 8 792; as exhorting the war-band in battle 313; as term for poet 87; in *Maxims I* 598; profession of 87, 496
scribes: scribal reading process 358
sea: concept of sea as 'covering' the earth 89; vocabulary relating to sea 341
The Seafarer 76, 199; as source for *Maxims* 13
Searle, J.R.: speech act theory 350
Serbo-Croatian charms 469
Serbo-Croatian oral tradition 312
Servius: theory of epithets 572
Seven Sleepers of Ephesus. *See* Charm 3, efficacy.
shamanism. *See also* Charms, performance.
short lines 279; in Charms 272; in *Maxims* 272; influence of proverbs 92; preferred over hypermetric lines 300. *See also* metrics.
Sigrdrífumál: as source for *Precepts* 20
similes 569
Simonides fragment 1: as analogue to *Fortunes* 183
Skírnismál: as analogue to Charms 320, 453
skothendingar: in *Maxims* 540
smith: in Charm 4 455
Smith, Thomas 216
Solomon and Saturn 1046–112. *See also under individual entries for* I, Prose section, *and* II.
———— authorship 134, 1061, 1095
———— comparative discussion: with *Adrian and Ritheus* 1047, 1057; with Chaucer, *The Book of the Duchess* 1094; with Cotton Vitellius A.xv *Solomon and Saturn* texts 1047, 1099; with Cynewulfian runic signatures 1104; with *Deor* 1102; with *Durham Ritual* 1089; with elegiac poetry 40; with European tradition 1050, 1053; with French analogues 1061; with Germanic tradition 1093; with Germanic verbal contests 1064, 1073; with medieval Latin works 1100; with

medieval contests of wit **29**; with Old
Norse riddles **183, 1049**; with *Proverbs
of Alfred* and *Proverbs of Hendyng*
1047; with Riddles **1103**; with
Scandinavian analogues **1061**; with
Scandinavian mythology **1077, 1088**;
with scholasticism **31**; with Solomon
and Marcolf tradition **102, 121, 109,
1047, 1056, 1069, 1073**; with
Vafþrúðnismál **320, 1047**; with
Vafþrúðnismál and *Alvíssmál* **351**
———— cultural significance: as witness to
Anglo-Saxon philosophy **47**; role of
superstitions in **16**; Saturn as Germanic
deity. *See* Saturn.
———— dating **5, 22, 31, 109, 203, 276,
1051, 1052, 1061, 1073**
———— editions **2, 6, 203, 1046, 1047,
1073, 1079, 1087**; excerpts **7, 63, 69,
72, 108, 153, 165**
———— genre **1103**; elegiac elements **47**;
Germanic verbal contests **61**; gnomic
elements **350**; in European context **121**;
incantatory elements **226**; riddle
elements **55, 350, 947**; riddle form
1073; Solomon and Marcolf genre
1087
———— language: auxiliary verbs **1101**;
dialect **215**; *ealand/igland* in sense of
'land bordering on water' **340**;
forscrifan **158**; *godspel* **151**;
identifications of names **1065**; Latin
vocabulary **141, 203**; *oferhygd* **254**;
prosaic vocabulary **276**; *warnung* **47**
———— literary qualities: as debate poem
1094; as didactic literature **34**; as
fantasy literature **1097**; cohesion **8, 25**;
dialogue form **136, 1064, 1073, 1094,
1108**; gnomic statements **77**; humour
74, 88; imagery of falling leaf **193,
1085**; imagery of heat and cold **1082**;
imagery of warfare **1106**; imagery of
wounds **1092**; literary merit **30, 52, 60,
88, 168, 300, 1049, 1061, 1073, 1083**;
persona **300**; personification of *yldo*
267; relation between the two poetic
sections **203**; rhyming **1105**;
Romanticism **103**; serious tone **1050**
———— localization **254**; Northumbria
1075; Wessex and Northumbria **1061**
———— metrics **92, 133, 272**; hypermetric
lines **15**
———— passages discussed in detail: lines

1 **340, 1107**; 2 **1112**; 3–4 **1107**; 7 **212**;
11 **1058**; 12 **258**; 16 **1058**; 25–8 **322**;
25a **198**; 34 **1058**; 39 **258**; 44–5 **212**;
46 **118**; 47 **1086**; 65 **151**; 81–2 **211**; 83
212; 89 **1100**; 90–1 **1075**; 93 **1083**;
94–5 **322, 1090**; 98–106 **256**; 99 **245**;
107 **226, 1058, 1065, 1067, 1100,
1111**; 108 **1058, 1065, 1083, 1091**;
111–17 **310, 322, 1090**; 129–30 **1090**;
130 **149**; 136 **212**; 138 **212, 1065,
1100**; 141–5 **1065**; 149–50 **163**; 151
178; 158 **243**; 163 **242**; 163–4 **1058**;
163–9 **242**; 167 **1058**; 179 **140**;
179–201 **1110**; 180 **1058**; 208 **308**;
212–24 **278, 300**; 213 **1071**; 214 **1058,
1066, 1071**; 236 **212, 1058, 1080,
1109**; 242 **1084**; 252 **1058**; 253–81
300; 264 **117**; 264–5 **147, 1070**; 267
1076; 269 **144**; 277 **1058**; 277–8 **1065**;
282–91 **1103**; 287 **1058**; 290 **129**; 299
128; 307 **1063**; 311 **1058**; 312–13 **134,
213**; 314 **285**; 327 **281**; 334 **227**; 336
218; 338–9 **243**; 339 **212, 1058, 1065,
1089, 1092, 1100**; 340 **218**; 341 **1058**;
344 **218**; 348 **218**; 353–8 **1082**; 360
212; 362–3 **652**; 367–9 **128**; 369 **212**;
389 **1075**; 396 **1058**; 429 **4**; 429a **47**;
430 **1084**; 437 **151, 342**; 437–50 **202**;
440 **151, 202**; 453 **204**; 457 **1088**;
459–60 **1078**; 460 **132**; 465 **212, 1058**;
478 **154, 155, 157, 212, 1075**; 478–9
1058; 479 **1067**; 482–3 **1058**; 482–98
319; 501 **1086**
———— scholarship **8, 1069, 1072, 1087,
1096**
———— sources: Æthicus Ister,
Cosmographia **1110**; Anglo-Saxon
poetic tradition **1080**; Bede, *Nomina
locorum* **1110**; Bible **1061**; Biblical
apocrypha **1059, 1068**; Cassiodorus,
Institutiones **1104**; *Collectanea Bedae*
1103; *Contradictio Salomonis* **1061,
1068**; early Christian-Manichean
debate literature **1096**; Germanic and
Oriental sources **5**; Germanic elements
355, 1047, 1049, 1055, 1061, 1073;
heathen literature **66**; Hisperic tradition
52; History of Solomon narratives
1061; influence of Riddles **79**; Isidore,
Etymologiae **1110**; Latin proximate
source **1057, 1073**; Legends of Cain
1062; *Letter of Alexander to Aristotle*

1097; *Liber Monstrorum* 1097; *Marvels of the East* 1097; Old Testament 7, 79; Oriental elements 74, 1047, 1048, 1049, 1053, 1061, 1064, 1070, 1073; origins and dissemination of source-material 1046; Prudentius, *Psychomachia* 1090, 1106; Scandinavian origins 1047; *The Evernew Tongue* 1068; tradition of Solomon dialogues 1047; Virgil, *Æneid* 1097
———— text: as Solomon anthology 1102; editorial policies 358, 1047, 1051, 1057, 1061; in context of CCCC 41 305; oral transmission 266; runes in Paternoster 216, 226, 230, 245, 1073, 1075, 1083, 1093, 1100, 1106; scribal accuracy 208; transcription 1051, 1052, 1054, 1061, 1081
———— themes: Cain and Abel 597; Christian doctrinal elements 1053, 1055, 1061, 1079, 1082, 1085, 1086, 1088, 1089, 1092, 1093, 1094, 1097, 1099, 1100, 1106; *Duodecim abusivis sæculi* 1086; Fate, as blend of Stoic and Christian 267; geography 340, 1107; Hell 97; identity of Saturn 1048, 1050, 1053, 1056, 1061, 1093; Last Judgement 1055, 1070; Lucifer's fall 222; Moloch 5; mysticism 31; Nimrod 1071; opposition to heathen beliefs 20, 274; Paternoster 55, 69, 88, 151, 178, 180, 203, 358, 474, 1049, 1056, 1061, 1065, 1068, 1073, 1079, 1083, 1091, 1098, 1104, 1108, 1111; psychomachia 319, 322; traveller recognizes his goal 1080; treatment of Hell 1082, treatment of Satan 1077, 1088; *Vasa Mortis* 211, 300, 1070, 1088, 1096, 1097; *weallende wulf* 300, 1056, 1068, 1071; wisdom on books 896; Wyrd 1060, 1061, 1073, 1074, 1077
———— translations: into English 1047; excerpts 7, 28, 29, 40, 62, 63, 102; into German 2, 1079; excerpts 69; into Italian 1087
Solomon and Saturn I
———— comparative discussion: in relation to psychomachia tradition 1106
———— theme: Christian doctrinal elements 1064
Solomon and Saturn Prose section 55,

1049, 1061, 1073, 1095; edition 1098; in relation to Cotton Vitellius A.xv prose *Solomon and Saturn* 1098; translation into Italian 1098
Solomon and Saturn II
———— comparative discussion: *De Consolatione Philosophiae* 1102
———— cultural significance: geography 1110
———— dating 8, 16
———— edition 300
———— literary qualities: cohesion 2; compositional mode 1110; dialogue form 2, 8, 74, 1050; structure 1096
———— sources 203
———— theme: temptation 1083
———— translation: into English 300
Solon fragment 13: as analogue to *Gifts* 183
sound as meaning: in OEW poems 306. *See also* onomatopoeia *in entries for individual poems.*
source studies: in relation to OEW poems 300; methods in 631
speech act theory: in relation to OEW poems 350
speeches 25. *See also* literary qualities: dialogue form *in entries for relevant individual poems.*
spell: as used in *Precepts* line 25 104
spiders 459, 487; as amulets 315; in Charm 3 492
St Germanus: in relation to Garmund in Charm 9 476
St Helen: in Charms 416
Stimmanalyse 551
structures of opposition 350
style 309; additive 614; in Riddles 671
sum 338; in *repetitio* 25, 229
sun worship: in Charm 1 278, 310, 420
superstition: as evidenced in Charms 374, 430; in *Solomon and Saturn* 16; relating to plants 98
swimming: as evidenced in *Gifts* 513
swords 242; in *Maxims* 242; in *Solomon and Saturn* 242
Symphosius
———— as source for Riddles 28, 65, 153, 251, 298, 658
———— literary merit 672
———— Enigma 1: in relation to Riddle 9 973
———— Enigma 2: as analogue to Riddle

60 **59, 298, 779, 833, 858, 871, 923, 946**
——— Enigma 4: as analogue to Riddle 91 **298**
——— Enigma 9: as analogue to Riddle 30 **672**
——— Enigma 12: as analogue to Riddle 85 **298**
——— Enigma 16: as analogue to Riddle 47 **298, 684, 898, 912**
——— Enigma 20: as analogue to Riddle 28 **298, 826**
——— Enigma 44: as analogue to Riddles **298**; as analogue to Riddle 65 **860**
——— Enigma 56: as analogue to Riddles **298**
——— Enigma 61: as analogue to Riddles **298**
——— Enigma 71: as analogue to Riddle 58 **298**
——— Enigma 73: as analogue to Riddles **298, 973**
——— Enigma 92: as analogue to Riddle 83 **298**
——— Enigma 95: as analogue to Riddle 86 **298, 938**
syncreticism **1093**
synecdoche **49**
syntax **218, 577**; auxiliary verbs **1101**; *hwonne* **253**; in *Order* **630**
systems theory **53**

Table of Nations: in relation to *Maxims I* **340**
Tacitus: in relation to *Maxims* **547**; on marriage **43**
Tatwine
——— as source for Riddles **298**; influence on Riddles **707, 737**
——— Enigmas 5 and 6: as analogues to Riddles **298**
technology **195**
tense usage **304**
theft: in Charms **416**
Theodore of Tarsus, *Penitential* **613**
Theognis, *Sentences*: resemblances to *Maxims* **65**
theology: in Riddles **661**
tirades (French verse-form): compared with quasi-stanzaic formations in OEW texts **101**
titles of poems **194**; abbreviations **33**; editorial titles **43**

translation process (medieval): in Riddles **350, 899**; into Old English verse **878**; translations of poems between Germanic dialects **275**
tristitia **267**
truth: in Anglo-Saxon thought **617**
Tryggðamál: compared to Old English gnomic poetry **183**

þula, plural *þulur*: compared with OEW texts **30**
Þunor: references in Charms **296**
þyrs **228, 587**; in *Maxims II* **570**

understatement **196, 849**

Vafþrúðnismál: compared with *Solomon and Saturn* **77**
Vainglory **1113–19**
——— audience: at mealtime recitation **1115**
——— comparative discussion: with Cassian **1114**; with *Homiletic Fragment I* **1119**; with Hroðgar's 'homily' in *Beowulf* **61, 284**; with Pomerius **1114**; with Psalm 9 **1115**; with Riddles **1119**
——— dating **17**
——— editions **2, 6, 65, 165, 188, 194, 270, 284, 300, 1115**; excerpts **68, 164, 217**
——— genre: elegiac elements **1119**
——— language: *hapax legomena* **270**; occurrence of *ofermod* in **254**; tense usage **304**; vocabulary **96**
——— literary qualities: ambiguity **1115**; didacticism **52**; imagery of warfare **1113, 1114**; literary merit **45, 60, 270**; realism **177**; reference to act of narration **343**; structure **270, 1115, 1116, 1119**; vagueness **300**
——— passages discussed in detail: lines 1–8 **1114**; 4 **147**; 8 **270, 631, 1116**; 9–12 **1116**; 10 **270, 1115**; 12 **122**; 13 **1115**; 14 **198, 270, 1115, 1118**; 16 **313**; 17 **198**; 24 **1115**; 25 **160**; 28 **160**; 28–9 **1116**; 32 **270**; 33 **1115**; 36 **1115**; 40 **308**; 44 **147**; 50b–66 **319**; 52–6 **1116**; 59 **147**; 70b **1114**; 71a **133**; 75 **276**; 77–80 **345**; 82a **133**; 83 **1115**
——— scholarship **7**
——— sources: 1 John 3 **1119**; absence of single clear source **194**; Augustine

1114; Bede, *In Epistolas Septem Catholicas* 1119; Caesarius of Arles 1116, 1119; Chrodegang of Metz, *Regula Canonicorum* 1116; Prudentius, *Psychomachia* 1113
—— text: facsimile 185; manuscript context 1119
—— theme 1115, 1119; Christian doctrinal elements 1113, 1114; figure of the scholar 1116; psychology of sin 290; psychomachia 319; Robertsonian interpretation 280; treatment of Lucifer 1117
—— translations: into English 65, 188, 270, 300; excerpts 7; into German 2, 70
valkyries 468; in Charm 4 197, 228, 460; in Charms 4 and 8 66, 109
variation technique 23, 54, 311
Vedic hymns: compared with Riddles 43
Venantius Fortunatus: influence on Old English elegy 199
vengeance: in Riddles 138
Vercelli, Biblioteca Capitolare CXVII (The Vercelli Book) 36; compilation of 54
versification. *See* metrics.
Versus Cuiusdam Scoti de Alphabeto: as analogue to *Rune Poem* 1033
vicissitudes of life 108
Vienna, Nationalbibliothek 751 36
Vikings: in frock-coats 155
Virgil
—— as source of literary exercises 584; influence on Riddles 109
—— *Æneid*: as source for *Solomon and Saturn* 1097
Völuspá: resemblance to Riddle 29 182

Wain constellation 314
The Wanderer 76, 199
Wanley, Humfrey 216. *See also* Rune Poem, text: Wanley.
war in heaven 319
warble-fly 315
warfare: ethic of 589; illustrated through OEW texts 13; ritual warfare 347; spiritual warfare 319
warrior ethos 177
water, holy 418, 430, 441, 483
water-elf. *See* Charm 7.
Wayland the smith: in relation to Charm 4 29, 381, 460
ways of death: theme in *Fortunes* 239

Wealas 138, 209
Weland. *See* Wayland.
Welsh gnomic poetry 259
Wessex: as localization for poetic composition 199
—— as localization for redaction of *Maxims II. See* Maxims II, localization.
—— as localization for redaction of *Maxims. See* Maxims, localization.
Widsith: compared with *Rune Poem* 30
Wild Hunt 262
Winfrid Proverb
—— comparative discussion: Bede, *Death Song* 203; legal formula 30
—— cultural significance 651
—— dating 295, 640
—— editions 2, 6, 64, 72, 91, 93, 203, 641, 642, 643, 644, 647, 649
—— language 683; *foreldit* 212, 652
—— localization 640
—— scholarship 653
—— text: facsimile 641; transcription 639
—— translations: into English 295, 640; into German and Gothic 641; into Latin 644, 647
winter: in Latin and Old English poetry 584
wisdom: association with age 333; definition of 301; early Germanic 155
wisdom poetry: Anglo-Saxon taste for 47; definition of genre 44; scholarship on 58, 300
witchcraft 178, 348, 433, 442, 456
wlanc 268, 294, 308, 335, 815, 899, 906
woðbora: as term for poet 87, 313
Woden: as discoverer of runes 1026; cult in England 262; in Charm 2 262, 429, 462, 465; in Charms 296, 432; in *Maxims I* 262; in *Maxims I*, contrasted with God 232; in *Solomon and Saturn*, compared with Saturn 43; in relation to *Gifts* 76; magical powers of 491
women: as heroes in Old English literature 334; authorship of OEW poems 352; women's hair, as described in OEW poems 114; women in *Maxims* 619; women in *Maxims I* 616; in relation to Charms 348; position of women in Anglo-Saxon England 325, 329, 348, 805, 901; transmission of folk wisdom by women 352; women's use of charms

or potions **600**; women's use of magic
613. *See also* female, feminine.
Wonders of the East. *See* Marvels of the
East.
wordplay: in *Maxims I* **623**; in relation to
runes **287**. *See also* paronomasia.
wounds: in Charms **370**
Wulf and Eadwacer
—— as 'Riddle 1' **2, 657, 662, 673, 679,
683, 684, 687, 699, 703, 728, 733, 737,
744, 766**
—— as 'charade' on the name
'Cynewulf' **71**
—— metrics: strophe-like form **101**

—— solved as 'the Christian preacher'
74
Wyrd: as fallen angel **151**; as heathen
goddess **202**; as principle of mutability
267; as subject to God **54**; as witch
156; associated with evil **267**;
compared with Christ **139**; definition of
158; in *Maxims* **151, 156**; in *Maxims II*
line 5 **222, 232, 559**; in *Solomon and
Saturn* **69, 151, 156, 222, 296**; survival
after Conversion **202**

Yggdrasill: in Old Norse mythology **226**;
in relation to Riddle 92 **897**

UNIVERSITY OF WINCHESTER
LIBRARY